PHILIP'S

G000294383

STREET ATLAS
Cheshire

First published in 1995 by

Philip's, a division of
Octopus Publishing Group Ltd
2-4 Heron Quays, London E14 4JP

Third colour edition 2005
First impression 2005

ISBN-10   0-540-08748-3 (spiral)
ISBN-13   978-0-540-08748-8 (spiral)

© Philip's 2005

Ordnance Survey®

This product includes mapping data licensed
from Ordnance Survey® with the permission of
the Controller of Her Majesty's Stationery Office.
© Crown copyright 2005. All rights reserved.
Licence number 100011710.

Printed and bound in Spain
by Cayfosa-Quebecor

Contents

III	**Key to map symbols**
IV	**Key to map pages**
VI	**Route planning**
VIII	**Administrative and Postcode boundaries**
1	**Street maps** at 3½ inches to 1 mile
237	**Street map of Chester city centre** at 7 inches to 1 mile
238	**Index** of towns and villages
241	**Index** of streets, hospitals, industrial estates, railway stations, schools, shopping centres, universities and places of interest

Digital Data

The exceptionally high-quality mapping found in this atlas is available as digital data in TIFF format, which is easily convertible to other bitmapped (raster) image formats.

The index is also available in digital form as a standard database table. It contains all the details found in the printed index together with the National Grid reference for the map square in which each entry is named.

For further information and to discuss your requirements, please contact Philip's on 020 7644 6932 or james.mann@philips-maps.co.uk

Key to map symbols

(22a)	**Motorway** with junction number
	Primary route – dual/single carriageway
	A road – dual/single carriageway
	B road – dual/single carriageway
	Minor road – dual/single carriageway
	Other minor road – dual/single carriageway
	Road under construction
	Tunnel, covered road
	Rural track, private road or narrow road in urban area
	Gate or obstruction to traffic (restrictions may not apply at all times or to all vehicles)
	Path, bridleway, byway open to all traffic, road used as a public path
	Pedestrianised area
DY7	**Postcode boundaries**
	County and unitary authority boundaries
	Railway, tunnel, railway under construction
	Tramway, tramway under construction
	Miniature railway
Walsall	**Railway station**
	Private railway station
South Shields	**Metro station**
	Tram stop, tram stop under construction
	Bus, coach station

◆	**Ambulance station**
◆	**Coastguard station**
◆	**Fire station**
◆	**Police station**
✚	**Accident and Emergency entrance to hospital**
H	**Hospital**
+	**Place of worship**
i	**Information Centre** (open all year)
🛒	**Shopping Centre**
P P&R	**Parking, Park and Ride**
PO	**Post Office**
⚑ 🚐	**Camping site, caravan site**
▶ ✕	**Golf course, picnic site**
Prim Sch	**Important buildings, schools, colleges, universities and hospitals**
	Built up area
	Woods
River Medway	**Water name**
	River, weir, stream
	Canal, lock, tunnel
	Water
	Tidal water
Church	**Non-Roman antiquity**
ROMAN FORT	**Roman antiquity**
87	**Adjoining page indicators and overlap bands** The colour of the arrow and the band indicates the scale of the adjoining or overlapping page (see scales below)
237	

Enlarged mapping only

	Railway or bus station building
	Place of interest
	Parkland

Abbr	Full	Abbr	Full	Abbr	Full
Acad	**Academy**	Inst	**Institute**	Recn Gd	**Recreation Ground**
Allot Gdns	**Allotments**	Ct	**Law Court**		
Cemy	**Cemetery**	L Ctr	**Leisure Centre**	Resr	**Reservoir**
C Ctr	**Civic Centre**	LC	**Level Crossing**	Ret Pk	**Retail Park**
CH	**Club House**	Liby	**Library**	Sch	**School**
Coll	**College**	Mkt	**Market**	Sh Ctr	**Shopping Centre**
Crem	**Crematorium**	Meml	**Memorial**	TH	**Town Hall/House**
Ent	**Enterprise**	Mon	**Monument**	Trad Est	**Trading Estate**
Ex H	**Exhibition Hall**	Mus	**Museum**	Univ	**University**
Ind Est	**Industrial Estate**	Obsy	**Observatory**	W Twr	**Water Tower**
IRB Sta	**Inshore Rescue Boat Station**	Pal	**Royal Palace**	Wks	**Works**
		PH	**Public House**	YH	**Youth Hostel**

■ The small numbers around the edges of the maps identify the 1 kilometre National Grid lines
■ The dark grey border on the inside edge of some pages indicates that the mapping does not continue onto the adjacent page

The scale of the maps on the pages numbered in blue is 5.52 cm to 1 km • 3½ inches to 1 mile • 1: 18103

0	¼	½	¾	1 mile
0	250 m	500 m	750 m	1 kilometre

The scale of the maps on pages numbered in red is 11.04 cm to 1 km • 7 inches to 1 mile • 1: 9051

0	220 yards	440 yards	660 yards	½ mile
0	125 m	250 m	375 m	½ kilometre

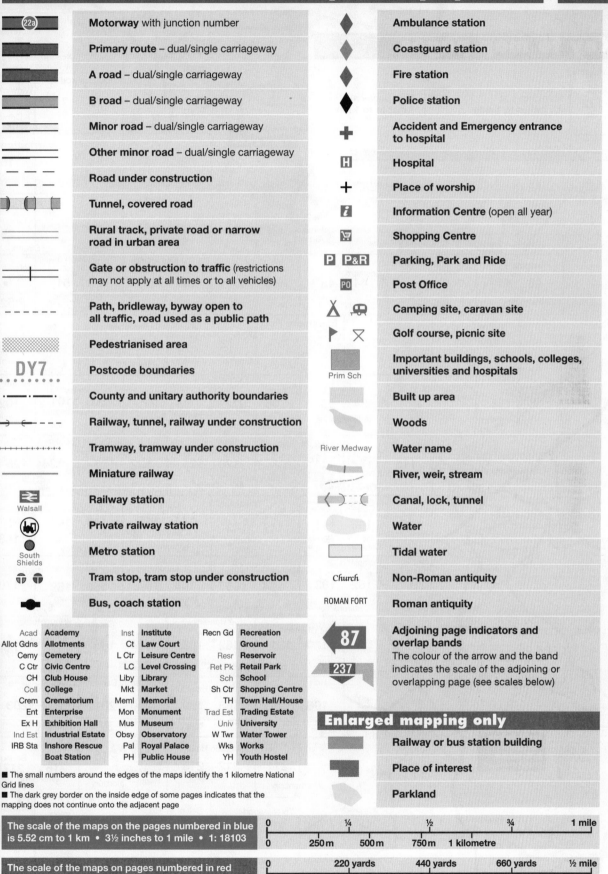

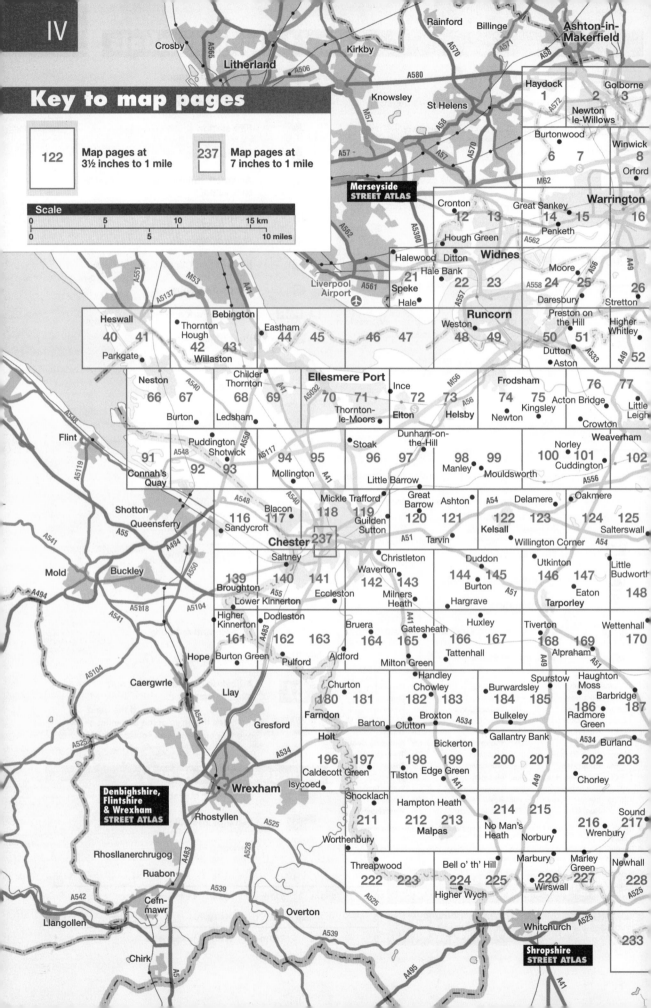

IV

Key to map pages

Crosby
Litherland
Rainford
Billinge
Ashton-in-Makerfield
Kirkby
Knowsley
St Helens
Haydock **1**
2 Golborne **3**
Newton le-Willows
Burtonwood
6 **7**
Winwick
8
Orford

Merseyside STREET ATLAS

Cronton
12 **13**
Great Sankey
14 **15** **Warrington** **16**
Penketh
Hough Green
Halewood Ditton **Widnes**
Hale Bank
21 **22** **23**
Speke
Hale
Moore
24 **25**
26
Daresbury
Stretton

Liverpool Airport
Runcorn
Weston **48** **49**
Preston on the Hill **50** **51**
Higher Whitley
Dutton Aston **52**

Heswall **40** **41**
Bebington
Thornton Hough **42** **43**
Willaston
Eastham **44** **45** **46** **47**
Parkgate

Neston **66** **67**
Childer Thornton **68** **69**
Ellesmere Port **70** **71**
Ince **72** **73**
Frodsham **74** **75** Acton Bridge **76** **77**
Burton
Ledsham
Thornton-le-Moors
Elton Helsby
Newton Kingsley
Crowton
Little Leigh

Flint
Puddington Shotwick **94** **95**
Stoak **96** **97**
Dunham-on-the-Hill
98 **99**
Manley Mouldsworth
Norley **100** **101**
Cuddington
Weaverham **102**

91
Connah's Quay **92** **93**
Mollington
Little Barrow

Shotton
Queensferry
Blacon **116** **117**
118
Mickle Trafford **119**
Great Barrow **120**
Ashton **121**
Delamere **122** **123** Oakmere **124** **125**
Sandycroft
Guilden Sutton
Kelsall
Salterswall

Mold
Buckley
Chester 237
Saltney **139** **140** **141**
Christleton
Waverton **142** **143**
Duddon **144** **145**
Utkinton **146** **147**
Little Budworth
Broughton
Lower Kinnerton
Eccleston
Milners Heath
Burton
Hargrave
Eaton **148**
Tarporley
Willington Corner
Tarvin

Higher Kinnerton **161**
Dodleston **162** **163**
Bruera **164** **165**
Huxley **166** **167**
Tiverton **168** **169**
Wettenhall **170**
Hope
Burton Green
Pulford
Aldford
Gatesheath
Tattenhall
Alpraham

Caergwrle
Llay
Churton **180** **181**
Handley Chowley **182** **183**
Burwardsley **184** **185**
Spurstow
Haughton Moss
Barbridge
Gresford
Farndon
Barton Clutton
Broxton **186** **187**
Radmore Green
Bulkeley

Hope
Holt **196** **197**
198 **199**
Bickerton
Gallantry Bank **200** **201**
202 **203** Burland
Caldecott Green
Tilston Edge Green
Chorley

Denbighshire, Flintshire & Wrexham STREET ATLAS

Rhostyllen
Isycoed
Shocklach **211**
Hampton Heath **212** **213**
Malpas
214 **215**
No Man's Heath Norbury
216 **217** Sound
Wrenbury

Rhosllanerchrugog
Ruabon
Worthenbury
Threapwood **222** **223**
Bell o' th' Hill **224** **225**
Marbury **226** **227** Marley Green
Newhall **228**
Higher Wych
Wirswall

Cefn-mawr
Llangollen
Overton
Whitchurch **233**

Chirk

Shropshire STREET ATLAS

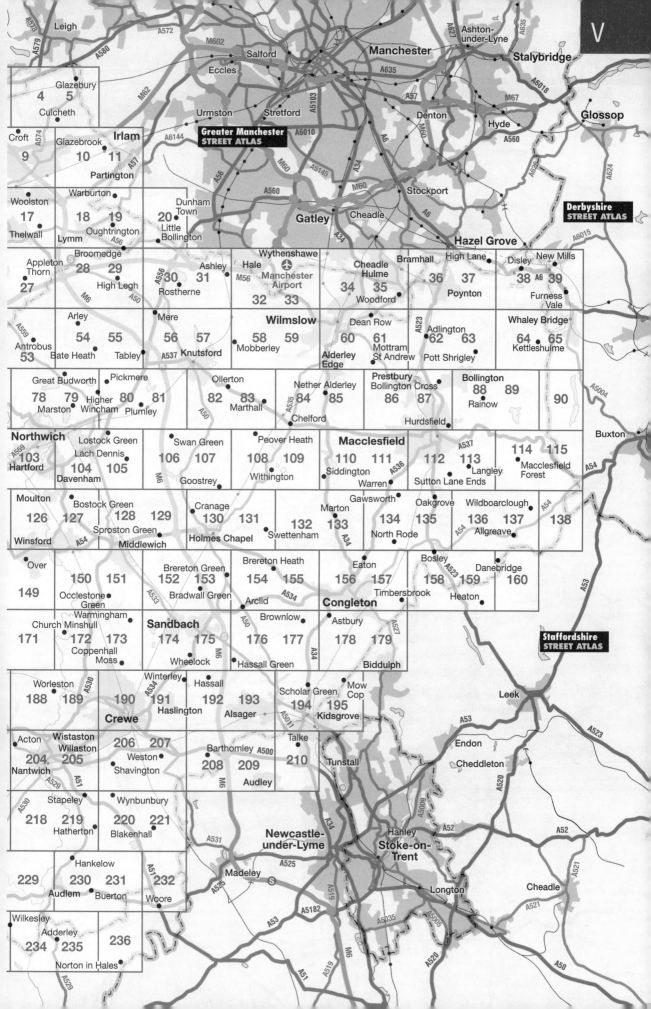

Leigh

A572

A580

A579

M602

Salford

Eccles

Manchester

A635

A627

Ashton-under-Lyne

A635

Stalybridge

A6018

M67

Glossop

A624

A6015

Glazebury

4 5

Culcheth

Urmston

Stretford

M62

Greater Manchester STREET ATLAS

A6010

Denton

A57

Hyde

A560

M60

Croft A574

9

Glazebrook

10 11

Irlam

A57

Partington

A6144

A56

Dunham Town

A6010

Gatley

A5145

A34

Stockport

A6

Derbyshire STREET ATLAS

Woolston

17

Thelwall

Warburton

18 19

Lymm

Oughtrington

A56

20

Little Bollington

M60

A560

Cheadle

Hazel Grove

Appleton Thorn

27

Broomedge

28 29

High Legh

M6

A50

A556

30

Rostherne

Ashley

31

M56

Hale

Wythenshawe

Manchester Airport

32 33

Cheadle Hulme

34 35

Woodford

Bramhall

36 37

Poynton

High Lane

Disley

38

A6

New Mills

39

Furness Vale

Arley

54 55

Antrobus

53

Bate Heath

A559

Tabley

Mere

56 57

A537

Knutsford

Wilmslow

58 59

Mobberley

Dean Row

60 61

Alderley Edge

Mottram St Andrew

A523

Adlington

62 63

Pott Shrigley

Whaley Bridge

64 65

Kettleshulme

Great Budworth

78 79

Marston

Pickmere

Higher 80 81

Wincham Plumley

A50

Ollerton

82 83

Marthall

Chelford

A535

Nether Alderley

84 85

Prestbury

Bollington Cross

86 87

Hurdsfield

Bollington

88 89

Rainow

90

A5004

Buxton

Northwich

A559

103

Hartford

Lostock Green

Lach Dennis

104 105

Davenham

Swan Green

106 107

M6

Goostrey

Peover Heath

108 109

Withington

Macclesfield

110 111

Siddington

Warren

A536

A537

112 113

Sutton Lane Ends

Langley

114 115

Macclesfield Forest

A54

Moulton

126 127

Winsford

A54

Bostock Green

128 129

Sproston Green

Middlewich

Cranage

130 131

Holmes Chapel

Swettenham

132 133

A34

North Rode

Gawsworth

134 135

Marton

Oakgrove

A54

Wildboarclough

136 137

Allgreave

138

A54

Over

149

150 151

Occleston Green

A533

Brereton Green

152 153

Bradwall Green

Brereton Heath

154 155

Arclid

A534

Eaton

156 157

Timbersbrook

Congleton

Bosley

158 159

A523

Heaton

Danebridge

160

A53

Church Minshull

171

172 173

Coppenhall Moss

Warmingham

Sandbach

174 175

Wheelock

M6

Brownlow

176 177

Hassall Green

Astbury

178 179

Biddulph

A527

A34

Staffordshire STREET ATLAS

Leek

A53

A523

Worleston

188 189

A530

Crewe

190

A534

Winterley

191

Haslington

Hassall

192 193

Alsager

A5011

Scholar Green

194 195

Kidsgrove

Mow Cop

Leek

Acton

204

Nantwich

Wistaston Willaston

205

A529

A51

206 207

Weston

Shavington

Barthomley

208 209

Audley

A500

M6

Talke

210

Tunstall

Endon

Cheddleton

A520

A523

Stapeley

218 219

Hatherton

A530

Wynbunbury

220 221

Blakenhall

A531

Newcastle-under-Lyme

A525

Madeley

A525

S

Hanley

Stoke-on-Trent

A52

A52

A521

A519

Hankelow

229

230 231

Audlem Buerton

A51

232

Woore

A525

A5182

A53

Longton

A5035

A5005

Cheadle

A521

A521

Wilkesley

Adderley

234 235

Norton in Hales

236

A529

M6

A519

A51

A520

A50

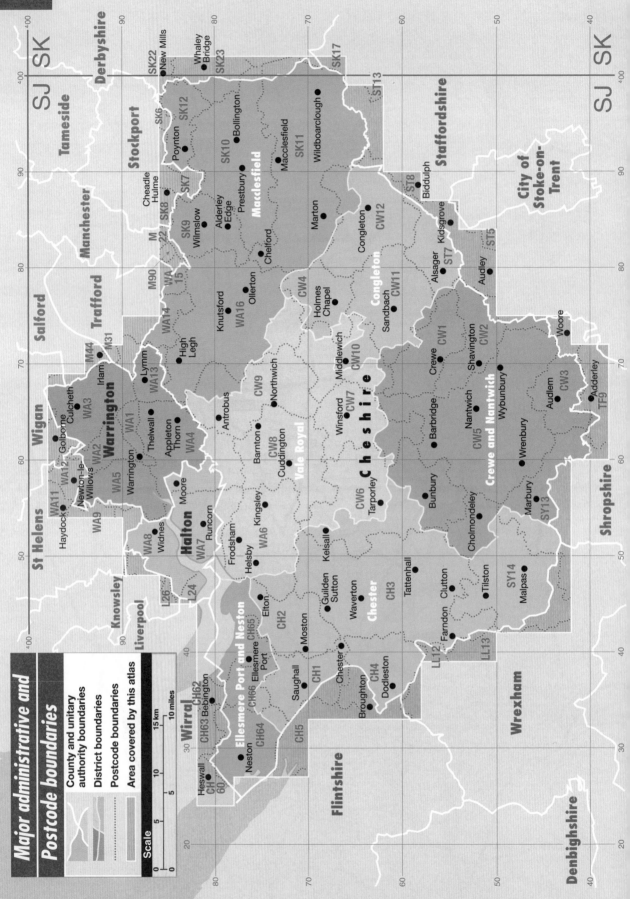

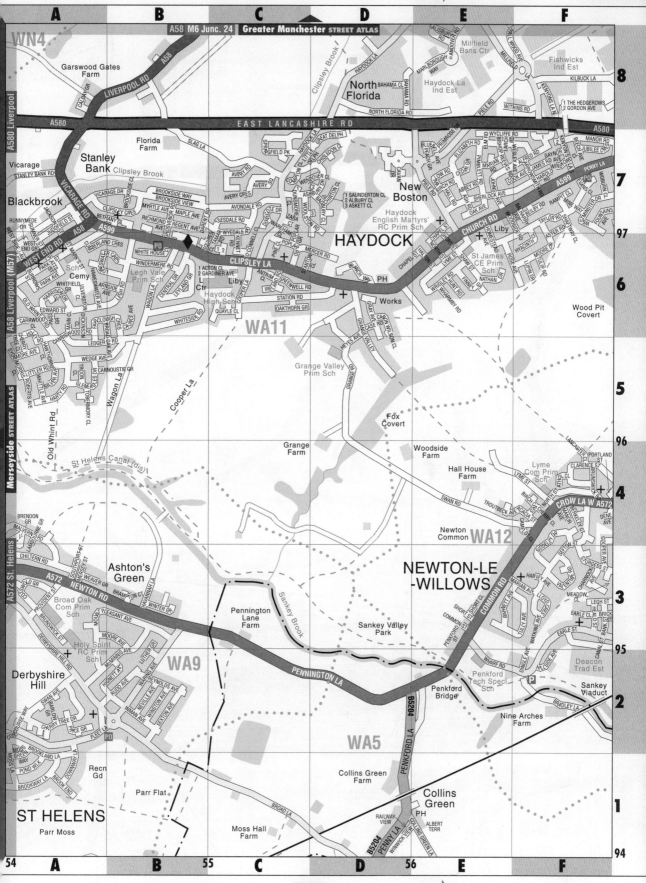

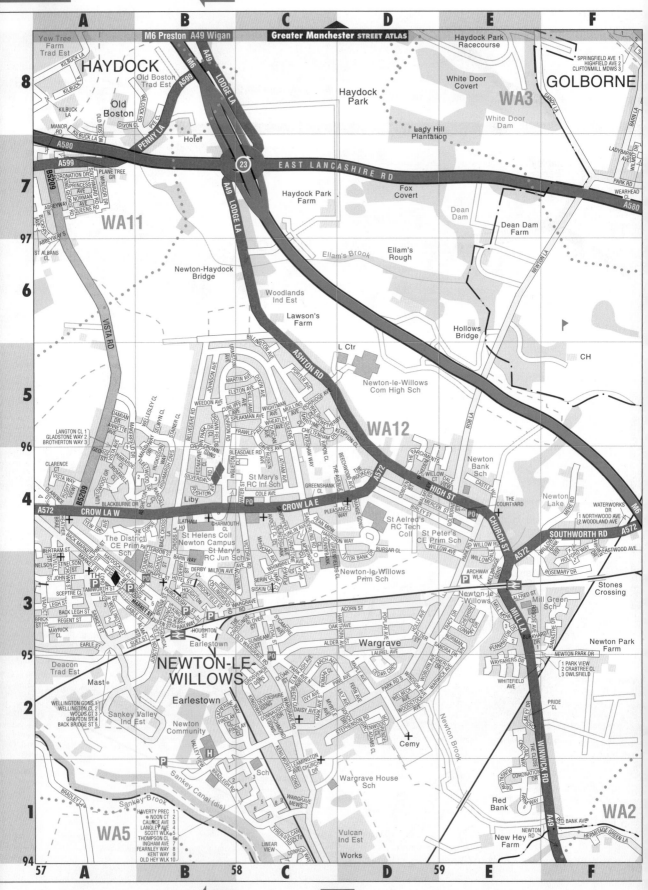

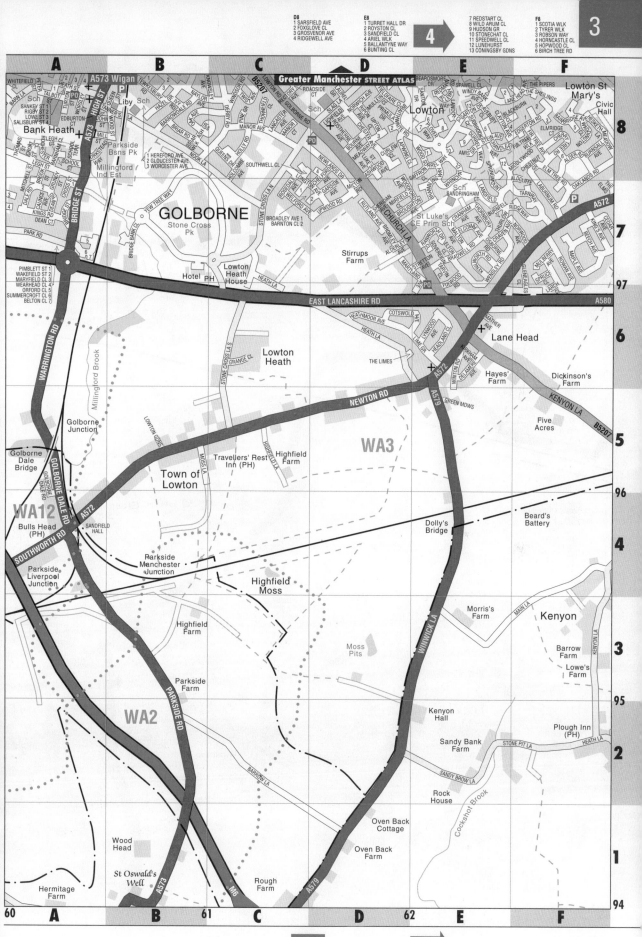

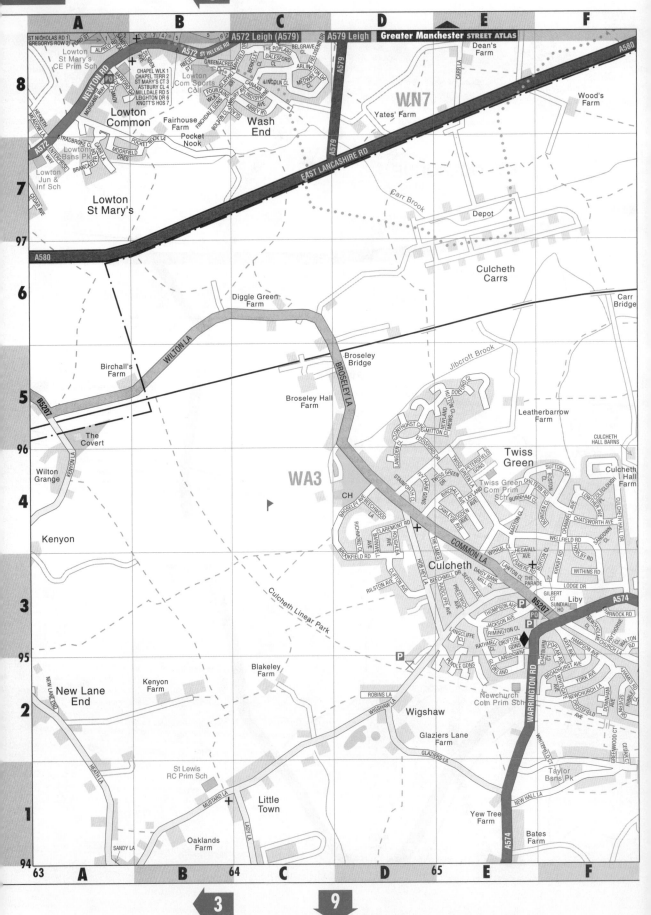

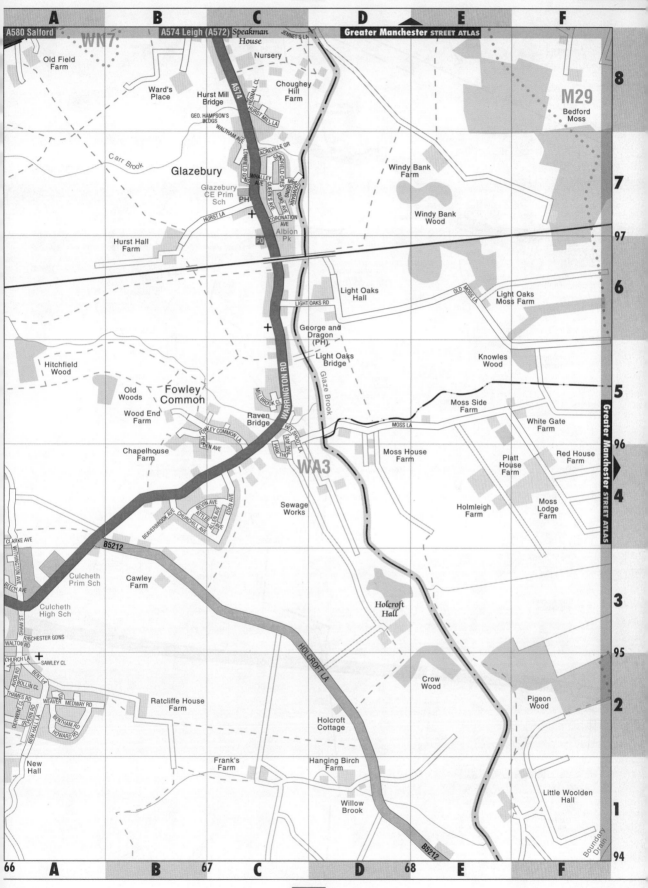

A   B   C   D   E   F

A580 Salford   A574 Leigh (A572)

WN7

Speakman House

JENNET'S LN

Nursery

Old Field Farm

Ward's Place

Hurst Mill Bridge

GEO. HAMPSON'S BLDGS

HESWALL CL

HURST MILL LA

WALTHAM AVE

Choughey Hill Farm

ACREVILLE GR

LOWFIELD GDNS

SANDFIELD CRES

MEADOWBANK

GLAZEBROOK

Glazebury

WHALLEY AVE

QUEEN'S AVE

DUKE AVE

CORONATION AVE

HURST LA

Carr Brook

Glazebury CE Prim Sch

PH

PO

Albion Pk

M29

Bedford Moss

Windy Bank Farm

Windy Bank Wood

8

7

97

Hurst Hall Farm

Light Oaks Hall

LIGHT OAKS RD

OLD MOSS LA

Light Oaks Moss Farm

6

Hitchfield Wood

George and Dragon (PH)

Light Oaks Bridge

WARRINGTON RD

Glaze Brook

Knowles Wood

Old Woods

Fowley Common

MILLBROOK LA

Wood End Farm

Raven Bridge

FOWLEY COMMON LA

HEBDEN AVE

EDEN AVE

HEY SHOOT LA

HAWTHO

Moss Side Farm

MOSS LA

White Gate Farm

Red House Farm

5

96

Chapelhouse Farm

BEVIN AVE

ATTLEE AVE

ATTLEE AVE

EDEN AVE

WA3

Moss House Farm

Platt House Farm

Moss Lodge Farm

Sewage Works

Holmleigh Farm

4

BEAVERBROOK AVE

CHURCHILL AVE

CLARKE AVE

WITHINGTON AVE

BEECH AVE

B5212

Culcheth Prim Sch

Cawley Farm

Holcroft Hall

Crow Wood

Pigeon Wood

3

95

Culcheth High Sch

ST SHAWS

RIBCHESTER GDNS

WALTON RD

CHURCH RD

Sawley Cl

AVON RD

BOLLIN CL

BENT LA

THAMES RD

DERWENT RD

WEAVER

MEDWAY RD

SEVERN RD

NEW HALL LA

BENTHAM RD

HOWARD RD

HOLCROFT LA

Ratcliffe House Farm

Holcroft Cottage

2

New Hall

Frank's Farm

Hanging Birch Farm

Willow Brook

B5212

Little Woolden Hall

Boundary Drain

1

66   A   B   67   C   D   68   E   F   94

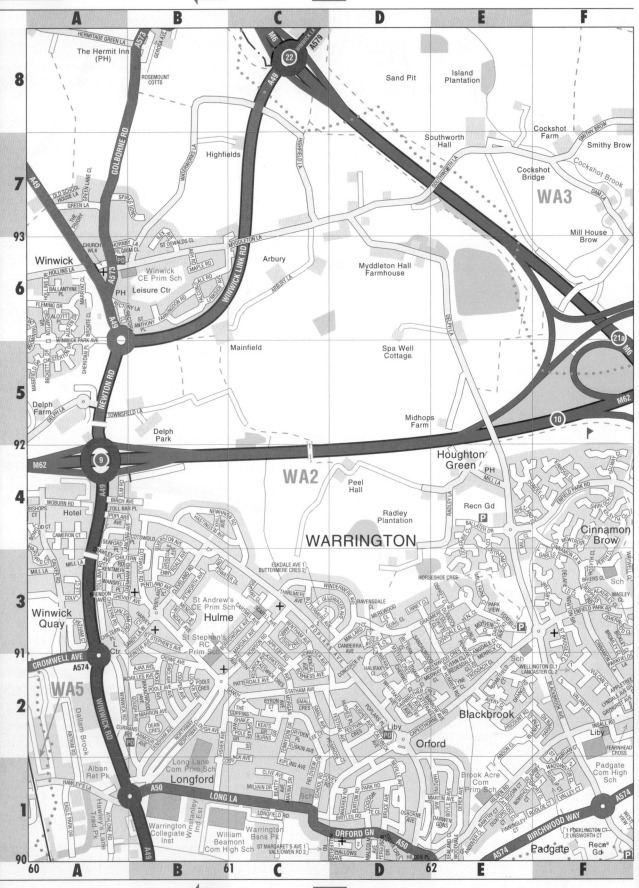

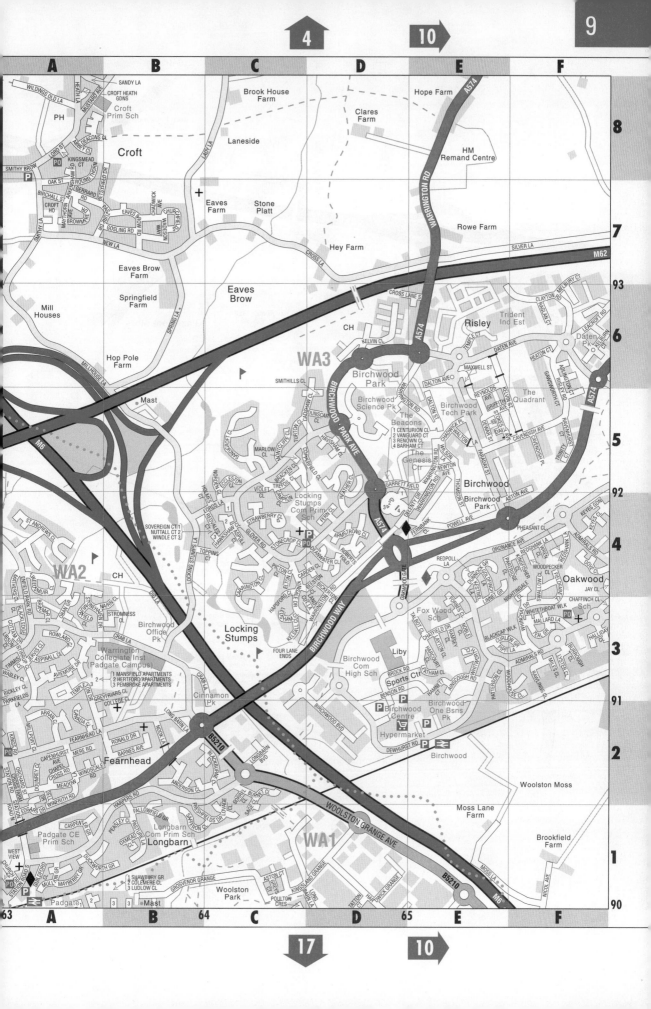

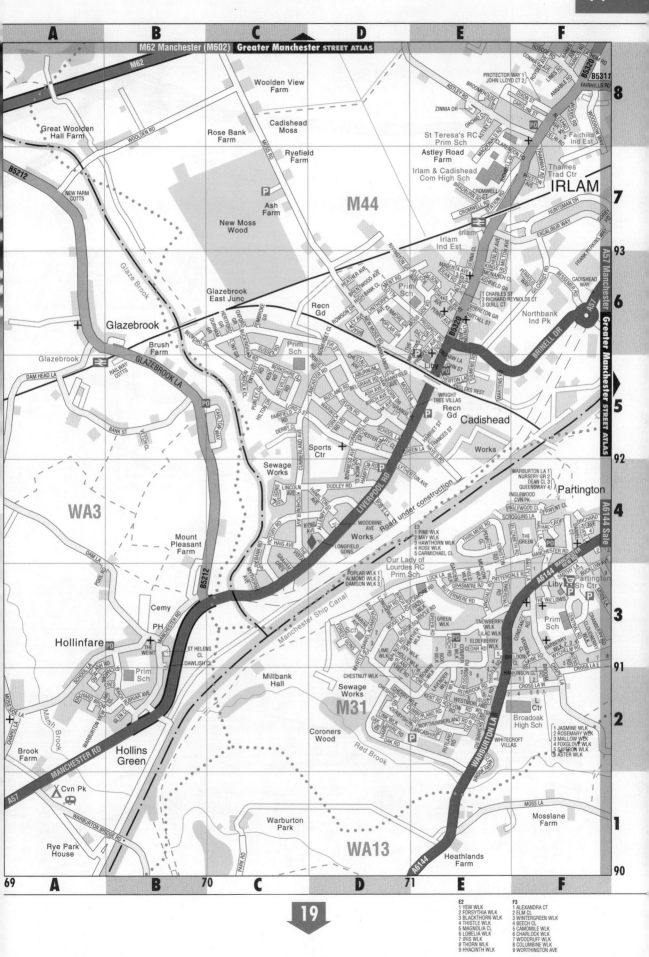

M62 Manchester (M602) **Greater Manchester** STREET ATLAS

M62

B5212

Great Woolden
Hall Farm

New Farm
Cotts

Woolden View
Farm

Cadishead
Moss

Rose Bank
Farm

Ryefield
Farm

Ash
Farm

New Moss
Wood

M44

WOOLDEN RD

MOSS RD

Glaze Brook

Glazebrook
East Junc

Glazebrook

Brush
Farm

Glazebrook

Railway
Cotts

Dam Head La

GLAZEBROOK LA

Bedford Gr

Durham Gr
Hertford Gr
Oxford Gr Buckingham Gr

Flint Gr
Norfolk Cl

Pembroke Gr

Recn
Gd

Prim
Sch

Sussex

B5212

Carlow Way

Veitch Cl

Bank St

PO

Berkshire Gr
Melville Cl
Kent Rd
Purley Cl
Hilton Dr

Dorset Rd
Lancaster Rd
Rutland Rd
Warwick Av

Belgrave Av

Chestnut
Rd

Birch Av
Grange Rd

Ash Av

Laburnum

Bakfield

Moss La

Sussex Rd

Fairfield
Rd

Lord's St

Derby Cl

Devon Rd

York Rd

School La

Chester Rd
Mary Cl

Pim Cl

Green La

Harriet St
Frances St

Prim
Sch

Rowson Dr
Rowson Cl

Level Av
Brookhouse Av
Nook Av

Heather Av
Brettwood Av
High Bank Cl

Kent Gr

Lynthorpe

Kenmore Gr
New Moss Rd

Poplar Gr

Dales Gr
Prospect Av

Rivington Rd

Nelson Dr

Magenta Av
Dean Rd
Drake Av

B5320

Kings Rd
Monarch Cl
Ashfield Gr

1 Charles St
2 Richard Reynolds Ct

Penry Av
Brereton Gr
Nuttall St

Denshaw La
John St

Atherton Rd
Anglers Rest

Wright
Tree Villas

Recn
Gd

Martens Rd

Cadishead

Works

Northbank
Ind Pk

BRINELL DR

A57

IRLAM

Roscoe Rd
Conway Rd
Royce Av

Lines Rd

B5320
B5311
FAIRHILLS RD

Astley Rd

Broomedge

Protector Way 1
John Lloyd Ct 2

Zinnia Dr
Orchid Dr

Caroline St
Dixon St

Delhi Rd

Clarendon Rd

Cromwell
Ct
Bradburn Gr
Station Rd

Cromwell Rd

Irlam
Ind Est

St Teresa's RC
Prim Sch

Astley Road
Farm

Irlam & Cadishead
Com High Sch

Macdonald Rd
Thorley Cl

Preston Av

Tramway Rd

Fairhills
Ind Est

Woodrow Way

Fairhills Way

Alexandra Av

Thames
Trad Ctr

Huntsman Dr

Excalibur Way

Frank Perkins Way

Derby Rd

Ferrous
Way

Gilchrist Rd
Bessemer Rd

Cadishead
Way

Irlam

Henley Av
Milton Av

Liby

Mount
Pleasant
Farm

WA3

Dam La

Pool Rd

Cemy

PH

PO

THE
WEINT

Manchester Rd

Hollinfare

School La

SCHOOL LA

Richard Brown Cres

Glen Cl
D Briar Av

Prim
Sch

St Helens
Cl

Dawlish Cl

Cheshire Rd

Millbank
Hall

Chestnut Wlk

Sewage
Works

M31

Coroners
Wood

Red Brook

Cvn Pk

Warburton Bridge Rd

Rye Park
House

A57

Marsh Brook

Chapel La

Moss Side La

Brook
Farm

**Hollins
Green**

PARK RD

Warburton
Park

WA13

Sewage
Works

LIVERPOOL RD

Victory Rd

Haig Av

Lincoln
Av
Kitchener Av

Hamilton Av

Byng Av
Allenby Rd

Seabank Rd

Sewage
Works

Sports
Ctr

Dudley Rd

Woodbine
Av

Works

Longfield
Gdns

Myrtle Av
Daniel Adams Av

Forest
Gdns

Marine
Av

Oak Rd

Lime
Wlks

Sycamore
Rd

Hazel
Wlk

Maple Rd

Cedar Rd

Larch
Rd

E3
1 Pine Wlk
2 May Wlk
3 Hawthorn Wlk
4 Rose Wlk
5 Carmichael Cl

Our Lady of
Lourdes RC
Prim Sch

Lock La

POPLAR WLK 1
ALMOND WLK 2
DAMSON WLK 3

Manchester Ship Canal

Patterdale Rd

Grasmere Rd

Buttermere Rd

Langdale Rd

Green
Wlk

Snowberry
Wlk
Lilac Wlk

Elderberry
Wlk

Redbrook Rd

Kent Rd

Lavender
Wlk

Cherry Wlk

Cumberland Rd
Westmorland

Derbyshire Rd
Northumberland Rd

Oak Rd

Rutland Rd

Warburton La 1
Nursery Gr 2
Dean Cl 3
Queensway 4

Inglewood
Cvn Pk

Inglewood Cl

Derwent Cl

Scroggins La

THE
GREEN

A6144

Manchester Rd

Smithy
Gr

Bucklow Av

Cranberry Rd
Cloudberry Rd

Central Rd

Cross La E

Constance Rd

Verbena
Av
Barberry Wlk
Wychelm Rd

Broom
Rd

Cross La W

Whitecroft
Villas

Broadoak
High Sch

L
Ctr

Partington

Liby

Partington
Sh Ctr

Prim
Sch

THE
WILLOWS

A6144 Sale

1 Alexandra Ct
2 Elm Cl
3 Wintergreen Wlk
4 Beech Wlk
5 Camomile Wlk
6 Charlock Wlk
7 Woodruff Wlk
8 Columbine Wlk
9 Worthington Av

1 Jasmine Wlk
2 Rosemary Wlk
3 Mallow Wlk
4 Foxglove Wlk
5 Saffron Wlk
6 Aster Wlk

WARBURTON LA

A6144

Heathlands
Farm

Mosslane
Farm

MOSS LA

E2
1 YEW WLK
2 FORSYTHIA WLK
3 BLACKTHORN WLK
4 THISTLE WLK
5 MAGNOLIA CL
6 LOBELIA WLK
7 IRIS WLK
8 THORN WLK
9 HYACINTH WLK

F3
1 ALEXANDRA CT
2 ELM CL
3 WINTERGREEN WLK
4 BEECH WLK
5 CAMOMILE WLK
6 CHARLOCK WLK
7 WOODRUFF WLK
8 COLUMBINE WLK
9 WORTHINGTON AVE

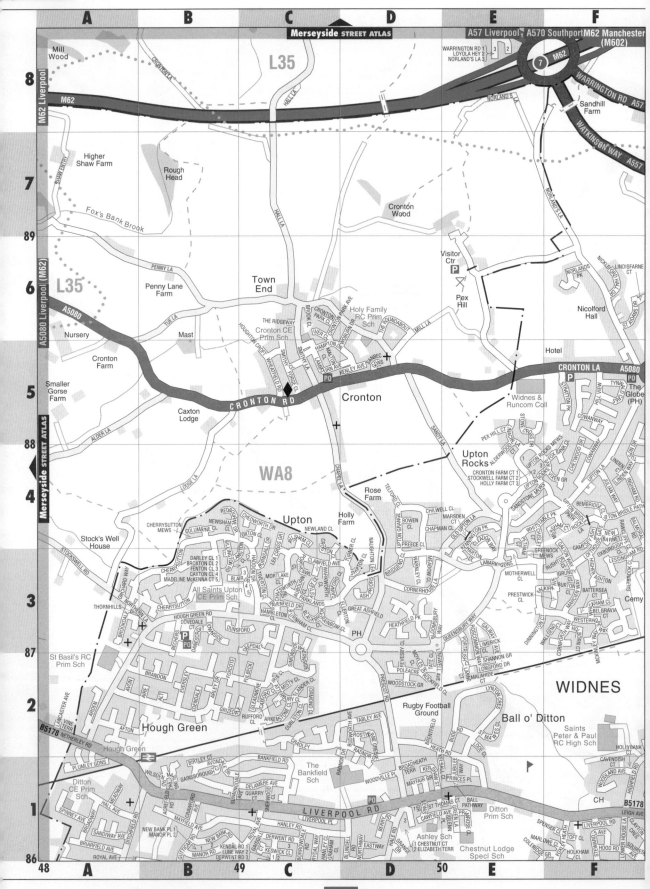

Merseyside STREET ATLAS

A569 St Helens (A570)

WA8

WA5

A1
1 CLAYTON CRES
2 HENDERSON RD
3 SQUIRES AVE
4 BRUNNER RD
5 MOND RD

B1
1 ALBERT SQ
2 ALBERT RD
3 BROOK ST
4 SAXON TERR

B2
1 HAWTHORN AVE
2 WILLOW AVE
3 LIME AVE
4 PINE AVE
5 MAPLE AVE
6 PLUMPTON CROSS

C1
1 PARR ST
2 RUNNYMEDE CT
3 CLIFFE ST
4 HENRY ST
5 RUNNYMEDE GDNS

C2
1 BROOKLANDS PK
2 KNOWLES ST
3 RUNNYMEDE WLK

D1
1 ASHFORD WAY
2 MELVILLE CL
3 KINGHAM CL
4 WILSON CL
5 HARGREAVES HO

A B C D E F

8

Eccles
Plantation

Finch's
Plantation

Lingley Mere
Bsns Pk

Lingley
Mere

South Park
Plantation

Lingley Green Ave

P

L Ctr

BILLINGTON CL

BAINBRIDGE CRES
STOCKPOOL CL
LONSDALE CL

MALHAM
CL

WENSLEYDALE CL

7

Bargyloo

A57

WARRINGTON RD

Park
Farm

ALVERSTONE
CL

Whittle Brook

Great Sankey
High Sch

Barrow Hall
Com Prim Sch

Brow
Farm

BLUE BRIDGE CL

HORNBY DALE AVE
BRANSDALE CL
FARNDALE DR
GISBURN DR
WIDDALE CL

AIREDALE CL

COVERDALE CL
TEESDALE CL
SWALEDALE CL
DEEP DALE
ALDERBANK

89

Dawson
House

Lingley
Green

FORELAND CL

CARWELL CL
TOTLAND CL

MAYFAIR CL

CRONULLA DR
WARWICK
STANLEY AVE
YORK AVE
PRINCESS AVE

PARK RD

HALL TERR
DRS DR
SUNNY'S

NORTH VIEW

CHESTNUT AVE
CONIFER
ROWAN CEDARS
VINE CRES

CHARLESDALE RD
WILMOT AVE

6

Hayfield
Farm

SANDY LA

SOUTH LANE ENTRY

Greenside
Farm

The
Trigger
Pond
(PH)

SHANKLIN CL

RUSCOM CL
MURIEL CL
ALDER CL
HILARY CL

PYCROFT CL

FRASER CL
PYCROFT RD
GEORGE
VICTORIA

LINGLEY
PH
KINTORE CL
SANDERSON CL
KEITH AVE
CRESC

WROXHAM RD

RANWORTH RD

SHERINGHAM RD
NORFOLK CL

WESBURY DR
LINGWOOD RD

CAMPBELL CRES

HAWTHORNE AVE

Laburnum
Farm

Liverpool Rd

HENDON CL
EDWARD
CLARENCE
FRIENDS LA

LIVERPOOL RD

YARMOUTH RD

Sankey
For
Penketh

A57

PO

5

WA8

Sandy Lane
Farm

WARRINGTON

LABURNUM

SOUTHWAY

ALBERT RD
BROOK CL

HADLEY

BRIGHTWELL
CL

FRIARS AVE

WALTON AVE

ST STEPHEN
THE DALE
ST MARY'S DR
ST MARY'S RD

CUNNINGHAM

THE
WILLOWS

SUSAN
DR
GROARKE
DR

DENISE
AVE
NORTON AVE

LARCH AVE

HELSTON CL
MEETING LA

HOLLY AVE
WINDMILL LA
ST ALBAN

WALSINGHAM RD

BURNHAM RD

HEATH RD

Sch

88

Camp
(dis)

A5080

SUNNY BANK
COTTS

Penketh Com
Prim Sch

KESWICK DR
CONISTON AVE
STOCKS LA

ACOMBE RD
PAIGNTON
CL
BIDEFORD RD
LYNTON
RD

JUBILEE AVE

WILLIAM PENN CL
HONITON WAY

AVON
AVE

CHERRY
TREE AVE

Liby

HILLSIDE
GR

AINSDALE RD
HESKETH

FORMBY CL

CORONATION DR
THE BROW

Recn
Gd

4

Four Top'd
Oak

SOUTH LA

Brook
Farm

FARNWORTH RD

Penketh

A5080

LAMERTON CL
TAVISTOCK RD

WITHCOMBE DR
ELLESMERE DR

Victoria
Rd

BANK
GDNS

BROAD OAK AVE
DAISY BANK RD

ARLINGTON DR
PORLOCK CL

DENEHURST

MARY RD
MARL HOOK
OAK RD
SOUTHLANDS
ONAMERE DR

ASH RD
MYRTLE CRES

MANSTON

A562

WARRINGTON RD

3

Fowl
Farm

MOWCROFT LA

BACK LA

Doe
Green

CUERDLEY RD
BEECH AVE

MENLYN GDNS
HAMLIN
GDNS

PENROSE
GDNS

THE PARK

FRAGAN DR
ST AUSTELL CL
PADSTOW

LAUNCESTON DR

BRAMBLE CL

FENHAM
DR

PERRYN
DR
BEADNELL DR

WELL LA

WOODLEY
FOLD

St Vincent's
RC Prim Sch

STANSTEAD AVE 1
HAMBLE DR 2

MANSTON

87

CUERDLEY GN

A562

Cuerdley
Cross

TAYLOR'S LA

Cross Lane Farm
Cottages

NEWSPAPER
HO

CAL STOCK CL

RAGLETT CL

FINLAY AVE
DITCHFIELD RD

Penketh South
Com Prim Sch

LC

PH

WRIGHTS LA

CH

WA5

FALMOUTH DR
ROTHAY DR
ROEBURN

WALKERS LA

POLPERRO CL
STATION RD
SALISBURY

CHAP
BRIMELOW
CRES

LC

Trans Pennine Trail

2

P

Marsh End
Farm

River Mersey

Ferry Inn
(PH)

Swing
Bridge

LC

1

Power
Station

LC

Riverside
Trad Est

Fiddler's
Ferry

St Helens Canal
(disused)

Fiddler's Ferry Reach

WA4

86

54 A 55 B C 56 D E F

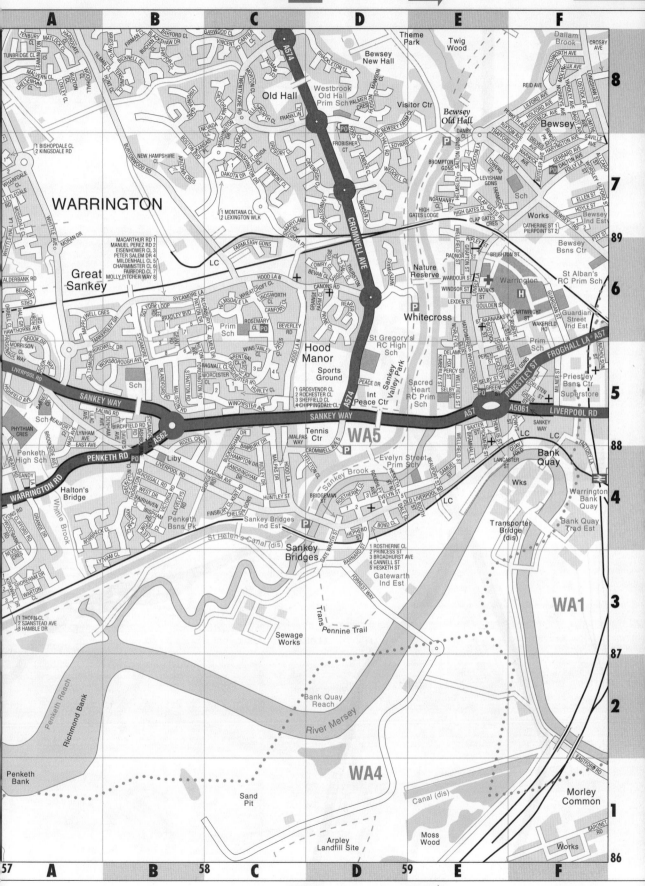

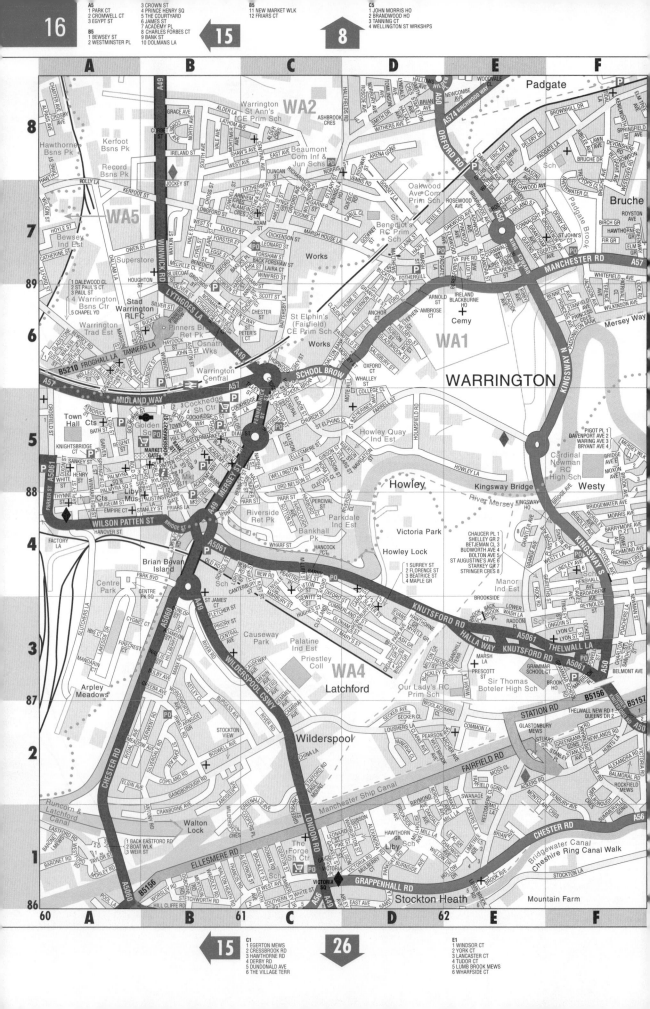

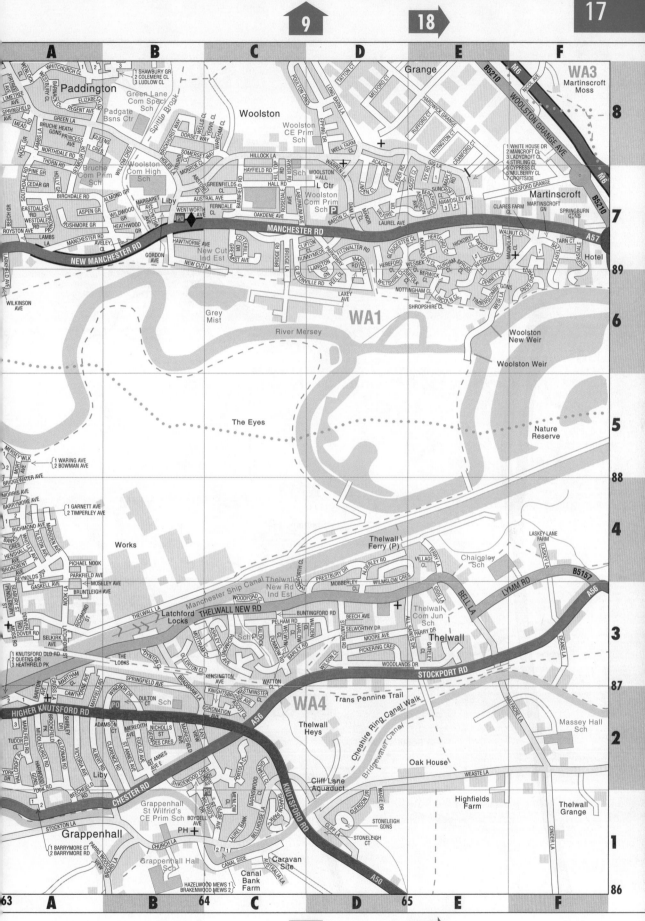

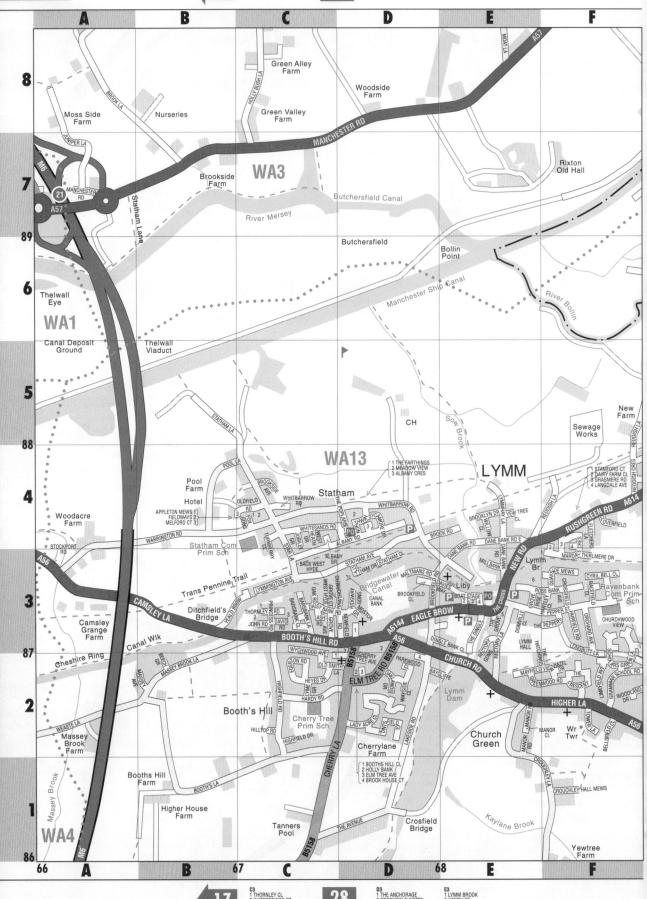

A B C D E F

C3
1 THORNLEY CL
2 WATERBRIDGE CT
3 BRIDGEWATER CT

D3
1 THE ANCHORAGE
2 BROOKFIELD COTTS
3 BOOTHS HILL HO

E3
1 LYMM BROOK
2 HENRY ST
3 LEGH ST
4 BRIDGEWATER ST
5 THIRLMERE LODGE
6 THE SQUARE

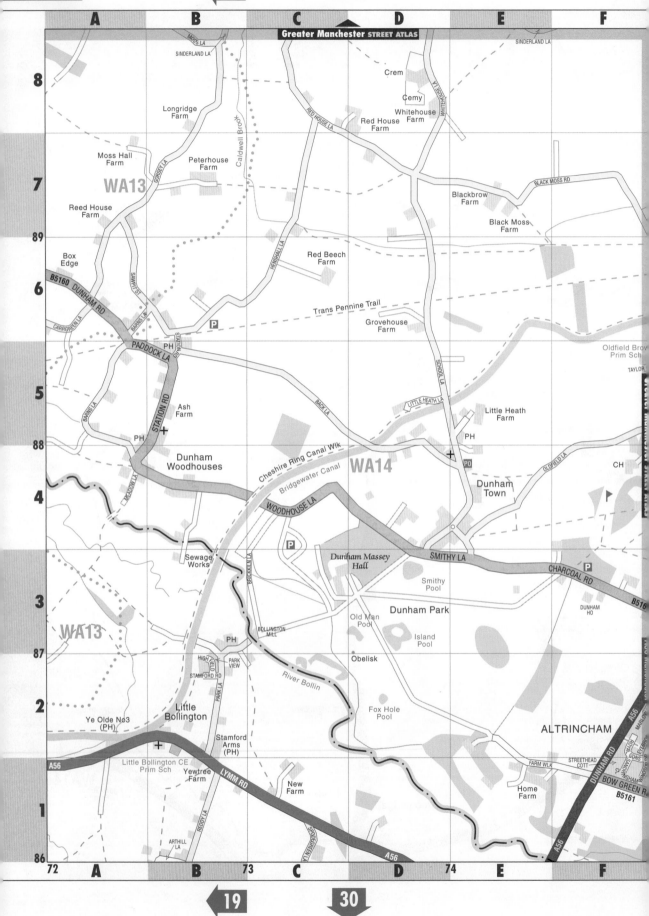

Greater Manchester STREET ATLAS

SINDERLAND LA

MOSS LA

Crem

Cemy

Whitehouse Farm

Red House Farm

Longridge Farm

RED HOUSE LA

Moss Hall Farm

Peterhouse Farm

GORSEY LA

Caldwell Brook

WA13

Blackbrow Farm

BLACK MOSS RD

Black Moss Farm

Reed House Farm

Box Edge

SAMPIT LA

HERSHALL LA

Red Beech Farm

89

6

B5160 DUNHAM RD

BARNS LA

CARROGREEN LA

PADDOCK LA

STATION RD

PH

P

Trans Pennine Trail

Grovehouse Farm

SCHOOL LA

Oldfield Brow Prim Sch

TAYLOR

5

Ash Farm

PH

BARNS LA

STATION RD

BACK LA

LITTLE HEATH LA

Little Heath Farm

PH

PO

CH

88

Dunham Woodhouses

MEDOCK LA

Cheshire Ring Canal Wlk

Bridgewater Canal

WA14

Dunham Town

OLDFIELD LA

4

WOODHOUSE LA

P

Dunham Massey Hall

SMITHY LA

CHARCOAL RD

B516

3

Sewage Works

BRICKKILN LA

Smithy Pool

Dunham Park

Old Man Pool

Island Pool

DUNHAM HO

WA13

PH

BOLLINGTON MILL

Obelisk

87

HIGH FIELD

PARK VIEW

STAMFORD RD

River Bollin

Fox Hole Pool

ALTRINCHAM

2

Ye Olde No3 (PH)

Little Bollington

PARK LA

Stamford Arms (PH)

DUNHAM RD

BOW GREEN RD

STREETHEAD COTT

FARM WLK

Home Farm

B5161

A56

Little Bollington CE Prim Sch

Yewtree Farm

LYMM RD

New Farm

A56

1

ARTHILL LA

REDDY LA

SPRINGFIELD LA

A56

86

72   73   74

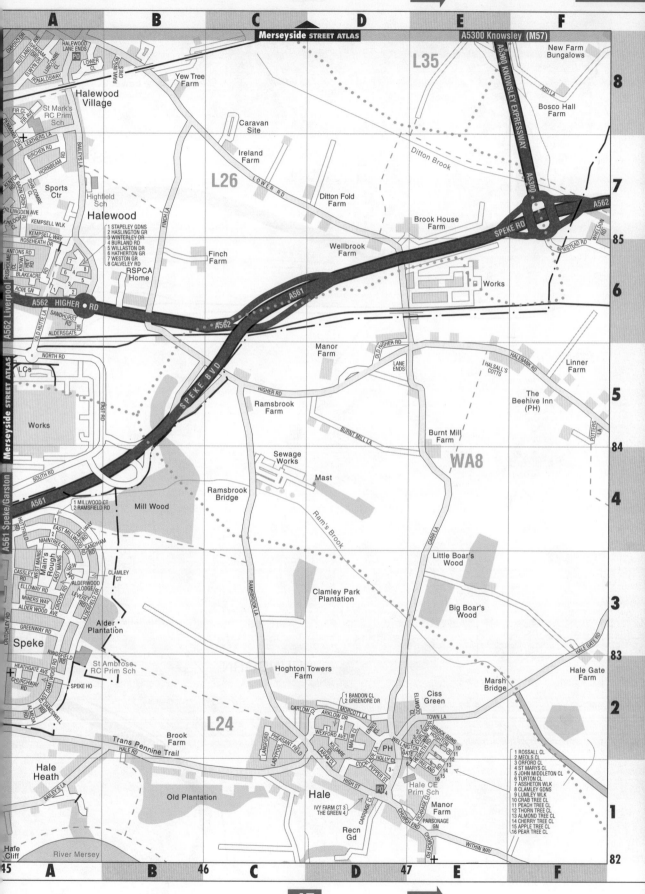

Merseyside STREET ATLAS

A5300 Knowsley (M57)

A B C D E F

New Farm
Bungalows

8

L35

Halewood
Village

Yew Tree
Farm

Caravan
Site

Bosco Hall
Farm

St Mark's
RC Prim
Sch

Ireland
Farm

L26

Ditton Brook

7

Sports
Ctr

Highfield
Sch

LOWER RD

Ditton Fold
Farm

A5300

A562

85

Halewood

Brook House
Farm

FINCH LA

1 STAPELEY GDNS
2 HASLINGTON GR
3 WINTERLEY DR
4 BURLAND RD
5 WILLASTON DR
6 HATHERTON GR
7 WESTON GR
8 CALVELEY RD

Finch
Farm

Wellbrook
Farm

SPEKE RD

A562

NEWSTEAD RD

WHELDON

6

RSPCA
Home

A561

Works

A562 HIGHER RD

A562

ALDERSGATE

NORTH RD

Manor
Farm

OLD HIGHER RD

HALEBANK RD

Linner
Farm

LCs

EAST RD

SPEKE BVD

HIGHER RD

LANE
ENDS

HALSALL'S
COTTS

The
Beehive Inn
(PH)

5

Works

Ramsbrook
Farm

BURNT MILL LA

Burnt Mill
Farm

POTTERS LA

84

SOUTH RD

WA8

A561

Sewage
Works

Mast

4

1 MILLWOOD CT
2 RAMSFIELD RD

Mill Wood

Ramsbrook
Bridge

Ram's Brook

RAMSBROOK LA

CARR LA

Little Boar's
Wood

Main's
Rough

CLAMLEY
CT

Clamley Park
Plantation

Big Boar's
Wood

HALE GATE RD

3

ALDERWOOD
LODGE

83

Speke

Alder
Plantation

St Ambrose
RC Prim Sch

SPEKE HO

Hoghton Towers
Farm

Marsh
Bridge

Ciss
Green

Hale Gate
Farm

2

L24

1 BANDON CL
2 GREENORE DR

MORCOTT LA

ELLWOOD

TOWN LA

BROOK GDNS

CARLOW CL

ARKLOW DR

WELLINGTON GDNS

Trans Pennine Trail

Brook
Farm

HALE RD

PHEASANT FIELD

WEXFORD AVE

MALIN CL

KILDARE

PH

HOLLY CL

IRELAND

1 ROSSALL CL
2 MEOLS CL
3 ORFORD CL
4 ST MARYS CL
5 JOHN MIDDLETON CL
6 TURTON CL
7 ASSHETON WLK
8 CLAMLEY GDNS
9 LUMLEY WLK
10 CRAB TREE CL
11 PEACH TREE CL
12 THORN TREE CL
13 ALMOND TREE CL
14 CHERRY TREE CL
15 APPLE TREE CL
16 PEAR TREE CL

Hale
Heath

HIGH ST

COCK PEPPER ST

Hale

PO

Hale CE
Prim Sch

Manor
Farm

1

Old Plantation

IVY FARM CT 3
THE GREEN 4

CARRIAGE CL

CHURCH RD

PARSONAGE
GN

Recn
Gd

CHURCH END

VICARAGE CL

Hale
Cliff

River Mersey

WITHIN WAY

82

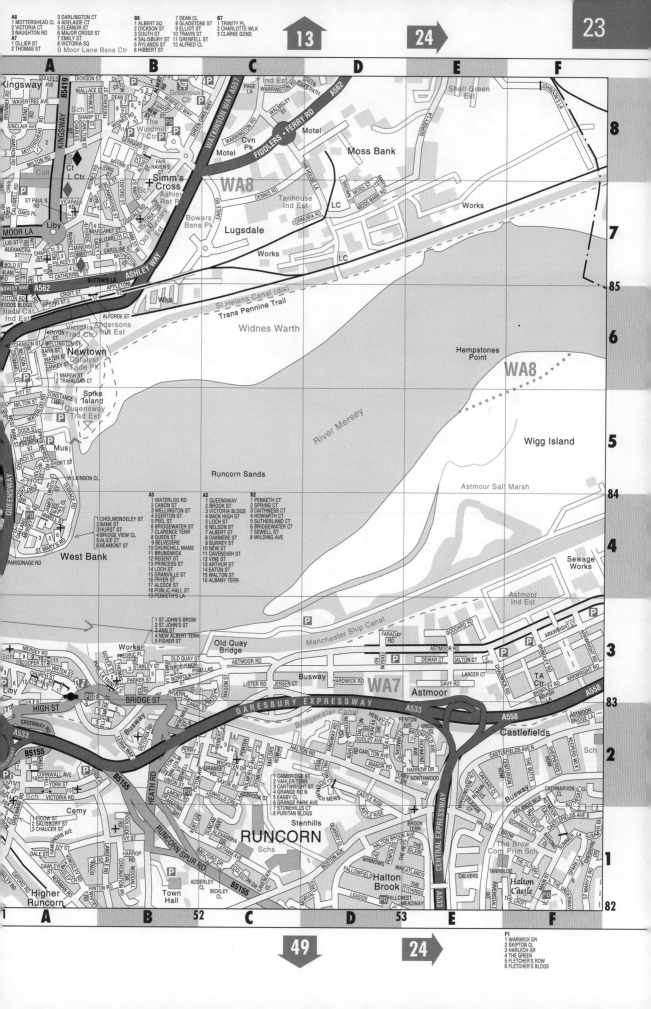

Fiddlers Ferry Power Station

St Helens Canal (disused)

Trans Pennine Way

WA5

WA8

Moss Side Farm

Moss Side

Norton Marsh

WA4

Upper Moss-Side Farm

MOSS SIDE LA

LAPWING LA

Cuerdley Marsh

River Mersey

WA7

Halton Moss

Manchester Ship Canal

EASTGATE RD

Wigg Island

Stonedelph Dock

PEMBROKE CT

CHANCELLOR RD

ROKEBY CT

Green Wood

BLACKHEATH LA

GREENWOOD DR

WARRINGTON RD

BEESTON CT

BERKELEY CT

Lodge Plantation

EVENWOOD CL

A558

BATSWATER CL

OAKMOORE

Sewage Works

WARRINGTON RD

CHRISTLETON CT

STUART RD

SARUS CT

HOWARD CT

MANOR PARK AVE

HAMPTON CT

MANOR FARM BARNS

Manor Farm

EASTGATE WAY

SUNNYSIDE LA

GODSTOW

CALMINGTON LA

WOODTHORN CL

KECKWICK LA

NEWMORE LA

1 CHASEWATER
2 FURNESS CT
3 SELBY CL
4 HERONS WAY
5 WALTHAM CT
6 BUCKFAST CT

ARKWRIGHT RD

BUSWAY

Astmoor Ind Est

ASTMOOR EAST INTC

Priory Cottages

LONGBENTON WAY

SEYMOUR CT

AXACON

Manor Park

Norton Priory Walled Gdn

TUDOR RD

BOLEYN CT

DARESBURY EXPRESSWAY

STEVENTON

GLASTONBURY CL

SHERBORNE CL

WHARFORD LA

PITTS HEATH LA

SAXON PK

SANDY M

Keckwick Brook

Poplar Farm

A558

P

P

Norton Priory (remains of)

Mus

Big Wood

WA7

Norton Townfield Bridge

LADY RICHELD CL

DURHAM WAY

RUDHEATH LA

SANDYMOOR LA

HONFORD MOSS

BISHAM PK

P

Haddock's Wood

Bridgewater Canal

RUNCORN

CANAL REACH

LOCKGATE

BRIDGEWAY

TOWNFIELD RD

WINDMILL HILL AVE N

TOWNFIELD

MALMESBURY CL

SHERIDAN WAY

WALSINGHAM WAY

Norton Bridge

Bog Wood

WA4

CASTLEFIELDS AVE N

KINGSHEAD CL

Sch

NIGEL WLK

FITZWILLIAM WLK

JOY ROW

CONWY CT

GREEN BRIDGE CL

CASTLEFIELDS AVE E

PRIORY WOOD

LOCKGATE W

BRIDGEMAN

STONE LEA

WINDMILL HILL AVE S

WINDMILL HILL AVE E

PO

SWINDEN CL

HARVARD CL

CHATTERIS PK

ELY PK

VILLAGE ST

P

ACHILLES CT

CHESTER CT

RICHARD CL

HERON HEY

PLANTATION CL

Sch

GREENBRIDGE RD

STONE LEA

EAST SLOPE

SOUTHWOOD AVE

WOODRIDGE

Windmill Hill Prim Sch

WINDMILL HILL AVE S

WINDMILL HILL AVE E

NORTON HILL

FORD CL

STANLEY CL

NEWBURGH CL

CHORLTON CL

Norton

1 WOLVERTON DR
2 MELLOR CL
3 SEAFORD CL

1 CONSTABLES CL
2 SUMMER CL
3 ST MARY'S RD

SPINNEY WLK

MEADOW ROW

PRIMROSE CL

MERLIN CL

Busway

WOODLAND WLK

KING ARTHUR'S WLK

Pickerings Rough

FERNWOOD

SANDALWOOD

TINNERS FOLD

COPPICE CL

COPPERWOOD

MILLWOOD

GLENWOOD

ELMWOOD

HORNBEAM CL

WHITEBEAM CL

NORTONWOOD LA

Windmill Hill

EALING CL 1
CAMDEN CT 2
GOOSEBERRY LA 3

HIGHGATE CL

ELSMORE CL

TWINTON

Cheshire Ring Canal Walk

Bridgewater Canal

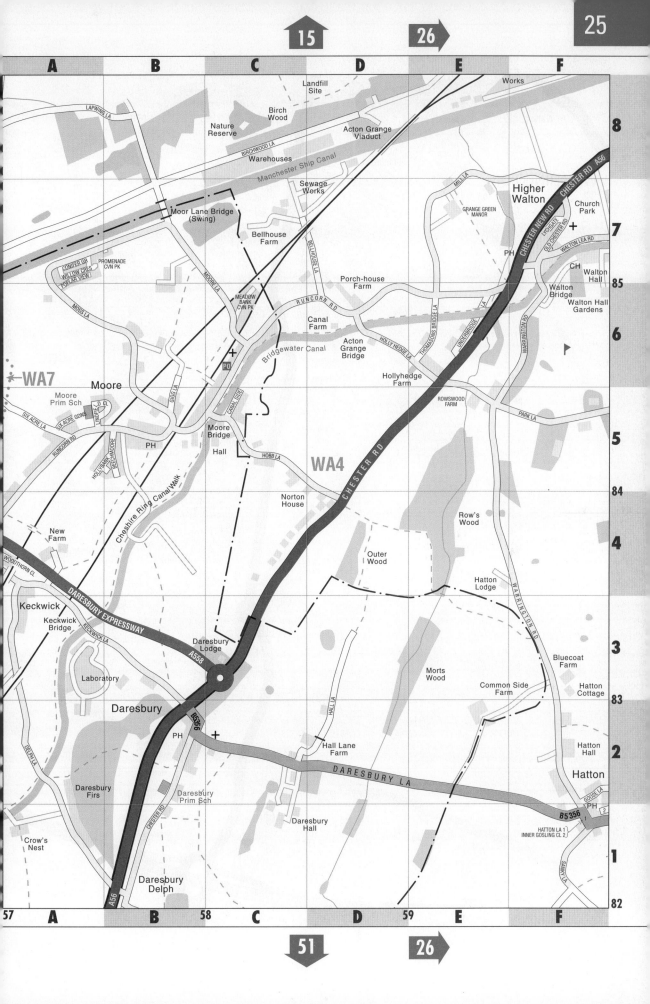

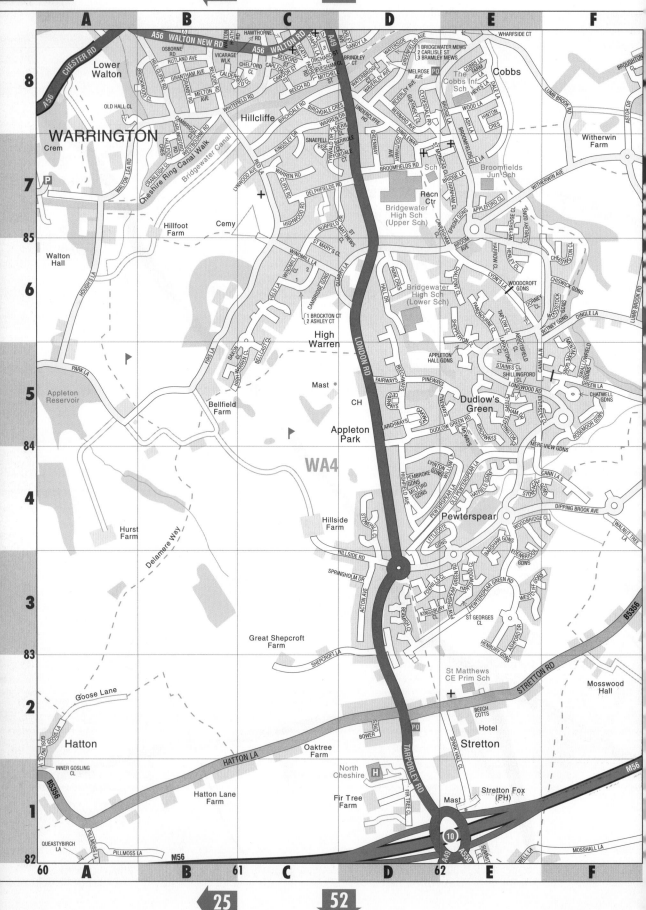

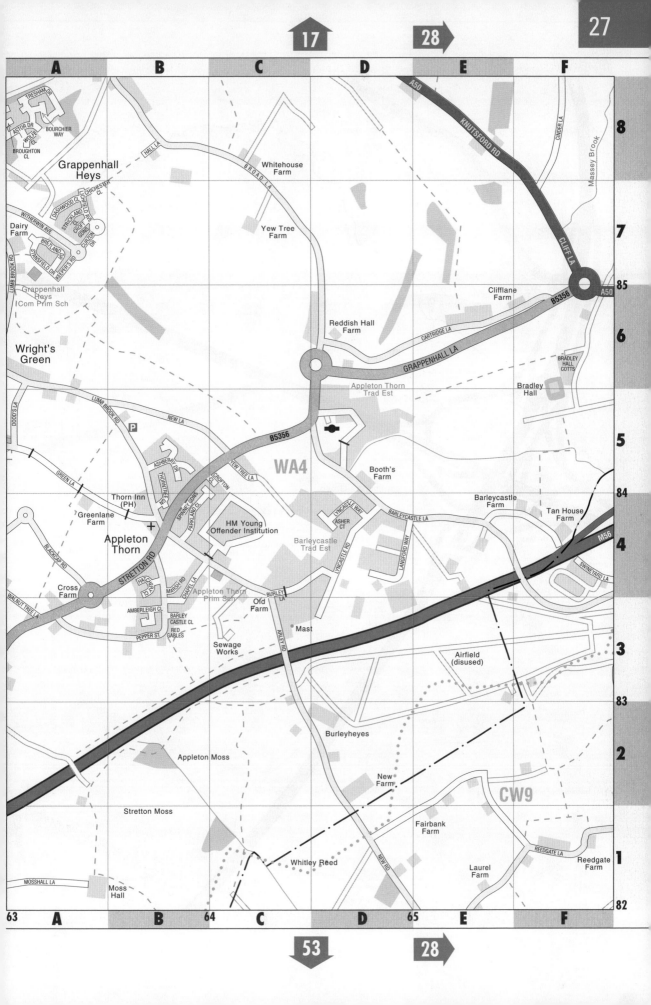

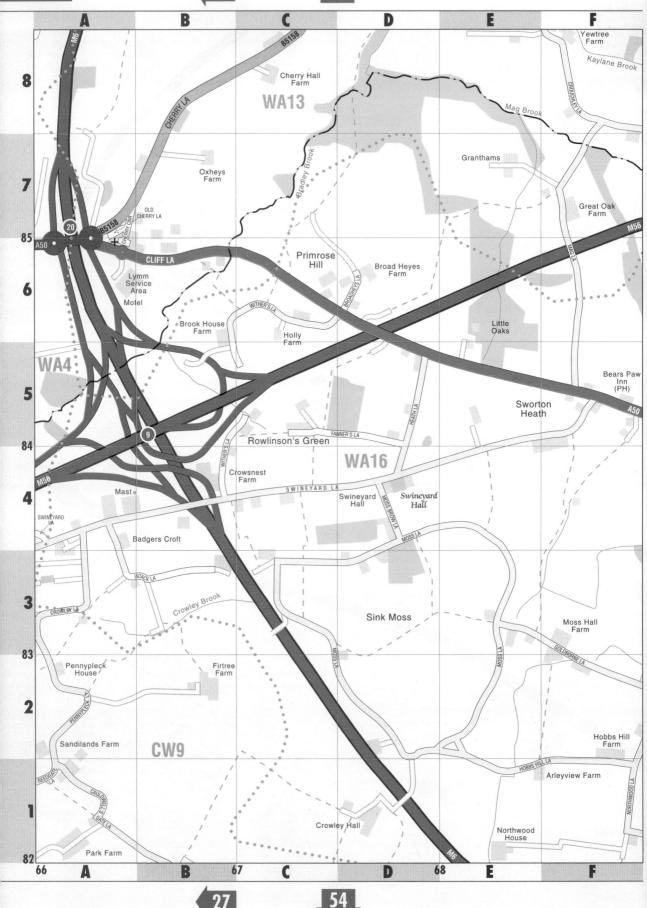
A   B   C   D   E   F

8

WA13

Cherry Hall
Farm

Yewtree
Farm

Kaylane Brook

Mag Brook

B5158

CHERRY LA

Oxheys
Farm

Granthams

7

Bradley Brook

CROUCHLEY LA

Great Oak
Farm

M56

20

B5158

OLD
CHERRY LA

CHERRY CNR

85

A50

CLIFF LA

Primrose
Hill

Broad Heyes
Farm

MAG LA

Lymm
Service
Area

BROADHEY'S LA

6

Motel

WITHER'S LA

Little
Oaks

Brook House
Farm

Holly
Farm

Bears Paw
Inn
(PH)

WA4

Sworton
Heath

5

HEATH LA

A50

9

FANNER'S LA

84

Rowlinson's Green

WITHER'S LA

WA16

Crowsnest
Farm

SWINEYARD LA

Swineyard
Hall

Swineyard
Hall

M56

Mast

MOSS BROW LA

4

SWINEYARD
LA

Badgers Croft

MOSS LA

INTACK LA

3

CROWLEY LA

Crowley Brook

Sink Moss

Moss Hall
Farm

MOSS LA

GOLDBORNE LA

83

Pennypleck
House

Firtree
Farm

PENNYPLECK LA

2

Sandilands Farm

CW9

Hobbs Hill
Farm

HOBBS HILL LA

Arleyview Farm

REEDGATE LA

CAULDWELL'S
GATE LA

NORTHWOOD LA

1

Crowley Hall

Northwood
House

M6

Park Farm

82

66   A   B   67   C   D   68   E   F

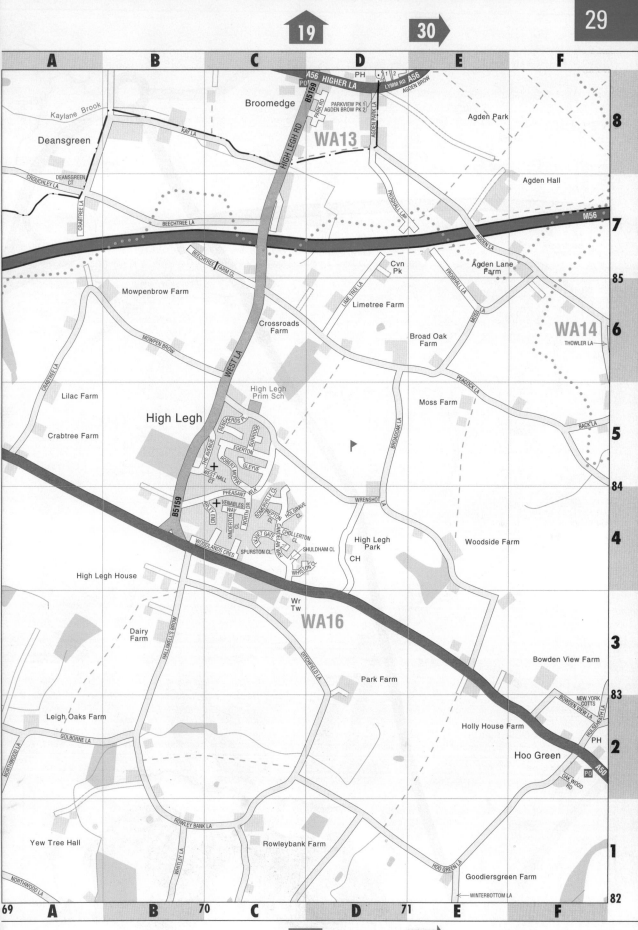

A B C D E F

Kaylane Brook

Broomedge

PARKVIEW PK 1
AGDEN BROW PK 2

A56 HIGHER LA PH

LYMM RD

A56 AGDEN BROW

Agden Park

Deansgreen

KAY LA

HIGH LEGH RD

B5159

PO

PARK RD

WA13

Agden Hall

CROUCHLEY LA

DEANSGREEN CT

CRABTREE LA

BEECHTREE LA

AGDEN PARK LA

FROGHALL LA

AGDEN LA

M56

8

7

85

BEECHTREE FARM CL

Mowpenbrow Farm

MOWPEN BROW

WEST LA

Crossroads
Farm

LIME TREE LA

Cvn
Pk

Limetree Farm

Broad Oak
Farm

FROGHALL LA

MOSS LA

Agden Lane
Farm

WA14

THOWLER LA

6

CRABTREE LA

Lilac Farm

High Legh

High Legh
Prim Sch

PREACHERDS PL

SURRIDGE

EGERTON

GLEYVE

Moss Farm

PEACOCK LA

BROADOAK LA

BACK LA

5

Crabtree Farm

THE AVENUE

ROBERT MOFFAT

WEST HALL CT

84

B5159

ARLEY END

PHEASANT WLK

VENABLES WAY

NORTH DR

KINDERTON CL

SOMERVILLE CL

REPTON CL

HOLGRAVE CL

Wrenshot La

WRENSHOT LA

High Legh
Park

CH

Woodside Farm

4

WOODLANDS CRES

LYMET GATE WAY

SPURSTON CL

CAMDEN WAY

CHOLLERTON
CL

SHULDHAM CL

WHISTON CL

High Legh House

Dairy
Farm

HALLIWELL'S BROW

DITCHFIELD LA

Wr
Tw

WA16

Bowden View Farm

3

Park Farm

NEW YORK
COTTS

83

Leigh Oaks Farm

GOLBORNE LA

NORTHWOOD LA

BOWDEN VIEW LA

HULSEHEATH LA

Holly House Farm

PH

Hoo Green

2

A50

PO

OAK WOOD RD

Yew Tree Hall

ROWLEY BANK LA

WHITLEY LA

Rowleybank Farm

HOO GREEN LA

1

NORTHWOOD LA

Goodiersgreen Farm

WINTERBOTTOM LA

82

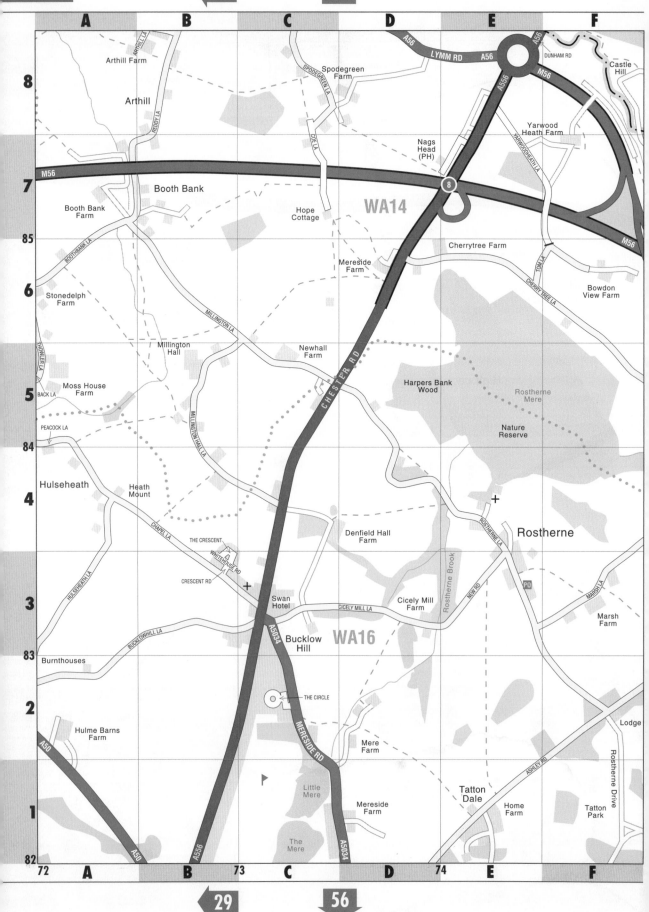

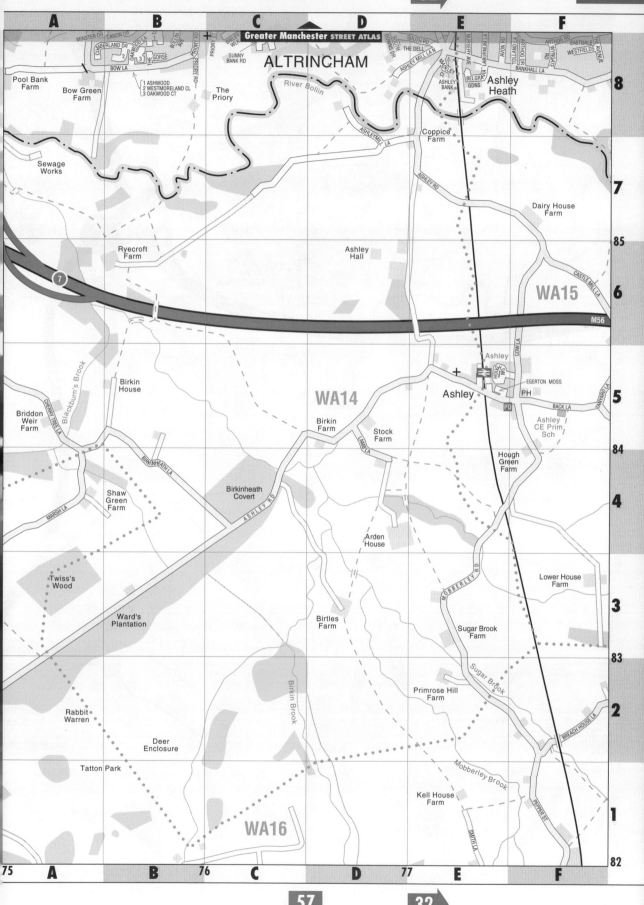

Greater Manchester STREET ATLAS

ALTRINCHAM

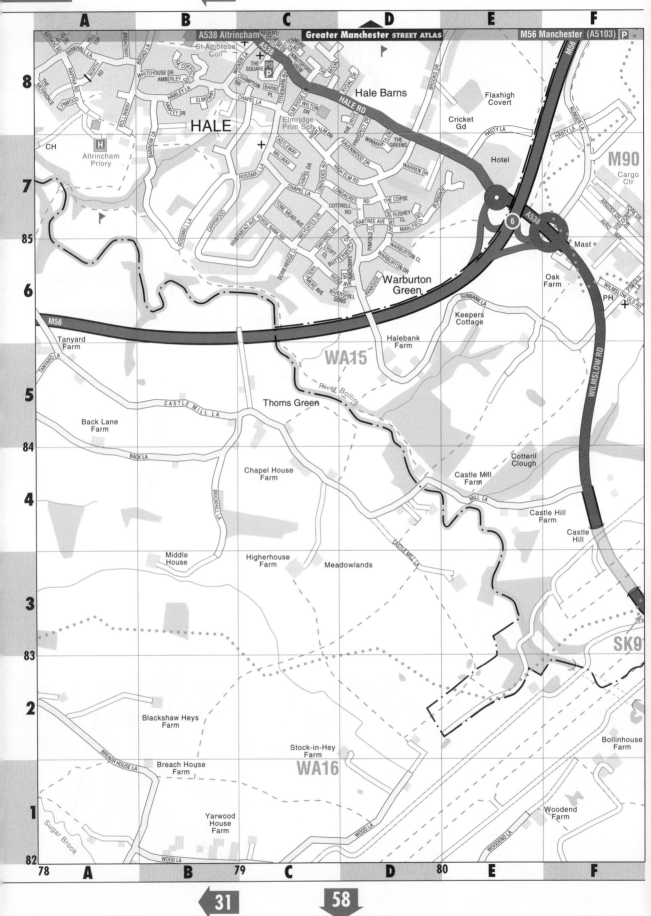

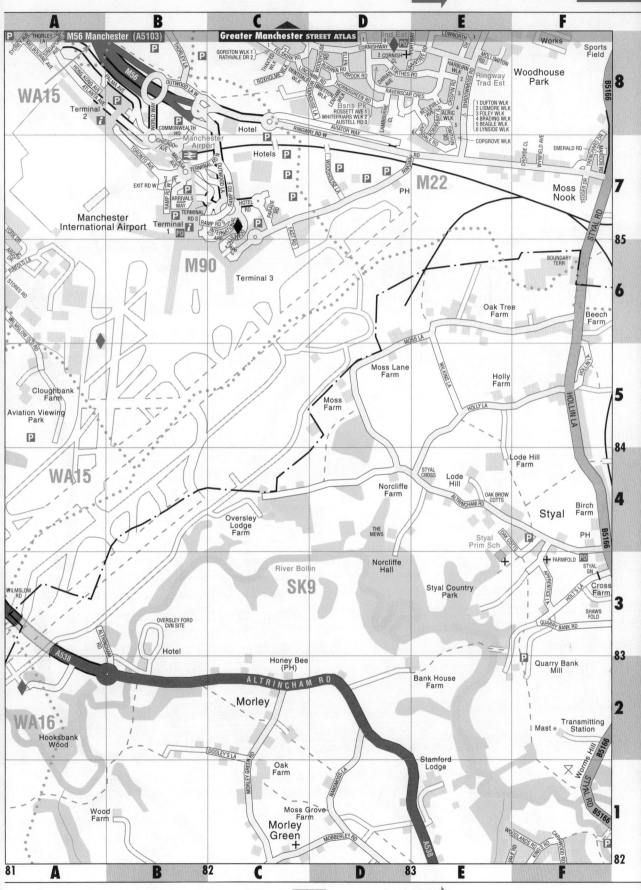

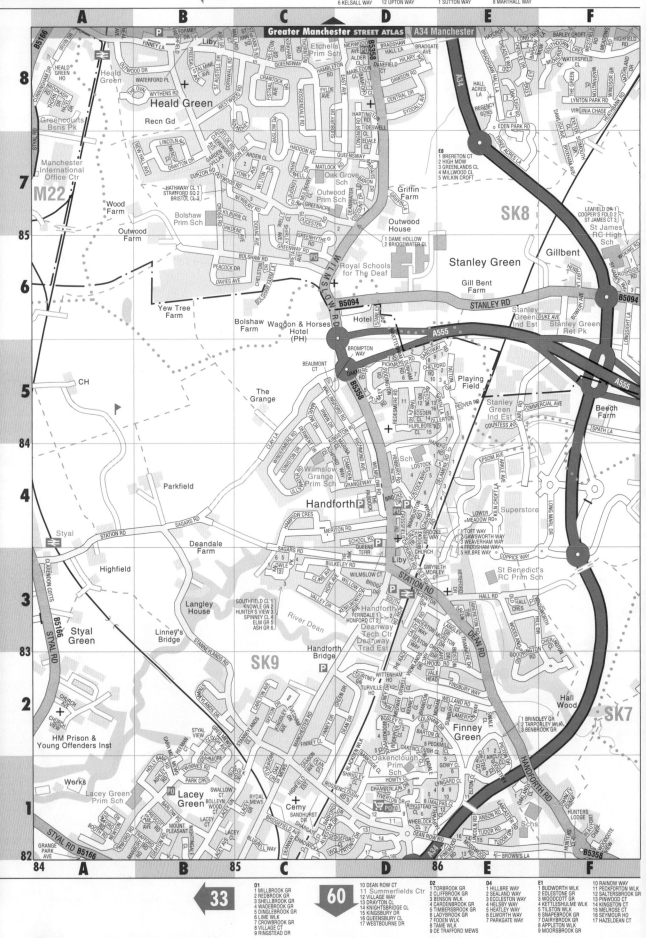

33

Greater Manchester STREET ATLAS A34 Manchester

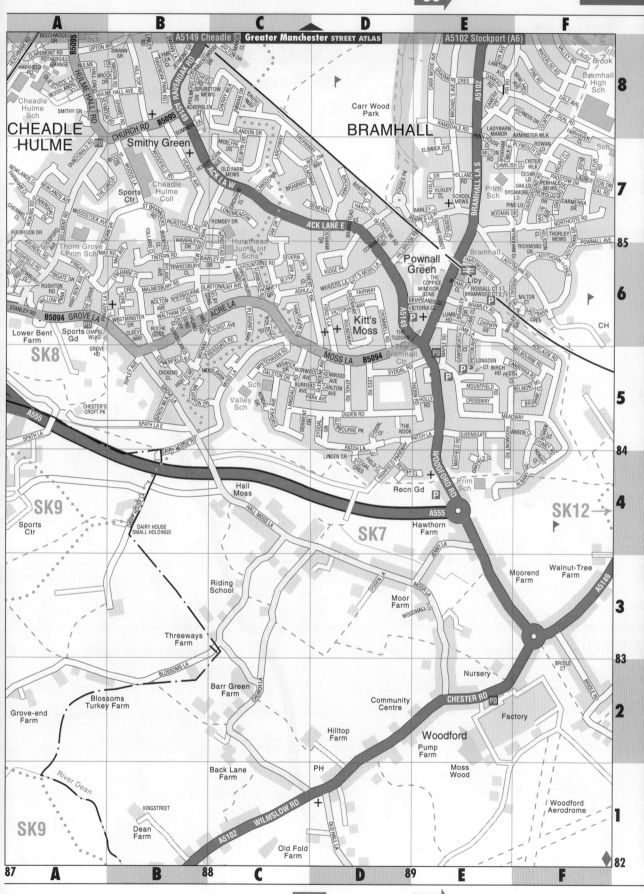

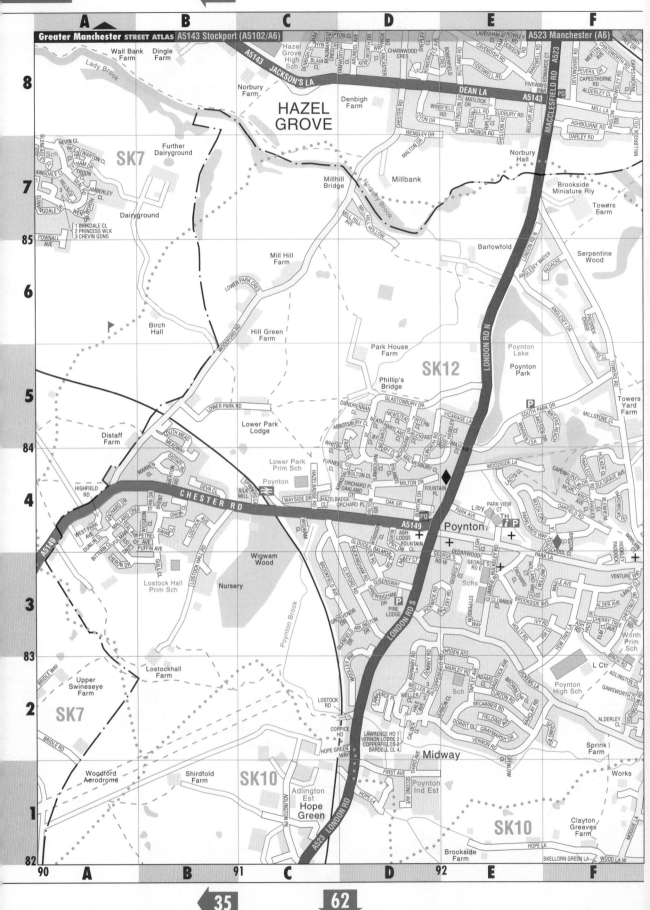

Greater Manchester STREET ATLAS A5143 Stockport (A5102/A6)

A523 Manchester (A6)

A B C D E F

8

7

85

6

5

84

4

3

83

2

1

82

90 A B 91 C D 92 E F

HAZEL GROVE

SK7

SK12

Poynton

SK7

SK10

SK10

Midway

Hope Green

38

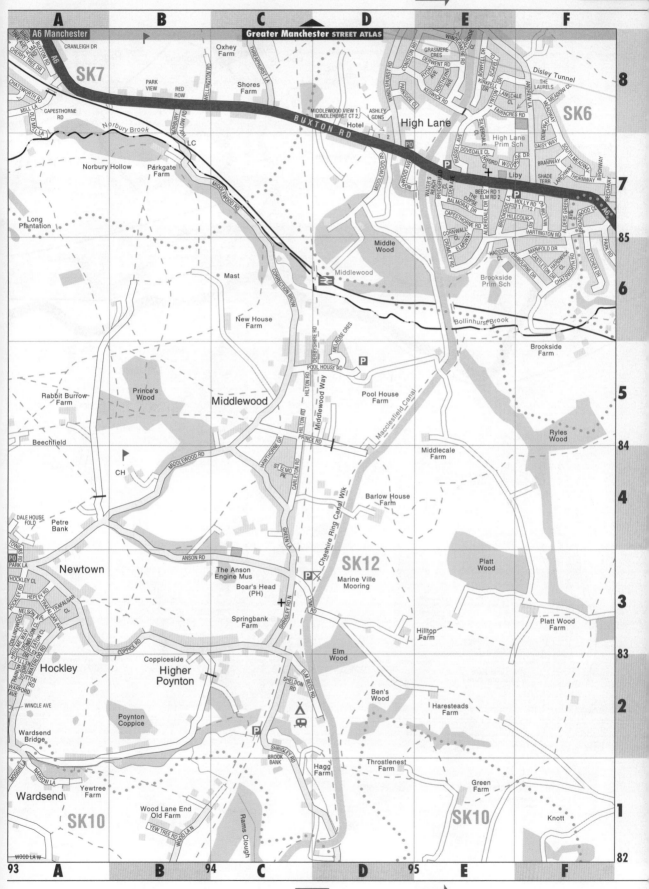

63   38

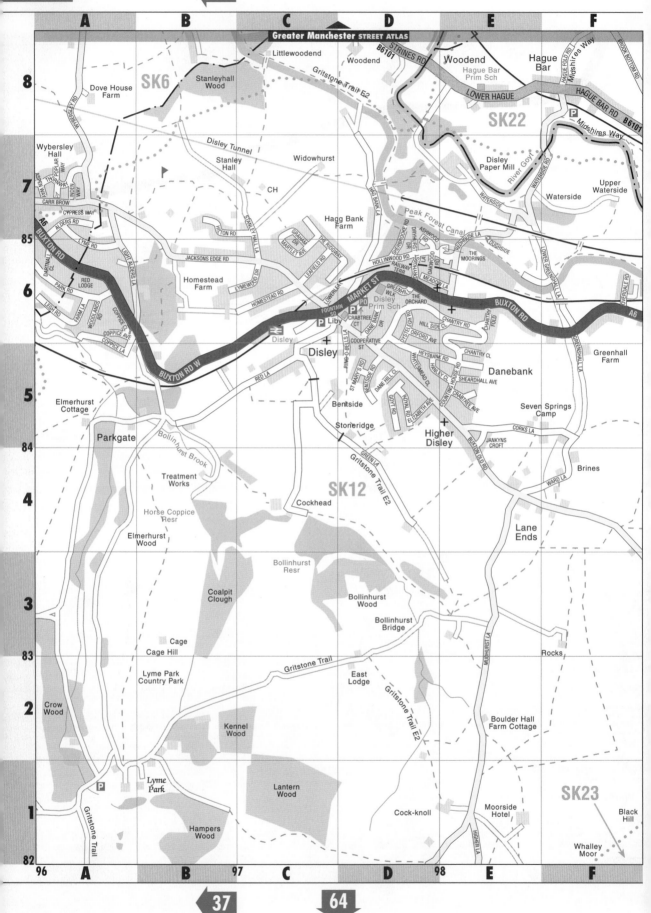

Greater Manchester STREET ATLAS

SK6

8

Dove House Farm

Littlewoodend

Woodend

B6101

STRINES RD

Woodend

Hague Bar Prim Sch

Woodend

Hague Bar

LOWER HAGUE

HAGUE BAR RD

B6101

SK22

Stanleyhall Wood

Gritstone Trail E2

HAGUE FOLD RD

Midshires Way

BROOK BOTTOM RD

Wybersley Hall

Disley Tunnel

Widowhurst

Disley Paper Mill

River Goyt

WATERSIDE RD

Upper Waterside

7

ASPEN WAY

POPLAR WAY

LINDEN WAY

THORNWAY

Stanley Hall

CH

HAG BANK LA

WATERSIDE

Waterside

CARR BROW

CYPRESS WAY

ALDERS RD

85

A6

BUXTON RD

LYME RD

LIGHT ALDERS LA

HIXTON RD

STANLEY HALL LA

JACKSONS EDGE RD

GRAHAM DR

MARTLET AVE

THE RIDGWAY

LEAFIELD RD

Hagg Bank Farm

HOLLINWOOD RD

SHERBROOKE RD

DRYHURST

ASHWOOD

OAKWOOD

REDHOUSE LA

CLOUGHSIDE

THE MOORINGS

LOWER GREENHALL LA

Peak Forest Canal

DARTMALL CL

PARK RD

RED LODGE

LEGH RD

FARM LA

SUNWOOD RD

COPPICE CL

HOMESTEAD DR

Homestead Farm

LYMEWOOD DR

HOMESTEAD RD

LOWER LEA

MARKET ST

FOUNTAIN SQ

PO

Disley Prim Sch

THE ORCHARD

MEADOW LA

GREENWAY WLK

HILL SIDE DR

ORFORD AVE

CHANTRY RD

CHANTRY FOLD

BUXTON RD

A6

GREENHALL LA

Greenhall Farm

6

COPPICE AVE

COPPICE LA

BUXTON RD W

Disley

RED LA

RING-O-BELLS LA

Liby

CRABTREE CT

DANE BANK DR

COOPERATIVE ST

Disley

ST MARYS RD

BENTSIDE RD

DANE HILL CL

HEYSBANK RD

WHITESMEAD CL

HANLEY CL

COUNTINT HOUSE RD

SHEARDHALL AVE

CRABTREE AVE

Danebank

CHANTRY CL

5

Elmerhurst Cottage

Bentside

GREEN LA

GOYT RD

ROYAL ELIZABETH AVE

Higher Disley

CORKS LA

Seven Springs Camp

Parkgate

Bollinhurst Brook

Stoneridge

Gritstone Trail E2

BUXTON OLD RD

JANKYNS CROFT

Brines

84

Treatment Works

Cockhead

SK12

WARD LA

Lane Ends

4

Horse Coppice Resr

Elmerhurst Wood

Bollinhurst Resr

3

Coalpit Clough

Bollinhurst Wood

Bollinhurst Bridge

MUDHURST LA

Rocks

Cage

Cage Hill

83

Gritstone Trail

East Lodge

Gritstone Trail E2

2

Crow Wood

Lyme Park Country Park

Kennel Wood

Boulder Hall Farm Cottage

SK23

Lyme Park

Lantern Wood

Cock-knoll

Moorside Hotel

HIGHER LA

Black Hill

1

Hampers Wood

Gritstone Trail

Whalley Moor

82

96

A

97

B

C

98

D

E

F

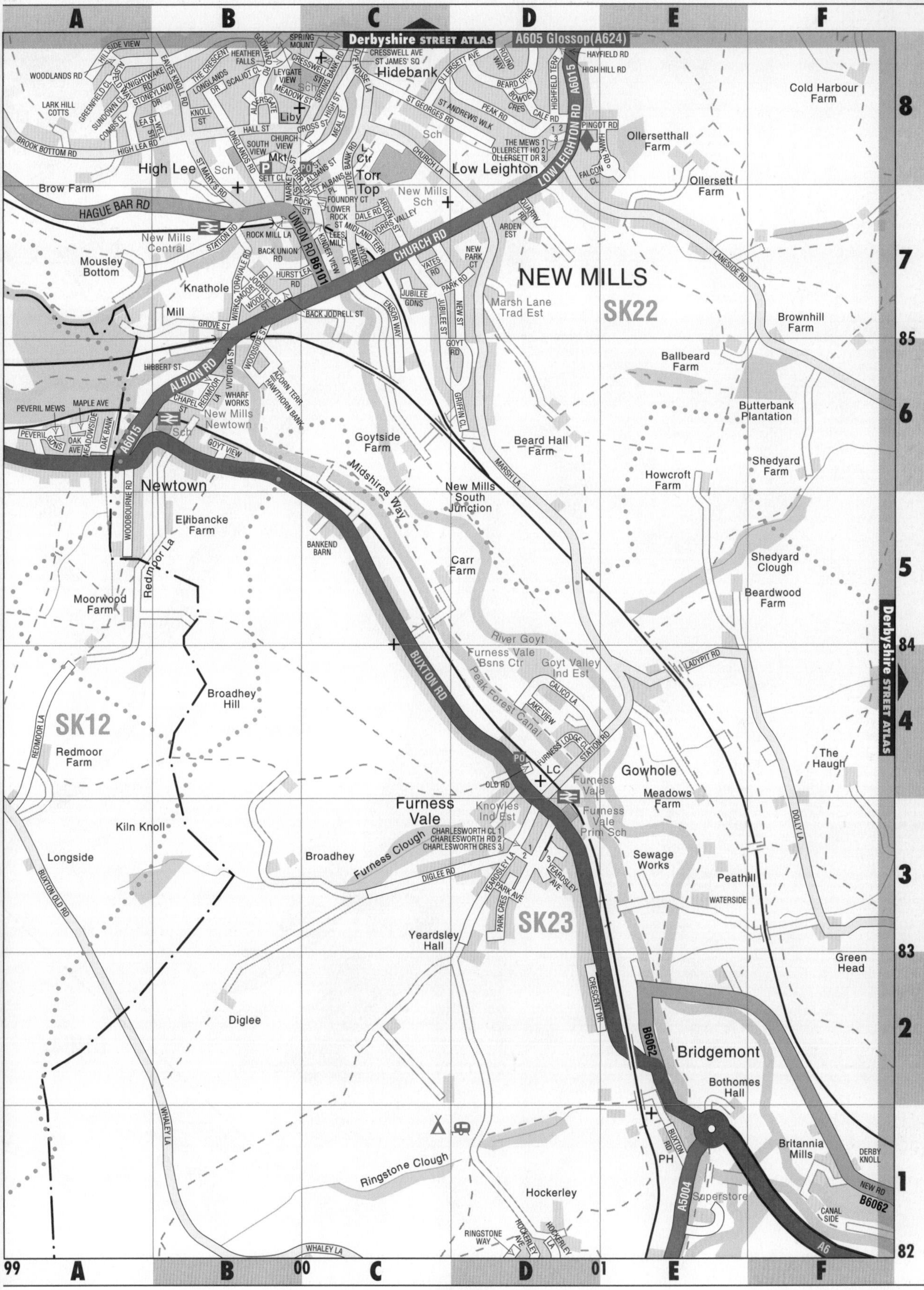

A B C D E F
Derbyshire STREET ATLAS
A605 Glossop(A624)
Hidebank
High Lee
Low Leighton
Torr Top
Brow Farm
HAGUE BAR RD
New Mills Central
Mousley Bottom
Knathole
Mill
NEW MILLS
SK22
Marsh Lane Trad Est
Cold Harbour Farm
Ollersetthall Farm
Ollersett Farm
Brownhill Farm
Ballbeard Farm
Butterbank Plantation
Shedyard Farm
Howcroft Farm
Beard Hall Farm
Goytside Farm
Midshires Way
New Mills South Junction
New Mills Newtown
Newtown
Ellibancke Farm
Moorwood Farm
Carr Farm
Shedyard Clough
Beardwood Farm
River Goyt
Furness Vale Bsns Ctr
Goyt Valley Ind Est
Peak Forest Canal
BUXTON RD
Broadhey Hill
SK12
Redmoor Farm
Kiln Knoll
Longside
Furness Vale
Knowles Ind Est
Gowhole
Meadows Farm
Broadhey
Furness Clough
Sewage Works
Peathill
SK23
Yeardsley Hall
The Haugh
Green Head
Diglee
Bridgemont
Bothomes Hall
Britannia Mills
Ringstone Clough
Hockerley
Superstore
A6015
A5004
B6062
B6101
A6
CHURCH RD
LOW LEIGHTON RD
ALBION RD
UNION RD
WHALEY LA
BUXTON OLD RD
DOLLY LA
LANESIDE RD
MARSH LA
8 7 6 5 4 3 2 1
85 84 83 82
99 00 01

Merseyside STREET ATLAS

A540 Hoylake

HESWALL

Heswall
Dales

Sewage
Works

Wirral Country
Park

The Pipers

CH60

Gayton
Cott

River Dee/Afon Dyfrdwy

Gayton Sands

CH64

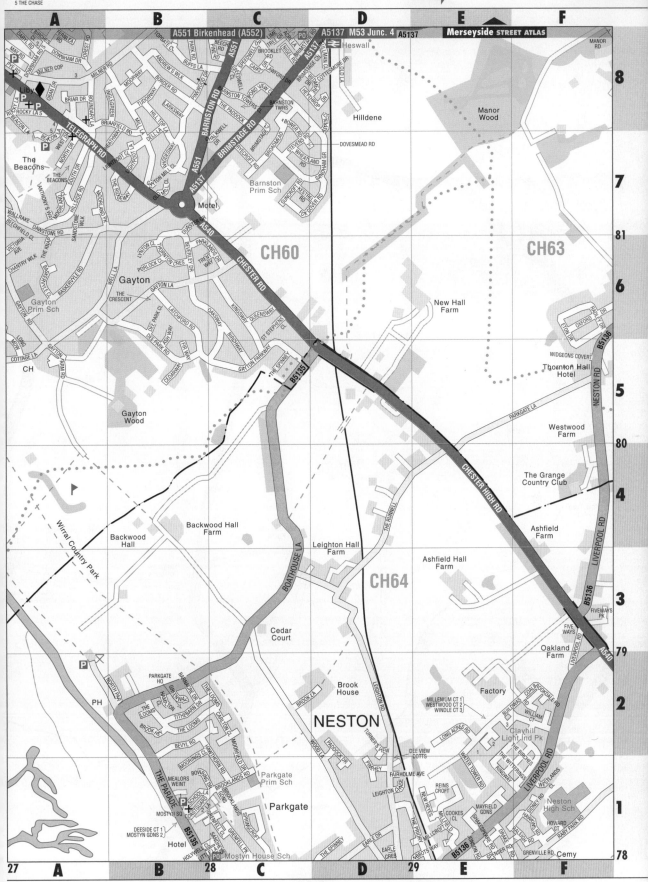

A8
1 DOWNHAM CT
2 BIRCHES HO
3 CHERRY TREE MEWS
4 BEACON CT
5 THE CHASE

Merseyside STREET ATLAS

CH60

CH63

CH64

NESTON

Parkgate

Wirral Country Park

Gayton

Gayton Wood

Backwood Hall

Backwood Hall Farm

Leighton Hall Farm

Manor Wood

New Hall Farm

Thornton Hall Hotel

Westwood Farm

The Grange Country Club

Ashfield Farm

Ashfield Hall Farm

Oakland Farm

Hilldene

Heswall

A551 Birkenhead (A552)

A5137 M53 Junc. 4

TELEGRAPH RD

CHESTER RD

CHESTER HIGH RD

NESTON RD

LIVERPOOL RD

BOATHOUSE LA

B5135

B5136

A540

THE PARADE

66

42

27   28   29

78

79

80

81

8

7

6

5

4

3

2

1

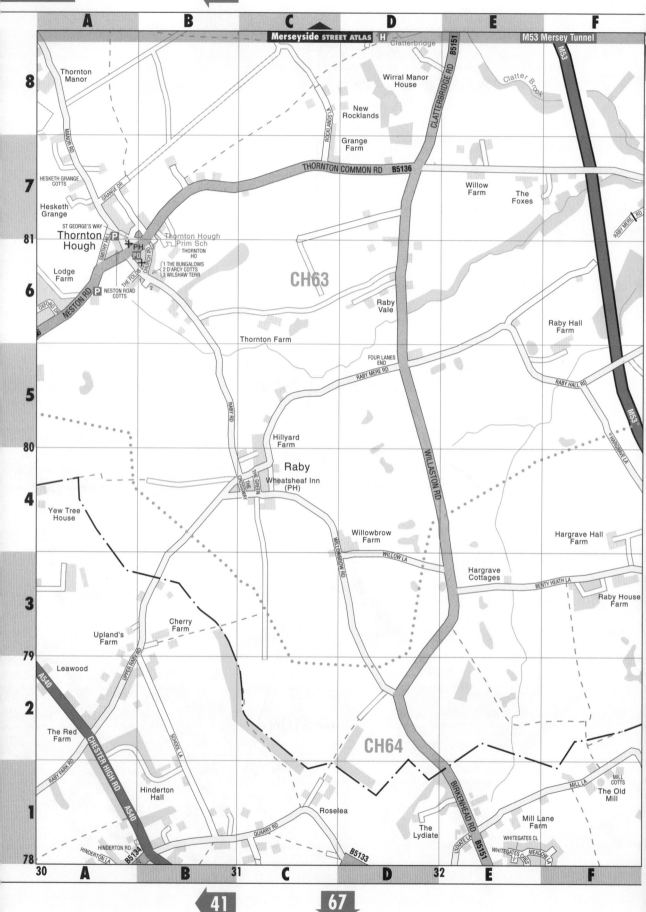

Merseyside STREET ATLAS H

Clatterbridge

M53 Mersey Tunnel

8

Thornton
Manor

Wirral Manor
House

Clatter Brook

New
Rocklands

MANOR RD

ROCKLANDS LA

CLATTERBRIDGE RD

B5151

M53

Grange
Farm

7

HESKETH GRANGE
COTTS

THORNTON COMMON RD   B5136

Willow
Farm

The
Foxes

Hesketh
Grange

GRANGE DR

RABY MERE RD

81

St GEORGE'S WAY

Thornton Hough
Prim Sch

Thornton
Hough

P + PH
SMITHY HILL

THORNTON
HO

CHURCH RD

1 THE BUNGALOWS
2 D'ARCY COTTS
3 WILSHAW TERR

CH63

6

Lodge
Farm

P

NESTON ROAD
COTTS

THE FOLDS

PO +

Raby
Vale

Raby Hall
Farm

OXFORD LA

NESTON RD

Thornton Farm

RABY RD

FOUR LANES
END

RABY MERE RD

WILLASTON RD

RABY HALL RD

HARGRAVE LA

5

80

Hillyard
Farm

Raby

THE CROSSWAY

THE GREEN

Wheatsheaf Inn
(PH)

4

Yew Tree
House

Willowbrow
Farm

WILLOWBROW RD

WILLOW LA

Hargrave Hall
Farm

3

Cherry
Farm

Hargrave
Cottages

BENTY HEATH LA

Raby House
Farm

Upland's
Farm

79

Leawood

UPPER RABY RD

A540

2

The Red
Farm

CHESTER HIGH RD

RABY PARK RD

A540

SCHOOL LA

CH64

BIRKENHEAD RD

MILL LA

MILL
COTTS

The Old
Mill

1

Hinderton
Hall

Roselea

The
Lydiate

Mill Lane
Farm

WHITEGATES CL

LYDIATE LA

B5151

78

HINDERTON RD

HINDERTON LA

B5134

QUARRY RD

B5133

WHITEGATES
CRES

MEADOW LA

Merseyside STREET ATLAS

River Mersey

Eastham Ctry Pk
Visitor Ctr
Eastham Ferry
Eastham Ferry Hotel
The Warrens Farm
Wirral Metropolitan Coll
WOOD HEATH WAY
Custom House
Eastham Locks
CHAPEL VIEW
CH
FERRY RD
LOCK RD
Queen Elizabeth II Dock
MAYFIELD DR
SEAVIEW AVE
CH62
ST DAVID RD
ST JOHN'S RD
CHRISTOPHER CLOR
Tanks
Tanks
Tanks
Oil Storage Depot
BANKFIELDS DR
VICARAGE ROW
Tanks
Sch
EASTHAM VILLAGE RD
STANLEY
CHURCH RD
B5132
Tanks
HALL FARM
EASTHAM HOUSE
EASTHAM MEWS
Tanks
Manchester Ship Canal
Tanks
LC
Hooton Park
B5132
David's Rough
ERIC FOUNTAIN RD
CH65
NORTH RD
Booston Wood
LC
5
RIVACRE RD
DUDLEY CRES
SEPTON RD
NEW CHESTER RD
Kennel Wood
6
RIVACRE RD
REDVERS AVE
VERNON AVE
Hooton WAY
HOOTON RD
B5133
CHRISTON CL
PENNANT DR
GRANGE CRES
CONISTON CL
HOOTON GN
Park Farm
Motor Vehicle Works
Hooton
A550
WELSH RD
CHESTER RD
A41
WOODCLOSE
NEW SCHOOL LA
HOOTON LA
CH66
7
M53
Rivacre Wood
B5132
B5132
SCHOOL LA

46

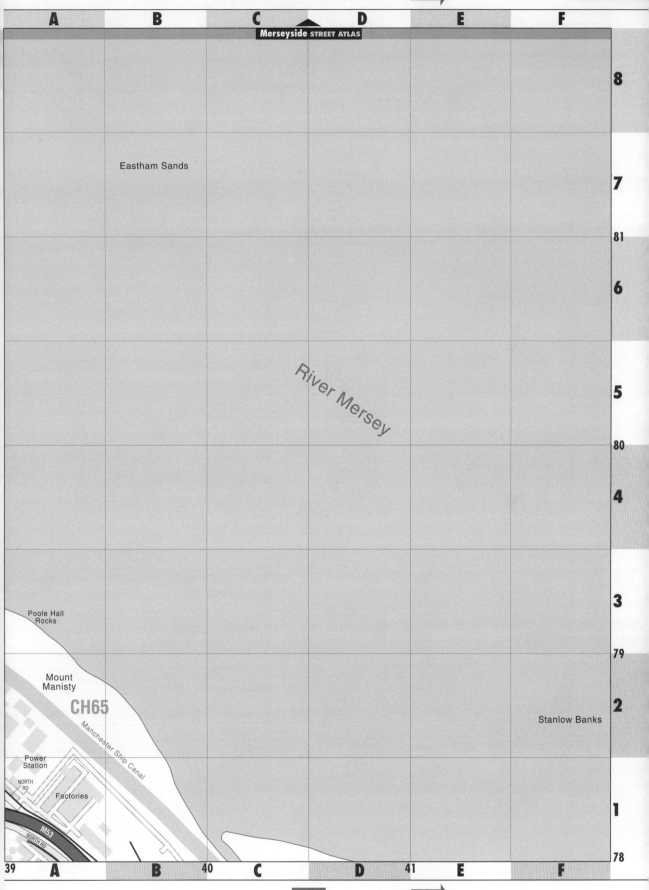

Merseyside STREET ATLAS

Eastham Sands

River Mersey

Poole Hall
Rocks

Mount
Manisty

CH65

Manchester Ship Canal

Power
Station

NORTH
RD

Factories

M53

NORTH RD

Stanlow Banks

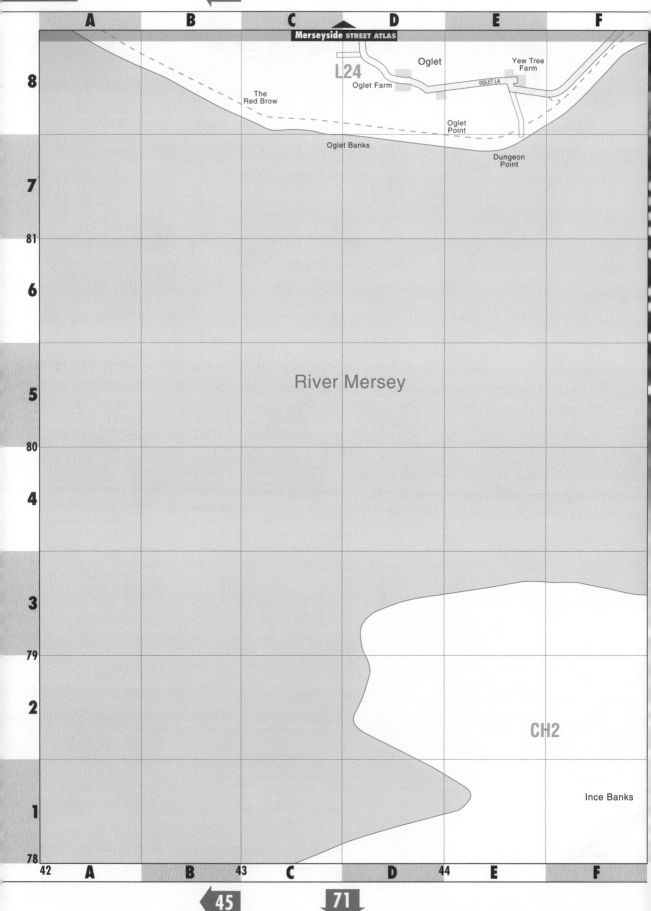

Merseyside STREET ATLAS

L24

Oglet

Yew Tree
Farm

The
Red Brow

Oglet Farm

OGLET LA

Oglet
Point

Oglet Banks

Dungeon
Point

River Mersey

CH2

Ince Banks

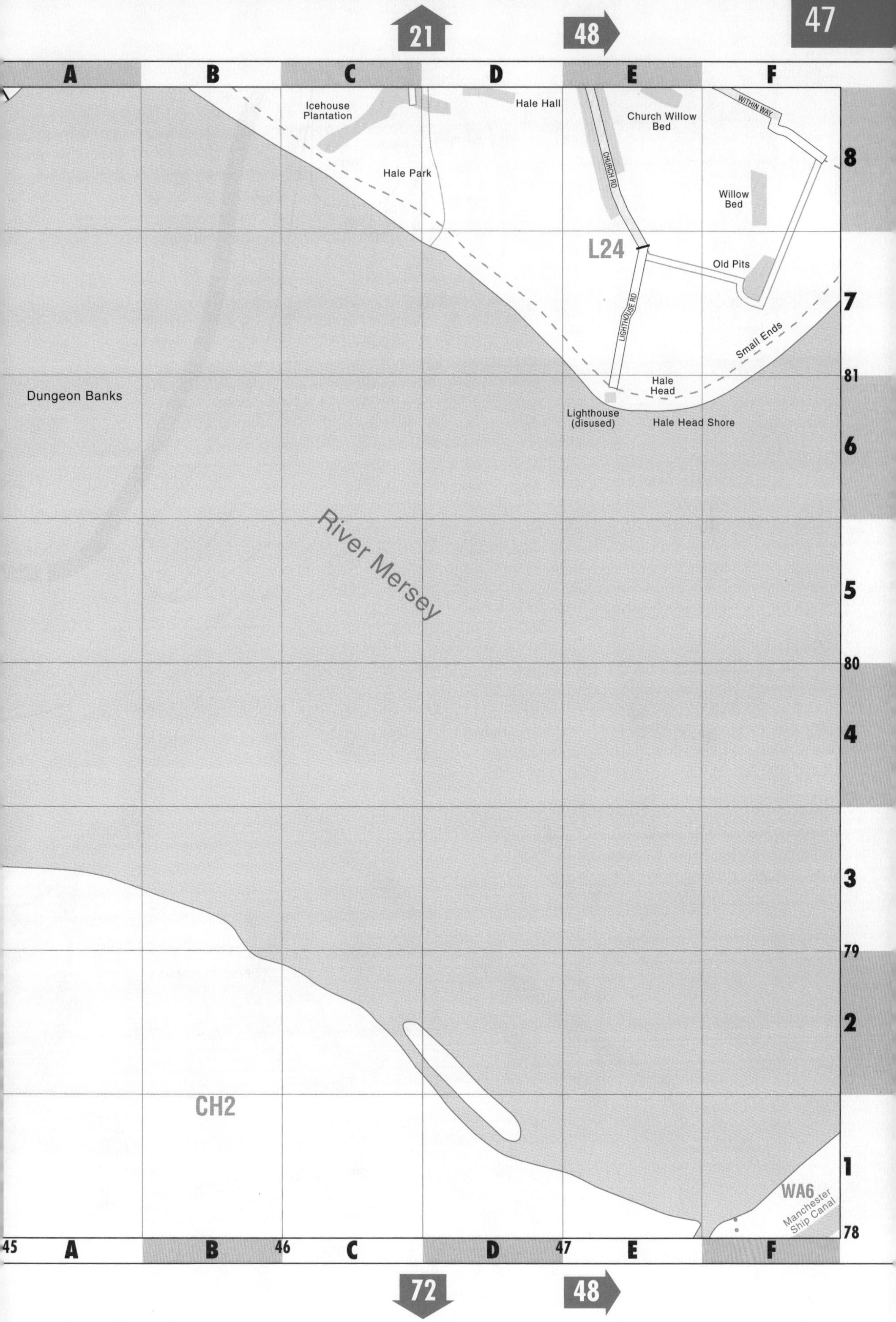

21
48

A　B　C　D　E　F

Icehouse
Plantation

Hale Hall

Church Willow
Bed

WITHIN WAY

8

Hale Park

Willow
Bed

L24

Old Pits

7

CHURCH RD

LIGHTHOUSE RD

Small Ends

81

Dungeon Banks

Hale
Head

Lighthouse
(disused)

Hale Head Shore

6

River Mersey

5

80

4

3

79

2

CH2

1

WA6

Manchester
Ship Canal

78

72
48

47
22

A B C D E F

8

L24

Docks

Works

Runcorn & Weston Canal (disused)

1 Lingfield Ho
2 Cunningham Ho
3 Cunningham Dr

BEACONSFIELD RD

HALE VIEW

HILLSIDE AVE

RUSSELL RD

HAZEL AVE

CAMERON AVE

MINSTER CT

SOUTHLANDS CT

JOHNS AVE

WHITLEY CT

Beacon Hill

ROYDEN AVE

Runcorn Hill (Public Park)

COOMBE DR

HIGHLANDS RD

PARK RD

P

HEATH PARK GR

Nature Reserve

Recn Gd

PERRIN AVE

LC

CLARKS TERR

PO

BEACON HILL VIEW

POST OFFICE LA

CANAL SIDE

CANAL SIDE

Swing Bridge

Weston Mersey Locks

Weston Point

WEST RD

SOUTH RD

SOUTH PAR

BAKER RD

KELLY RD

NETLY RD

CULLEN RD

LEONARD ST

SYDNEY ST

LYDIATE LA

MATHER AVE

SANDY LA

ROSCOE CRES

CASTNER AVE

CHESHYRE'S LA

LANCASTER AVE

WESTON RD

Weston Point Com Prim Sch

COLLIER'S ROW

WESTON CT PROSPECT ROW

COMPANY'S CL 1
MONTPELIER AVE 2
LAMBSICKLE CL 3

WA7

7

81

6

Manchester Ship Canal

Weaver Navigation

BANKS LA

LC

WESTON POINT EXPRESSWAY

Mast

Weston

ASHTON CL

CRESTA DR

LAMBSICKLE LA

MARION DR

DEATH RD S

WESTON CRES

TILDSLEY CRES

Works

PO

CAVENDISH FARM RD

A557

Works

5

Weaver Sluices

80

Weston Marsh Lock

4

River Weaver

3

79

Frodsham Marsh Farm

ALDER LA

Frodsham Marsh

Frodsham Score

Manchester Ship Canal

BROOK FURLONG

2

WA6

Canal Deposit Dump

Jetties

MOORDITCH LA

TANGERS LA

1

Canal Deposit Dump

MOORDITCH LA

78

River Mersey

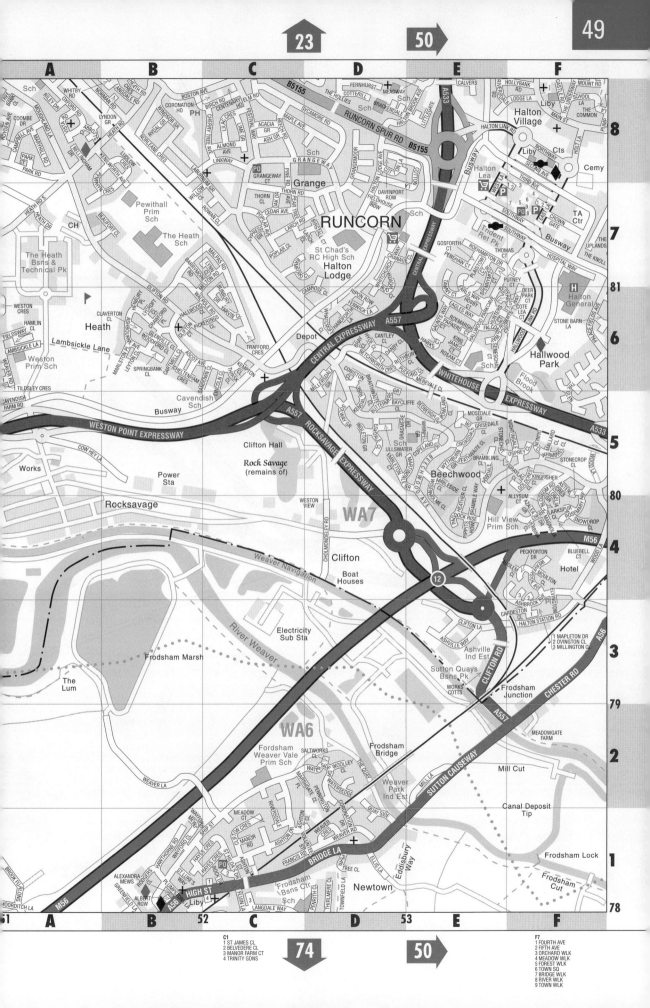

RUNCORN

Town Park

Murdishaw

WA4

Marina

Marina Village

Woodfalls Farm

Palace Fields

Busway Sch

Brookvale

Halton High Sch

Busway

Preston Brook

WA7

Whitehouse Ind Est

Sutton Lodge Farm

Sutton Weaver

Sutton Hall

Sutton Fields Farm

Stretche's Gorse

Aston Heath Farm

Birdswood Farm

Aston Heath

Four Winds

Bird's Wood

Lowe's Wood

Aston by Sutton Prim Sch

Beckett's Wood

Chapel Wood

Aston

Aston Lodge

Weaver View Cottages

WA6

1 SABRE CL
2 BARTON CL
3 SOVEREIGN CL
4 TALISMAN CL
5 DORRINGTON CL

6 ELLERBY CL
7 SAWLEY CL
8 BAYVIL CL
9 WOODEND
10 MORESBY CL

Sports Gd
1 CALVERLY CL
2 LINWOOD CL
3 WELLBROOK CL
4 HALSALL CL
5 GRANBY CL
6 ABINGTON WLK

A   B   C   D   E   F

8
7
81
6
5
80
4
3
79
2
79
1
78

RED BROW LA

CHESTER RD

A56

Hotel

Daresbury Pk

Mast

WINDMILL LA

Preston on the Hill

HILL TOP RD

Sumner's Farm

BARKERS HOLLOW RD

Preston Brook Tunnel

Dutton

PH

PENBURY PL

REDACRE CL

VALE CT

Bird's Wood

WA7

CHESTER RD A56

Little Manor Farm

NEWTON BANK

NEWTON LA

Daresbury Fruit Farm

Newtonbank Farm

Summer Lane Farm

SUMMER LA

New Manor Farm

NEW MANOR RD

White House Farm

Keckwick Brook

Turfland

Union Farm

Cheshire Ring Canal Walk

NORTHWICH RD

Longacre Wood

Dale Farm

Hill Farm

HILL TOP RD

Trent and Mersey Canal

Hall Cottage

Hope Farm

A533

Hallam Hall Farm

Newton Cross

MORPHANY LA

Morphany Hall

WA4

Thatched House Farm

HIGHER LA

Westbrook Farm

Meadow Farm

Lightwood Farm

MARSH LA

Oakbank

Owl's Nest

SANKEY LA

M56

NEWTON LA

Penkridge Lake Farm

Black Jane Farm

Brook House Farm

Glebe Farm

Whitley Brook

GREENHILL LA

Brook Lodge

Whitley Brook

Woodbank Farm

Seven Acre Wood

51
26

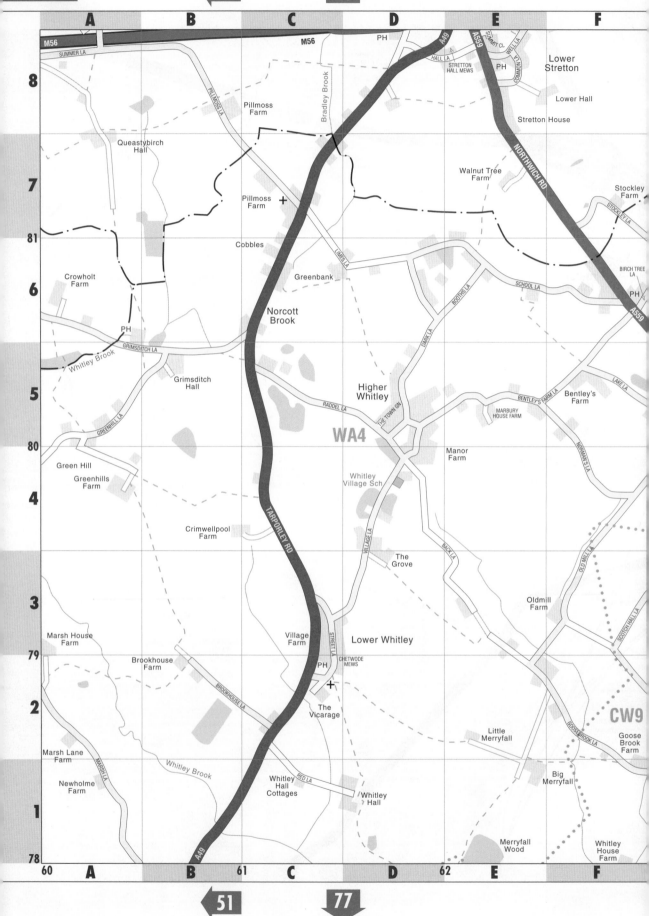

51
77

27
54

A B C D E F

8
7
81
6
5
80
4
3
79
2
1
78

Whitley Reed

Whitley
Reed Farm

NEW RD
REEDGATE LA

Parkmoss
Farm

ARLEY RD

Galemoss
Farm

Gale Brook

MOSS SIDE LA

Hill House

POOLS PLATT LA

Payne's Farm

WA4

STOCKLEY LA
BIRCH TREE LA

Fogg's
Farm

CH

Antrobus Farm

FOGG'S LA

Antrobus
House

Pools
Platt
Farm

HOLLINS LA

Antrobus
Hall

REED LA

BARBER'S LA

Nook
House

NOOK LA

Flash
Farm

Flash
Farm

FLASH LA

LODGE LA

Ashwood Brow
Farm

WEST
VIEW

BROW LA

LAKE LA

Potternell

CW9

OLD MILL LA

Lake Farm

WELL LA

80

KEEPERS LA

HOLLINS LA

MEGS LA

Manley Farm

Newall's
Rough

Antrobus

PH

Shawbrook

Pole Lane
Ends

MANLEY CL

THE OLD ORCHARD

PO

Foxley Brow
Farm

LOWE
CRES

KNUTSFORD RD

Firtree
Farm

Grandsires
Green

SCOTCH HALL LA

Well
Farm

WHEATSHEAF LA

Fox Farm

Antrobus
St Mark's CE
Prim Sch

SCHOOL LA

Old Pole
Farm

Frandley

Scotch Hall

NORTHWICH RD

OLD LA

The Folly

79

Frandley Brow
Farm

Frandley
Farm

Deakin Yard

Morris
Farm

SANDIWAY LA

Sandiway
Farm

Frandley
House

Frandley House

Thellow Heath
Farm

POLE LA

The Pole

Belmont
Dairy Farm

SCOTCH HALL LA

Seven
Oaks Farm

Cransley
Sch

Moat
Covert

GOOSEBROOK LA

Senna Green
Farm

Fields
Farm

Gibb
Hill

Belmont
Hall

BELMONT RD

HALL LA

SENNA LA

Senna Lane
Farm

GIBB HILL

A559

Cogshall
Hall

53
28

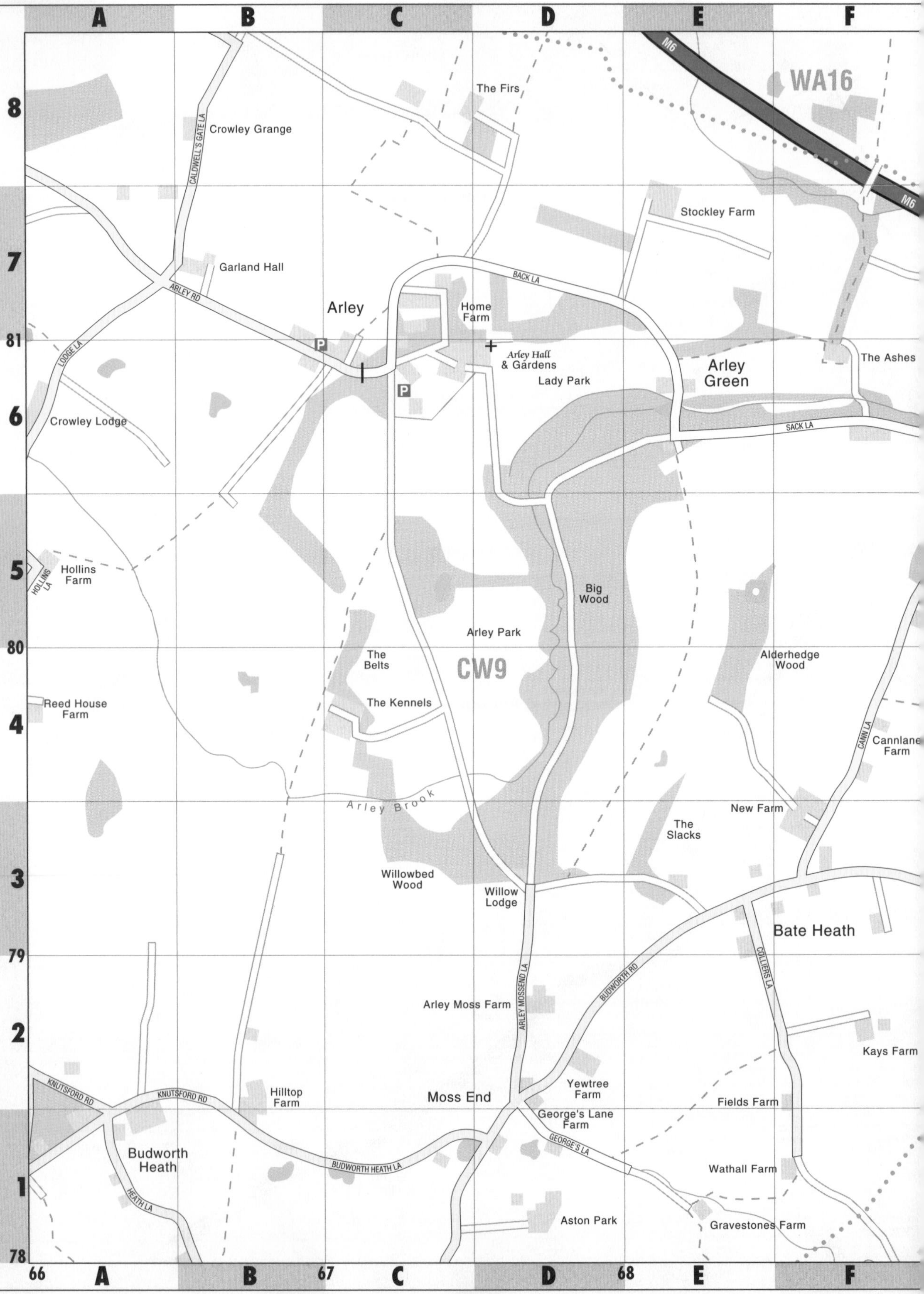

A **B** **C** **D** **E** **F**

8

WA16

Crowley Grange

CALDWELL'S GATE LA

The Firs

M6

Stockley Farm

7

Garland Hall

BACK LA

ARLEY RD

Arley

LODGE LA

81

Home Farm

Arley Hall & Gardens

Lady Park

Arley Green

The Ashes

P

P

SACK LA

6

Crowley Lodge

5

Hollins Farm

HOLLINS LA

Big Wood

Arley Park

Alderhedge Wood

80

The Belts

CW9

4

Reed House Farm

The Kennels

CANN LA

Cannlane Farm

Arley Brook

New Farm

The Slacks

3

Willowbed Wood

Willow Lodge

Bate Heath

79

ARLEY MOSSEND LA

BUDWORTH RD

CULLTERS LA

2

Arley Moss Farm

Kays Farm

KNUTSFORD RD

KNUTSFORD RD

Hilltop Farm

Moss End

Yewtree Farm

Fields Farm

George's Lane Farm

GEORGE'S LA

Budworth Heath

BUDWORTH HEATH LA

Wathall Farm

1

HEATH LA

Aston Park

Gravestones Farm

78

53
79

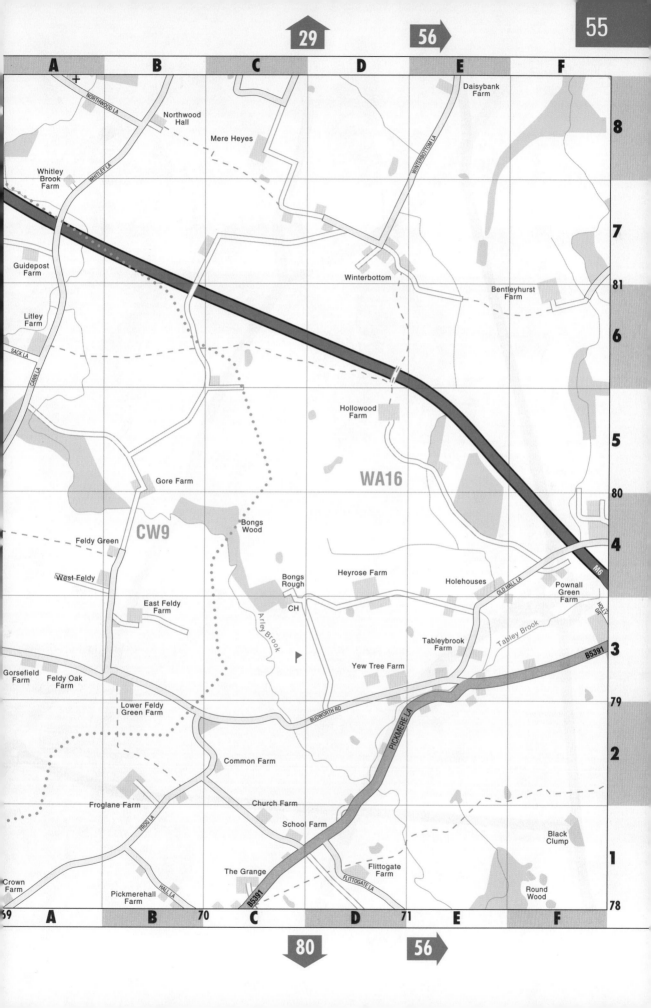

A B C D E F

8

Mere

The Mere

MERE HALL

MERE HOME FARM

CH

Mere Lodge

Lady Mary's Walk

Rostherne Drive

Tatton Hall

7

WARRINGTON RD

CHESTER RD

A50

A556

MERESIDE RD

CLAMHUNGER LA

ASHLEY RD

A5034

A5034

Mereheath Drive

Lodge

Melchett Mere

The Temple

81

Knowlespit Farm

Tatton Park

6

STEADINGS RISE

Moss Plantation

Moss Cottage

Mereheath Plantation

MEREHEATH LA

5

MOSS LA

Church Farm

Hotel

Over Tabley

Moss Farm

Roebuck Farm

80

Over Tabley Hall

TABLEY CT

WA16

Garage

MANCHESTER RD

GREEN LA

Bluebell Farm

4

OLD HALL LA

Dairy House Farm

Swains Walk

Playing Fields

M6

Cemy

Oakwood 1
Beechwood 2

19

PH

FRESHFIELDS

TABLEY CL

P

MEREHEATH PK

HOLLY GR

PICKMERE LA

3

B5391

Bank Farm

Tabley Hill Farm

Tabley Hill

QUEENSWAY

TABLEY RD

SUGAR PIT LA

WILLOW GN

1 2

B5083 GARDEN RD

VICTORIA ST

SPINNEY LA

79

TABLEY HILL LA

Tableyvale Farm

The Heath

ELIZABETH GASKELL CT 1
WINDSOR WAY 2
ROYCE CT 3
HEATHLANDS HO 4
WINSTANLEY HO 5

QUEEN ST

ALBERT ST

A50

2

Burnthouse Farm

Tableyvale Cottages

WARREN AVE

LADIES MILE

HEATH DR

WARREN AVE

A5033

Yewtree House

CHESTER RD

Villa Farm

A5033

NORTHWICH RD

NORTHFIELD RD

RACEFIELD RD

STANLEY RD

GASKELL AVE

Egerton Prim Sch

B5083

H

1

Belt Wood

Sudlow Farm

SUDLOW LA

M6

Knutsford High Sch (Lower Sch)

LILAC AVE

ACACIA AVE

TABLEY GR

WESTFIELD DR

SCHOOL AVE

MELLOR CRES

Knutsford High Sch (Upper Sch)

P

L Ctr

CROSSFIELD

CRANFORD AVE

ST JOHN'S AVE

HATTON ST JOHN'S RD

BEXTON RD

MEADOW DR

MEAD CL

MEADOW CL

LEE CL

ST PETER'S AVE

FLETCHER CT 1
EAST TERR 2
MASTERS CT 3
VICTORIA CT 4
COUNTY TERR 5

78

Knutsford Service Area

A556

72 A B 73 C D 74 E F

A B C D E F

8
7
81
6
5
80
4
79
2
1
78

Parkside Farm

Fourlane-ends

Mobberley Brook

PEPPER ST
SMALL LA
PINE TREE LA

PH

Mobberley

STATION RD
PH LC
HOBCROFT LA

LEYCESTER DR

SIDE LA
SMITH LA

Hanging Bank

Park Farm

Square Wood

Mobberley

BROADOAK LA

BEECH AVE

Smithlane Farm

Old Hall

Tatton Park

Boathouse Plantation

Witchcote Wood

Broad Oak Farm

Knutsford Drive

Tatton Mere

Shawheath Plantation

Birkin Brook

WA16

Sewage Works

Parkgate Farm

Tatton Mere Covert

Parkgate Trad Est

QUARMERFIELD RD
RAJAR COTTS

CUMBERFIELD RD

TOWN LA
B5085

MAYFIELD RD
SPRINGFIELD RD

Oak Tree Farm

KNUTSFORD RD

Dukenfield Hall

RYECROFT LA

BERNISDALE RD

PAVEMENT LA

MEADOWSWEET RD

Pavement Lane Farm

Water Works

Dog Wood

KNUTSFORD

CH

MERESIDE
LA

GARDEN RD

GEORGE ST

P
P
P

RUSKIN WAY
BRIAR CL
SILK MILL RD

COPPICE GR

MINSHULL ST

RUSKIN CT

DRURY LA

KING ST

PRINCESS ST
SILK MILL

PO

KING EDWARD RD
Sch
Lib

BEXTON RD

Civic Hall

P

STANLEY RD

GLEBELANDS CL
TREVONE CL

ST JOHN'S
ST JOHN'S RD

Stanley Rd Ind Est

A50

TOFT RD

ADAMS HILL

Knutsford

B5085

A537 BROOK ST

HOLLOW LA

LITTLE BROOK LA
KNUTSFORD CRES
HOLFORD AV

B5085

CHELFORD RD

LEGH RD

WOODVALE RD

BALMORAL CL

PARKHILL RD

GROVE PK

SPARROW LA

PO

MANOR PARK S

ROCKFORD LODGE

MOULTON CL

DELAMERE CL

HALLSIDE PK

WARWICK CL

SOUTH DOWNS

CARRWOOD

BUCKINGHAM GDNS

Over Knutsford

Booths Hall

FIR TREE AVE

Spring Wood

Springwood Farm

Booths Mere

St John's Wood Com Sch

LONGRIDGE

LICHFIELD RD

HIGHLANDS RD

HIGHER DOWNS

LINDOP

ASH GR

FOX CL

EAST BIRCH RD

BEECHWOOD

BROOKDALE AVE

Manor Park Prim Sch

Sch

THORNEYHOLME DR

WOODSIDE

MANCION DR

SANDIWAY

WOODLANDS DR

MOORDALE RD

MIDDLE WLK

VILLA RD

WLK

CHURCH MEWS

WOODLANDS CT

LINDEN DR

THE SHAMBLES

SHARSTON CRES

Cross Town

MANOR CRES

LOWE DR

MALT ST

HEYES LA

MALT RD

TEAL CL

GREEN LANE

MERLYN AVE

NORBURY CL

CHURCHFIELDS

SHAW DR

MAYFIELD

SHAW HEATH

St John's Ct

FORESTER AVE

BOOTHFIELDS

BELLINGHAM CL

KENILWORTH

TOWNFIELDS

MANOR RD

N WAY

Shaw Heath

LEGH CT

KEEPERS CL

Longridge Trad Est

MONTMORENCY RD

1 CHALFONT CT
2 SPRINGFIELDS
3 SUMMERFIELDS
4 SHAW HEATH VIEW

PO

MILL CL

LEGH CT

BIRKIN CT

MARDON CT

WOLFE

MONTGOMERY CL

MARLBOROUGH CL

HAIG CT

HAIG RD

THE GROVE

WELLINGTON

SPRINGWOOD AVE

MERIDIAN

OAKFIELD AVE

PARKGATE

BRAIDWOOD AVE

KESTREL AVE

BEWICK WLK

HESTON

LODGE RD

MALT RD

MOBBERLEY RD

PARKGATE LA

75 A B 76 C D 77 E F 78

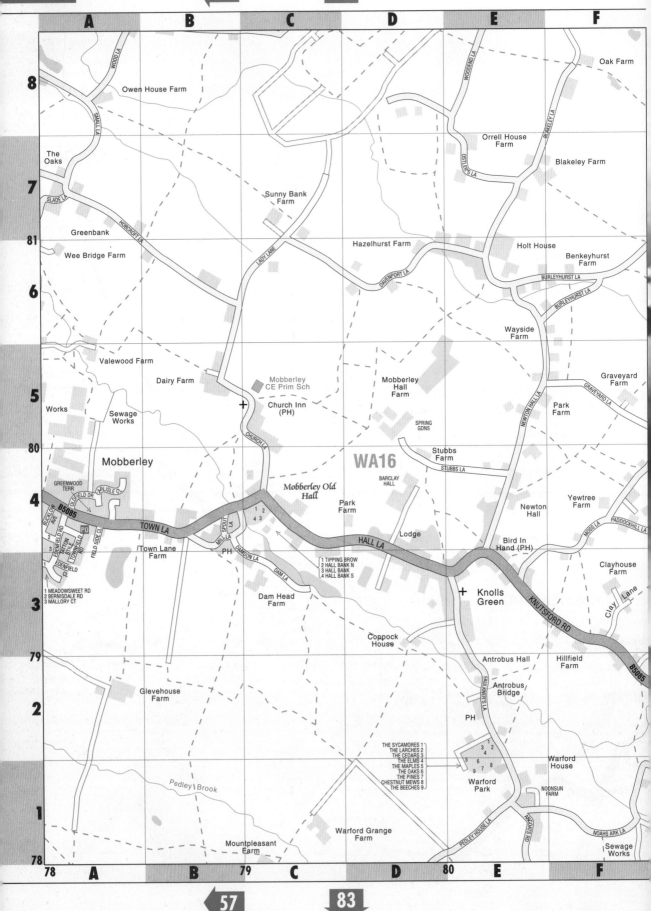

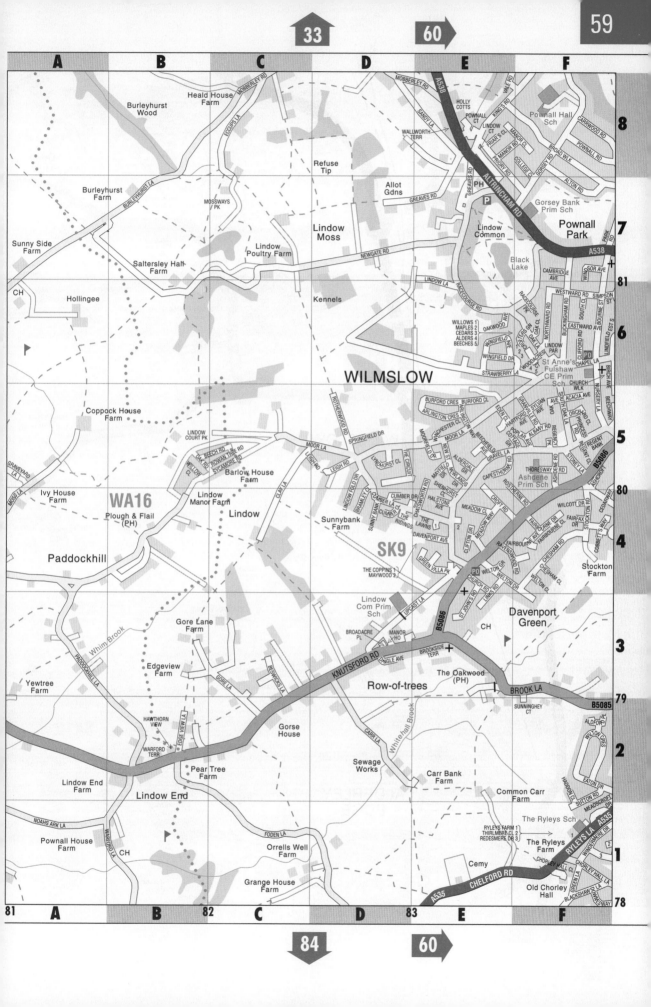

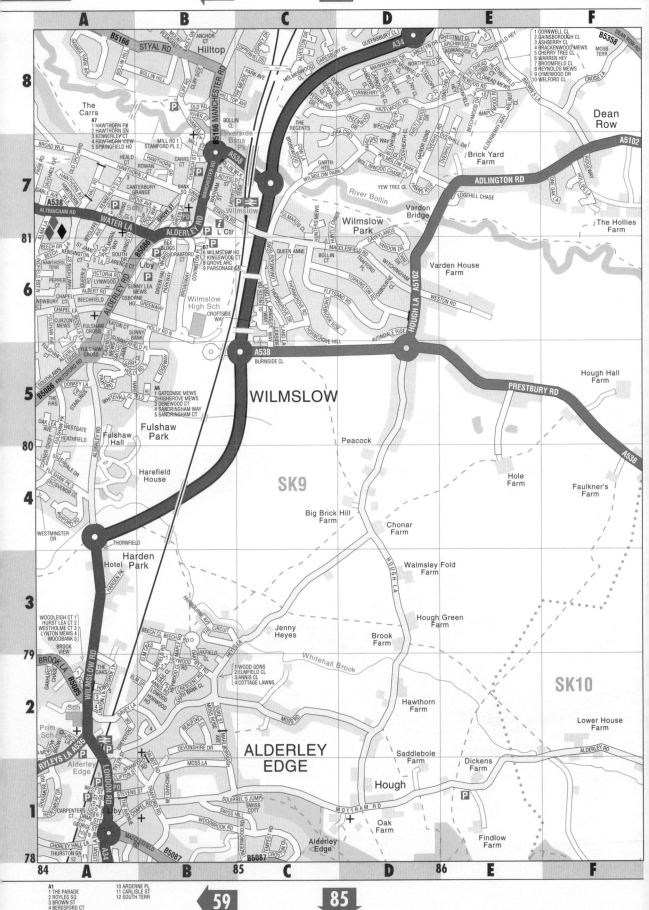

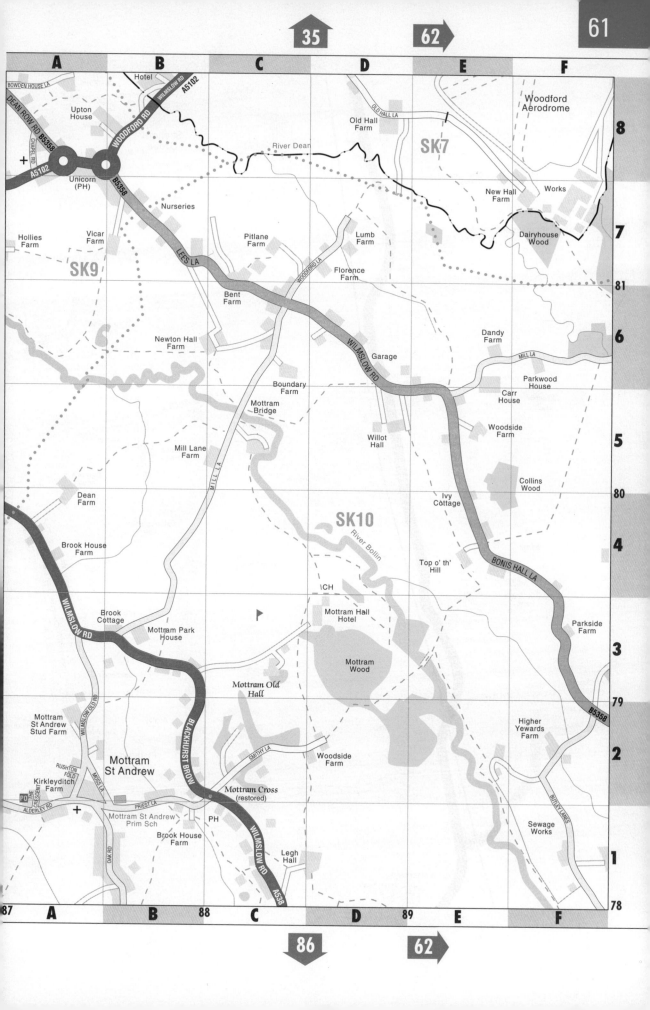

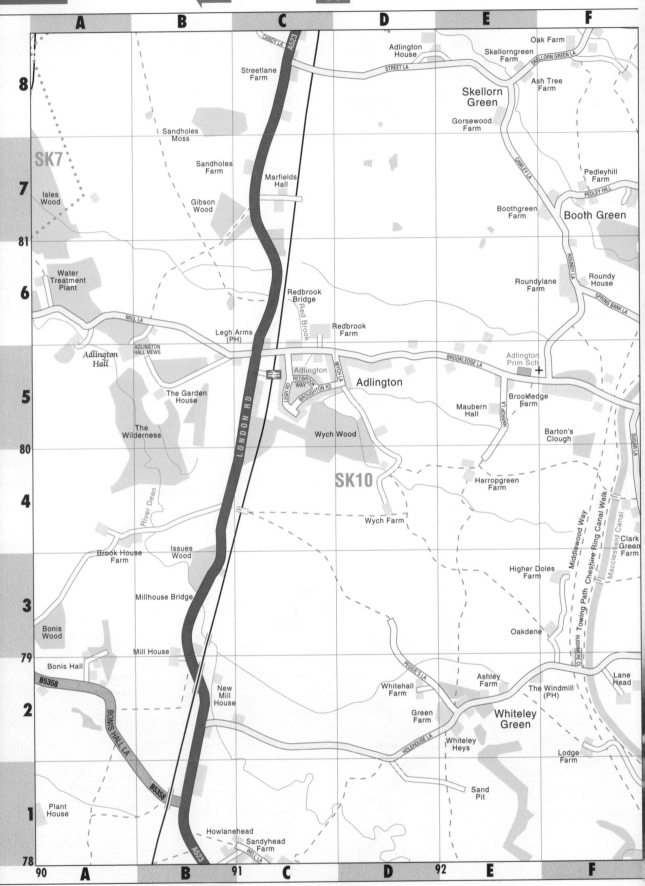

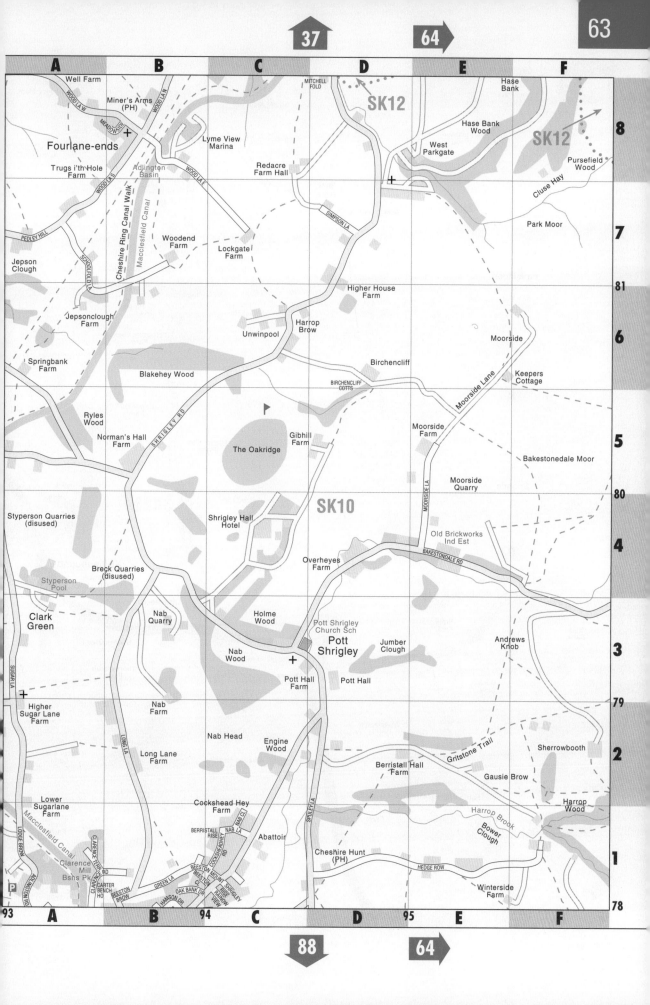

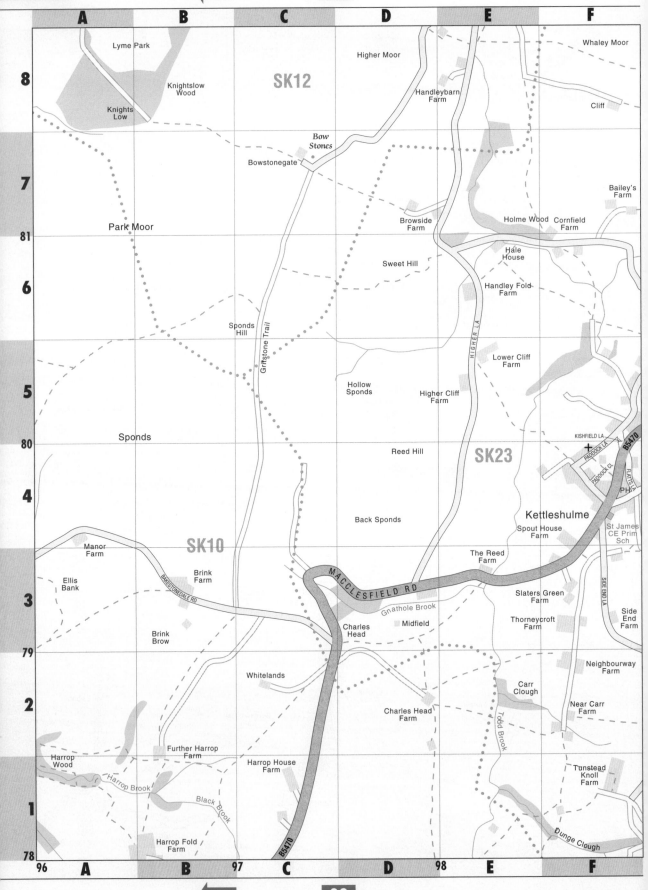

63
38

A B C D E F

8

Lyme Park

Knightslow
Wood

Knights
Low

SK12

Higher Moor

Handleybarn
Farm

Whaley Moor

Cliff

Bow
Stones

Bowstonegate

7

Park Moor

81

Browside
Farm

Sweet Hill

Bailey's
Farm

Holme Wood   Cornfield
Farm

Hale
House

6

Sponds
Hill

Gritstone Trail

Handley Fold
Farm

HIGHER LA

Lower Cliff
Farm

5

Hollow
Sponds

Higher Cliff
Farm

80

Sponds

Reed Hill

SK23

KISHFIELD LA

PADDOCK LA

PADDOCK CL

B5470

FLATTS LA

+

PH

4

Back Sponds

Kettleshulme

Spout House
Farm

St James
CE Prim
Sch

SK10

Manor
Farm

Brink
Farm

BAKESTONEDALE RD

MACCLESFIELD RD

The Reed
Farm

Slaters Green
Farm

SIDE END LA

3

Ellis
Bank

Brink
Brow

Gnathole Brook

Charles
Head

Midfield

Thorneycroft
Farm

Side
End
Farm

79

Whitelands

Charles Head
Farm

Todd Brook

Carr
Clough

Neighbourway
Farm

Near Carr
Farm

2

Further Harrop
Farm

Harrop House
Farm

Harrop
Wood

Harrop Brook

Black Brook

1

B5470

Tunstead
Knoll
Farm

Dunge Clough

Harrop Fold
Farm

78

96   A   97   B   97   C   98   D   98   E   F

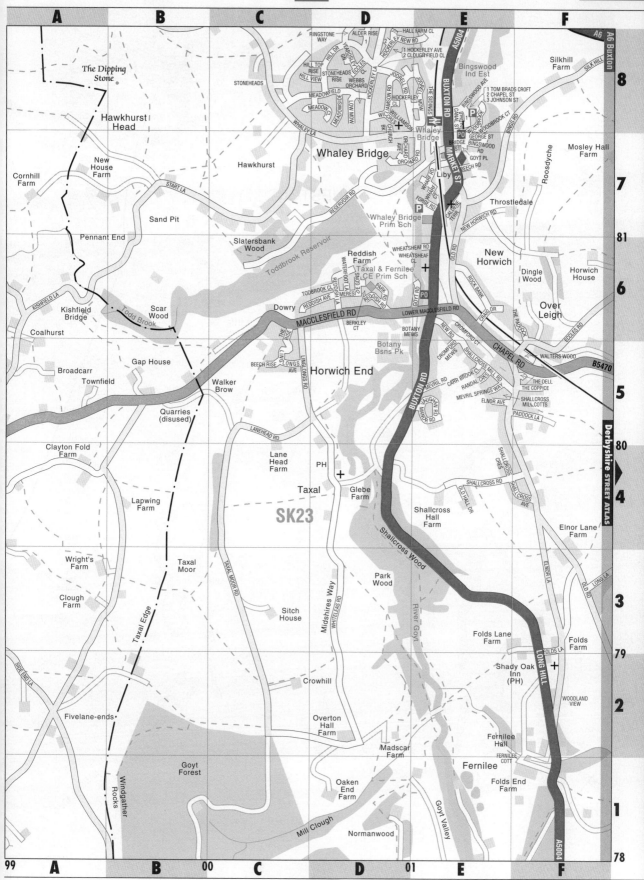

A6 Buxton

A6

Silkhill Farm

SILK HILL

The Dipping Stone

Bingswood Ind Est

Hawkhurst Head

1 TOM BRADS CROFT
2 CHAPEL ST
3 JOHNSON ST

Mosley Hall Farm

New House Farm

RINGSTONE WAY

ALDER RISE

HALL FARM CL

HOCKERLEY NEW RD

1 HOCKERLEY AVE
2 CLOUGFIELD CL

Roosdyche

Cornhill Farm

HILL TOP RISE

STONEHEADS

HILL DR

YEARDSLEY ECCLES

HOCKERLEY LA

JODREL

JOCKEY MDW

BUXTON RD

BINGSWOOD AVE

GEORGE ST

HILL VIEW

STONEHEADS

HOCKERLEY RISE

WEBBS ORCHARD

CANAL ST

WOODBROOK CT

START LA

MEADOW

MEADOWSIDE

WHALEY LA

WILLIAMSON RD

WILCKES

LOW MDW

WILCKES CHURCH

Whaley Bridge

ORCHARD

ORCHARD AVE

MARKET ST

Whaley Bridge

BRIDGE ST

BINGSWOOD RD

GOYT PL

BEECH RD

Liby

Throstledale

Sand Pit

Hawkhurst

RESERVOIR RD

WHARF RD

CALLOW TERR

New Horwich

Dingle Wood

Horwich House

Pennant End

Whaley Bridge Prim Sch

NEW HORWICH RD

Slatersbank Wood

Reddish Farm

WHEATSHEAF RD

WHEATSHEAF CL

Toddbrook Reservoir

Taxal & Fernilee CE Prim Sch

OLD RD

ROCK BANK

Over Leigh

Kishfield Bridge

KISHFIELD LA

Scar Wood

Todd Brook

TODDBROOK CL

REDDISH AVE

WATERFORD LA

MERSEY

SNOW LA

PARK RD

REDDISH RD

PO

GOYT RD

CRAIG DR

THE PADDOCK

ECCLES RD

Coalhurst

Dowry

Macclesfield Rd

Lower Macclesfield Rd

Botany Mews

CHAPEL RD

WALTERS WOOD

B5470

Broadcarr Townfield

Gap House

THE RISE

BERKLEY CT

Botany Bsns Pk

NEW RD

CROMFORD CT

SHALLCROSS MILL RD

CARR BROOK CL

THE DELL
THE COPPICE

Walker Brow

BEECH RISE

LONGS AVE

LING LONGS RD

Horwich End

BUXTON RD

CROMFORD MEWS

RANDAL CRES

MEVRIL SPRINGS WAY

ELNOR AVE

SHALLCROSS MILL COTTS

Quarries (disused)

LANEHEAD RD

MEVRIL RD

VAUGHAN RD

MANOR RD

PADDOCK LA

Clayton Fold Farm

Lane Head Farm

PH

Glebe Farm

SHALLCROSS CRES

SHALLCROSS RD

OLD HALL DR

SHALLCROSS AVE

Elnor Lane Farm

Lapwing Farm

Taxal

SK23

Shallcross Hall Farm

ELNOR LA

LONG LA

OLD RD

Wright's Farm

Taxal Moor

Taxal Moor Rd

Midshires Way

WHITELEAS RD

Park Wood

Shallcross Wood

River Goyt

Folds Lane Farm

LONG HILL

Folds Farm

Clough Farm

FOLDS LA

Sitch House

Shady Oak Inn (PH)

Taxal Edge

SIDE END LA

WOODLAND VIEW

Fivelane-ends

Crowhill

Overton Hall Farm

Fernilee Hall

FERNILEE COTT

Goyt Forest

Madscar Farm

Fernilee

Folds End Farm

Windgather Rocks

Oaken End Farm

Goyt Valley

Mill Clough

Normanwood

A5004

Derbyshire STREET ATLAS

E8
1 MARLOWE RD
2 POPLAR WEINT
3 SCHOLAR'S CT
4 HADDON HO
5 DENWALL HO
6 ASHFIELD HO

7 HARGREAVE HO
8 THE CROSS
9 The Royal Sh Arc
F7
1 NORMANS COTTS

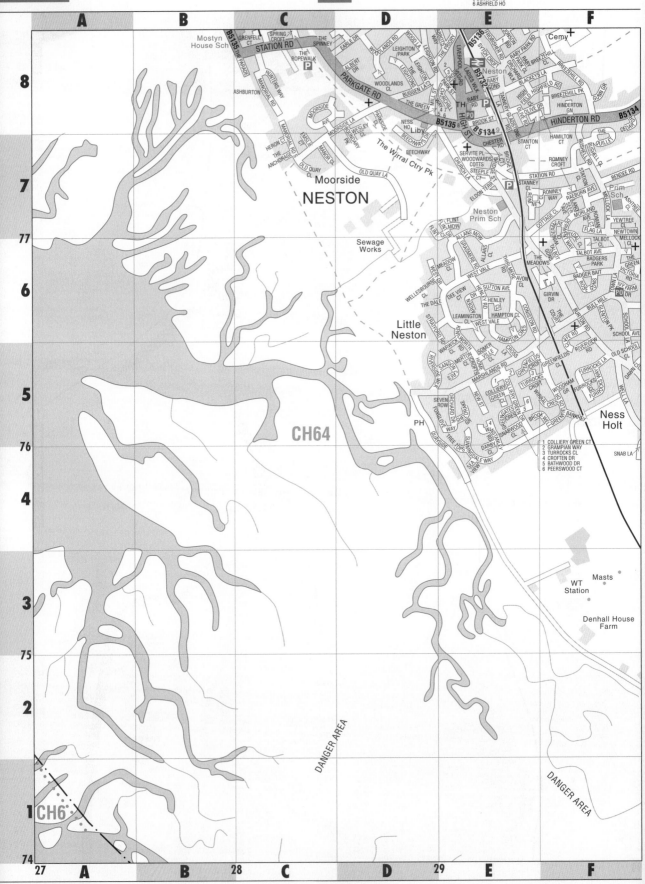

1 COLLIERY GREEN CT
2 GRAMPIAN WAY
3 TURROCKS CL
4 CROFTEN DR
5 BATHWOOD DR
6 PEERSWOOD CT

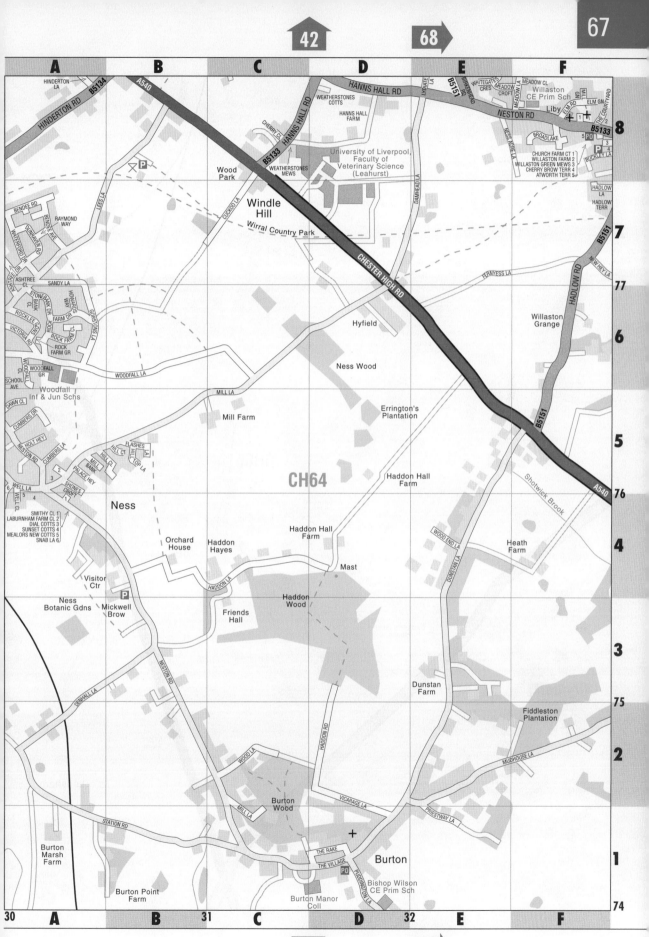

67 43

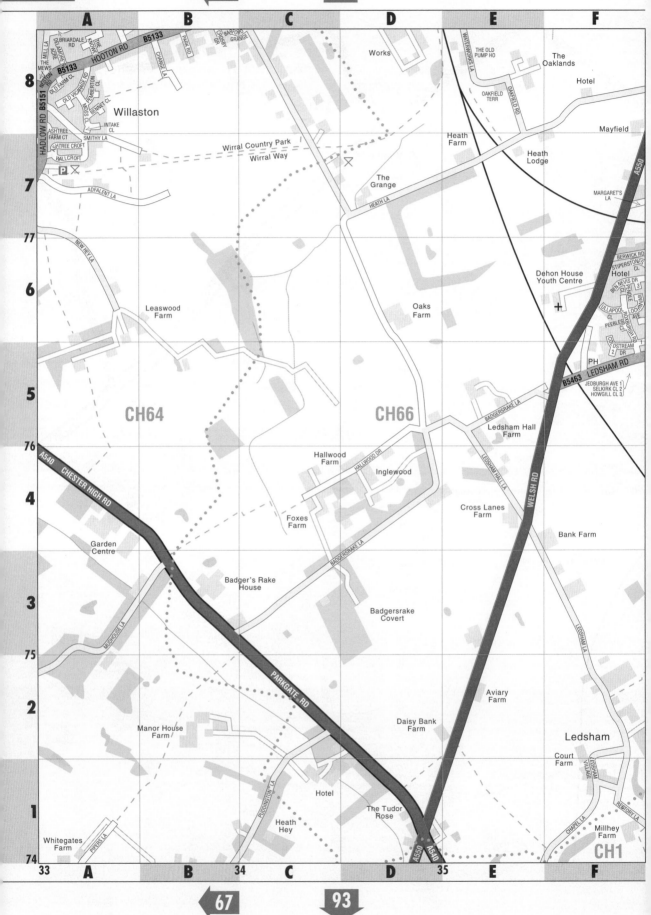

67 93

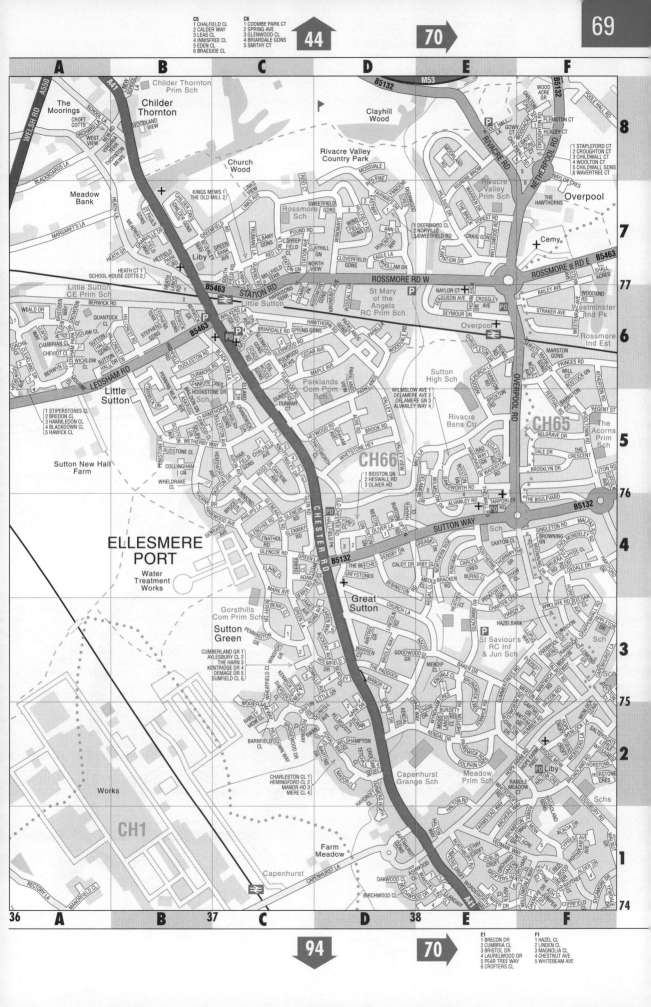

C6
1 WILKINSON STREET MEWS
2 CHURCH WLK
3 MARYVILLE CL
4 SUNNYSIDE
5 CHURCH PAR
6 WORCESTER WLK

69

C6
7 CRESSINGHAM GDNS
8 CHARLES PRICE GDNS
9 THE COURT HO
10 JOSEPH GROOME TWRS
11 HIGHFIELD RD N

45

C5
1 ASHFIELD RD N
2 WOODFIELD RD N
3 WELLINGTON CL
4 SHREWSBURY RD
5 WATERLOO CL
6 WELLESLEY WLK

ELLESMERE PORT

River Mersey

CH66

CH65

CH2

Whitby

Wolverham

Little Stanney

Whitbyheath

69

D2
1 BUCKINGHAM GDNS
2 SANDRINGHAM GDNS
3 FOTHERINGAY CT
4 CAERNARVON CT
C1
1 BARDSEY CL
2 ANGLESEY CL
3 ORKNEY CL
4 CUMBRAE DR

95

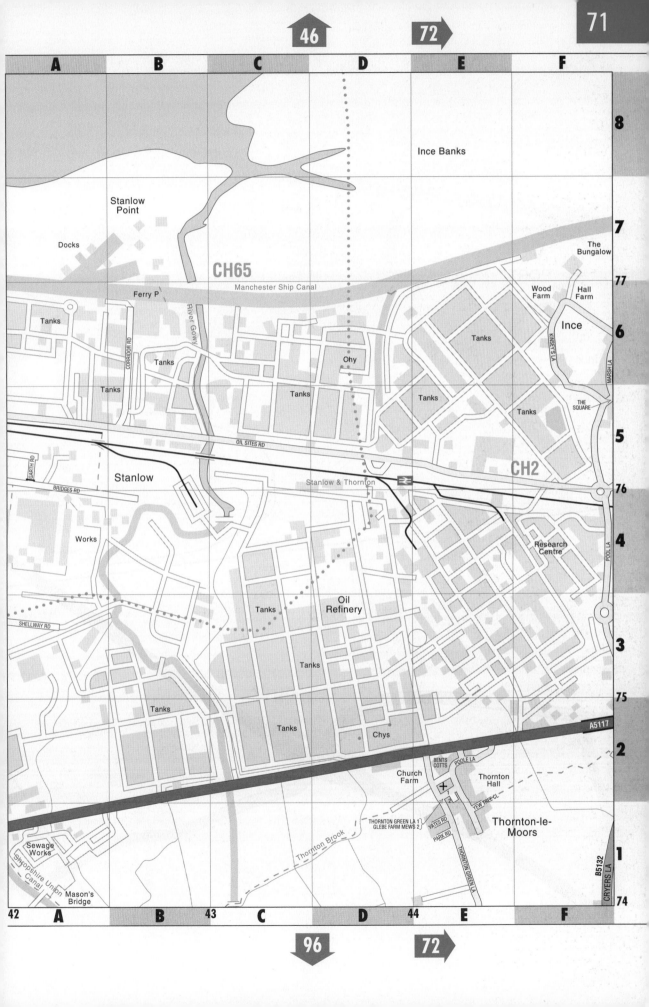

← 71
↑ 47

A B C D E F

8

Manchester Ship Canal

Canal Deposit
Dump

Works

7

Hoolpool Gutter

Holme
Farm

77

Works

Ince
Marshes

6

KINSEY'S
LA

LORDSHIP LA

RAKE LA

Ince
PH

THE
SQUARE

CH2

Works

5

STATION RD

LC

HOOLPOOL LA

Hornsmill Brook

76

PERIMETER RD

ELTON LA

INCE ORCHARDS
STATION RD
Ince &
Elton

CHERRY TREE CL

Helsby West Cheshire
Junction

M56

4

MOUNT
PLEASANT

PO

HIGHFIELD

ORCHARD PARK LA

HAPSFORD LA

TOWNFIELD
VILLAS

ORCHARD
PK

COPPICE GN

Elton
Prim Sch

Liby

DAIRY BANK

PH

CHAPEL
MEWS

MARSH LA

DOVE CL

REDWOOD DR

Sewage
Works

WA6

Elton

THE PADDOCK

FARMDALE DR

RYECROFT

WHITEFIELDS

GREENFIELD
GDNS

MANNA DR

HOLM

OSIER CL

MULBERRY
CL

1 BIRCHWOOD CL
2 SORBUS CL

3

DALEWOOD

GLENDALE
AVE

GLEBECROFT
AVE

SCHOOL LA

BRACKENDALE

LAWNSWOOD GR

HLYFIELD DR

INCE LA

PINEWOOD

ACACIA
CL

FIRBANK

MEADOW
VIEW

Elton
Green

FERNDALE AVE

PARKLAND DR

ALVANLEY VIEW

MANLEY
VIEW

75

POOL LA

POND
COTTS

LIME GR

POPLAR
GR

LAURELS
FARM CT

OLD HALL LA

WILLOW GR

Chester
Services

i

2

A5117

B5132

CRYERS LA

New Dairy
Farm

Motel

14

Nature
Reserve

Jessamine
Farm

HAPSFORD
MEWS

MOOR LA

Lower Hapsford
Hall

Sewage
Works

DALECROFT

HAPSDALE
VIEW

Hapsford

HAPSFORD LA

1

M56

COMMON LA

A5117

CHESTER
RD

A56

74

45 A B 46 C 47 D 47 E F

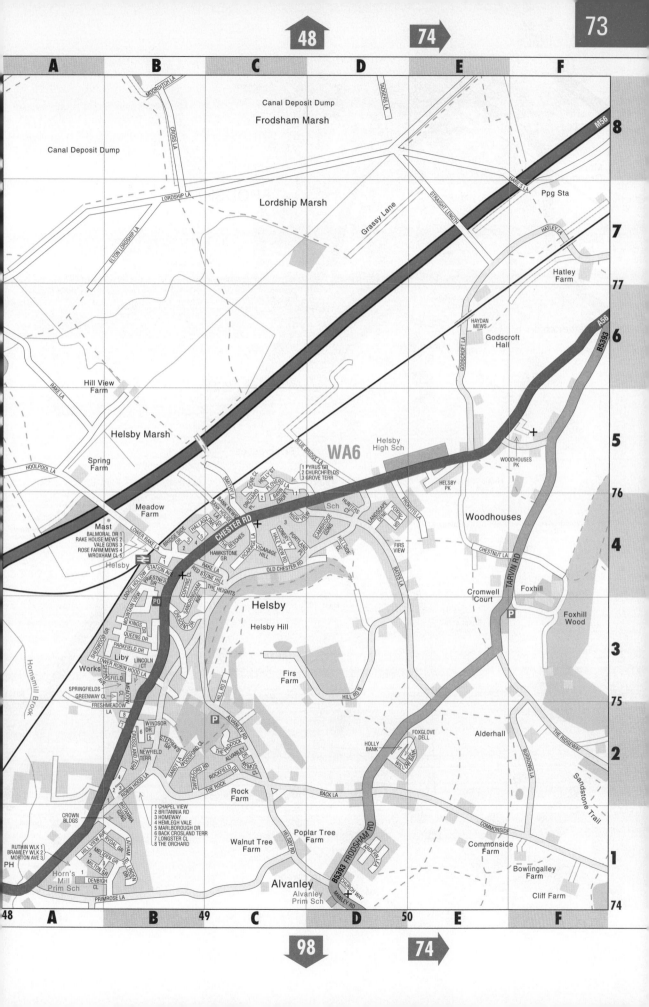

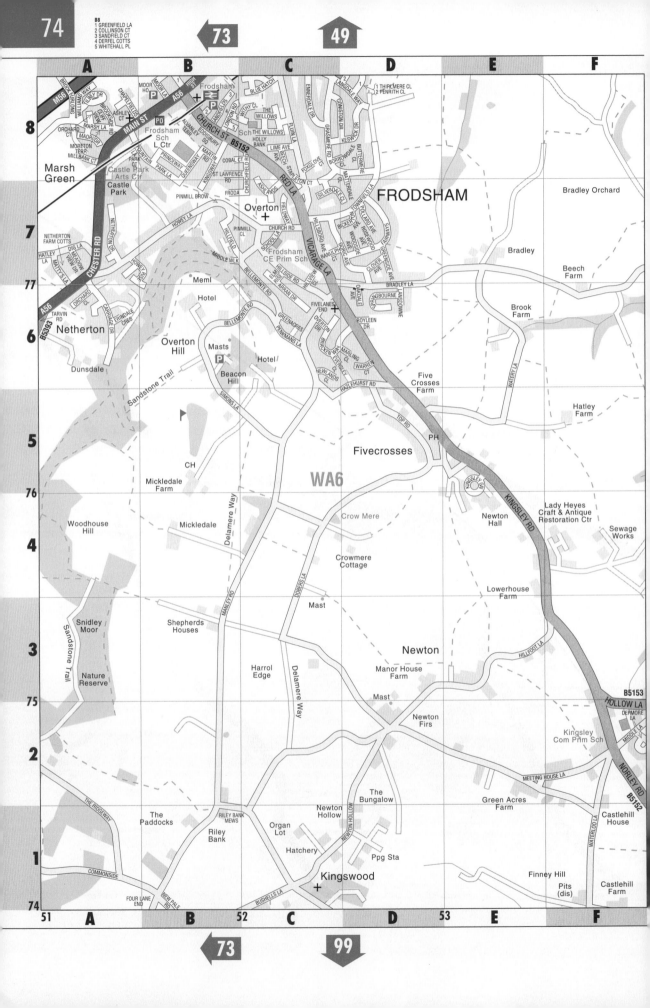

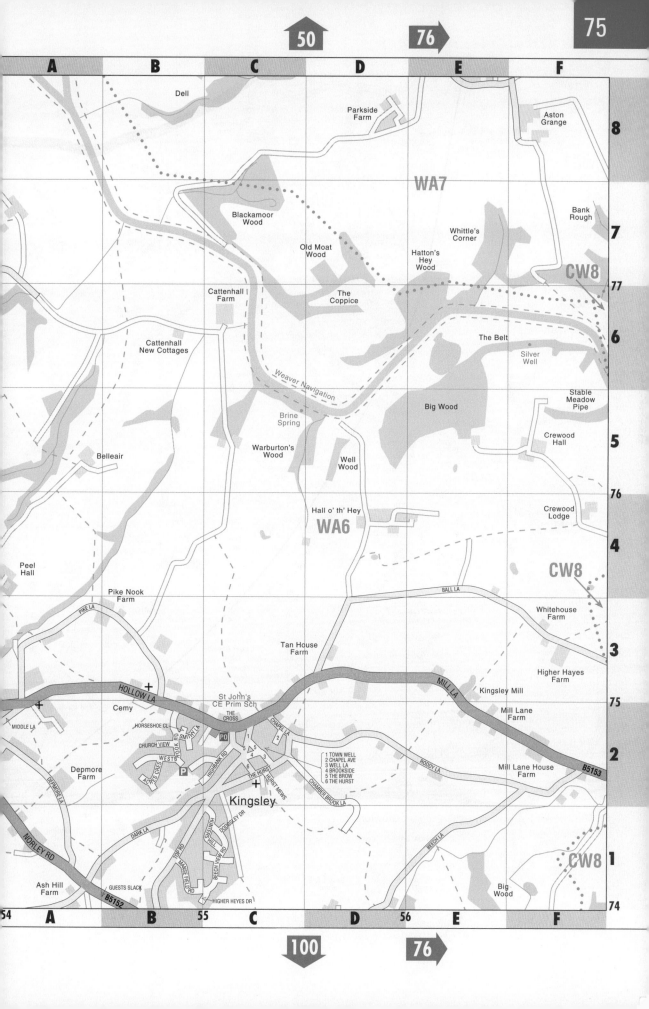

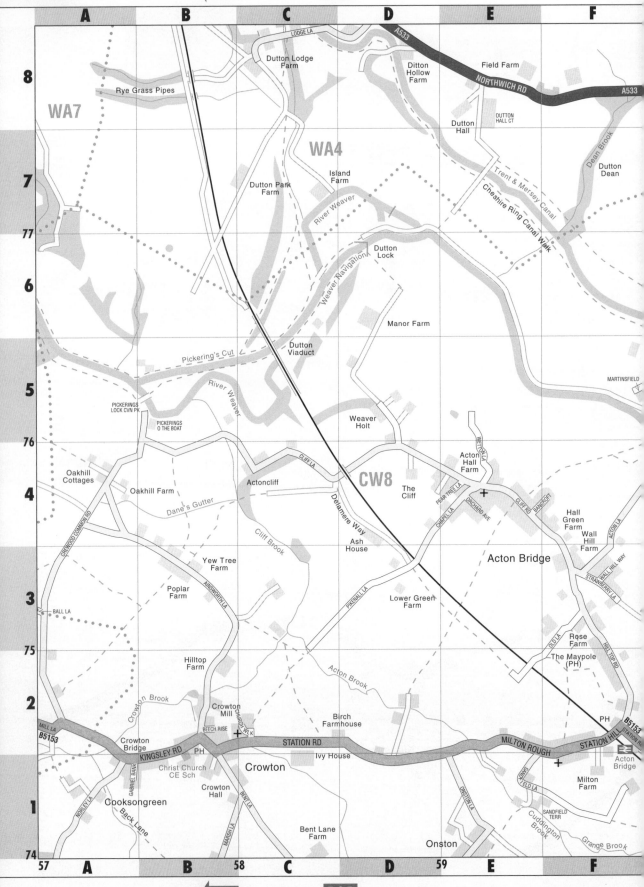

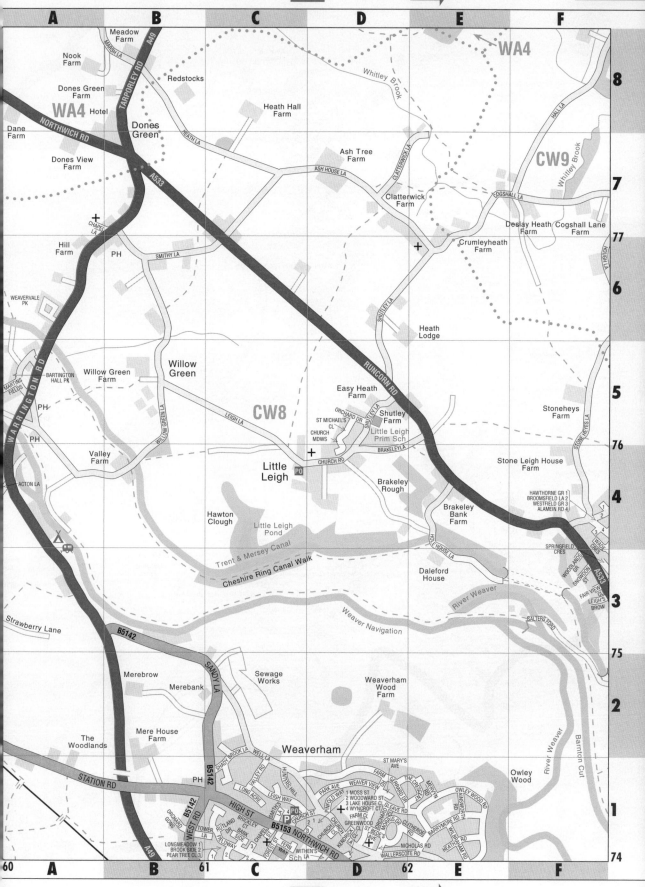

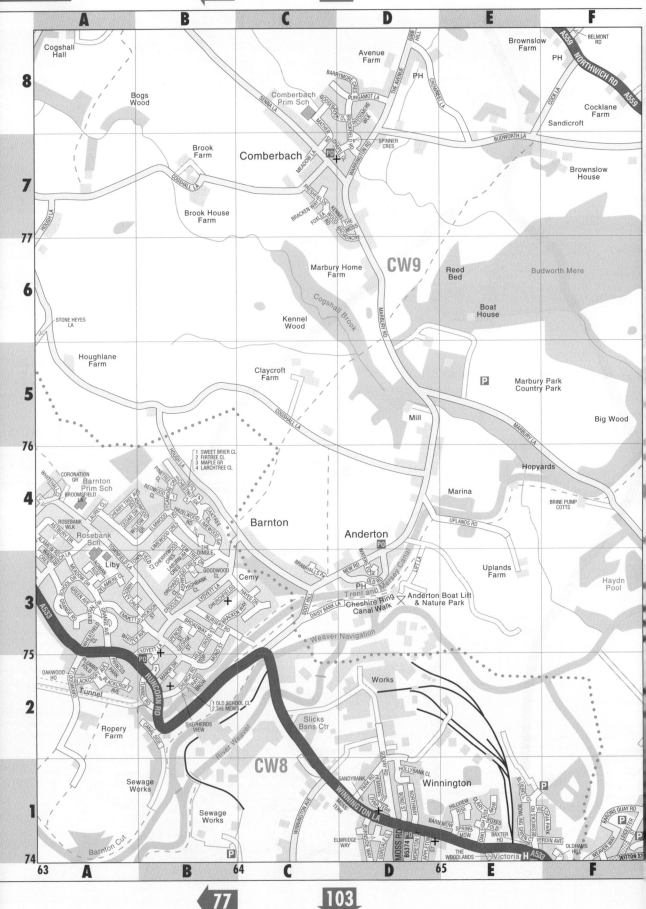

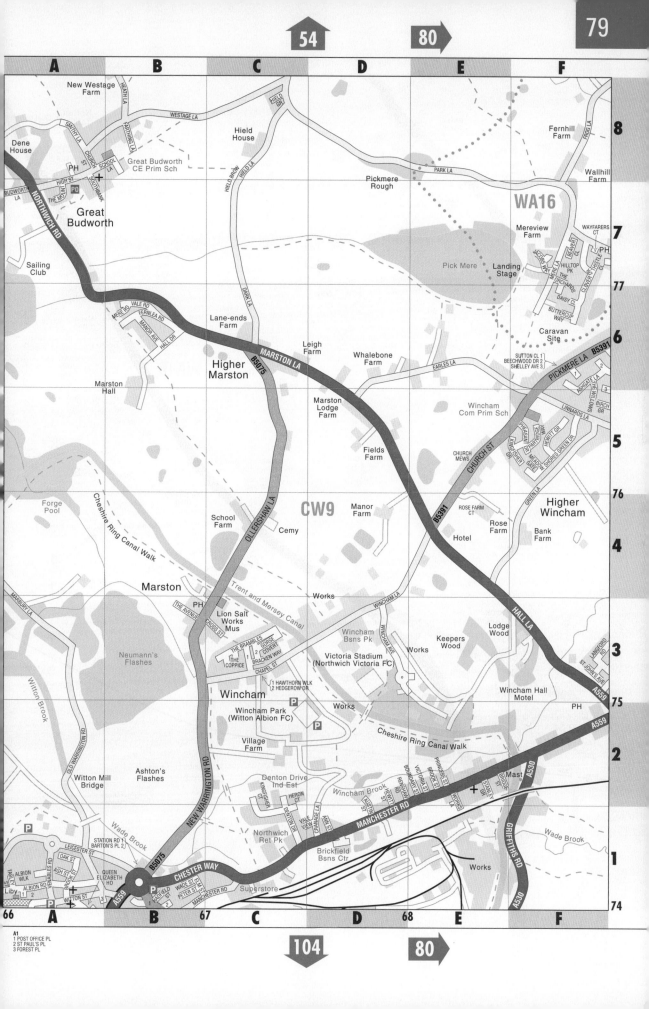

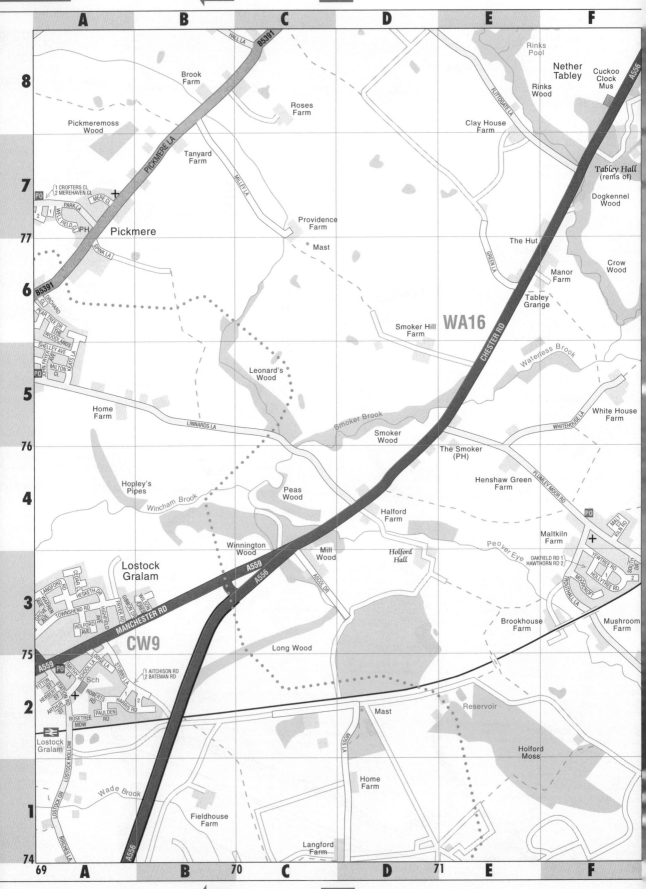

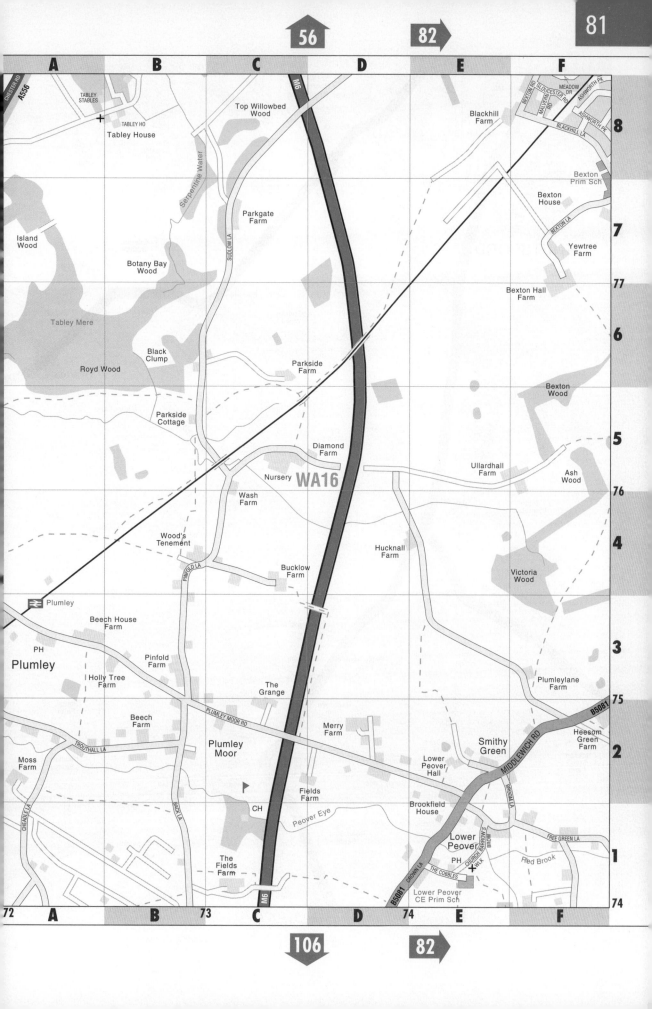

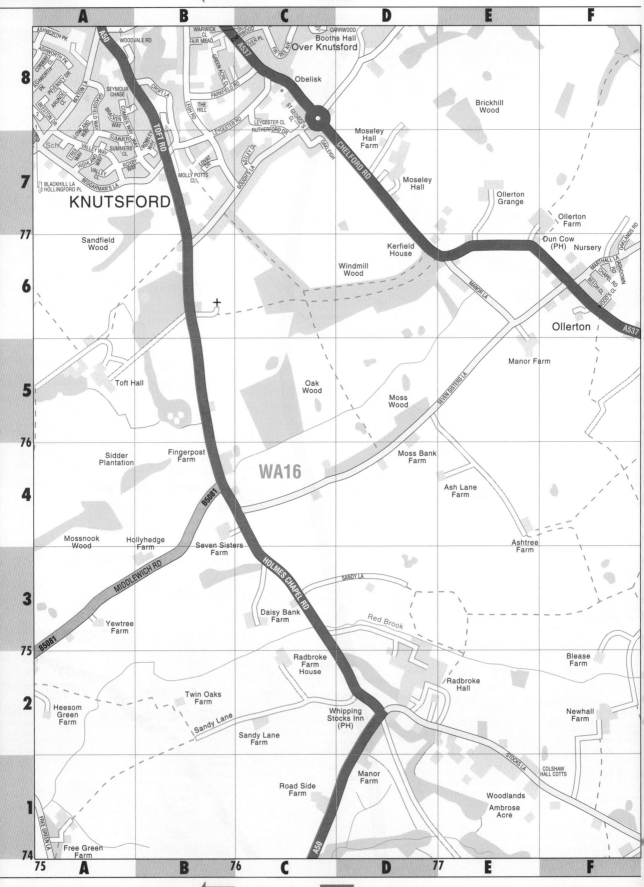

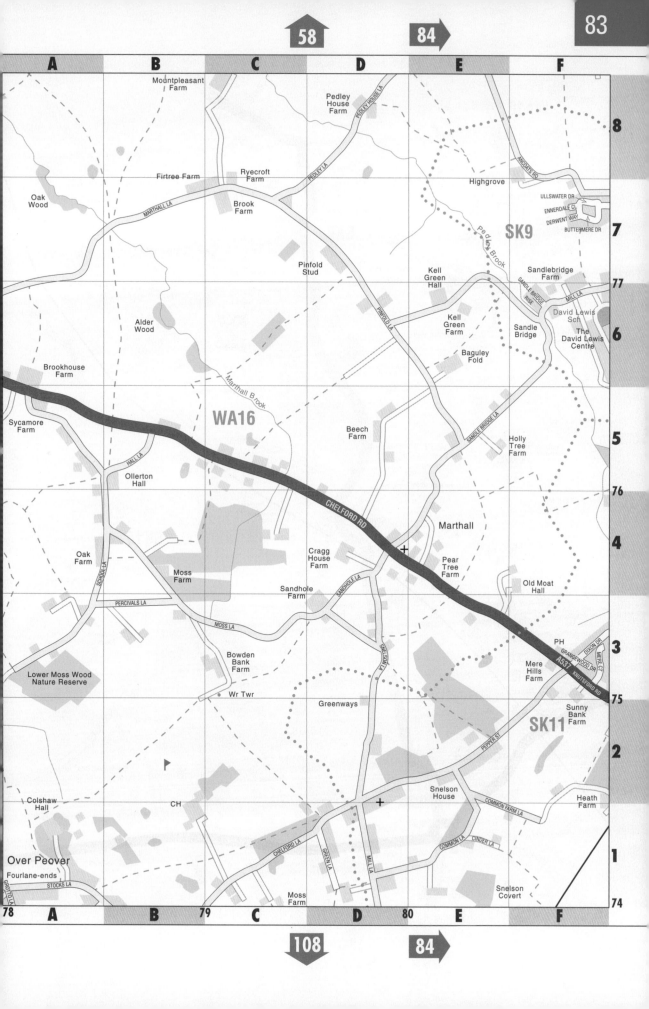

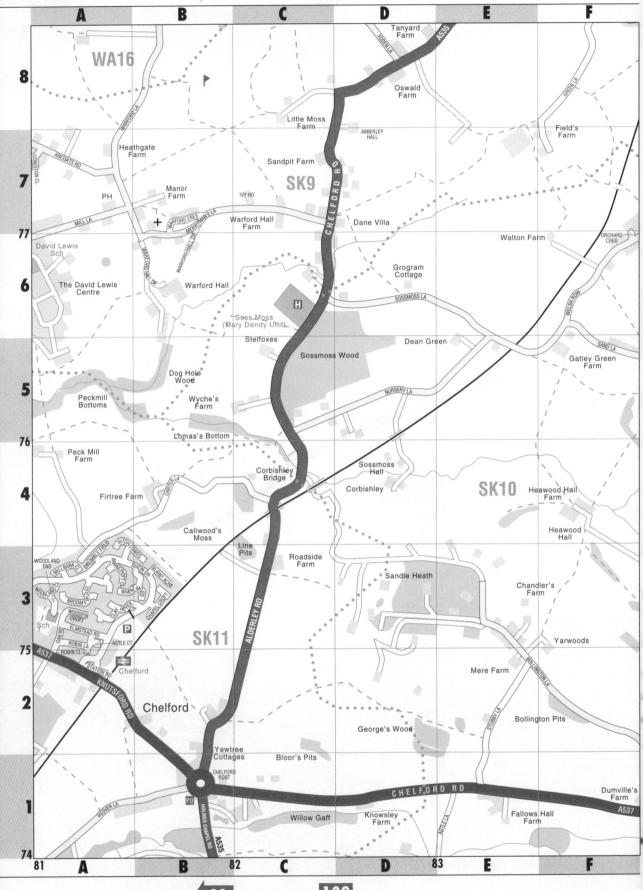

WA16

8

Tanyard
Farm

Oswald
Farm

Little Moss
Farm

ABBERLEY
HALL

Field's
Farm

Heathgate
Farm

Sandpit Farm

SK9

7

Manor
Farm

IVY HO

PH

Dane Villa

Walton Farm

ORCHARD
CRES

77

Warford Hall
Farm

David Lewis
Sch

Grogram
Cottage

The David Lewis
Centre

Warford Hall

SOSSMOSS LA

6

H

Soss Moss
(Mary Dendy Unit)

Dean Green

SAND LA

Stelfoxes

Sossmoss Wood

Gatley Green
Farm

Dog Hole
Wood

Peckmill
Bottoms

Wyche's
Farm

NURSERY LA

5

Lomas's Bottom

Peck Mill
Farm

Sossmoss
Hall

SK10

Heawood Hall
Farm

76

Corbishley
Bridge

Corbishley

Firtree Farm

CARTER LA

Heawood
Hall

4

Callwood's
Moss

Line
Pits

Roadside
Farm

Sandle Heath

Chandler's
Farm

WOODLAND
END

MILLBANK

3

Sch

ELMSTEAD RD

Yarwoods

SK11

ALDERLEY RD

75

A537

Chelford

Mere Farm

BOLLINGTON LA

2

Chelford

Bollington Pits

KNUTSFORD RD

STUBBY LA

Yewtree
Cottages

George's Wood

CHELFORD RDBT

ASTLE LA

Dumville's
Farm

1

CHELFORD RD

A537

Bloor's Pits

PEOVER LA

HOLMES CHAPEL RD

A535

Willow Gaff

Knowsley
Farm

Fallows Hall
Farm

74

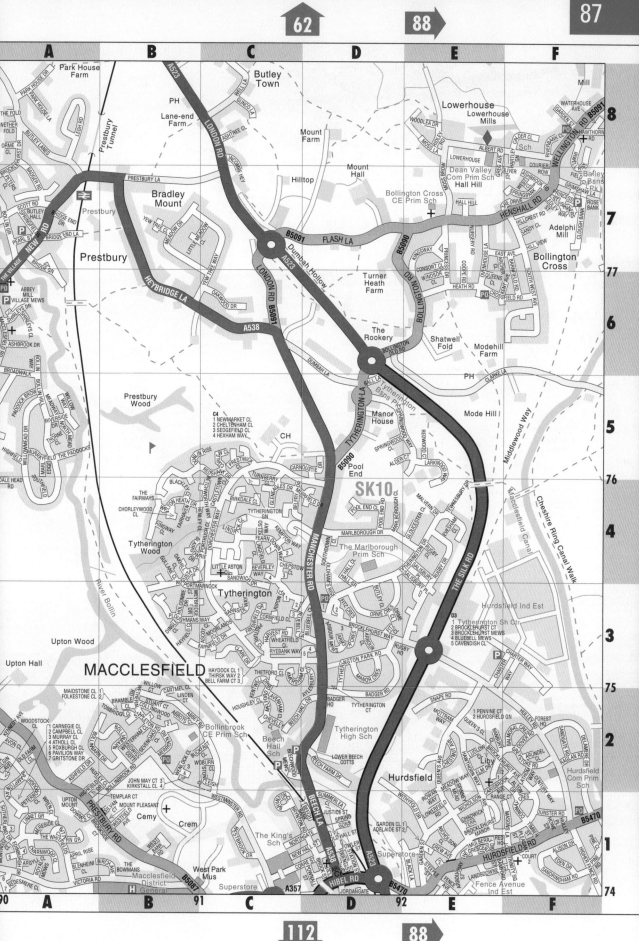

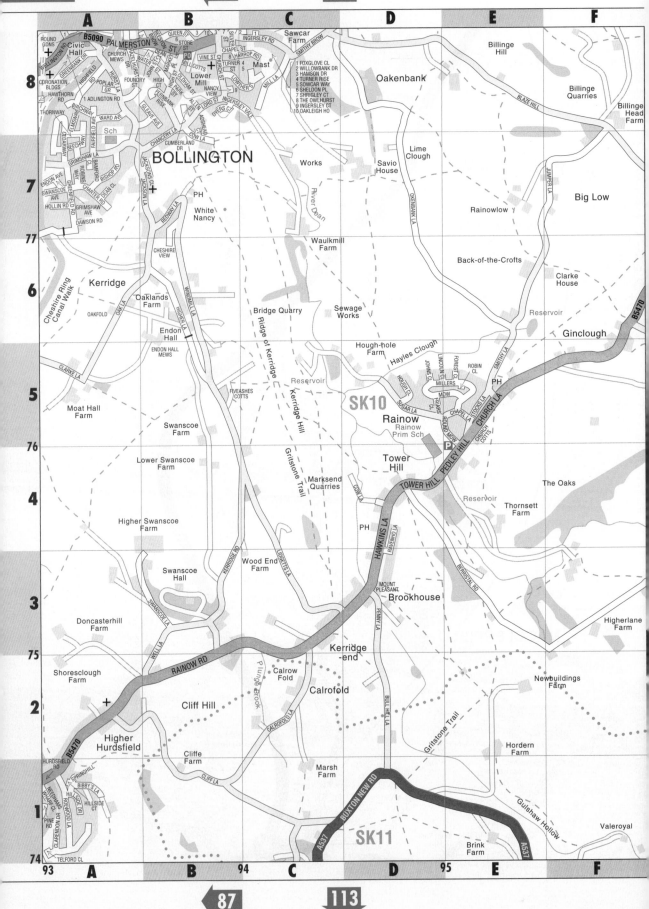

B5090 PALMERSTON
Civic Hall
CORONATION BLDGS
Round GDNS
BELLINGTON RD
GREENBANK DR
HAWTHORN RD
THORNWAY
BEECHWAY
ELMSHAW
BIRCHWAY
HIGHFIELD
CHURCH MEWS
DEAN
WATER ST
FOUNDRY ST
FERNBANK RISE
HURST LA
POPLAR GR
PARK
HIGH ST
OLD LA
BROOK
DEAN ST
MILL ST
STORE ST
QUEEN ST
Queen St
SILVER ST
CHAPEL ST
TURNER ST
HARROP RD
INGERSLEY RD
VINE ST
Lower Mill
NANCY VIEW
Mast
Sawcar Farm
Smithy Brow

1 FOXGLOVE CL
2 WILLOWBANK DR
3 HAMSON DR
4 TURNER RISE
5 SOWCAR WAY
6 SHELDON PL
7 SHRIGLEY CT
8 THE OWLHURST
9 INGERSLEY CT
10 OAKLEIGH HO

Billinge Hill

Oakenbank

Blaze Hill

Billinge Quarries

Billinge Head Farm

BOLLINGTON

Works

Savio House

Lime Clough

Big Low

Jumper La

PH

White Nancy

River Dean

Rainowlow

Kerridge

Cheshire Ring Canal Walk

Oaklands Farm

OAKFOLD

OAK LA

HIGHER LA

Waulkmill Farm

Bridge Quarry

Sewage Works

Back-of-the-Crofts

Clarke House

Reservoir

Ginclough

B5470

Endon Hall

ENDON HALL MEWS

WINDMILL LA

Ridge of Kerridge

Reservoir

Hough-hole Farm

Hayles Clough

HOUGH CL
SUGAR LA
JOHNS CL
LINCOLN CL
MILLERS
FRIARS CL
MDW
ROBIN CL
FOREST CL
CHAPEL LA
STOCKS LA
SMITHY LA

PH

SK10

Rainow
Rainow Prim Sch

Moat Hall Farm

Swanscoe Farm

Kerridge Hill

Gritstone Trail

FIVEASHES COTTS

Marksend Quarries

Tower Hill

TOWER HILL

PEDLEY HILL

CHURCH LA

CHURCH COTTS

Reservoir

The Oaks

Lower Swanscoe Farm

Higher Swanscoe Farm

CON LA

PH

HAWKINS LA

RAVENHO LA

Thornsett Farm

Swanscoe Hall

KERRIDGE RD

Wood End Farm

LIDGETTS LA

BERRISTALL RD

MOUNT PLEASANT

Brookhouse

Higherlane Farm

Doncasterhill Farm

SWANSCOE LA

WELL LA

RAINOW RD

Kerridge-end

PENNY LA

Newbuildings Farm

Shoresclough Farm

Plunge Brook

Calrow Fold

Calrofold

BULL HILL LA

Gritstone Trail

Hordern Farm

B5470

Higher Hurdsfield

Cliff Hill

CALROFOLD LA

Cliffe Farm

CLIFF LA

Marsh Farm

BUXTON NEW RD

Gulshaw Hollow

Valeroyal

HURDSFIELD RD
SPRINGHILL
BIBBY'S LA
HILLSIDE CT
PINE RD
NEEDHAMS
WHARF CT
CLARENDON DR
RICHMOND CT
TELFORD CL

A537

SK11

A537

Brink Farm

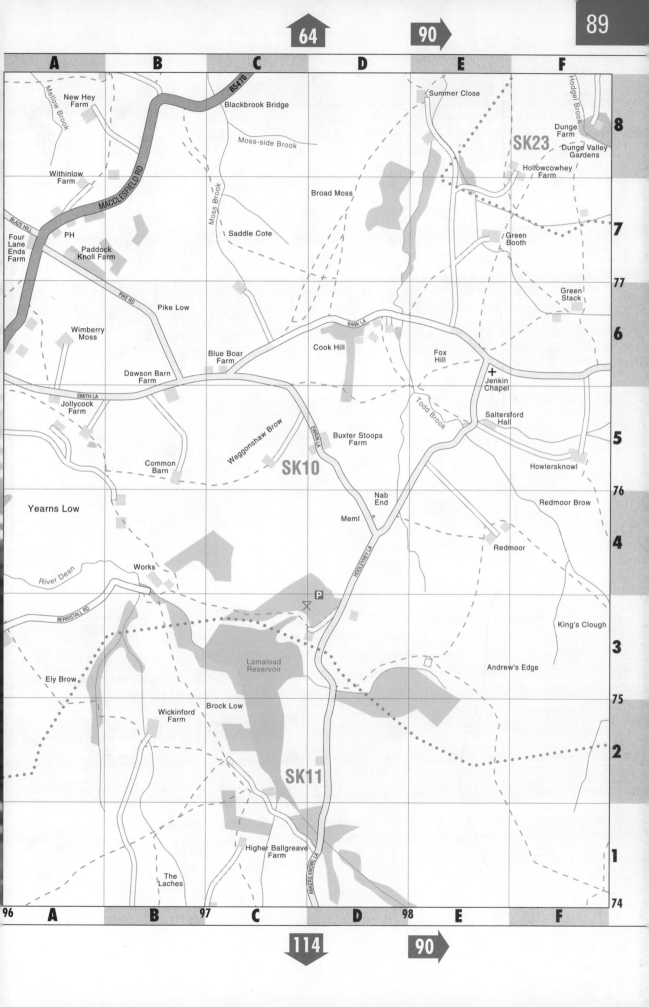

A B C D E F

8

Mellow Brook

New Hey Farm

B5470

Blackbrook Bridge

Summer Close

Hodgel Brook

Dunge Farm

SK23

Dunge Valley Gardens

Moss-side Brook

Hollowcowhey Farm

Withinlow Farm

MACCLESFIELD RD

Moss Brook

Broad Moss

Green Booth

7

BLAZE HILL

PH

Four Lane Ends Farm

Paddock Knoll Farm

Saddle Cote

77

Green Stack

PIKE RD

Pike Low

BANK LA

6

Wimberry Moss

Cook Hill

Fox Hill

Blue Boar Farm

Jenkin Chapel

Dawson Barn Farm

Saltersford Hall

SMITH LA

Todd Brook

Jollycock Farm

Waggonshaw Brow

EWRIN LA

Buxter Stoops Farm

5

SK10

Howlersknowl

Common Barn

76

Yearns Low

Nab End

Redmoor Brow

Meml

River Dean

Works

Redmoor

4

BERRISTALL RD

HOOLEYHEY LA

King's Clough

3

P

Andrew's Edge

Ely Brow

Lamaload Reservoir

75

Wickinford Farm

Brock Low

2

SK11

Higher Ballgreave Farm

1

ANKERS KNOWL LA

The Laches

74

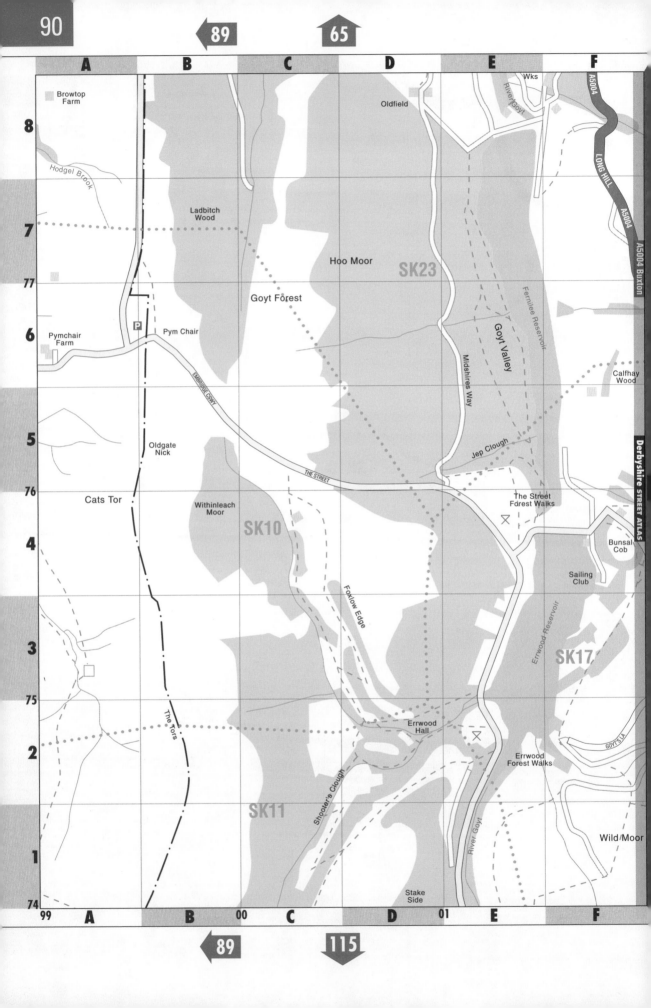

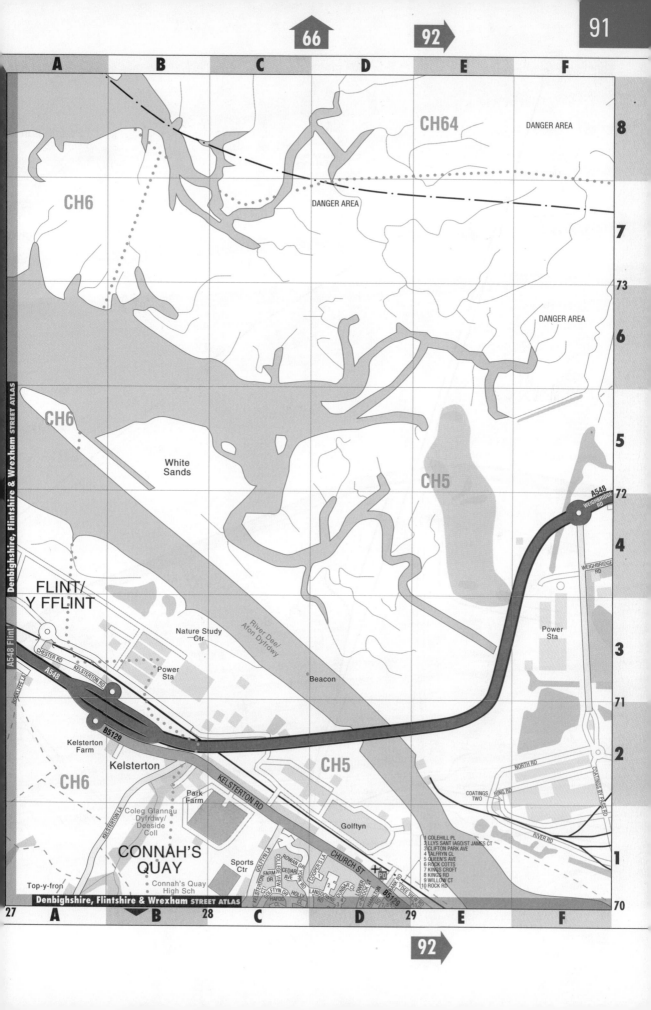

Puddington

The Mere

Marsh
Covert

Burton Mere
Fisheries

Barn
Farm

CH64

PUDDINGTON LA

PIPERS LA

Old
Hall

Puddington
Hall

Burton Point

DANGER AREA

Rifle Range

Platts
Covert

Reservoir

CH1 →

DANGER AREA

WEIGHBRIDGE RD

A548

LC

WEIGHBRIDGE RD

Works

SHOTWICK RD

A548

CH5

TENTH AVE

TENTH AVE

TENTH AVE

Mast

FOURTH AVE

SECOND AVE

SECOND AVE

Parc Ddiwydiannol
Glannau Dyfrdwy/
Deeside Ind Pk

FOURTH AVE

Newtech
Sq

Works

LC

FIRST AVE

SIXTH AVE

Parkway
Bsns
Ctr

THIRD AVE

Birkenhead
Junction

PARKWAY

RIVER RD

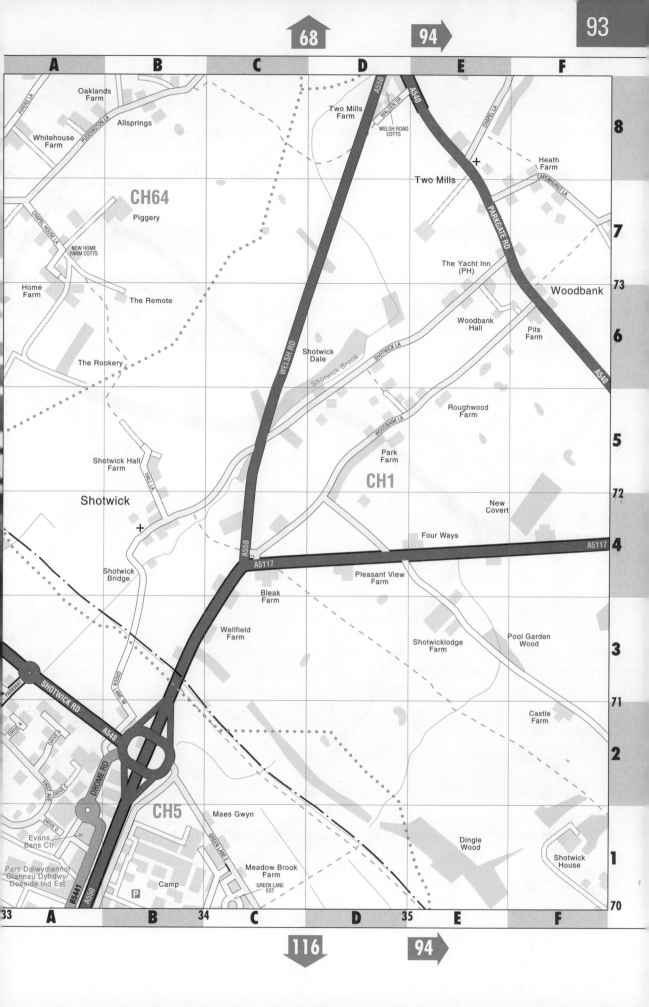

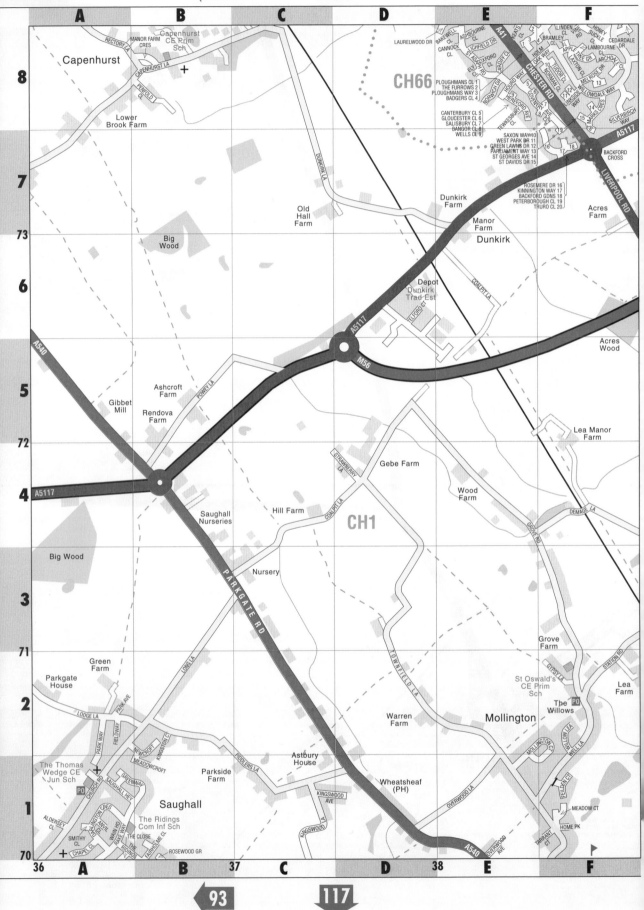

95

71

A **B** **C** **D** **E** **F**

8

Stoak Grange

Shropshire Union Canal

Dension's Bridge

Cryers Farm

B5132

Thornton Green La

Thornton Green Farm

7

PH

Little Stanney La

Church La

Heath La

Stoak

Croughton Rd

Bunbury Ct

Stoke Bridge

Spring Farm

Hallsgreen La

Cryers La

Hob La

73

M56

M56

Heath Farm

6

M53

15

Ashwood Farm Ct

Ashwood House

Ash Wood

Wimbolds Trafford

Ince La

Hall Farm

5

Ashwood La

River Gowy

CH2

Mill Brook

72

Park Farm

B5132

Wervin

Picton La

Landfill Site

4

Wervin New Hall

Hill Far

Hasnel La

A56

3

Woodside Farm

Picton

Green La

Picton Hall

PH

Trafford Bridge

Ashton House

Wervin Rd

71

The Shrewsbury Arms (PH)

2

New House Farm

Sewage Works

Warrington Rd

Ash Hey Farm

Green La

Ash Hay La

Saw Mill

1 HURLESTONE CL
2 WEAVER GR
3 DANE GR
4 ALYN RD
5 WOODLAND BANK
6 ST PETERS WAY
7 ST ANDREWS WLK

Cvn Site

1

Fox Covert La

M53

The Street

York Dr

Dee Rd

Stoak Rd

Plemstall La

Glebe Mdws

Linden Dr

Plemstall Way

A56

Acres La

70

42 **A** **B** **43** **C** **D** **44** **E** **F**

95

119

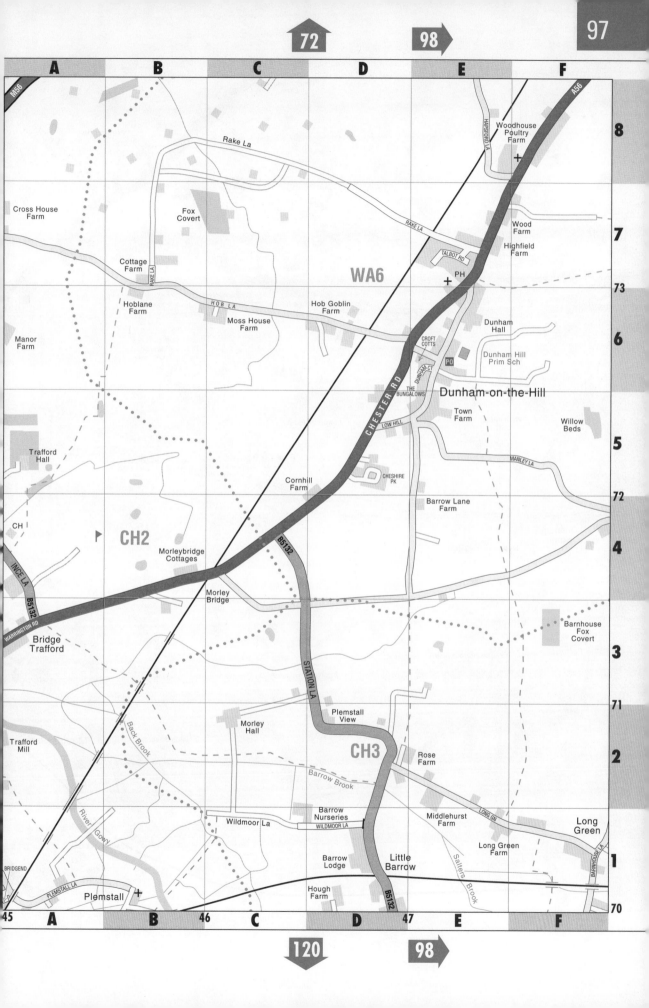

A **B** **C** **D** **E** **F**

8

Cross House Farm

Rake La

Fox Covert

Woodhouse Poultry Farm

Wood Farm

7

Cottage Farm

WA6

Talbot Rd

PH

Highfield Farm

73

Hoblane Farm

HOB LA

Moss House Farm

Hob Goblin Farm

Dunham Hall

6

Manor Farm

CROFT COTTS

Dunham Ct

PO

Dunham Hill Prim Sch

CHESTER RD

THE BUNGALOWS

LOW HILL

Dunham-on-the-Hill

Trafford Hall

Town Farm

Willow Beds

5

CH

CH2

Cornhill Farm

CHESHIRE PK

MANLEY LA

72

Morleybridge Cottages

B5132

Barrow Lane Farm

4

INCE LA

B5132

WARRINGTON RD

Morley Bridge

Barnhouse Fox Covert

Bridge Trafford

3

Back Brook

STATION LA

71

Morley Hall

Plemstall View

Trafford Mill

CH3

Rose Farm

2

River Gowy

Barrow Brook

Middlehurst Farm

LONG GN

Long Green

Wildmoor La

WILDMOOR LA

Barrow Nurseries

Long Green Farm

BARNHOUSE LA

1

BRIDGEND

PLEMSTALL LA

Plemstall

Barrow Lodge

Little Barrow

B5132

Hough Farm

Salters Brook

70

A B C D E F

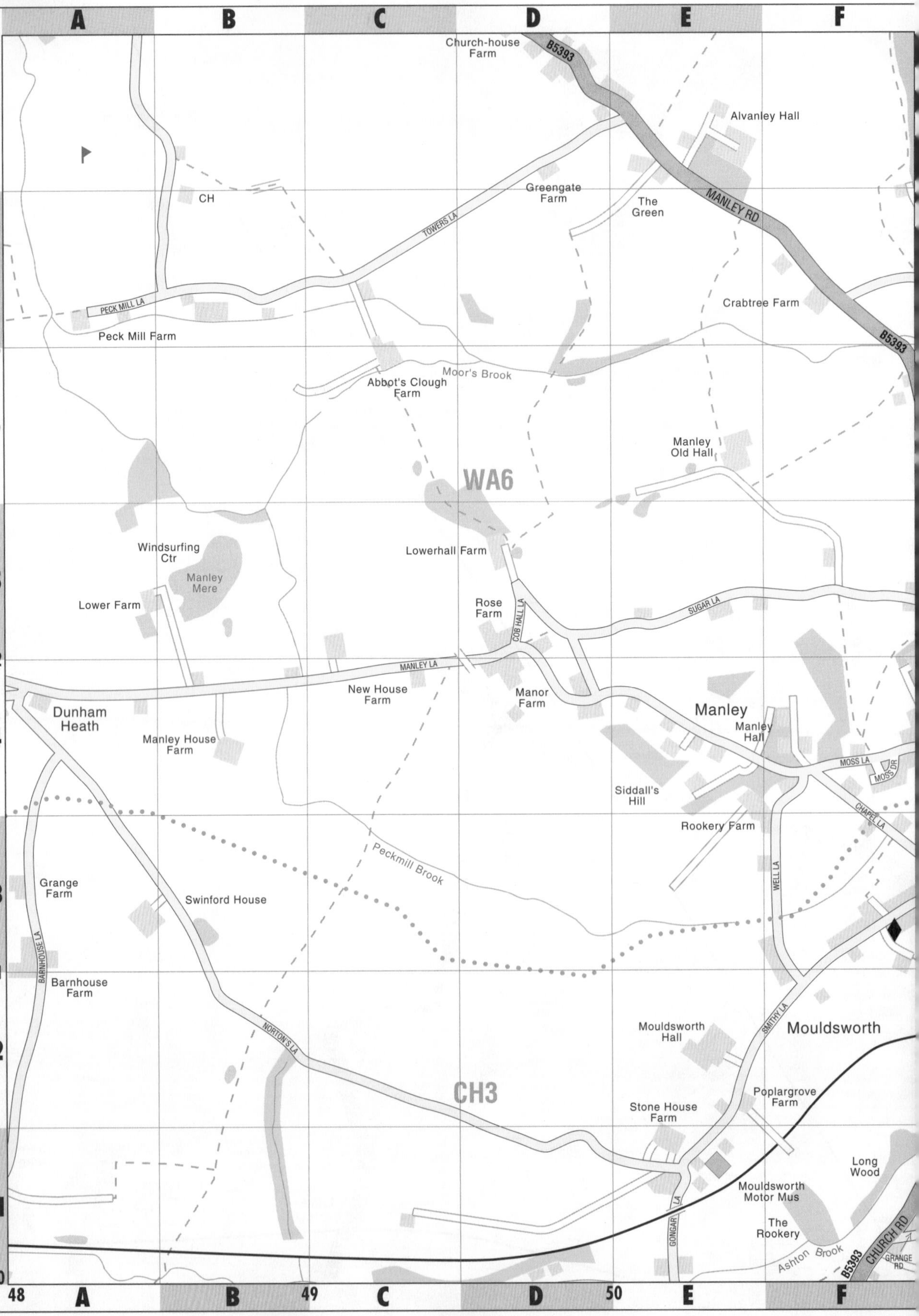

8

Church-house Farm

B5393

Alvanley Hall

CH

Greengate Farm

The Green

MANLEY RD

7

TOWERS LA

Crabtree Farm

PECK MILL LA

B5393

Peck Mill Farm

73

Moor's Brook

Abbot's Clough Farm

6

Manley Old Hall

WA6

Windsurfing Ctr

Lowerhall Farm

5

Manley Mere

Rose Farm

SUGAR LA

Lower Farm

COB HALL LA

72

MANLEY LA

New House Farm

Manor Farm

Manley

Dunham Heath

Manley Hall

4

Manley House Farm

MOSS LA

MOSS DR

Siddall's Hill

CHAPEL LA

Rookery Farm

WELL LA

Grange Farm

Swinford House

3

Peckmill Brook

BARNHOUSE LA

71

Barnhouse Farm

Mouldsworth Hall

SMITHY LA

Mouldsworth

2

NORTON'S LA

CH3

Poplargrove Farm

Stone House Farm

Long Wood

GONGAR LA

1

Mouldsworth Motor Mus

The Rookery

Ashton Brook

B5393

CHURCH RD

GRANGE RD

70

48 A 49 B C 49 D 50 E F

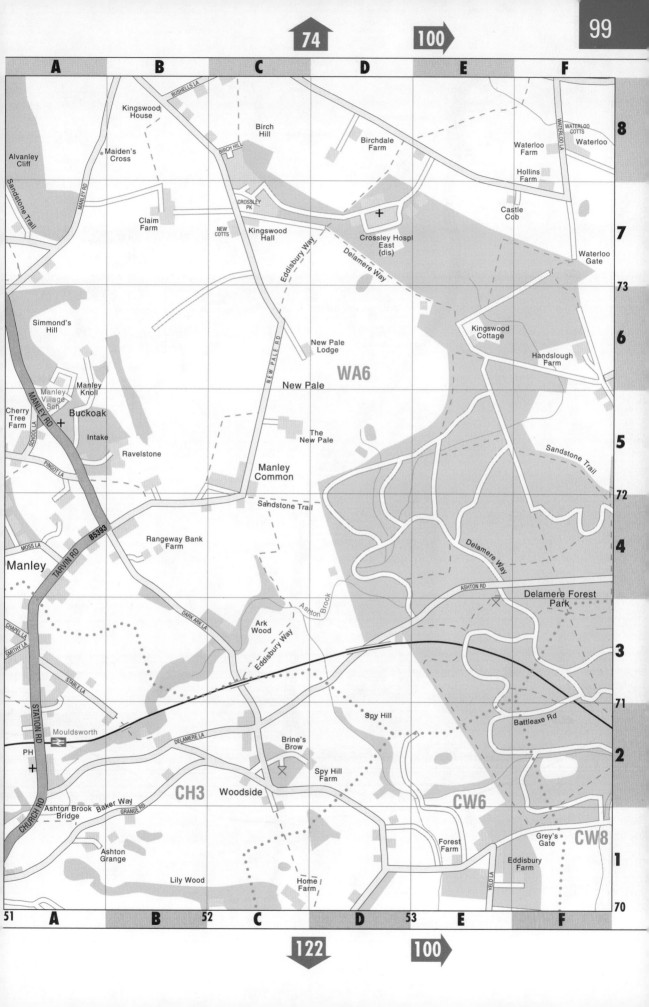

A   B   C   D   E   F

8

Alvanley
Cliff

Sandstone Trail

MANLEY RD

BUSHELLS LA

Kingswood
House

Maiden's
Cross

Claim
Farm

BIRCH HILL

Birch
Hill

Birchdale
Farm

NEW
COTTS

CROSSLEY
PK

Kingswood
Hall

Eddisbury Way

Delamere Way

Crossley Hospl
East
(dis)

Waterloo
Farm

Hollins
Farm

Castle
Cob

WATERLOO LA

WATERLOO
COTTS

Waterloo

Waterloo
Gate

7

73

Simmond's
Hill

NEW PALE RD

New Pale
Lodge

WA6

New Pale

Kingswood
Cottage

Handslough
Farm

6

Cherry
Tree
Farm

MANLEY RD

LA TOUCHS

Manley
Village
Sch

Manley
Knoll

Buckoak

Intake

Ravelstone

The
New Pale

Manley
Common

Sandstone Trail

Sandstone Trail

5

72

PINGOT LA

MOSS LA

TARVIN RD

B5393

Manley

Rangeway Bank
Farm

DARK ARK LA

Ashton Brook

Delamere Way

ASHTON RD

Delamere Forest
Park

4

3

71

CHAPEL LA

SMITHY LA

STABLE LA

STATION RD

PH

Ark
Wood

Eddisbury Way

Eddisbury Way

Spy Hill

Battleaxe Rd

CHURCH RD

Mouldsworth

DELAMERE LA

Brine's
Brow

Spy Hill
Farm

Woodside

CH3

Ashton Brook
Bridge

Baker Way

GRANGE RD

Ashton
Grange

Lily Wood

Home
Farm

Forest
Farm

Grey's
Gate

YELD LA

Eddisbury
Farm

CW6

CW8

2

1

70

51   A   B   52   C   D   53   E   F

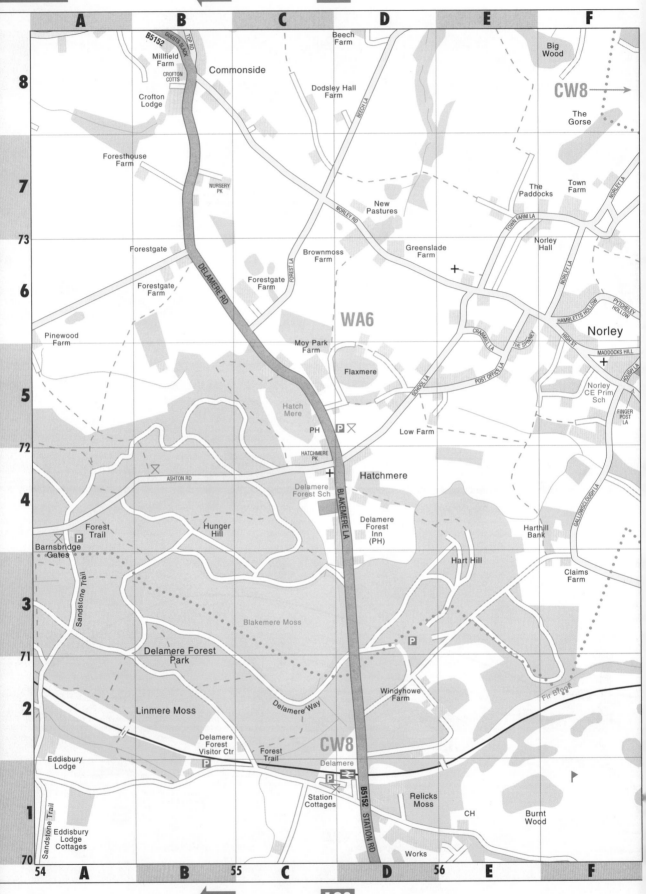

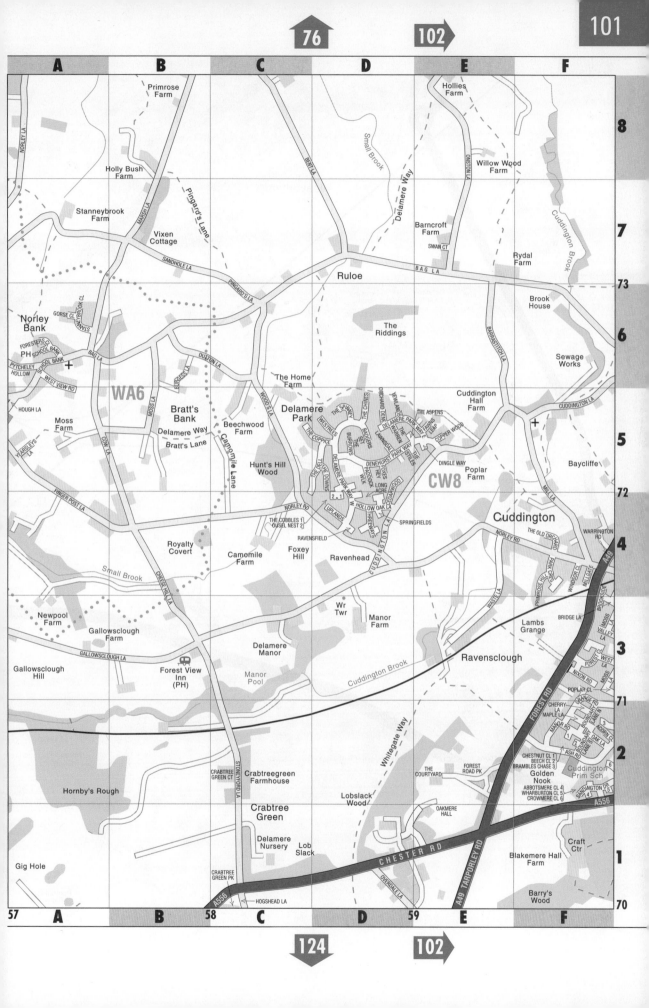

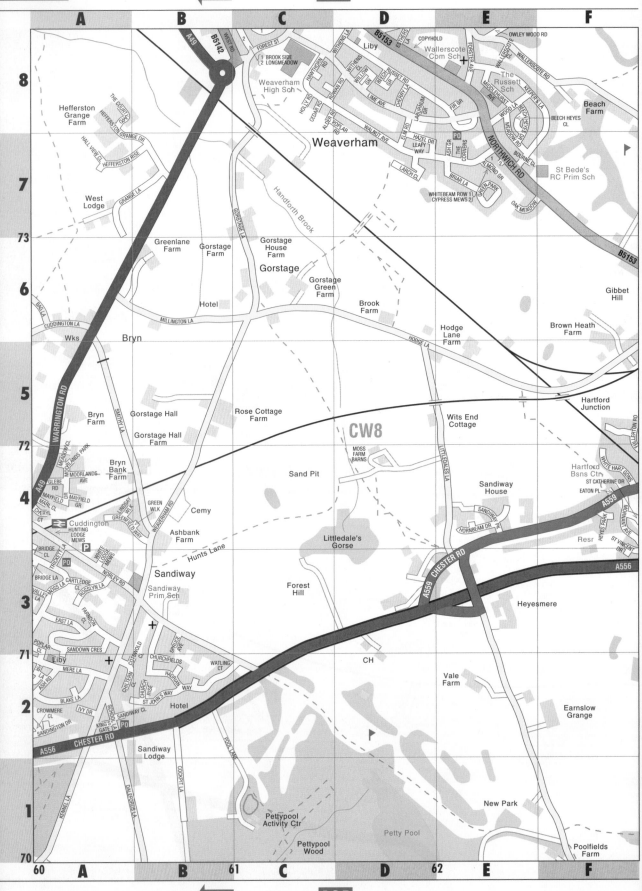

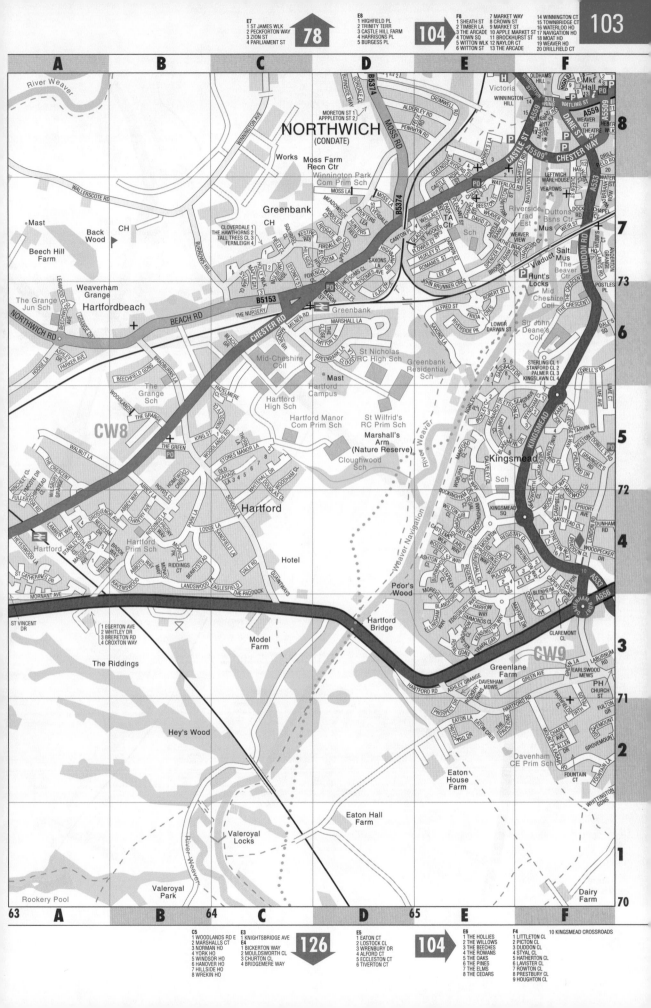

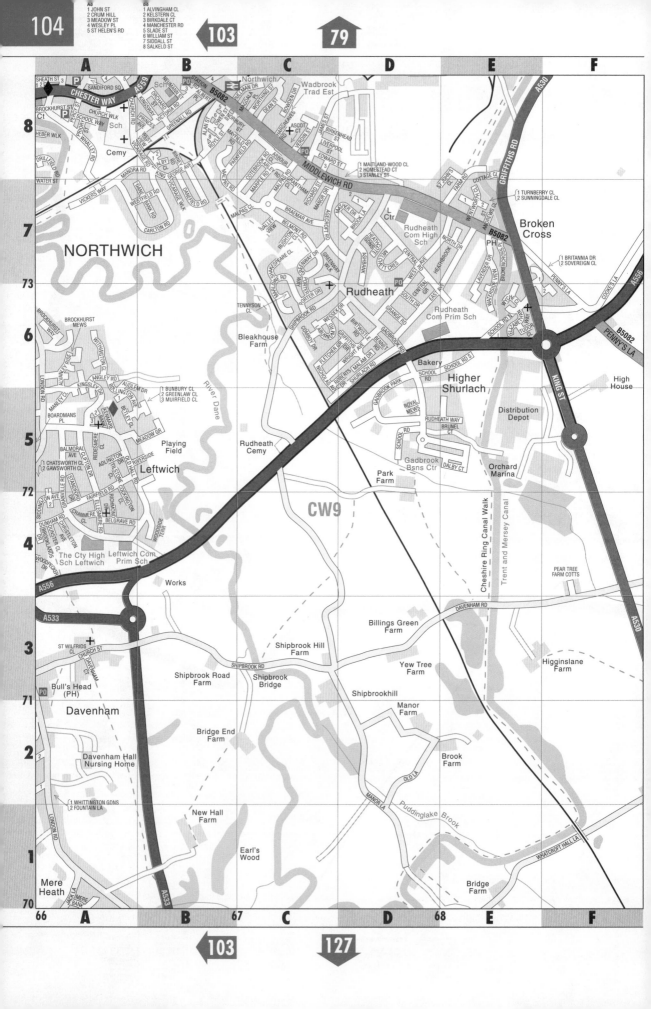

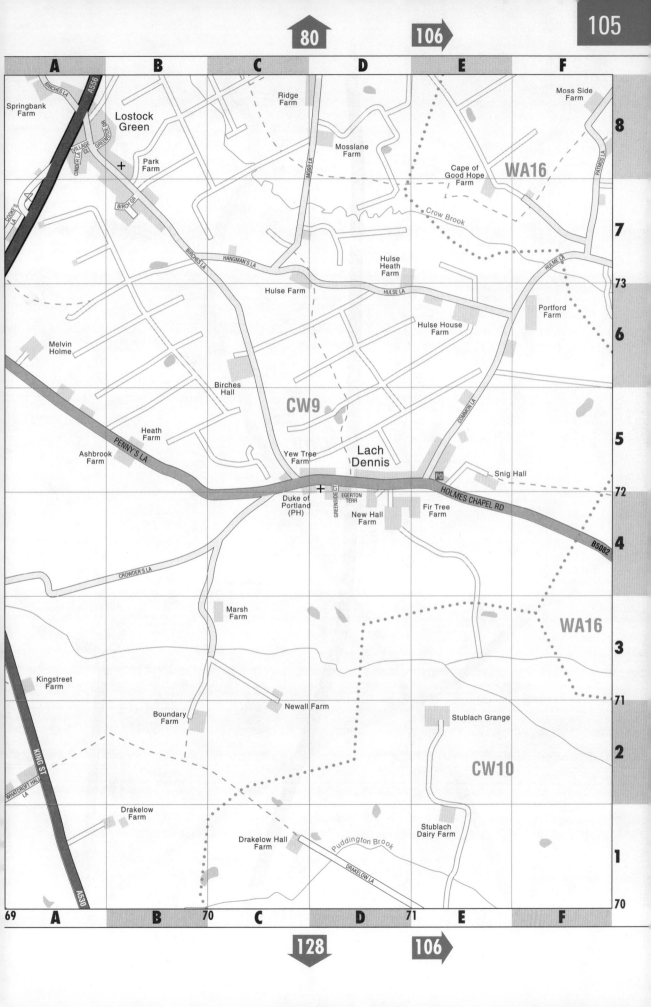

105
81

A **B** **C** **D** **E** **F**

8

Cheadle Farm

New Farm

CHEADLE LA

BACK LA

Back Lanes Farm

Crown Lane Farm

CROWN LA

B5081

Parkside Farm

Crown Inn (PH)

Swan Green

Yewtree Farm

Mill Bank Farm

Foxcovers

7

Backlane Farm

Millgate Farm

HULME LA

Mast

PO

SWAN GR

BIRCHWOOD DR

CHERRY WLK

HOLLY TREE DR

Birch Farm

Springfield

FOXCOVERT LA

Heath Farm

Peover Eye

73

Hulme Covert

BAKER'S LA

Bradshaw Brook

Springbank Farm

Bradshaw House

HEATH LA

SANDY LA

6

Graybrook Farm

Heath Farm

TOWNFIELD LA

CW9

Hulme Hall

Bradshawbrook Farm

Chapel Farm

WA16

MIDDLEWICH RD

+

Old Mill Farm

Townfield Farm

5

DAMS LA

72

HULME HALL LA

Washlone Farm

Hole La

Hole House

Hole House Wood

Motel

A50

4

B5082

Highfield House

Allostock Hall

Axon's Smithy Farm

WASH LA

CHAPEL LA

Chapel House Farm

Allostock

Brookhouse Farm

BROOK VIEW

3

HOLMES CHAPEL RD

Sculshaw Green Farm

Three Greyhounds (PH)

B5081

Shakerley Mere

PRINCESS RD

WOODLANDS CVN PK

LONDON RD

Widow's Home Farm

71

Sandhole Farm

2

Chestnut House Farm

The Croft

Woodlands Farm

Rudheath Woods

Newplatt Wood

CW4

1

Stublach Farm

CW10

Works

KING'S LA

King's Lane Farm

NORTHWICH RD

SANDY LA

NEW PLATT LA

KNUTSFORD RD

A50

Earnshaw House Farm

B5081

M6

Warrington Common

B5082

70

72 **A** **B** **73** **C** **D** **74** **E** **F**

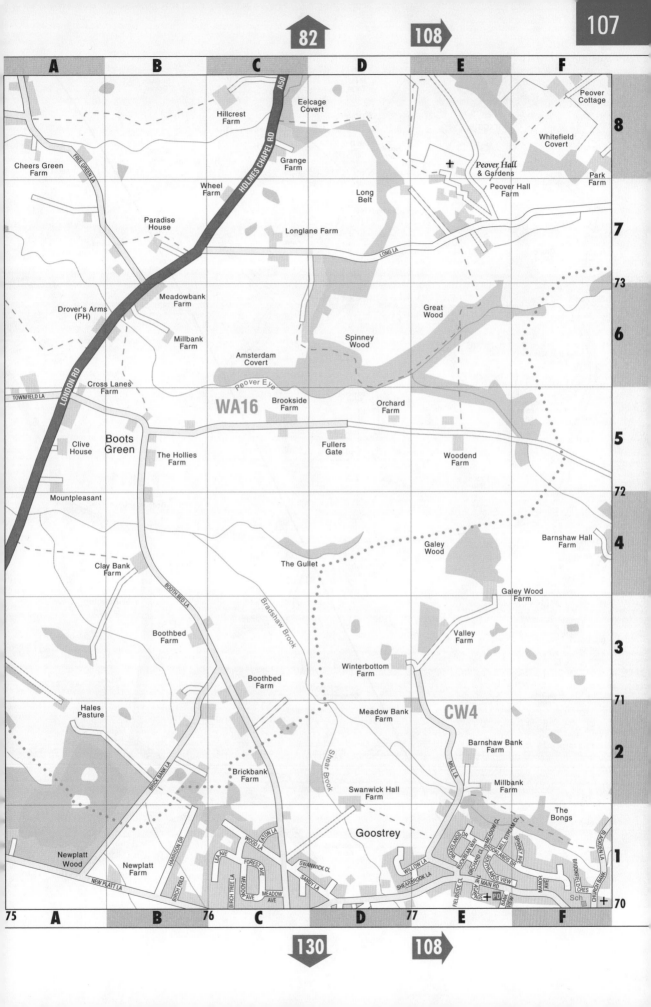

107
83

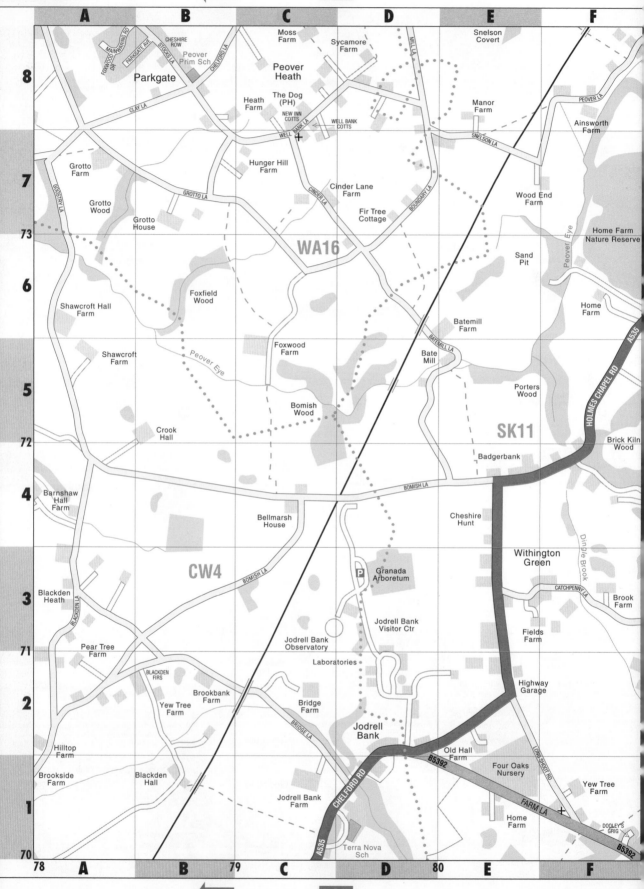

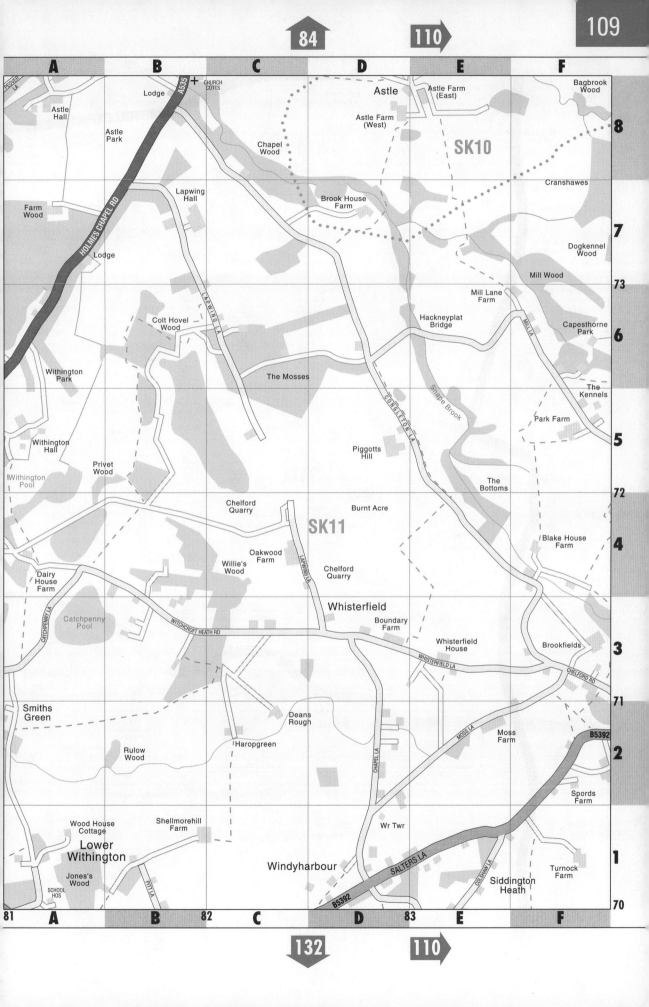

84
110
132
110

A B C D E F

8
7
73
6
5
72
4
3
71
2
1
70

PEOVER LA
Astle Hall
Astle Park
Lodge
A535
CHURCH COTTS
Chapel Wood
Astle
Astle Farm (East)
Astle Farm (West)
Bagbrook Wood
SK10
Cranshawes
Farm Wood
HOLMES CHAPEL RD
Lapwing Hall
Lodge
Brook House Farm
Dogkennel Wood
Mill Wood
LAPWING LA
Colt Hovel Wood
Mill Lane Farm
Hackneyplat Bridge
MILL LA
Capesthorne Park
Withington Park
The Mosses
CONGLETON LA
Snape Brook
The Kennels
Park Farm
Withington Hall
Privet Wood
Withington Pool
Piggotts Hill
The Bottoms
Blake House Farm
Chelford Quarry
SK11
Burnt Acre
72
4
Dairy House Farm
Oakwood Farm
Willie's Wood
LAPWING LA
Chelford Quarry
Whisterfield
Boundary Farm
Whisterfield House
Brookfields
CATCHPENNY LA
Catchpenny Pool
WITCHCROFT HEATH RD
WHISTERFIELD LA
CHELFORD RD
Smiths Green
Deans Rough
Haropgreen
CHAPEL LA
MOSS LA
Moss Farm
B5392
Rulow Wood
Spords Farm
Wood House Cottage
Shellmorehill Farm
Lower Withington
Wr Twr
SALTERS LA
Windyharbour
COLSHAW LA
Siddington Heath
Turnock Farm
PITT LA
SCHOOL HOS
Jones's Wood
B5392
B5392

81 A B 82 C D 83 E F

A **B** **C** **D** **E** **F**

8

Bagbrook Wood

Bridge Wood

Bagbrook Bridge

Bagbrook Farm

A34

A537

CHELFORD RD

Birtles Hill Farm

Birtles Bridge

WHIRLEY LA

Pale Farm

A537

Pale Lodge

SK10

Home Farm
North Lodge

Cranshawes

Big Wood

7

Park Plantation

Ley Plantation

73

Capesthorne Park

Henbury Hall

Marlheath Farm

6

Capesthorne Hall

East Lodge

Henbury Smithy

Smithy Wood

The Cave

SCHOOL LA

BEARHURST LA

Huntley Wood

CONGLETON RD

Lingards Farm

Sandbach Farm

5

MILL LA

Boathouse Covert

Lodge Farm

SK11

Henbury Moss

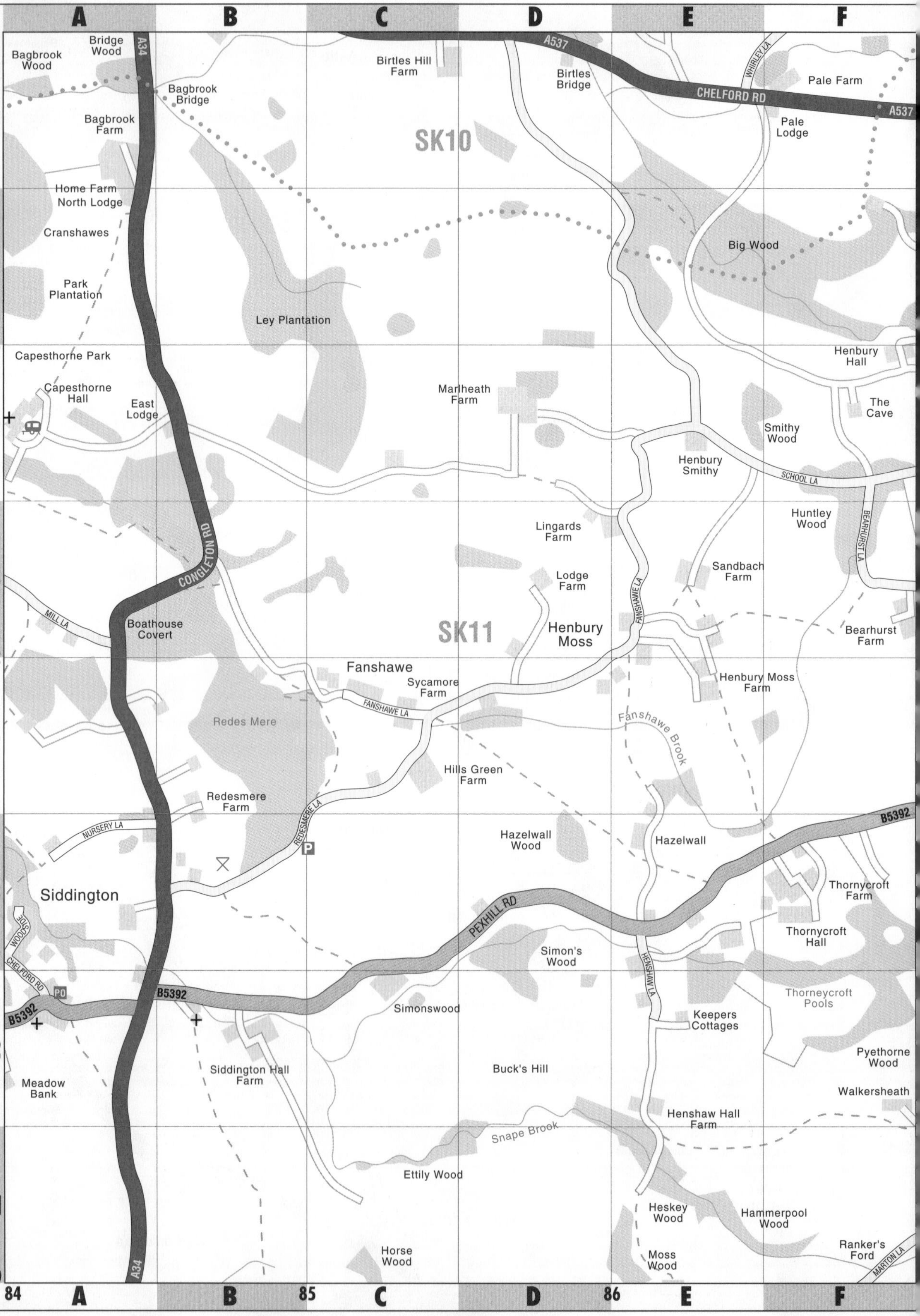

FANSHAWE LA

Bearhurst Farm

72

Fanshawe

Sycamore Farm

Henbury Moss Farm

Redes Mere

Fanshawe Brook

4

FANSHAWE LA

Hills Green Farm

Redesmere Farm

REDESMERE LA

Hazelwall Wood

Hazelwall

B5392

3

NURSERY LA

P

Thornycroft Farm

Siddington

PEXHILL RD

Thornycroft Hall

71

WOODS

CHELFORD RD

Simon's Wood

HENSHAW LA

Thorneycroft Pools

B5392

PO

Simonswood

Keepers Cottages

2

B5392

Meadow Bank

Siddington Hall Farm

Buck's Hill

Pyethorne Wood

Walkersheath

Henshaw Hall Farm

Snape Brook

1

Ettily Wood

Heskey Wood

Hammerpool Wood

Ranker's Ford

Horse Wood

Moss Wood

MARTON LA

70

84 **A** **B** **85** **C** **D** **86** **E** **F**

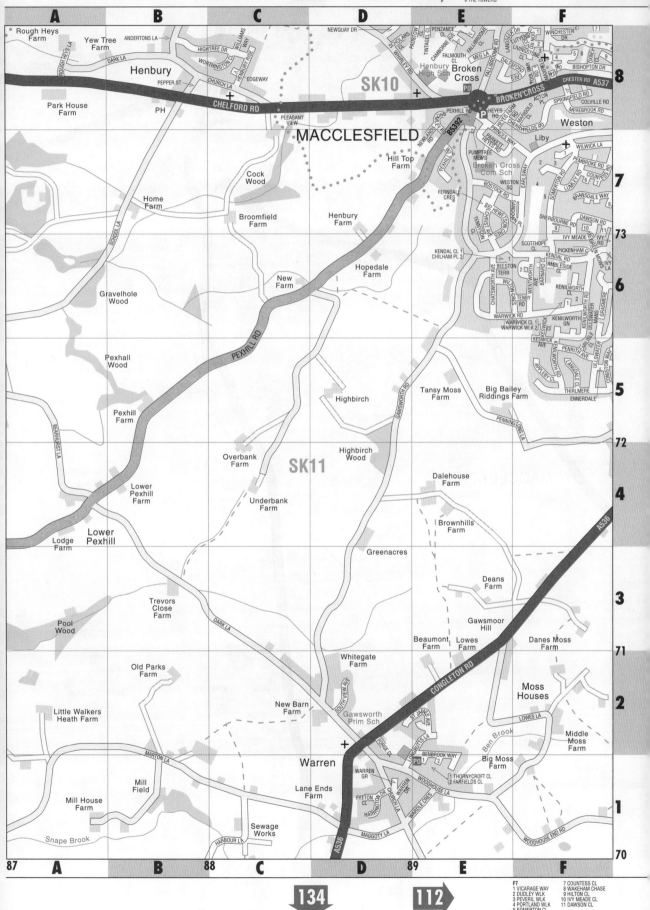

86

112

F8
1 ASHBOURNE MEWS
2 SHELBOURNE MEWS
3 ST LUKE'S HO
4 ALDERNEY CL
5 BLANDFORD DR
6 THE TOWERS
7 HEDINGHAM CL
8 MARLBOROUGH HO
9 ABINGDON CL
10 KENNET WAY

111

Rough Heys Farm
Yew Tree Farm
ANDERTONS LA
NEWQUAY DR
HIGHTREE DR
WILLIAMS WAY
HENBURY RISE
WORTHINGTON LA
EDGEWAY
DARK LA
ROUGH HEYS LA
Henbury
CHURCH LA
PEPPER ST
PH
Park House Farm
CHELFORD RD
PLEASANT VIEW
Home Farm
SCHOOL LA
Cock Wood
Broomfield Farm
New Farm
Henbury Farm
Hill Top Farm
SK10
MACCLESFIELD
WHIRLEY RD
SCHOLARS
PADSTOW
TINTAGEL CL
CAMBORNE AVE
CAMBORNE CL
PENZANCE
FALMOUTH CL
MEG LA
FALLIBROOME RD
LANDSEER DR
DALESFORD CRES
Henbury High Sch
Broken Cross
PO
WINCHESTER DR
BISHOPTON DR
CHESTER RD A537
8
B5392
PEXHILL RD
NEWLANDS RD
HEYES FARM RD
CHERRYFIELDS RD
MARIGOLD
ACTON PL
SPRINGFIELD RD
COLVILLE RD
MEREBROOK RD
Weston
7
73
6
5
72
4
3
71
2
1
70

Broken Cross Com Sch
PRINCES WAY
PARKETT
HEYES RD
PUMPTREE MEWS
WESTON SQ
EARL SWAY
BOSTOCK RD
Liby
WILWICK LA
SOMERTON RD
PEMBROKE RD
COUNTESS RD
LEAKEY RD
BRANSDALE WAY
SHERBOURNE RD
DAWSON RD
IVY MEADE RD
IVY RD
BRIER MOUNT
IVY LA
KENDAL CL
CHILHAM PL
SCOTTHOPE CL
PICKENHAM CL
KENDAL RD
AMBLESIDE CL
BEESTON AVE
CHATSWORTH AVE
WILTON CRES
TENNYSON CL
CHRIST CH
WARWICK RD
WARWICK CL
WARWICK WLK
WENTWORTH AVE
BARNARD CL
TENBY RD
KENILWORTH CL
KENILWORTH GN
CARLISLE
ULLSWATER MANS
GRASMERE
KESWICK AVE
KESWICK CL
PENRITH AVE
KENILWORTH RD
ULLSWATER CL
APPLEBY CL
LANGDALE CL
CONISTON WAY
THIRLMERE
ENNERDALE

Gravelhole Wood
Pexhall Wood
Pexhill Farm
PEXHILL RD
Highbirch
Highbirch Wood
SK11
Tansy Moss Farm
Big Bailey Riddings Farm
GAWSWORTH RD
PENNINGTON LA
Overbank Farm
Underbank Farm
Dalehouse Farm
Lower Pexhill Farm
BEARHURST LA
Lower Pexhill
Lodge Farm
Brownhills Farm
Greenacres
Deans Farm
A536
Gawsmoor Hill
Trevors Close Farm
Pool Wood
DARK LA
Beaumont Farm
Lowes Farm
Danes Moss Farm
71
Old Parks Farm
Whitegate Farm
CONGLETON RD
Moss Houses
Little Walkers Heath Farm
New Barn Farm
SOUTH VIEW AVE
Gawsworth Prim Sch
FORGE CL
ST JAMES AVE
LONGBUTTS LA
BENBROOK WAY
PO
Big Moss Farm
Ben Brook
LOWES LA
Middle Moss Farm
MARTON LA
Mill Field
Warren
WARREN GR
WARREN DRT
WOODHOUSE LA
1 THORNYCROFT CL
2 FARFIELDS CL
Mill House Farm
Snape Brook
Lane Ends Farm
FYTTON CL
HARRINGTON DR
CHURCH LA
WARDLE CRES
MAGGOTY LA
A536
WOODHOUSE END RD
Sewage Works
HARBOUR LA

F7
1 VICARAGE WAY
2 DUDLEY WLK
3 PEVERIL WLK
4 PORTLAND WLK
5 SOMERTON CL
6 WARDOUR CL
7 COUNTESS CL
8 WAKEHAM CHASE
9 HILTON CL
10 IVY MEADE CL
11 DAWSON CL

B6
1 ARMOURY TWRS
2 EVINGTON HO
3 BARRACKS SQ
4 ARMOURY COURT MEWS
5 QUEEN ANNES CT

C7
1 PETER STREET W
2 ATHEY STREET MILL
3 MARSDEN TERR
4 BACK PARADISE ST
5 HOLLAND ST
6 BLACKSHAW ST

111

7 ST JOHN'S RD
8 BAKER ST

D7
1 NEWGATE
2 DUKES CT
3 MARLBOROUGH CT
4 TOWNLEY ST

87

5 TOWNLEY PL
6 TOWNLEY MILL
7 WARDLE ST
8 TRAFALGAR CT
9 GRAPES ST
10 BROKEN BANKS
11 ST GEORGE'S PL
12 BRUNSWICK CT

E7
1 BAILEY CT
2 ST PAUL'S CT
3 ST PAUL'S RD
4 HALLEFIELD DR
5 HALLEFIELD CRES
6 BROOKSIDE MILL
7 THORNYCROFT ST
8 CAWLEY ST
9 PEARSON ST
10 LOWER BANK ST
11 BUCKLOW WLK
12 KNUTSFORD ROAD WLK
13 WILMSLOW WLK
14 ALDERLEY WLK
15 ELIZABETH HO
16 PLUMLEY CL
17 STUBBS TERR
18 WINLOWE

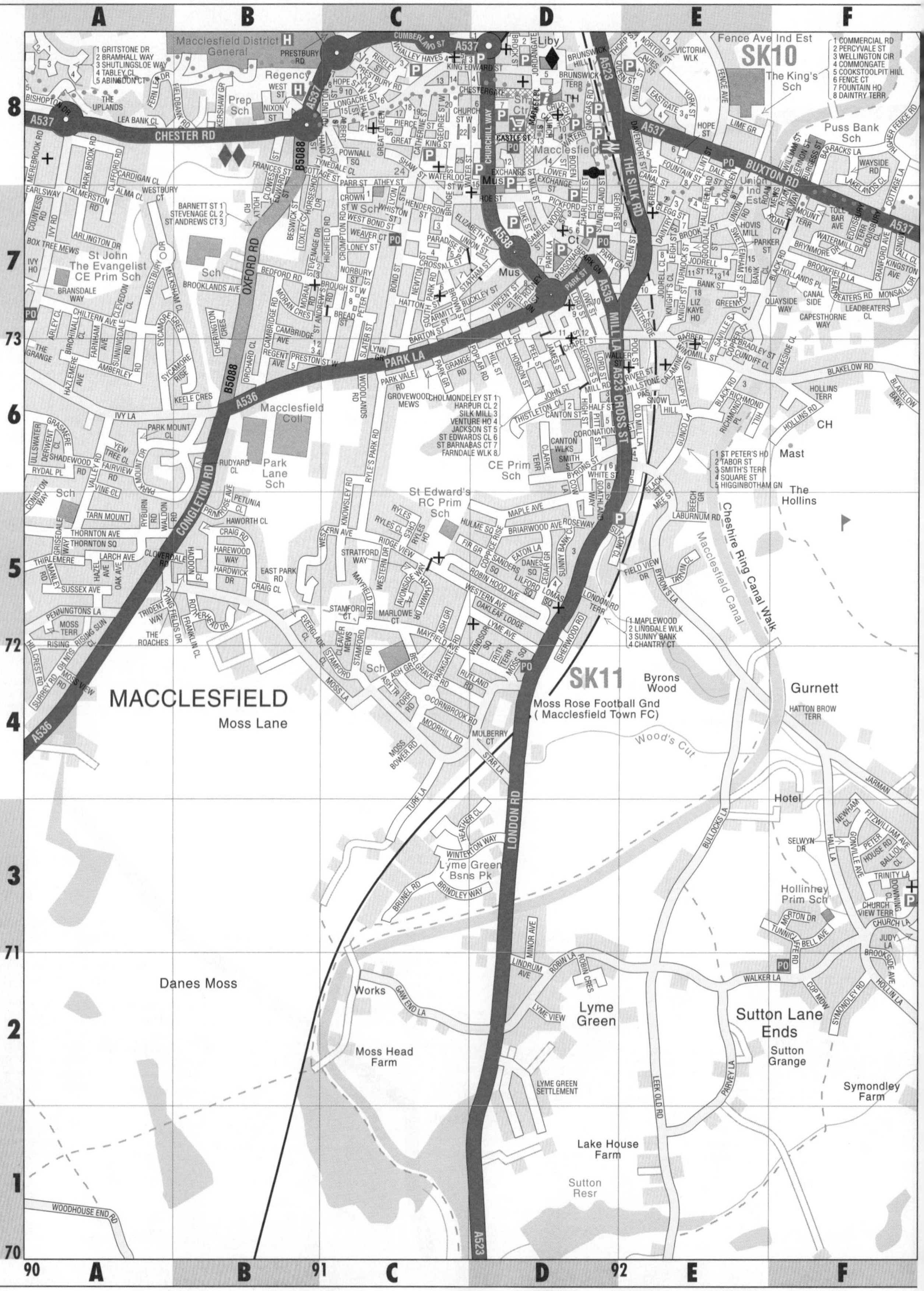

MACCLESFIELD
Moss Lane
Macclesfield District General
Macclesfield Coll
Park Lane Sch
St John The Evangelist CE Prim Sch
St Edward's RC Prim Sch
CE Prim Sch
The King's Sch
Puss Bank Sch
Fence Ave Ind Est
SK10
SK11
Moss Rose Football Gnd (Macclesfield Town FC)
Byrons Wood
Gurnett
Macclesfield Canal
Cheshire Ring Canal Walk
Lyme Green Bsns Pk
Danes Moss
Works
Moss Head Farm
Lyme Green
Lyme Green Settlement
Lake House Farm
Sutton Resr
Sutton Lane Ends
Sutton Grange
Symondley Farm
Hollinhey Prim Sch
Hotel
The Hollins
Mast
CHESTER RD
CONGLETON RD
OXFORD RD
PARK LA
LONDON RD
MILL LA
CROSS ST
THE SILK RD
BUXTON RD
A537
A536
A523
A538
B5088

111

C8
1 WILLERBY CL
2 WALKER ST
3 GROSVENOR ST
4 WESTMINSTER RD
5 STANLEY & BROCKLEHURST CT
6 COURT NO 4
7 MILLERS CT
8 MILLERS CROFT
9 BUCKDEN WAY

135

10 NEWBIGGIN WAY
11 SHARPLEY ST
12 BOOTHBY ST
13 GEORGES CT
14 WESTMINSTER ST
15 POYNTON ST
16 ANDERSON ST
17 SIMPSON'S CT
18 PINFOLD ST
19 REGENT & FOUNDRY CT
20 THE TOWER HO
21 LANGFORD ST
22 CHARLOTTE STREET W
23 CHARLTON ST
24 The Crown Ctr
25 EDGAR CT

D8
1 TUNNICLIFFE ST
2 CUMBERLAND ST
3 KING EDWARD RD
4 LITTLE ST
5 BRUNSWICK ST
6 CHURCH MEWS
7 STANLEY ST
8 UNICORN GATEWAY
9 CHATHAM ST
10 ST MICHAELS TERR
11 SHORT ST
12 EXCHANGE CL
13 BACK WALLGATE
14 QUEEN VICTORIA ST
15 WELLINGTON ST

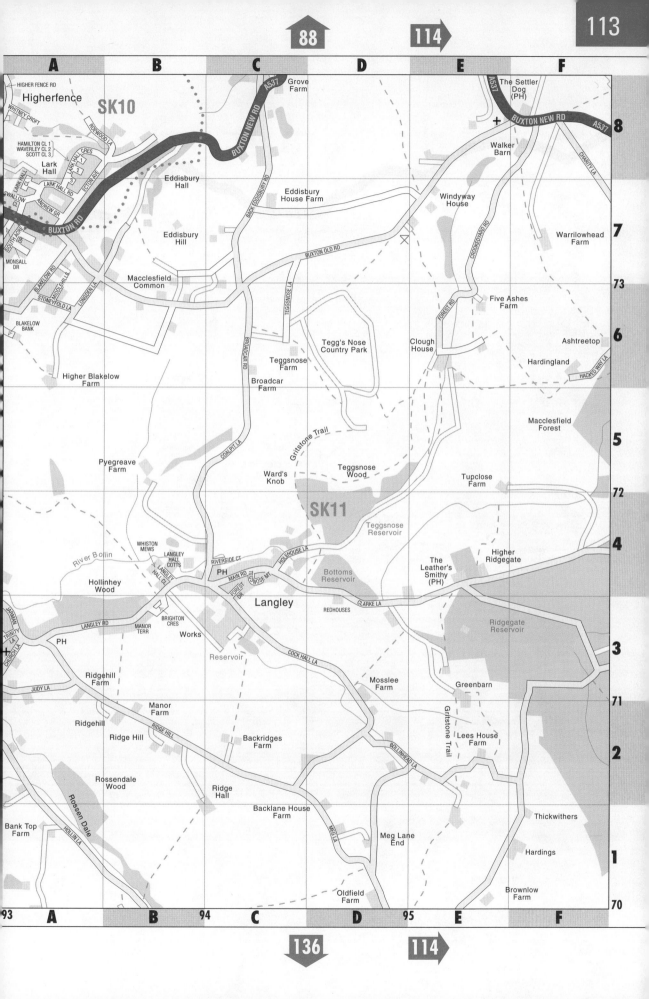

88
114

Higherfence

SK10

HIGHER FENCE RD
WHITNEY CROFT
ROEWOOD LA
HAMILTON CL 1
WAVERLEY CL 2
SCOTT CL 3
LARK HALL CRES
Lark
Hall
LARK HALL RD
ECTON AVE
LARK HALL
LARK HALL CT
ANDREW GR
SWALLOW CL
BUXTON RD
SOUTHACRE DR
MONSALL DR
BLAKELOW RD
MIDDLEHILLS
STONEYFOLD LA
LONGGILL LA
Blakelow
Bank
BLAKELOW
BANK
Higher Blakelow
Farm

Grove
Farm
A537
BUXTON NEW RD
Eddisbury
Hall
Eddisbury
House Farm
BACK EDDISBURY RD
Eddisbury
Hill
Macclesfield
Common
Buxton Old Rd
BUXTON OLD RD
BROADCAR RD
TEGGSNOSE LA
Teggsnose
Farm
Broadcar
Farm
COALPIT LA

The Settler
Dog
(PH)
A537
BUXTON NEW RD
A537
Walker
Barn
Windyway
House
CHARITY LA
Warrilowhead
Farm
Five Ashes
Farm
CROOKEDYARD RD
FOREST RD
Clough
House
Ashtreetop
Hardingland
HACKED WAY LA
Macclesfield
Forest

Tegg's Nose
Country Park

Gritstone Trail

Pyegreave
Farm

Ward's
Knob

SK11

Teggsnose
Wood

Teggsnose
Reservoir

Tupclose
Farm

The
Leather's
Smithy
(PH)

Higher
Ridgegate

River Bollin

WHISTON
MEWS
LANGLEY
HALL
COTTS
Langley
Hall Cl
RIVERSIDE CT
PH
MAIN RD
FOREST DR
NOSE MT
HOLEHOUSE LA
Bottoms
Reservoir
Langley
REDHOUSES
CLARKE LA
Hollinhey
Wood
Ridgegate
Reservoir
Greenbarn

LANGLEY RD
MANOR
TERR
BRIGHTON
CRES
Works
Reservoir
COCK HALL LA

JARMAN LA
TRINITY LA
CHURCH LA
PH
Ridgehill
Farm
JUDY LA
Manor
Farm
Ridgehill
RIDGE HILL
Ridge Hill
Backridges
Farm

Mosslee
Farm
BOLLINHEAD LA
Gritstone Trail
Lees House
Farm

Rossendale
Wood
Ridge
Hall

Backlane House
Farm

Thickwithers

Rossen Dale
HOLLIN LA
Bank Top
Farm
MEG LA
Meg Lane
End
Hardings

Oldfield
Farm

Brownlow
Farm

8
7
73
6
5
72
4
3
71
2
1
70

113
89

A **B** **C** **D** **E** **F**

8

Turnshawflat

A537

The Laches

Ankers Knowl Farm

BUXTON NEW RD

Fox Stake

Longclough Farm

A537

7

Hindsclough Farm

Fieldhead Farm

73

Greenways Farm

Brookhouse

HACKED WAY LA

CHARITY LA

6

Whitehills

Long Clough

Tor Brook

ANKERS LA

The Stanley Arms (PH)

Torgate Farm

5

Chapel House Farm

OVEN LA

Macclesfield Forest

Chambers Farm

72

Toot Hill

SK11

Bottom-of-the-Oven

Torgate Hill

Broughs Place

4

Macclesfield Forest

Bollin Brook

P

Clough Brook

Dryknowle Farm

3

Trentabank Reservoir

High Ash Farm

P Forest Walks

71

Ferriser

Yarnshaw Hill

2

Nessit Hill

Buxtors Hill

P

Yarnshaw Brook

Dingers Hollow

The Vicarage

1

High Moor

Highmoor Brook

Higher Barn

Vicarage Wood

70

96 **A** 97 **B** **C** 98 **D** **E** **F**

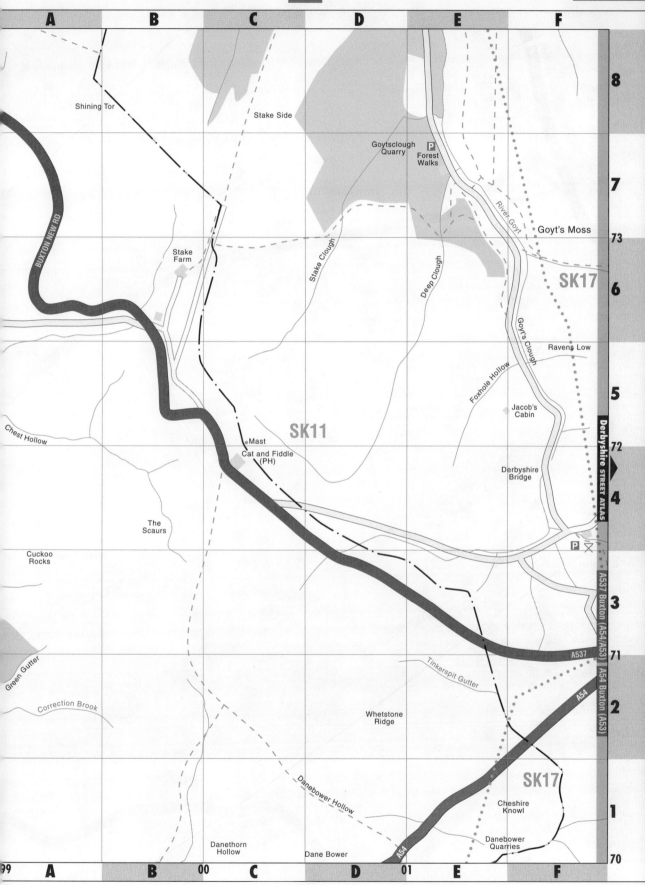

Shining Tor

Stake Side

BUXTON NEW RD

Goytsclough
Quarry

Forest
Walks

River Goyt

Goyt's Moss

SK17

Stake Farm

Stake Clough

Deep Clough

Goyt's Clough

Ravens Low

Chest Hollow

Foxhole Hollow

SK11

Jacob's
Cabin

Mast
Cat and Fiddle
(PH)

Derbyshire
Bridge

The Scaurs

Derbyshire STREET ATLAS

Cuckoo
Rocks

A537 Buxton (A54/A53)

A537

A54 Buxton (A53)

Green Gutter

Tinkerspit Gutter

A54

Correction Brook

Whetstone
Ridge

SK17

Danebower Hollow

Cheshire
Knowl

Danethorn
Hollow

Dane Bower

A54

Danebower
Quarries

Denbighshire, Flintshire & Wrexham STREET ATLAS

A B C D E F

8

7

69

6

5

68

4

3

67

2

1

66

33 34 35

Camp
Deva Bsns Pk
Old Marsh Farm
Old Marsh Farm Ho
GREEN LANE EST
Bridge Farm
FERNLEA CT
Seahill Farm
HAWTHORN VIEW
CEDAR AVE
CEDAR CL
WELSH RD
A550
A548
SEALAND RD
VILLA RD
Willow Farm
Brookfield Farm
LON YR ORSAF/STATION APP
LON YR YWEN/ YEW TREE AVE
STATION COTTS
B5441
A494
Brook Farm
SEALAND RD
St BARTHOLOMEWS CT
Sealand
CHURCH COTTS
A494 Queensferry
FOX'S DR
MANOR RD
MEADOW VIEW
WEST GDN
NORTH GDN
FERRY CL
Home Farm
Waterloo Farm
The Owl Ind Est
SOUTH GDN
EAST GDN
Church Farm
CH5
Sealand Manor
DEESIDE CRES
A548
Shooting School
Deeside Cottages
CH1
Engineer Pk
River Row Cottages
Deeside House
DEESIDE LA
THE BOWERY
Sealand Nursery
GLENDALE AVE
St Ives Pk
BABBAGE RD
WHITTLE CL
FACTORY RD
ALVIS RD
Works
OLD FARM COTTS
Glendale Bsns Pk
ST IVES WAY
RAILWAY
ASIATIC COTTS
Glendale Pk
BERNSDALE CL
CLAIR AVE
CROFTERS PK
HARRISON ST
PRINCE WILLIAM AVE
Wood Farm
HAMILTON AVE
EVANSLEIGH
PHOENIX ST
QUEEN'S AVE
NORTH ST
WATKIN ST
LAWRENCE CL
FAIRWAY
WOOD RD
PHILIP ST
STATION RD
Sandycroft
B5129
CH5
Bridge Inn (PH)
MOOR LA
ROSSLYN CL
CHESTER RD
The Beeches
CH4
CH4
Cop House Farm
B5129
RAKE LA
B5129
B5129
B5129

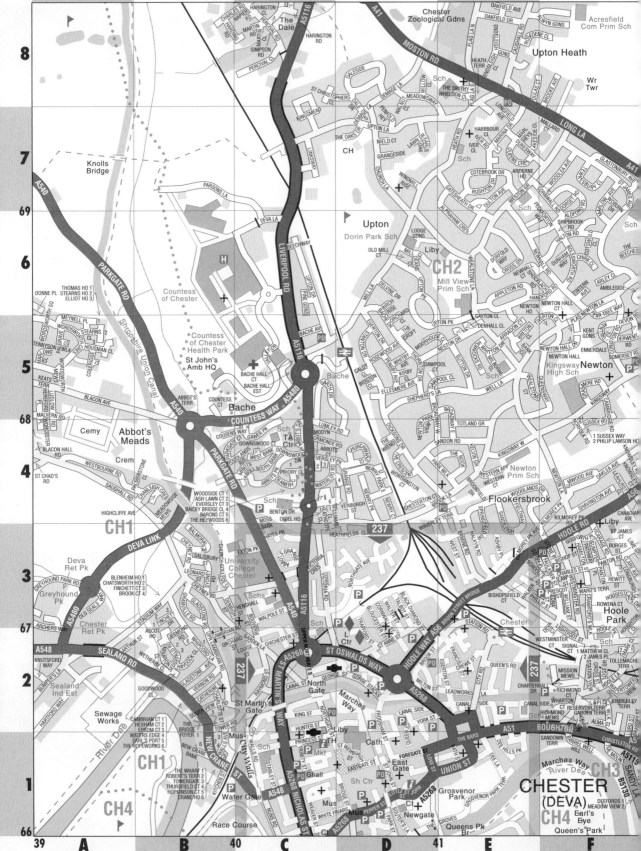

For full street detail of the highlighted area see page 237.

A1
1 MERECROFT
2 BOUGHTON LODGE
3 ORCHARD CT
4 KING EDWARD BLDGS
5 STOCKS AVE
6 WESTWARD RD
7 COTSWOLD CT
8 FAIRHOLME PL

B1
1 ARKLE CT
2 CHELFORD MEWS
3 HARTFORD MEWS
B2
1 MARLBOROUGH CT
2 VICARS CROSS CT

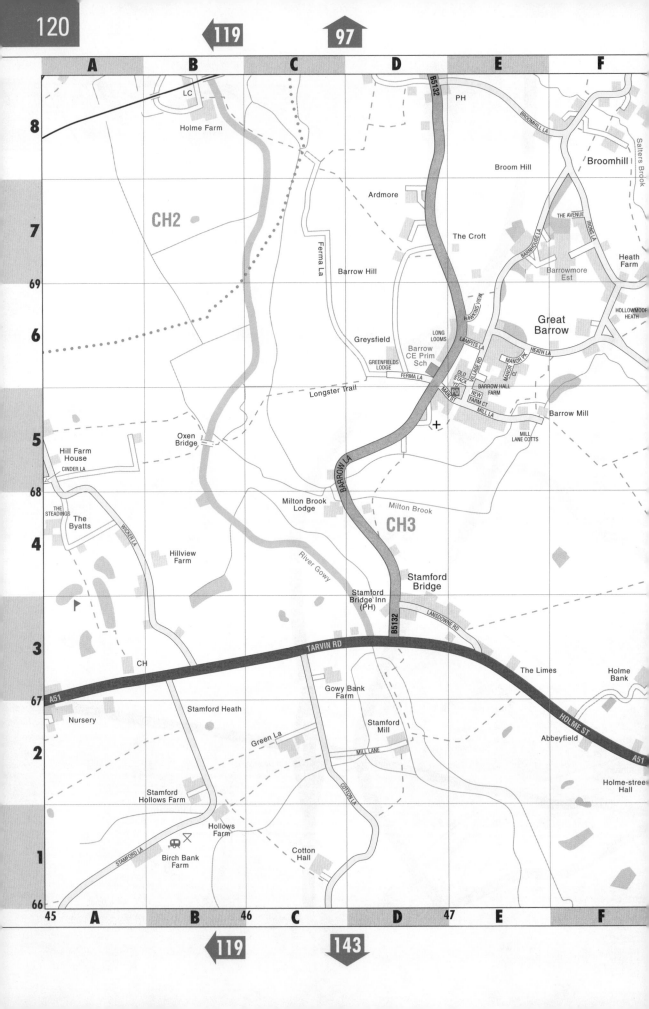

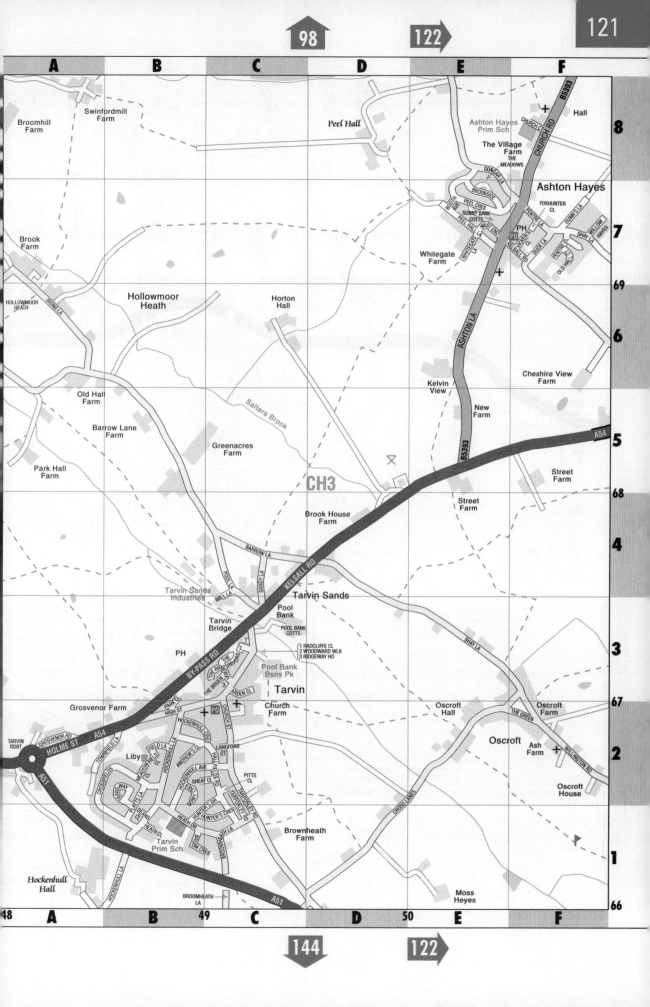

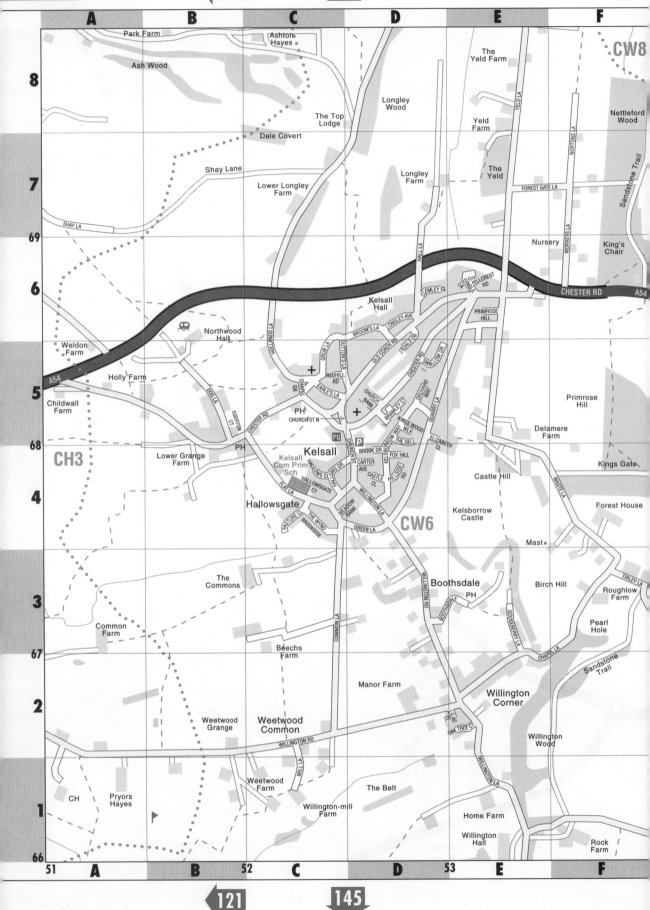

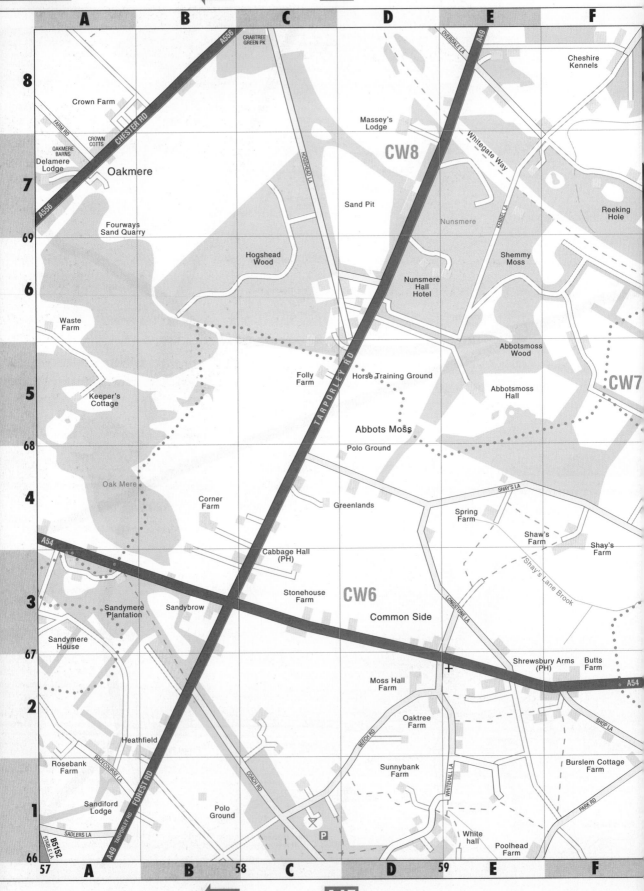

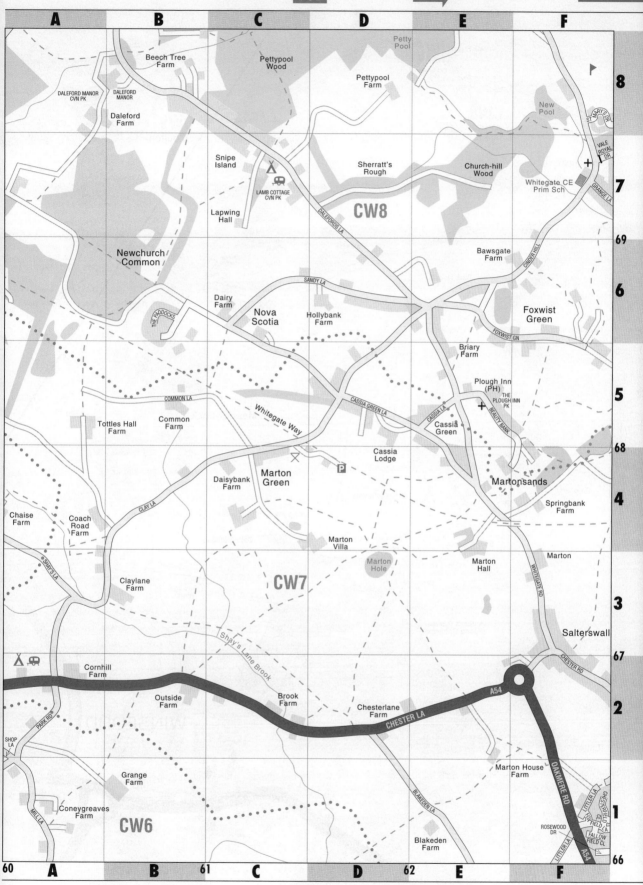

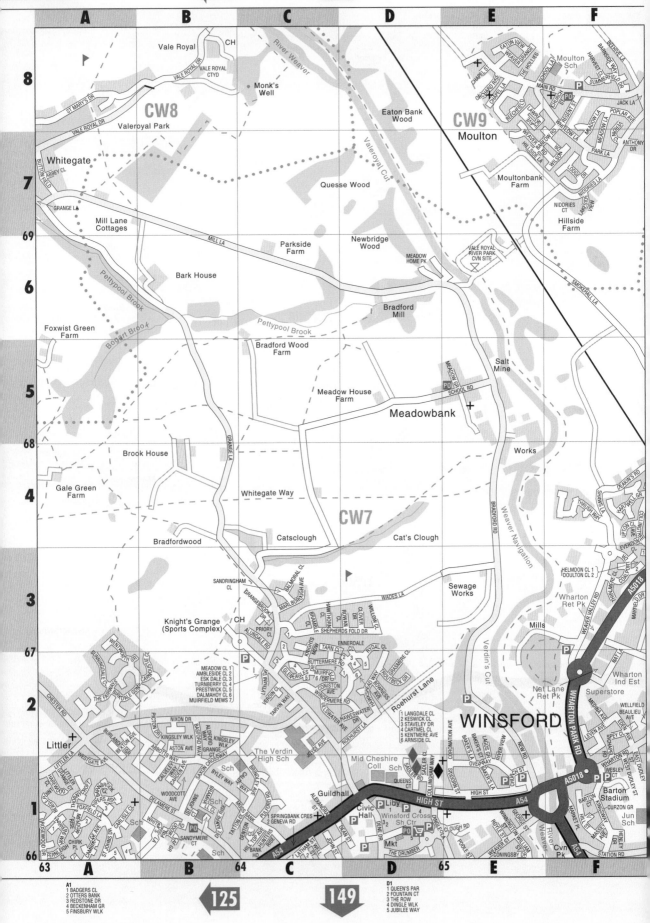

A1
1 BADGERS CL
2 OTTERS BANK
3 REDSTONE DR
4 BECKENHAM GR
5 FINSBURY WLK

D1
1 QUEEN'S PAR
2 FOUNTAIN CT
3 THE ROW
4 DINGLE WLK
5 JUBILEE WAY

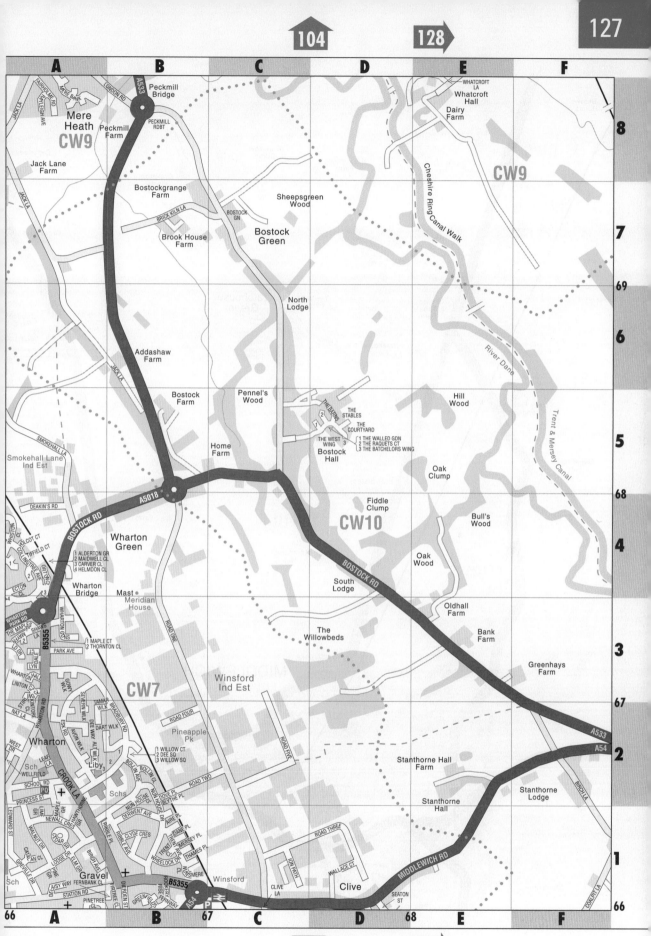

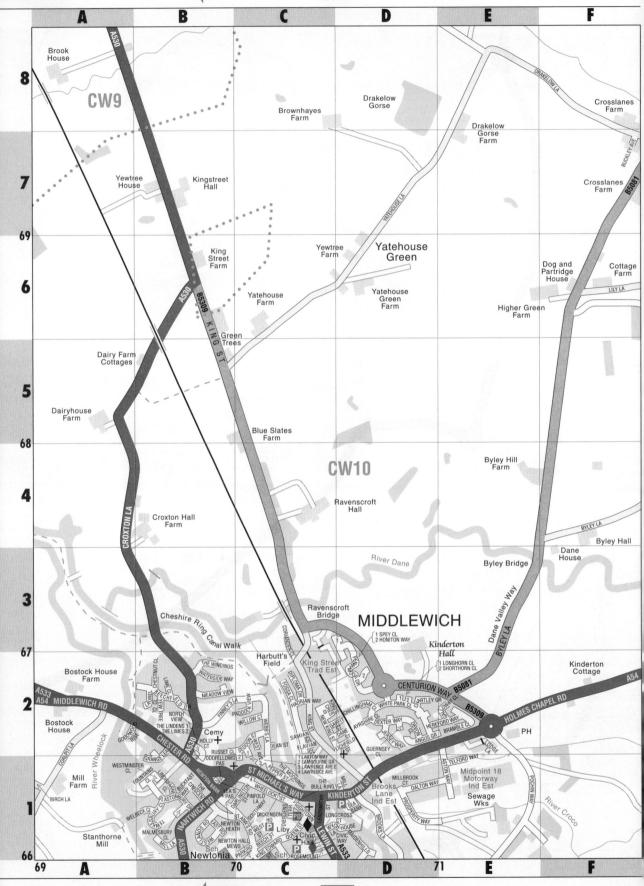

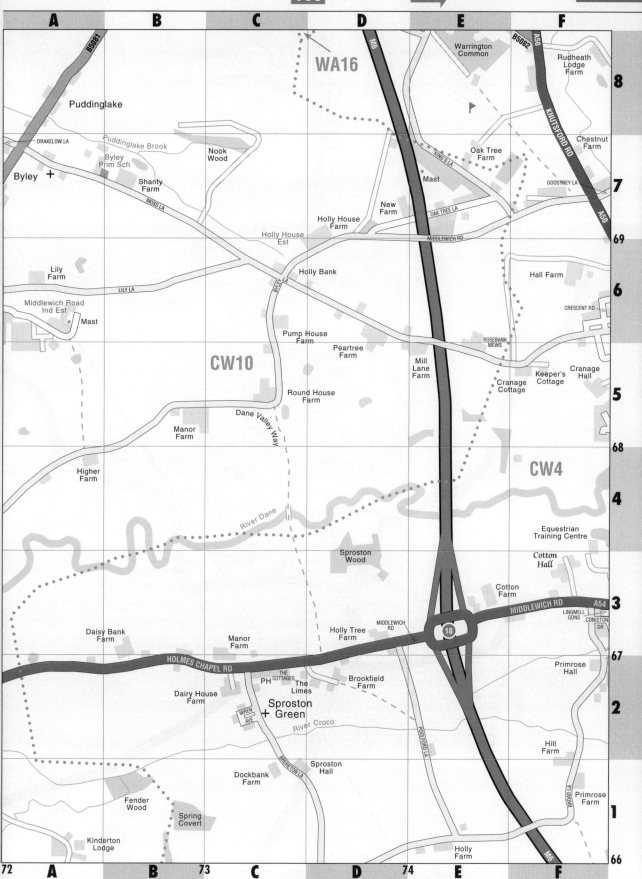

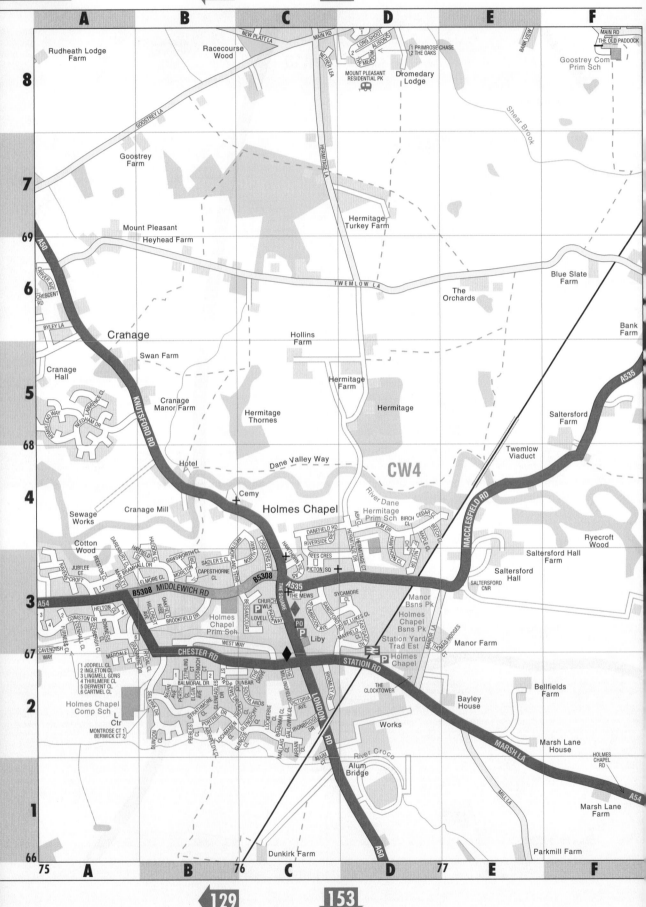

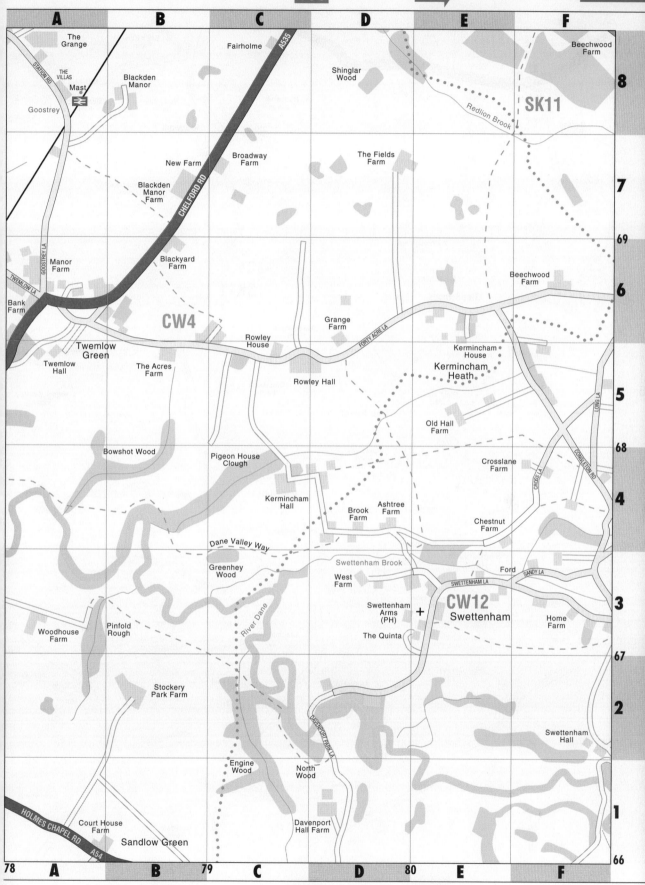

A B C D E F

8
7
69
6
5
68
4
3
67
2
1
66

The Grange
Fairholme
Shinglar Wood
Beechwood Farm
SK11

STATION RD
THE VILLAS
Mast
Blackden Manor
Goostrey

Redlion Brook

GOOSTREY LA
New Farm
Broadway Farm
The Fields Farm

CHELFORD RD
A535

Blackden Manor Farm

TWEMLOW LA
Manor Farm
Blackyard Farm
Beechwood Farm

Bank Farm

CW4
Grange Farm
Kermincham House

FORTY ACRE LA
Rowley House
Kermincham Heath

Twemlow Green
Twemlow Hall
The Acres Farm
Rowley Hall
Old Hall Farm

LONG LA

Bowshot Wood
Pigeon House Clough
Crosslane Farm
CROSS LA
CONGLETON RD

Kermincham Hall
Brook Farm
Ashtree Farm
Chestnut Farm

Dane Valley Way
Swettenham Brook
Ford
SANDY LA

Greenhey Wood
West Farm
SWETTENHAM LA
CW12
Swettenham

River Dane
Swettenham Arms (PH)
Home Farm

Woodhouse Farm
Pinfold Rough
The Quinta

Stockery Park Farm
Swettenham Hall

DAVENPORT PARK LA
Engine Wood
North Wood

HOLMES CHAPEL RD
A54
Court House Farm
Davenport Hall Farm

Sandlow Green

78 A B 79 C D 80 E F 66

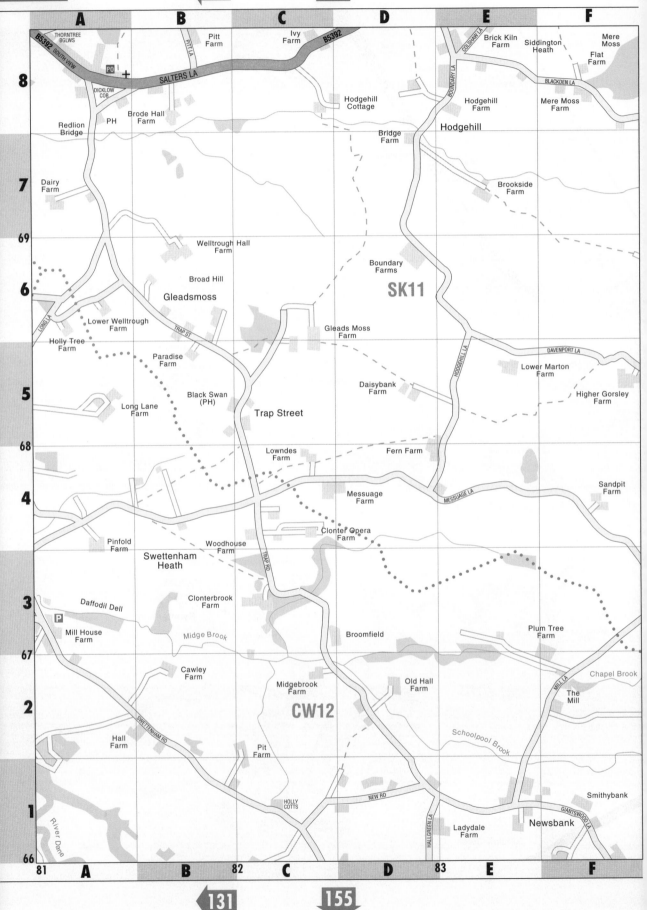

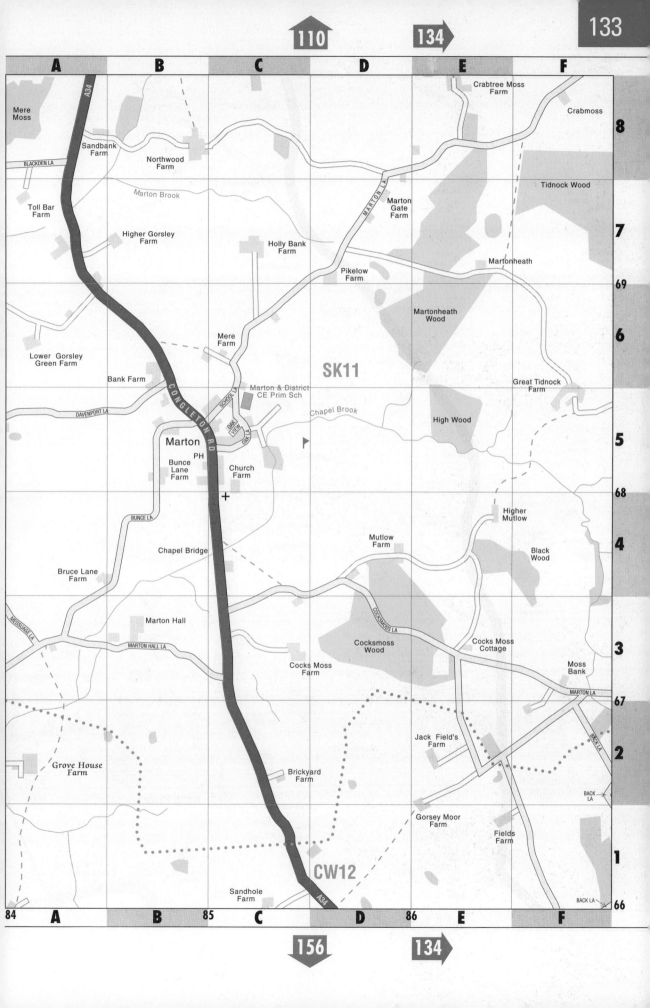

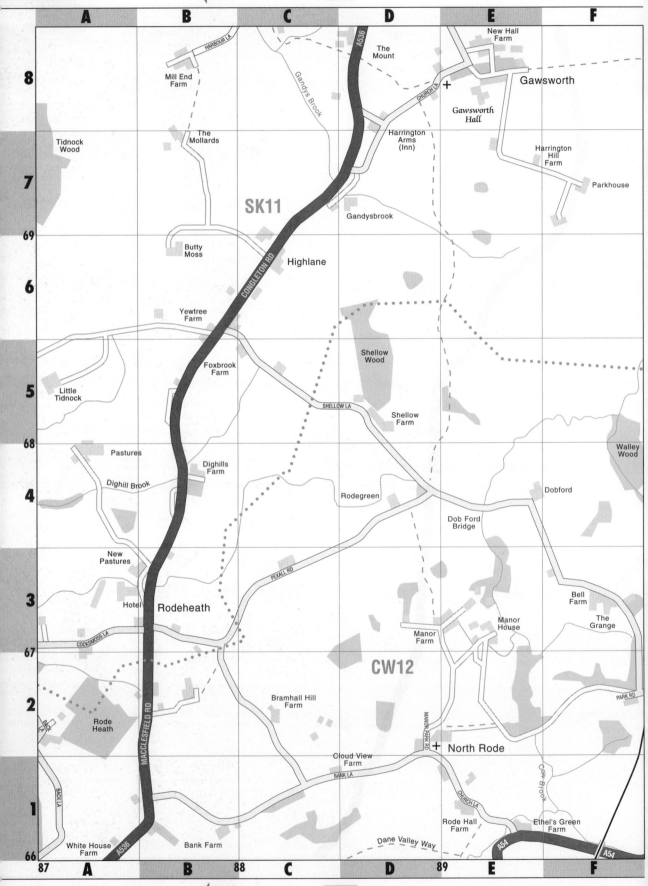

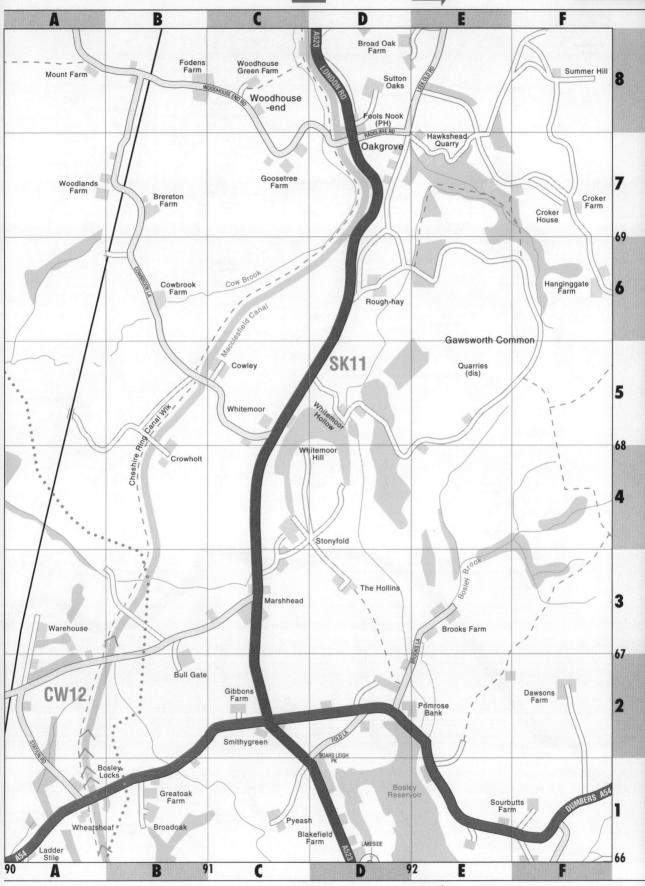

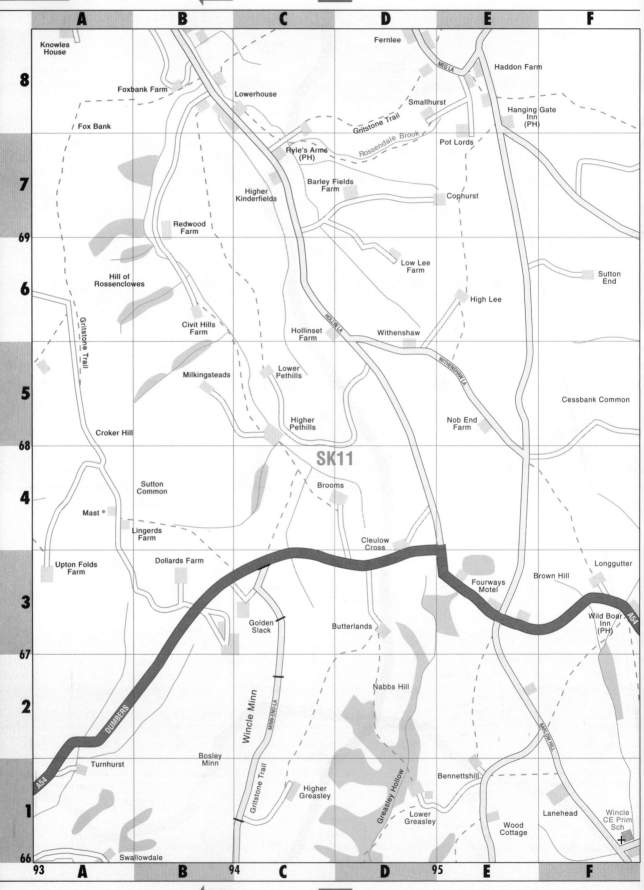

114
138

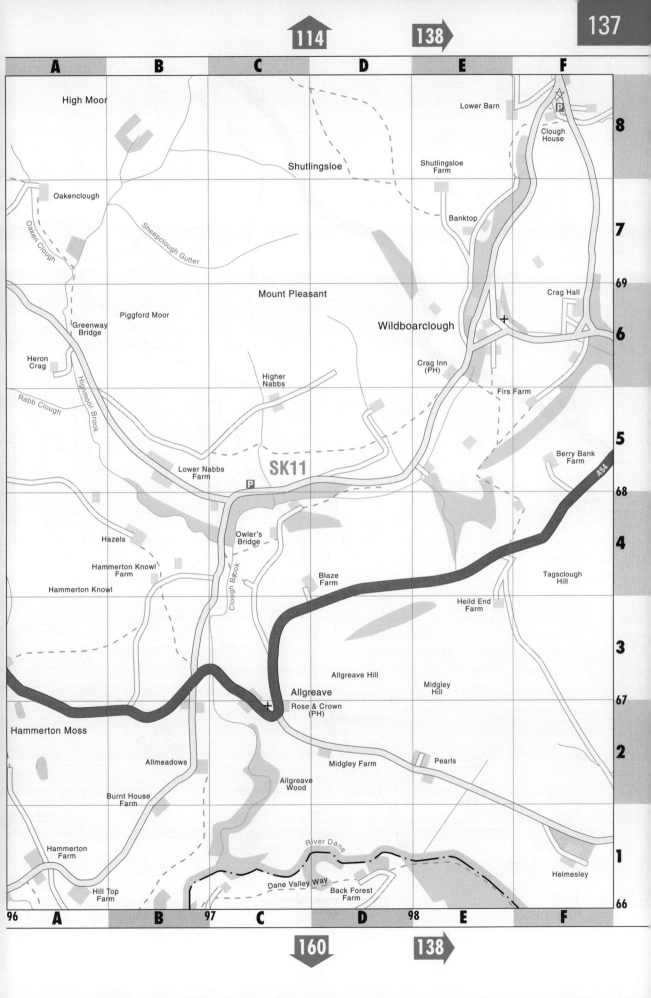

High Moor

Oakenclough

Oaken Clough

Sheepclough Gutter

Shutlingsloe

Lower Barn

Clough House

Shutlingsloe Farm

Banktop

Mount Pleasant

Greenway Bridge

Piggford Moor

Wildboarclough

Crag Hall

Heron Crag

Highmoor Brook

Rabb Clough

Higher Nabbs

Crag Inn (PH)

Firs Farm

Berry Bank Farm

A54

Lower Nabbs Farm

SK11

Hazels

Owler's Bridge

Hammerton Knowl Farm

Clough Brook

Blaze Farm

Heild End Farm

Tagsclough Hill

Hammerton Knowl

Allgreave Hill

Midgley Hill

Allgreave

Hammerton Moss

Rose & Crown (PH)

Allmeadows

Midgley Farm

Pearls

Allgreave Wood

Burnt House Farm

Hammerton Farm

River Dane

Helmesley

Hill Top Farm

Dane Valley Way

Back Forest Farm

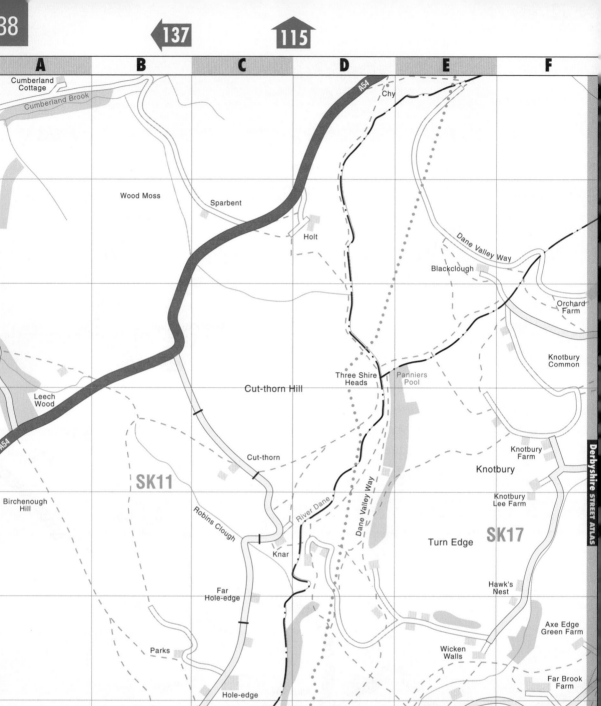

A   B   C   D   E   F

Cumberland
Cottage
Cumberland Brook

8

Wood Moss

Sparbent

7

Holt

A54

Chy

Dane Valley Way

Blackclough

Orchard
Farm

69

Knotbury
Common

6

Leech
Wood

Three Shire
Heads

Panniers
Pool

Cut-thorn Hill

A54

Knotbury
Farm

5

Cut-thorn

Knotbury

Birchenough
Hill

SK11

Knotbury
Lee Farm

68

Robins Clough

River Dane

Dane Valley Way

Turn Edge

SK17

4

Knar

Hawk's
Nest

Far
Hole-edge

Axe Edge
Green Farm

Parks

3

Wicken
Walls

Far Brook
Farm

Hole-edge

Bennettshitch

67

Spring
Head

2

Higher
Bangs

Lower
Bangs

New
Cottage

Burntcliff
Top

Greens

Wildstone
Rock

1

Midgleygate

P

Goosetree

Manor
Farm

The
Wash

Gradbach Mill
(YH)

Greenstitch

66

99   A   B   00   C   ▼   D   01   E   F

Derbyshire STREET ATLAS

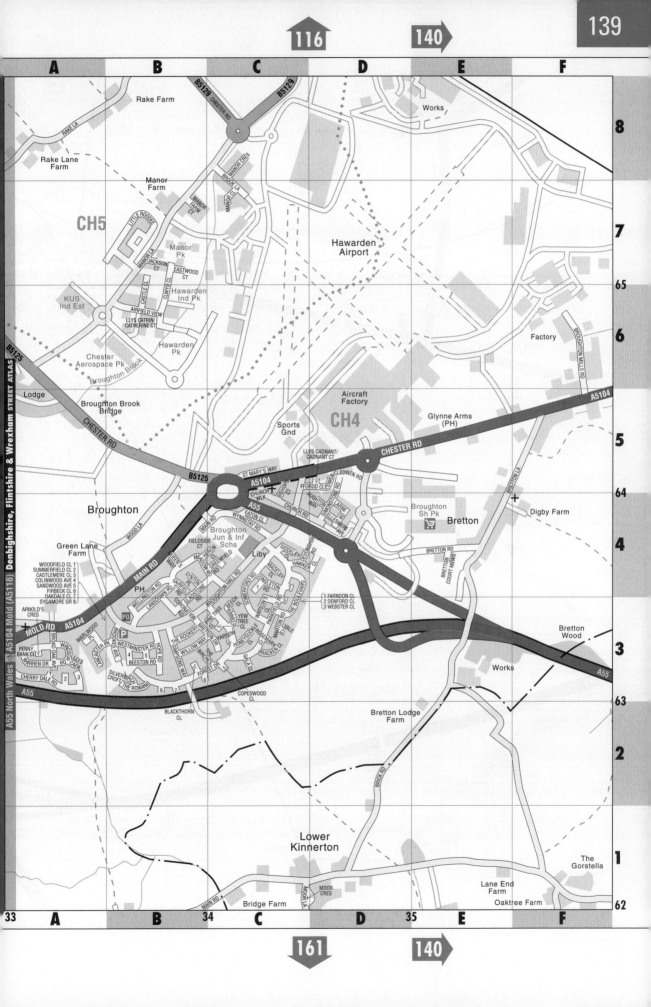

A B C D E F

8

7

65

6

5

64

4

3

63

2

1

62

A55 North Wales ◄ A5104 Mold (A5118) Denbighshire, Flintshire & Wrexham STREET ATLAS

B5129 CHESTER RD

B5129

Rake Farm

Works

Rake Lane Farm

CH5

Manor Farm

MANOR CRES

BROOK LA

MANOR CL

Hawarden Airport

LITTLE RODDEE

MANOR FARM CT

Manor Pk

MANOR LA

JACKSON CT

CASTLE CL

EASTWOOD CT

CLWYD CL

Hawarden Ind Pk

65

KUS Ind Est

AIRFIELD VIEW

LLYS CATRIN/ CATHERINE CT

Factory

Chester Aerospace Pk

Hawarden Pk

BROUGHTON MILLS RD

B5125

Broughton Brook

6

Lodge

Broughton Brook Bridge

CHESTER RD

Aircraft Factory

CH4

Glynne Arms (PH)

A5104

Sports Gnd

LLYS CADNANT/ CADNANT CT

CHESTER RD

5

Broughton

B5125

ST MARY'S WAY

A5104

CHURCH WLK

BISHOPS CL

FFORDD CLES

CLEDWEN RD

AUGHTON WAY

CHURCH RD

LARNE

Broughton Sh Pk

Bretton

Digby Farm

64

Green Lane Farm

WOOD LA

MAIN RD

EATON CL

WYNNSTAY RD

Broughton Jun & Inf Schs

FIELDSIDE CT

GREENFIELD

LIBY

SIDDELEY CL

LEYLAND RD

DEVONSHIRE RD

HAWKER CL

BRETTON RD

Bretton Court Mews

4

WOODFIELD CL 1
SUMMERFIELD CL 2
CASTLEMERE CL 3
COLINWOOD AVE 4
SANDWOOD AVE 5
FIRBECK CL 6
OAKDALE CL 7
SYCAMORE GR 8

MAIN RD

QUEEN'S WAY

HERON CL

LINTON PL

GLADSTONE

FAIRFIELD RD

CORONATION RD

BROUGHTON HALL RD

GREENFIELD

MAGELEY CL

CONGLETON RD

SOMERFORD RD

WATSON'S CL

PARKFIELD

MARTIN VALE

Liby

1 FARNDON CL
2 DENFORD CL
3 WEBSTER CL

ARNOLD'S CRES

MOLD RD

A5104

MARLWOOD

WELLINGTON RD

LANSDOWN RD

ASH GR

OYSTER PK

BROOKES AVE

THE ROOKERY

BRETTON LA

PHIL TREE CL

BEECH CL

HONEYSUCKLE

WINSFORD

RUSSEBARY CL

PH

PO

Bretton Wood

Works

PENNY BANK CL

BROAD OAK AVE

WINDSOR HO

LLYS CAER

WESTMINSTER RD

HOPE RD

SIMPSONS WAY

WILLOW WAY

THE BIRCHES

YARROW

GALA RD

BRACKEN CL

A55

3

WARREN DR

CHERRY DALE RD

BEESTON RD

SILVERBIRCH CROFT

THE ROWANS

COPESWOOD CL

Bretton Lodge Farm

63

A55

BLACKTHORN CL

2

Lower Kinnerton

BROOK RD

The Gorstella

1

Bridge Farm

MAIN RD

MOOR LA

MOOR CRES

Lane End Farm

Oaktree Farm

62

A B C D E F

8

7

65

6

5

64

4

3

63

2

1

62

36 A B 37 C D 38 E F

B5129

Higher Ferry La
Ferry House

CH1

Top Farm

Border House

North St

Saltney Terr
Ewart St

River Dee/Afon Dyfrdwy

Bumper's La

Facit Glen Ind Est

MONTROSE CT 1
CHURCHSIDE WLK 2
GLAN ABER DR 3
DONNINGTON WAY 4

SALTNEY FERRY RD

Bradshaw La

Parc Ddiwydiannol Y Ffin/
The Borders Ind Pk

Brymau Four Est

Brymau Three Est

River La
Ketlan Ct

Brymau Two Est

Brymau One Est

CWAT ERWAIN

Saltney Bsns Ctr

A5104

CHESTER ST

P

Mwynain Ave
Kynaston Dr
Belmont Dr
Idelta Ct
Major Ave
St David's Terr

Chesterbank Bsns Pk

Bridge St

St Davids Ret Pk

Central Trad Est

MARLEY WAY

HIGH ST

Libby

Sch

Wks

Henry Wood Ct

CORLTON GN

MOUNT PLEASANT

Shrewsbury Way
Telford Way
Coronation
Hope St
Newbury
Bray Cl
St Marks Rd
Shrewsbury Rd
Wenlock Rd
Windsor Rd
Henley Rd
Hemel Rd
Wrexham Rd

Saltney Ferry Prim Sch

Leyland Dr

PO

CHESTER RD

B5129

Carlton Ave
Howard Rd
Norton Ave

Engleed Ave
Linden Gr
Lime Gr

Moorcroft Mews

The Orchards

Salisbury Ave

The Nook

Scholars Cl

Ashleigh Cl

Maes-y-Coed

Mercer Way
Nesbin Way
Westbury Way

Newby Cl
Stafford Cl
Loxdale Ct
Lynton Cl
Oxford Cl
Willow Cl
Redhill Rd

Well House Farm

Wyrmy Rd

Belgrave Ave

Moss Gr

George Kenyon Way

Isabella Cl

Ranmore Way

Poplar Rd

Sandy La

Celyn Cres
Conway Cl

Douglas Cl

Larch Way

Redwood

Oak Rd

PO

Sch

Sandy Lane Farm

Beechwood

Victoria Rd

Irving's Cres
Laburnum Way

Mountain View

Elms Gr

Eaton Gr

Beaumont

Barrwoods

F6
1 GUILDFORD CL
2 DOWNSFIELD RD
3 SUNBURY CRES
4 ABINGDON CRES
5 LLYS RHUDDLAN/
RHUDDLAN CT

Kings Cl
Danefield Rd
Clover La
Clover Cl
Leyfield Cl

CHESTER
(DEVA)

Probyn Cres
Teg-aled Wyn

Maple Gr

Boundary La
Echo

Halkett Cl
Shannon Dr

Beaver Cl

Stanley Park Dr

Weybourne Cl

Beech Cl

Birch Rd

Lache
COLCHESTER SQ

Medlar Cl

Larkspur Cl

64

Greenlane Crossing

Capeland Cl

Tatton Cl

Elder Cl

Avonlea Cl

Sycamore Dr
Dorchester Rd
Winchester Cl

Circular Dr

Lonsdale Ct

Rowcliffe Ave
Marton Cl
Whaddon Rd
Greenacre Rd

Sheringham Cl

CH4

Balderton Brook

Green La

Lache Hall Cres

Baron Way

Forge Way

Smithy Pathway

Ramsden Ct
Haymakers Ct

Bretton Hall

The Lache Eyes

A55

Bretton Wood

Lache La

Decoy Farm

A55

Common Farm

Roughlyn Cres

Two Mile

Balderton

Balderton Lodge

LC

Lache La

Marleston Ct

Roughhill

Gorstella

Balderton Dr

A483 WREXHAM RD

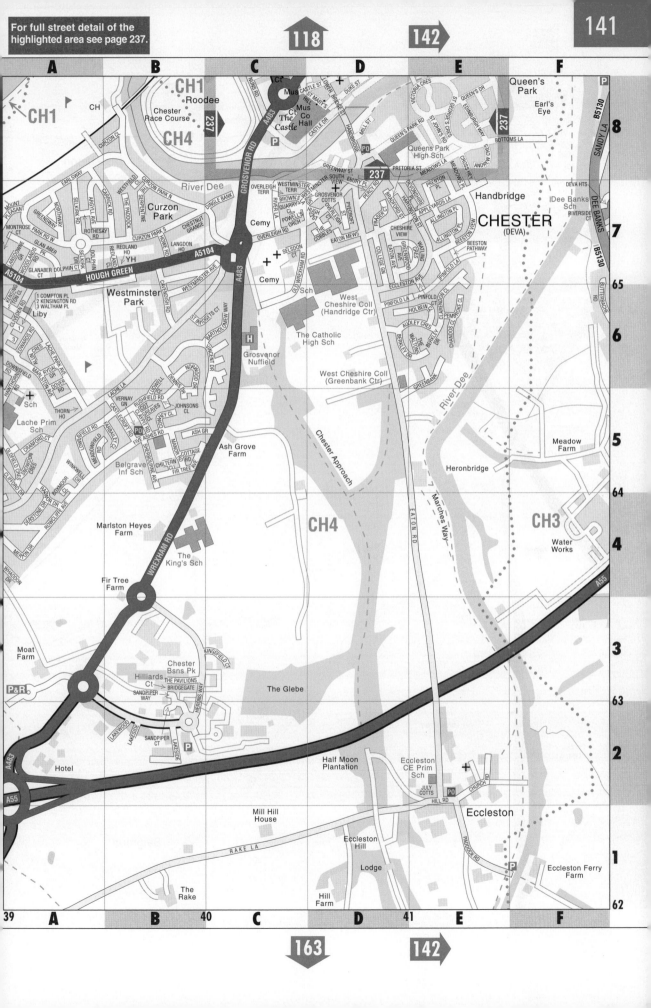

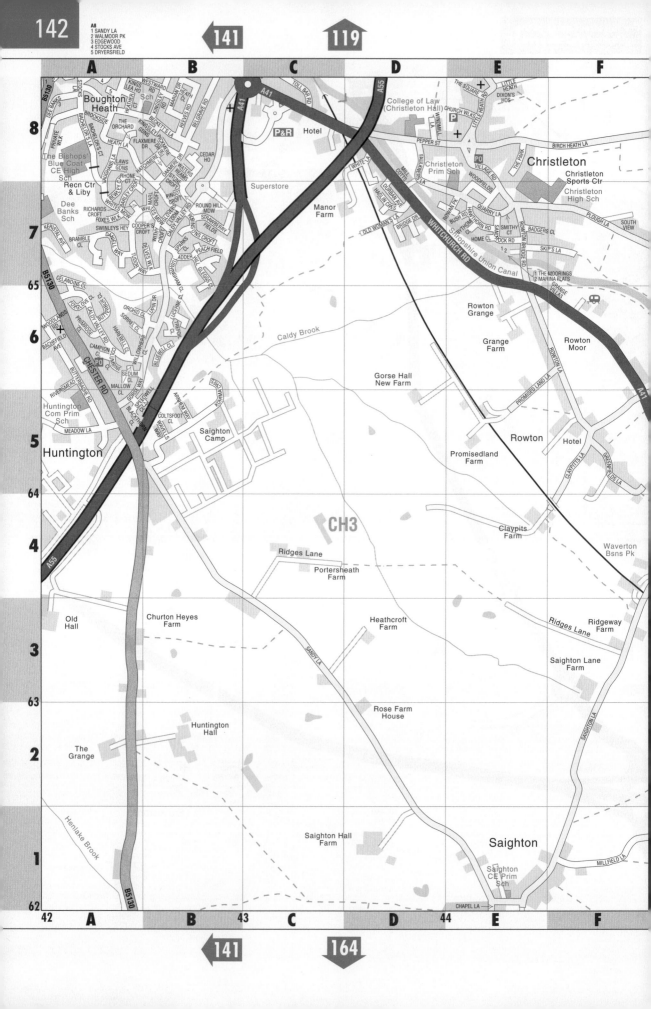

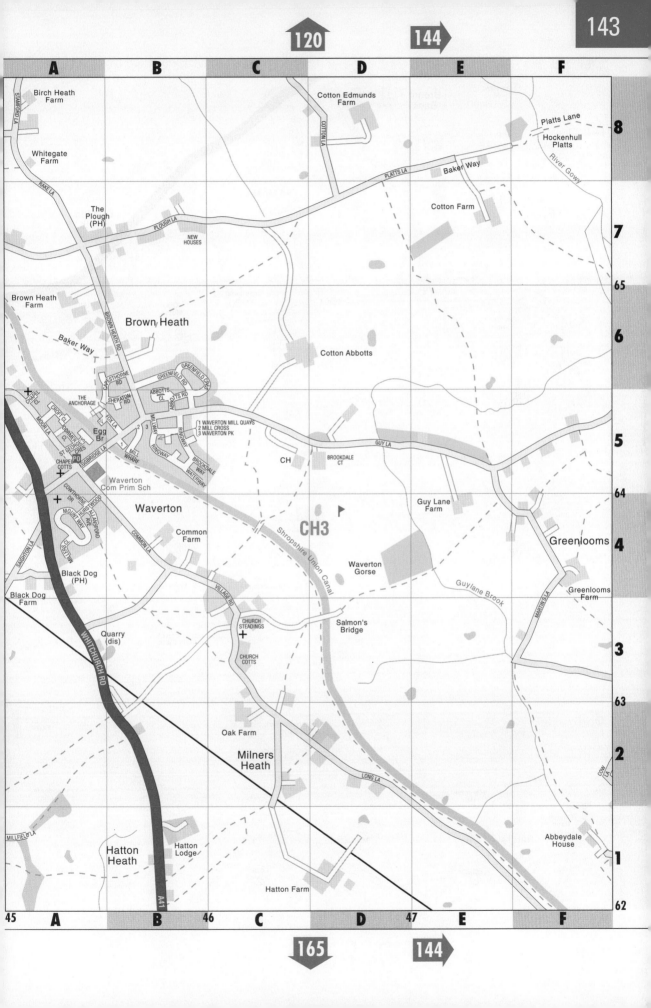

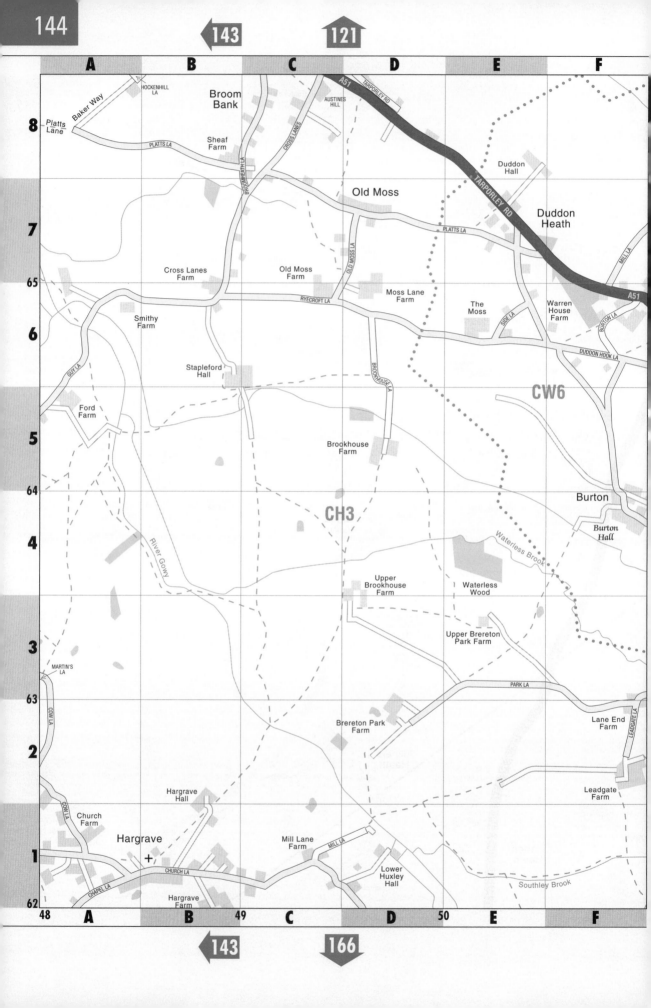

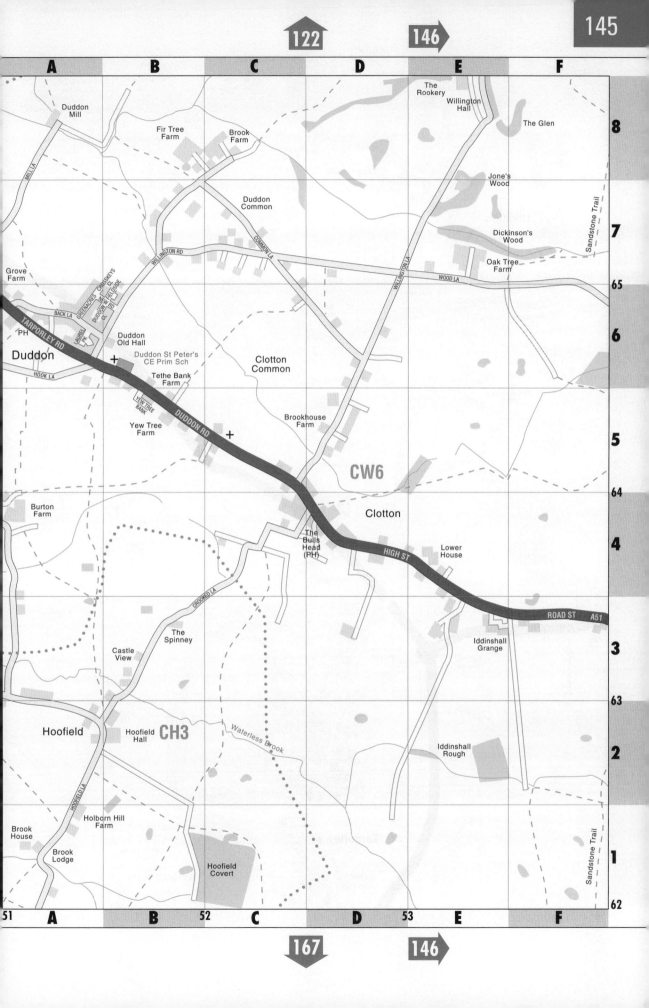

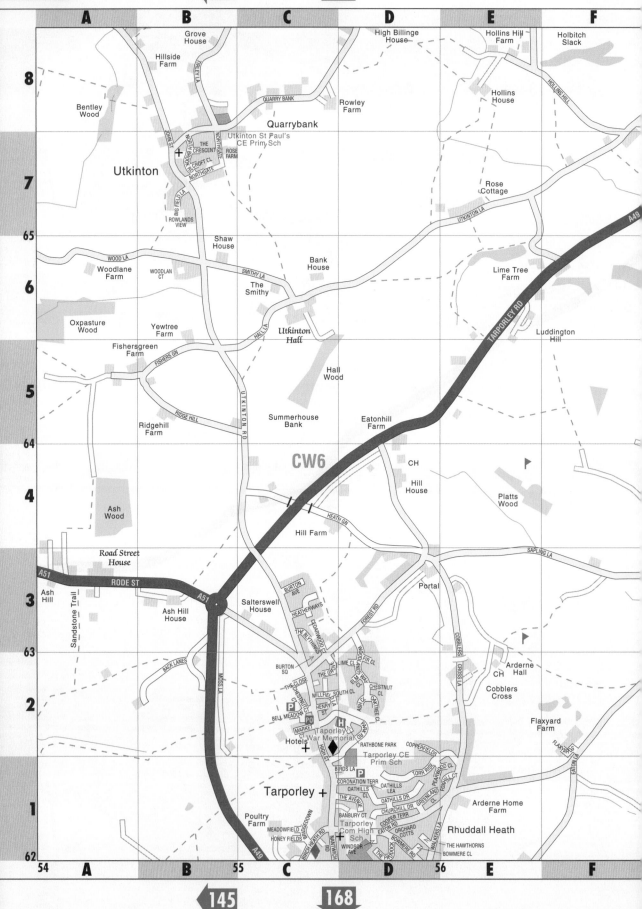

147
125

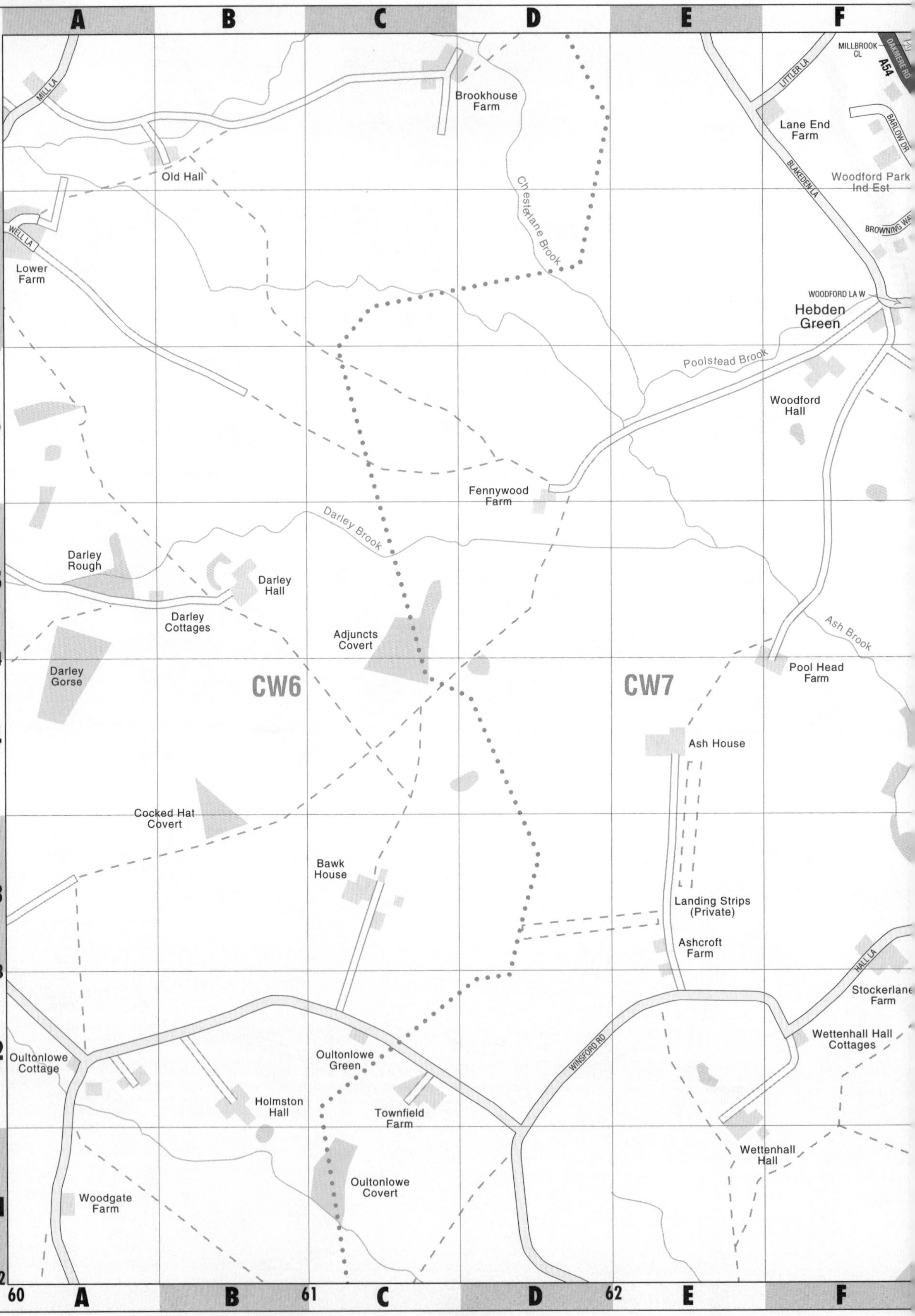

A B C D E F

8

Brookhouse Farm

MILL LA

Old Hall

MILLBROOK CL

OAKMERE RD

A54

LITTLER LA

Lane End Farm

Woodford Park Ind Est

BLAKEDEN LA

BROWNING WA

7

WELL LA

Lower Farm

Chesterlane Brook

WOODFORD LA W

Hebden Green

65

Poolstead Brook

Woodford Hall

6

Fennywood Farm

Darley Brook

Ash Brook

5

Darley Rough

Darley Hall

Darley Cottages

Adjuncts Covert

Pool Head Farm

64

Darley Gorse

CW6

CW7

4

Cocked Hat Covert

Ash House

Landing Strips (Private)

3

Bawk House

Ashcroft Farm

63

HALL LA

Stockerlane Farm

2

Oultonlowe Cottage

Oultonlowe Green

WINSFORD RD

Wettenhall Hall Cottages

Holmston Hall

Townfield Farm

Wettenhall Hall

1

Woodgate Farm

Oultonlowe Covert

62

60 A 61 B C 61 D 62 E F

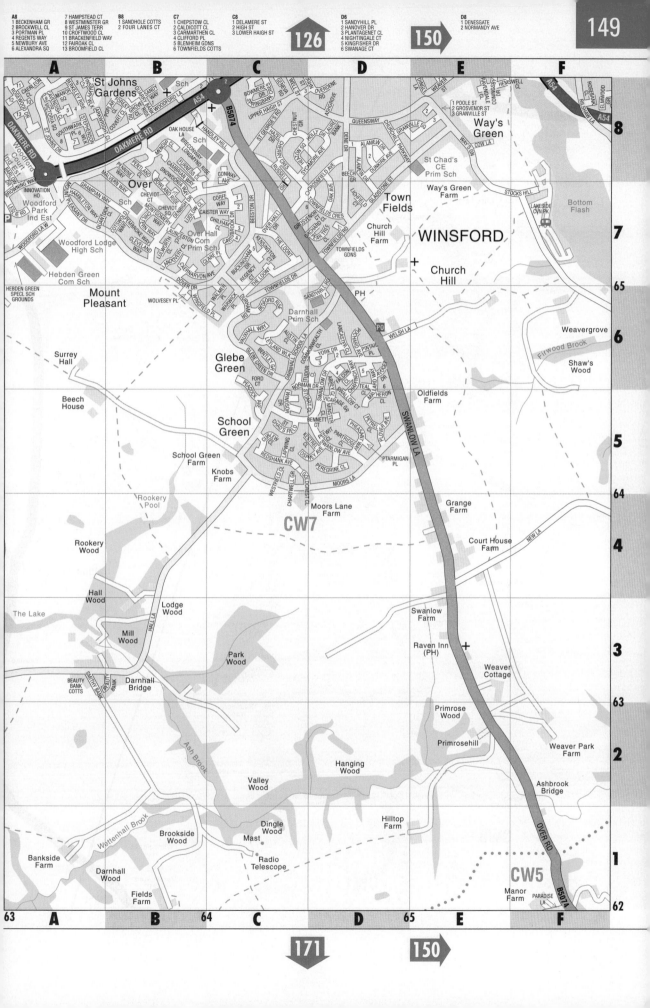

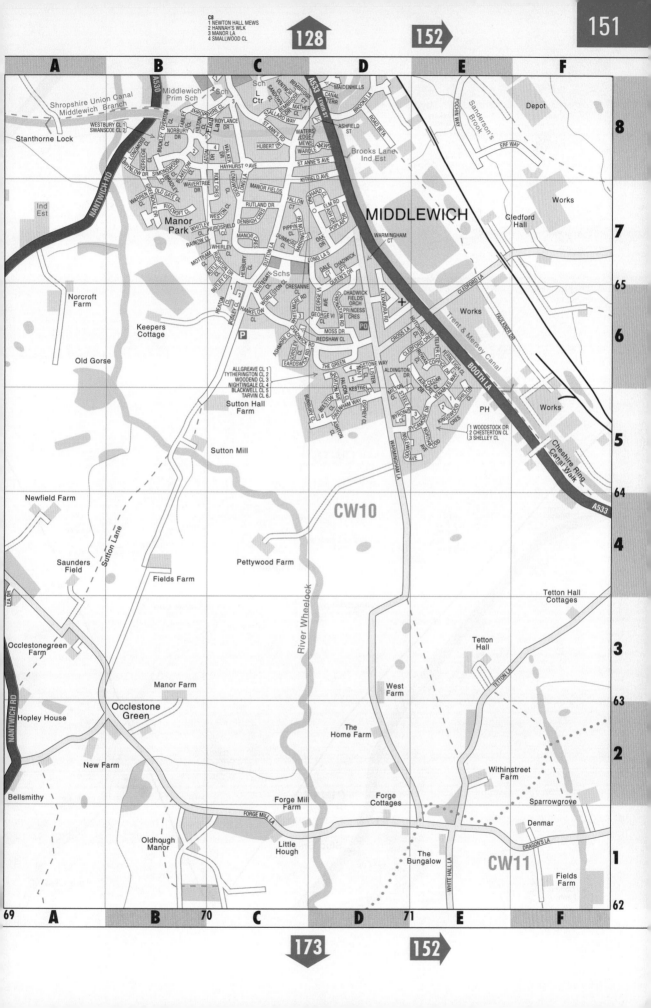

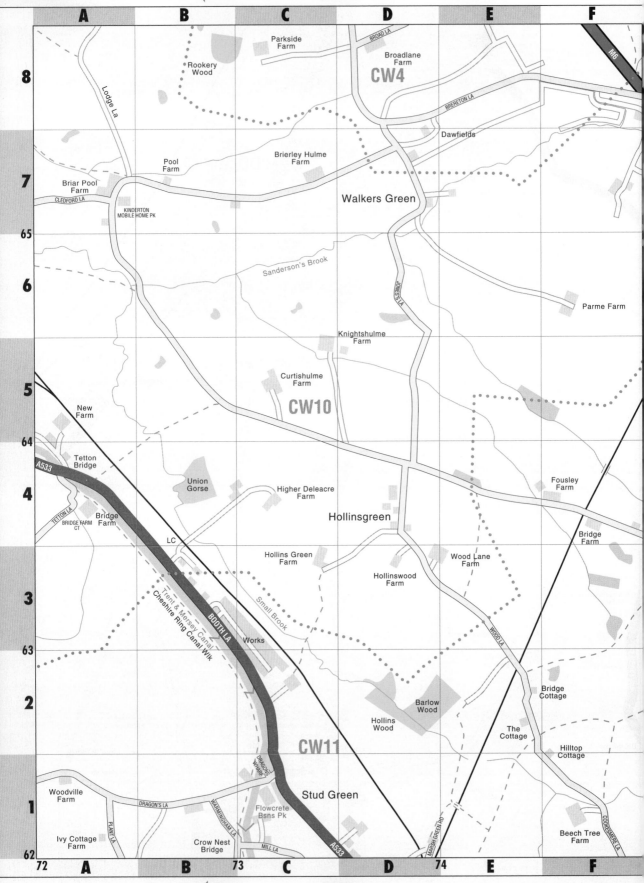

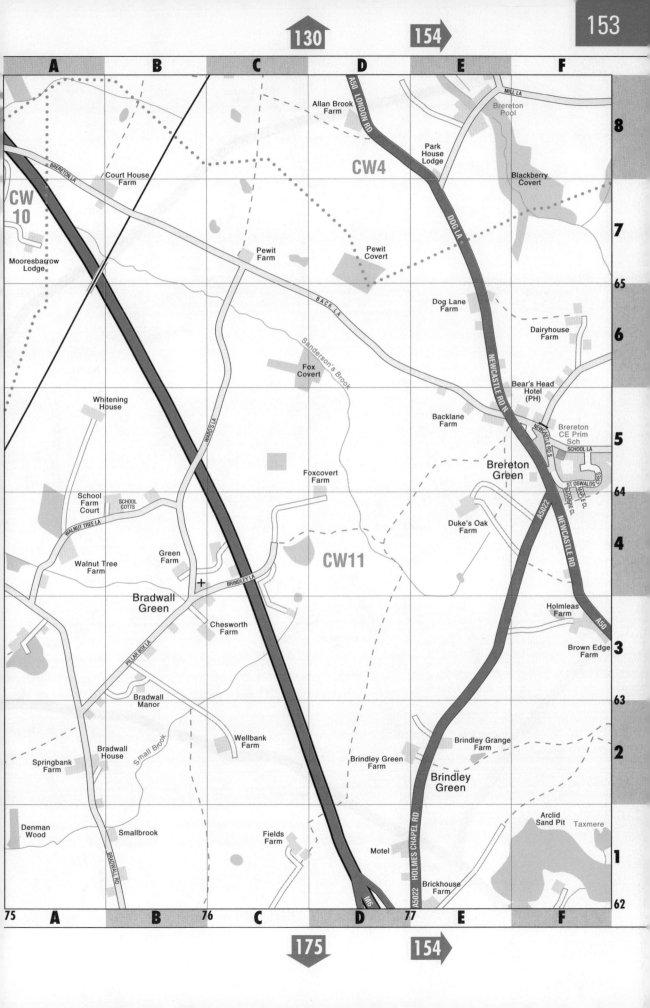

153 131

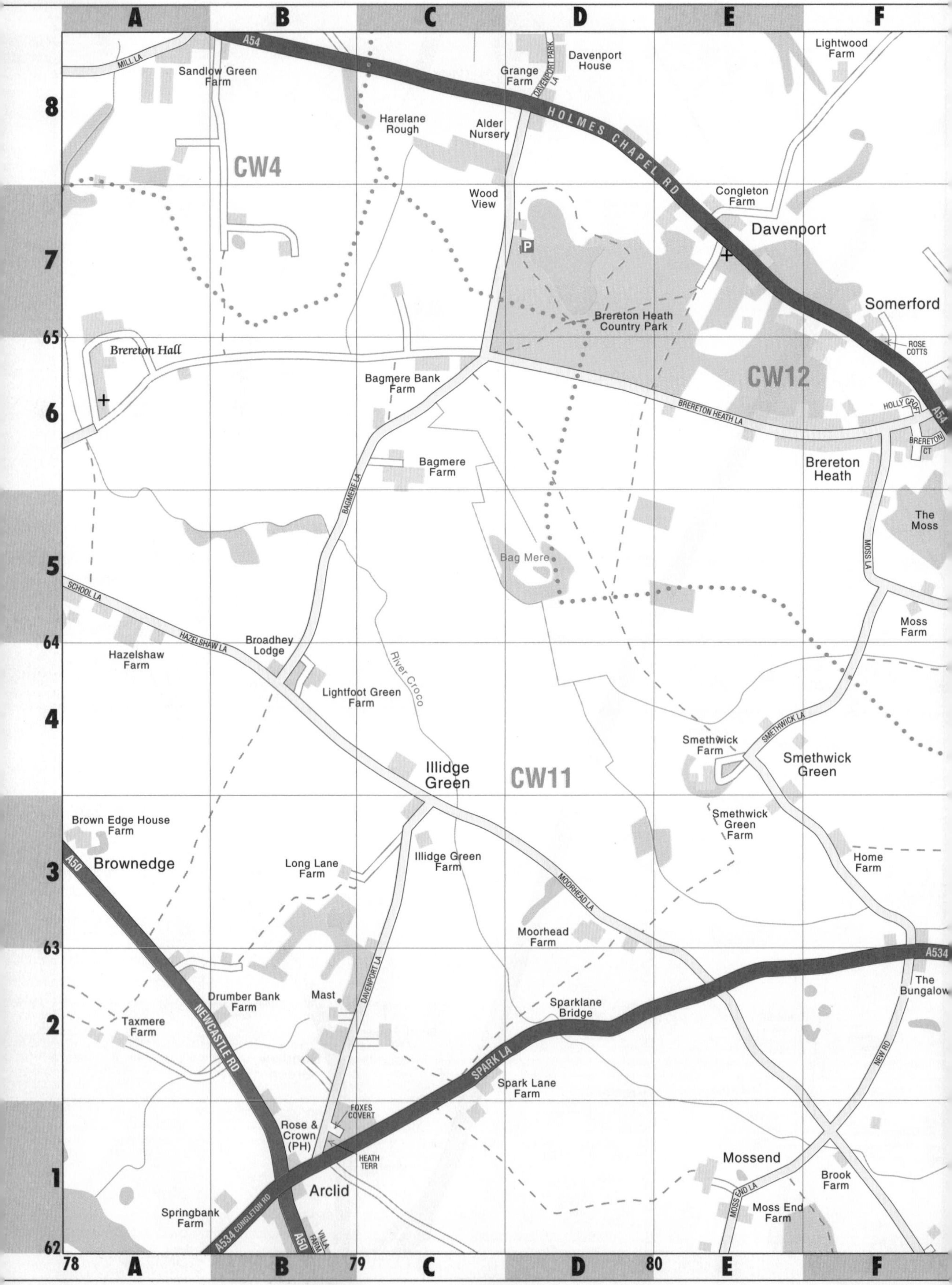

A **B** **C** **D** **E** **F**

8

MILL LA
A54
Sandlow Green Farm
Harelane Rough
Grange Farm
Davenport House
Davenport House
DAVENPORT PARK LA
Alder Nursery
HOLMES CHAPEL RD
Lightwood Farm

CW4

7

Wood View
P
Congleton Farm
Davenport
+

65

Brereton Hall
Brereton Heath Country Park
Somerford
ROSE COTTS

6

+
Bagmere Bank Farm
BRERETON HEATH LA
CW12
HOLLY CROFT
A54
BRERETON CT
Brereton Heath

Bagmere Farm
The Moss
BAGMERE LA
MOSS LA

5

SCHOOL LA
Bag Mere
Moss Farm

64

Hazelshaw Farm
HAZELSHAW LA
Broadhey Lodge
River Croco

4

Lightfoot Green Farm
Smethwick Farm
SMETHWICK LA
Smethwick Green

Illidge Green
CW11
Smethwick Green Farm

Brown Edge House Farm
Long Lane Farm
Illidge Green Farm
Home Farm

3

A50
Brownedge
DAVENPORT LA
MOORHEAD LA
Moorhead Farm
A534

63

Drumber Bank Farm
Mast
Sparklane Bridge
The Bungalow

2

Taxmere Farm
NEWCASTLE RD
SPARK LA
Spark Lane Farm
NEW RD
Mossend

FOXES COVERT
Rose & Crown (PH)
HEATH TERR
Brook Farm

1

Springbank Farm
A534 CONGLETON RD
Arclid
VILLA FARM
A50
Moss End Farm
MOSS END LA

62

78 **A** **B** 79 **C** **D** 80 **E** **F**

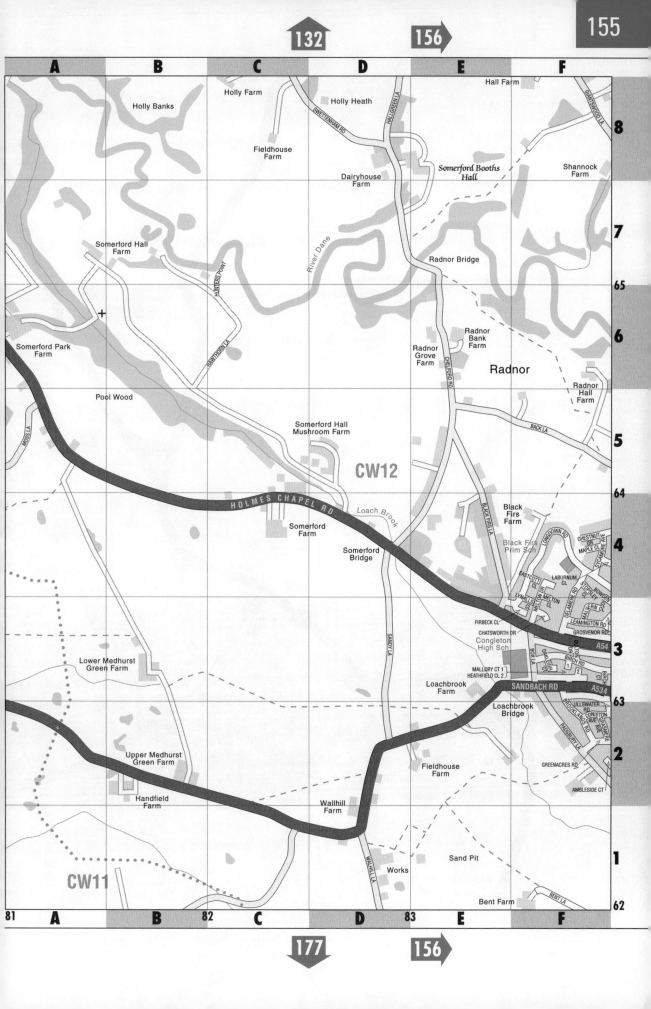

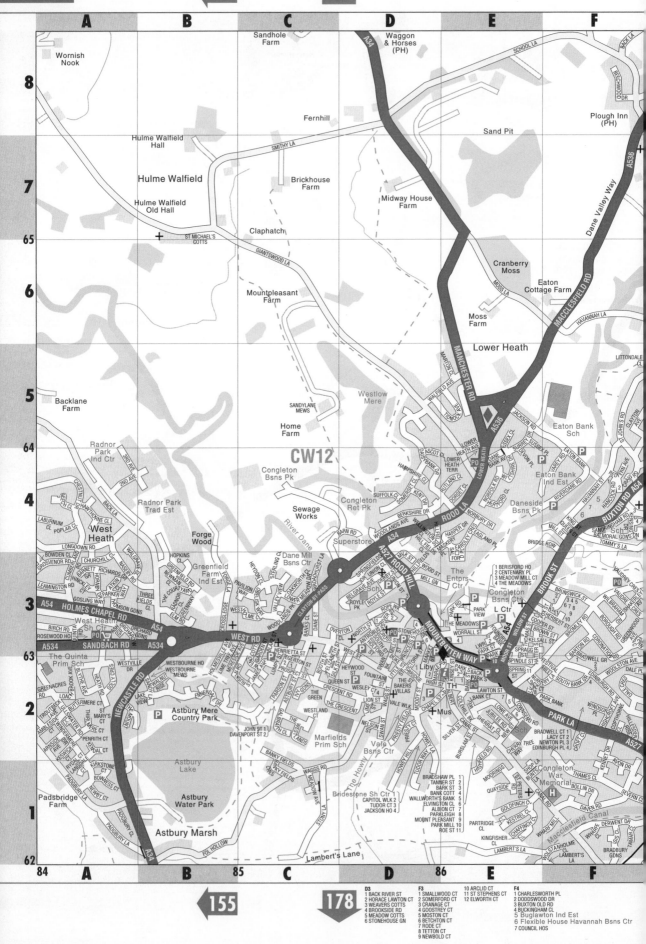

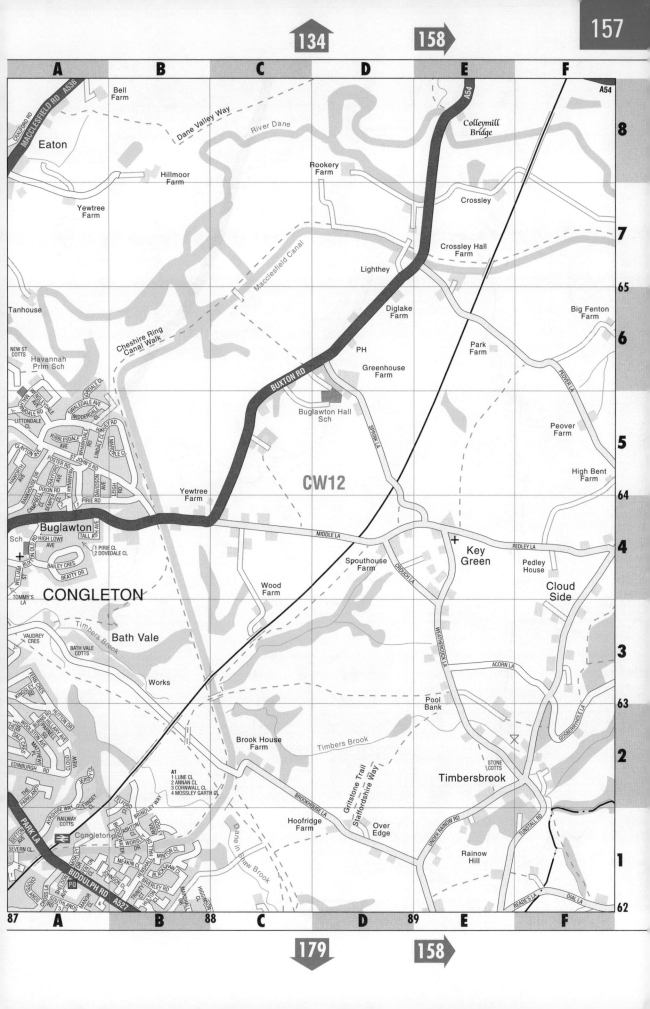

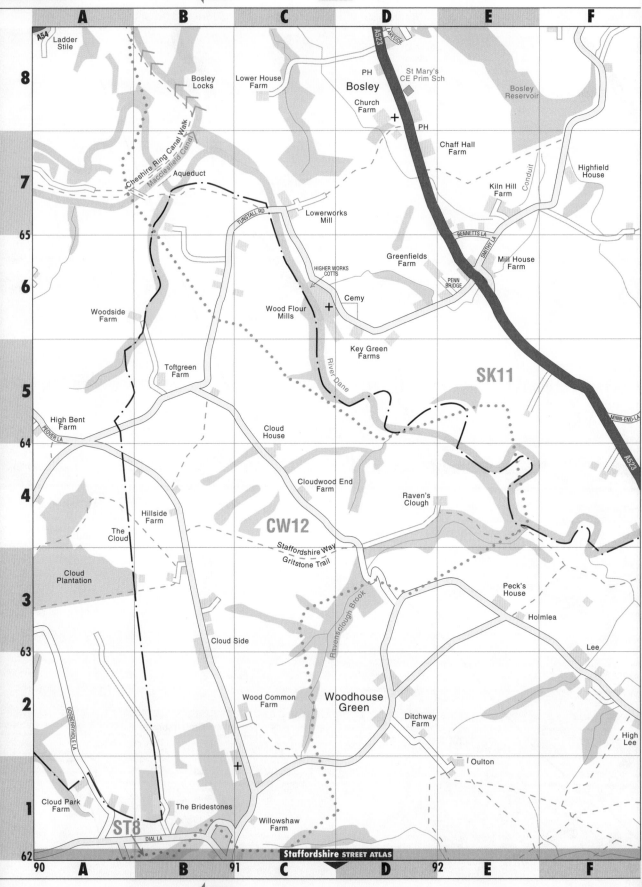

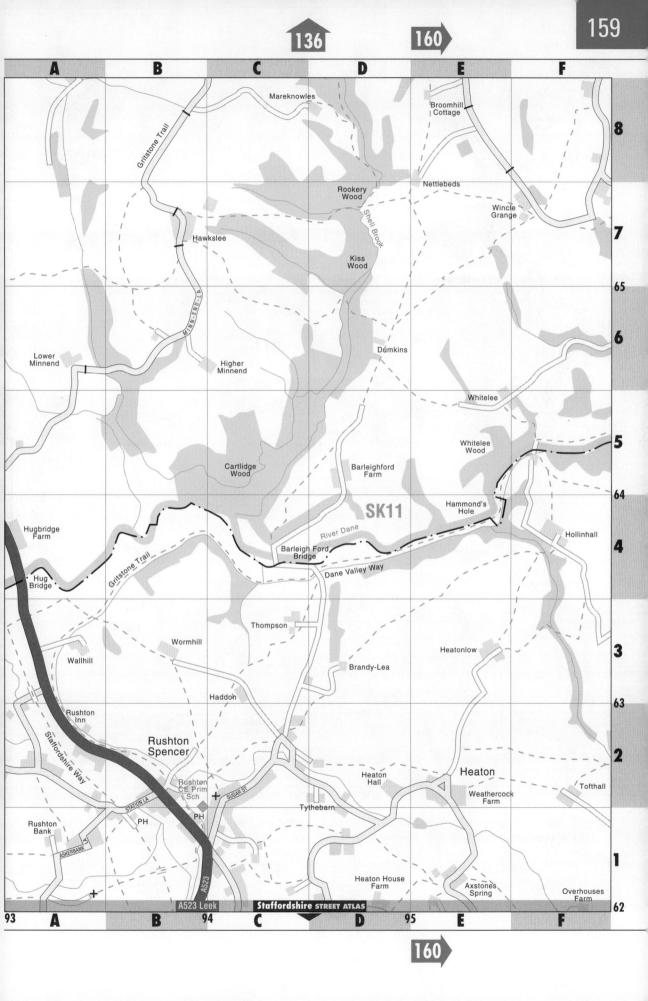

A   B   C   D   E   F

8

Mareknowles

Broomhill
Cottage

Gritstone Trail

Rookery
Wood

Nettlebeds

7

Shell Brook

Wincle
Grange

Hawkslee

65

6

MINN END LA

Kiss
Wood

Lower
Minnend

Dumkins

Higher
Minnend

Whitelee

5

Cartlidge
Wood

Barleighford
Farm

Whitelee
Wood

64

SK11

Hammond's
Hole

Hollinhall

Hugbridge
Farm

River Dane

4

Gritstone Trail

Barleigh Ford
Bridge

Dane Valley Way

Hug
Bridge

Thompson

Wormhill

Heatonlow

3

Wallhill

Brandy-Lea

Haddon

63

Rushton
Inn

2

Staffordshire Way

Rushton
Spencer

Rushton
CE Prim
Sch

Heaton
Hall

Heaton

Tofthall

SUGAR ST

STATION LA

Weathercock
Farm

PH

PH

Tythebarn

Rushton
Bank

1

ASKERBANK

A523

Heaton House
Farm

Axstones
Spring

Overhouses
Farm

62

A   **B**   **C**   **D**   **E**   **F**

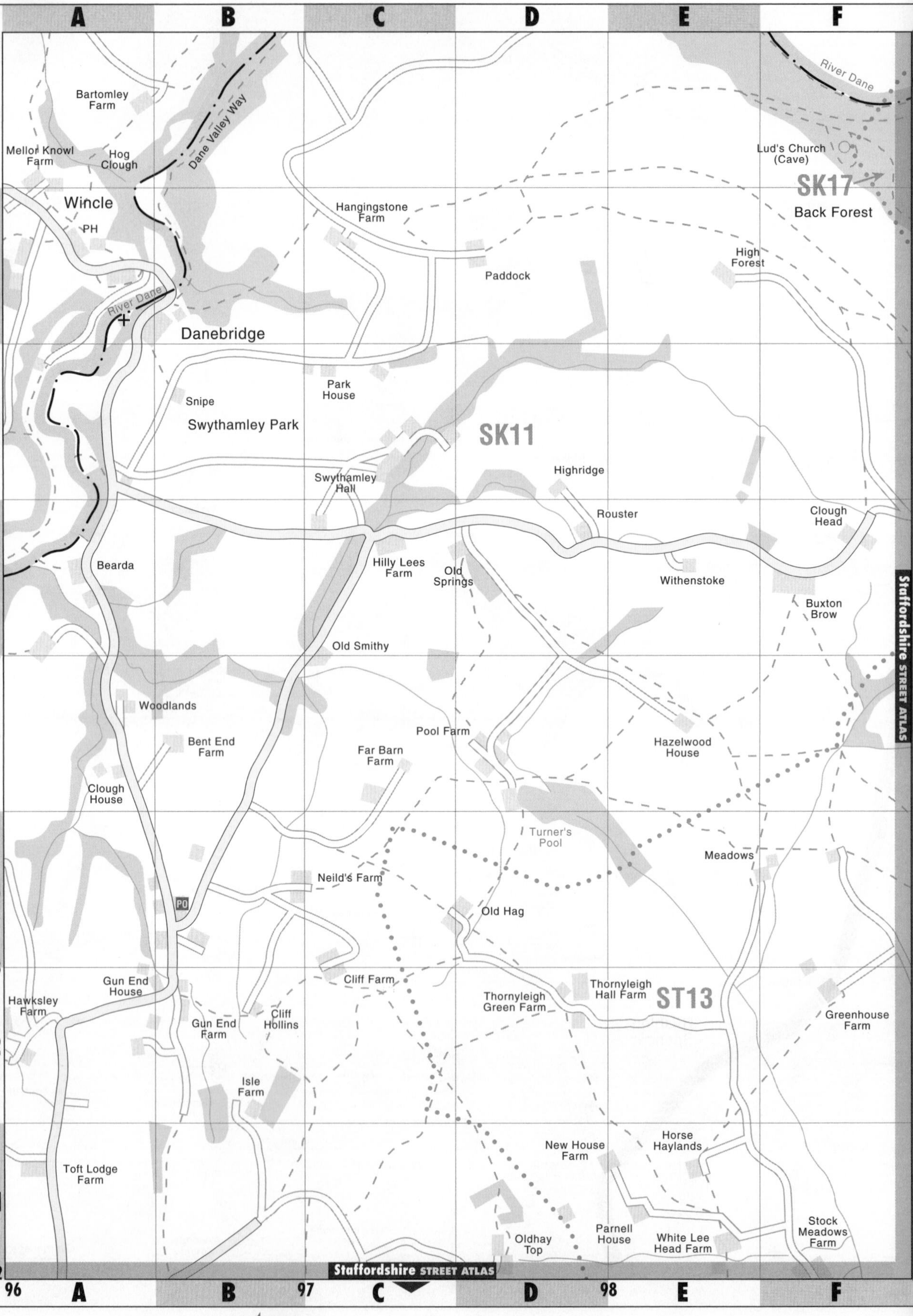

River Dane

8

Bartomley Farm

Mellor Knowl Farm

Hog Clough

Dane Valley Way

Lud's Church (Cave)

SK17

Back Forest

Wincle

PH

High Forest

7

Hangingstone Farm

Paddock

River Dane

65

Danebridge

Park House

Snipe

Highridge

Clough Head

6

Swythamley Park

SK11

Swythamley Hall

Rouster

Withenstoke

Bearda

Hilly Lees Farm

Old Springs

Buxton Brow

5

Old Smithy

64

Woodlands

Pool Farm

Hazelwood House

4

Bent End Farm

Far Barn Farm

Meadows

Clough House

Turner's Pool

3

Neild's Farm

Old Hag

63

Hawksley Farm

Gun End House

Cliff Farm

Thornyleigh Hall Farm

ST13

Greenhouse Farm

2

Gun End Farm

Cliff Hollins

Thornyleigh Green Farm

Isle Farm

New House Farm

Horse Haylands

1

Toft Lodge Farm

Stock Meadows Farm

62

Oldhay Top

Parnell House

White Lee Head Farm

Staffordshire STREET ATLAS

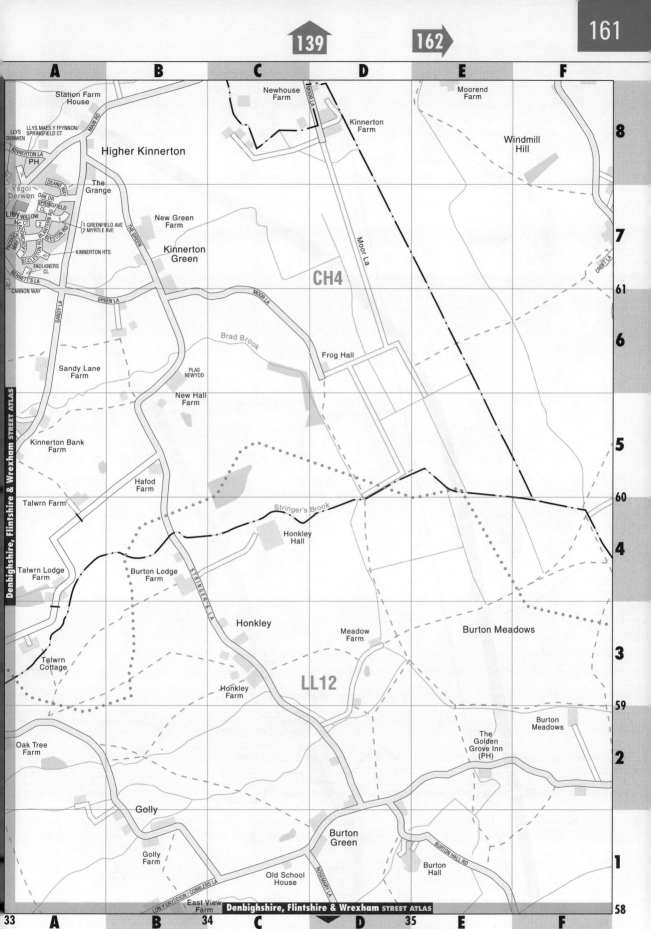

A   B   C   D   E   F

Station Farm House
LLYS MAES Y FFYNNON/ SPRINGFIELD CT
LLYS DERWEN
KINNERTON LA
PH
Higher Kinnerton
Newhouse Farm
MOOR LA
Kinnerton Farm
Moorend Farm
Windmill Hill
8

Ysgol Derwen
DEANS WAY
The Grange
OAK DR
SPRINGFIELD CL
WILLOW
1
New Green Farm
Liby
McCT
2
PADDOCK WAY
OAK DR
BLAENTERN RD
MEADOWCROFT
ECCLESTON RD
BEESTON RD
1 GREENFIELD AVE
2 MYRTLE AVE
KINNERTON HTS
THE GREEN
Kinnerton Green
7

FAULKNERS CL
BENNETT'S LA
CANNON WAY
SANDY LA
GREEN LA
MOOR LA
Moor La
CH4
61

Sandy Lane Farm
PLAS NEWYDD
Brad Brook
Frog Hall
6

New Hall Farm
5

Kinnerton Bank Farm
Hafod Farm
Stringer's Brook
60

Talwrn Farm
Honkley Hall
Talwrn Lodge Farm
Burton Lodge Farm
STRINGER'S LA
Honkley
Meadow Farm
Burton Meadows
4

Talwrn Cottage
Honkley Farm
LL12
59
3

Oak Tree Farm
The Golden Grove Inn (PH)
Burton Meadows
2

Golly
Golly Farm
Burton Green
BURTON HALL RD
Burton Hall
1

LON Y CRYDDION/ COBBLERS LA
ROSEMARY LA
Old School House
East View Farm
58

33   A   B   34   C   D   35   E   F

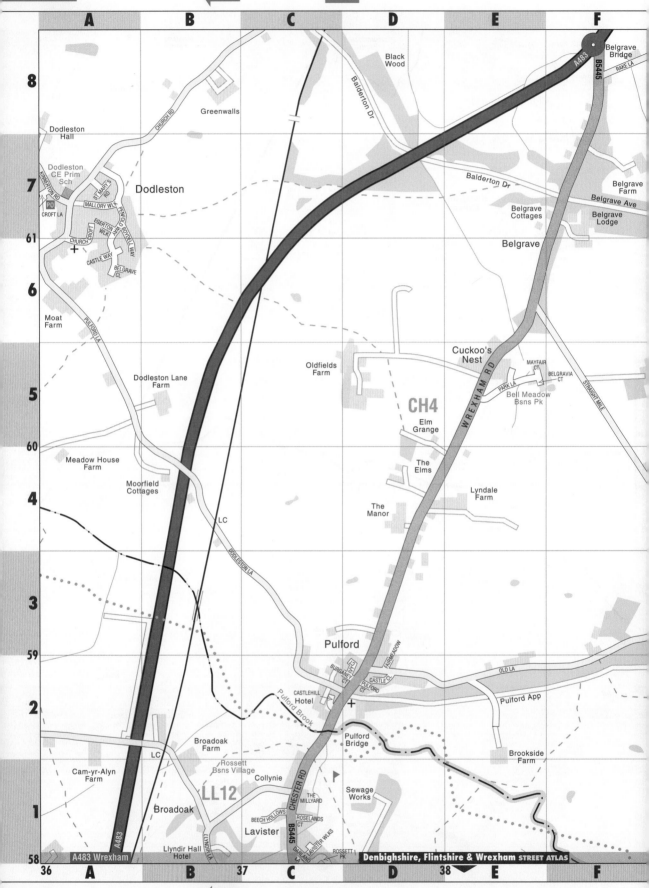

A483

B5445

Belgrave
Bridge

RAKE LA

Black
Wood

Balderton Dr

Balderton Dr

Belgrave
Farm

Belgrave Ave

Belgrave
Cottages

Belgrave
Lodge

Greenwalls

CHURCH RD

Dodleston
Hall

Dodleston
CE Prim
Sch

KINNERTON RD

PO

CROFT LA

ST MARY'S RD

MALLORY WLK

PENFOLD ROYDELL WAY

Dodleston

Belgrave

EGERTON WLK

CHURCH

CASTLE WAY

BELGRAVE CL

Moat
Farm

PULFORD LA

Dodleston Lane
Farm

Oldfields
Farm

Cuckoo's
Nest

WREXHAM RD

MAYFAIR CT

PARK LA

BELGRAVIA CT

Bell Meadow
Bsns Pk

STRAIGHT MILE

CH4

Elm
Grange

Meadow House
Farm

Moorfield
Cottages

The
Elms

Lyndale
Farm

LC

DODLESTON LA

The
Manor

Pulford

FAIRMEADOW

OLD LA

Pulford App

BURGANIC CT

PULFORD CT

CASTLE CT

CHESTER RD

CASTLEHILL
Hotel

Pulford Brook

Pulford
Bridge

Brookside
Farm

Broadoak
Farm

Rossett
Bsns Village

LC

Collynie

Cam-yr-Alyn
Farm

LL12

LLYNDIR LA

Lavister

BEECH HOLLOWS

B5445

THE
MILLYARD

ROSELANDS
CT

Sewage
Works

Broadoak

DARLAND

LAVISTER WLKS

ROSSETT
PK

A483

Llyndir Hall
Hotel

A483 Wrexham

58

Denbighshire, Flintshire & Wrexham STREET ATLAS

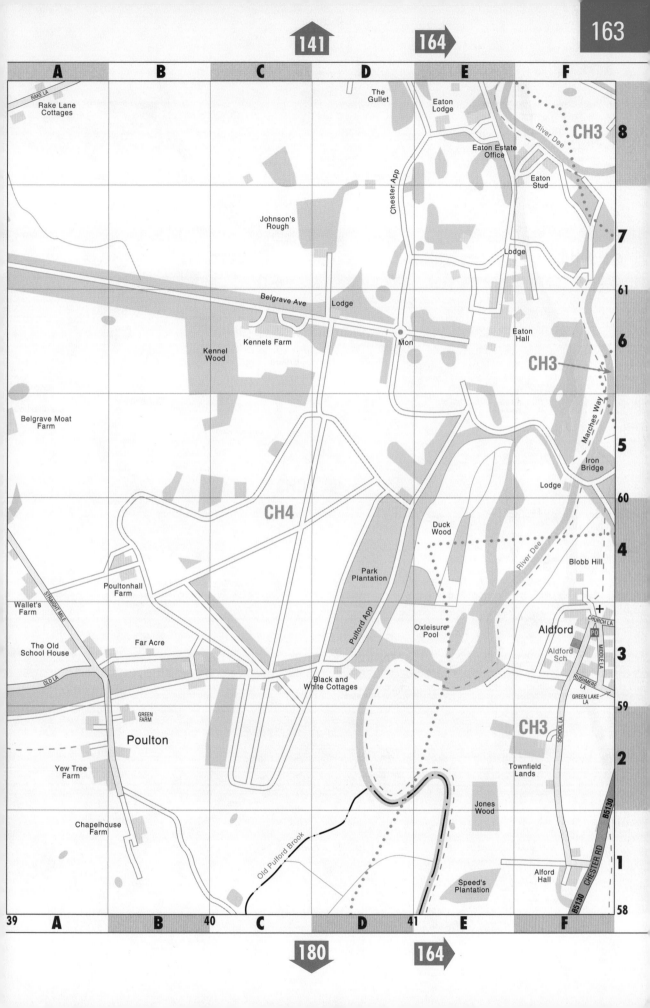

141
164

A B C D E F

Rake La

Rake Lane
Cottages

The
Gullet

Eaton
Lodge

River Dee

CH3

8

Chester App

Eaton Estate
Office

Eaton
Stud

Johnson's
Rough

Lodge

7

Belgrave Ave

Lodge

61

Kennels Farm

Eaton
Hall

6

Mon

Kennel
Wood

CH3

Matches Way

Belgrave Moat
Farm

Iron
Bridge

5

Lodge

60

CH4

Duck
Wood

River Dee

Blobb Hill

4

Park
Plantation

Pulford App

Poultonhall
Farm

Wallet's
Farm

Oxleisure
Pool

Aldford

Church La

Aldford
Sch

Middle La

3

The Old
School House

Straight Mile

Far Acre

Old La

Black and
White Cottages

Rushmere La

Green Lake La

School La

59

Green
Farm

CH3

Poulton

2

Yew Tree
Farm

Townfield
Lands

Chapelhouse
Farm

Jones
Wood

B5130

1

Old Pulford Brook

Speed's
Plantation

Alford
Hall

Chester Rd

B5130

58

39 A B 40 C D 41 E F

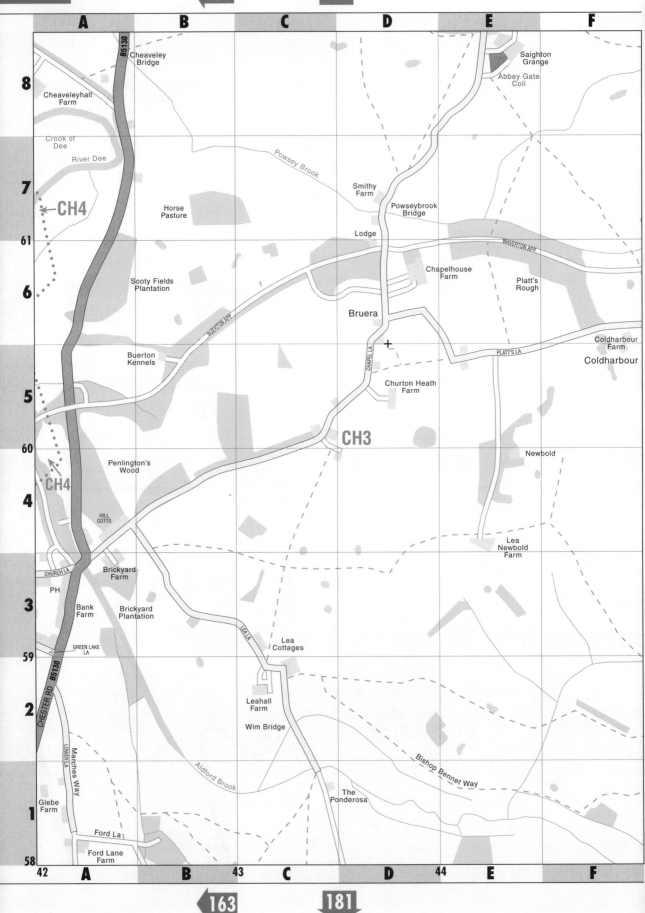

143
166

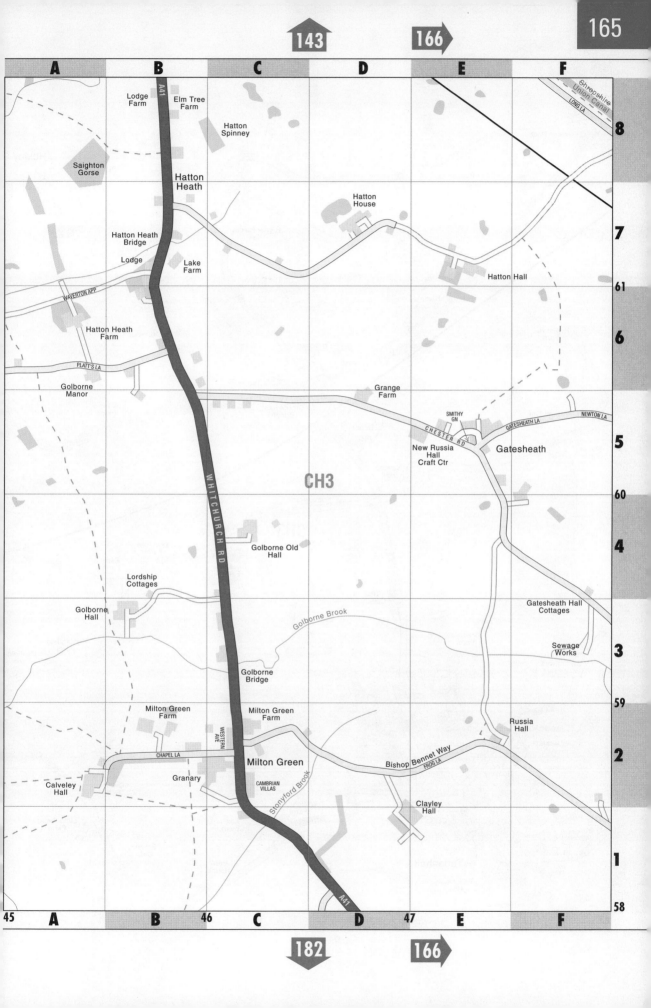

182
166

165
144

A B C D E F

8

7

61

6

5

60

4

3

59

2

1

58

CHAPEL LA

Golden Nook Farm

The Poplars

LONG LA

MILL LA

Green Farm

PH

Huxley

Huxley Bridge

Higher Huxley Hall

River Gowy

Pool Bank Farm

Nixon's Bridge

Shropshire Union Canal

RED LA

Mill Farm

Poplar Hall Farm

Mast

CROW'S NEST COTTS

Crow's Nest Cotts

Millfields

Works

Birch Tree Farm

Depot PH

Crow's Nest Bridge

Dutton's Bridge

Manor Farm

Newton Hall

NEWTON COTTS

Bishop Bennet Way

NEWTON LA

CH3

Yew Tree Farm

Newton

The Cedars

Cheshire Farm

Ford Farm

FORD LA

Greaves Farm

Springfield Farm

Oakfield Farm

Brook Hall

CHESTER RD

TATTENHALL RD

Keys Brook

RAVENSHOLME LA

GREENLANDS

OAKLANDS CL

OAKLANDS AVE

ROOKERY RD

KEYSBROOK

CASTLEFIELDS

SMITHFIELDS

HARDING AVE

KEYSBROOK AVE

TATTENHALL LA

RAVENSHOLME CT

Park Prim Sch

Liby

The Rookery

PARK AVE

REAN MDW

Owler Hall

Frog Hall Farm

MILLBROOK END

COVERT RISE

BARNWELL RD

Mill Brook

HALL VIEW

CHURCH BANK

CROOKES CT

THE NINE HOS

MILLBANK COTTS

PO

PLACKA CT

FIELD LA

Whitehead Farm

Little Owler Farm

GORSEFIELD

SPRINGY

NEWALL CL

HIGH ST

OLD MILL PL

PH

BURWARDSLEY RD

Fox Covert

BROCKWAY E

BROCKWAY W

ROSEMARY ROW

BARBOUR SQ

Tattenhall

Bank House

Broad Oak

BIRDS LA

CARRS LA

FROG LA

ROSE CNR

ROCKY LA

Tattenhall Hall

EDGECROFT

BOLESWORTH RD

A 48 B 49 C D 50 E F

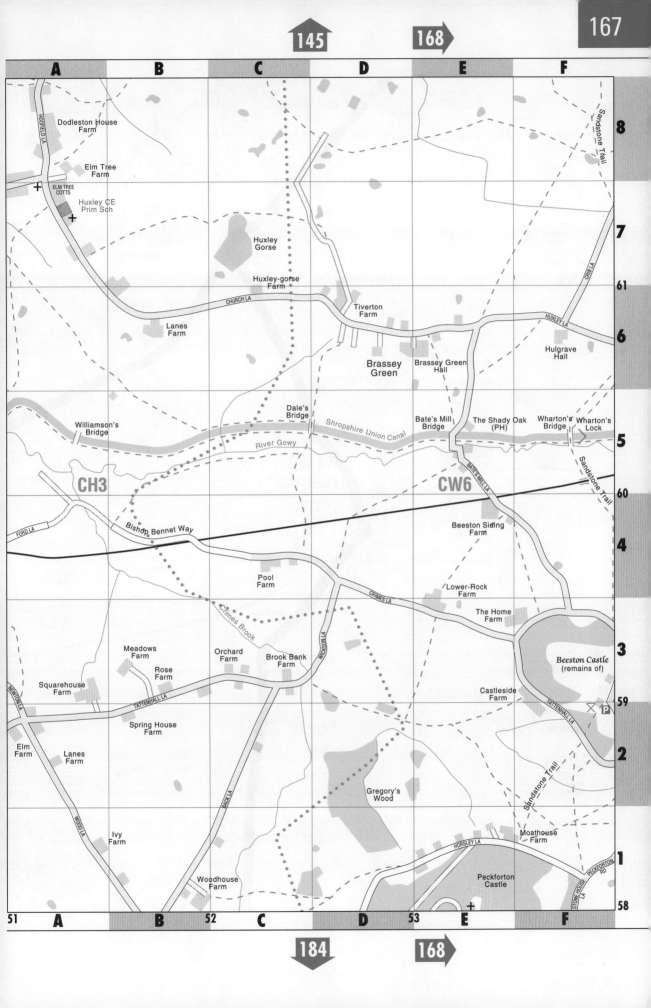

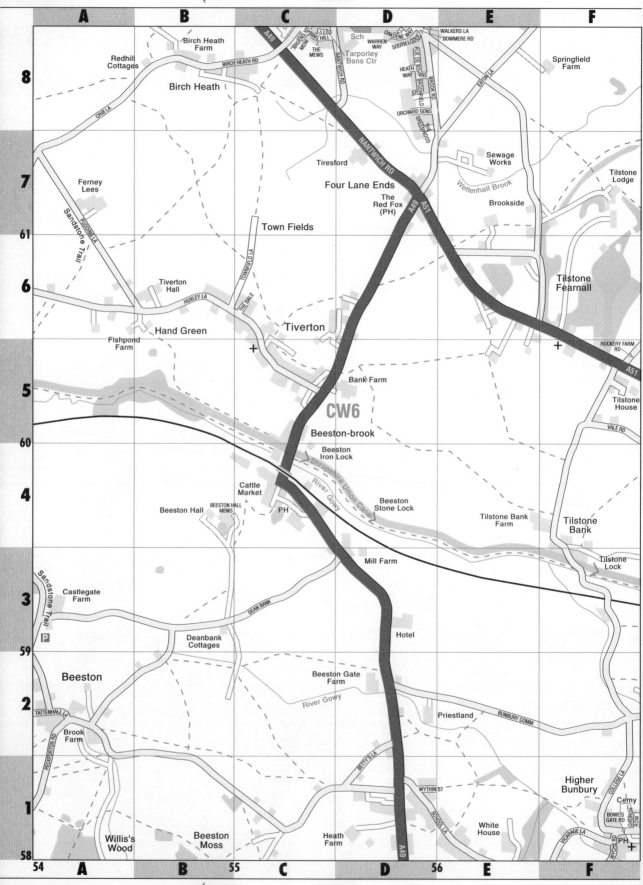

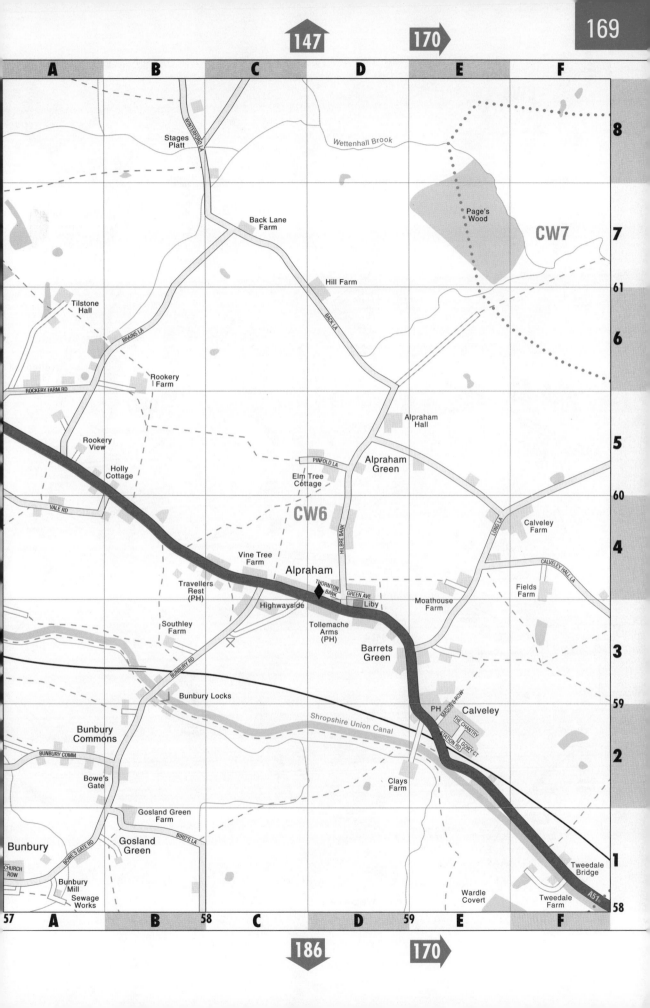

169
148

A B C D E F
8 7 6 5 4 3 2 1
61 60 59 58
CW6
Wettenhall Brook
Bridge Farm
Towns Green Cottages
EATON RD
Holme Farm
Corner Farm
Towns Green
Cornhill Farm
PH
Wettenhall
Village Farm
Manor Farm
Long Lane Farm
WINSFORD RD
LONG LA
Bankside Wood
New Farm
Bankside Brook
Wettenhall Green
South View
DOUGLAS LA
CW7
Ankersplatt Brook
Bankside
PH
Calveley Green Farm
Fox Covert
Brooklands Farm
CHAPEL CL
Cholmondeston
Gale Farm
Cross Road Farm
CROWTON COTTS
CALVELEY GREEN LA
Crowton Brook
The Woodlands
The Elms Farm
CW6
Calveley Hall Farm
Calveley Prim Sch
Ladyacre Wood
Old Covert
Rosebank Farm
SOUTH VIEW LA
CALVELEY HALL LA
Bank Farm
South View Farm
TOP FARM LA
Highbank Farm
Greenbank Farm
Parkfield House Farm
CW5
Top Farm
A51
Wardle Bank
60 61 62

169
187

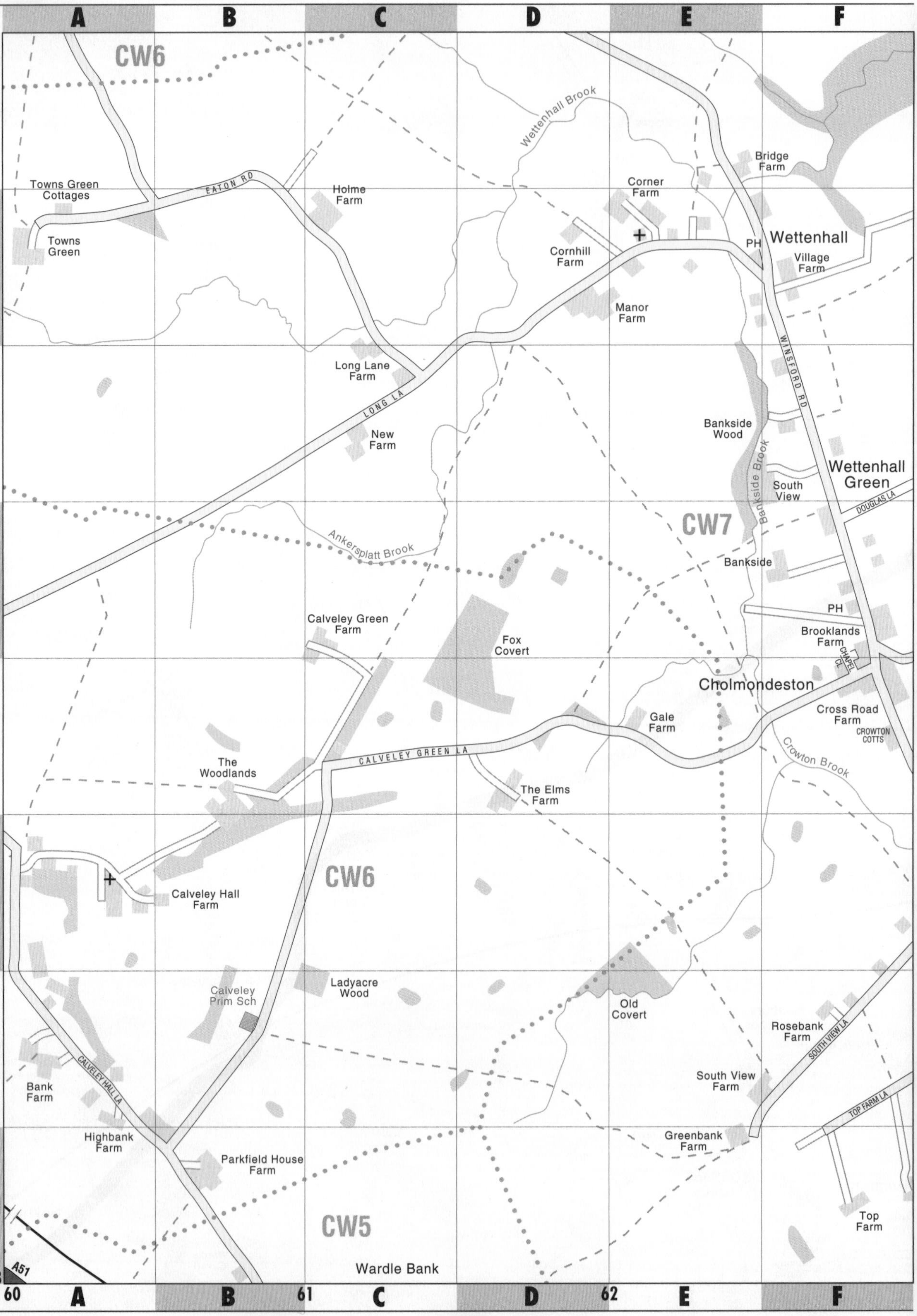

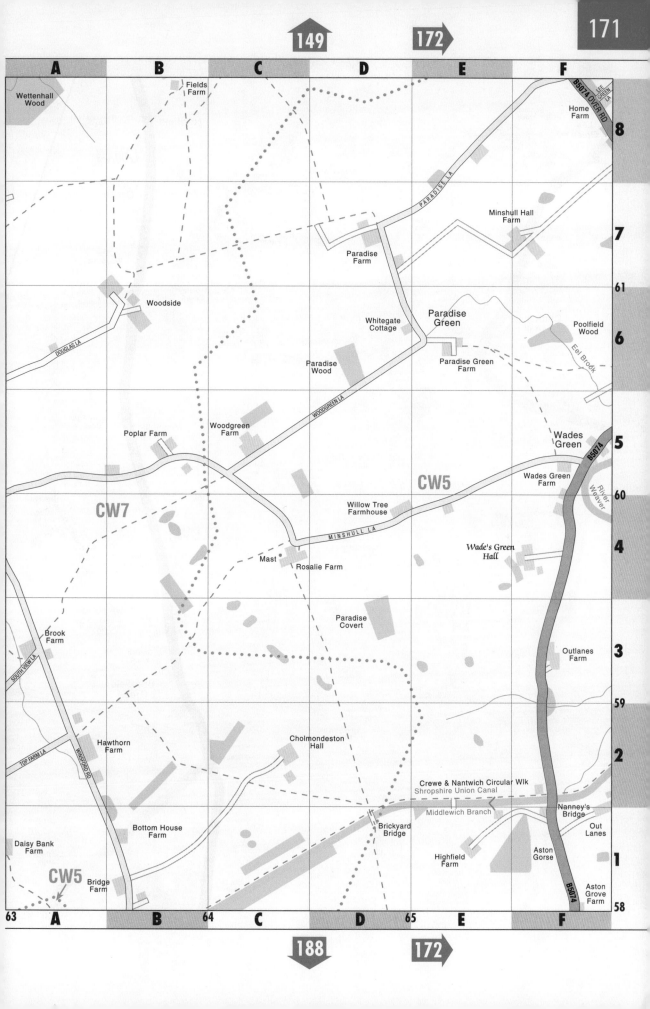

171
150

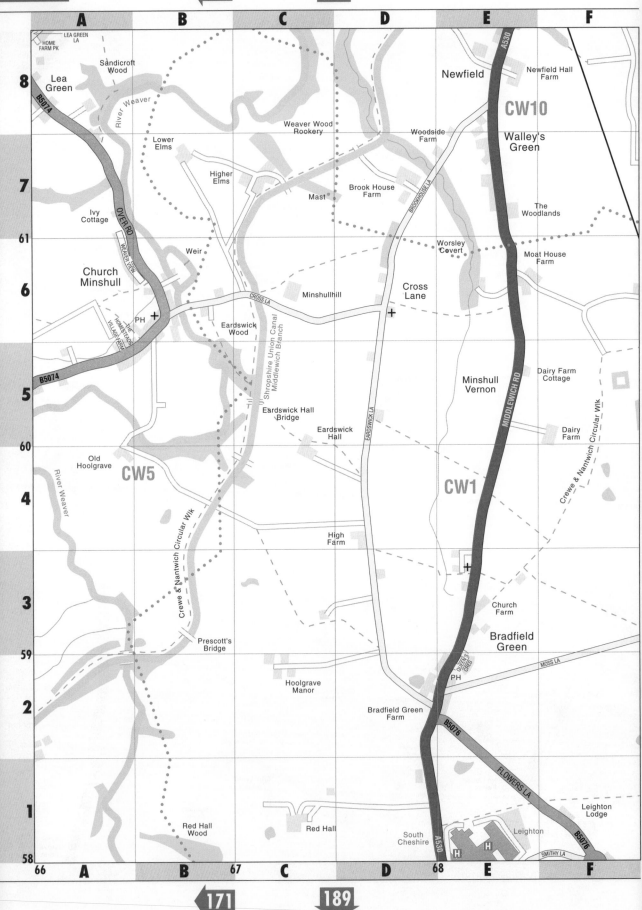

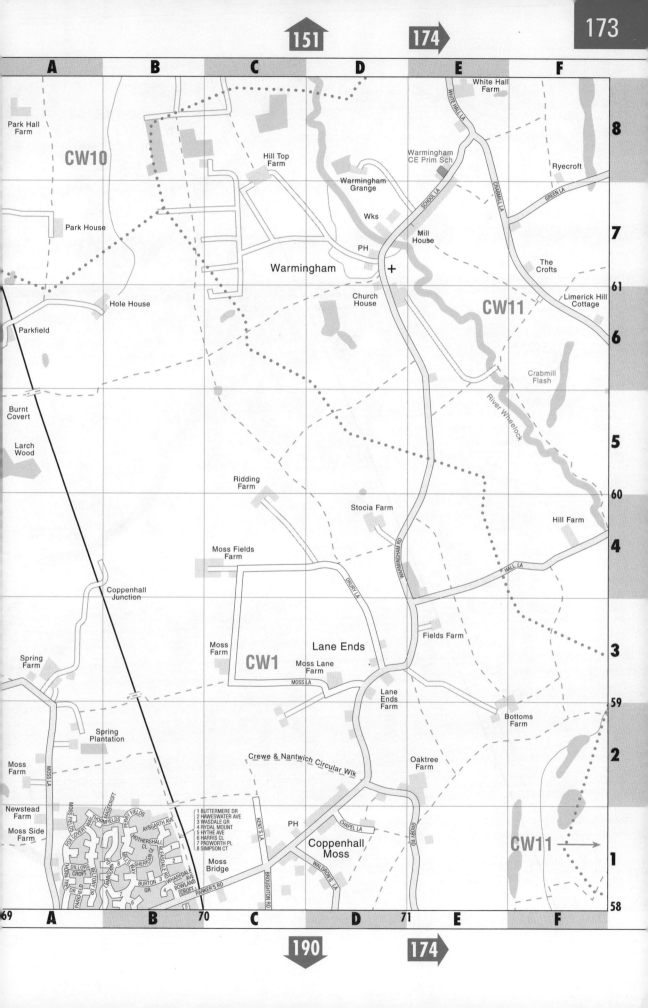

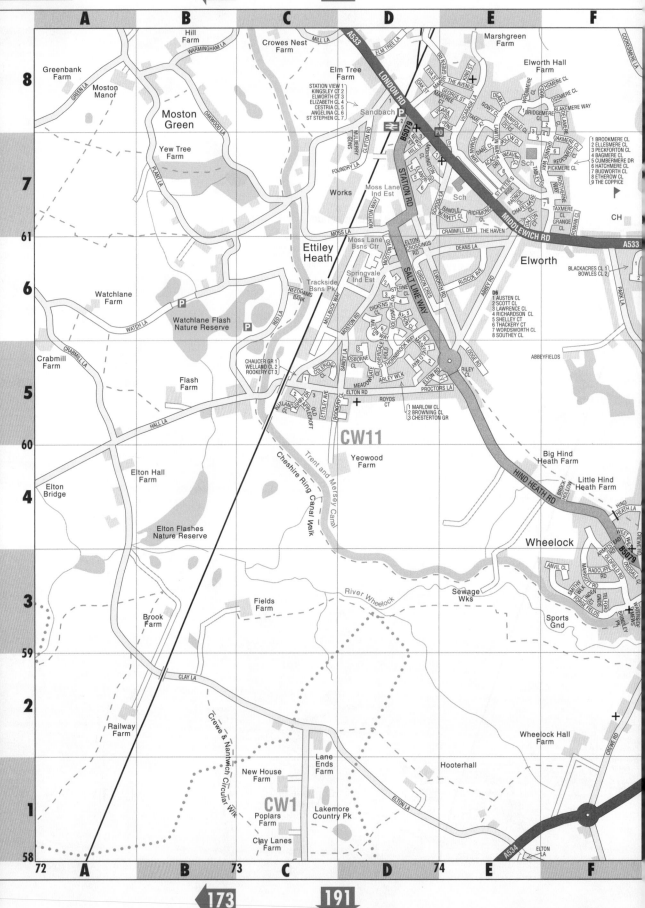

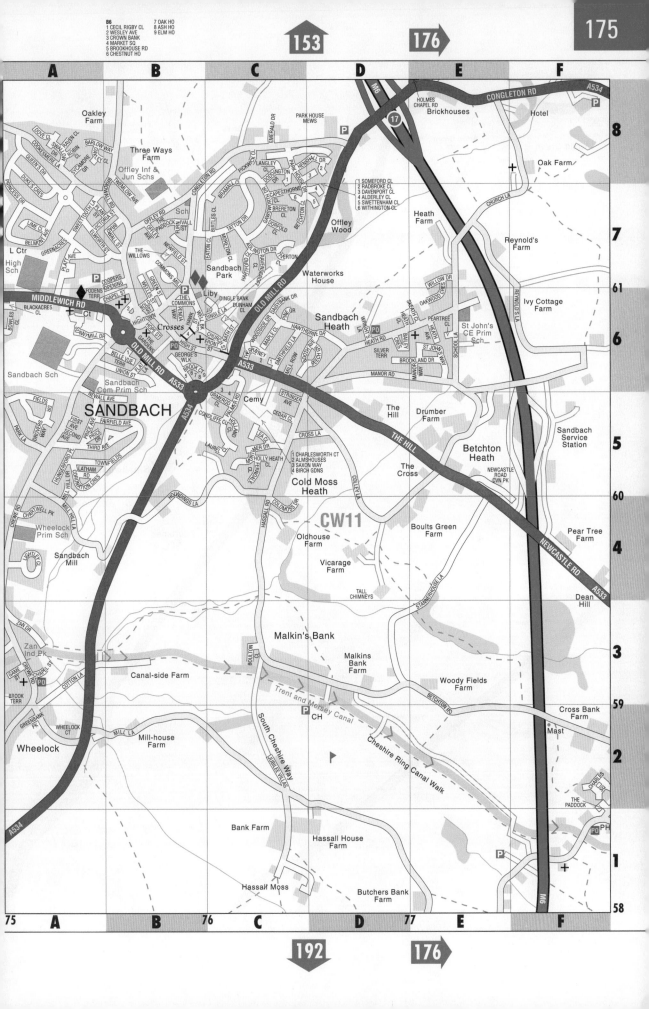

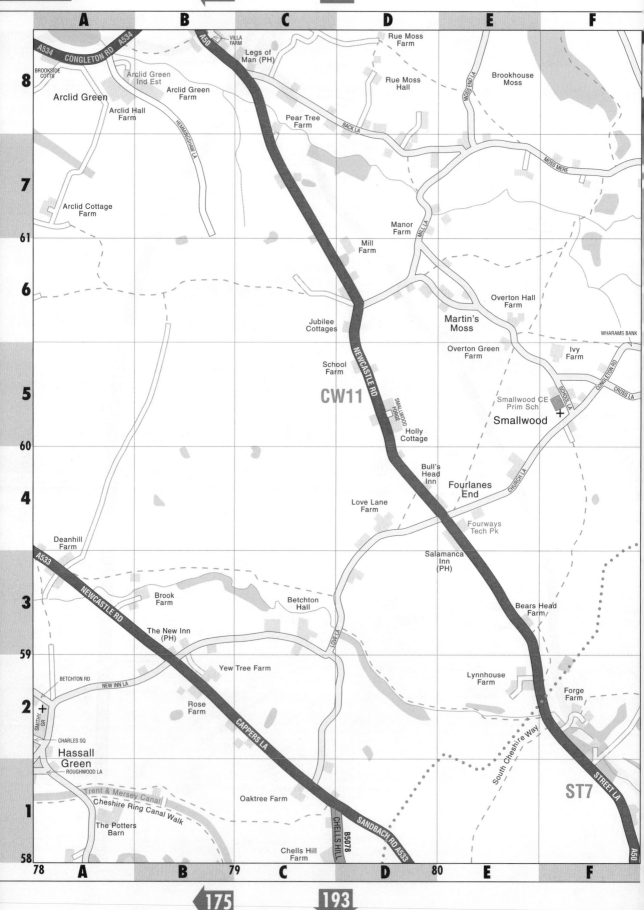

A534 CONGLETON RD A534

A50

VILLA FARM

Legs of Man (PH)

Rue Moss Farm

Rue Moss Hall

Brookhouse Moss

BROOKSIDE COTTS

Arclid Green Ind Est

Arclid Green

Arclid Green Farm

Arclid Hall Farm

Pear Tree Farm

HEMMINGSHAW LA

BACK LA

MOSS END LA

MOSS MERE

Arclid Cottage Farm

Manor Farm

Mill Farm

MILL LA

Overton Hall Farm

Martin's Moss

WHARAMS BANK

Jubilee Cottages

Overton Green Farm

Ivy Farm

School Farm

NEWCASTLE RD

CW11

SMALLWOOD FORGE

Smallwood CE Prim Sch

SCHOOL LA

CONGLETON RD

CROSS LA

Smallwood

Holly Cottage

Bull's Head Inn

Fourlanes End

CHURCH LA

Love Lane Farm

Fourways Tech Pk

Salamanca Inn (PH)

Deanhill Farm

A533

NEWCASTLE RD

Brook Farm

Betchton Hall

Bears Head Farm

The New Inn (PH)

LOVE LA

BETCHTON RD

NEW INN LA

Yew Tree Farm

Lynnhouse Farm

Forge Farm

SMITHY GR

Rose Farm

CHARLES SQ

Hassall Green

ROUGHWOOD LA

CAPPERS LA

South Cheshire Way

ST7

STREET LA

Trent & Mersey Canal

Cheshire Ring Canal Walk

Oaktree Farm

SANDBACH RD A533

A50

The Potters Barn

CHELLS HILL

B5078

Chells Hill Farm

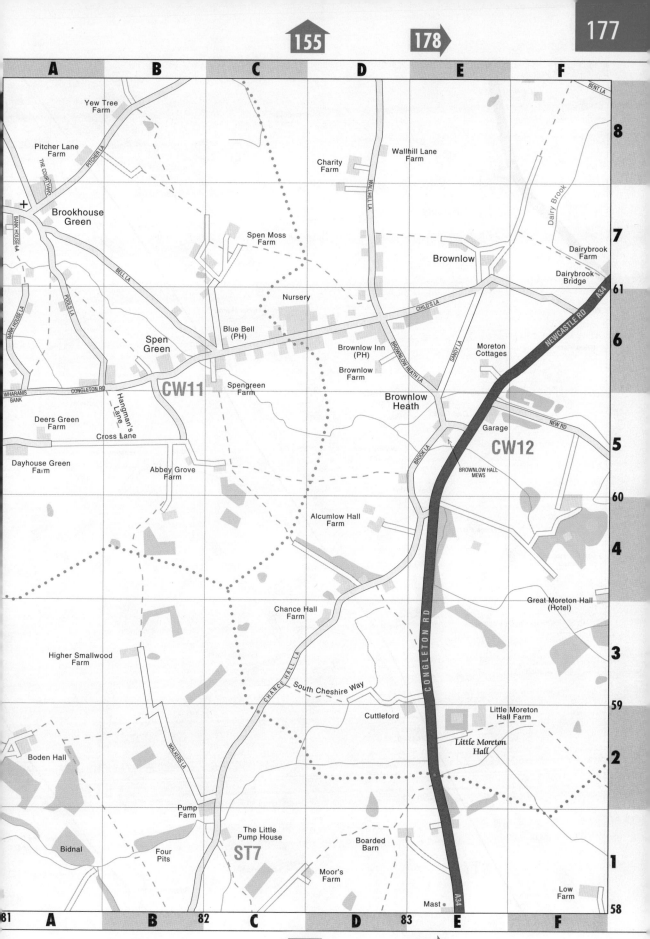

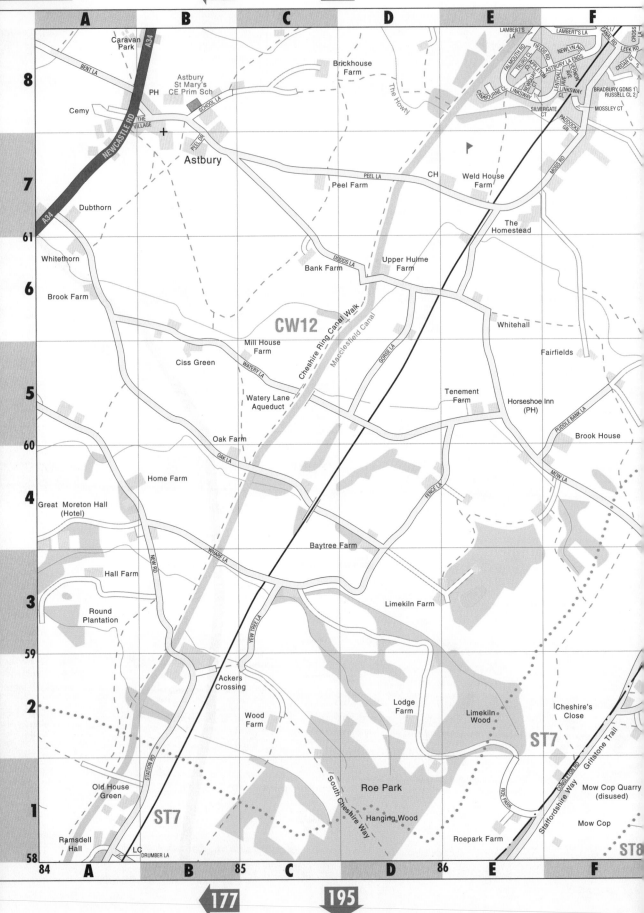

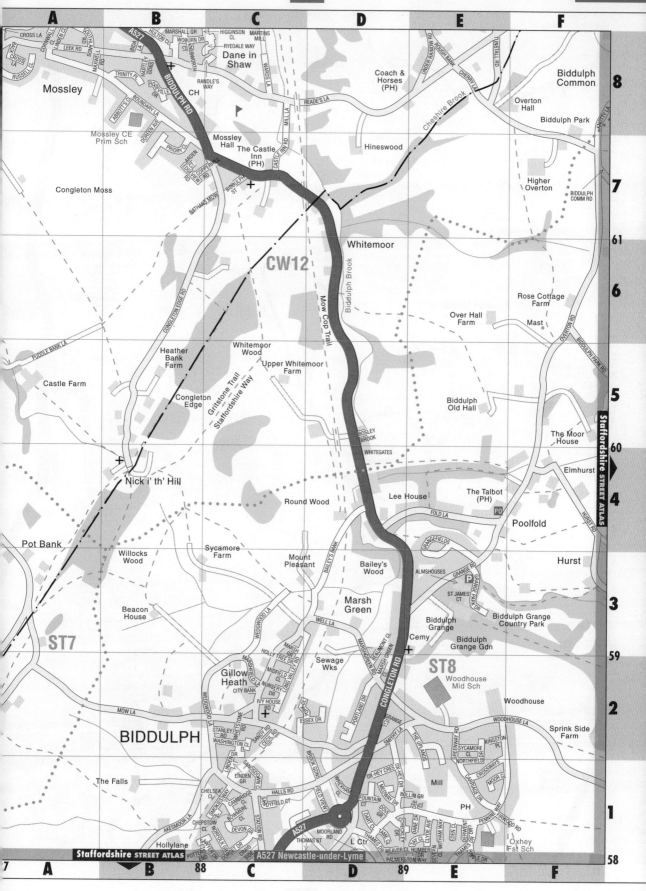

A B C D E F

8
7
61
6
5
60
4
59
3
2
1
58

Mossley

Cross La
Cornwall
Lindley Cl
Leek Rd
South Ave
Mayfield Cl
Cross La
Russell Cl

Dane in Shaw

Marshall Gr
Higginson Cl
Martins Mill
Woburn Dr
Knebworth
Ryedale Way

A527
Hulton Cl
Birds La
Hartley Gdns
Rossville Dr
Trinity Pl
Abbott's Cl
Boundary La
Doreen Ave
Priory Cl
Garden Court
Copperhill
Nathans Mow

BIDDULPH RD

CH
Randle's Way
Mossley Hall

Mossley CE
Prim Sch
Congleton Moss

The Castle Inn
(PH)

Mossley
St
Biddulph
St

Castle Rd
Mill La
Wards La
Reade's La

Coach &
Horses
(PH)

Under Rough Bank
Cherry La
Tunstall Rd

Biddulph
Common

Hineswood

Cheshire Brook

Overton
Hall
Biddulph Park

Higher
Overton

BIDDULPH
COMM RD

Whitemoor

CW12

Biddulph Brook

Mow Cop Trail

Over Hall
Farm

Rose Cottage
Farm

Mast

Overton Rd
BIDDULPH PARK RD

Puddle Bank La
Castle Farm

Congleton Edge Rd

Heather
Bank
Farm

Whitemoor
Wood

Upper Whitemoor
Farm

Gritstone Trail
Staffordshire Way

Congleton
Edge

Biddulph
Old Hall

The Moor
House

Staffordshire STREET ATLAS

Nick i' th' Hill

Bosley Brook

WHITEGATES

Elmhurst

Hurst Rd

Pot Bank

Round Wood

Lee House

The Talbot
(PH)

PO

Poolfold

Hurst

ST7

Willocks
Wood

Sycamore
Farm

Mount
Pleasant

Bailey's
Wood

Bailey's Bank

FOLD LA

Grangefields

Almshouses

Grange Rd
Grange Park Dr

Biddulph
Grange

Biddulph Grange
Country Park

Beacon
House

Wedgwood La

Marsh
Green

WELL LA

St James
Ct

P

St James
Ct

Cemy

Biddulph
Grange Gdn

ST8

Mow La

Gillow
Heath

Marsh Gr
Marshfield La
Holly Tree Ct
Midfield Cl
Long Valley Rd
Nursery La
Beaumont Cl

Sewage
Wks

Mansergh Green
Portland Dr

Congleton Rd

Smith's La

Woodhouse
Mid Sch

Woodhouse

WOODHOUSE LA

Sprink Side
Farm

BIDDULPH

Wedgwood
Stanley
Rd
Washington Cl
Linden
Cl
Linden
Gr
Chelsea
Cl
Cambridge
Cl
Bowmere
Cl
Chepstow
Cl
Devon
Cl

Ivy House
Rd
Ridestone
Sandy Rd
Cecil Rd

City Bank

Essex Dr

Halls Rd
Soyfield Ct

Grange
Ct

Brook Gdns

Field View

Ox-Hey Cres
Oxhey Dr
Medway Dr
Bollin Gr
Dove
Dee Cl

The Uplands

Freeway Rd
Sycamore
Cl
Northfield
Kingston
Pl
Crossways

Moor Ct

The Falls

Mill

PH

Pennine
Firwood Rd

Sandygate
Smokes Way
Norfolk Cl
Station Rd
Dorset Cl
Craig
Side

A527
Moorland
Rd
Thomas St

Fountain

Dart Cl
Tame Cl

Lay Cl
Dane Dr
Checkley
Weaver Cl
Palmerston Way

Humber
Clyde Ave
Witham Cl
Thames Dr Dr
Derwent
Eden Cl
Severn Cl
Ribble Dr

Oxhey
Fst Sch

Hollylane

Akesmoor La
Potters
End

L Ctr

163

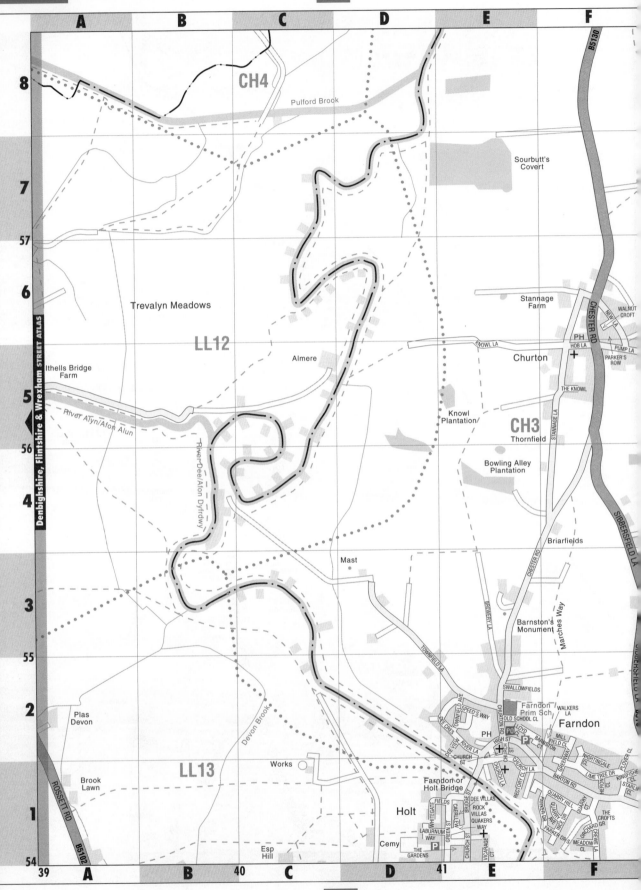

Denbighshire, Flintshire & Wrexham STREET ATLAS

CH4

Pulford Brook

Sourbutt's
Covert

Trevalyn Meadows

LL12

Almere

Ithells Bridge
Farm

River Alyn/Afon Alun

River Dee/Afon Dyfrdwy

Stannage
Farm

CHESTER RD

B5130

WALNUT
CROFT

NEW LA

PH

HOB LA

PUMP LA

PARKER'S
ROW

KNOWL LA

Churton

THE KNOWL

STANNAGE LA

Knowl
Plantation

CH3

Thornfield

Bowling Alley
Plantation

Mast

Briarfields

CHESTER RD

BREWERY LA

TOWNFIELD LA

Barnston's
Monument

Marches Way

SIBBERSFIELD LA

Devon Brook

SWALLOWFIELDS

Farndon
Prim Sch

OLD SCHOOL CL

SPEED'S WAY

TOWNFIELD AVE

CHURTON RD

WALKERS
LA

Farndon

Plas
Devon

DEE CRES

RIVER LA

DEE VIEW

PH

P

LLOYD
CRES

HIGH ST

P.O.

BARNSTON

MILL
FIELD CL

GREENWAY

NIGHTINGALE
CL

FLOWER CL

CHURCH
CT

CHURCH LA

RICE LA

RECTORY CL

CHURCH CL

BARTON RD

LIME TREE DR

KINGSFIELD CL

STARLING CL

LL13

Works

Farndon or
Holt Bridge

WHITEGATE
FIELDS

LABURNUM
WAY

THE
GARDENS

GREEN ST

CAERLLEW

CHURCH ST

DEE VILLAS

ROCK
VILLAS

QUAKERS
WAY

VICARAGE
CT

RECTORY CL

PARKER LA

PARKER DR S

QUARRY HILL

QUARRY
AVE

QUARRY
CL

HERON CL

ORCHARD CR

MEADOW CL

CREWE LA

THE
CROFTS

Brook
Lawn

ROSSETT RD

B5102

Holt

Cemy

P

Esp
Hill

39   40   41

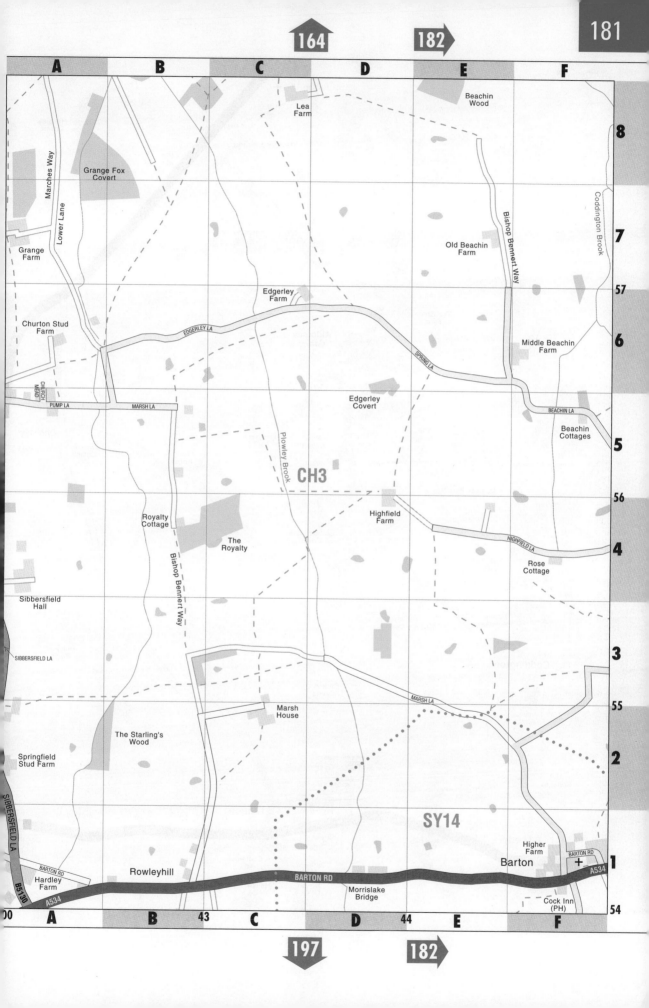

A   B   C   D   E   F

8

Stonyford Brook

Rectory   +

A41

Well Farm

Handley   PH   WHITCHURCH RD

Mill Hill

Handley Covert

Smellmoor Wood

ROCKY LA

7

Mere Brook

Pigeonhouse Farm

Aldersey Brook

57

CH

The Green Farm

Aldersey Green

WHITCHURCH RD

6

Coddington Brook

Pump Lane Wood

PUMP LA

Square Covert

A41

Smithy Farm

ALDERSEY LA

CHOWLEY OAK LA

Pool Covert

The Cottage

New Covert

CH3

Chowley

5

Aldersey Park

Chowley Collina

GREEN LA

56

HIGHFIELD LA

BEACHIN LA

Lodge

Slobbercrofts Covert

DOG LA

Holywell Brook

4

Holywell Farm

Holywell Gorse

Yewtree Farm

+   Crook Aldersey

3

Coddington

Holywell Gorse

Whitegates Farm

Clutton Coverts

55

Mill Cottages

LOWER HALL MBWS 1
BARNABY CHASE 2
MEADOW RISE 3
BARN CT 4
ASHLEY GDNS 5
SCHOOL GN 6

CHAILEY RISE

HOLYWELL LA

2

Pool Plantation

1 2 3 4
LOWER HALL
5 6

HIGH CROSS LA

FOX LA

Clutton

Clutton Hall Farm

Broxton Bridge

A534

SY14

Pool Plantation

BROXTON RD

Broxton Bridge

☓   P

1

A534   BARTON RD

Carden Brook

TOWNSHIP CL

Clutton CE Prim Sch

Parker's Hill

Clutton Hill

Hotel

Barton Plantation

Park House

54

45   A   B   46   C   D   47   E   F

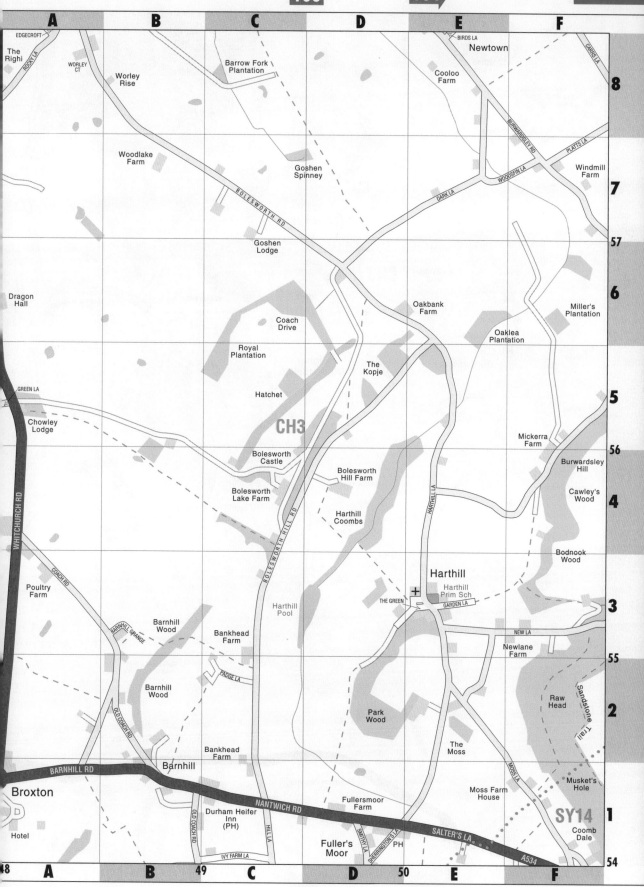

A **B** **C** **D** **E** **F**

8

Honeyend Farm

Wood Farm

WOOD BACK LA

Pennsylvania Wood

The Table Rock

Stanner Nab

Lodge

CARRS LA

PLATTS LA

Fly Fishery

7

Outlanes Farm

Spring House Farm

OUT LA

57

Burwardsley Hall

PENNSYLVANIA LA

River Gowy

BURWARDSLEY RD

Hall

CH3

6

Broad Rough

PO

HARTHILL RD

SCHOOL LA

Cheshire Candle Workshops

ROCK LA

PH

Waste Hill

HILL LA

Quarry Bank Cotts

QUARRYBANK

Curdlands House

CHURCH RD

Burwardsley

Willow Hill

BARRACKS LA

Higher Burwardsley

Peckforton

PECKFORTON HALL LA

5

SARRA LA

FOWLERS BENCH LA

Sandstone Trail

Peckforton Hills

CW6

56

Willow Hill

Stone House

4

Cawley Lodge Farm

Grig Hill Farm

Peckforton Gap

Hillside Farm

STONE HOUSE LA

3

NEW LA

Droppingstone Farm

Sycamore Farm

Bulkeley Hill

Cottenham Farm

Rawhead Farm

55

Bulkeley Mill

2

SY14

COPPERMINE LA

Bickerton Hill

MILL LA

MILL GR.

YEW TREE CL.

MILL VIEW CL.

Bulkeley

WREXHAM RD

Bridg Farm

A53

The Bickerton Poacher (PH)

SANDY LA

White House Farm

HITCHENS LA

CHOLMONDELEY LA

1

Tower Wood

Chiflik Farm

A534

WREXHAM RD

The Grange

54

51 **A** **B** 52 **C** **D** 53 **E** **F**

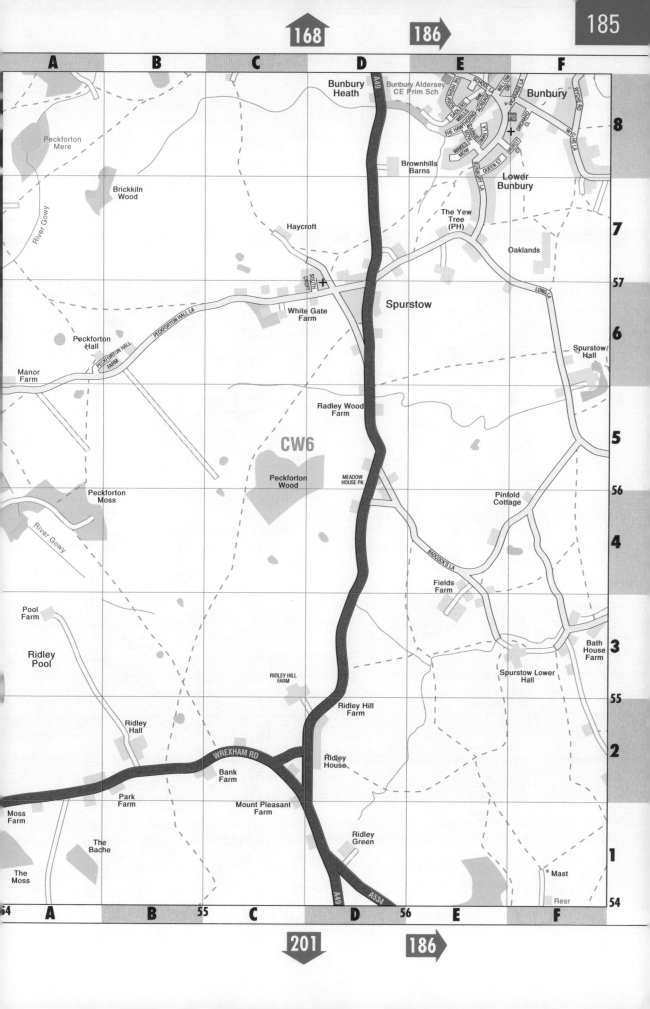

A B C D E F

Peckforton Mere

River Gowy

Brickkiln Wood

Peckforton Hall

Peckforton Hall Farm

Manor Farm

Peckforton Moss

River Gowy

Pool Farm

Ridley Pool

Ridley Hall

WREXHAM RD

Bank Farm

Park Farm

Moss Farm

The Bache

The Moss

Mount Pleasant Farm

Ridley Green

Ridley House

Ridley Hill Farm

RIDLEY HILL FARM

CW6

Peckforton Wood

Radley Wood Farm

MEADOW HOUSE PK

White Gate Farm

SOUTH CROFT

Haycroft

PECKFORTON HALL LA

Bunbury Heath

A49

Bunbury Aldersey CE Prim Sch

SCHOOL LA

THE THORNS

VICARAGE LA

WILLOW CL

Bunbury

WYCHE RD

SADLERS

WELLS

THE HAWTHORNS

JANE SEDDON

ASPEN

HURST CL

ORCHARD CL

PO

BUNBURY LA

WAKES

MOW

QUEEN ST

Lower Bunbury

Brownhills Barns

The Yew Tree (PH)

Oaklands

LONG LA

Spurstow

Spurstow Hall

Pinfold Cottage

BADCOCK'S LA

Fields Farm

Spurstow Lower Hall

Bath House Farm

Mast

Resr

A49

A534

8

7

57

6

56

5

4

3

55

2

1

54

54 55 56

A B C D E F

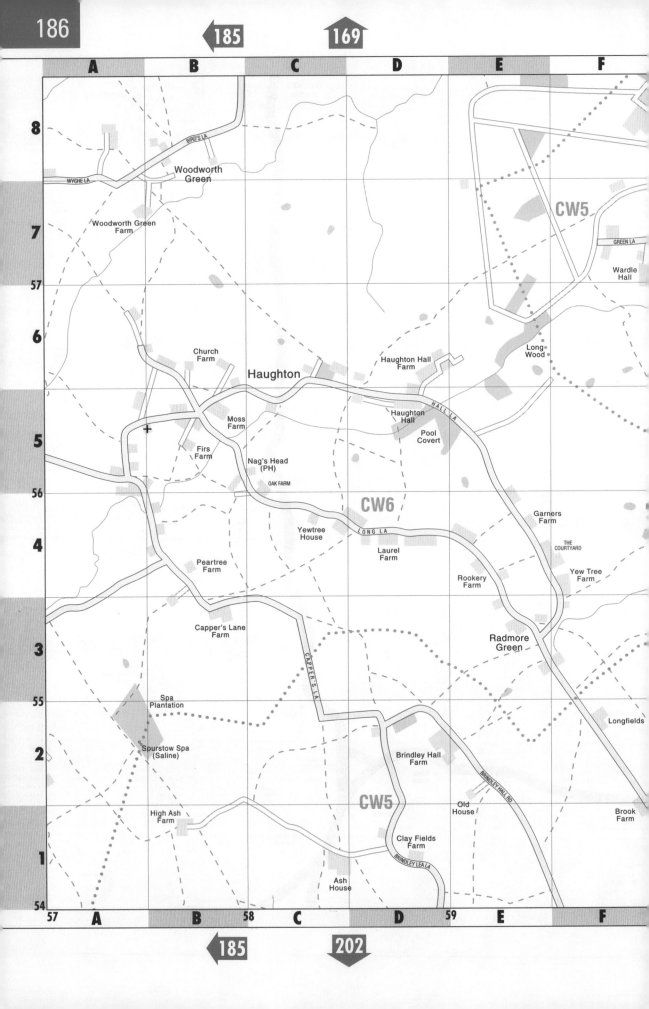

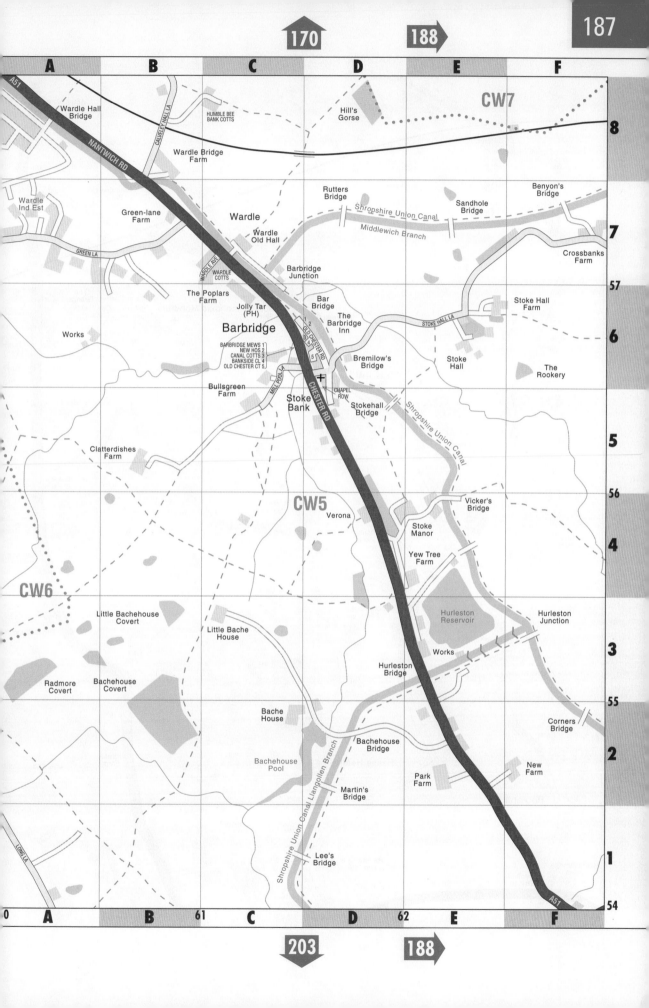

170
188

A B C D E F

CW7

A51

Wardle Hall
Bridge

NANTWICH RD

CALVELEY HALL LA

HUMBLE BEE
BANK COTTS

Hill's
Gorse

8

Wardle Bridge
Farm

Benyon's
Bridge

Wardle
Ind Est

Green-lane
Farm

Wardle

Rutters
Bridge

Shropshire Union Canal

Sandhole
Bridge

7

GREEN LA

Wardle
Old Hall

Middlewich Branch

Crossbanks
Farm

WARDLE AVE

WARDLE
COTTS

Barbridge
Junction

57

The Poplars
Farm

Bar
Bridge

Stoke Hall
Farm

Jolly Tar
(PH)

STOKE HALL LA

Works

Barbridge

The
Barbridge
Inn

6

OLD CHESTER RD

BARBRIDGE MEWS 1
NEW HOS 2
CANAL COTTS 3
BANKSIDE CL 4
OLD CHESTER CT 5

Stoke
Hall

The
Rookery

Bremilow's
Bridge

Bullsgreen
Farm

MILL POOL LA

Stoke
Bank

CHESTER RD

CHAPEL
ROW

Stokehall
Bridge

Shropshire Union Canal

5

Clatterdishes
Farm

56

CW5

Verona

Vicker's
Bridge

Stoke
Manor

4

CW6

Yew Tree
Farm

Little Bachehouse
Covert

Hurleston
Reservoir

Hurleston
Junction

Little Bache
House

Works

3

Radmore
Covert

Bachehouse
Covert

Hurleston
Bridge

55

Bache
House

Corners
Bridge

2

Shropshire Union Canal Llangollen Branch

Bachehouse
Bridge

Bachehouse
Pool

Park
Farm

New
Farm

Martin's
Bridge

Lee's
Bridge

1

A51

54

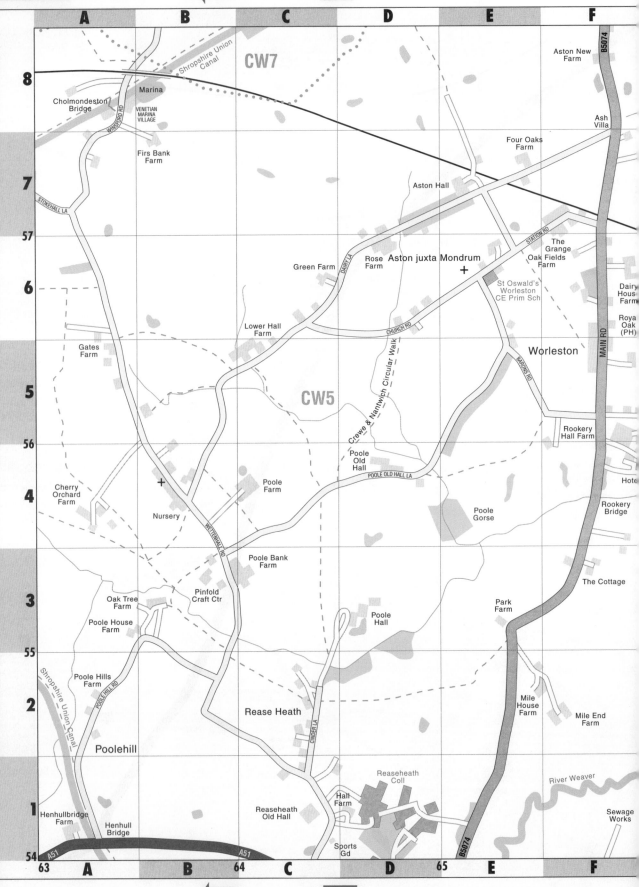

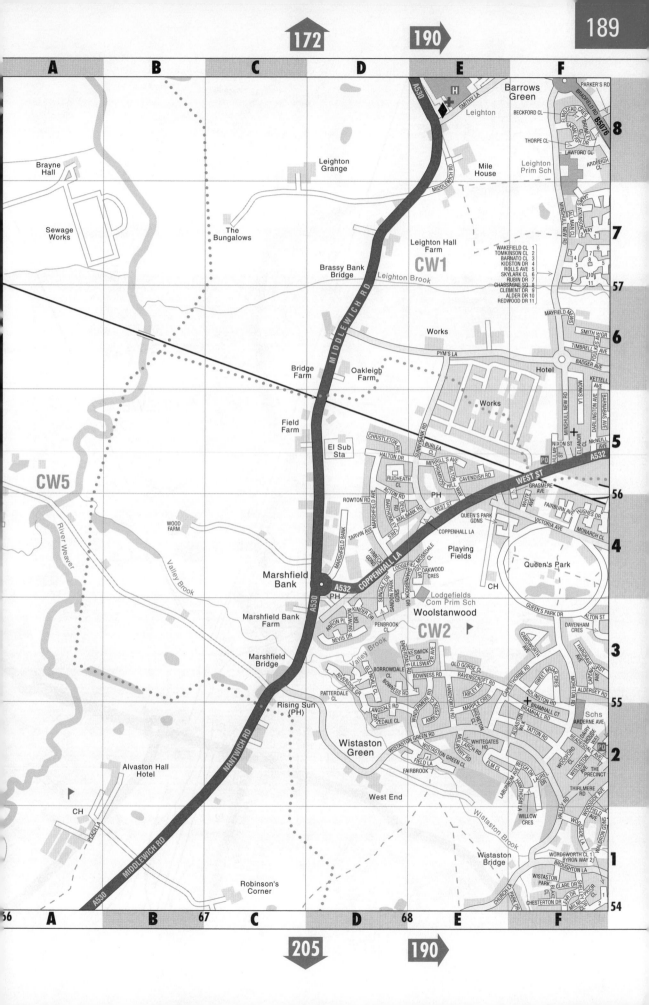

191
175

A B C D E F

8

Whitehall Farm

Wheelockheath Farm

Daisy Bank House

Fingerpost Farm

MILL LA

HASSALL RD

M6

Wheelock Heath

School Farm

ALSAGER RD

Holly Tree Farm

Day Green

COPPICE RD

SANDY LA

Hassall Pool

7

Walnut Tree Farm

Hassall

CW11

Hassall Hall

POOL LA

HASSALL RD

57

Bridgehouse Farm

Bostock House

6

South Cheshire Way

Green Bank Farm

Dunnock's Fold Farm

Moss Cottage

5

Castle Farm

DUNNOCKSFOLD RD

56

Homeshaw Farm

Oakhanger Hall

Moss End Farm

WINDSOR DR

4

Woodside Farm

Stockton Farm

ST7

SPENCER CL

CRANBERRY

DELAMERE CT

Heathfield Farm

Oakhanger Farm

KENSINGTON CL

CLOSE LA

CRANBERRY CT

Hall o' the Heath

CW1

Gate Farm

Ashfields

3

HOLMSHAW LA

Rose Tree Farm

Mast

NURSERY RD

Spartan Wood Farm

55

TAYLORS LA

Peartree Farm

Oakhanger Moss

White Moss Farm

White Moss

2

Butterton Lane Farm

BUTTERTON LA

Moss Farm

CREWE RD B50

B5078

Oakhanger

Mast

Radway Green

RADWAY GREEN RD

B5078

B5017

BUTTERTON LA

MILL LA

LC

NO 1 ROAD N

Works

NO 2 ROAD N

CENTRAL

1

DUNN'S COTTS

M6

Radway Green Bsns & Tech Ctr

CW2

B5078

54

CW2

75 A B 76 C D 77 E F

193
177

Townsend Farm

CHANCE HALL LA

Rode Mill

POOL SIDE

Holehouse Farm

HOLEHOUSE LA

Rode Pool

Old Wood

Rode Hall

Home Farm

Works

CHURCH LA

Scholar Green

Kent Green Farm

FOUNDRY LA

FOUNDRY PH

BARLEYCROFT TERR

Swing Bridge

BARNBRIDGE CL

STATION RD

HOLLINSHEAD CL

A34

Bank Farm

Big Barr

Lunts Moss Farm

LUNTS MOSS

WAVERTREE AVE

MEAD AVE

BARBER DR

MARGERY AVE

CINDER HILL LA

DREWELL RD

Cheshire Ring Canal Walk

Macclesfield Canal

A50

OLD DRAGON RD

Snape's Aqueduct

Bratt's Wood

Brick House Farm

ALMA CL

THE MOUNT

Scholar Green Prim Sch

PORTLAND DR

Little-moss

OAKS MORETON PL

CONGLETON RD N

MEADOW WAY

CHERRY TREE AVE

OAKWOOD AVE

BRATTSWOOD DR

BROWN AVE

WOODGATE AVE

Church Lawton Prim Sch

Ashbank Farm

Hall Green

PH

BLEEDING WOLF

LITTLE MOSS LA

NURSERY RD

LAWTONGATE EST

THE GREEN

GROVE AVE

Summer House Plantation

ST7

Mill Lane Plantation

LAWTON COPPICE

WOODSIDE LA

THE SPINNEY

MOSS LA

Moss House Farm

A50

THE GROVE

GROVE PARK AVE

ELMWOOD AVE

CROSSKEYS CL

DAIRY LANDS RD

Lawton-gate

LIVERPOOL RD W

CHURCH LA

Lawton Hall

Gritstone Trail

KNOWSLEY LA

A5011

Bridge Farm

Church Lawton

LAWTON AVE

Red Bull

LINLEY GR

FODEN AVE

LC

HAZEL GR

LINLEY RD

Rye Low

Cheshire Ring Canal Walk

Trent and Mersey Canal

CONGLETON RD S

Sewage Works

Red Bull Aqueduct

WOODLANDS

Playing Field

LIVERPOOL RD E

GLOUCESTER RD

ESSEX DR

LIME KILN LA

Pool-lock Aqueduct

Works

Gas Works Ind Est

SOMERSET AVE

LINCOLN RD

NORFOLK RD

VICTORIA AVE

WHITEHALL AVE

LINLEY LA

Toll Gate Farm

Slum Wood

OLD BUTT LA

SLACKEN LA

PICKMERE PL

WOODLANDS AVE

HARDINGS MDW

HADDINGSWOOD RD

Harding's Wood

STATION RD

Kidsgrove

Liby

MEADOWS RD

A5

PO

Linley Hall

WEST AVE

Butt Lane

Nelson Ind Est

CHURCH ST

LEBRET ST

SKELLERN ST

CHAPEL ST

LONGFIELD

OLD BUTT

WOODLANDS AVE

MILLSTONE AVE

WOODSHUTT'S ST

SECOND AVE

THIRD AVE

FIFTH AVE

BYTH AVE

FOURTH AVE

Sch

CORONATION CRES

ST JOHN WOOD

A5011

LINLEY RD

The Reginald Mitchell Prim Sch

ST SAVIOUR'S ST

St Saviour's CE Prim Sch

Linley Trad Est

B5371

CEDAR AVE

BANBURY ST

MILL NURSERY

ORCHARD CRES

MITCHELL DR

BRINDLEY CL

HARECASTLE AVE

HOLLINS CRES

ASH RD

GROVE AVE

FIRST AVE

B5371

Woodshutts

MILL RD

A34

CONGLETON RD

PO

THE AVENUE

ST JOHN WOOD

193
210

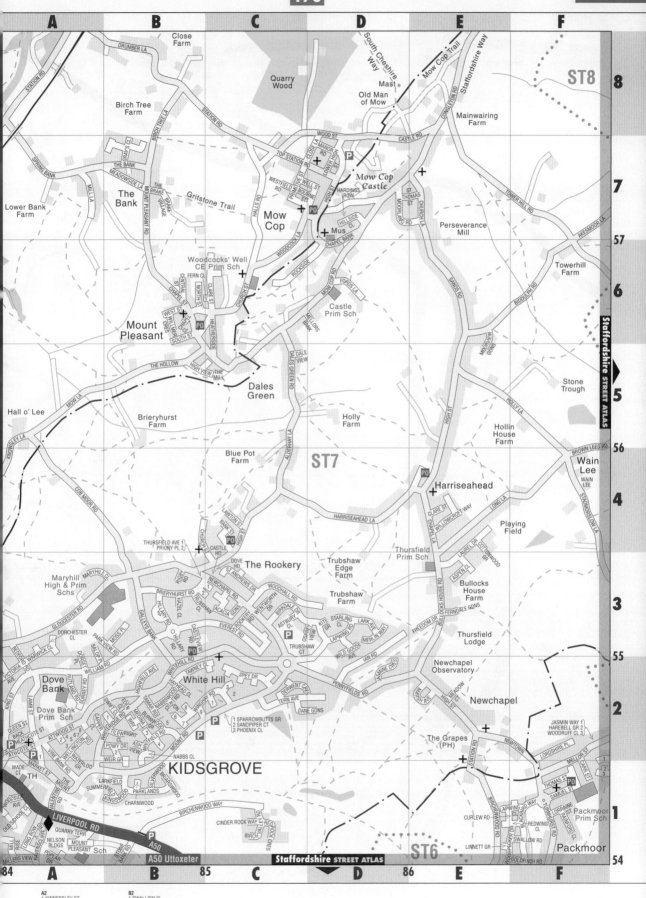

ST8

Mast
Old Man
of Mow
Mainwairing
Farm

Close
Farm

Quarry
Wood

Drumber La

Birch Tree
Farm

Station Rd

Spring Bank

Lower Bank
Farm

The Bank

The
Brake

Gritstone Trail

Mow Cop
Castle

Mow Cop

Perseverance
Mill

Towerhill
Farm

Woodcocks' Well
CE Prim Sch

Mus

Castle
Prim Sch

Mount
Pleasant

Dales
Green

Brieryhurst
Farm

Holly
Farm

Hall o' Lee

Blue Pot
Farm

ST7

Stone
Trough

Wain
Lee

Hollin
House
Farm

Harriseahead

Harriseahead La

Thursfield
Prim Sch

Playing
Field

Bullocks
House
Farm

Maryhill
High & Prim
Schs

The Rookery

Trubshaw
Edge
Farm

Trubshaw
Farm

Thursfield
Lodge

Newchapel
Observatory

Newchapel

Dove
Bank

Dove Bank
Prim Sch

White Hill

1 SPARROWBUTTS GR
2 SANDPIPER CT
3 PHOENIX CL

The Grapes
(PH)

JASMIN WAY 1
HAREBELL GR 2
WOODRUFF CL 3

KIDSGROVE

Packmoor
Prim Sch

Liverpool Rd

A50 Uttoxeter

Staffordshire STREET ATLAS

ST6

Packmoor

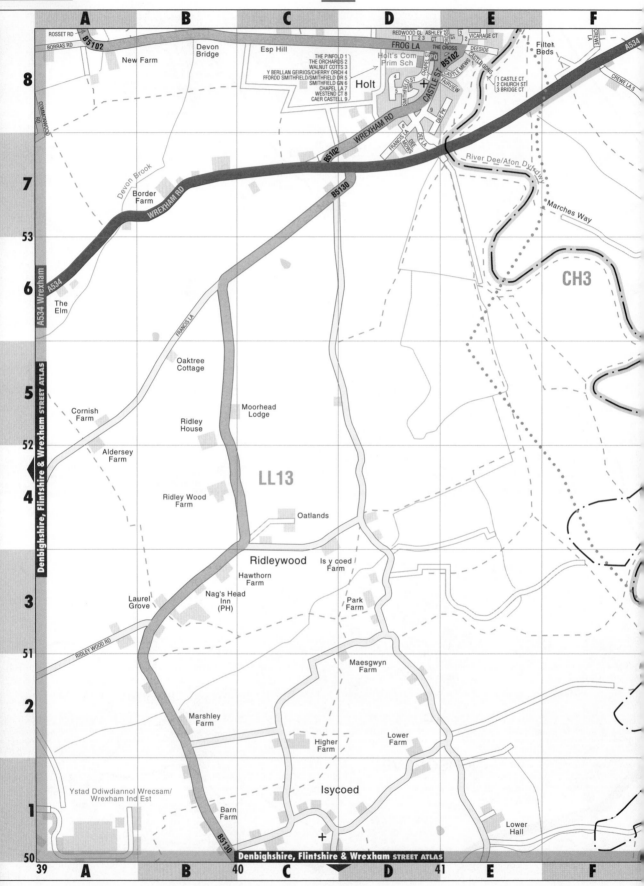

A B C D E F

8

7

53

6

5

52

4

3

51

2

1

50

39 A B 40 C D 41 E F

Denbighshire, Flintshire & Wrexham STREET ATLAS

ROSSET RD
BORRAS RD
B5102
New Farm
Devon Bridge
Esp Hill

REDWOOD CL   ASHLEY
VICARAGE CT
FROG LA
THE CROSS
DEESIDE
Filter Beds
CREWE LA
A534

THE PINFOLD 1
THE ORCHARDS 2
WALNUT COTTS 3
Y BERLLAN GEIRIOS/CHERRY ORCH 4
FFORDD SMITHFIELD/SMITHFIELD DR 5
SMITHFIELD GN 6
CHAPEL LA 7
WESTEND CT 8
CAER CASTELL 9

Holt's Com
Prim Sch
Holt
1 CASTLE CT
2 CHURCH ST
3 BRIDGE CT
CASTLE MEWS
CASTLE GDNS
CASTLE ST

Devon Brook
Border Farm
WREXHAM RD
B5102
WREXHAM RD
B5130
River Dee/Afon Dyfrdwy
Marches Way

A534 Wrexham
A534
The Elm

FRANCIS LA

CH3

Oaktree Cottage

Cornish Farm
Ridley House
Moorhead Lodge

Aldersey Farm

LL13

Ridley Wood Farm

Oatlands

Ridleywood
Is y coed Farm

Hawthorn Farm
Laurel Grove
Nag's Head Inn (PH)
Park Farm

RIDLEY WOOD RD

Maesgwyn Farm

Marshley Farm

Higher Farm
Lower Farm

Ystad Ddiwdiannol Wrecsam/
Wrexham Ind Est

Barn Farm
B5130
Isycoed

Lower Hall

Denbighshire, Flintshire & Wrexham STREET ATLAS

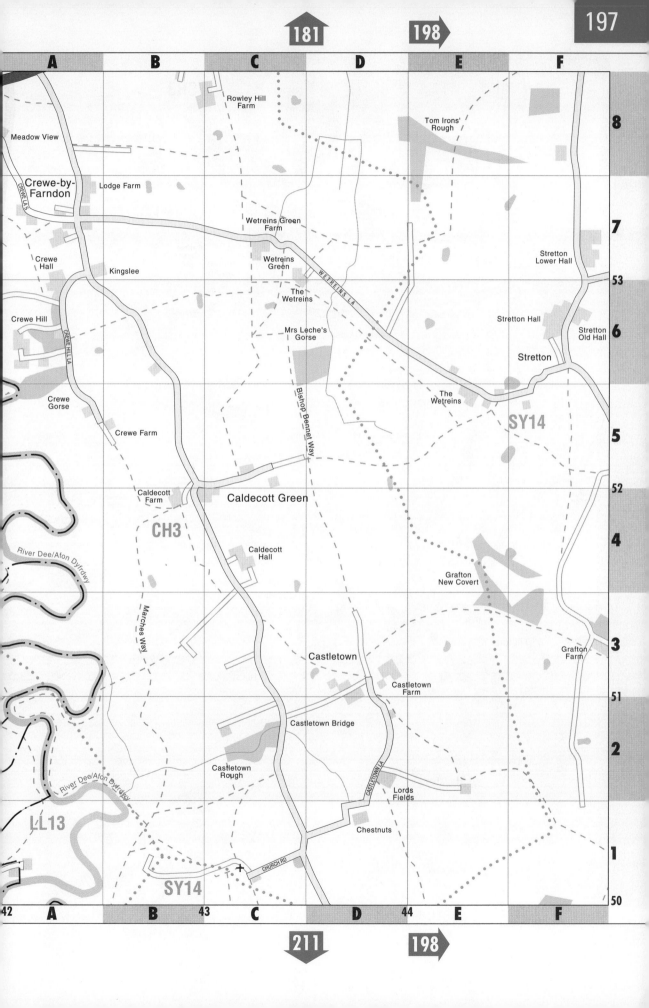

A   B   C   D   E   F

8

Meadow View

Crewe-by-
Farndon

Lodge Farm

Rowley Hill
Farm

Tom Irons'
Rough

7

Wetreins Green
Farm

Crewe
Hall

Kingslee

Wetreins
Green

Stretton
Lower Hall

53

The
Wetreins

Crewe Hill

Mrs Leche's
Gorse

Stretton Hall

Stretton
Old Hall

6

Stretton

Crewe
Gorse

The Wetreins

SY14

Crewe Farm

Bishop Bennet Way

5

Caldecott
Farm

52

Caldecott Green

CH3

Caldecott
Hall

4

Grafton
New Covert

Marches Way

Grafton
Farm

3

Castletown

Castletown
Farm

51

Castletown Bridge

2

Castletown
Rough

Lords
Fields

LL13

River Dee/Afon Dyfrdwy

Chestnuts

1

SY14

CHURCH RD

50

River Dee/Afon Dyfrdwy

CREWE LA S

CREWE HILL LA

WETREINS LA

CASTLETOWN LA

A B C D E F

8

CH3

The Birches

Golborne's Wood

Round Hill

Moor Gorse

Garden Plantation

The Quarries

Cliffe Bank

Mill Coppice

Home Farm

Hotel

7

Carden Marsh

Stretton Mill

Higher Carden

53

HIGHER CARDEN LA

Laurel Grove

Lower Carden

6

Lower Farm

Hook's Rough

Hook's Brook

5

Lower Carden Hall

Stone House

Grafton Lodge

52

SY14

4

The Heir's Wood

Isle Farm

Hobb Hill Farm

Hobb Hill

Carden Arms Inn (PH)

Grafton Farm

Tilston

PO

GREENWAY RD

HOLLY TERR

INVERESK RD

LOWCROSS LA

Finsdale Farm

GRANGE LA

3

WYNTER LA

ROOKERY RD

Ford

Lowcross Hill

Edge Grange

WYNTER CL

LONG LA

CHURCH RD

Tilston CE Prim Sch

51

Yewtree Farm

2

Frog Hall

The Old Rectory

Quarry (dis)

Lowcross Gorse

SCAR LA

The Cape

Lowcross Farm

Dyer's Farm

1

Church Croft

Lower Wood

50

45 A B 46 C D 47 E F

A41 WHITCHURCH RD A41

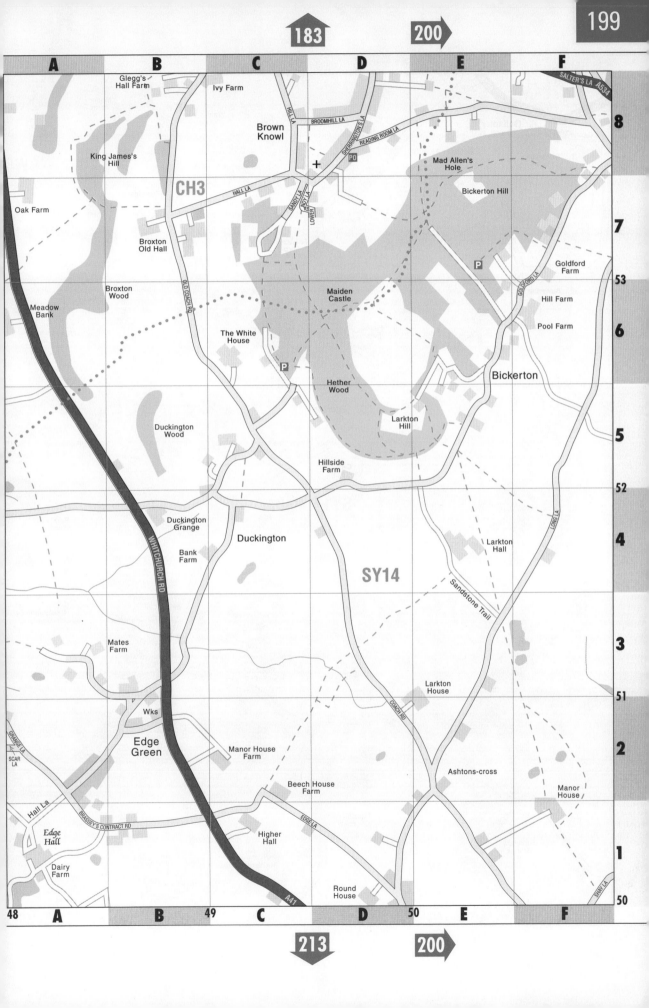

199 184

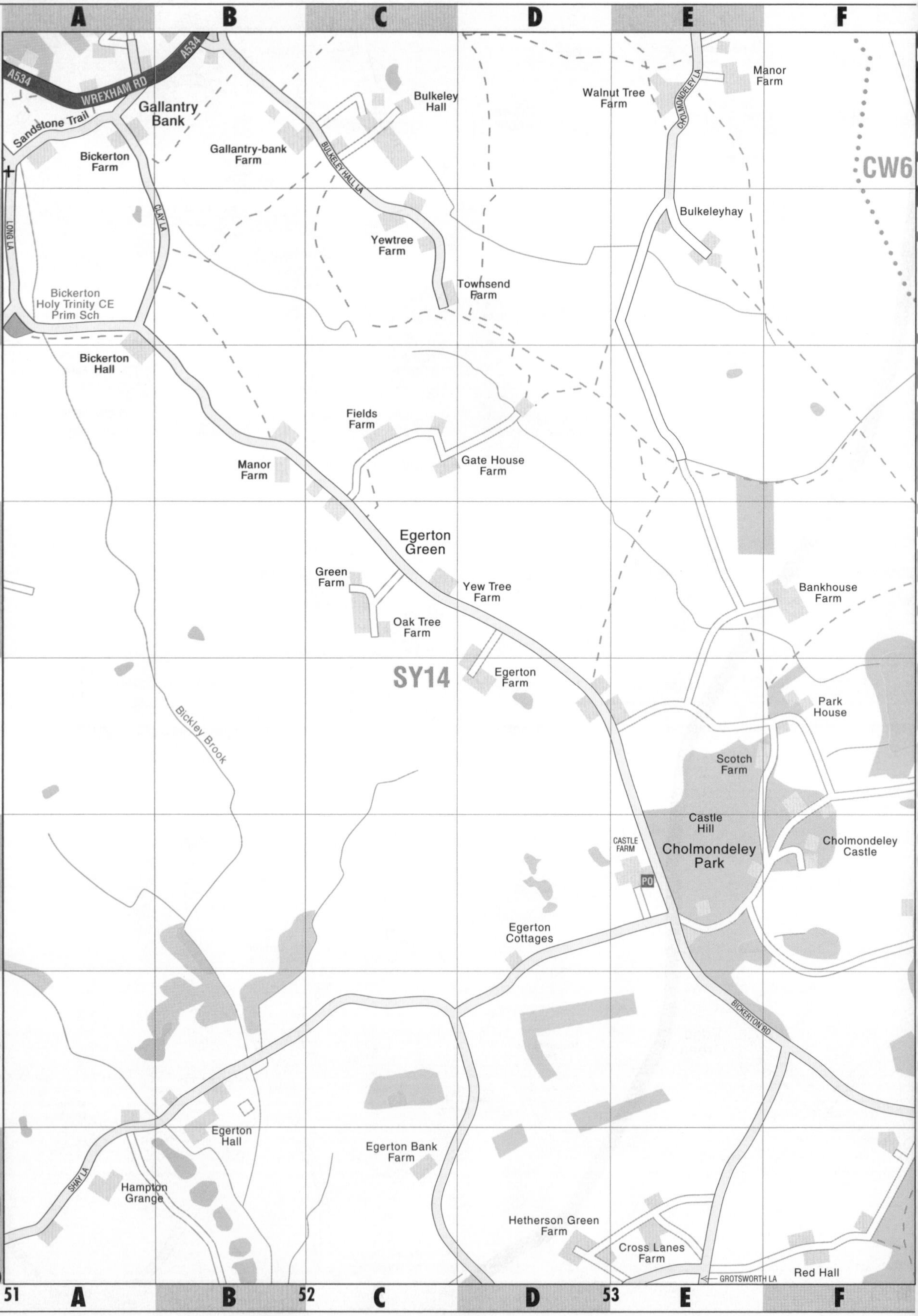

A
B
C
D
E
F
8
7
6
5
4
3
2
1
53
52
51
50
51
52
53
A534
WREXHAM RD
A534
Gallantry Bank
Sandstone Trail
Bickerton Farm
Gallantry-bank Farm
Bulkeley Hall
BULKELEY HALL LA
Walnut Tree Farm
CHOLMONDELEY LA
Manor Farm
CW6
Bulkeleyhay
LONG LA
CLAY LA
Yewtree Farm
Townsend Farm
Bickerton Holy Trinity CE Prim Sch
Bickerton Hall
Fields Farm
Manor Farm
Gate House Farm
Egerton Green
Green Farm
Yew Tree Farm
Oak Tree Farm
Bankhouse Farm
SY14
Egerton Farm
Park House
Bickley Brook
Scotch Farm
Castle Hill
CASTLE FARM
Cholmondeley Park
Cholmondeley Castle
PO
Egerton Cottages
BICKERTON RD
Egerton Hall
Egerton Bank Farm
SHAY LA
Hampton Grange
Hetherson Green Farm
Cross Lanes Farm
GROTSWORTH LA
Red Hall

199 214

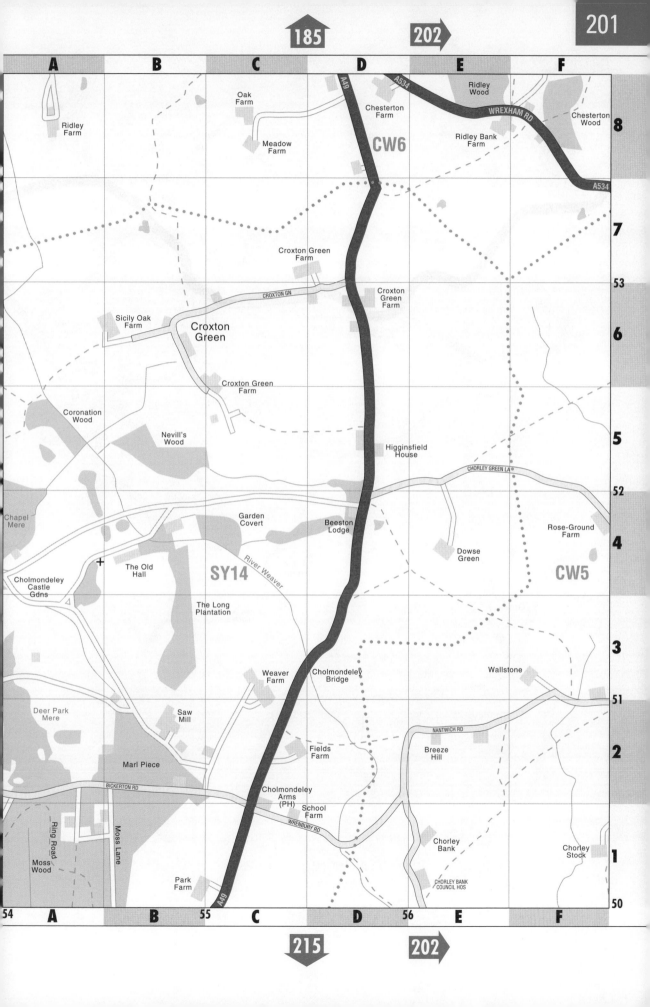

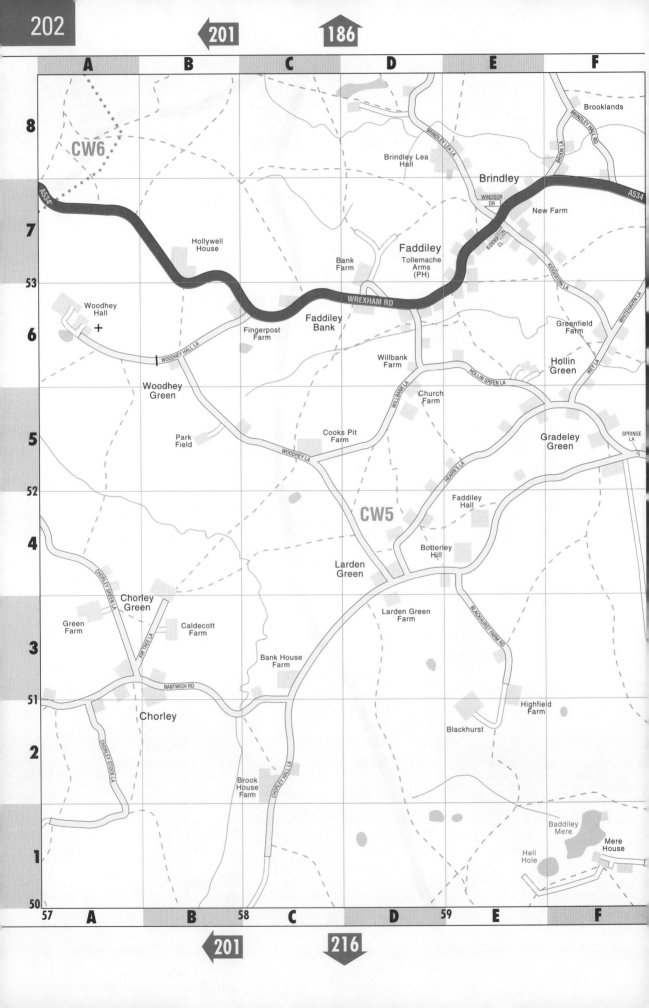

A B C D E F

8

CW6

A534

7

Brooklands

Brindley Hall Rd

Brindley Lea La

Brindley Lea Hall

Brindley

Windsor Dr

New Farm

A534

Brook La

53

Hollywell House

Bank Farm

Faddiley

Tollemache Arms (PH)

Kidderton Cl

Kidderton La

Whitehaven La

6

Woodhey Hall

Fingerpost Farm

Faddiley Bank

Willbank Farm

Hollin Green La

Greenfield Farm

Hollin Green

Woodhey Hall La

Wch La

Woodhey Green

Willbank La

Church Farm

5

Park Field

Woodhey La

Cooks Pit Farm

Hearn's La

Gradeley Green

Springe La

52

CW5

Faddiley Hall

4

Larden Green

Botterley Hill

Chorley Green La

Chorley Green

Caldecott Farm

Larden Green Farm

Blackhurst Farm Rd

3

Green Farm

Fir Tree La

Bank House Farm

Highfield Farm

51

Nantwich Rd

Chorley

Blackhurst

2

Chorley Stock La

Chorley Hall La

Brook House Farm

Baddiley Mere

Mere House

1

Hell Hole

50

57 A B 58 C D 59 E F

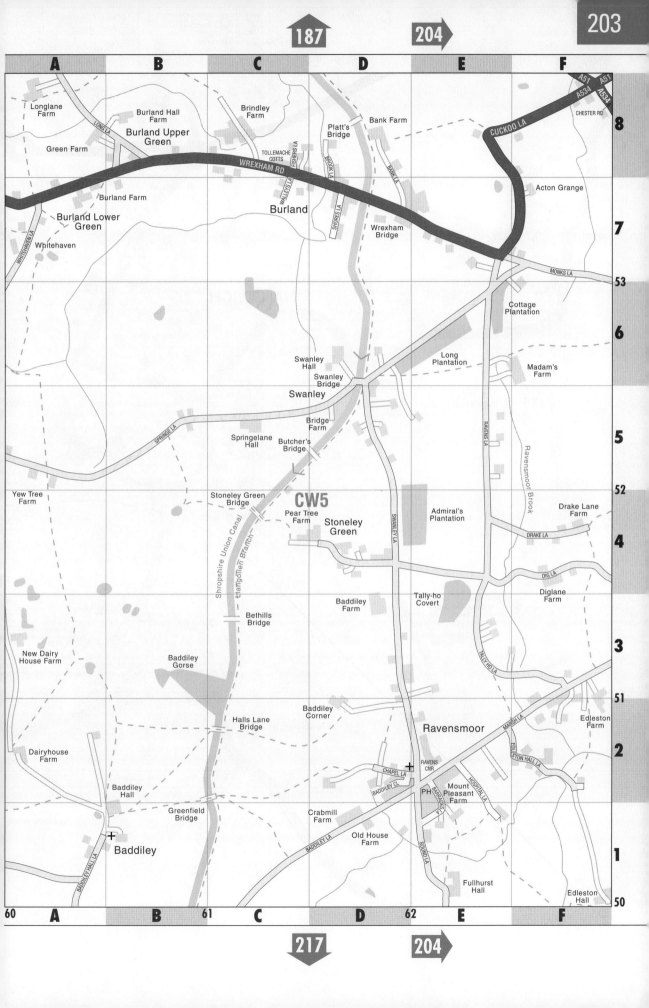

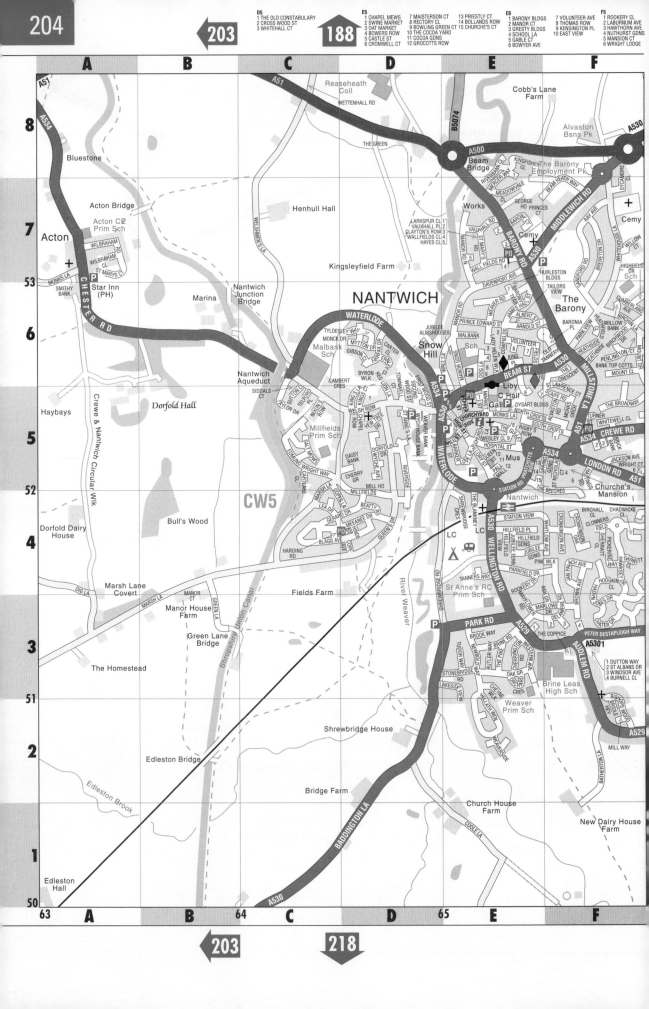

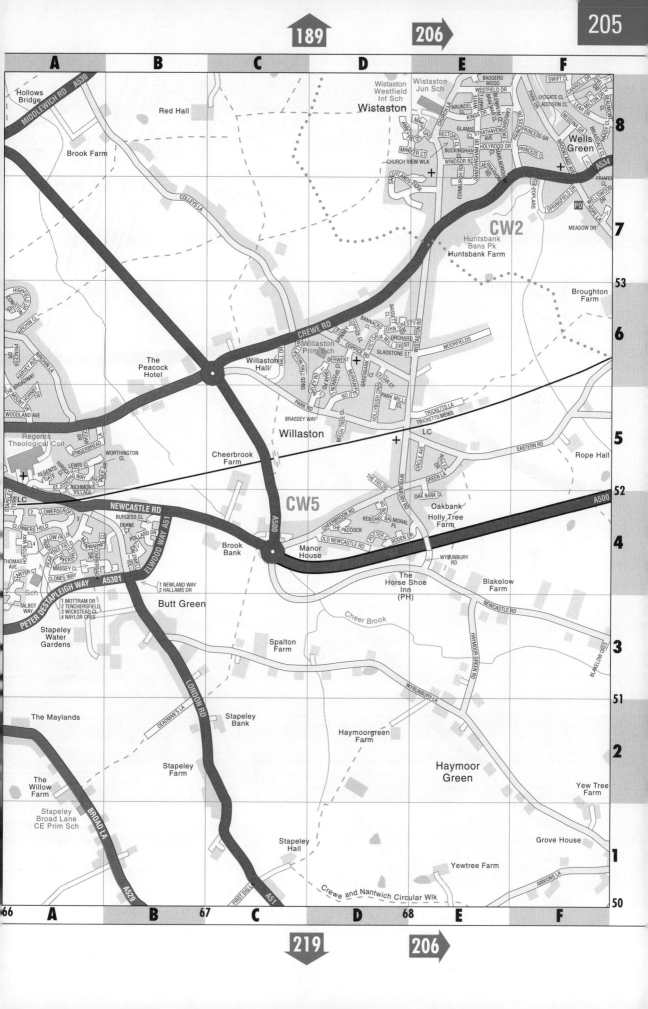

A B C D E F

8

7

53

6

5

52

4

3

51

2

1

50

CW1

Basford Hall
Sorting Sidings

CREWE RD

A534

A500

B5071

GRESTY RD

1 COLLINBROOK AVE
2 BALMORAL AVE

Sch

FIRWOOD WLK
HEYWOOD GN
ARTLE RD
SMALLBROOK WLK
DAVENPORT AVE
BASFORD RD
HOWBECK WLK
BIRCHALL WLK
BROOKSIDE GN
NORTHBANK WLK
FANSHAWE WLK
BARNETT WLK
BIRCHS WLK
HUTTON WLK
CLOUGH
SNAPE RD
CHENEY WLK
SANDERSON CL
CHARLCOTE CRES
CHILWORTH
MELFORD
BROADLEIGH WAY
WESTHOLME CL
ARLINGTON
WILDERHOPE
ASHBURNHAM

Mill

Gresty Green
Farm

LC

PH

Greenbank
Farm

HUNTER AVE

GRESTY GREEN RD

GRESTY LA

The Berkeley
Prim Sch

Broughton
Farm

EASTERN RD

Ropegreen
Bridge

ROPE LA

Brook
Farm

Green Farm

Shavington
Sports Ctr

Shavington
High Sch

Rope Farm

Soccer
Ctr

Shavington
House

Shavington

CREWE RD

WEST WAY
MORTH WAY
PARK ESTATE

Shavington
Hall

Basford

Basford
Hall

WESTON LA

Sutch Farm

CHESTNUT AVE
NORTHFIELD PL
WESTON CT
WOODNOTH DR
SOUTHBANK AVE
VINE TREE AVE
EDWARDS
EDWARDS CL
OSBORNE GR
BURLEA DR

RICHARDSON CL
MEADOW CL

Shavington
Prim Sch

P

PO

THE HOLLIES

Shavington
Farm

BROOK AVE
THE ORCHARDS

CW2

LARCH AVE

HOLLY MOUNT

Swill Brook

BACK LA

CASEY LA

Puseydale
Farm

PH

MAIN RD

LORDS MILL RD
STEWART ST
TALBOT CL
MEDINA
CRES
WINDSOR DR
CROMWELL
CAMELOT GR
Shavington Green
Farm

Hough
Cotts

PH

BUCK LA

1 ELLWOOD GN
2 MARTON CL
3 NORBURY CL
4 THE BROOKLANDS

Hough

HEAWARD CL
GREENFIELDS AVE
WINCHESTER GR
WESSEX CL
ASHCROFT
PAGE GR
MONTROSE CL
KNIGHTS CL
CL REGENT
ENFIELD
CAMERON AVE

B5071

GOODALL'S
CNR

NURSERY CL

NEWCASTLE RD

CHURTON CL
BICKLEY CL
RIDLEY DR
RUSHTON DR
WOODSTON CL
WAVERTON CL

WESTGATE

HUNTERSFIELD

DIG LA

Hough
Manor

Wybunbury
Grange

STOCK LA

CW5

Clannor Heath

Moss
Farm

COCKSHADES
FARM

Crewe and Nantwich Circular Wlk

Hough
Hall

ALDFORD CL
PIT LA
WOODCOTT
CL

KINGS MDW
TILSTONE
CL

Hough Common

CROSS LA
BIRCH LA

South Cheshire Way

Yew Tree Farm

Pinfold Farm

WYBUNBURY
LA

ANNIONS LA
MAIN RD
RIDDINGS
DR
CHADS
GREEN

Pinfold Corner

B5071

MOORLANDS
DR

Wybunbury Moss

Dove House
Farm

Highfield Farm

69 A B 70 C D 71 E F

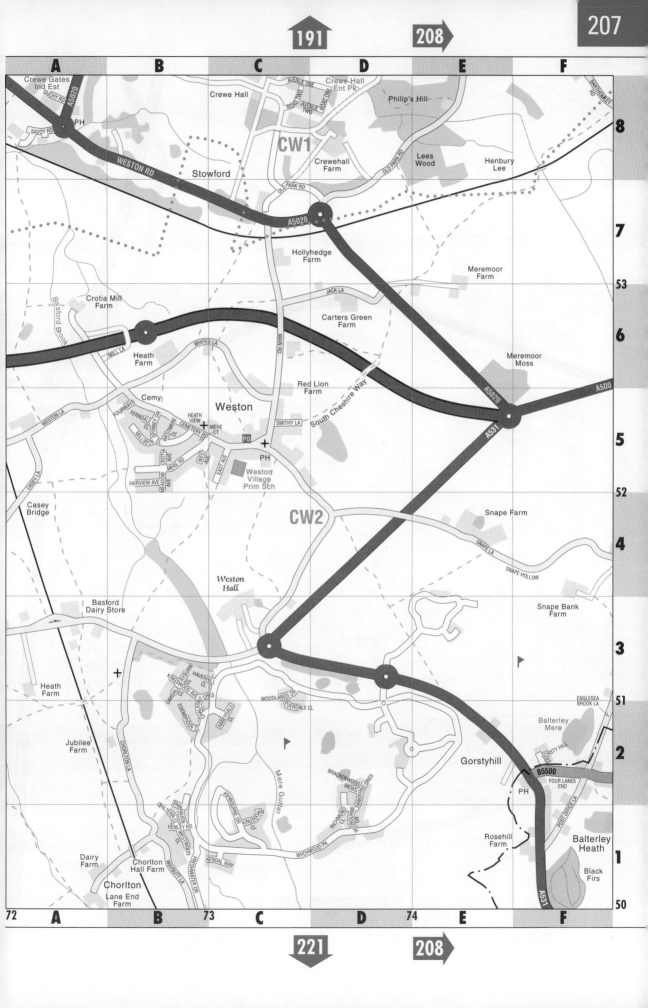

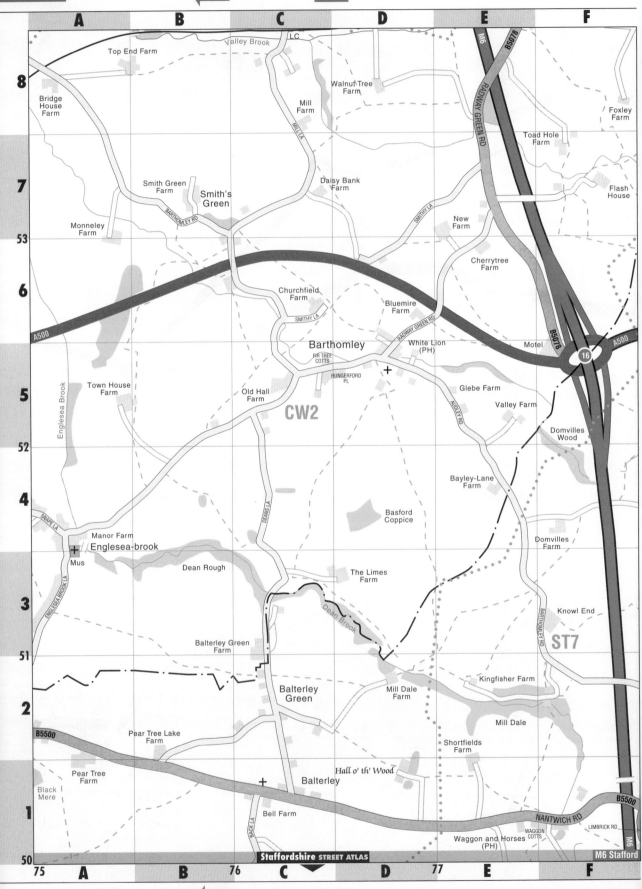

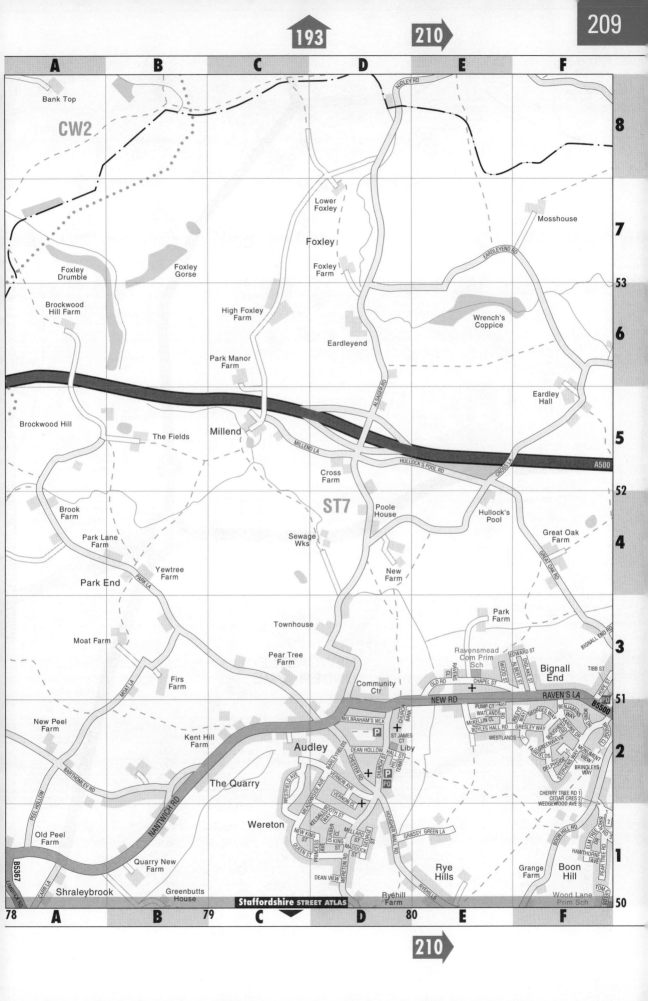

A   B   C   D   E   F

Bank Top

CW2

8

Lower Foxley

Mosshouse

Foxley

7

EARDLEYEND RD

Foxley Drumble

Foxley Gorse

Foxley Farm

53

Brockwood Hill Farm

High Foxley Farm

Wrench's Coppice

6

Eardleyend

ALSAGER RD

Park Manor Farm

Brockwood Hill

The Fields

Millend

Eardley Hall

5

MILLEND LA

HULLOCK'S POOL RD

CROSS LA

A500

52

Cross Farm

ST7

Poole House

Hullock's Pool

Brook Farm

Park Lane Farm

Sewage Wks

Great Oak Farm

4

PARK LA

Yewtree Farm

New Farm

GREAT OAK RD

Park End

Townhouse

Park Farm

BIGNALL END RD

3

Moat Farm

Pear Tree Farm

Ravensmead Com Prim Sch

EDWARD ST

Bignall End

TIBB ST

MOAT LA

Firs Farm

RAVENS CL

WOOD ST

ALBERT ST

DIGLAKE ST

OLD RD

CHAPEL ST

HOPE ST

PO

Community Ctr

NEW RD

RAVEN'S LA

B5500

51

New Peel Farm

Kent Hill Farm

WILBRAHAM'S WLK

P

BANK

ST JAMES CT

PUMP CT

WATLANDS RD

MILEYS WAY

GEORGES WAY

BENJAMINS WAY

IKINS DR

BRIDGE ST

BARTHOMLEY RD

BARLEY FIELDS

DEAN HOLLOW

CHURCH ST

HALL ST

Liby

McKELLIN CL

BOYLES HALL RD

GRESLEY WAY

WESTLANDS

BOUGHEY RD

AARONS DR

MONUMENT VIEW

GREENWAYS RD

2

Audley

WESTFIELD AVE

MEADOWSIDE AVE

VERNON AVE

P

PO

ST JAMES TERR

FAIRFIELDS

STEPHENS WAY

DELPHSIDE

BRINDLEYS WAY

NANTWICH RD

The Quarry

VERNON CL

CHERRY TREE RD 1

CEDAR CRES 2

WEDGEWOOD AVE 3

PEEL HOLLOW

KELSALL WAY

BOOTH ST

DURBER CL

MELLARD ST

GEORGE ST

GRASSY GREEN LA

BOON HILL RD

ELM TREE DR

PEAR TREE RD

Wereton

NEW KING ST

PRINCESS AVE

KING ST

MADDOCK ST

HOUGHER WALL RD

HAWTHORNE AVE

B5367

Old Peel Farm

QUEEN ST

WERETON RD

Rye Hills

Grange Farm

Boon Hill

LIMBRICK RD

CARR LA

Shraleybrook

DEAN VIEW

Greenbutts House

RYEHILLS

Ryehill Farm

Wood Lane Prim Sch

50

78   A   B   79   C   D   80   E   F

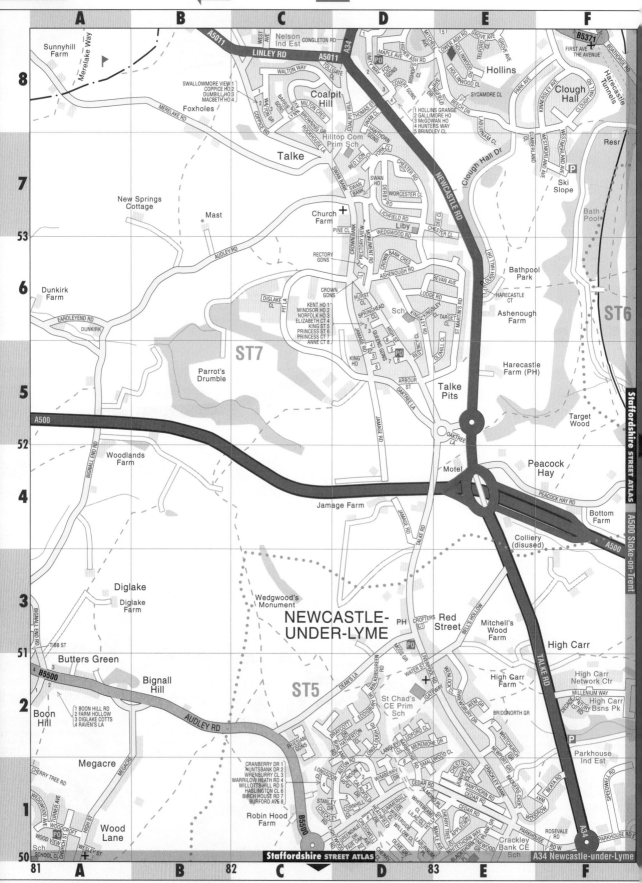

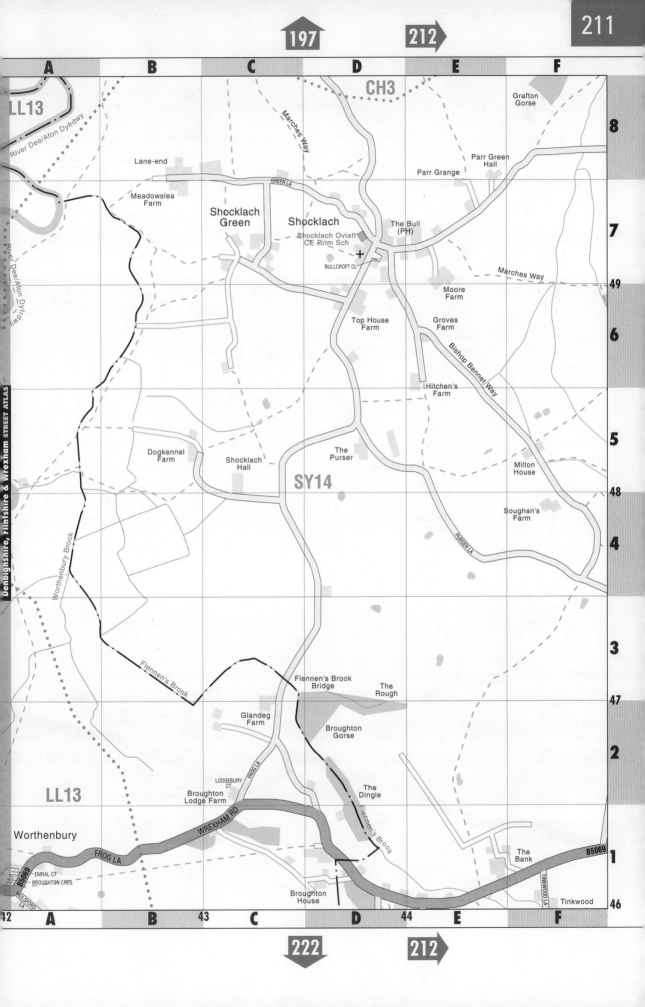

CH3

Grafton
Gorse

8

Lane-end

Parr Green
Hall

Meadowslea
Farm

GREEN LA

Parr Grange

The Bull
(PH)

Shocklach
Green

Shocklach

7

Shocklach Oviatt
CE Prim Sch

BULLCROFT CL

49

Moore
Farm

Marches Way

6

Top House
Farm

Groves
Farm

Bishop Bennet Way

Hitchen's
Farm

Dogkennel
Farm

The
Purser

5

Shocklach
Hall

SY14

Milton
House

48

Soughan's
Farm

4

PURSER LA

Worthenbury Brook

3

Flennen's Brook

Flennen's Brook
Bridge

The
Rough

47

Glandeg
Farm

Broughton
Gorse

2

FROG LA

LODGEBURY
CT

The
Dingle

LL13

Broughton
Lodge Farm

WREXHAM RD

Worthenbury

Flennen's Brook

B5069

The
Bank

B5069

FROG LA

1

EMRAL CT

B5069

BROUGHTON CRES

TINKWOOD LA

MULSFORD LA

Broughton
House

Tinkwood

46

Denbighshire, Flintshire & Wrexham STREET ATLAS

River Dee/Afon Dyfrdwy

LL13

211
198

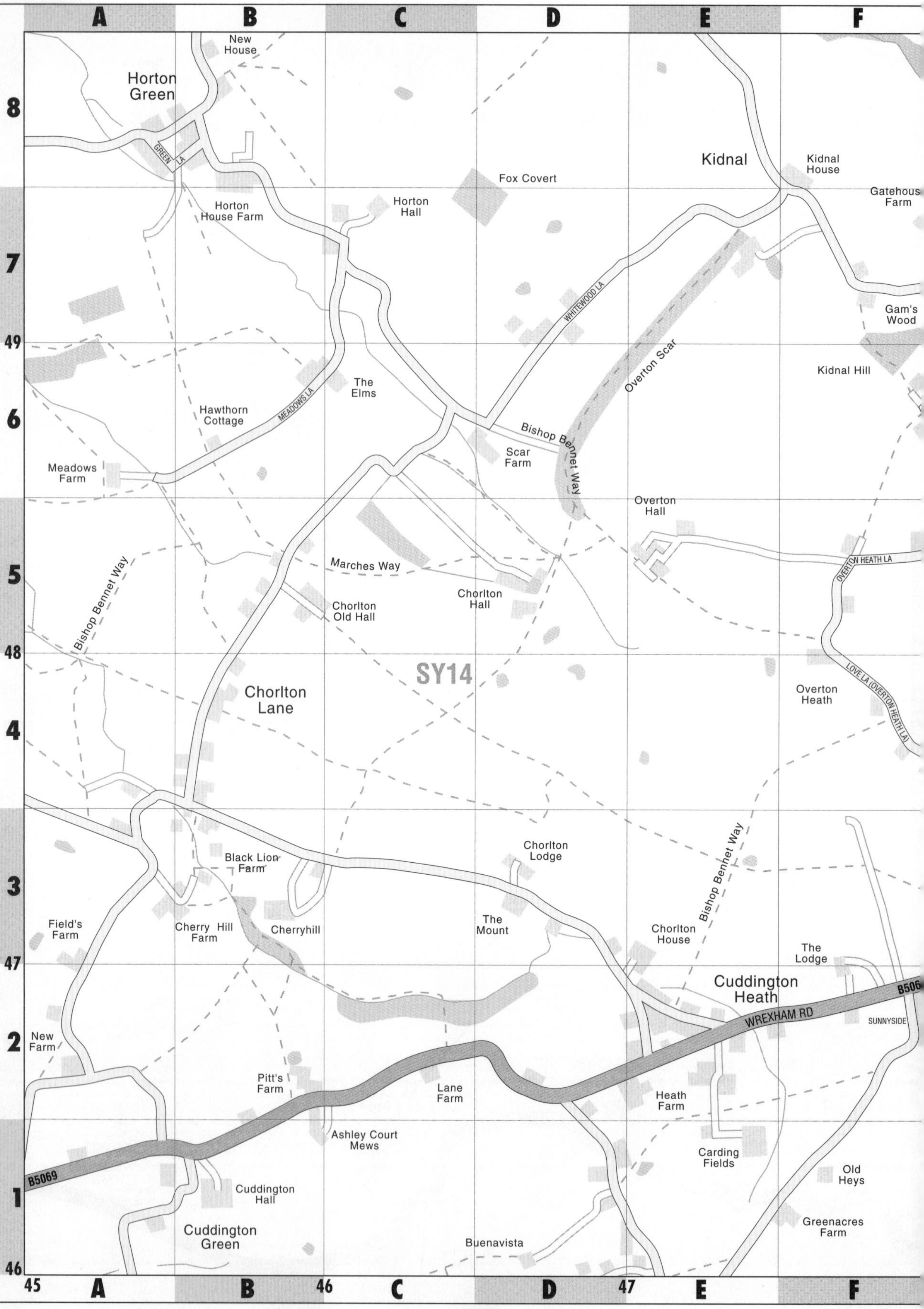

	A	B	C	D	E	F

8

New House

Horton Green

GREEN LA

Horton House Farm

Kidnal

Kidnal House

Gatehouse Farm

7

Fox Covert

Horton Hall

WHITEWOOD LA

Overton Scar

Gam's Wood

49

Kidnal Hill

The Elms

6

Hawthorn Cottage

MEADOWS LA

Bishop Bennet Way

Scar Farm

Meadows Farm

Overton Hall

5

Bishop Bennet Way

Marches Way

Chorlton Old Hall

Chorlton Hall

OVERTON HEATH LA

48

SY14

4

Chorlton Lane

Overton Heath

LOVE LA (OVERTON HEATH LA)

3

Black Lion Farm

Chorlton Lodge

Chorlton House

Bishop Bennet Way

Field's Farm

Cherry Hill Farm

Cherryhill

The Mount

The Lodge

47

Cuddington Heath

B5069

2

New Farm

Pitt's Farm

Lane Farm

WREXHAM RD

SUNNYSIDE

Heath Farm

1

B5069

Ashley Court Mews

Cuddington Hall

Carding Fields

Old Heys

Cuddington Green

Buenavista

Greenacres Farm

46

45	A	B	46	C	D	47	E	F

211
223

199
214

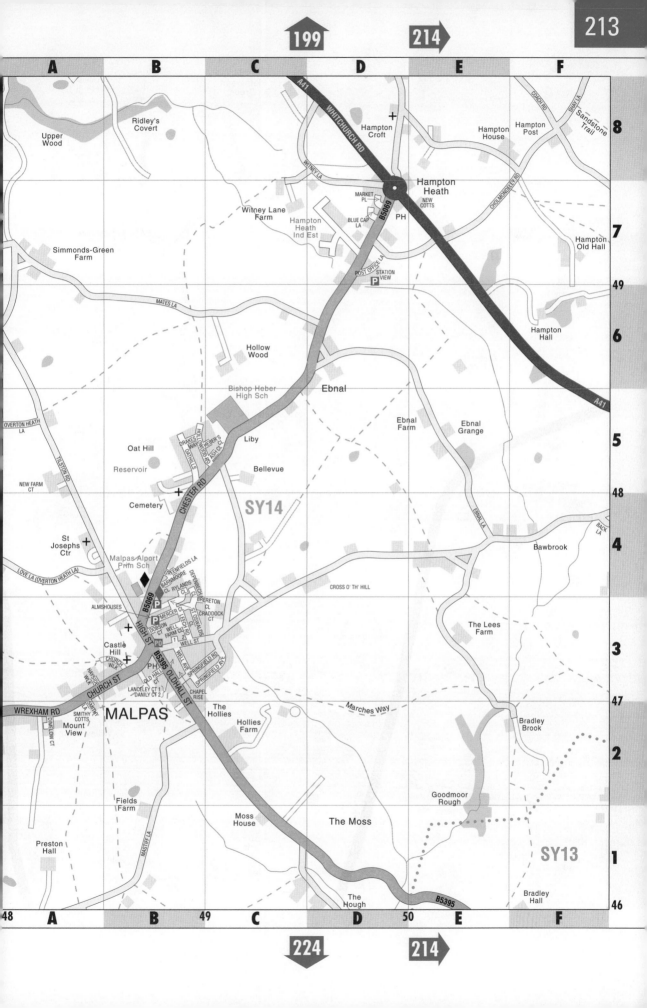

A B C D E F

8
7
49
6
5
48
4
3
47
2
1
46

Upper Wood

Ridley's Covert

Simmonds-Green Farm

OVERTON HEATH LA

TILSTON RD

NEW FARM CT

St Josephs Ctr

LOVE LA (OVERTON HEATH LA)

ALMSHOUSES

Castle Hill

CHURCH WLK

HAYSIDE WLK

WREXHAM RD

SMITHY COTTS

Mount View

DIMELOW CT

Preston Hall

Fields Farm

MASTIFF LA

MALPAS

CHURCH ST

B5395 OLD HALL ST

OLD HALL CT

LANCELEY CT 1
DANILY CT 2

PH

HIGH ST

B5069

P

PO

DOBSON CT

MERCER CT

WELL ST

WELL ST

TECH CL

ST OSWALDS

FARM CL

RYLANDS CL

BARNMOORE CL

GREENFIELDS LA

DEPERBECH CL

BRERETON CL

CRADDOCK CT

WELL AVE

SPRINGFIELD RD

SPRINGFIELD AVE

CHAPEL RISE

Malpas Alport Prim Sch

Oat Hill

Reservoir

Cemetery

CHESTER RD

Bishop Heber High Sch

HOLLINWOOD RD

DRAKES WAY

OATHILLS

HEBER'S CL

ASH CL

Liby

Bellevue

SY14

Hollow Wood

WITNEY LA

Witney Lane Farm

MATES LA

A41

WHITCHURCH RD

Hampton Croft

MARKET PL

Hampton Heath Ind Est

BLUE CAP LA

B5069

PH

POST OFFICE LA

STATION VIEW

P

Hampton Heath

NEW COTTS

CHOLMONDELEY RD

COACH RD

SHAY LA

Sandstone Trail

Hampton House

Hampton Post

Hampton Old Hall

Hampton Hall

Ebnal

Ebnal Farm

Ebnal Grange

EBNAL LA

BACK LA

Bawbrook

CROSS O' TH' HILL

The Lees Farm

The Hollies

Hollies Farm

Marches Way

Bradley Brook

Goodmoor Rough

SY13

The Moss

Moss House

The Hough

B5395

Bradley Hall

48 A B 49 C D 50 E F

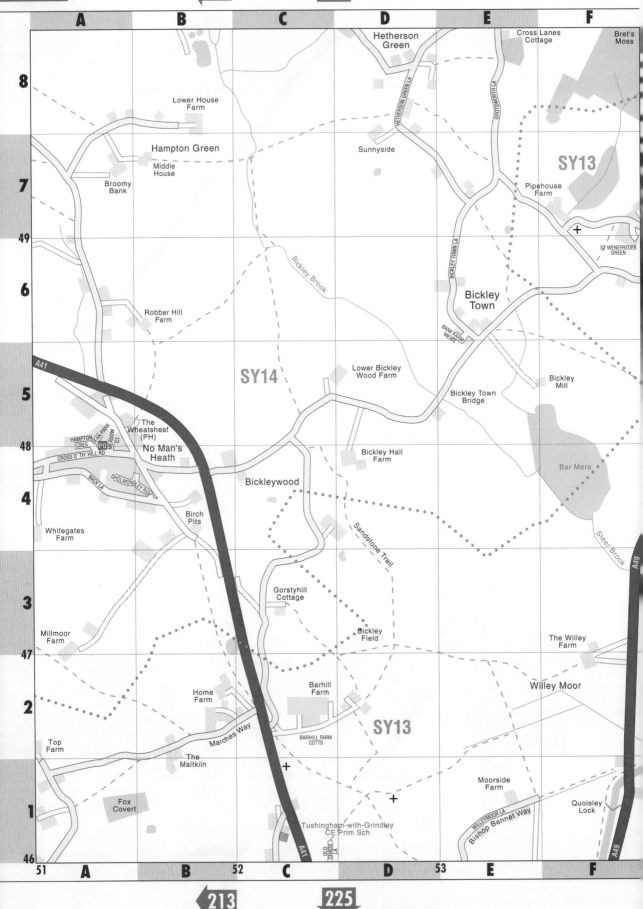

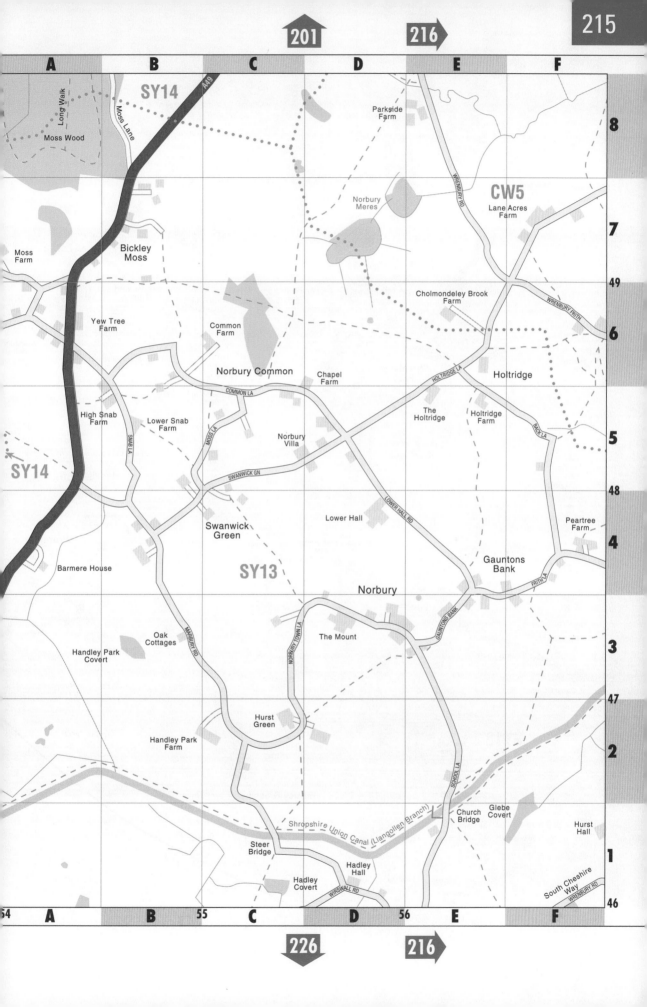

A **B** **C** **D** **E** **F**

8

Chorley Hall

Baddiley Resr

Frith Green Farm

Wrenbury Wood

7

Frith Farm

New Covert

WRENBURY FRITH

49

Wrenbury Wood

Sprostonwood Farm

6

COUNCIL HOUSES

Bank Farm

The Heald

Heald Covert

Sprostonwood House

Wrenbury Hall

Ivy House Farm

Wrenbury Frith

CHOLMONDELEY RD

CW5

Sproston Hill Farm

5

Wrenbury Church Bridge

Starkey's Bridge

Wrenbury Bridge

48

Porter's Hill

WATERSIDE COTTS

Cotton Arms (PH)

Wrenbury House

4

Wrenbury Frith Bridge (Draw-bridge)

FRITH LA

CHURCH FARM

THE GREEN

PO

Wrenbury

OAK VILLAS 1
OAK COTTS 2

Wrenbury Prim Sch

Frith-hall Farm

MARLE CL

NANTWICH RD

SANDFIELD CT

OAKFIELD CT

OAKFIELD AVE

1 2

Thomason's Bridge

Shropshire Union Canal (Llangollen Branch)

Sandfield House

STATION RD

Ryebank

Marbury Brook

3

River Weaver

Hill Farm

South Cheshire Way

Smeaton Hall

Canal Covert

47

NEW RD

SY13

2

Marbury Heyes

Pinsley Green

PINSLEY GREEN RD

Hurst Hall

Smeaton Wood Farm

1

Townley Farm

Hewitt's Moss

WRENBURY RD

MARLEY GN

HOLLYHURST RD

Yew Tree Farm

46

Townley Cottage

57 **A** **B** **58** **C** **D** **59** **E** **F**

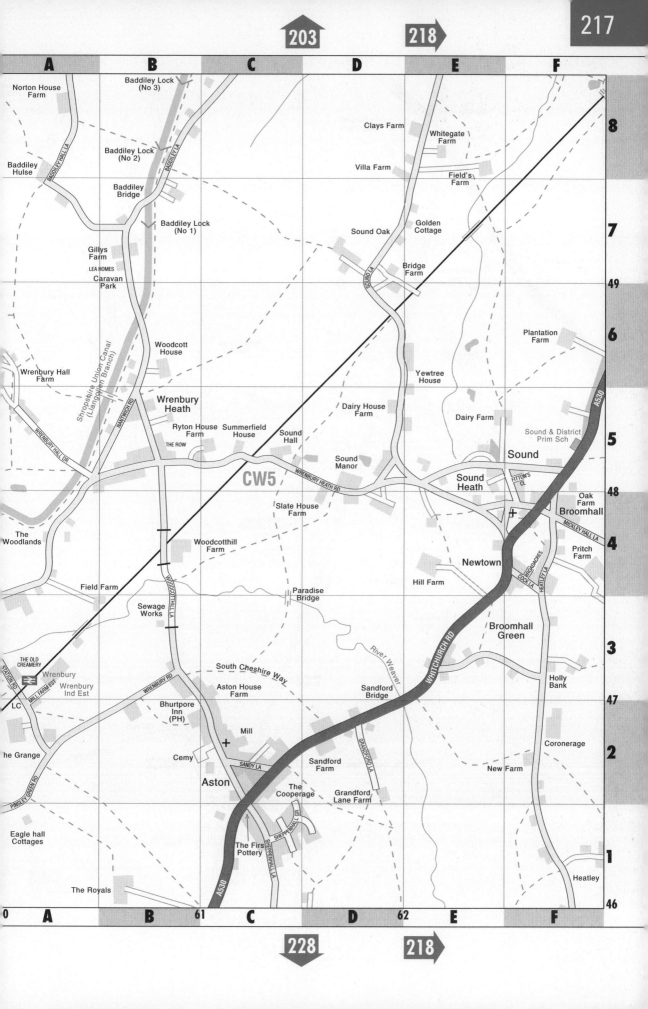

203
218
228
218

A **B** **C** **D** **E** **F**

8
7
49
6
5
48
4
3
47
2
1
46

Norton House Farm
Baddiley Lock (No 3)
Clays Farm
Whitegate Farm
Villa Farm
Field's Farm
Baddiley Hulse
Baddiley Lock (No 2)
Baddiley Bridge
Sound Oak
Golden Cottage
Gillys Farm
LEA HOMES
Caravan Park
Baddiley Lock (No 1)
Bridge Farm
Woodcott House
Yewtree House
Plantation Farm
Wrenbury Hall Farm
Shropshire Union Canal (Llangollen Branch)
Wrenbury Heath
Dairy House Farm
Dairy Farm
Sound & District Prim Sch
NANTWICH RD
Ryton House Farm
Summerfield House
Sound Hall
Sound
BADDILEY HALL LA
THE ROW
Sound Manor
Sound Heath
FITTON'S CL
Oak Farm
Broomhall
CW5
WRENBURY HEATH RD
MICKLEY HALL LA
WRENBURY HALL DR
The Woodlands
Slate House Farm
Woodcotthill Farm
Newtown
BROADACRES
Pritch Farm
COCK LA
HEATLEY LA
A530
Field Farm
Hill Farm
Broomhall Green
Sewage Works
WOODCOTTHILL LA
Paradise Bridge
River Weaver
WHITCHURCH RD
THE OLD CREAMERY
South Cheshire Way
Holly Bank
STATION RD
Wrenbury
Wrenbury Ind Est
Aston House Farm
Sandford Bridge
MILL FARM EST
LC
Bhurtpore Inn (PH)
WRENBURY RD
Coronerage
The Grange
Mill
Sandford Farm
New Farm
PINSLEY GREEN RD
Cemy
SANDY LA
GRANDFORD LA
Aston
The Cooperage
Grandford Lane Farm
Eagle hall Cottages
SHEPPENHALL GR
SHEPPENHALL LA
The Firs Pottery
A530
Heatley
The Royals

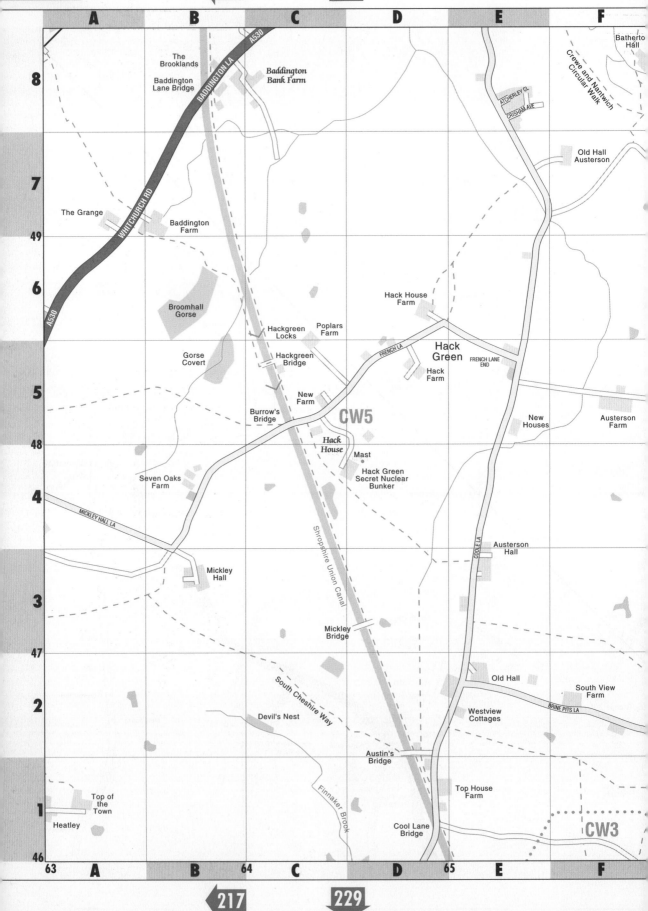

A B C D E F

8

7

49

6

5

48

4

47

3

2

1

46

63 A B 64 C D 65 E F

The Brooklands
Baddington Lane Bridge
Baddington Bank Farm
Baddington Farm
The Grange
Broomhall Gorse
Gorse Covert
Hackgreen Locks
Hackgreen Bridge
Poplars Farm
New Farm
Burrow's Bridge
Hack House Farm
Hack Green
French Lane End
Hack Farm
New Houses
Austerson Farm
CW5
Hack House
Mast
Hack Green Secret Nuclear Bunker
Seven Oaks Farm
Mickley Hall La
Mickley Hall
Shropshire Union Canal
Coole La
Austerson Hall
Mickley Bridge
South Cheshire Way
Old Hall
South View Farm
Brine Pits La
Westview Cottages
Devil's Nest
Finnaker Brook
Austin's Bridge
Top House Farm
Top of the Town
Heatley
Cool Lane Bridge
CW3
Whitchurch Rd
A530
Baddington La
Atcherley Cl
Crisham Ave
Old Hall Austerson
Batherto Hall
Crewe and Nantwich Circular Walk

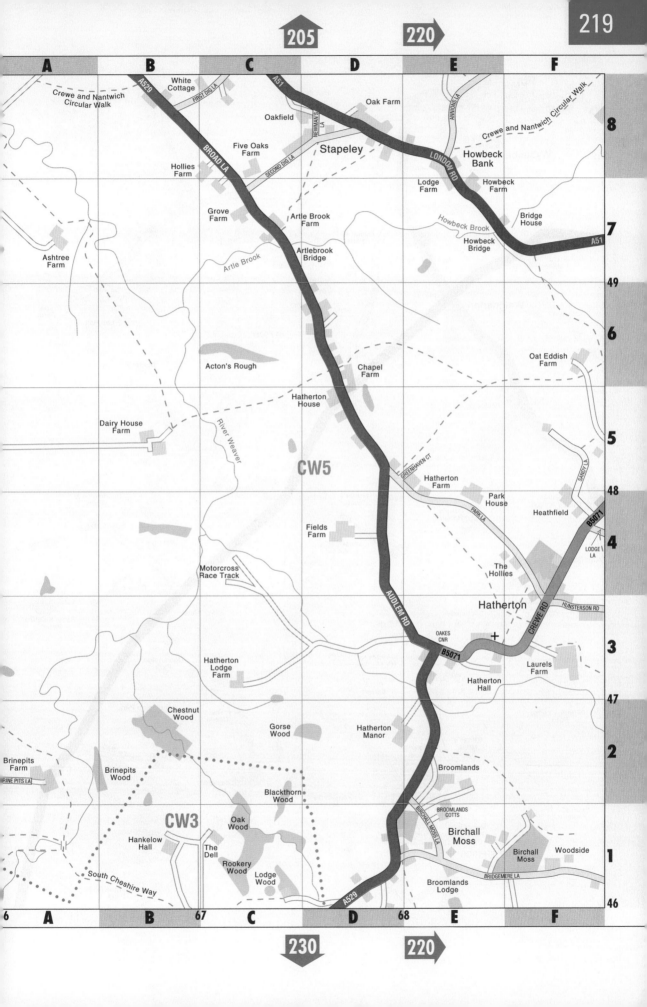

A B C D E F

8

7

49

6

5

48

4

3

47

2

1

46

Crewe and Nantwich Circular Walk

White Cottage

A529

FIRST DIG LA

BROAD LA

A51

Oakfield

NEWMAN'S LA

Oak Farm

Stapeley

SECOND DIG LA

Five Oaks Farm

Hollies Farm

Grove Farm

Artle Brook Farm

Artlebrook Bridge

Ashtree Farm

Artle Brook

Crewe and Nantwich Circular Walk

ANNIONS LA

Howbeck Bank

LONDON RD

Lodge Farm

Howbeck Farm

Howbeck Brook

Bridge House

Howbeck Bridge

A51

Oat Eddish Farm

SANDY LA

Acton's Rough

Chapel Farm

Hatherton House

Dairy House Farm

River Weaver

CW5

GREENHAVEN CT

Hatherton Farm

Park House

Heathfield

B5071

48

Fields Farm

PARK LA

The Hollies

LODGE LA

Motorcross Race Track

Hatherton

CREWE RD

HUNSTERSON RD

AUDLEM RD

OAKES CNR

B5071

Laurels Farm

Hatherton Lodge Farm

Hatherton Hall

Chestnut Wood

Gorse Wood

Hatherton Manor

Brinepits Farm

BRINE PITS LA

Brinepits Wood

Blackthorn Wood

Broomlands

CW3

Oak Wood

BIRCHALL MOSS LA

BROOMLANDS COTTS

Birchall Moss

Woodside

Hankelow Hall

The Dell

Rookery Wood

Lodge Wood

Birchall Moss

South Cheshire Way

A529

Broomlands Lodge

BRIDGEMERE LA

6 A B 67 C D 68 E F

219
206

A B C D E F

8
The Riddings
B5071
RIDDINGS LA
VALEBROOK DR
HIGH BECK CRES
CORSEY BANK CRES
GLEBE CL
CHURCH WAY
MAIN RD
FIELDS VIEW CL
CHURCHFIELDS
PO
SCHOOL BANK
Red Lion (PH)
1 ST CHADS CL
2 SOUTHFIELDS CL
3 MOORLANS DR
Cemy
Hall Bank
Cobb's Moss
CW2
Ellesmere Farm

Wybunbury
Brook House
BRIDGE ST
Wybunbury Delves CE Prim Sch

7
A51
Manor Farm
WYBUNBURY RD
Hough Mill Farm
BACK LA
Sand Pit
The Cliffe
Jerusalem
WRINEHILL RD
COBBS LA

49
Walgherton
PH
Jericho
Lea Forge Farm
Lea Hall
Lea Farm

6
CREWE RD
Lodge Farm
The Oaks
Forge Bank
Hunter's Hill

Poolbank
Trout Farm

5
CW5
Lea Park

48
B5071
Dagfields Craft & Antique Ctr
Perry's Rough
George's Wood
Whispey Hill
Doddington Mill Farm

4
Northwood
LODGE LA
Hatherton Lodge
Birchenhill Wood
South Cheshire Way
Speakman's Moss
George's Wood
LONDON RD
MILL LA
Mill Covert
Black Mere
Robin Knight's Rough

3
Sewage Works
Demesne House
Doddington Park

47
Hatherton Lodge Farm
HUNSTERSON RD
Black Covert
The Castle
Doddington Park House

2
Glover's Moss
Ridley's Pool
Wilbraham's Walk
Lake Lodge
Doddington Pool

Bearcat Fields
Chapel Wood
Pepperstreet Moss
Doddington Hall

1
Manor Farm
Hunsterson
The Duckery
Ley Groun Farm

46
BRIDGEMERE LA
HUNSTERSON RD
PEWIT LA
Doddington Park Farm
A51

69 A B 70 C D 71 E F

219
231

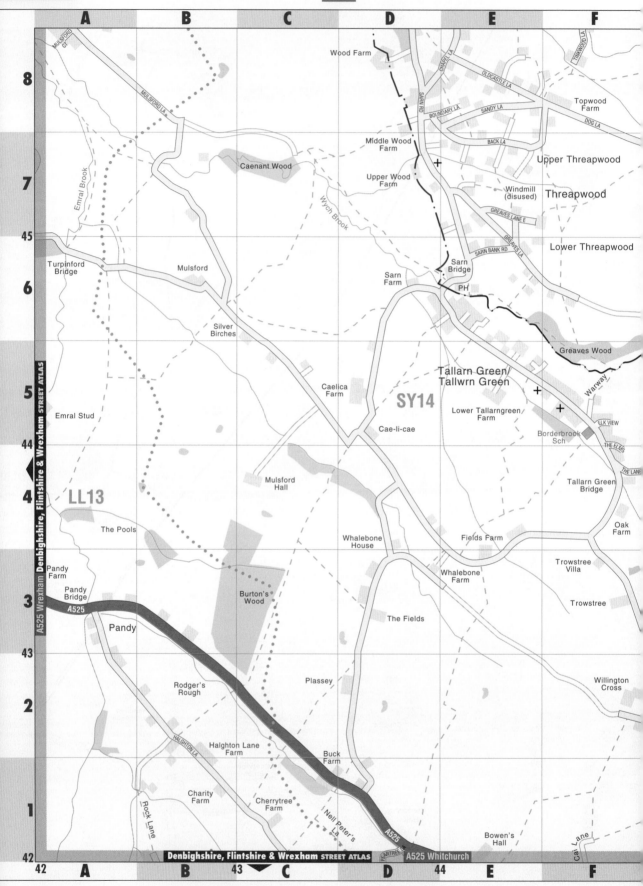

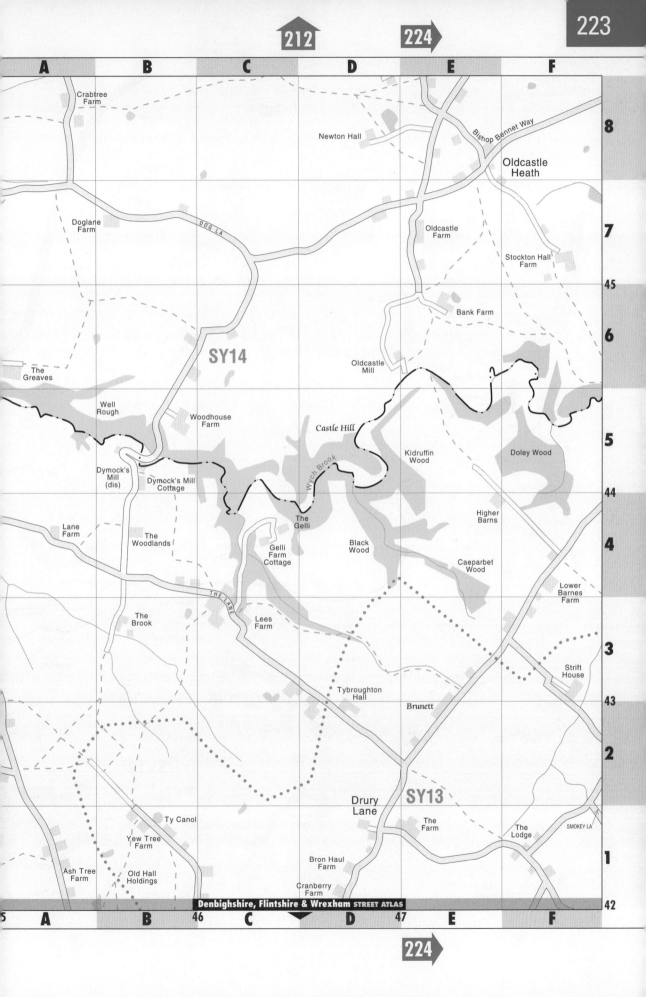

A   B   C   D   E   F

Crabtree
Farm

Newton Hall

Bishop Bennet Way

8

Oldcastle
Heath

Doglane
Farm

DOG LA

Oldcastle
Farm

7

Stockton Hall
Farm

45

Bank Farm

6

The
Greaves

SY14

Oldcastle
Mill

Well
Rough

Woodhouse
Farm

Castle Hill

Kidruffin
Wood

Doley Wood

5

Dymock's
Mill
(dis)

Dymock's Mill
Cottage

Wych Brook

44

The
Gelli

Higher
Barns

Lane
Farm

The Woodlands

Gelli
Farm
Cottage

Black
Wood

Caeparbet
Wood

Lower
Barnes
Farm

4

The
Brook

THE LANE

Lees
Farm

Strift
House

3

Tybroughton
Hall

Brunett

43

2

Drury
Lane

SY13

Ty Canol

The
Farm

The
Lodge

SMOKEY LA

Yew Tree
Farm

Bron Haul
Farm

1

Ash Tree
Farm

Old Hall
Holdings

Cranberry
Farm

42

5   A   B   46   C   D   47   E   F

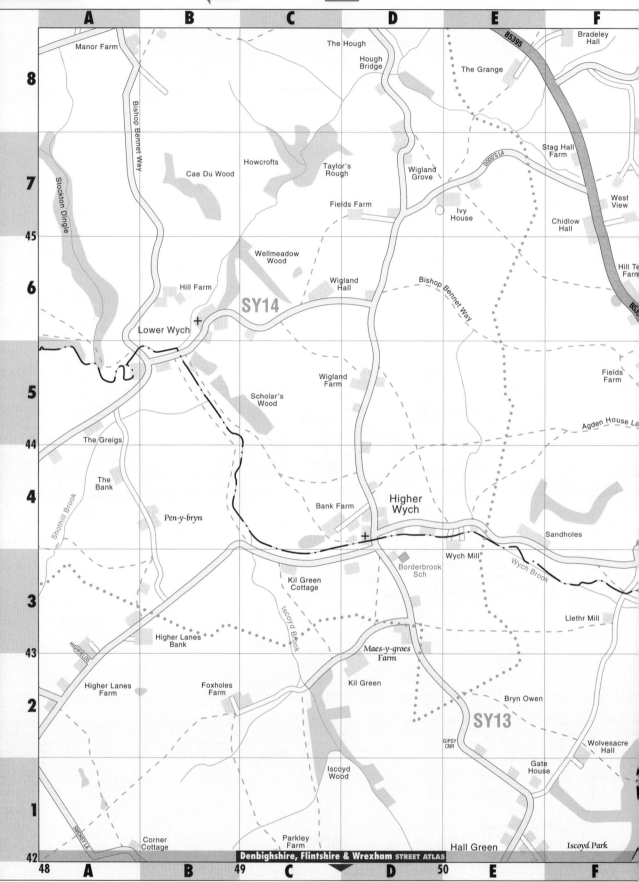

Manor Farm

Bishop Bennet Way

Stockton Dingle

The Hough

Hough Bridge

The Grange

B5395

Bradeley Hall

Cae Du Wood

Howcrofts

Taylor's Rough

Wigland Grove

DODD'S LA

Stag Hall Farm

West View

Fields Farm

Ivy House

Chidlow Hall

Hill Te Farm

Wellmeadow Wood

Hill Farm

SY14

Wigland Hall

Bishop Bennet Way

B5

Lower Wych

Scholar's Wood

Wigland Farm

Fields Farm

The Greigs

Agden House La

Shothill Brook

The Bank

Pen-y-bryn

Bank Farm

Higher Wych

Sandholes

Wych Brook

Llethr Mill

Kil Green Cottage

Borderbrook Sch

Wych Mill

Iscoyd Brook

Higher Lanes Bank

HIGHFIELDS

Maes-y-groes Farm

Bryn Owen

SY13

Higher Lanes Farm

Foxholes Farm

Kil Green

Wolvesacre Hall

GIPSY CNR

Iscoyd Wood

Gate House

SMOKER LA

Corner Cottage

Parkley Farm

Hall Green

Iscoyd Park

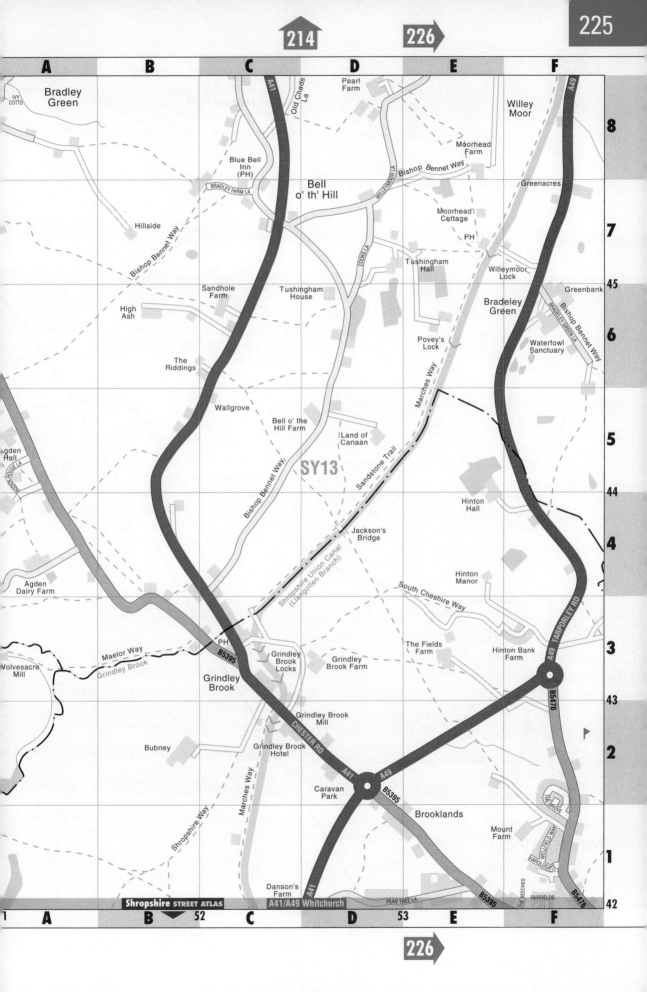

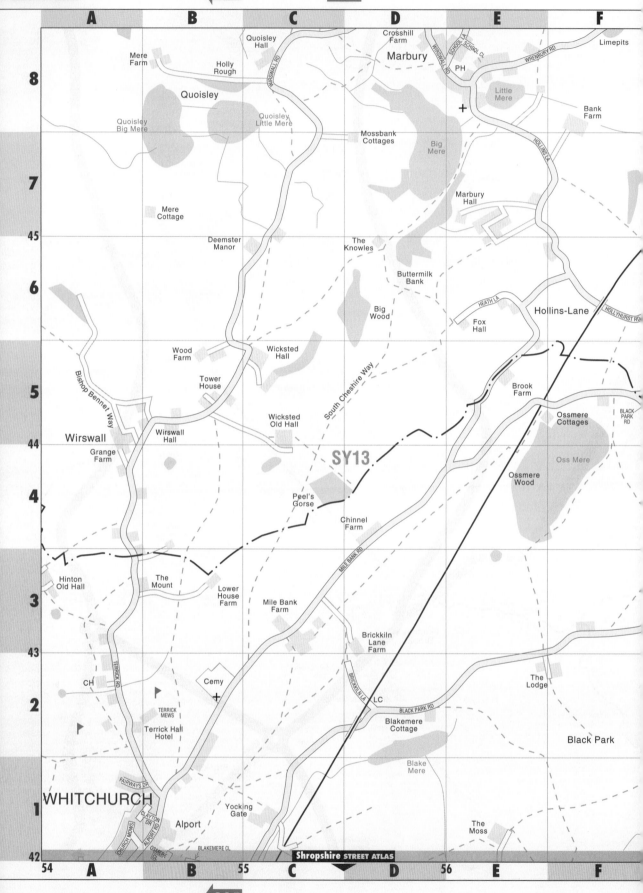

Limepits

Marbury

Crosshill Farm

PH

SCHOOL LA
SCHOOL CL
WRENBURY RD

Little Mere

Bank Farm

Mere Farm

Holly Rough

Quoisley Hall

WIRSWALL RD

HOLLINS LA

Quoisley

Quoisley Big Mere

Quoisley Little Mere

Mossbank Cottages

Big Mere

Mere Cottage

Deemster Manor

The Knowles

Buttermilk Bank

Marbury Hall

HEATH LA

Fox Hall

Hollins-Lane

HOLLYHURST RD

Big Wood

Wood Farm

Wicksted Hall

Tower House

SOUTH CHESHIRE WAY

Brook Farm

Ossmere Cottages

BLACK PARK RD

Bishop Bennet Way

Wirswall

Wirswall Hall

Wicksted Old Hall

SY13

Ossmere Wood

Oss Mere

Grange Farm

Peel's Gorse

Chinnel Farm

Hinton Old Hall

The Mount

Lower House Farm

Mile Bank Farm

MILE BANK RD

Brickkiln Lane Farm

TERRICK RD

CH

Cemy

BRICKKILN LA

LC

The Lodge

TERRICK MEWS

Terrick Hall Hotel

BLACK PARK RD

Blakemere Cottage

Black Park

FAIRWAYS DR

WHITCHURCH

Yocking Gate

Blake Mere

CLAYTON MDWS
CLAYTON DR
ALPORT RD
CHURCH MDWS
OSMERE CL

Alport

The Moss

BLAKEMERE CL

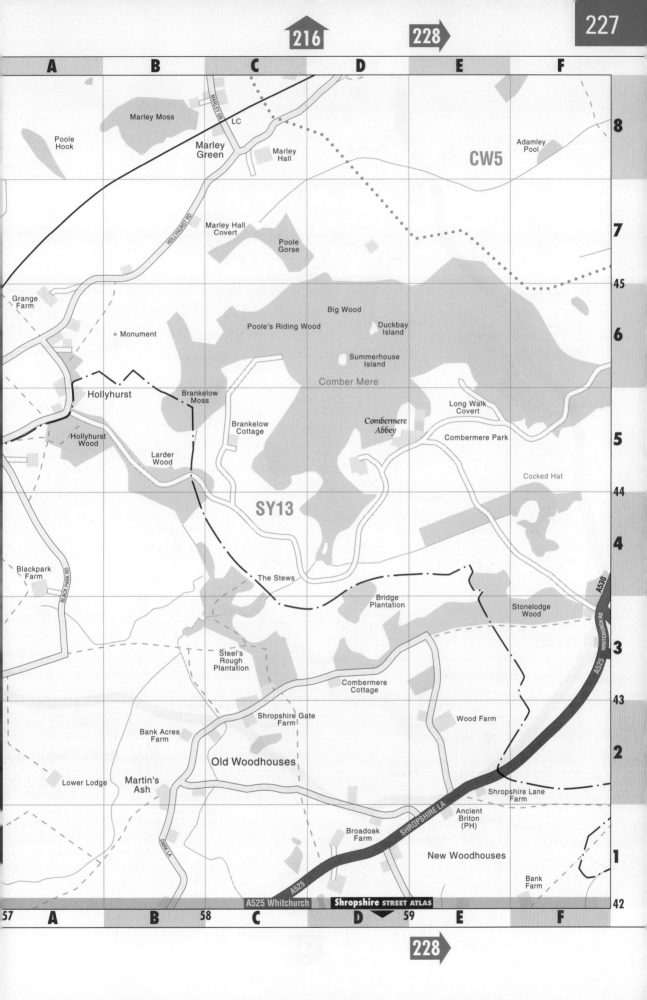

A   B   C   D   E   F

8
Poole Hook
Marley Moss
MARLEY GRN
LC
Marley Green
Marley Hall
CW5
Adamley Pool

7
Hollyhurst Rd
Marley Hall Covert
Poole Gorse
45

Grange Farm
Big Wood
Monument
Poole's Riding Wood
Duckbay Island
6
Summerhouse Island

Hollyhurst
Brankelow Moss
Comber Mere
Long Walk Covert
Combermere Abbey
Combermere Park
5
Hollyhurst Wood
Brankelow Cottage
Larder Wood
Cocked Hat
44

SY13
4
Black Park Rd
Blackpark Farm
The Stews
Bridge Plantation
Stonelodge Wood
A530
A525
WHITCHURCH RD
3
Steel's Rough Plantation
Combermere Cottage
43

Shropshire Gate Farm
Wood Farm
Bank Acres Farm
2
Old Woodhouses
Shropshire Lane Farm

Lower Lodge
Martin's Ash
Shropshire La
Ancient Briton (PH)
Dark La
Broadoak Farm
1
A525
New Woodhouses
Bank Farm
42

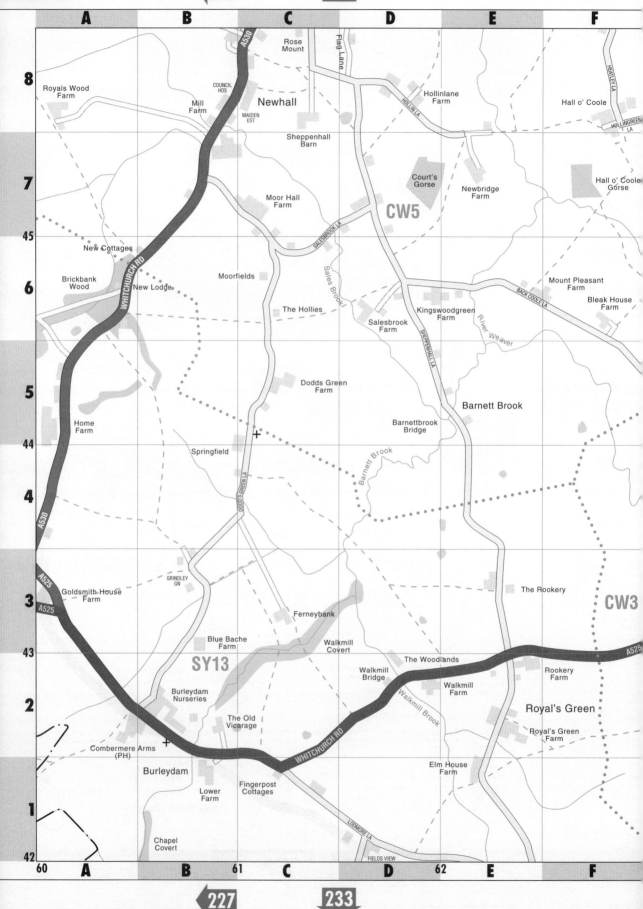

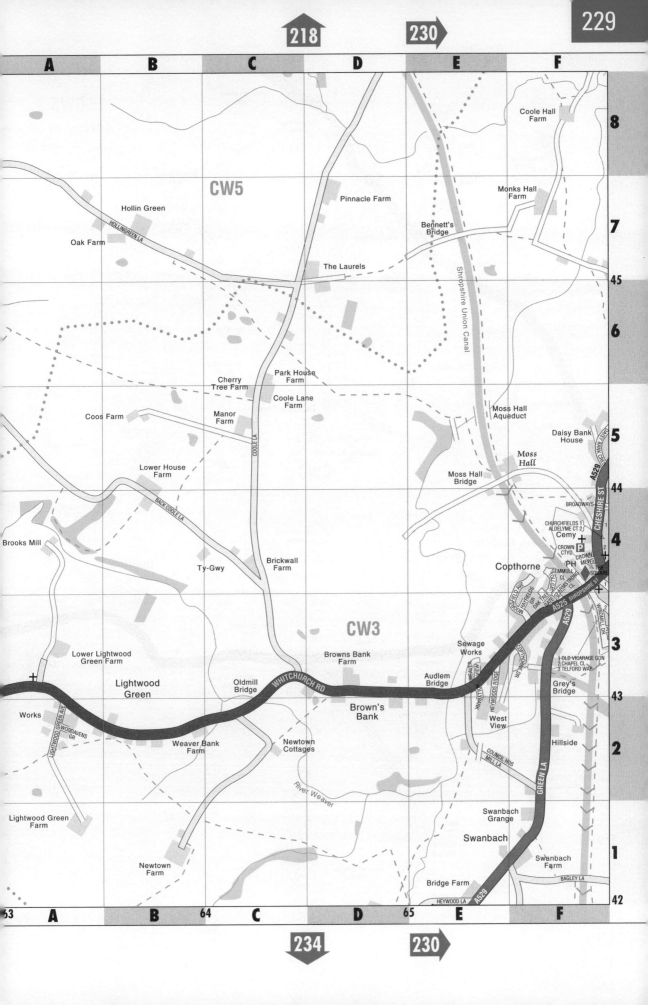

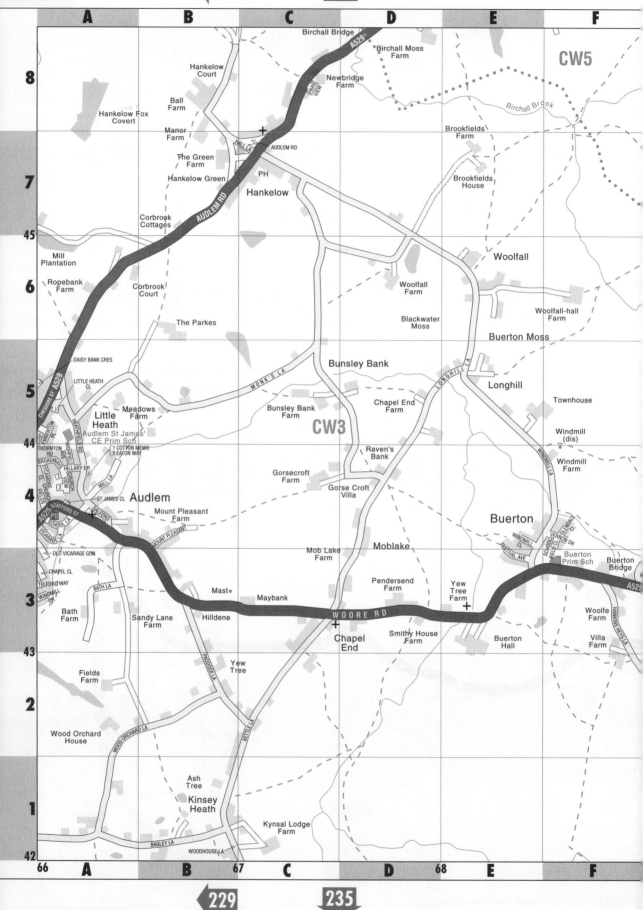

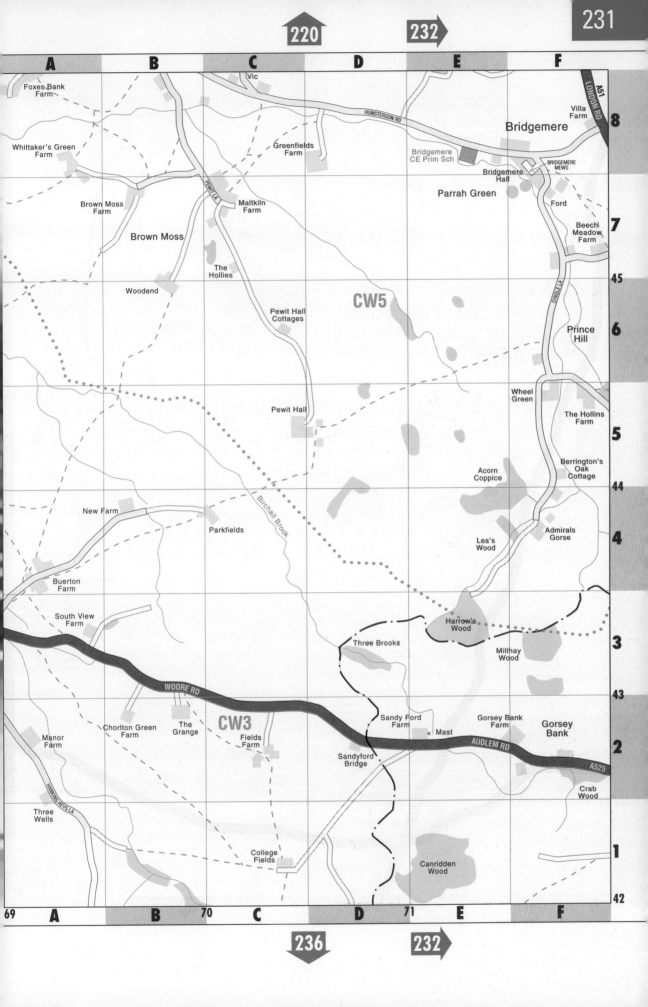

A   B   C   D   E   F

8

7

45

6

5

44

4

43

3

2

42

1

A51 LONDON RD

Foxes Bank Farm

Whittaker's Green Farm

Brown Moss Farm

Brown Moss

Vic

Greenfields Farm

HUNSTERSON RD

Bridgemere

Villa Farm

Bridgemere CE Prim Sch

Bridgemere Hall

BRIDGEMERE MEWS

Parrah Green

Ford

Beech Meadow Farm

PENY LA

Maltkiln Farm

The Hollies

Woodend

Pewit Hall Cottages

CW5

DINGLE LA

Prince Hill

Wheel Green

The Hollins Farm

Pewit Hall

Berrington's Oak Cottage

Acorn Coppice

Admirals Gorse

New Farm

Parkfields

Birchall Brook

Lea's Wood

Buerton Farm

South View Farm

Harrow's Wood

Millhay Wood

Three Brooks

WOORE RD

CW3

Sandy Ford Farm

Mast

Gorsey Bank Farm

Gorsey Bank

Manor Farm

Chorlton Green Farm

The Grange

Fields Farm

Sandyford Bridge

AUDLEM RD

A525

Crab Wood

HAWKINS HEYS LA

Three Wells

College Fields

Canridden Wood

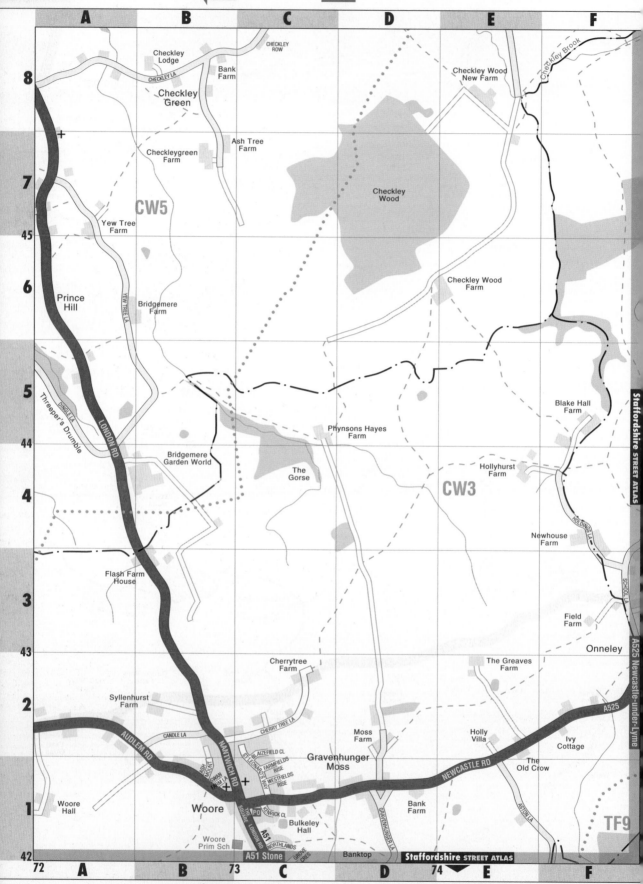

A	B	C	D	E	F

8

Checkley Row

Checkley
Lodge

Bank
Farm

CHECKLEY LA

Checkley Wood
New Farm

Checkley Brook

7

Checkley
Green

Ash Tree
Farm

Checkleygreen
Farm

Checkley
Wood

CW5

45

Yew Tree
Farm

6

Prince
Hill

Bridgemere
Farm

Checkley Wood
Farm

YEW TREE LA

5

DINGLE LA

Threeper's Drumble

LONDON RD

Blake Hall
Farm

44

Bridgemere
Garden World

Phynsons Hayes
Farm

Hollyhurst
Farm

4

The
Gorse

CW3

HOLDINGS LA

Newhouse
Farm

3

Flash Farm
House

SCHOOL LA

Field
Farm

43

Cherrytree
Farm

The Greaves
Farm

Onneley

2

Syllenhurst
Farm

Moss
Farm

Holly
Villa

Ivy
Cottage

A525

AUDLEM RD

CANDLE LA

CHERRY TREE LA

NANTWICH RD

BLAIZEFIELD CL
ST LEONARDS WAY

FARMFIELDS
RISE

WESTFIELDS
RISE

Gravenhunger
Moss

NEWCASTLE RD

The
Old Crow

ASTON LA

A525 Newcastle-under-Lyme

Staffordshire STREET ATLAS

1

Woore
Hall

THE SQUARE
FROG LA
SWAN LA
ASH LA

Woore

PO

KENRICK CL

Bulkeley
Hall

GRAVENHUNGER LA

Bank
Farm

TF9

42

Woore
Prim Sch

A51 Stone

NORTHLANDS

LONDON RD

GROVE DRES

Banktop

72	A	B	73	C	D	74	E	F

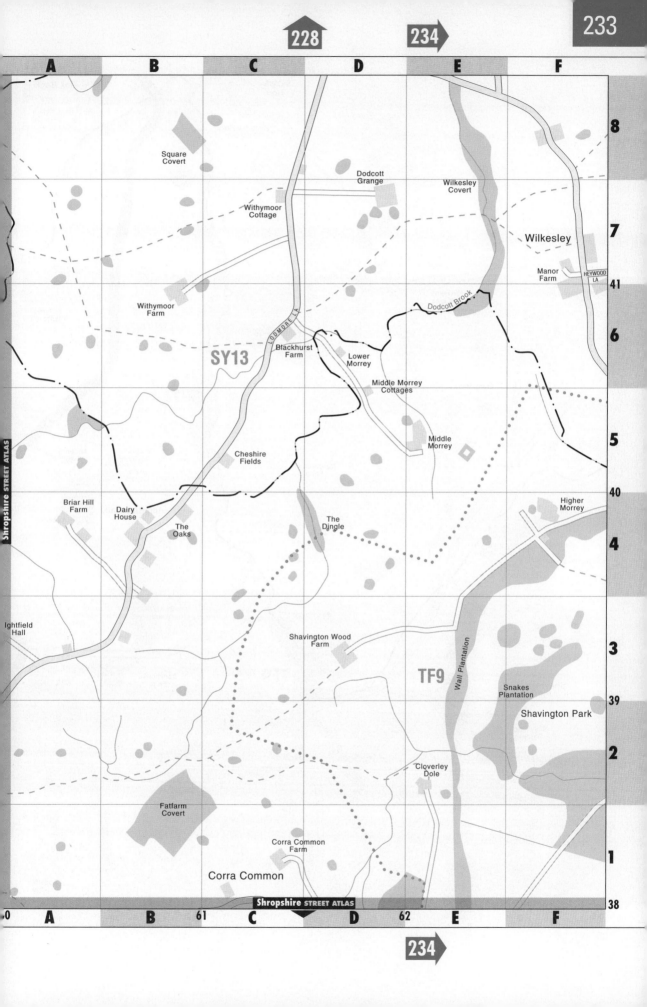

A   B   C   D   E   F

8

Square
Covert

Dodcott
Grange

Wilkesley
Covert

7

Wilkesley

Withymoor
Cottage

Manor
Farm

HEYWOOD LA

41

Withymoor
Farm

Dodcott Brook

6

SY13

LODMORE LA

Blackhurst
Farm

Lower
Morrey

Middle Morrey
Cottages

Cheshire
Fields

Middle
Morrey

5

40

Briar Hill
Farm

Dairy
House

The
Oaks

The
Dingle

Higher
Morrey

4

Ightfield
Hall

Shavington Wood
Farm

TF9

Wall Plantation

Snakes
Plantation

3

Shavington Park

39

2

Cloverley
Dole

Fatfarm
Covert

Corra Common
Farm

1

Corra Common

38

0   A   B   61   C   D   62   E   F

A **B** **C** **D** **E** **F**

8

Butterley
Heys

Cox Bank

Butterley Heys
Cottages

GREEN LA

Heywood
Farm

Lane
Farm

Coxbank Brook

Shropshire Union Canal

Duckow
Wood

7

SY13

CW3

A529

HEYWOOD LA

Park Farm

41

Heyfields
Farm

Wilkesley
Farm

Heyfields
Cottages

Yewtree
Plantation

6

Kent's
Rough

Ferny Heys

Nethermost
Wood

Adderley
CE Prim
Sch

5

Northwood's
Farm

River Duckow

Black
Covert

Adderley
Hall

A529

40

Adderley Park

Adderley
Hall
Farm

4

Yew Tree
Farm

Bawhill
Wood

A529

Gas House

SHAVINGTON
HOME FARM

3

The
Spinneys

Gas House
Plantation

TF9

Bankhouse
Farm

Shavington
Park

39

Shavington
Gardens

2

Big Pool

1

Big Wood

Tittenley
Pool

Adderley
Lodge

38

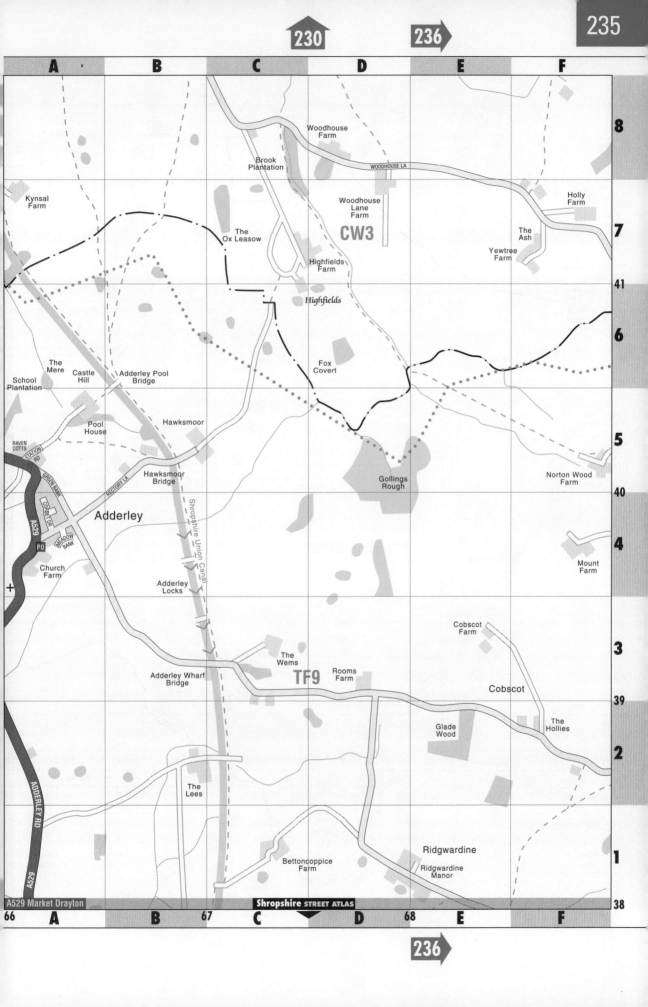

A   B   C   D   E   F

8

Woodhouse
Farm

Brook
Plantation

WOODHOUSE LA

Kynsal
Farm

Woodhouse
Lane
Farm

Holly
Farm

The
Ox Leasow

CW3

The
Ash

7

Yewtree
Farm

41

Highfields
Farm

Highfields

6

The
Mere

Castle
Hill

Adderley Pool
Bridge

Fox
Covert

School
Plantation

RAVEN
COTTS

Pool
House

Hawksmoor

Norton Wood
Farm

5

Hawksmoor
Bridge

Gollings
Rough

40

Adderley

Mount
Farm

4

A529

Church
Farm

Adderley
Locks

Cobscot
Farm

3

The
Wems

Adderley Wharf
Bridge

TF9

Rooms
Farm

Cobscot

39

Glade
Wood

The
Hollies

2

The
Lees

Ridgwardine

1

Bettoncoppice
Farm

Ridgwardine
Manor

38

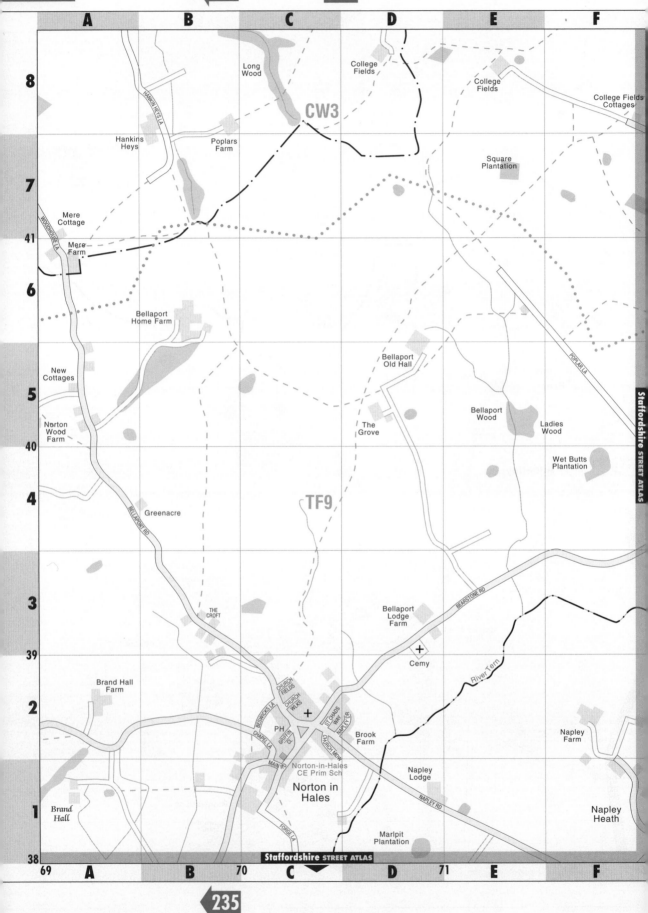

CW3

Long
Wood

College
Fields

College
Fields

College Fields
Cottages

HANKIN HEYS LA

Hankins
Heys

Poplars
Farm

Square
Plantation

Mere
Cottage

WOODHOUSE LA

Mere
Farm

Bellaport
Home Farm

Bellaport
Old Hall

POPLAR LA

New
Cottages

Bellaport
Wood

Ladies
Wood

Norton
Wood
Farm

The
Grove

Wet Butts
Plantation

TF9

BELLAPORT RD

Greenacre

BEARSTONE RD

THE
CROFT

Bellaport
Lodge
Farm

Cemy

River Tern

Brand Hall
Farm

CHURCH
FIELDS

CHURCH
WLKS

BESNICKS LA

ST CHADS WAY

NAPLEY DR

PH

GRIFFIN
CL

CHAPEL LA

CHURCH MDW

Brook
Farm

Napley
Farm

MAIN RD

Norton-in-Hales
CE Prim Sch

Napley
Lodge

Norton in
Hales

NAPLEY RD

Brand
Hall

FORGE LA

Marlpit
Plantation

Napley
Heath

Staffordshire STREET ATLAS

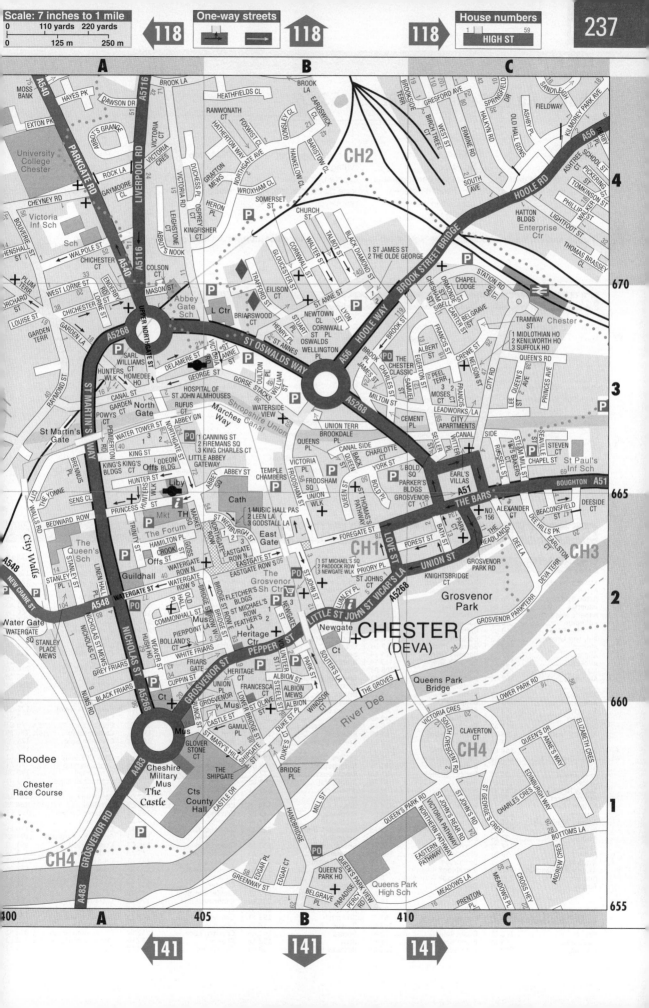

Index

Church Rd 6 Beckenham BR2..........**53** C6

Place name	Location number	Locality, town or village	Postcode district	Page and grid square
May be abbreviated on the map	Present when a number indicates the place's position in a crowded area of mapping	Shown when more than one place has the same name	District for the indexed place	Page number and grid reference for the standard mapping

Public and commercial buildings are highlighted in magenta   **Places of interest** are highlighted in blue with a star★

Abbreviations used in the index

Acad	Academy	Comm	Common	Gd	Ground	L	Leisure	Prom	Prom
App	Approach	Cott	Cottage	Gdn	Garden	La	Lane	Rd	Road
Arc	Arcade	Cres	Crescent	Gn	Green	Liby	Library	Recn	Recreation
Ave	Avenue	Cswy	Causeway	Gr	Grove	Mdw	Meadow	Ret	Retail
Bglw	Bungalow	Ct	Court	H	Hall	Meml	Memorial	Sh	Shopping
Bldg	Building	Ctr	Centre	Ho	House	Mkt	Market	Sq	Square
Bsns, Bus	Business	Ctry	Country	Hospl	Hospital	Mus	Museum	St	Street
Bvd	Boulevard	Cty	County	HQ	Headquarters	Orch	Orchard	Sta	Station
Cath	Cathedral	Dr	Drive	Hts	Heights	Pal	Palace	Terr	Terrace
Cir	Circus	Dro	Drove	Ind	Industrial	Par	Parade	TH	Town Hall
Cl	Close	Ed	Education	Inst	Institute	Pas	Passage	Univ	University
Cnr	Corner	Emb	Embankment	Int	International	Pk	Park	Wk, Wlk	Walk
Coll	College	Est	Estate	Intc	Interchange	Pl	Place	Wr	Water
Com	Community	Ex	Exhibition	Junc	Junction	Prec	Precinct	Yd	Yard

Index of localities, towns and villages

A

Abbot's Meads 118 A4
Acton 204 A7
Acton Bridge 76 E3
Adderley 235 B4
Adder's Moss 85 F6
Adlington 62 D5
Alderley Edge 60 C2
Aldersey Green 182 C6
Aldford 163 F3
Allgreave 137 C3
Allostock 106 E3
Alport 226 B1
Alpraham 169 C4
Alsager 193 E5
Altrincham 31 C8
Alvanley 73 C1
Anderton 78 D4
Antrobus 53 C4
Appleton 13 A2
Appleton Park 26 D5
Appleton Thorn 27 B4
Arclid 154 B1
Arclid Green 176 A8
Arley 54 C7
Arley Green 54 E6
Ashley 31 E5
Ashley Heath 31 E8
Ashton Hayes 121 F7
Ashton's Green 1 B3
Astbury 178 B7
Astbury Marsh 156 B1
Astle 109 D8
Astmoor 23 E3
Aston Nantwich 217 C2
Aston Runcorn 50 D1
Aston Heath 50 E2
Aston juxta Mondrum ..188 E6
Audlem 230 B4
Audley 209 D2

B

Bache 118 C5
Backford 95 A4
Baddiley 203 B1

Balderton 140 C1
Ball o' Ditton 12 E2
Balterley 208 C1
Balterley Green 208 C2
Balterley Heath 207 F1
Bank Heath 3 A8
Bank Quay 15 F4
Barbridge 187 C6
Barnett Brook 228 E5
Barnhill 183 B1
Barnton 78 C4
Barrets Green 169 D3
Barrows Green 189 F8
Barrow's Green 13 E4
Barthomley 208 D5
Barton 181 F1
Basford 206 E5
Bate Heath 54 F3
Bath Vale 157 B3
Bebington 43 A7
Beechwood 49 E5
Beeston 168 A2
Beeston-brook 168 C5
Belgrave 162 E6
Bell o' th' Hill 225 D7
Betchton Heath 175 E5
Betley 221 F8
Betley Common 221 E6
Bewsey 15 F8
Bickerton 199 E6
Bickley Moss 215 B7
Bickley Town 214 E6
Bicklewood 214 C4
Biddulph 179 B2
Biddulph Common 179 F8
Bignall End 209 F3
Birchall Moss 219 E1
Birch Heath 168 B8
Birchwood 9 E5
Blackbrook Haydock 1 A7
Blackbrook Warrington ..8 E2
Blacon 117 F3
Blakenhall 221 A4
Bold Heath 13 E7
Bollington 88 B7
Bollington Cross 87 F7
Boon Hill 209 F1
Booth Bank 30 B7
Booth Green 62 F7
Boothsdale 122 E3

Booth's Hill 18 C2
Boots Green 107 B5
Bosley 158 D8
Bostock Green 127 C7
Boughton 119 A2
Boughton Heath 142 A8
Bradeley Green 225 F6
Bradfield Green 172 E3
Bradley Green 225 A8
Bradley Mount 87 B7
Bradwall Green 153 B3
Bramhall 35 D8
Brassey Green 167 D6
Bratt's Bank 101 B5
Brereton Green 153 F5
Brereton Heath 154 F6
Bretton 139 E4
Bridgemere 231 F8
Bridgemont 39 E2
Bridge Trafford 97 A3
Brindley 202 E7
Brindley Green 153 E2
Broadoak 162 B1
Broken Cross Macclesfield
...................111 E8
Broken Cross Northwich .104 E7
Brookhouse 88 D3
Brookhouse Green 177 A7
Brookhurst 43 C5
Brooklands 225 E1
Brookvale 50 B5
Broom Bank 144 B8
Broomedge 19 C1
Broomhall 217 F4
Broomhall Green 217 E3
Broomhill 120 F8
Broughton 139 B4
Brownedge 154 A3
Brown Heath 143 B6
Brownhill 147 B6
Brown Knowl 199 C8
Brownlow 177 E7
Brownlow Heath 177 E5
Brown Moss 231 B7
Brown's Bank 229 D2
Broxton 183 A1
Bruche 16 F7
Bruera 164 D6
Bryn 102 A6
Bucklow Hill 30 C3

Buckoak 99 A5
Buddileigh 221 F7
Budworth Heath 54 A1
Buerton 230 E4
Buglawton 157 A4
Bulkeley 184 E2
Bunbury 185 F8
Bunbury Commons 169 A2
Bunbury Heath 185 D8
Bunsley Bank 230 C5
Burland 203 C7
Burland Lower Green ..203 A7
Burland Upper Green ..203 B8
Burleydam 228 B1
Burton Duddon 144 F4
Burton Neston 67 D1
Burton Green 161 D1
Burtonwood 6 E6
Burwardsley 184 B5
Butley Town 87 C8
Butters Green 210 A2
Butt Green 205 B3
Butt Lane 194 D1
Byley 129 A7

C

Cadishead 11 E5
Caldecott Green 197 C4
Calrofold 88 C2
Calveley 169 E2
Capenhurst 94 A8
Castlefields 23 F2
Castletown 197 D3
Chapel End 230 D3
Cheadle Hulme 35 A8
Checkley 221 C1
Checkley Green 232 B8
Chelford 84 B2
Chester 237 B2
Childer Thornton 69 B8
Cholmondeston 170 F4
Chorley 202 B2
Chorley Green 202 A3
Chorlton 207 B1
Chorlton Lane 212 B4
Chowley 182 F5
Christleton 142 F8

Church Green 18 E2
Church Hill 149 E7
Church Lawton 194 C3
Church Minshull 172 A6
Churton 180 E5
Cinnamon Brow 8 F4
Clark Green 63 A3
Clifton 49 D4
Clive 150 C8
Clive Green 150 D6
Clotton 145 D4
Cloud Side 157 F4
Clough Hall 210 F8
Clutton 182 D1
Coalpit Hill 210 C8
Cobbs 26 E8
Cobscot 235 E3
Coddington 182 A3
Coldharbour 164 F5
Cold Moss Heath 175 D5
Collins Green 1 E1
Comberbach 78 C7
Commonside 100 B8
Common Side 124 D3
Congleton 157 A4
Connah's Quay 91 B2
Cooksongreen 76 A1
Coppenhall 190 D7
Coppenhall Moss 173 D1
Copthorne 229 F4
Cotebrook 147 A8
Cox Bank 234 F8
Crabtree Garden 101 C1
Cranage 130 A6
Crewe 190 E5
Crewe-by-Farndon 197 A7
Crewe Green 191 B3
Croft 9 B4
Cronton 12 D5
Cross Lane 172 D6
Cross Town 57 B2
Croughton 95 F5
Crowton 76 C1
Crow Wood 13 D3
Croxton Green 201 B6
Cuckoo's Nest 162 E5
Cuddington 101 F4
Cuddington Green 212 B1
Cuddington Heath 212 E2
Cuerdley Cross 14 A2

Culcheth 4 E3
Culcheth Carrs 4 E6
Curzon Park 141 B7

D

Dales Green 195 C5
Danebank 38 E5
Danebridge 160 B7
Dane in Shaw 179 C8
Daresbury 25 B2
Daresbury Delph 25 B1
Davenham 104 C4
Davenport 154 E7
Davenport Green 59 F3
Day Green 192 F8
Dean Row 60 F8
Delamere 123 D6
Delamere Park 101 C5
Derbyshire Hill 1 A2
Diglake 210 A3
Disley 38 C5
Ditton 22 C8
Ditton Marsh 22 D6
Dodleston 162 A7
Dones Green 77 B8
Dove Bank 195 A2
Drury Lane 223 D2
Duckington 199 C4
Duddon 145 A6
Duddon Heath 144 E7
Dudlow's Green 26 C4
Dukesfield 22 E3
Dunham Heath 98 A4
Dunham-on-the-Hill 97 E5
Dunham Town 20 B4
Dunham Woodhouses 20 B4
Dunkirk 94 E6
Dutton 51 A4

E

Earlestown 2 B2
Eastham 43 F7
Eastham Ferry 44 B8
Eaton Congleton 157 A8
Eaton Tarporley 147 B4
Ebnal 213 D6
Eccleston 141 E1
Edge Green 199 B2
Egerton Green 200 C5
Ellesmere Port 70 A7
Elton .72 C3
Elworth 174 E6
Englesea-brook 208 A4
Ettiley Heath 174 C6

F

Faddiley 202 D7
Faddiley Bank 202 C6
Fanshawe 110 C4
Farndon 180 F2
Farnworth 13 A3
Fearnhead 9 B2
Fernilee 65 E1
Finney Green 34 E2
Fivecrosses 74 D5
Flint/Y Fflint 91 A3
Flookersbrook 118 E4
Fourlane-ends 63 A8
Four Lane Ends 168 D7
Fourlanes Ends 176 E4
Fowley Common 5 B5
Foxley 209 D7
Foxwist Green 125 F6
Frandley 53 A4
Frodsham 74 D7
Frodsham Marsh 48 E2
Fuller's Moor 183 D1
Fulshaw Park 60 B5
Furness Vale 39 C3

G

Gallantry Bank 200 A8
Gatesheath 165 E5
Gauntons Bank 215 E4
Gawsworth 134 E8
Gayton 41 B6
Gemini .7 D3
Gibb Hill 53 D1
Gillbent 34 F6
Gillow Heath 179 C2
Ginclough 88 A6
Glazebrook 11 B6
Glazebury 5 B7
Gleadsmoss 132 B6
Glebe Green 149 C6
Golborne 3 B7
Golly .161 B1
Goostrey 107 D1
Gorse Covert 10 B5
Gorstage 102 C6
Gorstella 140 A1

Gorstyhill 207 E2
Gosland Green 169 B1
Gowhole 39 E4
Gradeley Green 202 F5
Grange Runcorn 49 D7
Grange Warrington 17 E8
Grappenhall 17 A1
Grappenhall Heys 27 A8
Gravel 127 A1
Great Barrow 120 E6
Great Budworth 79 A7
Great Sankey 15 A6
Great Sutton 69 D3
Greenbank 103 C7
Greendale 86 E7
Greenlooms 143 F4
Grindley Brook 225 C3
Guilden Sutton 119 E5
Gurnett 112 F4

H

Hack Green 218 D8
Hague Bar 38 F8
Hale Altrincham 32 B8
Hale Speke 21 D1
Hale Bank 22 A4
Hale Barns 32 D8
Hale Heath 21 A1
Halewood Village 21 A8
Hall Green Kidsgrove 194 E5
Hall Green Whitchurch 224 E1
Hallowsgate 122 C4
Hallwood Park 49 F6
Halton Brook 23 D1
Halton Lodge 49 D7
Halton Moss 24 F6
Halton View 13 C1
Halton Village 49 F8
Hampton Green 214 B7
Hampton Heath 213 E7
Handbridge 141 E7
Handforth 34 C4
Hand Green 168 B6
Handley 182 D8
Hankelow 230 C7
Hapsford 72 E1
Harden Park 60 A3
Harding's Wood 194 E2
Hargrave 144 A4
Harriseahead 195 E4
Hartford 103 C4
Hartfordbeach 103 B6
Harthill 183 E3
Haslington 191 D4
Hassall 192 C7
Hassall Green 176 A1
Hatchmere 100 D4
Hatherton 219 E3
Hatton 26 A2
Hatton Heath 143 B1
Haughton 186 C6
Haydock 1 D6
Haymoor Green 205 E2
Heald Green 34 B8
Heath .49 B6
Heatley 19 C5
Heaton 159 E2
Hebden Green 148 F7
Helsby 73 C3
Henbury 111 B8
Henfold 113 A8
Hetherson Green 214 D8
Hidebank 39 C8
High Carr 210 F3
Higher Bunbury 168 F1
Higher Burwardsley 184 C5
Higher Carden 198 D7
Higher Disley 38 D5
Higherfence 113 A8
Higher Hurdsfield 88 B2
Higher Kinnerton 161 B8
Higher Marston 79 C6
Higher Poynton 37 B2
Higher Runcorn 23 A1
Higher Shurlach 104 E6
Higher Walton 25 F7
Higher Whitley 52 D5
Higher Wincham 79 F4
Higher Wych 224 D4
Highlane 134 C6
High Lane 37 D8
High Lee 39 B8
High Legh 29 B5
High Warren 26 C6
Hillcliffe 26 C8
Hilltop 60 B8
Hobb Hill 198 D3
Hockley 37 A2
Hodgehill 132 E8
Hollinfare 11 A3
Hollin Green 202 F6
Hollins 210 E8
Hollinsgreen 152 D4
Hollins Green 11 B2
Hollins-Lane 226 E6
Hollyhurst 227 A5
Holmes Chapel 130 C4
Holt 196 D6
Holtridge 215 E6
Honkley 161 C3

Hood Manor 15 D5
Hoofield 145 A2
Hoo Green 29 F2
Hoole .119 A3
Hoole Bank 119 C7
Hoole Park 118 F3
Hooton 44 A1
Hooton Park 44 C4
Hope Green 36 C1
Horton Green 212 A8
Hough Alderley Edge 60 D1
Hough Crewe 206 F3
Hough Green 12 B2
Houghton Green 8 E4
Howbeck Bank 219 E8
Howley 16 D5
Hulme 8 B3
Hulme Walfield 156 B7
Hulseheath 30 A4
Hunsterson 220 B1
Huntington 142 A5
Hurdsfield 87 E2
Hurst .179 F3
Huxley 166 F8

I

Illidge Green 154 C4
Ince 72 A6
Inchyra 11 F7
Iscoyed 196 C1

J

Jodrell Bank 108 D2

K

Keckwick 25 A3
Kelsall 122 C4
Kelsterton 91 B2
Kermincham Heath 131 E5
Kerridge 88 A6
Kerridge-end 88 C3
Kettleshulme 64 F4
Key Green 157 E4
Kidnal 212 E8
Kidsgrove 195 B1
Kingsley 75 C2
Kingsmead 103 E5
Kingsway 23 A8
Kingswood Frodsham 74 C1
Kingswood Warrington 7 B2
Kinnerton Green 161 B7
Kinsey Heath 230 B1
Kitt's Moss 35 D6
Knolls Green 58 E3
Knotbury 138 F5
Knutsford 57 A3

L

Lacey Green 34 B1
Lach Dennis 105 D5
Lache .140 F5
Lane Ends Crewe 173 D3
Lane Ends Disley 38 E4
Lane Head 3 E6
Langley 113 C3
Larden Green 202 D4
Latchford 16 D3
Lavister 162 C1
Lawton-gate 194 A4
Lawton Heath 193 E6
Lawton Heath End 193 C6
Lea Green 172 A8
Ledsham 68 F2
Leftwich 104 B5
Leightwood Green 229 B3
Lindow 59 C4
Lindow End 59 B2
Lindow Moss 59 D7
Lingley Green 14 C7
Little Barrow 97 D1
Little Bollington 20 B2
Little Budworth 147 F7
Little Heath 230 A5
Little Leigh 77 C4
Little-moss 194 E6
Little Neston 66 D6
Littler .126 A2
Little Stanney 70 E1
Little Sutton 69 B5
Littleton 119 E1
Little Town 4 C1
Locking Stumps 9 C3
Longbarn 9 B1
Longford 8 B1
Long Green 97 F1
Longhill 230 E5
Longmoss 86 C1
Lostock Gralam 80 A3
Lostock Green 105 B8

Lowcross Hill 198 D3
Lower Bunbury 185 E7
Lower Carden 198 C6
Lower Heath 156 B5
Lowerhouse 87 E8
Lower House 22 E8
Lower Kinnerton 139 D1
Lower Peover 81 E1
Lower Pexhill 111 A4
Lower Stretton 52 F8
Lower Threapwood 222 F6
Lower Walton 26 A8
Lower Whitley 52 D3
Lower Withington 109 A1
Lower Wych 224 B6
Low Leighton 39 D8
Lowton .3 E8
Lowton Common 4 A8
Lowton Heath 3 C6
Lowton St Mary's 3 C7
Lugsdale 23 C7
Lunts Heath 13 C5
Lyme Green 112 D2
Lymm 18 E4

M

Macclesfield 112 B4
Macclesfield Forest 114 D5
Malkin's Bank 175 C3
Malpas 213 B2
Manley 99 A4
Manor Park Middlewich . . .151 B7
Manor Park Runcorn 24 B3
Marbury 226 D8
Marley Green 227 C8
Marshfield Bank 189 C4
Marsh Green Biddulph 179 D3
Marsh Green Frodsham 74 A8
Marston 79 B4
Marthall 83 E4
Martin's Ash 227 B2
Martinscroft 17 F7
Martin's Moss 176 E6
Marton 133 B5
Marton Green 125 C4
Martonsands 125 F4
Maw Green 190 E7
Meadowbank 126 E5
Megacre 210 A1
Mere 56 B8
Mere Heath 104 A1
Mickle Trafford 119 E8
Middlewich 128 D3
Middlewood 37 C5
Midway 36 D2
Milend 209 C5
Milners Heath 143 C2
Milton Green 165 C2
Minshull Vernon 172 E5
Mobberley 57 F7
Moblake 230 D4
Mollington 94 E2
Monks Heath 85 A1
Moore .25 B6
Moorside 65 C7
Morley .33 C2
Morley Common 15 F1
Morley Green 33 C1
Moss Bank 23 B8
Mossbrow 19 E7
Mossend 154 E1
Moss End 54 C2
Moss Houses 111 F2
Moss Lane 112 B4
Mossley 179 A8
Moss Nook 33 F7
Moston 95 C1
Moston Green 174 B8
Mottram St Andrew 61 B2
Mouldsworth 98 F2
Moulton 126 E7
Mount Pleasant Kidsgrove
. . . . .195 B6
Mount Pleasant Winsford
. . . . .149 B6
Mow Cop 195 C7
Murdishaw 50 D7

N

Nantwich 204 D6
Ness 67 B4
Ness Holt 66 F5
Neston 66 C7
Nether Alderley 85 A6
Nether Tabley 80 F8
Netherton 74 A6
New Boston 1 E7
Newcastle-under-Lyme
. . . . .210 D3
Newchapel 195 B2
New End Lane 4 A2
Newfield 172 E6
New Horwich 65 E6
New Mills 39 D7
New Pale 99 C6
Newsbank 132 F1
Newton Chester 118 F5

Newton Frodsham 74 D3
Newton Tattenhall 166 E4
Newtonia 128 B1
Newton-le-Willows 2 B2
Newtown Frodsham 49 D1
Newtown New Mills 39 B6
Newtown Poynton 37 A3
Newtown Sound 217 E4
Newtown Widnes 23 A6
New Woodhouses 227 E1
Nick i' th' Hill 179 B4
No Man's Heath 214 B4
Norbury 215 D4
Norbury Common 215 C6
Norcott Brook 52 C6
Norley 100 F6
Norley Bank 101 A6
North Florida 1 D8
North Rode 134 E2
Northwich 103 D8
Norton in Hales 236 C1
Nova Scotia 125 C6

O

Oakenbank 88 D8
Oakgrove 135 D7
Oakhanger 192 C2
Oakmere 124 A7
Oakwood 9 F4
Occlestone Green 151 B2
Oglet 46 D8
Old Boston 2 A8
Oldcastle Heath 223 F8
Old Hall 15 C8
Old Moss 144 D7
Old Woodhouses 227 C2
Ollerton 82 F6
Onneley 232 F3
Orford 8 D2
Oscroft 121 E2
Oughtrington 19 C4
Over 149 B7
Over Knutsford 57 C1
Over Leigh 65 F6
Over Peover 83 A1
Overpool 69 F7
Over Tabley 56 A5
Overton 74 C7

P

Packmoor 195 F1
Paddington 17 A8
Paddockhill 59 A4
Padgate 8 F1
Palace Fields 50 A6
Pandy 222 A3
Paradise Green 171 E6
Park End 209 A4
Parkgate Chelford 108 B8
Parkgate Disley 38 A5
Parkgate Neston 41 C1
Partington 11 F4
Peacock Hay 210 F4
Peckforton 184 F5
Penketh 14 D4
Peover Heath 108 C8
Pewterspear 26 E4
Pickmere 80 A7
Picton .96 C3
Pinsley Green 216 D2
Piper's Ash 119 D4
Plemstall 97 A1
Plumley 81 A3
Plumley Moor 81 C2
Poolehill 188 A2
Poolfold 179 F4
Pot Bank 179 A4
Pott Shrigley 63 D3
Poulton 163 B2
Pownall Green 35 E6
Pownall Park 59 F7
Poynton 36 E4
Prestbury 87 B7
Preston Brook 50 F5
Preston on the Hill 51 A6
Primrose Hill 28 C6
Puddinglake 129 B8
Puddington 92 F8
Pulford 162 D3

Q

Quarrybank 146 C8
Queen's Park 141 F8
Quoisley 226 B8

R

Raby 42 C4
Raby Mere 43 B7
Radmore Green 186 E3
Radnor 155 E6
Radway Green 192 F1

Rainow 88 D5
Ravensclough 101 E3
Ravensmoor 203 E2
Rease Heath 188 C2
Red Bull 194 E3
Red Street 210 E3
Rhuddall Heath 146 E1
Ridgwardine 235 E1
Ridleywood 196 C3
Risley 9 E6
Rocksavage 49 B4
Rodeheath 134 B3
Rode Heath 193 E7
Roodee 141 B8
Rostherne 30 E4
Roughhill 140 E1
Rowleyhill 181 B1
Rowlinson's Green 28 C5
Row-of-trees 59 D3
Rowton 142 E5
Royal's Green 228 E2
Rudheath 104 D6
Rudheath Woods 106 E2
Ruloe 101 D7
Runcorn 23 C1
Rushgreen 19 A4
Rushton 147 C5
Rushton Spencer 159 B2
Rye Hills 209 E1

S

Saighton 142 E1
St Johns Gardens 149 B8
Salterswall 125 F3
Saltney 140 D6
Sandbach 175 B5
Sandbach Heath 175 D6
Sandiway 102 B3
Sandlow Green 131 B1
Sandycroft 116 B2
Sankey Bridges 15 C4
Saughall 94 B1
Scholar Green 194 E8
School Green 149 C5
Sealand 116 E6
Shavington 206 C5
Shaw Heath 57 D3
Shell Green 13 E1
Shocklach 211 D7
Shocklach Green 211 C7
Shotwick 93 B4
Shraleybrook 209 A1
Siddington 110 A3
Siddington Heath ...109 E1
Simm's Cross 23 B7
Skellorn Green 62 E8

Slaughter Hill 191 D3
Smallwood 176 E5
Smethwick Green 154 F4
Smith's Green 208 B7
Smithy Green Bramhall ..35 B7
Smithy Green Knutsford ..81 E2
Snow Hill 204 D6
Somerford 154 F7
Sound 217 F5
Sound Heath 217 E5
Spen Green 177 B6
Sproston Green 129 C2
Spurstow 185 D6
Stamford Bridge ...120 D4
Stanley Bank 1 A7
Stanley Green 34 E6
Stanlow 71 B5
Stapeley 219 D8
Stoak 96 A7
Stockton Heath 16 D1
Stoke Bank 187 C5
Stoneley Green 203 D4
Stowford 207 B8
Stretton 197 F6
Stretton 26 E2
Stud Green 152 C1
Styal 33 F4
Styal Green 34 A3
Sutton Green 69 C3
Sutton Lane Ends ..112 F2
Sutton Weaver 50 B3
Swanbach 229 E1
Swan Green 106 D8
Swanley 203 C5
Swanwick Green ...215 C4
Swettenham 131 E3
Swettenham Heath ..132 B3
Sworton Heath 28 E5
Sydney 191 A5

T

Tabley Hill 56 D3
Talke 210 C7
Talke Pits 210 E5
Tallarn Green/Tallwrn
  Green 222 E5
Tarporley 146 C1
Tarvin 121 C3
Tarvin Sands 121 C4
Tattenhall 166 B1
Tatton Dale 30 E1
Taxal 65 D4
The Bank 195 B7
The Barony 204 F6
Thelwall 17 E3
The Quarry 209 C2

The Rookery 195 C3
The Valley 190 A3
Thorns Green 32 C5
Thornton Hough 42 A7
Thornton-le-Moors ..71 F1
Threapwood 222 F7
Thurlwood 193 E7
Tilston 198 B3
Tilstone Bank 168 F4
Tilstone Fearnall ..168 F6
Timbersbrook 157 E2
Tiverton 168 C6
Torr Top 39 C8
Town End 12 C6
Town Fields 149 D7
Town of Lowton ...3 B5
Trap Street 132 C5
Twemlow Green ...131 A5
Twiss Green 4 E4
Two Mills 93 E8
Tytherington 87 C3

U

Upper Threapwood 222 F7
Upton Chester 118 D6
Upton Widnes 12 C4
Upton Heath 118 F8
Upton Rocks 12 E4
Utkinton 146 B7

V

Vicarscross 119 E2
Vulcan Village 7 C8

W

Wades Green 171 F5
Wain Lee 195 F4
Walgherton 220 B6
Walkers Green 152 D7
Walley's Green 172 E7
Warburton 19 C8
Warburton Green ..32 D6
Wardle 187 C7
Wardsend 37 A1
Wargrave 2 D3
Warmingham 173 D7
Warren 111 D1
Warrington 16 E6
Wash End 4 C8
Waverton 143 B4

Way's Green 149 E8
Weaverham 77 C2
Weetwood Common ...122 C2
Wells Green 205 F8
Wereton 209 C1
Wervin 96 A4
West Bank 23 A4
Westbrook Centre ...7 B1
West Heath Betley ..221 E8
West Heath Congleton ..156 A4
Westminster Park ...141 B6
Weston Crewe 207 C5
Weston Macclesfield ..111 F8
Weston Runcorn 48 F6
Weston Point 48 D7
Westy 16 F5
Wettenhall 170 F7
Wettenhall Green ..170 F6
Whaley Bridge 65 D7
Wharton 127 A2
Wharton Green 127 B4
Wheelock 174 F4
Wheelock Heath ...192 A8
Whirley Grove 86 D3
Whisterfield 109 D3
Whitby 70 A4
Whitchurch 226 A1
Whitecross 15 E6
Whitegate 126 A7
White Hill 195 B2
Whiteley Green ...62 E2
Whitley Reed 53 D8
Widnes 22 E7
Wigshaw 4 D2
Wildboarclough ...137 E6
Wilderspool 16 C2
Wilkesley 233 F7
Willaston Ellesmere Port ..68 A8
Willaston Nantwich ..205 C5
Willington Corner ..122 E2
Willow Green 77 B5
Wilmslow 60 C5
Wilmslow Park 60 D7
Wimboldsley 150 F4
Wimbolds Trafford ..96 F6
Wincham 79 C3
Wincle 160 A7
Windle Hill 67 C7
Windmill Hill 24 C1
Windyharbour 109 D1
Winnington 78 D1
Winsford 126 E2
Winterley 191 F7
Winwick 8 A6
Winwick Quay 8 A3
Wirswall 226 A5
Wistaston 205 D8
Wistaston Green ..189 D2
Withington Green ..108 E3

Wolverham 70 D4
Woodbank 93 F6
Woodend 38 E8
Woodford 35 E2
Woodhey Green ...202 B6
Woodhouse-end ...135 C8
Woodhouse Green ..158 D2
Woodhouse Park ...33 F8
Woodhouses 73 E4
Wood Lane 210 A1
Woodshutts 194 F1
Woodworth Green ..186 B8
Woolfall 230 E6
Woolstanwood 189 E3
Woolston 17 C8
Woore 232 B1
Worleston 188 F5
Worthenbury 211 A1
Wrenbury 216 F4
Wrenbury Frith ..216 C6
Wrenbury Heath ..217 B5
Wright's Green ..27 A6
Wybunbury 220 A8

Y
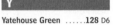

Yatehouse Green 128 D6

2

2nd Ave CW12 . . . . .156 A4

3

3rd Ave CW12 . . . . .156 A4

1

1875 Bakers Ct CH1,
CH3 . . . . .237 C3

A

Aarons Dr ST7 . . . . .209 F2
Abberley Hall SK9 . . . . .84 D7
Abbey Cl Croft WA3 . . . . .9 A8
Whitegate CW8 . . . . .126 A7
Widnes WA8 . . . . .22 C8
Winsford CW7 . . . . .149 D5
Abbey Ct SK12 . . . . .36 D3
Abbey Fields CW2 . . . . .205 E8
Abbey Gate Coll CH3 . . . . . .164 E8
Abbey Gate Sch CH2 . . . . . .237 A3
Abbey Gn CH1 . . . . .237 A3
Abbey Hey WA7 . . . . .50 F4
Abbey La Delamere CW8 . . .123 E5
Hartford CW8 . . . . .103 B4
Abbey Mill SK10 . . . . .87 A6
Abbey Pl WA7 . . . . .190 D6
Haydock WA11 . . . . .1 E7
Macclesfield SK10 . . . . .87 B2
Sandbach CW11 . . . . .174 E6
Widnes WA8 . . . . .22 C8
Abbey Sq CH1 . . . . .237 B3
Abbey St CH1 . . . . .237 B3
Abbey Way CW8 . . . . .103 B4
Abbeydale CW2 . . . . .207 C2
Abbeyfield Ho
2 Crewe CW2 . . . . .190 D2
Ellesmere Port CH65 . . . . . . .70 A3
Abbeyfields CW11 . . . . .174 F5
Abbeyway N WA11 . . . . .2 A7
Abbeyway S WA11 . . . . .2 A7
Abbot's Dr CH2 . . . . .118 C4
Abbot's Grange CH2 . . . . . .237 A4
Abbot's Nook CH2 . . . . .237 A4
Abbot's Terr CH1 . . . . .118 B5
Abbots Cl SK10 . . . . .87 B2
Abbots Ct CH2 . . . . .118 C4
Abbots Knoll CH2 . . . . .118 C4
Abbots Mews CH65 . . . . .70 B6
Abbots Pk CH2 . . . . .118 C4
Abbots Way
Hartford CW8 . . . . .103 B4
Neston CH64 . . . . .41 E1
Abbotsbury Cl
Poynton SK12 . . . . .36 D5
Wistaston CW2 . . . . .206 B8
Abbotsfield Cl WA4 . . . . .26 E6
Abbotsmere Cl CW8 . . . . . .101 F2
Abbott's Cl CW12 . . . . .179 B8
Abbotts Cl Runcorn WA7 . . .49 A8
Waverton CH3 . . . . .143 B5
Abbotts Rd CH3 . . . . .143 B5
Abbotts Way CW7 . . . . .126 B2
Aberdare Cl WA5 . . . . .7 C1
Aberdaron Dr CH1 . . . . . . .117 E3
Aberdeen Wlk SK10 . . . . . . .86 F3
Aberfeldy Cl CW4 . . . . .130 B2
Abingdon Ave WA1 . . . . .17 E7
Abingdon **9** SK11 . . . . . .111 F8
Abingdon Cres **4** CH4 . . . .140 F6
Abington Rd CW1 . . . . .190 D6
Abington Wlk WA7 . . . . .50 C5
Abstone Cl WA1 . . . . .17 B7
Acacia Ave
Knutsford WA16 . . . . .56 E1
Warrington WA1 . . . . .17 D7
Widnes WA8 . . . . .13 B3
Wilmslow SK9 . . . . .59 F5
Acacia Cl CW1 . . . . .72 C3
Acacia Cres CW2 . . . . .190 E6
Acacia Dr
Ellesmere Port CH66 . . . . . . .69 F1
Sandbach CW11 . . . . .174 E7
Acacia Gdns ST7 . . . . .195 C3
Acacia Gr WA7 . . . . .49 C6
Acacia St WA12 . . . . .1 F4
Academy Pl **7** WA1 . . . . . .16 B5
Academy St WA1 . . . . .16 B5
Academy Way WA1 . . . . .16 B5
Acer Ave CW1 . . . . .190 E7
Achilles Ave WA2 . . . . .8 A2
Achilles Ct WA7 . . . . .24 A2
Ack La E SK7 . . . . .35 D7
Ack La W SK8 . . . . .35 C7
Ackerley Cl WA2 . . . . .8 F3
Ackers La WA4 . . . . .16 E1
Ackers Rd WA4 . . . . .16 E2
Ackersley Ct SK8 . . . . .35 B8
Acorn Bank Cl CW2 . . . . . .206 B7
Acorn Cl Cuddington CW8 . .101 F2
Winsford CW7 . . . . .150 A8
Acorn Dr CH65 . . . . .70 B1
Acorn La CW12 . . . . .157 C3
Acorn St WA12 . . . . .2 D3
Acorn Terr SK22 . . . . .39 B6
Acorns Prim Sch The
CH65 . . . . .69 F5
Acre Gn L26 . . . . .21 A6
Acre La Bebington CH62 . .43 D8

Acre La continued
Cheadle Hulme SK8 . . . . . . .35 C6
Heswall CH60 . . . . .41 C8
Acre Rd CH66 . . . . .69 D5
Acreage The
Bunbury CW6 . . . . .185 E8
Goostrey CW4 . . . . .107 E1
Acrefield Rd WA8 . . . . .12 B1
Acres Cres WA6 . . . . .75 B2
Acres La CH2 . . . . .119 A8
Acresfield Com Prim Sch
CH2 . . . . .118 B4
Acton CW11 . . . . .1 C6
Acton Ave CW4 . . . . .26 D3
Acton Bridge Sta CW8 . . . . .76 F1
Acton CE Prim Sch
CW5 . . . . .204 A7
Acton Cl WA11 . . . . .1 C6
Acton La CW8 . . . . .76 F4
Acton Pl SK11 . . . . .111 F8
Acton Rd Burtonwood WA5 . . .6 C6
Crewe CW2 . . . . .189 D4
Acton Way ST7 . . . . .193 D6
Adam Ave
Ellesmere Port CH66 . . . . . . .69 D3
Ellesmere Port,Great Sutton
CH66 . . . . .69 C4
Adam Cl CH66 . . . . .69 D4
Adam St WA2 . . . . .16 C7
Adams Cl
Newton-le-W WA12 . . . . .2 D2
Poynton SK12 . . . . .36 E2
Adams Hill WA16 . . . . .57 A1
Adamson Ct WA4 . . . . .17 B2
Adamson St WA4 . . . . .16 B3
Adaston Ave CH62 . . . . .43 F4
Adder Hill CH3 . . . . .142 B7
Adderley CE Prim Sch
TF9 . . . . .234 F5
Adderley Cl WA7 . . . . .23 C1
Adderley Rd TF9 . . . . .235 A2
Addingham Ave WA8 . . . . . .22 C7
Addison Cl CW2 . . . . .205 F8
Addison Sq WA8 . . . . .13 A1
Adela Rd WA7 . . . . .22 F2
Adelaide Ct **4** WA3 . . . . . .23 A7
Bramhall SK7 . . . . .35 F5
Adelaide Sch CW1 . . . . .190 C5
Adelaide St Crewe CW1 . . . .190 C6
Macclesfield SK10 . . . . .87 E1
Adey Rd WA13 . . . . .19 A5
Adfalent La CH64 . . . . .68 A7
Adlington Cl SK12 . . . . .36 F2
Adlington Ct WA3 . . . . .9 F6
Adlington Dr
Northwich CW9 . . . . .104 A5
Sandbach CW11 . . . . .175 C7
Adlington Est SK10 . . . . .36 C1
Adlington Hall Mews
SK10 . . . . .62 B5
Adlington Pk SK10 . . . . .36 C1
Adlington Prim Sch SK10 . .62 E5
Adlington Rd
Bollington SK10 . . . . .63 A1
Crewe CW2 . . . . .189 F3
Runcorn WA7 . . . . .24 D2
Wilmslow SK9 . . . . .60 E7
Adlington St SK10 . . . . .112 C8
Adlington Sta SK10 . . . . .62 C5
Admirals Rd WA3 . . . . .9 F4
Adshead Ct SK10 . . . . .88 B7
Adwell Cl WA3 . . . . .4 A8
Afton WA8 . . . . .12 A2
Agden Brow WA13 . . . . .19 E1
Agden Brow Pk
Broomedge WA13 . . . . .19 D1
Lymm WA13 . . . . .29 D8
Agden House La SY13 . . . .225 A5
Agden La
Broomedge WA13 . . . . .19 E1
Little Bollington WA13 . . . . . .29 E7
Agden Park La WA13 . . . . . .29 D8
Agecroft Rd CW9 . . . . .104 C7
Ainley Cl WA7 . . . . .50 A5
Ainscough Rd WA3 . . . . .9 E3
Ainsdale Cl
Bebington CH63 . . . . .43 C5
Bramhall SK7 . . . . .36 A7
Warrington WA5 . . . . .14 F4
Ainsworth La WA3 . . . . .76 B3
Ainsworth Rd CW8 . . . . .77 E1
Aintree Gr CH66 . . . . .69 D3
Airdrie Cl CH62 . . . . .43 D3
Aire WA8 . . . . .12 A2
Aire Cl CH65 . . . . .70 A7
Aire Pl WA7 . . . . .127 B1
Airedale Cl WA5 . . . . .14 F7
Airfield View CH5 . . . . .139 B6
Aitchison Rd CW9 . . . . .80 A2
Ajax Ave WA2 . . . . .8 B2
Akesmoor La
Biddulph ST8 . . . . .179 B1
Kidsgrove ST7 . . . . .195 F7
Alamein Cres WA2 . . . . .16 C7
Alamein Dr CW7 . . . . .149 D8
Alamein Rd Barnton CW8 . . .78 A4
Chester CH2 . . . . .95 B1
Alan Dr WA15 . . . . .32 A8
Alan St CW9 . . . . .104 B8
Alban Ret Pk WA2 . . . . .8 A1
Alban St CW1 . . . . .190 C5
Albany Cres WA13 . . . . .18 D4
Albany Gdns CH66 . . . . .69 C4
Albany Gr WA13 . . . . .18 C4
Albany Rd Bramhall SK7 . . . .35 F4
Lymm WA13 . . . . .18 D4
Wilmslow SK9 . . . . .59 F5

Albany Terr **16** WA7 . . . . .23 A2
Albert Dr Neston CH64 . . . . . .66 D8
Warrington WA5 . . . . .14 D6
Albert Pl Congleton CW12 . .156 E2
Northwich CW9 . . . . .104 B8
Warrington WA4 . . . . .17 A2
2 Widnes WA8 . . . . .13 B1
Wilmslow SK9 . . . . .60 A6
Albert Row WA6 . . . . .49 A6
Albert Sq **1** WA8 . . . . .23 B8
Albert St Audley ST7 . . . . . .209 F3
Chester CH1 . . . . .237 C3
Crewe CW1 . . . . .190 C5
Irlam M44 . . . . .11 E6
Knutsford WA16 . . . . .56 F2
Macclesfield SK11 . . . . .112 C8
Nantwich CW5 . . . . .204 E6
7 Runcorn WA7 . . . . .23 A2
Albert Terr WA5 . . . . .1 E1
Albion Ct CW12 . . . . .156 E2
Albion Mews CH1 . . . . .237 B2
Albion Pk WA3 . . . . .5 C7
Albion Pl CH1 . . . . .237 B1
Albion Rd New Mills SK22 . . .39 B6
Northwich CW9 . . . . .79 A1
Albion St Chester CH1 . . . . .237 B2
Crewe CW2 . . . . .190 A3
Albion Wlk CW9 . . . . .79 A1
Albright Rd WA8 . . . . .22 A6
Albury Cl WA11 . . . . .1 D7
Alcock St WA7 . . . . .23 A3
Alconbury Cl WA5 . . . . .15 B6
Alcott Pl WA2 . . . . .8 A6
Aldcliffe WA3 . . . . .3 B8
Aldelyme Ct CW3 . . . . .229 F4
Alder Ave Poynton SK12 . . . .36 F3
Widnes WA8 . . . . .13 B3
Alder Cl SK8 . . . . .34 D8
Alder Cres CW2 . . . . .16 C8
Alder Ct SK10 . . . . .87 E5
Alder Dr CH66 . . . . .69 F1
Alder Gr CH2 . . . . .119 B4
Alder La
Burtonwood WA2,WA5 . . . . . .7 C7
Cronin WA8,L35 . . . . .12 A5
Frodsham WA6,WA7 . . . . . . .48 D3
Warrington WA2 . . . . .16 B8
Alder Rd Golborne WA3 . . . . .3 F8
Warrington WA1 . . . . .17 D7
Weaverham WA8 . . . . .102 D8
Alder Rise SK23 . . . . .65 D8
Alder Root La WA2 . . . . .7 F6
Alder St WA12 . . . . .2 C3
Alder Wood Ave L24 . . . . . . .21 A3
Alderbank Rd WA5 . . . . .15 A6
Alderdale Dr SK6 . . . . .37 E7
Alderdale Gr SK9 . . . . .59 E5
Alderfield Dr L24 . . . . .21 A3
Alderhay La ST7 . . . . .195 C4
Alderley Ave CW9 . . . . .3 D7
Alderley Cl
Hazel Grove SK7 . . . . .36 F8
Poynton SK12 . . . . .36 F2
Sandbach CW11 . . . . .175 C7
Alderley Edge Prim Sch
SK9 . . . . .60 A2
Alderley Edge Sch for Girls
SK9 . . . . .60 A2
Alderley Edge Sta SK9 . . . . .60 A2
Alderley Lodge SK9 . . . . .60 A5
Alderley Pl CH1 . . . . .117 E6
Alderley Rd
Alderley Edge SK10,SK9 . . . .60 A2
Chelford SK10 . . . . .84 C3
Northwich CW8 . . . . .103 E8
Prestbury SK10 . . . . .86 E3
Warrington WA4 . . . . .17 D4
Wilmslow SK9 . . . . .60 A6
Alderley Wlk **14** SK11 . . . .112 E7
Alderman Bolton Prim Sch
WA4 . . . . .16 F3
Alderney Cl
Ellesmere Port CH65 . . . . . . .70 C1
4 Macclesfield SK11 . . . .111 F8
Alderney Ho CH2 . . . . .119 B4
Alders SK9 . . . . .59 F6
Alders Green Ave SK6 . . . . . .37 F3
Alders Rd SK12 . . . . .38 A7
Alders Way SK10 . . . . .86 F6
Aldersey Cl Runcorn WA7 . . .24 D1
Saughall CH1 . . . . .94 A1
Aldersey La CH3 . . . . .182 C5
Aldersey Rd CW2 . . . . .190 A2
Aldersgate SK22 . . . . .39 B8
Aldersgate Ave WA7 . . . . . . .50 D8
Aldersgate Dr L26 . . . . .21 A6
Aldersgate Rd SK8 . . . . .35 C5
Alderton Gr CW7 . . . . .127 A4
Alderwood Ct WA8 . . . . .12 E4
Alderwood Lodge L24 . . . . . .21 A3
Aldewood Cl WA3 . . . . .10 A6
Aldford Cl Bebington CH63 . .43 B6
Hough CW2 . . . . .206 E2
Aldford Pl SK9 . . . . .59 F2
Aldford Rd CH2 . . . . .118 F6
Aldford Sch CH3 . . . . .163 F3
Aldford Way CW7 . . . . .126 B2
Aldgate CH65 . . . . .70 A5
Aldington Dr CW10 . . . . . . .151 D5
Aldridge Dr WA5 . . . . .6 F7
Aled Way CH4 . . . . .140 D5
Alexander Ct CH3 . . . . .237 C2
Alexander St WA2 . . . . .16 B7
Alexandra Ct **1** M31 . . . . . .11 F3
Alexandra Ind Est WA8 . . . .22 F7
Alexandra Mews WA4 . . . . . .49 B1
Alexandra Pl CW1 . . . . .190 B5
Alexandra Rd
Middlewich CW10 . . . . .151 D6
Warrington WA4 . . . . .16 F2
Warrington, Stockton Heath
WA4 . . . . .16 D1
Alexandra Sq **6** CW7 . . . .149 A8
Alexandra St
Ellesmere Port CH65 . . . . . . .70 C7
Warrington WA1 . . . . .16 E7
Widnes WA8 . . . . .23 A7
Winsford CW7 . . . . .126 C1
Alford Ct **4** CW9 . . . . .103 E5
Alforde St WA8 . . . . .23 A7
Alfred Ct **12** WA8 . . . . .23 B8
Alfred Rd Golborne WA3 . . . . .4 A8
Haydock WA11 . . . . .1 F7
Newton-le-W WA12 . . . . .2 E3
Northwich CW9 . . . . .103 C6
Widnes WA8 . . . . .23 B8
Alfred St Irlam M44 . . . . .11 E6
Warrington WA2 . . . . .16 C7
Algernon St Runcorn WA7 . .22 F3
Warrington, Stockton Heath
WA4 . . . . .16 C1
Alice Ct WA8 . . . . .23 A4
Alison Dr Goostrey CW4 . . . .130 D8
Macclesfield SK10 . . . . .87 F1
Alistair Dr CH63 . . . . .43 C6
All Hallows RC High Sch
SK11 . . . . .112 B7
All Saints Dr WA4 . . . . .17 E3
All Saints RC Prim Sch
WA3 . . . . .3 B8
All Saints Upton CE Prim Sch
WA8 . . . . .12 B3
Allans Cl CH64 . . . . .66 E6
Allans Mdw CH64 . . . . .66 E7
Allansford Ave CH3 . . . . . . .143 A4
Allcard St WA5 . . . . .15 F7
Allen Ave WA3 . . . . .5 C4
Allen Dr CW9 . . . . .103 F2
Allen Pl CW1 . . . . .190 B5
Allen Rd WA7 . . . . .48 D7
Allen St Bollington SK10 . . . .88 B8
Macclesfield SK11 . . . . .112 F7
Warrington WA2 . . . . .16 A6
Allenby M44 . . . . .11 D4
Allendale WA7 . . . . .50 B6
Allerby Way WA3 . . . . .3 E8
Allerton Rd WA8 . . . . .13 C3
Allgreave Cl CW10 . . . . .151 C6
Allington Pl CH4 . . . . .141 E7
Allman Cl CW1 . . . . .189 F7
Allotment Rd M44 . . . . .11 D6
Allport La CH62 . . . . .43 D8
Allport Rd CH62,CH63 . . . . . .43 D7
Allports The CH62 . . . . .43 D7
Allysum St WA7 . . . . .49 F4
Alma Ave CW1 . . . . .190 C6
Alma Cl
Macclesfield SK11 . . . . .112 A7
Scholar Green ST7 . . . . .194 D8
Alma La SK9 . . . . .60 A7
Alma St Chester CH2 . . . . . .118 F2
Newton-le-W WA12 . . . . .2 B3
Almeda Rd L24 . . . . .21 A2
Almer Dr WA5 . . . . .15 C5
Almond Ave Crewe CW1 . . . .190 D6
Runcorn WA7 . . . . .49 C8
Almond Dr WA5 . . . . .6 F6
Almond Gr
Warrington WA1 . . . . .17 D7
Weaverham CW8 . . . . .102 E7
Widnes WA8 . . . . .22 D8
Almond Pl ST5 . . . . .210 D1
Almond Tree Cl L24 . . . . . . .21 C1
Almond Wlk M31 . . . . .11 D3
Almshouses
Biddulph ST8 . . . . .179 E3
Malpas SY14 . . . . .213 B3
Sandbach CW11 . . . . .175 C6
Alnwick Dr CH65 . . . . .70 D2
Alpass Ave WA5 . . . . .16 A8
Alpine St WA12 . . . . .2 A3
Alport Rd SY13 . . . . .226 B1
Alpraham Cres CH2 . . . . . . .118 C6
Alpraham Gn CW6 . . . . .169 E5
Alric Wlk M22 . . . . .33 E8
Alsager Highfields Com Prim
Sch ST7 . . . . .193 D4
Alsager Rd Audley ST7 . . . . .209 F6
Haslington CW11 . . . . .192 C7
Alsager Sch ST7 . . . . .193 B8
Alsager Sta ST7 . . . . .193 E3
Alsfeld Way SK22 . . . . .39 A8
Alt WA8 . . . . .12 A2
Alt Wlk CW7 . . . . .127 A2
Alton Dr SK10 . . . . .87 F1
Alton Rd SK9 . . . . .59 F7
Alton St CW2 . . . . .190 B3
Altrincham Priory Hospl
WA15 . . . . .32 A7
Altrincham Rd Styal SK9 . . . .33 E4
Wilmslow SK9 . . . . .33 C2
Alum Ct CW4 . . . . .130 C2
Alumbrook Ave CW4 . . . . . .130 C3
Alun Cres CH4 . . . . .141 A6
Alundale Rd CW7 . . . . .126 C3
Alvanley Dr WA6 . . . . .73 C2
Alvanley Prim Sch WA6 . . . . .73 D1
Alvanley Rd
Ellesmere Port CH66 . . . . . . .69 D4
Helsby WA6 . . . . .73 C2
Alvanley Rise CW9 . . . . . . .104 A6
Alvanley Terr WA6 . . . . .74 B8

Alvanley View CH2 . . . . .72 B3
Alvanley Way CH66 . . . . .69 E4
Alvaston Bsns Pk CW5 . . . .204 F8
Alvaston Rd CW5 . . . . .204 F5
Alvaston Wlk CW2 . . . . .189 C2
Alverstone Cl WA5 . . . . .14 C7
Alverton CI WA8 . . . . .22 D8
Alveston Cl SK10 . . . . .86 F1
Alveston Dr SK9 . . . . .60 C8
Alvingham Cl **1** CW9 . . . . .104 B8
Alvis Rd CH5 . . . . .116 B3
Alwyn Gdns CH2 . . . . .118 F8
Alyn Rd CH2 . . . . .96 F1
Alyndale Rd CH4 . . . . .140 D6
Amberley Cl WA4 . . . . .27 B3
Amberley Dr WA15 . . . . .32 B8
Amberley Rd SK11 . . . . .112 A6
Ambleside CH2 . . . . .119 A6
Ambleside Cl
Bebington CH62 . . . . .43 E7
Crewe CW2 . . . . .189 D3
Macclesfield SK11 . . . . .111 F6
Runcorn WA7 . . . . .49 C6
Winsford CW7 . . . . .126 C3
Ambleside Cres WA2 . . . . . . .8 C3
Ambleside Ct CW12 . . . . . . .156 A2
Ambleside Rd CH65 . . . . . . .70 C2
Ambrose Ct WA1 . . . . .16 D6
Ambuscade Cl CW1 . . . . . . .190 E5
Amelia Ct WA8 . . . . .13 B4
Amelia St WA2 . . . . .16 C7
Amersham Ct SK10 . . . . .87 C3
Amis Gr WA3 . . . . .3 E8
Amy St CW2 . . . . .190 C3
Anchor Ct WA7 . . . . .50 D6
Anchor Ct
Warrington WA1 . . . . .16 D6
Wilmslow SK9 . . . . .60 B8
Anchorage The
1 Lymm WA13 . . . . .18 D3
Neston CH64 . . . . .66 C7
Waverton CH3 . . . . .143 A5
Ancoats Rd WA16,SK9 . . . . .83 F8
Anderson Cl Crewe CW1 . .191 A4
Warrington WA2 . . . . .9 B2
Anderson Ct CW2 . . . . .9 B2
Anderson St **16** SK10 . . . . .112 C8
Andersons Ind Est WA8 . . . .23 A6
Anderton Grange CW9 . . . . .103 F7
Anderton Way SK9 . . . . .34 D3
Andertons La SK10,SK11 . . .86 B1
Andover Cl WA2 . . . . .8 E1
Andover Rd WA11 . . . . .1 E7
Andrew Cl WA8 . . . . .22 C8
Andrew Cres CH4 . . . . .237 C1
Andrew Gr SK10 . . . . .113 A7
Andrew La SK6 . . . . .37 F8
Andrew's Cl CH3 . . . . .121 B2
Andrew's Wlk CH60 . . . . . . .41 B8
Andromeda Way WA9 . . . . . . .6 B7
Anemone Way WA9 . . . . .6 A7
Angelina Cl CW11 . . . . .174 D7
Anglers Rest M44 . . . . .11 E5
Anglesey Cl **2** CH65 . . . . . .70 C1
Anglesey Dr SK12 . . . . .36 F6
Anglesey Water SK12 . . . . . .36 E6
Angus Gr CW10 . . . . .128 D2
Angus Rd CH63 . . . . .43 C6
Angus Wlk SK10 . . . . .86 F2
Ankers Knowl La SK11 . . . .114 D6
Ankers La SK11 . . . . .114 D6
Ann Cl CH66 . . . . .69 D7
Ann St Northwich CW9 . . . . .79 D1
Runcorn WA7 . . . . .23 B3
Ann St W WA8 . . . . .23 B7
Annable Rd M44 . . . . .11 F8
Annan Cl **2** CW12 . . . . . . .157 A1
Anne Ct ST7 . . . . .210 D6
Anne's Way CH4 . . . . .237 C1
Annette Ave WA12 . . . . .2 A5
Annie St WA2 . . . . .16 C6
Annions La CW5 . . . . .205 F1
Annis Cl SK9 . . . . .60 B2
Annis Rd SK9 . . . . .60 B2
Ansdell Rd WA8 . . . . .13 C2
Anson Cl Bramhall SK7 . . . . .35 F5
Warrington WA2 . . . . .8 E2
Anson Engine Mus The★
SK7 . . . . .37 C3
Anson Rd Handforth SK9 . . . .34 F1
Poynton SK12 . . . . .37 B3
Anthony Dr CW9 . . . . .126 F7
Anthony's Way CH60 . . . . . . .41 A7
Antons Rd L26 . . . . .21 A6
Antony Rd WA4 . . . . .16 B1
Antrim Cl WA11 . . . . .1 C6
Antrim Dr CH66 . . . . .69 F2
Antrim Rd WA2 . . . . .8 A2
Antrobus St CW12 . . . . .156 D3
Anvil Cl Elton CH2 . . . . .72 B4
Haslington CW11 . . . . .174 D3
Saughall CH1 . . . . .94 A1
Apple Market St **10**
CW9 . . . . .103 F8
Apple Tree Cl L24 . . . . .21 E1
Apple Tree Gr CH66 . . . . . . .94 F8
Appleby Cl
Macclesfield SK11 . . . . .111 F5
Widnes WA8 . . . . .22 C8
Appleby Gr CH62 . . . . .43 D6
Appleby Rd WA3 . . . . .9 D5
Appleby Wlk **5** WA8 . . . . . .22 C8
Applecroft ST5 . . . . .210 E1

Applecross CI WA3 . . . . . . .10 A6
Appledale Dr CH66 . . . . . .95 A8
Applefield CW8 . . . . .103 D7
Appleford CI WA4 . . . . .26 E7
Appleton CI CW12 . . . . . .178 E8
Appleton Dr CH65 . . . . . . .69 F3
Appleton Hall Gdns WA4 .26 E5
Appleton Mews WA13 . . . .18 C4
Appleton Rd
  Chester CH2 . . . . .118 E6
  Widnes WA8 . . . . .13 B1
Appleton St Widnes WA8 .23 B7
  Winnington CW8 . . . . .78 D1
Appleton Thorn Prim Sch
  WA4 . . . . .27 C4
Appleton Thorn Trad Est
  WA4 . . . . .27 D5
Appleton Village WA8 . .13 B1
Appleton Wlk 8 SK9 . . . .34 E1
Appletree Gr WA2 . . . . .8 F2
Appleyards La CH4 . . . . .141 E7
April Rise SK10 . . . . .87 A1
Arabis Gdns WA9 . . . . .6 F3
Aragon Ct WA7 . . . . .24 C3
Aragon Gn CH1 . . . . .117 E6
Aran CI L24 . . . . .21 D1
Arbour Cl
  Macclesfield SK10 . . . . . . .87 D3
  Northwich CW9 . . . . .104 C8
Arbour Cres SK10 . . . . . . .87 D3
Arbour Mews SK10 . . . . . .87 D3
Arbour St SK17 . . . . .210 D5
Arbourhay St SK10 . . . . . .87 E1
Arbury La WA2 . . . . .8 C6
Arcade The
  Ellesmere Port CH65 . . . . .70 A5
  13 Northwich CW8 . . . . .103 F8
Archer Ave WA4 . . . . .16 E2
Archer CI SK10 . . . . .87 E7
Archers Gn CH62 . . . . . . .43 E3
Archers Way Blacon CH1 118 A2
  Ellesmere Port CH66 . . . . .69 E1
Archway Wlk WA1 . . . . .2 E3
Arclid CI SK9 . . . . .34 E1
Arclid 10 CW12 . . . . .156 F3
Arclid Green Ind Est
  CW11 . . . . .176 A8
Arden WA8 . . . . .12 A2
Arden CI Heald Green SK8 .34 C7
  Tarvin CH3 . . . . .121 C3
  Warrington WA3 . . . . .10 B6
Arden Ct CW12 . . . . .179 B7
Arden Dr CH64 . . . . .66 E6
Arden Est S22 . . . . .39 D7
Arden St SK22 . . . . .39 C7
Ardenbrook Rise SK10 . .86 F6
Ardern Lea WA3 . . . . .73 D1
Arderne Ave CW2 . . . . . .190 A2
Arderne Ho CH2 . . . . . . .118 F7
Arderne PI 10 SK9 . . . . . .60 A1
Ardleigh CI CW1 . . . . . . .189 F8
Arena Gdns WA2 . . . . .16 D8
Argosy Dr M90 . . . . .32 F7
Argyle Ct 9 WA16 . . . . . .57 A2
Argyll Ave Bebington CH62 43 D4
  Chester CH4 . . . . .141 A7
Argyll CI SK10 . . . . .87 A1
Ariel Wlk 4 WA3 . . . . .3 E8
Arizona Cres WA5 . . . . . .15 B7
Arkenshaw Rd WA3 . . . . . .9 A8
Arkenstone CI WA8 . . . . .12 C2
Arkle Ave SK9 . . . . .34 E1
Arkle Ct 1 CH3 . . . . .119 B1
Arklow Dr L24 . . . . .21 D2
Arkwright CI CW7 . . . . . .149 A8
Arkwright Ct WA7 . . . . . . .23 F3
Arkwright Rd WA7 . . . . . . .23 F3
Arley Ave WA4 . . . . .26 D8
Arley CI Alsager ST7 . . . .193 C3
  Chester CH2 . . . . .118 F6
  Macclesfield SK11 . . . . . .112 A7
Arley Dr WA8 . . . . .12 B2
Arley End WA16 . . . . .29 C4
Arley Hall & Gdns* CW9 54 D6
Arley Mossend La CW9 . .54 D2
Arley PI CW2 . . . . .206 A8
Arley Rd Antrobus CW9 . . .54 B7
  Appleton Thorn WA4 . . . . .27 C3
  Northwich CW9 . . . . .104 C8
Arley Wlk CW11 . . . . .174 D5
Arlington CI CW2 . . . . . .206 C8
Arlington Cres SK9 . . . . . .59 E5
Arlington Dr Golborne WN7 4 C1
  Macclesfield SK11 . . . . . .112 A7
  Poynton SK12 . . . . .36 D3
  Warrington WA5 . . . . .14 E4
Arlington Way SK9 . . . . . .59 E5
Armistead Way CW4 . . . .130 A5
Armistead Rd CW11 . . . .174 F4
Armitt St SK11 . . . . .112 C7
Armour Ave WA2 . . . . .8 B2
Armoury Court Mews 4
  SK11 . . . . .112 B6
Armoury Twrs 1 SK11 .112 B6
Armstrong Cl
  Audlem CW3 . . . . .229 F4
  Warrington WA3 . . . . .9 D4
Armthorpe Dr CH66 . . . . .69 C5
Arncliffe Dr WA5 . . . . .6 F4
Arndale WA7 . . . . .49 E5
Arnhem Cres WA2 . . . . . .16 C7
Arnhem Way CH3 . . . . . .142 B5
Arnold PI WA8 . . . . .22 C7
Arnold St Nantwich CW5 .204 E6

Arnold St continued
  Warrington WA5 . . . . .16 D6
Arnold's Cres CH4 . . . . . .139 A3
Arnside Ave
  Congleton CW12 . . . . . . .156 A2
  Haydock WA11 . . . . .1 B6
Arnside CI High Lane SK6 .37 E8
  Winsford CW7 . . . . .126 D2
Arnside Gr WA1 . . . . .16 B2
Arpley Rd WA1 . . . . .16 B4
Arpley St WA1 . . . . .16 A4
Arradon Ct CH2 . . . . .118 E5
Arran Ave CH65 . . . . .70 C1
Arran Cl
  Holmes Chapel CW4 . . . .130 C2
  Warrington WA2 . . . . .9 A2
Arran Dr WA6 . . . . .74 C6
Arron PI CW2 . . . . .189 D3
Arrowcroft Rd CH3 . . . . .119 F5
Arrowsmith Dr ST7 . . . . .193 B3
Arrowsmith Rd WA11 . . . .1 F7
Arthill La
  Little Bollington WA14 . . . .20 B1
  Rostherne WA14 . . . . .30 B8
Arthog Dr WA15 . . . . .31 F8
Arthog Rd WA15 . . . . .31 F8
Arthur Ave CH65 . . . . .70 C5
Arthur St Chester CH1 . . .118 A2
  3 Crewe CW2 . . . . .190 D2
  Lostock Gralam CW9 . . . . .80 A2
  13 Runcorn WA7 . . . . .23 A2
  Warrington WA2 . . . . .16 A6
Artists La SK10 . . . . .85 C7
Artle Rd CW2 . . . . .206 C8
Arundel Ave WA7 . . . . . . .36 D8
Arundel Cl
  Knutsford WA16 . . . . .82 A8
  Macclesfield SK11 . . . . . . .87 F2
  Wistaston CW2 . . . . .205 E8
Arundel CI CH65 . . . . .70 E3
Arundel Rd SK8 . . . . .35 A6
Arundell CI WA5 . . . . .6 F6
Ascol Dr WA16 . . . . .80 C3
Ascot Ave WA7 . . . . .49 B6
Ascot CI Congleton CW12 156 D4
  Macclesfield SK10 . . . . . . .87 C3
  Warrington WA4 . . . . .17 C2
  Warrington, Martinscroft
  WA1 . . . . .17 E7
Ascot Ct CW9 . . . . .104 C8
Ascot Dr CH66 . . . . .69 D3
Ascot Ho CH1 . . . . .118 B2
Ash Ave Irlam M44 . . . . . .11 D5
  Newton-le-W WA12 . . . . . .2 C2
Ash CI Ellesmere Port CH66 69 F1
  Holmes Chapel CW4 . . . .130 D4
  Malpas SY14 . . . . .213 C5
  Tarporley CW6 . . . . .146 D2
Ash Ct 14 WA16 . . . . .57 A2
Ash Gr Chester CH4 . . . . .141 B5
  Congleton CW12 . . . . . . .156 A3
  Ellesmere Port CH66 . . . . .69 C6
  Golborne WA3 . . . . .3 B8
  Handforth SK9 . . . . .34 C3
  Heald Green SK8 . . . . .34 B8
  Knutsford WA16 . . . . .57 D1
  Macclesfield SK11 . . . . . .112 C4
  Nantwich CW5 . . . . .204 F3
  Rode Heath ST7 . . . . .193 F7
  Runcorn WA7 . . . . .49 C8
  Warrington WA4 . . . . .16 D3
  Weaverham CW8 . . . . . . .102 E7
  Widnes WA8 . . . . .22 D8
Ash Grove Prim Sch
  SK11 . . . . .112 C6
Ash Hay La
  Hoole Bank CH2 . . . . . . .119 C8
  Picton CH2 . . . . .96 C2
Ash Ho 8 WA14 . . . . . . .175 B6
Ash House La CW8 . . . . . .77 D7
Ash La Warrington WA4 . . .26 E8
  Widnes WA8 . . . . .22 A8
Ash Lawn Ct CH2 . . . . . .118 C4
Ash Lodge SK12 . . . . .36 D4
Ash Mount CW3 . . . . .232 B1
Ash Priors WA8 . . . . .12 D3
Ash Rd Crewe CW1 . . . . .190 D6
  Cuddington CW8 . . . . . . .101 F2
  Elton CH2 . . . . .72 C3
  Haydock WA11 . . . . .1 E7
  Hollinfare WA3 . . . . .11 A2
  Lymm WA13 . . . . .18 C3
  Partington M31 . . . . .11 D3
  Poynton SK12 . . . . .36 F3
  Warrington WA5 . . . . .14 F4
  Winwick WA2 . . . . .8 A6
Ash St CW9 . . . . .79 A1
Ash Terr ST7 . . . . .112 C4
Ash Vlew ST7 . . . . .195 B2
Ash Way CH60 . . . . .41 B6
Ashbank CW8 . . . . .104 D7
Ashberry CI SK9 . . . . .60 D8
Ashberry Dr WA4 . . . . . . .27 B5
Ashbourne Ave WA7 . . . .49 B6
Ashbourne CI CH66 . . . . .94 E8
Ashbourne Dr
  Chorlton CW2 . . . . .207 C1
  High Lane SK6 . . . . .37 C6
Ashbourne Mews 1
  SK10 . . . . .111 F8
Ashbourne Rd
  Hazel Grove SK7 . . . . .36 F8
  Warrington WA5 . . . . .15 B5
Ashbrook Ave WA3 . . . . . .49 F3
Ashbrook Cres WA2 . . . .16 D8
Ashbrook Dr SK10 . . . . . .87 A6

Ashbrook Rd
  Bollington SK10 . . . . .87 F7
  Nether Alderley SK10 . . . .85 F6
Ashburton CH64 . . . . .66 C8
Ashbury CI WA7 . . . . .24 C2
Ashbury Dr WA11 . . . . .1 D7
Ashby Dr CW11 . . . . .174 C5
Ashby PI CH2 . . . . .237 C4
Ashcroft SK9 . . . . .59 F5
Ashcroft Ave CW2 . . . . . .206 B3
Ashcroft Rd WA13 . . . . . . .19 B4
Ashdale CI ST7 . . . . .193 C6
Ashdene Prim Sch SK9 . .59 F5
Ashdene Rd SK9 . . . . .59 F5
Ashdown La WA3 . . . . .10 B5
Ashdown Rd WA16 . . . . . .82 F6
Ashenhurst Rd ST7 . . . . .193 F3
Ashenough Rd ST7 . . . . .210 D6
Asher Ct WA4 . . . . .27 D4
Ashfield CI WA13 . . . . .19 B4
Ashfield Cres
  Bebington CH62 . . . . .43 D8
  Blacon CH1 . . . . .117 D5
Ashfield Dr SK10 . . . . .87 A2
Ashfield Gr M44 . . . . .11 E6
Ashfield Ho 6 CH64 . . . .66 E8
Ashfield Rd
  Bebington CH62 . . . . .43 C8
  Ellesmere Port CH65 . . . . .70 C5
Ashfield Rd N 1 CH65 . .70 C5
Ashfield St CW10 . . . . . . .151 D8
Ashford CI SK9 . . . . .34 C4
Ashford Dr WA4 . . . . .26 E3
Ashford Rd SK9 . . . . .60 A4
Ashford Way 1 WA8 . . . .13 D1
Ashgate La CW9 . . . . .79 F6
Ashgrove CW7 . . . . .149 D8
Ashlands WA6 . . . . .74 C7
Ashlea Dr SK9 . . . . .205 E5
Ashleigh CI CH4 . . . . .140 E6
Ashley Bank WA14 . . . . . .31 E8
Ashley CE Prim Sch
  WA15 . . . . .31 F5
Ashley CI WA4 . . . . .17 C3
Ashley Ct Frodsham WA6 . .74 B4
  Holt LL13 . . . . .196 D8
  Warrington WA4 . . . . .26 C6
Ashley Dr Bramhall SK7 . . .35 C6
  Hartford CW8 . . . . .103 A6
Ashley Gdns Clutton CH3 182 C1
  High Lane SK6 . . . . .37 D8
Ashley Gn WA8 . . . . .22 B8
Ashley Grange CW9 . . . .103 E3
Ashley Mdw CW1 . . . . . . .191 D5
Ashley Mill La N WA14 . .31 E8
Ashley Rd
  Ashley WA14,WA15,WA16 .31 C4
  Ashley,Ashley Heath WA14,
  WA15 . . . . .31 E7
  Handforth SK9 . . . . .34 B1
  Mere WA16 . . . . .56 D8
  Runcorn WA7 . . . . .23 D2
Ashley Ret Pk WA8 . . . . . .23 B7
Ashley Sch WA8 . . . . .12 D1
Ashley Sta WA15 . . . . .31 E5
Ashley Way W WA8 . . . . . .22 F7
Ashley Way WA8 . . . . .23 B7
Ashleymill La WA14 . . . . .31 D7
Ashley Rd
  Ashworth Pk WA16 . . . . . .81 F8
  Asiatic Cotts CH5 . . . . . .116 B3
Askerbank La SK11 . . . . .159 A1

Askett CI WA11 . . . . .1 C7
Askrigg Ave CH66 . . . . . . .69 B5
Aspen Cl
  Ellesmere Port CH66 . . . . .69 E1
  Heswall CH60 . . . . .41 D8
  Kidsgrove ST7 . . . . .195 E3
Aspen Gr Saughall CH1 . . .17 A7
  Warrington WA2 . . . . .8 A7
Aspen Way Chester CH2 . .119 B4
  High Lane SK6 . . . . .38 A4
Aspens The CW8 . . . . . . .101 E5
Aspinall CI WA7 . . . . .9 A3
Aspull CI WA3 . . . . .9 C4
Asquith CI CW1 . . . . .191 C5
Assheton CI WA12 . . . . . . .2 B4
Assheton Wlk L24 . . . . . . .21 E2
Astbury CI Crewe CW1 . .190 A7
  Golborne WA3 . . . . .4 B8
  Kidsgrove ST7 . . . . .195 C5
Astbury Dr CW8 . . . . .78 A4
Astbury Lane Ends
  CW12 . . . . .178 F8
Astbury Mere Ctry Pk*
  CW12 . . . . .156 B2
Astbury St CW12 . . . . . . .156 C2
Astbury St Mary's CE Prim
  Sch CW12 . . . . .178 B8
Aster Cres WA7 . . . . .49 F5
Aster Rd WA11 . . . . .1 F7
Aster Wlk M31 . . . . .11 F2
Astle CI CW10 . . . . .151 C7
Astle Ct SK11 . . . . .84 A3
Astle La SK11 . . . . .84 E1
Astley CI Knutsford WA16 .82 C7
  Warrington WA4 . . . . .16 B3
  Widnes WA8 . . . . .12 C3
Astley Ct M44 . . . . .11 E8
Astley Rd M44 . . . . .11 E8
Astmoor Bridge La WA7 .23 F2
Astmoor East Intc WA7 .24 A3
Astmoor Ind Est WA7 . . .23 F3
Astmoor La WA7 . . . . .23 F1
Astmoor Prim Sch WA7 . .23 F3
Astmoor Rd Runcorn WA7 23 C3
  Runcorn WA7 . . . . .23 A2
Aston Ave Warrington WA3 . .9 F4
  Winsford CW7 . . . . .126 B2
Aston by Sutton Prim Sch
  WA7 . . . . .50 C2
Aston Ct WA1 . . . . .9 C1
Aston Fields Rd WA7 . . . .50 E4
Aston Gn WA7 . . . . .50 E6
Aston La Runcorn WA7 . . . .50 F5
  Sutton WA7 . . . . .50 C2
  Woore CW3 . . . . .232 E1
Aston La N WA7 . . . . .50 E4
Aston La S WA7 . . . . .50 E3
Aston Rd ST5 . . . . .210 D1
Aston Way
  13 Handforth SK9 . . . . . . .34 D5
  Middlewich CW10 . . . . . .128 E1
Astor Dr WA4 . . . . .26 F8
Atcherley CI CW5 . . . . . . .218 E8
Athelbrae CI CW8 . . . . . .103 F7
Atherton La M44 . . . . .11 E5
Atherton Rd CH65 . . . . . . .69 F6
Athey St SK11 . . . . .112 C8
Athey Street Mill 2
  SK11 . . . . .112 C7
Athlone Rd WA2 . . . . .8 A1
Athol CI Bebington CH62 . .43 E5
  Newton-le-W WA12 . . . . . .1 F4
Athol Dr CH62 . . . . .43 E5
Athol Rd SK7 . . . . .35 D5
Atholl Ave CW2 . . . . .190 C1
Atholl CI SK10 . . . . .87 A1
Atkin CI CW12 . . . . .156 A3
Atlanta Ave M90 . . . . .33 A8
Atterbury CI WA8 . . . . . . .12 C2
Attlee Ave WA3 . . . . .5 C4
Attwood CI CW1 . . . . . . .191 C4
Attwood St ST7 . . . . .195 A2
Atworth Terr CH64 . . . . . .67 F8
Auburn CI WA8 . . . . .12 C3
Auckery Ave CH66 . . . . . .69 D3
Auckland Rd CH1 . . . . . .117 D4
Audlem CI WA7 . . . . .49 F4
Audlem Dr CW9 . . . . .104 A6
Audlem Rd
  Hankelow CW3 . . . . .230 C7
  Hatherton CW5 . . . . .219 D3
  Nantwich CW5 . . . . .204 F3
Audlem St James' CE Prim
  Sch CW3 . . . . .230 A5
Audley Cres CH4 . . . . . . .141 E6
Audley Rd Alsager ST7 . . .193 C1
  Barthomley CW2 . . . . . . .208 E5
  Newcastle-u-Lyme ST7,
  ST5 . . . . .210 B2
  Talke ST7 . . . . .210 B6
Audley St CW1 . . . . .190 D5
Audley St W CW1 . . . . . . .190 D5
Audre CI WA4 . . . . .14 D6
Aughton Way CH4 . . . . . .139 D4
Augusta Dr SK10 . . . . .87 B4
Augusta Ho CH1 . . . . . . .117 F6
Austell Rd M22 . . . . .33 D8
Austen CI 1 CW11 . . . . .174 D6
Austen Dr WA2 . . . . .8 A6
Austen Ho SK10 . . . . .86 F1
Austin CI CW7 . . . . .149 C6
Austin St CW9 . . . . .79 D1
Austins Hill CH3 . . . . .144 C8
Austral Ave WA1 . . . . .17 C2
Australia La WA4 . . . . .17 C1
Autumn Ave WA16 . . . . . .57 C2
Avebury CI Golborne WA3 . .3 C8
  Widnes WA8 . . . . .13 F3

Aveley CI WA1 . . . . .17 B7
Avens Rd M31 . . . . .11 F3
Avenue One CW1 . . . . . .207 C8
Avenue The
  Alderley Edge SK9 . . . . . . .60 A1
  Alsager ST7 . . . . .193 D4
  Altrincham WA15 . . . . . . .31 F8
  Bebington CH62 . . . . .43 C8
  Comberbach CW9 . . . . . . .78 D8
  Great Barrow CH3 . . . . . .120 F7
  High Legh WA16 . . . . .29 C5
  Kidsgrove ST7 . . . . .194 F1
  Lymm WA13 . . . . .18 D1
  Marston CW9 . . . . .79 B3
  Newton-le-W WA12 . . . . . .2 D4
  Sandbach CW11 . . . . . . .174 E8
  Tarporley CW6 . . . . .146 D1
Avenue Two CW1 . . . . . .207 C8
Avery CI WA11 . . . . .8 E2
Avery Cres WA11 . . . . .1 C7
Avery Rd WA11 . . . . .1 C7
Avery Sq WA11 . . . . .1 C7
Aviator Way M22 . . . . .33 D8
Aviemore Dr WA3 . . . . .9 A3
Avocet CI
  Newton-le-W WA12 . . . . . .2 C4
  Warrington WA2 . . . . .8 D3
Avocet Dr CW7 . . . . .149 D6
Avon WA8 . . . . .12 A2
Avon Ave WA5 . . . . .14 F4
Avon CI Kidsgrove ST7 . . .195 B2
  Macclesfield SK10 . . . . . . .87 A2
  Neston CH64 . . . . .66 E6
Avon Ct ST7 . . . . .193 C5
Avon Dr Congleton CW12 .156 F1
  Crewe CW1 . . . . .191 A5
Avon Rd Altrincham WA15 .31 F8
  Culcheth WA3 . . . . .5 A2
  Heald Green SK8 . . . . .34 C7
Avon Wlk CW7 . . . . .127 A2
Avondale CH65 . . . . .70 B2
Avondale Ave CH62 . . . . .43 F5
Avondale Dr WA8 . . . . . . .12 B1
Avondale Rd WA11 . . . . . . .1 C7
Avondale Rise SK9 . . . . . .60 D6
Avonlea CI CH4 . . . . .140 E4
Avonside Way SK11 . . . .112 C5
Avro Way M90 . . . . .32 F7
Axminster Wlk SK7 . . . . . .35 E7
Aycliffe Wlk 6 WA8 . . . . .22 C8
Aylesbury CI
  Ellesmere Port CH66 . . . . .69 C3
  Macclesfield SK10 . . . . . . .87 D3
Aylesby CI WA16 . . . . .57 B1
Aylsham CI WA8 . . . . .12 C4
Ayrshire CI SK10 . . . . . . .128 D2
Ayrshire Way CW12 . . . . .157 A1
Aysgarth Ave CW1 . . . . .173 B1
Azalea Gdns WA9 . . . . .6 A7
Azalea Gr WA7 . . . . .49 F4

B

Babbacombe Rd WA5 . . .14 E4
Babbage Rd CH5 . . . . . . .116 A4
Bache Ave CH2 . . . . .118 C5
Bache Dr CH2 . . . . .118 D5
Bache Hall Ct CH2 . . . . .118 C5
Bache Hall Est CH2 . . . .118 C5
Bache Sta CH2 . . . . .118 D5
Bachefield Ave CH3 . . . .142 A6
Bachelor's Ave CH3 . . . .142 A8
Bachelor's La CH3 . . . . .142 A8
Back Bridge St WA12 . . . .2 B3
Back Brook PI WA4 . . . . . .16 E3
Back Coole La CW3 . . . .229 B4
Back Crosland Terr WA6 .73 B2
Back Cross La
  Congleton CW12 . . . . . . .179 C8
  Newton-le-W WA12 . . . . . .2 B4
Back Eastford Rd WA4 . . .16 A1
Back Eddisbury Rd
  SK11 . . . . .113 C7
Back Forshaw St WA2 . . .16 C7
Back Heathcote St ST7 .195 A2
Back High St 4 WA7 . . . .23 A2
Back Jodrell St SK22 . . . .39 B7
Back La Alpraham CW6 . .169 C6
  Altrincham WA15 . . . . . . .32 B4
  Bate Heath CW9 . . . . .54 D7
  Betley CW2 . . . . .208 C3
  Brereton Green CW11 . . .153 D6
  Burtonwood WA5 . . . . .6 D7
  Congleton CW12 . . . . . . .156 A4
  Duddon CW6 . . . . .145 A6
  Helsby WA6 . . . . .73 D2
  High Legh WA14 . . . . .29 F5
  Marton CW12,SK11 . . . . .133 F2
  No Man's Heath SY14 . . .214 A4
  Norbury SY13 . . . . .215 F5
  Partington WA14 . . . . .20 C5
  Plumley WA16 . . . . .81 B1
  Shavington CW2 . . . . . . .206 E4
  Smallwood CW11 . . . . . .176 D8
  Swan Green WA16 . . . . . .106 B8
  Tattenhall CH3 . . . . .167 C2
  Threapwood SY14 . . . . . .222 E7
  Warrington WA5 . . . . .14 A3
  Wybunbury CW5 . . . . . . .220 C6
Back Lanes CW6 . . . . . . .146 B2
Back Legh St WA12 . . . . . .2 A3
Back Market St WA12 . . . .2 A3
Back Paradise St 4
  SK11 . . . . .112 C7
Back Park St CW12 . . . . .156 E2
Back Queen St CH1 . . . .237 B3

Back Rathbone St WA12 ..2 A3
Back River St **1** CW12 .156 D3
Back Union Rd SK22 ....39 C7
Back Wallgate **13** SK11 .112 D8
Backford Cl WA7 .....50 C5
Backford Cross CH66 ...94 F7
Backford Gdns CH1 ....94 F7
Backlands CW1 ......190 C6
Badbury Cl WA11 ......1 D7
Badcock's La CW6 ....185 E4
Baddeley Cl CW5 ....203 D2
Baddiley Hall La CW5 .217 A8
Baddiley La CW5 ....203 D1
Baddington La CW5 ...204 C1
Badger Ave CW1 .....190 B5
Badger Bait CH64 .....66 F6
Badger Cl WA7 ....50 A6
Badger Ho SK10 ......87 D2
Badger Rd
  Macclesfield SK10 ....87 D2
  Prestbury SK10 ......87 A7
Badgers Cl
  Christleton CH3 .....142 E7
  Ellesmere Port CH66 ..94 F8
  1 Winsford CW7 ....126 A1
Badgers Croft ST5 ...210 E1
Badgers Pk CH64 .....66 F6
Badgers Set CW8 ....101 D5
Badgers Wlk CW8 ....205 E8
Badgers Wood CW3 ..95 E2
Badgersrake La CH66 ..68 D3
Bag La
  Cuddington CW8,WA6 .101 C4
  Norley WA6 ....101 A6
Bagley La CW3 ......230 B1
Bagmere Cl
  Brereton Green CW11 .153 F4
  Sandbach CW11 .....174 F7
Bagmere La CW11 ....154 B5
Bagnall Cl WA5 ......15 C5
Bagot Ave WA12 ......1 E3
Bagstock Ave SK12 ...36 E2
Baguley Ave WA8 ....22 A5
Bahama Cl WA11 ......1 D8
Bahama Rd WA11 ......1 D8
Baildon Gn CH66 .....69 B5
Bailey Ave CH65 .....69 F6
Bailey Bridge Cl CH2 .118 D4
Bailey Bsns Pk SK11 ..87 F7
Bailey Cl CW1 ......190 C7
Bailey Cres
  Congleton CW12 ....157 A4
  Sandbach CW11 ....175 D6
Bailey Ct Alsager ST7 .193 E2
  1 Macclesfield SK10 .112 E7
Bailey M31 ....11 F8
Bailey's Bank ST8 ...179 D3
Bailey's La L24 ......21 A1
Baileys Cl WA8 ......13 A5
Baileys La L26 ......21 A7
Bainbridge Ave WA3 ...3 F8
Bainbridge Cres WA5 ..14 E4
Baines Ave M44 ......11 F8
Baker Cl CW2 ....190 A2
Baker Dr CH66 ......69 E3
Baker Rd WA7 ....48 D7
Baker St **8** SK11 ...112 C4
Baker's Ct CW7 .....126 E1
Baker's La
  Swan Green WA16 ...106 D6
  Winsford CW7 .....126 E1
Bakers Pl WA2 ....16 B7
Bakers Villas The CW12 .156 D2
Bakestonedale Rd SK10 .63 E8
Bakewell Cl CH66 ....94 E8
Bakewell Rd
  Burtonwood WA5 .....7 A7
  Hazel Grove SK7 ....36 E8
Bala Cl WA5 ....7 E2
Baldock Cl WA4 .....17 C3
Balfour Cl CW1 .....191 C4
Balfour St WA7 ......22 F1
Balham Cl WA8 ......13 A4
Balharry Ave WA11 ....1 E7
Ball La Bollington SK10 .87 D5
  Kingsley WA6 ....75 E4
Ball Pathway WA1 ....12 E1
Ballantyne Pl WA2 .....8 A6
Ballantyne Way **5** WA3 ..3 E8
Ballater Cres WA3 ...119 B2
Ballater Dr WA2 ......8 E4
Ballerat Cl CH1 .....117 D4
Balliol Cl SK11 .....112 E3
Balmoral Ave
  Crewe CW2 ....190 B1
  Northwich CW9 .....104 A5
Balmoral Cl
  Knutsford WA16 .....57 B1
  Winsford CW7 .....126 C3
Balmoral Cres SK10 ..87 F2
Balmoral Dr Helsby WA6 .73 B4
  High Lane SK6 ......37 F7
  Holmes Chapel CW4 .130 B2
  Poynton SK12 ......36 D3
Balmoral Gdns
  Congleton CW12 ....156 F4
  Ellesmere Port CH65 ..70 D3
Balmoral Pk CH1 ....118 B3
Balmoral Pl CW5 ....205 D4
Balmoral Rd
  Warrington WA4 .....16 F2
  Widnes WA8 ....13 A4
Balmoral Way SK9 ...60 A6
Bamburgh Ct CH65 ...70 E3
Bamford Cl
  Bollington SK10 .....88 A7
  Heald Green SK8 ....34 D8

Bamford Cl continued
  Runcorn WA7 ....49 C7
Bamford St SK10 .....87 E1
Banastre Dr WA12 .....2 F3
Banbury Cl SK10 ......87 E2
Banbury Ct CW6 .....146 D1
Banbury St ST7 .....194 D1
Bancroft CW8 ....76 F4
Bancroft Rd WA8 .....13 D2
Bandon Cl L24 ....21 D2
Banff Ave CH63 ......43 D5
Bangor Cl CH66 ......94 F8
Bank Cl Chester CH2 ..118 E5
  Neston CH64 ....67 A6
Bank Cott CW12 .....156 D2
Bank Ct **5** ST7 .....195 A8
Bank Farm Mews SY14 .214 E6
Bank Gdns WA5 ......14 E4
Bank Ho CW7 ......126 C1
Bank House La
  Helsby WA6 ....73 C4
  Smallwood CW11 ....177 A6
Bank La Burland CW5 ..203 D7
  Congleton CW12 ....134 C1
  Rainow SK10 ....89 D6
Bank Mews WA5 ......73 C4
Bank Rd CH5 ....91 D1
Bank Side CW8 ......77 C1
Bank Sq SK9 ....60 B7
Bank St Congleton CW12 .156 D2
  Hollinfare WA3 ......11 B5
  Kidsgrove ST7 .....195 C4
  Macclesfield SK11 ...112 E7
  Newton-le-W WA12 ....1 F3
  9 Warrington WA1 ..16 B5
  Widnes WA8 ....23 A4
Bank The ST7 ......195 B7
Bank Top Cotts CW5 .204 F6
Bank View CW7 .....107 E1
Bankend Barn SK23 ...39 C5
Bankes' La
  Runcorn,Weston WA7 .48 F5
  Runcorn,Weston Point WA7 .48 E6
Bankfield Ave Irlam M44 .11 D5
  Wistaston CW2 .....206 A4
Bankfield Rd WA8 ....12 C1
Bankfield Sch The WA8 .12 D1
Bankfields Dr CH2 ....44 B5
Bankhall La WA14,WA15 .31 F8
Bankhall Pk WA1 .....16 C4
Bankhouse Dr CW12 .157 A5
Banklands Cl M44 .....11 D5
Banks Cl CW12 .....156 C3
Banks Cres WA4 ......16 F4
Banks Rd CH60 ......40 D8
Bankside Altrincham WA15 .32 D6
  Runcorn WA7 ....50 E7
Bankside Cl
  Handforth SK9 ......34 D1
Bankside Ct ST7 ....193 E5
Banky Fields CW12 ..156 C2
Banky Fields Cres
  CW12 ....156 C1
Bannacks Cl CW5 ...205 D6
Barbauld St WA1 .....16 B5
Barber Dr ST7 .....194 E7
Barber St SK11 .....112 E7
Barber's La Antrobus CW9 .53 D6
  Northwich CW8 .....103 E8
Barberry Wlk M31 ....11 F3
Barbondale Rd WA5 ...14 F7
Barbour Sq CH3 ....166 B1
Barbridge Mews CW5 .187 D6
Barbridge Rd ST5 ...210 D2
Barclay Hall WA16 ...58 D4
Barclay Rd SK12 .....36 E2
Bardell Cl SK12 ......36 D2
Bardsey Cl **1** CH65 ..70 C1
Bardsley Ave WA5 .....7 F1
Barford Cl WA5 ....7 B1
Barford Dr Golborne WA3 .4 A8
  Handforth SK9 ......34 C1
Barford Grange CH64 .68 B8
Barham Ct WA3 ....9 D4
Barhill Farm Cotts SY13 .214 C2
Barington Dr WA7 ....50 E7
Baristow Cl CH2 ....237 B4
Bark St WA12 ....156 E2
Barker St Crewe CW2 .190 D1
  Nantwich CW5 .....204 E5
Barker's Hollow Rd WA4 .51 A5
Barkhill Rd CH1 .....119 B3
Barley Castle Cl WA4 ..27 B3
Barley Croft Alsager ST7 .193 E2
  Cheadle Hulme SK8 ...34 F8
  Chester CH3 ....142 A7
Barley Dr SK7 ....35 E7
Barley Mow Cl CH66 ..69 C2
Barley Rd WA4 ......17 C3
Barleycastle La WA4 ..27 D4
Barleycastle Trad Est
  WA4 ....27 D4
Barleycroft Terr ST7 .194 F7
Barleyfields ST7 ....209 D2
Barleywood Cl CW2 ..206 B8
Barlow Dr CW7 .....148 F8
Barlow Gr WA9 ....1 A2
Barlow Hill SK11 ....136 F2
Barlow Rd Handforth SK9 .34 B1
  Moulton CW9 ......126 F7
Barlow Way CW11 ...175 A8
Barmouth Cl WA5 .....7 E2
Barn Croft WA6 ......73 C4

Barn Croft Rd L26 ....21 A7
Barn Ct CH3 ....182 C2
Barn La WA3 ....2 F8
Barn Mdw CW8 ......78 E1
Barn Rd CW12 .....156 D4
Barn Way WA8 ......23 A6
Barn Way WA12 ......2 B3
Barnabas Ave CW1 ..189 F5
Barnaby Chase CH3 .182 C2
Barnaby Rd SK12 ....36 D2
Barnack Cl WA1 .....17 A8
Barnacre Dr CH64 ....41 B3
Barnard St WA5 .....15 D3
Barnato Cl CW1 ....189 F7
Barnbridge Cl ST7 ..194 E7
Barnbrook Cl CW7 ..126 A1
Barncroft WA7 ......50 D7
Barncroft Cl SK11 ....84 A3
Barnes Ave WA2 ......9 B2
Barnes Cl Blacon CH1 .117 F6
  Haslington CW1 ....191 C4
  Widnes WA5 ....15 A5
  Widnes WA8 ....13 D2
Barnes Rd WA8 ......13 C2
Barneston Rd WA8 ...13 B3
Barnett Ave WA12 .....1 E3
Barnett Gr CW2 ....156 A3
Barnett St SK11 ....112 B7
Barnett Wlk CW2 ...206 C8
Barnfield CH3 ......166 A4
Barnfield Ave WA7 ...50 D7
Barnfield Cl CH66 ....69 C2
Barnfield Rd
  Bollington SK10 .....87 F6
  Warrington WA1 .....17 C7
Barnham Cl WA3 ......3 A8
Barnhill Grange CH3 .183 B3
Barnhill Rd CH3 ....183 A1
Barnhouse La
  Great Barrow CH3 ..120 E7
  Mouldsworth CH3 ....98 A3
Barnmoore Cl SY14 ..213 B4
Barns La WA3,WA14 ..20 A5
Barns Pl WA15 ......32 C8
Barns The WA7 .....127 D5
Barnside Way
  Macclesfield SK10 ...87 C3
  Moulton CW9 .....126 F8
Barnston Ave CH65 ...69 F5
Barnston Ct CH3 ....180 E2
Barnston Prim Sch CH60 .41 C7
Barnston Rd CH60 ....41 C6
Barnston Towers Cl
  CH60 ....41 C8
Barnston Twrs CH60 ..41 C8
Barnswood Cl WA4 ...17 C1
Barnton WA3 ....3 D7
Barnton Prim Sch CW8 .78 A4
Barnwell Ave WA3 .....4 D4
Barnwell Cl CW2 ...206 B8
Baron Cl WA1 ....17 D7
Baron Gn SK8 ....34 D7
Baron's Cl WA8 ......22 C8
Baronet Mews WA4 ...16 A1
Baronet Rd WA4 .....16 A1
Baronia Pl CW5 ....204 F6
Barons Cl WA7 ....23 F1
Barons Ct CH2 .....118 C4
Barons Quay Rd CW9 .78 C1
Barons Rd
  Shavington CW2 ....206 A4
  Worleston CW5 ....188 C5
Barony Bldgs **1** CW5 .204 E6
Barony Ct CW5 .....204 E7
Barony Employment Pk The
  CW5 ....204 F8
Barony Rd CW5 .....204 E7
Barony Terr CW5 ...204 E6
Barony Way CH4 ....140 E4
Barracks La
  Burwardsley CH3 ...184 C5
  Macclesfield SK10 ...112 F6
  Ravensmoor CW5 ...203 E1
Barracks Sq **3** SK11 .112 B6
Barrastitch La CW8 ..101 E6
Barratt Rd ST7 .....193 F3
Barrel Well Hill CH2 .118 F1
Barrie Gdns ST7 ....210 C8
Barrie Gr CW1 .....190 E4
Barrington Dr CW10 .151 C7
Barrow Ave WA2 ......8 E2
Barrow CE Prim Sch
  CH3 ....120 D6
Barrow Hall Com Prim Sch
  WA5 ....14 E7
Barrow Hall Farm CH3 .120 E5
Barrow Hall La WA5 ..14 E7
Barrow La
  Altrincham WA15 .....32 B7
  Golborne WA2 ....3 C2
  Great Barrow CH3 ..120 C5
  Tarvin CH3 ....121 C4
Barrow Mdw SK8 ....34 E8
Barrow's Brow WA16 .81 E1
Barrow's Green La WA8 .13 E3
Barrow's Row WA8 ...13 B4
Barrowdale Rd WA3 ...3 B8
Barrowmore Est CH3 .120 F7
Barrows Ct CW1 ....190 A8
Barrule Cl WA4 ......26 D7
Barry Cl CH65 ....95 C8
Barry St WA4 ....16 C4
Barrymore Ave WA4 ..16 A1
Barrymore Cres CW9 .78 D8
Barrymore Ct WA1 ...17 A1

Barrymore Rd
  Runcorn WA7 ....49 B7
  Warrington WA4 .....17 A1
  Weaverham WA8 ....77 C1
Barrymore Way CH63 .43 B6
Bars The CH1,CH3 ...237 C2
Barsbank Cl WA13 ...18 C3
Barsbank La WA13 ...18 C3
Barshaw Gdns WA4 ...26 A4
Bartholomew Way CH4 .141 C6
Bartholomew Cres CW2 .189 D4
Barthomley Rd
  Barthomley CW2 ...208 B7
  Betley ST7 ....208 F3
Bartington Hall Pk CW8 .77 A5
Bartlegate WA7 ......50 B5
Barton Ave WA4 .....17 A2
Barton Cl Handforth SK9 .34 D2
  Runcorn WA7 ....50 C7
Barton Rd
  Barton CH3,SY14 ...181 D1
  Congleton CW12 ....156 F3
  Farndon CH3 ......180 F1
Barton St SK11 .....112 C7
Barton Stad CW7 ...126 F1
Barton's Pl CW9 .....79 B1
Barwood Ave ST7 ...194 A5
Barwoods Dr CH4 ...140 F6
Basford Rd CW7 ....206 D8
Basford Way CW7 ...126 B2
Baskervyle Cl CH60 ..41 A6
Baskervyle Rd CH60 ..41 A6
Baslow Dr Hazel Grove SK7 .36 F8
  Heald Green SK8 ....34 C8
Bassett Cl CW5 ....205 D6
Batchelors Wing The
  CW10 ....127 D5
Bate's Mill La CW6 ..167 E5
Bateman Rd CW9 .....80 B2
Batemans Ct CW2 ...206 B8
Batemill Cl SK10 .....86 F1
Batemill La WA16,SK11 .108 C5
Bates La WA3 ....73 D4
Bath Cres SK8 ......35 B6
Bath La WA3 ....230 A3
Bath St Chester CH1 .237 B2
  Sandbach CW11 ....175 C6
  Warrington WA1 .....16 A5
Bath Vale Cotts CW12 .157 A3
Batherton Cl WA8 ....23 B7
Batherton La CW5 ...204 F2
Bathwood Dr CH64 ...66 E5
Batterbee Cl CW1 ...191 D5
Battersby La WA2 ....16 C6
Battersea Ct WA8 ....12 F3
Battery La WA1 ......17 F7
Bawtry Cl WA2 ....8 E1
Baxter Cl WA7 ....50 D7
Baxter Ho WA8 ......78 E1
Baxter St WA5 ......15 E5
Baycliffe WA13 ......18 D2
Baycliffe Cl WA7 .....49 D5
Bayley Rd CW5 .....205 D6
Bayswater Cl WA7 ...24 F4
Baytree Cl CH66 .....69 F1
Bayvil Cl WA7 ....50 E7
Beach Gr CW8 ......103 C6
Beach Rd CW8 ......103 B6
Beachin La CH3 ....182 A4
Beacon Ct **4** CH60 ..41 A8
Beacon Hill View WA7 .48 D7
Beacon La CH60 .....41 A7
Beacons The
  Heswall CH60 ......41 A7
  Warrington WA3 ......9 D5
Beaconsfield Cres WA8 .13 A4
Beaconsfield Gr WA8 .13 B4
Beaconsfield Rd
  Runcorn WA7 ....22 E1
  Widnes WA8 ....13 B4
Beaconsfield St CH3 .237 C2
Beadnell Dr WA5 .....14 F3
Beagle Point CW7 ...126 A1
Beagle Wlk M22 .....33 E8
Beam Heath Way CW5 .204 F7
Beam St CW5 ......204 E6
Beamish Cl WA4 .....26 D3
Beamont St WA8 .....23 A4
Beard Cres SK22 .....39 D8
Beardsmore Dr WA3 ...3 E8
Bearhurst La SK11 ...111 A5
Bearstone Rd TF9 ..236 E3
Beasley Cl CH66 .....69 D3
Beata Rd ST5 ......210 F1
Beatrice St WA4 .....16 D4
Beatty Ave WA8 ......8 C1
Beatty Dr CW12 ....157 A4
Beatty Rd CW5 .....204 D4
Beaufort Chase SK9 ..34 F1
Beaufort Cl
  Alderley Edge SK9 ...60 B2
  Runcorn WA7 ....49 B7
  Warrington WA5 .....15 A5
  Widnes WA8 ....22 A8
Beaufort St WA5 .....15 E4
Beaulieu Ave CW7 ..126 F2
Beaumaris Cres SK7 ..36 C8
Beaumaris Dr CH65 ..70 D2
Beaumont Cl
  Biddulph ST8 ......179 D3
  Chester CH4 ......140 E6
  Wistaston CW2 ....205 F8
Beaumont Com Inf & Jun
  Schs WA2 ....16 C7
Beaumont Ct SK9 ....34 C5
Beauty Bank
  Whitegate CW7 ....125 E5

Beauty Bank continued
  Winsford CW7 .....149 A3
Beauty Bank Cotts CW7 .149 A3
Beaver Cl Chester CH4 .140 E5
  Pickmere WA16 .....79 F7
Beaver Ctr The CW9 .103 F7
Beaverbrook Ave WA3 ...5 B4
Bebington Rd CH66 ..69 D4
Becconsall Cl CW1 ..190 A8
Becconsall Dr CW1 ..190 A8
Bechers WA8 ....12 B3
Beckenham Gr **4** CW7 .126 A1
Beckett Ave CW7 ...150 D8
Beckett Dr Lymm WA13 ..19 B8
  Winwick WA2 ....8 A4
Beckett's La CH3 ...142 A8
Beckford Cl CW1 ...189 F8
Becks La SK10 ....86 F2
Bedells La SK9 ......60 A6
Bedford Ave CH65 ...70 A2
Bedford Ave E CH65 ..70 B2
Bedford Cl CW2 ....190 D1
Bedford Gdns CW2 ..190 C1
Bedford Gn M44 .....11 B6
Bedford Gr ST7 ....193 B5
Bedford Pl CW2 ....190 C1
Bedford Rise CW7 ..149 C6
Bedford St
  Kidsgrove ST7 .....195 A3
  Macclesfield SK11 ...112 B7
Bedford Rise CW7 ..149 C6
Bedford St Crewe CW2 .190 C1
  Warrington WA4 .....26 C8
Bedward Row CH1 ..237 A2
Beech Ave Culcheth WA3 ..5 A3
  Frodsham WA6 ......74 C5
  Golborne WA3 ....3 F7
  Haydock WA11 ......1 F7
  Mobberley WA16 ....57 E6
  Rode Heath ST7 ....193 F8
  Warrington WA5 .....14 C3
  Warrington, Thelwall WA4 ..17 F5
Beech Cl
  Alderley Edge SK9 ...60 B3
  Congleton CW12 ....156 A4
  Cuddington CW8 ....101 F2
  Holmes Chapel CW4 .130 D4
  Newton-le-W WA12 ....2 C2
  Ollerton WA16 ......82 F6
  4 Partington M31 ...11 F3
Beech Cotts
  Alderley Edge SK9 ...85 A8
  Stretton WA4 ....26 E1
Beech Cres SK12 .....36 E4
Beech Dr Crewe CW2 .189 F2
  Knutsford WA16 .....57 C2
  Talke ST7 ....210 E8
Beech Farm Dr SK10 ..87 D2
Beech Gr Chester CH2 .119 A3
  Crewe CW1 ....190 E5
  Ellesmere Port CH66 ..95 A8
  Lymm WA13 ....18 B2
  Macclesfield SK11 ...112 E5
  Sandbach CW11 ....175 D6
  Warrington WA1 .....17 A7
  Warrington, Latchford WA4 .16 D3
  Weaverham WA8 ....102 D8
  Wilmslow SK9 ......60 A6
  Winsford CW7 .....149 D8
Beech Hall Dr SK10 ..87 C2
Beech Hall Sch SK10 ..87 C2
Beech Hey La CH64 ..43 B1
Beech Heyes Cl CW8 .102 E8
Beech Heyes Dr CW8 .102 E8
Beech Hollows LL12 .162 C1
Beech La Barnton CW8 ..78 A3
  Eaton CW6 ....147 B6
  Macclesfield SK10 ...87 D1
  Norley WA6 ....75 E1
  Wilmslow SK9 ......60 A6
Beech Rd
  Alderley Edge SK9 ...60 B3
  Heswall CH60 ......41 C8
  High Lane SK6 ......37 F7
  Little Budworth CW6 .124 D2
  Morley Green WA16 ..59 C5
  Runcorn WA7 ....49 C8
  Sutton WA7 ....50 B4
  Warrington WA4 .....26 C8
  Whaley Bridge SK23 ..65 C5
Beech Rise Crowton CW8 .76 B2
  Whaley Bridge SK23 ..65 C5
Beech St Crewe CW1 .190 C4
  Middlewich CW10 ...128 C1
Beech Tree Cl CW5 ..205 D5
Beech View Rd WA6 ..75 C1
Beechcroft Ave CW2 .206 B7
Beechcroft Dr CH65 ..70 B2
Beeches The
  Chester CH2 ....119 A6
  Ellesmere Port CH66 ..69 D4
  Helsby WA6 ....73 C4
  Mobberley WA16 ....58 E1
  Nantwich CW5 .....204 F5
  3 Northwich CW9 ..103 E6
  Whitchurch SY13 ...225 F1
Beechfield Moulton CW9 .126 E8
  Wilmslow SK9 ......60 A6
Beechfield Ave SK9 ...59 E5
Beechfield Cl CH60 ...41 A7
Beechfield Dr CW10 .128 B2
Beechfield Gdns CW8 .103 B6
Beechfield Rd
  Alderley Edge SK9 ...85 B8

Beechfield Rd continued
Cheadle Hulme SK8 ......35 B8
Ellesmere Port CH65 ......70 B5
Warrington WA4 ......17 A2
Beechfields CW7 ......150 B8
Beechlands Ave CH3 ...119 A1
Beechmill Dr WA3 ......4 E3
Beechmoore WA4 ......25 B5
Beechmuir CH1 ......117 E3
Beechtree Farm Cl WA16 29 C7
Beechtree La WA13 ......29 B7
Beechway Bollington SK10 .88 D7
Chester CH2 ......118 C6
High Lane SK6 ......37 F7
Neston CH64 ......66 D7
Wilmslow SK9 ......59 F5
Beechways WA4 ......26 D5
Beechways Dr CH64 ......66 D7
Beechwood
Knutsford WA16 ......56 F3
Knutsford,Cross Town
WA16 ......57 C2
Beechwood Ave
Hartford CW8 ......103 A6
Newton-le-W WA12 ......2 D4
Runcorn WA7 ......49 E5
Warrington WA5 ......14 F5
Warrington,Padgate WA1 ...16 E7
Beechwood Dr
Alsager ST7 ......193 B4
Eaton (nr Congleton)
CW12 ......156 F8
Ellesmere Port CH66 ......69 D1
Higher Wincham CW9 ...79 F6
Wilmslow SK9 ......60 E8
Beechwood Gr SK8 ......35 A8
Beechwood La WA3 ......4 E4
Beechwood Mews SK10 .87 C2
Beechwood Prim Sch
WA7 ......49 E5
Beechwood Rd
Bebington CH62 ......43 C8
Saltney CH4 ......140 C5
Beechwood Sch CW1 .190 C5
Beecroft Cl WA5 ......7 D1
Beehive La CW9 ......126 F8
Beeston Castle★ CW6 ..167 F3
Beeston Cl Bollington SK10 63 C1
Holmes Chapel CW4 ......130 A3
Middlewich CW10 ......151 D5
Warrington WA3 ......9 D4
Beeston Ct WA7 ......24 C4
Beeston Dr Alsager ST7 ...193 C3
Knutsford WA16 ......82 A8
Winsford CW7 ......149 C7
Beeston Gn CH66 ......69 E5
Beeston Hall Mews
CW6 ......168 B4
Beeston Mount SK10 ...63 C1
Beeston Pathway CW1 .141 E7
Beeston Rd
Broughton CH4 ......139 B3
Handforth SK9 ......34 D5
Higher Kinnerton CH4 ...161 A7
Beeston St CW8 ......103 E7
Beeston Terr SK11 ......111 E6
Beeston View CW7 ......141 E7
Beggarman's La WA16 ..82 A7
Begonia Gdns WA9 ......6 A7
Beilby Rd WA11 ......1 C7
Belfry Cl SK9 ......60 D8
Belfry Dr SK10 ......87 C4
Belgrave Ave
Alsager ST7 ......193 D5
Congleton CW12 ......156 D3
Saltney CH4 ......140 E6
Warrington WA1 ......16 E7
Belgrave Cl
Dodleston CH4 ......162 A6
Golborne WN7 ......4 C8
Widnes WA8 ......13 E3
Belgrave Dr CH65 ......69 F5
Belgrave Inf Sch CH4 ...141 B5
Belgrave Pl CH4 ......237 B1
Belgrave Rd Chester CH3 142 A7
Crewe CW2 ......190 B2
Irlam M44 ......11 D5
Macclesfield SK11 ......112 C4
Northwich CW9 ......104 A4
Belgrave St CH1 ......237 C3
Belgravia Ct Pulford CH4 162 E5
Widnes WA8 ......12 F3
Belgravia Gdns WA15 ...31 E8
Bell Ave SK11 ......112 F3
Bell Farm Ct SK10 ......87 C3
Bell House Rd WA8 ......13 C1
Bell La Smallwood CW11 .177 B7
Warrington WA4 ......17 E3
Bell Meadow Bsns Pk
CH4 ......162 E5
Bell Meadow Ct WA4 ..146 C2
Bell's Hollow ST5 ......210 E3
Bellaport Rd TF9 ......236 A4
Bellard Dr CH2 ......119 A4
Bellcast Cl WA4 ......26 C5
Belle Vue Terr CW11 ...175 B6
Bellemonte Rd WA6 ...74 C6
Belleville Ave M22 ......33 E8
Bellevue La CH3 ......119 E4
Bellhouse La
Higher Walton WA4 ......25 D7
Warrington WA4 ......17 C1
Bellingham Cl WA16 ...57 C2
Bellingham Dr WA7 .....49 A8

Bellsfield Cl WA13 ......18 F2
Belmont Ave
Macclesfield SK10 ......86 C1
Sandbach CW11 ......175 A7
Warrington WA4 ......16 F3
Belmont Cres WA5 ......15 A6
Belmont Dr CH4 ......140 C6
Belmont Rd Bramhall SK7 .35 F5
Great Budworth CW9 ...53 F1
Northwich CW9 ......104 C7
Widnes WA8 ......13 E2
Belton Cl WA3 ......3 A7
Beltony Dr CW1 ......173 A1
Belvedere 9 WA7 ......23 A3
Belvedere Cl 2 WA6 ...49 C1
Belvedere Dr CH1 ......117 E4
Belvedere Rd WA12 ......2 B5
Belvedere Terr ST7 ......193 F7
Belvoir Ave SK7 ......36 E8
Belvoir Rd
Warrington WA4 ......26 B8
Widnes WA8 ......13 B1
Bembridge Cl
Widnes WA8 ......12 F4
Warrington WA5 ......14 C7
Bembridge Ct CW10 ....151 C8
Bembridge Dr CW10 ....151 C8
Ben Nevis Dr CH66 ......68 F6
Benbrook Gr SK9 ......34 E2
Benbrook Way SK11 ....111 E1
Bendee Ave CH64 ......67 A7
Bendee Rd CH64 ......67 A7
Benjamins Way ST7 ....209 F2
Bennet Cl CH64 ......68 A8
Bennet Rd CW9 ......104 D6
Bennett Ave WA1 ......16 F6
Bennett Cl CW1 ......190 E4
Bennett Ct CW7 ......149 D5
Bennett St WA1 ......16 B5
Bennett's La
Higher Kinnerton CH4 ...161 A7
Widnes WA8 ......13 E1
Bennetts La SK11 ......158 E7
Benson Rd WA3 ......9 D3
Benson Wlk 3 SK9 ......34 D2
Bent La Astbury CW12 ...178 A8
Culcheth WA3 ......5 A2
Lymm WA13 ......19 C6
Norley WA6 ......101 C8
Bentham Ave WA2 ......8 C3
Bentham Rd WA3 ......5 A2
Bentinck St WA7 ......22 F3
Bentley Dr CW1 ......191 A5
Bentley Gr CW7 ......149 C6
Bentley's Farm La WA4 .52 E5
Benton Dr CH2 ......118 C4
Bents Cotts CH2 ......71 E2
Bentside Rd SK12 ......38 D5
Benty Heath La CH64,
CH66 ......43 B3
Beresford Ct 4 SK9 ......60 A1
Beresford St WA1 ......16 E7
Berisford Ho CW12 ....156 E3
Berkeley Ave ST7 ......193 D5
Berkeley Cl WN7 ......4 C8
Berkeley Cres CW2 ....206 A8
Berkeley Ct
Newton-le-W WA12 ......1 F4
Runcorn WA7 ......24 D4
Berkeley Prim Sch The
CW2 ......206 B7
Berkeley Rise CW7 .....149 A8
Berkley Cl SK23 ......65 D6
Berkley Dr CH4 ......141 E6
Berkshire Dr
Congleton CW12 ......156 D4
Irlam M44 ......11 C5
Warrington WA1 ......17 E7
Bermondsey Gr WA8 ...13 D4
Bernard Ave WA4 ......26 D8
Bernisdale Rd WA16 ....57 F4
Bernsdale Cl CH5 ......116 A3
Berristal Rd SK10 ......88 E3
Berristall Rise SK10 ....63 C1
Berry Cl
Ellesmere Port CH66 ......69 C3
Wilmslow SK9 ......60 A5
Berry Dr CH66 ......69 C3
Berry Rd WA8 ......12 D1
Berrystead CW8 ......103 B4
Bertram St WA12 ......2 A4
Berwick Ave CH62 ......43 E4
Berwick Cl
Macclesfield SK10 ......86 F2
Warrington WA1 ......17 E6
Berwick Ct CW4 ......130 B2
Berwick Gdns CH66 ...69 B6
Berwick Rd CH66 ......69 A6
Berwyn Cl CH66 ......69 A6
Bessancourt CW4 ......130 C3
Bessemer Rd M44 ......11 F6
Beswick St SK11 ......112 B7
Beswicks La
Norton in Hales TF9 ....236 C2
Row-of-trees SK9 ......59 C3
Beswicks Rd CW8 ......78 C1
Betchton Cl CW11 ......175 C7
Betchton Ct 6 CW12 ...156 F3
Betchton Rd CW11 ....175 E3
Betchworth Cres WA4 ..49 D6
Betchworth Way SK10 ..87 C4
Bethany Cl WA11 ......1 B7
Betjeman Cl WA4 ......16 F4
Betjeman Way CW1 ....190 F5
Betley Cl CW9 ......104 A5
Betley St CW1 ......190 C4

Betsyfield Dr WA3 ......9 A8
Bettisfield Ave CH62 ...43 D6
Betty's La CW6 ......168 D1
Bevan Ave ST7 ......210 E6
Bevan Cl WA5 ......15 D6
Beverley Ave WA4 ......26 D8
Beverley Dr CH60 ......41 B6
Beverley Rd WA5 ......15 C6
Beverley Way
Ellesmere Port CH66 ......69 B7
Macclesfield SK10 ......87 C4
Bevin Ave WA3 ......5 B4
Bevyl Rd CH64 ......41 B2
Bewick Wlk WA16 ......57 B3
Bewley Ct CH3 ......142 A7
Bewsey Bsns Ctr WA5 ..15 F7
Bewsey Farm Cl WA5 ..15 D8
Bewsey Ind Est WA5 ...16 A7
Bewsey Lodge Prim Sch
WA5 ......15 F7
Bewsey Park Cl WA5 ...15 F7
Bewsey Rd WA2,WA5 ...16 A6
Bewsey St 1 WA4 ......16 B5
Bexhill Ave WA2 ......8 B4
Bexington Dr CW1 ......190 B8
Bexton Ave CW7 ......126 A2
Bexton La WA16 ......82 A8
Bexton Prim Sch WA16 ...82 B7
Bexton Rd WA16 ......56 F1
Bibby Ave WA1 ......16 E6
Bibby St ST7 ......193 E6
Bibby's La ST7 ......88 A1
Bickerton Ave WA6 ....74 D7
Bickerton Cl WA3 ......9 D4
Bickerton Holy Trinity CE
Prim Sch SY14 ......200 A7
Bickerton Rd SY14 ....201 B2
Bickerton Way 1 CW9 .103 E4
Bickley Cl Hough CW2 ..206 E2
Northwich CW9 ......103 E5
Runcorn WA7 ......23 C1
Bickley Town La SY14 ..214 E6
Bicknell Cl WA5 ......15 B8
Bida La CW12 ......179 B8
Biddulph Common Rd
ST8 ......179 F7
Biddulph Grange Ctry Pk★
ST8 ......179 F3
Biddulph Grange Gdn★
ST8 ......179 F3
Biddulph Park Rd ST8 ..179 F5
Biddulph Rd
Biddulph ST7 ......195 F6
Congleton CW12 ......179 B8
Biddulph St CW12 ......179 C7
Bideford Rd WA5 ......14 E4
Bidston Cl CW2 ......118 D5
Bidston Dr SK9 ......34 E2
Bidston Gn CH66 ......69 D4
Bidvale Way CW1 ......190 D7
Big Field La CW6 ......146 B7
Biggin Cl WA2 ......8 E1
Bignall End Rd
Audley ST7 ......210 A3
Newcastle-u-Lyme ST7 ..210 A4
Billington Ave WA12 ....2 C5
Billington Cl Crewe CW2 190 A1
Warrington WA5 ......14 E8
Billington Rd WA8 ......12 B3
Bilton Cl WA8 ......13 E2
Bilton Way CW2 ......189 E5
Bings Rd SK23 ......65 F8
Bingswood Ave SK23 ...65 E8
Bingswood Ind Est SK23 .65 E8
Bingswood Rd SK23 ...65 E7
Binney Rd CW9 ......104 B8
Binyon Way CW1 ......191 A4
Birch Ave Alsager ST7 ..193 E2
Crewe CW1 ......190 F5
Irlam M44 ......11 D5
Macclesfield SK10 ......87 B1
Warrington WA2 ......8 A4
Wilmslow SK9 ......59 F6
Winsford CW7 ......127 A1
Birch Brook Rd WA13 ..19 C5
Birch Cl Crewe CW1 ....190 F5
Holmes Chapel CW4 ....130 D3
Birch Cres WA12 ......1 F4
Birch Ct CW12 ......155 F3
Birch Fold CW7 ......107 B1
Birch Gdns CW11 ......175 C5
Birch Gr
Ellesmere Port CH66 ......70 A1
Higher Wincham CW9 ...79 F5
Knutsford WA16 ......57 D2
Lostock Green CW9 ......105 B7
Warrington,Bruche WA1 ...16 F7
Warrington,Latchford WA4 .16 D3
Birch Heath La CH3 ...142 F8
Birch Heath Rd CW6 ...168 C8
Birch Hill WA6 ......99 C8
Birch Ho SK7 ......35 E5
Birch House Rd ST5 ...210 D1
Birch La Hough CW2 ...206 F2
Winsford CW10 ......127 F2
Birch Rd Audley ST7 ...209 F1
Chester CH4 ......140 F5
Congleton CW12 ......155 F3
Haydock WA11 ......1 E7
Hollinfare WA3 ......11 B2
Partington M31 ......11 D3
Poynton SK12 ......36 F2
Runcorn WA7 ......49 C8
Widnes WA8 ......13 B3
Birch Rise CH2 ......118 D6
Birch Tree Ave SK7 ....37 A8
Birch Tree Ct CH2 ......237 C4

Birch Tree La
Antrobus CW4 ......53 A6
Goostrey CW4 ......107 C1
The Bank ST7 ......195 B8
Birch Tree Rd 6 WA3 ....3 F8
Birch Valley Rd ST7 ...195 C1
Birch Way SK10 ......86 E6
Birchall Ave WA3 ......4 E4
Birchall Moss La CW5 .219 E1
Birchall St WA3 ......9 A7
Birchall Wlk CW2 ......206 D8
Birchdale Cres WA4 ....26 C8
Birchdale Rd
Warrington WA4 ......26 C8
Warrington,Paddington
WA1 ......17 A7
Birchen Rd L26 ......21 A7
Birchencliff Cl SK10 ...63 D6
Birchenwood Rd ST6,
ST7 ......195 E1
Birchenwood Way ST7 .195 E1
Birches Cl CH60 ......41 A8
Birches Croft Dr SK10 ..86 F1
Birches Ho 2 CH60 ....41 A8
Birches La CW9 ......105 B7
Birches The
Broughton CH4 ......139 B3
Crewe CW2 ......206 C8
Neston CH64 ......41 F2
Birches Wlk 7 ST7 ....195 B2
Birchfield Ave
Rode Heath ST7 ......193 F7
Widnes WA8 ......13 A2
Birchfield Rd Lymm WA13 .19 B4
Warrington WA5 ......15 B5
Widnes,Appleton WA8 ...13 A1
Widnes,Farnworth WA8 ..13 A3
Birchgate Cl SK10 ......86 E1
Birchhall Cl WA5 ......204 F4
Birchin Cl CW5 ......205 A6
Birchin La CW5 ......205 A6
Birchinall Cl SK11 ......112 A7
Birchmuir CH1 ......117 E3
Birchmuir Cl CW1 ......190 B6
Birchway Bollington SK10 .88 A8
Bramhall SK7 ......35 D7
Heswall CH60 ......41 C5
High Lane SK6 ......37 F7
Birchways WA4 ......26 C5
Birchwood Bvd WA3 ....9 D2
Birchwood CE Prim Sch
WA3 ......9 F3
Birchwood Cl
Ellesmere Port CH66 ......69 D1
Elton CH2 ......72 C3
Birchwood Com High Sch
WA3 ......9 D3
Birchwood Dr
Nantwich CW5 ......204 F6
Swan Green WA16 ....106 D7
Wilmslow SK9 ......60 D8
Birchwood Forest Pk
WA3 ......10 A5
Birchwood La WA4 ....25 C8
Birchwood Office Pk WA3 9 B3
Birchwood One Bsns Pk
WA3 ......9 A3
Birchwood Park Ave WA3 .9 F3
Birchwood Science Pk
WA3 ......9 D5
Birchwood Sh Ctr WA3 ..9 D2
Birchwood Sta WA3 ....9 E3
Birchwood Tech Pk WA3 .9 E5
Birchwood Way WA2,WA3 .9 D3
Bird's La CW6 ......186 B8
Birds La Tarporley CW6 .146 C1
Tattenhall CH3 ......166 E1
Birdwell Dr WA5 ......15 A5
Birkdale Ave CH63 ....43 A7
Birkdale Cl Bramhall SK7 .36 A7
Macclesfield SK10 ......87 C4
Birkdale Ct 3 CW9 ....104 B8
Birkdale Dr ST7 ......195 C3
Birkdale Gdns CW7 ....126 A2
Birkdale Rd
Warrington WA5 ......14 F4
Widnes WA8 ......13 B5
Birkenhead Rd CH64 ...42 E1
Birkenhead St CW4 ....104 C8
Birkett Ave CH65 ......70 C2
Birkin Cl WA16 ......57 D4
Birkinheath La WA14 ...31 B4
Birley St WA12 ......2 D4
Birstall Ct WA7 ......49 D7
Birtles Cl CW11 ......175 C7
Birtles Hall SK10 ......85 D2
Birtles La SK10 ......85 E2
Birtles Rd
Macclesfield SK10 ......86 D1
Warrington WA2 ......8 D1
Birtles Way 4 SK9 ....34 D5
Birtley Ct WA8 ......12 B1
Birtwistle Rd CW9 .....104 C6
Bisham Pk WA7 ......24 D2
Bishop Heber High Sch
SY14 ......213 C5
Bishop Rd CH1 ......88 A7
Bishop Reeves Rd WA11 ...1 C7
Bishop St CH2 ......118 F2
Bishop Wilson CE Prim Sch
CH64 ......67 D1
Bishop's Cl ST7 ......210 D8
Bishopdale Cl WA5 ....14 F7
Bishopgates Dr CW9 ...103 E4
Bishops Ct
Broughton CH4 ......139 C4
Warrington WA2 ......8 A4
Bishops Gate CH2 ......119 A3

Bishops Gdns CH65 ....70 A5
Bishops Way WA8 ......13 D3
Bishops Wood CW5 ...204 D5
Bishops' Blue Coat CE High
Sch The CH3 ......142 B3
Bishopsfield Ct CH2 ...118 F3
Bishopton Dr SK11 ....111 F8
Bispham Rd WA5 ......15 B4
Bittern Cl Poynton SK12 ...36 A4
Runcorn WA7 ......50 D3
Warrington WA2 ......9 B3
Bittern Gr SK10 ......87 A1
Black Cat Ind Est WA8 ..23 A6
Black Denton's Pl WA8 .13 C1
Black Diamond St CH1 .237 B4
Black Firs La CW12 ....155 E4
Black Firs Prim Sch
CW12 ......155 F4
Black Friars CH1 ......237 A2
Black Lion La CH66 ....69 C6
Black Moss Rd WA14 ..20 F7
Black Park Rd SY13 ...226 D2
Black Rd SK11 ......112 F7
Blackacres Cl CW11 ...174 F6
Blackbird Way ST7 ....195 E1
Blackboards La CH66 ..69 A8
Blackbrook Ave WA2 ....8 F2
Blackbrook Cl WA8 ....12 C3
Blackburn Cl WA3 ......3 E8
Blackburne Ave WA8 ...22 B5
Blackburne Cl WA2 ......9 C2
Blackburne Dr WA12 ...2 A4
Blackcap Rd WA4 ......27 A4
Blackcap Wlk WA3 ......9 E3
Blackcroft Ave CW8 ....78 A2
Blackden Firs CW4 ....108 B2
Blackden La
Goostrey CW4 ......108 A3
Siddington SK11 ......132 F3
Blackden Wlk SK9 ......34 D1
Blackdown Cl CH66 ...69 A5
Blackeys La CH64 ......66 E8
Blackheath La WA7 ....24 F5
Blackhill La WA16 ......81 F8
Blackhurst Brow SK10 ..61 B2
Blackhurst Farm Rd
CW5 ......202 E3
Blackhurst St WA1 .....16 B5
Blackledge Cl WA2 ......9 A3
Blackley Cl
Macclesfield SK10 ......87 B4
Warrington WA2 ......16 D3
Blackshaw Cl CW12 ...157 B1
Blackshaw Dr WA5 ......7 B1
Blackshaw La SK9 ......59 F1
Blackshaw St 6 SK11 ..112 C7
Blackthorn Cl
Broughton CH4 ......139 B3
Huntington CH3 ......142 A5
Wistaston CW2 ......206 A8
Blackthorn Pl ST5 .....210 E1
Blackthorn Wlk 3 M31 ..11 E2
Blackthorne Ave CH66 .95 A8
Blackwell Cl CW10 ....151 D6
Blacon Ave CH1 ......118 A5
Blacon Hall Jun Sch
CH1 ......117 E5
Blacon Hall Rd CH1 ...117 E5
Blacon High Sch CH1 .117 D4
Blacon Inf Sch CH1 ...117 E5
Blacon Point Rd CH1 ..117 E3
Bladon Cl CW9 ......103 F4
Bladon Cres ST7 ......193 C5
Blagg Ave CW5 ......204 C4
Blair Cl SK7 ......36 C8
Blair Dr WA8 ......12 C3
Blairgowrie Dr SK10 ...87 B4
Blaizefield Cl CW3 ....232 C2
Blake Cl Blacon CH1 ...117 F6
Crewe CW2 ......189 F1
Blake La CW8 ......102 A2
Blake St CW12 ......156 C3
Blakeacre Rd L26 ......21 A6
Blakeley Brow CH63 ...43 A6
Blakeley Ct CH63 ......43 A6
Blakeley Dell CH63 ....43 B6
Blakeley Dene CH63 ...43 B7
Blakeley La WA16 ......58 F8
Blakeley Rd CH63 ......43 A6
Blakelow Bank SK11 ...112 F6
Blakelow Cl CW10 ....151 B8
Blakelow Cres CW5 ...205 F3
Blakelow Rd SK11 .....112 F6
Blakemere Cl SY13 ...226 B1
Blakemere Ct CH65 ....70 C7
Blakemere Dr CW9 ....103 E5
Blakemere La WA6 ...100 D4
Blakemere Way CW11 .174 F8
Blandford Dr
5 Macclesfield SK11 ...111 F8
Northwich CW9 ......103 E3
Blandford Rd WA5 ......15 B5
Blankney The CW5 ....204 E6
Blantern Rd CH4 ......161 A7
Blantyre St WA7 ......22 F3
Blaze Hill SK10 ......88 B8
Bleadale Cl SK9 ......34 D1
Bleasdale Rd
Crewe CW1 ......173 B1
Newton-le-W WA12 ......2 C4
Bleeding Wolf La ST7 ..194 E5
Blenheim Cl
Macclesfield SK10 ......87 A1
Northwich CW9 ......103 F4
Poynton SK12 ......36 F4
Warrington WA2 ......8 F2

Blenheim Cl *continued*
Wilmslow SK9 ....60 D7
Wistaston CW2 ....205 E8
Blenheim Ct ST7 .....193 D5
Blenheim Gdns 5 CW7 .149 C7
Blenheim Ho CH1 .....118 B3
Bloomsbury Way WA8 ..12 D3
Blossom Hts CW8 .....103 D7
Blossom Rd M31 ....11 E2
Blossoms La SK7 ....35 B2
Blue Bridge La WA6 ...73 C5
Blue Cap La SY14 .....213 D7
Blue Hatch WA6 ....74 C8
Blue Planet Aquarium★
CH65 ....70 D1
Blue Ridge Cl WA5 .....14 E7
Bluebell Ave WA11 ....1 E7
Bluebell Cl
Huntington CH3 ....142 B6
Macclesfield SK10 .....87 D3
Winnington CW8 ....78 E1
Bluebell Ct WA7 ....49 F4
Bluebell La SK10 ....87 C3
Bluebell Mews 4 SK10 .87 D3
Bluebell Way
Alsager ST7 ....193 B3
Handforth SK9 ....34 C1
Bluecoat St WA2 ....16 B7
Blundell Rd WA8 ....22 D8
Blunstone Cl CW2 .....199 A8
Blyth Cl Macclesfield SK10 .86 E1
Runcorn WA7 ....50 D5
Blyth Rd CH63 ....43 C7
Blythe Bramhall SK7 ...35 C6
Congleton CW12 ......156 A2
Widnes WA8 ....13 B5
Blythe Pl CW7 ....127 B2
Blythes The CW6 ......146 C3
Boardmans Pl CW9 ....104 A5
Boars Leigh Pk SK11 ..135 D1
Boat Mus The★ CH65 ...70 C7
Boat Stage WA13 ....18 E3
Boat Wlk WA4 ....16 A1
Boathorse Rd ST7 ......210 F8
Boathouse La CH64 .....41 C3
Bob's La M44 ....11 D4
Boden Dr CW5 ....205 D4
Boden St SK11 ....112 D8
Bodiam Ct CH65 ....70 E2
Bodmin Ave SK10 ......86 E1
Bodmin Cl WA7 ....50 B6
Bodmin Dr SK7 ....35 E7
Bodnant Cl CW7 ....190 A8
Bold Bsns Ctr WA9 ......6 B7
Bold Cross WA8 ....13 E7
Bold Ind Est WA8 ......13 C5
Bold Ind Park WA9 ......6 B6
Bold La WA5,WA9 ....6 C7
Bold Pl CH1 ....237 B3
Bold Sq CH1 ....237 C3
Bold St Haslington CW1 .191 C4
Runcorn WA7 ....23 B3
Sandbach CW11 ......175 B6
Warrington WA1 ....16 A5
Widnes WA8 ....23 C2
Bolesworth Hill Rd CH3 183 C4
Bolesworth Rd
Chester CH2 ....118 F6
Tattenhall CH3 ....183 C7
Boleyn Cl CH1 ....117 E6
Boleyn Ct WA7 ....24 C3
Bolland's Ct CH1 ......237 A2
Bollands Row 14 CW5 ..204 E5
Bolleyn Wood Ct SK9 ...34 B1
Bollin Ave
Altrincham WA14 ......31 B8
Winsford CW7 ....127 B2
Bollin Cl Alsager ST7 .192 F3
Culcheth WA3 ....5 A2
Lymm WA13 ....19 A4
Sandbach CW11 ......174 E7
Wilmslow SK9 ....60 B8
Winsford CW7 ....127 B2
Bollin Ct Lymm WA13 ...19 C5
Wilmslow SK9 ....60 C6
Bollin Dr Congleton CW12 156 F1
Lymm WA13 ....19 A4
Prestbury SK10 ....87 A7
Bollin Gr Biddulph ST8 .179 E1
Bollin Hill Prestbury SK10 .87 A5
Wilmslow SK9 ....60 B8
Bollin Mews SK10 ....86 F7
Bollin Way SK10 ....87 A6
Bollin Wlk SK9 ....60 C7
Bollinbarn SK10 ....87 B2
Bollinbarn Dr SK10 .....87 A2
Bollinbrook CE Prim Sch
SK10 ....87 B2
Bollinbrook Rd SK10 ....87 B2
Bollington Ave CW9 ...104 A5
Bollington Cross CE Prim Sch
SK10 ....87 E7
Bollington La SK10 .....84 E2
Bollington Mill WA14 ...20 C3
Bollington Old Rd SK10 .87 D6
Bollington Rd SK10 .....87 E6
Bollinhead La SK11 ....113 D2
Bollinway WA15 ....32 A4
Bollinwood Chase SK9 ..60 D7
Bolshaw Cl WA5 ....190 A4
Bolshaw Farm La SK8 ...34 C6
Bolshaw Prim Sch SK8 ..34 B7
Bolshaw Rd SK8 ....34 C6
Bolton Ave
Cheadle Hulme SK8 ....35 B6
Warrington WA4 ....16 F4
Bolton Cl Golborne WA3 ..4 B8
Poynton SK12 ....36 D4

Bomish La CW4,SK11 ...108 C3
Bond Cl WA5 ....15 D4
Bond St
Macclesfield SK11 ....112 C7
Winnington CW8 ....78 D1
Bonis Hall La SK10 .....61 F4
Boon Hill Rd ST7 ......209 F1
Booth Ave
Ashton Hayes CH3 ....121 E7
Little Budworth CW6 .147 F7
Sandbach CW11 ......175 C6
Booth Bed La WA16,
CW4 ....107 B4
Booth La
Middlewich CW10 .....151 B5
Middlewich,Stud Green
CW10,CW11 ....152 B3
Booth Rd Handforth SK9 .34 A1
Hartford CW8 ....103 A4
Booth St Audley ST7 ...209 D1
Congleton CW12 ......156 C2
Warrington WA5 ....15 E4
Booth's Hill Rd WA13 ...18 C3
Booth's La WA13 ....18 B1
Boothbank La WA14 .....30 A6
Boothby St 12 SK10 ....112 C8
Boothfields WA16 ....57 C2
Booths Hill Cl WA13 ....18 C2
Booths La WA4 ....52 E6
Boothsdale CW6 ....122 D3
Boothsmere Cl CW11 ..174 F8
Border Rd CH60 ....41 B8
Border Way CH3 ....119 C1
Borderbrook Sch
Drury Lane SY14 ......224 D3
Tallarn Green/Tallwrn Green
SY14 ....222 F5
Borders Ind Pk The/Parc
Ddiwydiannol Y Ffin
CH4 ....140 C7
Borough Rd CW12 ......156 F3
Borras Rd LL13 ....196 A8
Borron Rd WA12 ....2 B5
Borrowdale Ave WA2 .....8 C3
Borrowdale Cl
Crewe CW2 ....189 E3
Frodsham WA6 ....74 D8
Borrowdale Rd WA8 .....22 C8
Bosden Cl SK9 ....34 D5
Bosley Brook CW12 ....179 D5
Bosley Cl Handforth SK9 .34 D2
Middlewich CW10 .....151 C6
Bosley Dr SK12 ....37 A3
Bosley View CW12 ......157 B1
Bostock Gn
Bostock Green CW9 ...127 C7
Ellesmere Port CH65 ..69 F6
Bostock Hall CW10 ....127 D5
Bostock Rd
Macclesfield SK11 ....111 E7
Winsford CW7 ....127 A4
Bostock St WA5 ....15 E6
Boston Ave WA7 ....23 D1
Boston Bvd WA5 ....15 B7
Boston Ct Bramhall SK7 .35 D7
Culcheth WA3 ....4 F4
Boswell Ave WA4 ....16 B2
Botany Bsns Pk SK23 ...65 D5
Botany Mews SK23 ......65 C6
Boteler Ave WA5 ....15 F7
Bottoms La CH4 ....141 F8
Boughey Rd ST7 ....209 F2
Boughton CH2,CH1 .....118 F2
Boughton Hall Ave CH3 119 A1
Boughton Hall Dr CH3 .119 A1
Boughton Heath Prim Sch
CH3 ....142 B8
Boughton Lodge 2
CH3 ....119 A1
Boulevard The
Broughton CH4 ....139 C3
Ellesmere Port CH65 ..69 F4
Boulting Ave WA5 ....7 F1
Boulton Cl CW11 ....175 C3
Boundary La
Chester CH4 ....140 E5
Congleton CW12 ......179 B8
Heswall CH60 ....41 A8
Over Peover WA16,SK11 .108 D7
Siddington SK11 ......132 E8
Threapwood SY14 ....222 E8
Boundary Lane N CW8 .101 F2
Boundary Lane S CW8 .101 F2
Boundary Pk CH64 .....66 D7
Boundary St
Northwich CW9 ....79 C2
Warrington WA1 ....16 E7
Boundary Terr SK9 ......33 F6
Bourchier Way WA4 .....27 A8
Bourne Ave WA3 ....3 D8
Bourne Cl CW8 ....102 E7
Bourne Rd ST7 ....194 F2
Bourne St Mow Cop ST7 .195 C7
Wilmslow SK9 ....59 F6
Bournemouth Cl WA7 ...50 D6
Bouverie St CH1 ....237 A4
Boverton Cl WA5 ....7 E1
Bow Green Rd WA14 ....20 F1
Bow La WA14 ....31 B8
Bowden Cl
Congleton CW12 ......156 A3
Culcheth WA3 ....4 F4
Bowden Cres SK22 ......39 C8
Bowden Dr CW9 ....104 C8
Bowden House La SK9 ..61 A8
Bowden View La WA16 ..29 F2
Bowdon Cl WA1 ....16 F8

Bowe's Gate Rd CW6 ...169 A1
Bowen Cl Bramhall SK7 ..35 F5
Widnes WA8 ....12 B4
Bowen Cooke Ave CW1 .190 A5
Bowen St CW2 ....190 A3
Bower Cres WA4 ....26 D2
Bower Rd CH60 ....41 C8
Bower St WA8 ....13 C1
Bowerfield Ave SK7 .....36 D8
Bowerfield Cres SK7 ....36 E8
Bowers Bsns Pk WA8 ...23 B7
Bowers Row 4 CW5 ....204 E5
Bowery Ave SK8 ....34 F6
Bowery The CH1 ....116 D4
Bowfell Cl CH62 ....43 D3
Bowfell Dr SK6 ....37 E8
Bowkers Croft CW11 ...191 F8
Bowland Cl Runcorn WA7 .49 C5
Warrington WA3 ....10 B5
Bowland Croft CW1 ....173 B1
Bowland Rise CW7 .....149 B7
Bowles Cl CW11 ....175 A6
Bowling Green Ct
9 Nantwich CW5 .....204 E5
Winnington CW8 ....78 E1
Bowman Ave WA4 ....17 A5
Bowmans The SK10 .....87 B1
Bowmere Cl
Biddulph ST8 ....179 C1
Tarporley CW6 ....146 D1
Bowmere Dr CW7 ......149 C8
Bowmere Rd CW6 ......146 D1
Bowness Ave
Bebington CH63 ....43 C5
Irlam M44 ....11 D4
Warrington WA2 ....11 D4
Bowness Cl CW4 ....130 A3
Bowness Ct CW12 ......156 A1
Bowness Rd CW2 ......189 E3
Bowood Ct WA2 ....8 A4
Bowring Dr CH64 ....41 B1
Bowyer Ave 6 CW5 ....204 E6
Box La CW5 ....155 F3
Box Tree Mews SK11 ...112 A7
Box Wlk M31 ....11 E3
Boxgrove Cl WA8 ....13 B3
Boxmoor Cl CH4 ....141 A5
Boydell Ave
Warrington WA4 ....17 B2
Warrington,Westy WA4 .16 F4
Boydell Way CH4 ......162 A6
Boyle Ave WA2 ....8 E1
Boyles Hall Rd ST7 ....209 E2
Bracken Cl
Broughton CH4 ....139 C3
Macclesfield SK10 .....86 F1
Rode Heath ST7 ......193 F8
Warrington WA3 ....9 C5
Bracken Rd CH66 ....69 E4
Bracken Way
Barnton CW8 ....78 B3
Comberbach CW9 .....78 C7
Frodsham WA6 ....74 C6
Knutsford WA16 ....82 A8
Wincham CW9 ....79 C3
Brackendale Elton CH2 ..72 B3
Runcorn WA7 ....49 D8
Brackenfield Way 11
CW7 ....149 A8
Brackenwood Cl CW2 ..206 B8
Brackenwood Dr WA8 ...22 A8
Brackenwood Mews
Chorlton CW2 ....207 D2
Wilmslow SK9 ....60 E8
Brackley Ave M44 ....11 D6
Brackley St Runcorn WA7 .22 F3
Warrington WA4 ....16 C1
Bradburn Rd M44 ....11 E7
Bradburns La CW8 .....103 B6
Bradbury Gdns CW12 ..156 F1
Bradbury Rd CW7 ......127 B2
Braddon Cl CW9 ....103 F4
Bradeley Green La SY13 225 F6
Bradeley Hall Rd CW1 .191 B5
Bradeley Rd CW1 ......191 C4
Bradfield Rd CW1 ......190 B7
Bradford La SK10 ....85 C6
Bradford Rd CW7 ......126 E4
Bradford St CH4 ....141 D7
Bradgate Ave SK8 ......34 D8
Brading Wlk M22 ....33 E8
Bradlegh Rd WA12 ....2 B1
Bradley Bvd WA5 ....15 B6
Bradley Cl CW10 ....151 B7
Bradley Farm La SY13 ..225 C7
Bradley La Frodsham WA6 74 D7
Newton-le-W WA5,WA12 ..2 A1
Bradley St SK11 ....112 E6
Bradley Way WA8 ....13 B1
Bradmoor Rd CH62 .....43 D8
Bradshaw Com Prim Sch
WA4 ....17 B2
Bradshaw Hall La
Cheadle Hulme SK8 ....34 E8
Heald Green SK8 ......34 D8
Bradshaw La Lymm WA13 .19 D3
Warrington WA4 ....17 B3
Bradshaw Pl CW12 .....156 E2
Bradshaw St WA8 ....13 A2
Bradwall Rd CW11 .....175 B7
Bradwall St CW11 .....175 B7
Bradwell Cl CH65 ....70 A4
Bradwell Dr SK8 ....34 C7
Bradwell Gr CW12 .....156 F2

Bradwell Rd Golborne WA3 .3 E7
Hazel Grove SK7 ......36 E8
Braemar Ave CW9 ......104 C7
Braemar Cl Chester CH3 .119 C3
Holmes Chapel CW4 ...130 C2
Warrington WA2 ....9 A3
Wistaston CW2 ....205 E8
Braemar Ct CH65 ....70 E3
Braeside
6 Ellesmere Port CH66 ..69 C5
Macclesfield SK11 ....112 F6
Braidwood Ave WA16 ...57 C3
Brains La CW6 ....169 B6
Braintree Rd M22 ....33 E8
Braithwaite Cl WA7 .....49 D5
Braithwaite Rd WA3 ......3 D8
Brake The ST7 ....195 B7
Brake Village ST7 .....195 B7
Brakeley La CW8 ....77 D4
Brakenwood Mews WA4 .17 C1
Bramall Cl CW11 ......175 C7
Macclesfield SK10 .....87 B2
Middlewich CW10 .....128 E2
Warrington WA5 ....14 E3
Winsford CW7 ....126 C3
Bramble Way WA7 ......49 E4
Brambles Chase CW8 ..101 F2
Brambles The
Burtonwood WA5 ....7 A7
Haslington CW1 ....191 B4
Wincham CW9 ....79 C3
Brambling Cl WA7 ......49 F5
Brambling Way WA3 ......3 E7
Bramhall Cl CW7 ......126 B1
Macclesfield SK10 .....87 B2
Middlewich CW10 .....128 E2
Warrington WA5 ....14 E3
Winsford CW7 ....126 C3
Bramhall Ctr The SK7 ...35 E6
Bramhall Dr
Bebington CH62 ....43 F4
Holmes Chapel CW4 ..130 A3
Bramhall High Sch SK7 ..35 F8
Bramhall La S SK7 ......35 E7
Bramhall Rd CW2 ......189 F2
Bramhall St WA5 ....15 E5
Bramhall Sta SK7 ....35 E6
Bramhall Way SK10 .....112 A8
Bramhalls Pk CW9 ......78 C5
Bramley Cl Bramhall SK7 .35 E6
Ellesmere Port CH66 ..94 F8
Wilmslow SK9 ....59 D4
Bramley Ct CW6 ....122 D5
Bramley Dr SK7 ....35 E6
Bramley Mews WA4 .....26 C8
Bramley Rd SK7 ....35 E6
Bramley Wlk WA6 ....73 A1
Brampton Ave SK10 .....87 A2
Brampton Ct WA9 ....1 B3
Bramshill Cl WA3 ....10 A6
Bramway Bramhall SK7 ..35 C7
High Lane SK6 ....37 F7
Bramwood Ct SK7 ....35 E6
Brancaster Dr WA3 ......4 A7
Brancepeth Ct CH65 ....70 E3
Branch Way WA11 ....1 D6
Brancote Gdns CH62 ...43 D7
Branden Dr WA16 ....57 B1
Brandon WA8 ....12 B2
Brandon Cl SK9 ....34 D2
Brandwood Ave WA2 .....8 B2
Brandwood Ho 2 WA1 ...16 C5
Bransdale Cl WA5 ....14 F7
Bransdale Way SK11 ...111 F7
Brantfield Ct WA2 ....8 E2
Brassey St CH3 ....118 F1
Brassey Way CW5 .....205 D5
Brassey's Contract Rd
SY14 ....199 A1
Brassington Terr CW3 ..221 F3
Brathay Cl WA2 ....8 C3
Brattswood Dr ST7 ....194 A5
Bray Cl Crewe CW1 ....190 E5
Runcorn WA7 ....49 D6
Bray Rd CH4 ....140 F6
Breach House La WA16 ..32 A1
Bread St SK11 ....112 C6
Breck Rd WA8 ....13 B1
Breck The CH66 ....69 E7
Brecon Cl SK12 ....36 F4
Brecon Ct WA5 ....7 E2
Brecon Dr 1 CH66 ......69 E1
Brecon Way CW2 ......206 A7
Breconway CW7 ....149 B8
Bredon Cl CH66 ....69 A6
Breen Cl CH3 ....166 B1
Breezehill Cl CH64 ......66 F8
Breezehill Pk CH64 .....66 F8
Breezehill Rd CH64 .....66 F8
Brendon Ave WA2 ....8 A3
Brendon Gr WA9 ....1 A4
Brennus Pl CH1 ....237 A3
Brent Cl SK12 ....36 B4
Brentfield WA8 ....12 D2
Brentnall Cl WA5 ....15 C5
Brentwood Ave M44 ....11 D6
Brentwood Rd CH1 .....117 E5
Brereton CE Prim Sch
CW11 ....153 F5
Brereton Cl Crewe CW2 .189 F2
Malpas SY14 ....213 B3
Runcorn WA7 ....50 A8
Sandbach CW11 ......175 C7
Brereton Ct
1 Cheadle Hulme SK8 ..34 E8
Brereton Dr CW5 ......204 F5
Brereton Gn M44 ....11 E6
Brereton Heath Ctry Pk★
CW12 ....154 D7

Brereton Heath La
CW11,CW12 ....154 E6
Brereton La CW4 ......152 E8
Brereton Rd
Handforth SK9 ....34 E3
Hartford CW8 ....103 A4
Bretland Dr WA4 ....27 A7
Breton Cl CH2 ....118 E5
Bretton Court Mews
CH4 ....139 E4
Bretton Dr CH4 ....139 B3
Bretton La CH4 ....139 F5
Bretton Rd CH4 ....139 E4
Bretton Wlk M22 ....33 D8
Brewery La CH3 ....180 E3
Brian Ave Warrington WA2 16 B8
Warrington, Stockton Heath
WA4 ....16 E1
Briar Ave WA3 ....11 B2
Briar Cl WA16 ....57 A3
Briar Dr CH60 ....41 A8
Briar La CW8 ....102 E3
Briar Rd WA3 ....3 B8
Briar Wlk WA3 ....3 B8
Briardale Cl CW2 ......205 F8
Briardale Rd
Ellesmere Port CH66 ..69 C6
Willaston CH64 ....43 A1
Briarfield Ave WA8 ......12 A1
Briarfield Rd
Ellesmere Port CH65 ..70 B5
Heswall CH60 ....41 B8
Briarlands Cl SK7 ....35 D6
Briarstead Cl SK7 ....35 D7
Briarswood ST7 ....195 B1
Briarswood Ct CH1 ....237 B3
Briarwood Runcorn WA7 ..50 B8
Wilmslow SK9 ....60 C7
Briarwood Ave
Macclesfield SK11 ....112 D5
Warrington WA1 ....16 E7
Brick Bank CW5 ....204 F5
Brick Bank La WA16,
CW4 ....107 B2
Brick Kiln La CW10 ....127 B7
Brick Rd CH4 ....139 D2
Brick St Newton-le-W WA12 ..1 B4
Warrington WA3 ....16 C5
Brickfield Bsns Ctr CW9 .79 D1
Brickfield La CH3 ......119 F2
Brickhill La WA15 ....32 B4
Brickhurst Way WA1 ....17 B8
Brickkiln La
Little Bollington WA14 ..20 C3
Whitchurch SY13 .....226 D1
Brickley Ct CW8 ....77 C1
Bridestone Sh Ctr
CW12 ....156 D2
Bridge Ave WA4 ....16 F4
Bridge Ave E WA4 ......16 F5
Bridge Bank Cl WA3 .....3 B7
Bridge Cl Audley ST7 ..209 F2
Cuddington CW8 ......102 A3
Lymm WA13 ....19 B4
Wistaston CW2 ......206 A7
Bridge Ct Chester CH2 .119 A2
Holt LL13 ....196 E8
Neston CH64 ....66 E7
Bridge Dr
Christleton CH3 ....142 D7
Handforth SK9 ....34 D3
Bridge End Dr SK10 .....87 A7
Bridge End La SK10 .....87 A7
Bridge Farm Ct CW10 ..152 A4
Bridge Foyer The CH1 ..118 B2
Bridge Gn SK10 ....87 B7
Bridge La
Cuddington CW8 ......101 F3
Frodsham WA6 ....49 D1
Goostrey CW4 ....108 C2
Warrington WA4 ....26 A5
Warrington WA4 ....26 E8
Warrington,Woolston WA1 .17 C7
Bridge Mdw CH66 ....69 F2
Bridge Pl CH1 ....237 B1
Bridge Rd WA1 ....17 C7
Bridge Row CW12 .....156 F4
Bridge Side Dr WA6 ....73 B4
Bridge St Chester CH1 .237 B2
Congleton CW12 ......156 D2
Golborne WA3 ....3 A7
Holt LL13 ....180 E1
Macclesfield SK11 ....112 C7
Neston CH64 ....66 E7
Newton-le-W WA12 .....2 B3
Northwich CW9 ....79 E2
Runcorn WA7 ....23 B2
Saltney CH4 ....140 D7
Warrington WA1 ....16 B4
Warrington WA1 ....16 B5
Whaley Bridge SK23 ...65 E7
Wybunbury CW5 .....220 B8
Bridge St Row E CH1 ...237 B2
Bridge St Row W CH1 ..237 B2
Bridge Terr CH3 ....119 B2
Bridge View WA8 ....23 A4
Bridge Wlk 7 WA7 ......49 F7
Bridgedown CW6 ......146 C2
Bridgefield Ave SK9 .....34 C1
Bridgefield Cl SK6 ......37 E7
Bridgegate CH4 ....141 B3
Bridgeman Rd CH1 .....117 C3
Bridgeman St WA5 ......15 D4

246 Bri – Bul

Bridgemere CE Prim Sch
CW5 .....231 E8
Bridgemere Cl CW11 ..174 F8
Bridgemere Garden World*
CW5 .....232 B4
Bridgemere La CW5 ..219 E1
Bridgemere Mews CW5 231 E8
Bridgemere Way [4]
CW9 .....103 E4
Bridgend CH2 .....97 A1
Bridgend Cl WA8 .....12 D3
Bridges Rd CH65 .....70 F5
Bridgewater Ave WA4 ..16 F4
Bridgewater Cl
Congleton CW12 .....157 B1
Heald Green SK8 .....34 D7
Bridgewater Ct
[3] Lymm WA13 .....18 C3
[6] Runcorn WA7 .....23 B2
Bridgewater Dr CH3 ..119 C2
Bridgewater Grange
WA7 .....50 F5
Bridgewater High Sch (Lower Sch) WA4 .....26 D6
Bridgewater High Sch (Upper Sch) WA4 .....26 D7
Bridgewater Mews WA4 .26 C8
Bridgewater St
[4] Lymm WA13 .....18 E3
[6] Runcorn WA7 .....23 A4
Bridgeway E WA7 .....24 C2
Bridgeway W WA7 .....24 C2
Bridgewood Dr CH66 ..69 C2
Bridgnorth Gr ST5 .....210 E2
Bridle Cl CH62 .....43 E7
Bridle Ct Bramhall SK7 ..35 F2
Crewe CW2 .....190 B4
Bridle Hey CW5 .....204 F2
Bridle Pk CH62 .....43 E7
Bridle Rd Bebington CH62 .43 E6
Crewe CW2 .....190 B4
Woodford SK7 .....35 F2
Bridle Way
Ellesmere Port CH66 .....69 D3
Woodford SK7 .....36 A2
Bridlemere Ct WA1 .....16 E8
Briedden Way CH66 .....69 A6
Brierley Bsns Ctr CW1 .190 D4
Brierley Prim Sch CW1 .190 D4
Brierley Rd CW12 .....157 B1
Brierley St CW1 .....190 D4
Briers Cl WA2 .....8 F3
Brieryhurst Rd ST7 .....195 B3
Briggs Ave CW2 .....190 D1
Bright St WA1 .....190 B5
Brighton Cres SK11 .....113 B3
Brighton St WA5 .....15 E6
Brights Ave [6] ST7 .....195 B2
Brightwell Cl WA5 .....14 E5
Brimelow Cres WA5 .....14 E3
Brimstage Cl WA1 .....16 E8
Brimstage Gn CH60 .....41 D8
Brimstage Rd CH60 .....41 C7
Brindley Ave
Warrington WA4 .....16 F4
Winsford CW7 .....126 C1
Brindley Cl
Kidsgrove ST7 .....194 E1
Talke ST7 .....210 E8
Brindley Ct WA4 .....26 D8
Brindley Gr SK9 .....34 E2
Brindley Hall Rd CW5 ..186 E2
Brindley La CW11 .....153 C4
Brindley Lea La CW5 ..186 D1
Brindley Pk CW11 .....174 F8
Brindley Rd WA7 .....23 F3
Brindley St WA7 .....22 F3
Brindley Way
Congleton CW12 .....157 B1
Macclesfield SK11 .....112 C3
Brindley Wharf WA4 .....50 F6
Brindleys Way ST7 .....209 F2
Brine Leas High Sch
CW5 .....204 F3
Brine Pits La CW5 .....218 F2
Brine Pump Cotts CW9 ..78 F4
Brine Rd CW5 .....204 E3
Brinell Dr M44 .....11 F6
Brinley Cl CH62 .....43 D5
Brinton Cl WA8 .....22 E8
Brisbane Cl SK7 .....35 F5
Brisbane Rd CH1 .....117 C4
Bristol Ave WA7 .....50 E6
Bristol Cl Blacon CH1 ..117 C4
Heald Green SK8 .....34 C7
Bristol Dr [3] CH66 .....69 E1
Bristow Cl WA5 .....15 B8
Britannia Dr CW9 .....104 E7
Britannia Gdns WA6 .....73 B1
Britannia Rd WA6 .....73 B2
Brixham Ave SK8 .....34 F7
Brixham Wlk SK7 .....35 E7
Broad Ct SK9 .....85 B8
Broad La Altrincham WA15 .32 B8
Appleton Thorn WA4 .....27 C8
Burtonwood WA5 .....6 E8
Haydock WA5,WA9 .....1 C1
Heswall CH60 .....40 C8
Holmes Chapel CW4 .....129 F1
Stapeley CW5 .....205 A1
Broad Oak Ave
Broughton CH4 .....139 A3
Haydock WA11 .....1 A6
Warrington WA5 .....14 E4

Broad Oak Com Prim Sch
WA9 .....1 A3
Broad St CW1 .....190 C6
Broad Street Inf Sch
CW1 .....190 C6
Broad Wlk SK9 .....59 F8
Broadacre CW9 .....78 D6
Broadacre Pl SK9 .....59 D3
Broadacres CW5 .....217 F4
Broadbent Ave WA4 .....16 F4
Broadcar Rd SK11 .....113 C6
Broadfields WA7 .....50 C8
Broadheath Terr WA8 ..12 D1
Broadheys La WA16 .....28 D6
Broadhurst Ave
Culcheth WA3 .....4 F2
Warrington WA5 .....15 D4
Broadhurst La CW12 ..156 C3
Broadlake CH64 .....67 F8
Broadland Gdns CH66 ..69 F2
Broadland Rd CH66 .....69 F2
Broadleigh Way CW2 ..206 C8
Broadley Ave WA3 .....3 C7
Broadmead Chester CH3 119 C2
Heswall CH60 .....41 C7
Broadoak High Sch M31 ..11 F3
Broadoak La
High Legh WA16 .....29 D5
Mobberley WA16 .....57 E6
Broadwalk SK10 .....87 A5
Broadway
Altrincham WA15 .....32 A8
Barnton CW8 .....78 B3
Widnes WA8 .....12 A1
Wilmslow SK9 .....60 B6
Broadway E CH2 .....118 E5
Broadway The CW5 .....204 F5
Broadway W CH2 .....118 D5
Broadways CW3 .....230 A4
Broadwood Cl SK6 .....37 F7
Broady Ct [5] CW2 .....190 D2
Brock Gdns L24 .....21 E2
Brock Hollow CW11 .....174 F4
Brock Rd WA3 .....9 D3
Brock St
Macclesfield SK10 .....112 D8
Macclesfield SK10 .....87 D1
Brockhurst Mews CW9 .104 A6
Brockhurst St CW9 .....104 A6
Brockhurst Way CW9 ..104 A6
Brocklebank Dr CW8 ..103 E7
Brocklehurst Ave SK10 ..87 D2
Brocklehurst Ct [2] SK10 .87 D3
Brocklehurst Dr SK10 ..87 A7
Brocklehurst Manor
SK10 .....87 E1
Brocklehurst Mews [3]
.....87 D3
Brocklehurst Way SK10 .87 D3
Brockton Ct WA4 .....26 C6
Brockway E CH3 .....166 A1
Brockway W CH3 .....166 A1
Brockwell Cl [2] CW7 ..149 A8
Brodie Cl CH2 .....95 C1
Brogden Ave WA3 .....4 E4
Broken Banks [10] SK11 ..112 D7
Broken Cross SK11 .....111 F8
Broken Cross Com Sch
SK11 .....111 E7
Brokencross Pl CW9 ..104 E7
Bromborough Rake Sta
CH62 .....43 C8
Bromborough Sta CH63 .43 C7
Bromborough Village Rd
CH62 .....43 B8
Bromley Ave WA3 .....3 D7
Bromley Cl Crewe CW1 .189 F8
Heswall CH60 .....40 E7
Warrington WA2 .....8 F3
Bromley Dr CW4 .....130 C2
Bromley Rd
Congleton CW12 .....156 F3
Macclesfield SK10 .....111 E8
Brompton Gdns WA5 ..15 E7
Brompton Way
Ellesmere Port CH66 .....69 E1
Handforth SK9 .....34 C5
Bronington Ave CH62 ..43 D6
Bronte Cl WA2 .....8 A6
Brook Acre Com Prim Sch
WA2 .....8 E1
Brook Ave
Shavington CW2 .....206 C5
Warrington, Stockton Heath
WA4 .....16 E1
Warrington, Westy WA4 ..16 F5
Brook Bank SK12 .....37 C2
Brook Bottom Rd SK22 ..39 A8
Brook Cl Crewe CW1 ..190 F4
Cronton WA8 .....12 C6
Brook Ct Chester CH1 ..118 B3
Sandbach CW11 .....175 B6
Brook Dr Kelsall CW6 ..122 D4
Warrington WA5 .....15 A5
Brook End WA9 .....1 A1
Brook Farm Cl M31 .....11 F2
Brook Furlong WA6 .....48 F2
Brook Gdns ST8 .....179 D1
Brook Hey WA6 .....41 B2
Brook Ho WA4 .....16 F3
Brook House Ct WA13 ..18 D2
Brook La Alderley Edge SK9 59 F3
Astbury CW12 .....177 E5
Broughton CH5 .....139 C7
Burland CW5 .....203 D8
Chester CH2 .....118 E4
Faddiley CW5 .....202 F8

Brook La continued
Knutsford WA16 .....57 B1
Neston CH64 .....41 C2
Northwich WA9 .....104 D7
Warrington WA3 .....18 A8
Brook Pl Chester CH1 ..237 B3
Warrington WA4 .....16 E3
Brook Rd
Ellesmere Port CH66 .....69 D5
Lymm WA13 .....18 E4
Tarporley CW6 .....168 D8
Brook Side CW8 .....102 C8
Brook St Chester CH1 ..237 B3
Congleton CW12 .....156 F3
Crewe CW2 .....190 D3
Golborne,Bank Heath WA3 ..3 A8
Knutsford WA16 .....57 B1
Macclesfield SK11 .....112 F7
Neston CH64 .....66 E8
Northwich CW9 .....79 A1
Northwich, Lostock Gralam
CW9 .....79 E2
[2] Runcorn WA7 .....23 A2
[3] Widnes WA8 .....13 B1
Brook Terr Runcorn WA7 ..23 E1
Sandbach CW11 .....175 A3
Brook View
Alderley Edge SK9 .....60 A3
Allostock WA16 .....106 F3
Brook Villas ST7 .....193 E3
Brook Way Hartford CW8 103 B4
Nantwich CW5 .....204 E3
Warrington WA5 .....15 A5
Brook Well CH64 .....66 F5
Brookash Rd M22 .....34 A8
Brookdale WA8 .....12 A3
Brookdale Ave WA16 ..57 C2
Brookdale Ct CH3 .....143 D5
Brookdale Pk CW2 .....190 A3
Brookdale Pl CH1 .....237 B3
Brookdale Way CH3 .....143 B5
Brooke Ave Chester CH2 .118 F8
Handforth SK9 .....34 D4
Brooke Dean Com Sch
SK9 .....34 D4
Brooke Dr SK9 .....34 D4
Brooke Ho SK10 .....86 F1
Brooke Way SK9 .....34 D4
Brookes Ave CH4 .....139 B3
Brookfield Ave
Poynton SK12 .....36 C3
Runcorn WA7 .....23 E2
Brookfield Cl Lymm WA13 18 D3
Tarporley CW6 .....168 D8
Brookfield Cotts [2]
WA13 .....18 D3
Brookfield Cres CW4 ..107 F1
Brookfield Ct CW1 .....190 B5
Brookfield Dr
Alsager ST7 .....193 C5
Chester CH2 .....118 E4
Holmes Chapel CW4 .....130 B3
Brookfield La SK11 .....112 F7
Brookfield Pk WA4 .....17 A2
Brookfield Rd
Comberbach CW9 .....78 D8
Culcheth WA3 .....4 D3
Lymm WA13 .....18 D3
Brookfield St WA12 .....2 B3
Brookfields Sch WA8 ..13 D2
Brookhouse Cl SK11 ..86 F1
Brookhouse Dr CW2 ..206 C8
Brookhouse La
Church Minshull CW1,
CW10 .....172 D7
Congleton CW12 .....157 C2
Duddon CH3 .....144 D6
Lower Whitley WA4 .....52 B2
Brookhouse Rd
Alsager ST7 .....193 D3
[5] Sandbach CW11 .....175 B6
Brookhurst Ave CH63 ..43 C5
Brookhurst Cl CH63 .....43 C5
Brookhurst Prim Sch
CH63 .....43 C6
Brookhurst Rd CH63 ..43 C5
Brookland Ave CW2 .....205 F8
Brookland Dr CW11 .....175 E6
Brookland La WA9 .....1 A1
Brookland St WA1 .....16 E7
Brooklands Ave SK11 ..112 B7
Brooklands Dr
Goostrey CW4 .....107 F1
Northwich CW9 .....104 A4
Brooklands Gdns CH64 ..41 C1
Brooklands Gr CW1 .....190 A6
Brooklands Pk [1] WA8 ..13 C2
Brooklands Rd
Congleton CW12 .....155 F2
Neston CH64 .....41 C1
Brooklands The CW2 ..206 E3
Brookledge La SK10 .....62 E5
Brooklet Rd CH60 .....41 C8
Brooklyn Dr
Ellesmere Port CH65 .....69 F5
Lymm WA13 .....18 E4
Brooklyn St CW2 .....190 C2
Brookmere Cl CW11 ..174 E8
Brooks Dr WA15 .....32 D8
Brooks La Bosley SK11 ..135 E2
Middlewich CW10 .....128 D1
Brooks Lane Ind Est
Middlewich CW10 .....128 D1
Middlewich CW10 .....151 D8

Brookside
Ashton Hayes CH3 .....121 E7
Chester CH3 .....142 A8
Cuddington CW8 .....101 F3
Kelsall CW6 .....122 C4
Kingsley WA6 .....75 C2
Warrington WA4 .....16 E3
Brookside Ave
Lymm WA13 .....18 C4
Poynton SK12 .....36 E3
Sutton Lane Ends SK11 ..112 F2
Warrington WA5 .....15 A4
Warrington, Stockton Heath
WA4 .....16 D1
Brookside Cl WA11 .....1 B7
Brookside Cotts CW11 .176 A8
Brookside Ct SK10 .....87 A1
Brookside Gn [2] CW2 .206 C8
Brookside La SK6 .....37 E7
Brookside Mill [6] SK11 .112 F7
Brookside Miniature Rly*
SK12 .....36 F7
Brookside Prim Sch
Ellesmere Port CH66 .....69 E4
High Lane SK6 .....37 E6
Brookside Rd
[4] Congleton CW12 .....156 D3
Frodsham WA6 .....74 A8
Brookside Terr
Chester CH3 .....237 C4
Wilmslow SK9 .....59 E3
Brookside View [1] WA11 ..1 B7
Brookside Way WA11 ..1 B7
Brookvale Ave N WA7 ..50 B6
Brookvale Ave S WA7 ..50 B5
Brookvale Cl WA5 .....6 F6
Brookvale Prim Sch WA7 50 B5
Brookview Cl CW2 .....206 C8
Brooway La WA9 .....1 A1
Broom Ave WA4 .....26 C6
Broom Cres CH3 .....121 B1
Broom La WA16 .....81 F2
Broom Rd M31 .....11 F2
Broom St CW1 .....190 A6
Broom's La CW6 .....122 D6
Broome Ct WA7 .....50 B5
Broomehouse Ave M44 ..11 E8
Broomfield Cl
Chelford SK11 .....84 A3
Wilmslow SK9 .....60 E8
Broomfields WA4 .....26 E7
Broomfields Jun Sch
WA4 .....26 E7
Broomfields La CW8 .....77 F4
Broomfields Rd WA4 ..26 D7
Broomheath La
Tarvin CH3 .....121 C1
Tarvin CH3 .....144 C7
Broomhill La
Brown Knowl CH3 .....199 D8
Great Barrow CH3 .....120 E8
Broomlands CH60 .....40 E8
Broomlands Cotts CW5 .219 E1
Broomsfield La CW8 .....78 A4
Broseley Ave WA3 .....4 D4
Broseley La WA3 .....4 D5
Brotherton Cl CH62 .....43 C8
Brotherton Way WA12 ..2 B4
Brough St W SK11 .....112 C7
Broughton Ave WA3 .....3 D7
Broughton Cl WA4 .....26 E8
Broughton Cres SY14 ..211 A1
Broughton Hall Rd CH4 139 C4
Broughton Inf Sch CH4 .139 C4
Broughton Jun Sch
CH4 .....139 C4
Broughton La CW1 .....189 F1
Broughton Mills Rd
CH4 .....139 F6
Broughton Rd
Adlington SK10 .....62 C5
Crewe CW1 .....190 D4
Broughton Sh Pk CH4 .139 E4
Broughton Way WA8 ..22 B5
Brow Com Prim Sch The
WA7 .....23 E1
Brow La Antrobus CW9 ..53 D5
Heswall CH60 .....40 F7
Brow The WA6 .....75 C2
Browmere Dr WA3 .....9 A7
Brown Ave
Lawton-gate ST7 .....194 A5
Nantwich CW5 .....204 F4
Brown Heath Rd CH3 ..143 B6
Brown Lees Cl CW2 .....190 B1
Brown Lees Rd ST7 .....195 F4
Brown St
[3] Alderley Edge SK9 .....60 A1
Congleton CW12 .....156 E3
Macclesfield SK11 .....112 C7
Widnes WA8 .....23 D7
Brown's La Chester CH4 .141 C7
Wilmslow SK9 .....60 E8
Brownhill Dr WA1 .....16 F8
Brownhills Rd CW6 .....147 C6
Browning Ave WA8 .....22 F8
Browning Cl Blacon CH1 .117 F6
Sandbach CW11 .....174 D5
Browning Dr
Ellesmere Port CH65 .....69 F4
Winwick WA2 .....8 A6
Browning Gn ST7 .....210 C8
Browning St CW1 .....190 C4
Browning Way CW7 .....149 A7
Brownlow Cl SK12 .....36 E2

Brownlow Hall Mews
CW12 .....177 E5
Brownlow Heath CW12 .177 E5
Brownlow Heath La
CW12 .....177 D6
Broxton Ave CW10 .....151 D6
Broxton Cl WA8 .....12 C3
Broxton Rd Clutton CH3 .182 D1
Ellesmere Port CH66 .....69 E5
Bruce Ave WA2 .....8 D1
Bruce Cres CH63 .....43 C6
Bruce Dr CH66 .....69 C4
Bruce Rd WA1 .....16 F8
Bruche Com Prim Sch
WA1 .....17 A7
Bruche Dr WA1 .....16 F8
Bruche Heath Gdns WA1 17 A8
Bruen The CH3 .....121 C3
Bruera Rd CH65 .....69 F4
Brunel Ct CW9 .....104 E5
Brunel Rd SK11 .....112 C3
Brunner Gr CW5 .....205 A5
Brunner Rd WA8 .....23 A3
Brunsborough Cl CH62 ..43 C6
Brunswick [11] WA7 .....23 A3
Brunswick Cres CH66 ..69 E3
Brunswick Ct [12] SK11 .112 C7
Brunswick Hill SK10 .....112 D8
Brunswick Rd WA12 .....1 F4
Brunswick St
Congleton CW12 .....156 F3
[5] Macclesfield SK10 .....112 D8
St Helens WA9 .....1 A3
Brunswick Terr SK10 ..112 D8
Bruntleigh Ave WA4 ..17 A3
Bryant Ave WA4 .....16 F5
Brymau Four Est CH4 ..140 D7
Brymau One Est CH4 ..140 D7
Brymau Three Est CH4 ..140 D7
Brymau Two Est CH4 ..140 D7
Brynlow Dr CW10 .....151 B8
Brynmore Dr SK11 .....112 F7
Brynn St WA8 .....23 B8
Brynton Cl SK10 .....87 C1
Brynton Rd SK10 .....87 C1
Buchan Cl WA5 .....15 B8
Buchan Gr CW2 .....190 B3
Buck La CW2 .....206 E3
Buckbean Way CW4 ..107 E1
Buckden Way [9] SK10 .112 C8
Buckfast Ave WA11 .....2 A7
Buckfast Cl
Cheadle Hulme SK8 .....35 B6
Macclesfield SK10 .....87 C2
Poynton SK12 .....36 D5
Warrington WA5 .....14 E3
Buckfast Ct WA7 .....24 E3
Buckfast Way [10] WA8 .128 B1
Buckingham Ave
Chester CH3 .....119 B2
Widnes WA8 .....13 A4
Buckingham Cl
[4] Congleton CW12 .....156 F4
Wistaston CW2 .....205 E8
Buckingham Dr
Knutsford WA16 .....57 B1
Northwich CW9 .....103 E4
Warrington WA5 .....15 C4
Warrington CW7 .....149 C7
Buckingham Gdns [1]
CH65 .....70 D2
Buckingham Rd
Irlam M44 .....11 C6
Poynton SK12 .....36 D3
Wilmslow SK9 .....59 F6
Buckland Cl WA8 .....22 D7
Buckley Ave CW10 .....128 F7
Buckley Cl CW10 .....151 B8
Buckley St
Macclesfield SK11 .....112 D7
Warrington WA1 .....16 B6
Bucklow Ave
Mobberley WA16 .....58 A4
Partington M31 .....11 F3
Bucklow Gdns WA13 ..19 A4
Bucklow Wlk [11] SK11 .112 C8
Bucklowhill La WA16 ..30 B3
Buckton St WA1 .....16 D7
Bude Cl Alsager ST7 .....193 B3
Bramhall SK7 .....35 F7
Crewe CW1 .....190 B8
Bude Rd WA8 .....12 E2
Budworth Ave
Warrington WA4 .....16 F4
Widnes WA8 .....12 D2
Budworth Cl
Runcorn WA7 .....49 D7
Sandbach CW11 .....174 F7
Budworth Heath La CW9 54 C1
Budworth La CW9 .....78 E7
Budworth Rd
Bate Heath CW9 .....54 E2
Ellesmere Port CH66 .....69 E2
Over Tabley WA16 .....55 C2
Budworth Wlk [1] SK9 ..34 E1
Buerton App CH3 .....164 B6
Buerton Prim Sch CW3 .230 F3
Buffs La CH60 .....41 B8
Buggen La CH64 .....66 D8
Buglawton Hall Sch
CW12 .....157 D5
Buglawton Ind Est [5]
CW12 .....156 F4
Buglawton Prim Sch
CW12 .....157 A4
Buildwas Rd CH64 .....66 E8
Bulkeley Hall La SY14 ..200 C8

Bulkeley Rd
  Handforth SK9 ....34 D3
  Poynton SK12 ....36 E3
Bulkeley St Chester CH3 .119 A1
  Crewe CW1 ....190 E3
Bull Hill CH64 ....66 F6
Bull Hill La SK10 ....88 D2
Bull Ring CW9 ....103 F8
Bull Ring The CW10 .....128 C1
Bullcroft Cl SY14 ....211 D7
Bullocks House Rd WA5 .195 E3
Bullocks La SK11 ....112 C3
Bumper's La CH1 ....117 F1
Bunbury Aldersey CE Prim
  Sch CW6 ....185 E8
Bunbury Cl
  Middlewich CW10 .....151 D5
  Northwich CW9 ....104 A5
  Stoak CH2 ....96 A7
Bunbury Comm CW6 ....168 E2
Bunbury Dr WA7 ....49 C6
Bunbury Gn CH65 ....70 D2
Bunbury La CW6 ....185 E8
Bunbury Mill* CW6 .....169 A1
Bunbury Rd CW6 ....169 B3
Bunce La SK11 ....133 B4
Bunce St CH1 ....237 A1
Bungalow Rd WA12 ....2 E1
Bungalows The
  Dunham-on-t-H WA6 ....97 C6
  Thornton Hough CH63 ..42 B6
Bunting Cl **6** WA3 ....3 E8
Buntingford Rd WA4 .....17 C3
Bunts La CW12 ....156 E1
Burdett Rd CH66 ....69 E2
Burfield Dr WA4 ....26 D7
Burford Ave Bramhall SK7 .35 D5
  Newcastle-u-Lyme ST5 ..210 D1
Burford Cl SK9 ....59 E5
Burford Cres SK9 ....59 E5
Burford La WA13 ....19 C2
Burgamot La CW9 ....78 D8
Burges St CH2 ....118 F3
Burgess Ave WA4 ....16 B2
Burgess Cl CW5 ....205 B4
Burgess Dr CH1 ....117 A5
Burgess La WA6 ....101 B6
Burgess Pl **6** CW8 .....103 E8
Burgess St SK10 ....112 E8
Burjen Way CW1 ....190 B6
Burkhardt Dr WA12 ....2 E1
Burland Cl WA7 ....22 F1
Burland Gr CW7 ....126 A2
Burland Rd Halewood L26 .21 A6
  Newcastle-u-Lyme ST5 ..210 D1
Burlea Cl CW2 ....189 E5
Burlea Dr CW2 ....206 B5
Burley La WA4 ....27 C4
Burleyhurst La SK9,WA16 .59 B7
Burnell Cl CW5 ....204 F3
Burnell Rd CH65 ....70 E4
Burnet Cl WA2 ....9 C4
Burnfell WA3 ....3 E7
Burnham Cl Culcheth WA3 ..4 F3
  Warrington WA5 ....14 F5
  Widnes WA8 ....12 C3
Burnham Rd CH4 ....140 F6
Burns Cl
  Ellesmere Port CH66 ....69 E4
  Rode Heath ST7 ....193 E8
Burns Cres WA8 ....22 F8
Burns Dr CW1 ....190 F4
Burns Gr WA2 ....8 C2
Burns Rd CW12 ....157 A2
Burns Way CW11 ....117 E6
Burnsall Ave WA3 ....3 E1
Burnsall Dr WA8 ....12 C3
Burnside WA15 ....32 D7
Burnside Ave WA4 ....16 D1
Burnside Cl SK9 ....60 C6
Burnside Way
  Northwich CW8 ....103 D8
  Winnington CW8 ....78 D1
Burnt Acre SK11 ....84 B3
Burnt Mill La WA8 ....21 D5
Burnwood Gr ST7 ......195 B2
Burran Rd M22 ....33 D8
Burrough Cl WA3 ....9 F3
Burrows Hill CW8 ....103 B7
Burrows La WA6 ....73 F2
Burrows St WA11 ....1 A6
Burrows The CW8 ......101 D5
Bursar Cl WA12 ....2 D4
Burslam St CW12 ....156 E2
Burton Ave CW6 ....146 C3
Burton Cl Culcheth WA3 ....4 F3
  Widnes WA8 ....12 C3
Burton Dr SK12 ....36 D4
Burton Gn CH66 ....69 D4
Burton Gr CW1 ....173 B1
Burton Hall Rd LL12 ....161 E1
Burton La CW6 ....144 F6
Burton Manor Coll CH64 .67 D1
Burton Rd Blacon CH1 ...117 E5
  Neston CH64 ....66 F6
  Warrington WA2 ....8 D1
Burton Sq CW6 ....146 C2
Burtonwood Com Prim Sch
  WA5 ....6 E1
Burtonwood Ind Ctr WA5 .6 E7
Burtonwood Rd WA5 .....7 A2
Burwardsley Rd CH3 ....166 D1
Burwardsley Way CW9 ..103 E4
Bush Rd Christleton CH3 .142 E7
  Widnes WA8 ....22 F5
Bush Way CH60 ....40 D8
Bushell Cl CH64 ....66 F7

Bushell Rd CH64 ....66 F7
Bushells La WA6 ....99 B8
Butler Way CW5 ....204 D3
Butley Cl
  Macclesfield SK10 ....87 D3
  Middlewich CW10 ......151 C7
Butley Hall SK10 ....87 A7
Butley Lanes SK10 ....61 F1
Butterbache Rd CH3 ....142 A6
Butterbur Cl CH3 ......142 A6
Buttercup Way WA10 ....79 F6
Buttermarket St WA1 ....16 B5
Buttermere Ave
  Ellesmere Port CH65 ....70 C3
  Warrington WA2 ....8 C3
Buttermere Cl WA6 ......74 D8
Buttermere Cres WA2 ....8 C3
Buttermere Ct CW12 ...156 A2
Buttermere Dr
  Alderley Edge SK9 ....83 F7
  Altrincham WA15 ....32 D6
  Crewe CW1 ....173 B1
Buttermere Gr WA7 .....49 D5
Buttermere Rd
  Partington M31 ....11 E3
  Winsford CW7 ....126 C2
Butterton La Crewe CW1 .192 C1
  Oakhanger CW1 ....192 B2
Button Field CW8 ....126 A7
Butts Gn WA5 ....7 A3
Butts The Alsager ST7 ...193 D4
  Runcorn WA7 ....23 F2
Buxton Ave WA5 ....190 E4
Buxton Cl WA5 ....15 A8
Buxton New Rd
  Macclesfield SK11 ....88 E1
  Macclesfield Forest SK11 .114 D7
Buxton Old Rd
  Congleton CW12 ....157 A4
  Disley SK12 ....38 E4
  Macclesfield SK11 ......113 D7
Buxton Rd
  Congleton CW12 ......157 C6
  Disley SK12 ....38 E4
  High Lane SK6,SK7,SK12 .37 D8
  Macclesfield SK10,SK11 .113 A7
  New Mills SK22,SK23 ....39 C4
  Whaley Bridge SK23 ....65 E8
  Whaley Bridge, New Horwich
  SK23 ....65 E5
Buxton Rd W SK12 ......38 B5
By-Pass Rd CH3 ....121 B3
Bye Pass The CH3 ......119 C2
Byland Ave SK8 ....35 B6
Byland Cl WA8 ....13 C5
Bylands Cl SK12 ....36 D4
Byley La
  Cranage CW4,CW10 ...129 C6
  Middlewich CW10 .....128 C3
Byley Prim Sch CW10 ..129 B7
Byley Way CW7 ....126 B1
Byng Ave M44 ....11 D4
Byron Cl Blacon CH1 ...117 F6
  Crewe CW1 ....190 F4
  Middlewich CW10 .....151 D5
  Rode Heath ST7 ....193 E7
  Sandbach CW11 ....174 D6
Byron Ct WA2 ....8 C2
Byron St WA7 ....23 A1
Byron Way CW2 ....190 A1
Byron Wlk CW5 ....204 D6
Byron's La SK11 ....112 E5
Byrons St SK11 ....112 D6
Bythom Cl CH3 ....142 E7

C

Cabot Cl WA5 ....7 C1
Cabul Cl WA2 ....16 D7
Cadishead Prim Sch M44 .11 E6
Cadishead Way M44 .....11 F6
Cadnant Cl CH1 ....117 D3
Cadnant Ct/Llys Cadnant
  CH4 ....139 D5
Cadshaw Cl WA3 ....9 D5
Caer Castell LL13 ......196 D8
Caerleon Cl CW7 ......149 A8
Caerllew LL13 ....180 E1
Caernarvon Ave CW7 ..149 B7
Caernarvon Cl WA7 .....23 F2
Caernarvon Ct **4** CH65 .70 D2
Caernarvon Rd CW2 ...205 E8
Caesars Cl WA7 ....23 E2
Cairns Cres CH1 ....117 D4
Cairo St WA1 ....16 B5
Caister Way CW7 .....149 C2
Caithness Dr **3** WA7 ...23 B2
Calamine St SK11 ......112 E6
Calday Gr WA11 ....1 A8
Caldbeck Ave WA2 ....8 C3
Caldene Terr SK23 ......65 E7
Calder Ave CW1 ....191 A5
Calder Cl Bollington SK10 .87 F8
  Poynton SK12 ....36 D2
  Widnes WA8 ....13 F3
Calder Way **2** CH65 ....69 C5
Calderfield Cl WA4 ......26 B8
Caldicott Ave CH62 .....43 D7
Caldicott Cl **2** CW7 ...149 C7
Caldwell Ave WA5 ....7 F2
Caldwell Cl CW5 ......205 B4
Caldwell Rd WA8 ....23 A7
Caldwell's Gate La CW9 .54 B8
Caldy Cl CH3 ....118 D5
Caldy Dr CH66 ....69 D4
Caldy Rd Alsager ST7 ..193 C4
  Handforth SK9 ....34 D3

Caldy Valley Rd
  Chester CH3 ....142 B7
  Huntington CH3 ....142 A6
Caldy Way CW7 ....126 C1
Cale Rd SK22 ....39 D8
Calico La SK23 ....39 D4
California Cl WA5 ....15 C8
Callands Prim Sch WA5 ..7 E2
Callands Rd WA5 ....7 D2
Calmington La WA7 .....24 F4
Calrofold Dr ST5 ......210 D1
Calrofold La SK10 ....88 C2
Calstock Cl WA5 ....14 E3
Calveley Ave CH62 ......43 F4
Calveley Cl CW9 ....103 E5
Calveley Green La CW6,
  CW7 ....170 C4
Calveley Hall La CW5,
  CW6 ....170 A2
Calveley Prim Sch CW6 170 B2
Calveley Rd Halewood L26 21 A6
  Macclesfield SK10 ....86 F1
Calveley Way CW7 .....126 B1
Calver Rd WA2 ....8 A3
Calverley Cl **3** SK9 ....60 C8
Calverly Ct WA7 ....50 C5
Calvers WA7 ....23 E1
Camberley Cl SK7 ....36 A7
Camberwell Park Rd
  WA8 ....13 D4
Camborne Ave SK10 ...111 E8
Camborne Cl
  Congleton CW12 ......178 E8
  Runcorn WA7 ....50 C6
Cambourne Rd WA5 .....6 F6
Cambrai Ave WA4 ......16 C2
Cambrian Ave CH3 ....119 B2
Cambrian Cl CH66 ......69 A6
Cambrian Ct CH1 ......118 B2
Cambrian Rd CH1 .....118 B2
Cambrian Villas CH3 ...165 C2
Cambrian Way CW7 ...149 B8
Cambridge Ave
  Macclesfield SK11 ......112 B7
  Wilmslow SK9 ....59 F7
  Winsford CW7 ....126 A1
Cambridge Cl
  Biddulph ST8 ....179 C1
  Warrington WA4 ....26 B7
Cambridge Gdns
  Helsby WA6 ....73 D4
  Warrington WA4 ....26 C6
Cambridge Rd
  Bebington CH62 ....43 E8
  Chester CH2 ....118 F5
  Ellesmere Port CH65 ....70 D5
  Macclesfield SK11 ......112 B7
Cambridge Road Com Prim
  Sch CH65 ....70 C5
Cambridge St
  Runcorn WA7 ....23 C2
  Widnes WA8 ....23 B7
Camden Ct WA7 ....24 D1
Camden Rd CH65 ....70 A5
Camden St CW1 ......190 D4
Camellia Gdns WA9 .....6 B7
Camelot Cl WA12 ....1 F4
Camelot Gr CW2 ......206 C4
Camelot Way WA7 ......50 A8
Cameron Ave
  Runcorn WA7 ....48 E3
  Shavington CW2 ......206 B3
Cameron Cl WA2 ....8 A4
Cameron Rd WA8 ....23 A8
Camm St CW2 ....190 D2
Camomile Wlk **5** M31 ..11 F3
Campbell Ave WA7 .....49 A8
Campbell Cl
  Congleton CW12 ......157 A4
  Haslington CW1 ......191 C4
  Macclesfield SK10 ......87 A1
  Northwich CW9 ....103 F4
Campbell Cres WA5 .....14 F6
Campden Way SK9 ......34 D4
Campion Cl
  Huntington CH3 ......142 A6
  Warrington WA3 ....9 C4
Campsey Ash WA8 .....12 F4
Camrose Cl WA7 ....49 C6
Camsley La WA13 ....18 B3
Canaan WA3 ....4 C8
Canada Cl WA2 ....9 A2
Canadian Ave CH2 ....119 A3
Canal Bank WA13 ....18 D3
Canal Bridge Ent Pk
  CH65 ....70 D6
Canal Cotts CW5 ......187 D6
Canal Rd CW12 ....156 F1
Canal Reach WA7 ......24 C2
Canal Side Barnton CW8 .78 B2
  Chester CH1 ....237 C3
  Macclesfield SK11 ......112 F7
  Moore WA4 ....25 C5
  Runcorn WA7 ....48 D7
  Warrington WA4 ....17 C1
  Whaley Bridge SK23 ....39 F1
Canal Side Cotts WA7 ...50 F6
Canal St Chester CH1 ..237 A3
  Congleton CW12 ......156 E2
  Macclesfield SK10 ......112 E6
  Newton-le-W WA12 ......1 F5
  Runcorn WA7 ....23 B2
  Whaley Bridge SK23 ....65 D6
Canal Terr CW10 ......151 D8
Canalside CH65 ....70 D6
Canberra Ave WA3 ......8 D3
Canberra Rd SK7 ....35 F5
Canberra Sq WA2 ....8 D2

Canberra Way CH1 ....117 D4
Candelan Way WA16 ....29 C4
Candle La CW3 ....232 B2
Candleston Cl WA5 ......7 E1
Candy La SK10 ....62 C8
Canford Cl Crewe CW1 .190 B8
  Warrington WA5 ....15 C6
Cann La CW9 ....55 A6
Cann La N WA4 ....26 E5
Cann La S WA4 ....26 E5
Cannell Ct WA7 ....50 A6
Cannell St WA5 ....15 D4
Canning St CH1 ....237 A3
Canniswood Rd WA11 ....1 A6
Cannock Cl CH66 ....94 E8
Cannon St CH65 ....70 A5
Cannon Way CH4 ......161 A7
Cannonbury Cl WA7 ....50 A8
Canon Dr WA14 ....31 B8
Canon St WA7 ....22 F3
Canon Wilson Cl WA11 ...1 D6
Canons Rd WA5 ....15 D6
Canterbury Cl CH66 ....94 E8
Canterbury Grange
  CH65 ....60 B7
Canterbury Rd
  Blacon CH1 ....117 F5
  Widnes WA8 ....22 C8
Canterbury St WA4 .....16 C4
Cantley Cl WA7 ....49 D6
Canton Pl CW8 ....103 D7
Canton St CW11 ....112 C6
Canton Wlks CW11 ....112 D6
Canute Pl **11** WA16 ....57 A2
Capeland Cl CH4 ......140 C5
Capenhurst Ave
  Crewe CW2 ....190 A3
  Warrington WA2 ....9 A2
Capenhurst CE Prim Sch
  CH1 ....94 B8
Capenhurst Cl SK12 ....36 F4
Capenhurst Gdns CH66 .69 D1
Capenhurst Grange Sch
  CH66 ....69 E2
Capenhurst La
  Capenhurst CH1 ....94 B8
  Ellesmere Port CH65 ....70 A3
  Woodbank CH1 ....93 F7
Capenhurst Sta CH1 ....69 C1
Capesthorne Cl
  Alsager ST7 ....193 C3
  Hazel Grove SK7 ......36 F8
  Holmes Chapel CW4 ..130 B3
  Northwich CW9 ....103 F4
  Sandbach CW11 ....175 C7
  Widnes WA8 ....22 E8
Capesthorne Hall*
  SK11 ....110 A6
Capesthorne Rd
  Crewe CW2 ....189 F3
  Hazel Grove SK7 ......36 F8
  High Lane SK6 ....37 E7
  Warrington WA2 ....8 D2
  Waverton CH3 ....143 B6
  Wilmslow SK9 ....59 E5
Capesthorne Way **16**
  SK11 ....112 F7
Capitol Wlk CW12 .....156 D2
Capper Cl ST7 ....195 A2
Capper's La CW5,CW6 .186 C3
Cappers La CW11 .....176 C2
Car St CH1 ....237 C3
Carden Ave CW7 ......126 B1
Cardenbrook Gr **4** SK9 .34 D2
Cardeston Cl WA7 ......49 F3
Cardiff Cl CH66 ....94 E8
Cardigan Cl
  Macclesfield SK11 ......112 A8
  Warrington WA2 ....7 D2
Cardinal Newman RC High
  Sch WA4 ....16 F5
Cardway Bsns Pk ST7 .193 F3
Carey St WA8 ....13 C1
Cargo Ctr M90 ....32 F7
Carisbrook Ave SK10 ...87 E2
Carisbrook Dr CW7 ...149 C7
Carisbrooke Cl CW2 ..205 E8
Carleton Rd SK12 ......37 C4
Carlett Bvd CH62 ......43 F5
Carlingford Rd WA4 ....26 B7
Carlisle Cl
  Macclesfield SK11 ......111 F5
  Mobberley WA16 ......58 A4
  Winsford CW7 ....126 A1
Carlisle Rd CH1 ....117 E5
Carlisle St
  11 Alderley Edge SK9 .60 A1
  Crewe CW2 ....190 B2
  Warrington WA4 ....26 C8
Carlow Cl L24 ....21 D2
Carlton Ave Bramhall SK7 .35 D5
  Handforth SK9 ....34 C2
  Runcorn WA7 ....23 D2
  Saltney CH4 ....140 D6
Carlton Cl
  Mickle Trafford CH2 ...119 E8
  Neston CH64 ....41 C2
Carlton Cres CH66 .....69 F8
Carlton Pl CH2 ....119 A4
Carlton Rd Lymm WA13 ..19 B5
  Northwich CW9 ....104 B7
Carlton St
  Warrington WA4 ....26 C8
  Widnes WA8 ....23 A7
Carlton Way M44 ....11 C5
Carlyle Cl ST7 ....193 E8
Carlyle Cres CH66 .....69 C4

Carmarthen Cl
  Warrington WA5 ....7 D2
  3 Winsford CW7 ......149 C7
Carmel Cl CH1 ....117 D3
Carmel Ct WA8 ....13 B4
Carmenna Dr SK7 ......35 F7
Carnegie Cl SK10 ....87 A1
Carnoustie Cl
  Wilmslow SK9 ....60 D8
  Winsford CW7 ....126 B2
Carnoustie Dr SK10 ....87 D5
Carnoustie Gr WA11 .....1 A5
Carol Dr CH60 ....41 C8
Carol St WA4 ....16 D4
Caroline Ho CH1 ......117 E6
Caroline St Irlam M44 ..11 C8
  Widnes WA8 ....23 B7
Carpenter Gr WA2 ......9 A1
Carpenters Ct SK9 .....60 A1
Carr Brook Ct SK23 ....65 E5
Carr Brow SK6 ....38 A7
Carr La Alderley Edge SK9 .59 D2
  Audley ST7 ....209 A1
  Golborne WA3 ....4 A7
  Golborne,Wash End WN7 .4 E8
  Hale L24,WA8 ....21 E4
Carr Mill Mews SK9 ....34 B1
Carr St ST7 ....195 F1
Carr Wood Ave SK7 ....35 E8
Carrgreen La WA13 ....19 F6
Carriage Cl L24 ....21 D1
Carriage Dr Biddulph ST8 179 E1
  Frodsham WA6 ....74 A6
Carrick Dr CH65 ....70 B2
Carrick Rd CH4 ......141 B7
Carrington Cl WA3 ......9 C4
Carrington Way CW1 ..190 B8
Carroll Dr CW2 ....205 F8
Carrs Ct SK9 ....60 B7
Carrs La CH3 ....166 F1
Carrwood
  Altrincham WA15 ......32 B7
  Knutsford WA16 ....57 C1
Carrwood Cl WA11 ......1 A6
Carrwood Rd SK9 ......59 F8
Carsdale Rd M22 ....33 E8
Carter Ave CW6 ......122 D4
Carter Bench Ho SK10 ..63 A1
Carter Cl CW5 ....204 D6
Carter La CW11 ....84 B4
Carter St CH1 ....237 C3
Cartier Cl Warrington WA5 15 C8
  Warrington,Old Hall WA5 .7 C1
Cartlake Cl WA5 ......204 C5
Cartledge Cl CW8 .....102 A3
Cartmel Ave WA2 ....8 C3
Cartmel Cl
  Holmes Chapel CW4 ..130 A3
  Macclesfield SK10 ......87 B2
  Warrington WA5 ....7 E2
  Winsford CW7 ....126 D2
Cartmel Dr CH66 ....69 F2
Cartmell Cl WA7 ....49 B6
Cartridge La WA4 ......27 E6
Cartwright Rd CW1 ...191 D5
Cartwright St
  Runcorn WA7 ....23 C2
  Warrington WA5 ....15 E6
Carver Ave CW4 ......130 A6
Carver Cl CW7 ....127 A4
Case Rd WA5 ....1 D6
Casey La CW2 ....206 C4
Cassia Green La CW7 ..125 D5
Cassia La CW7,CW8 ..125 E5
Cassley Rd L24 ....21 A3
Casson St CW1 ....190 B5
Castle Bank CW8 .....103 E7
Castle Cl Broughton CH5 .139 B6
  Kelsall CW6 ....122 D4
  Pulford CH4 ....162 D2
Castle Ct Holt LL13 ...196 E8
  Northwich CW8 ......103 E7
Castle Dr Chester CH1 ..237 B1
  Ellesmere Port CH65 ....70 A3
  Heswall CH60 ....40 F8
Castle Farm SY14 .....200 E3
Castle Gdns LL13 .....196 E8
Castle Gn WA5 ....7 B2
Castle Hill
  Newton-le-W WA12 ......2 E4
  Prestbury SK10 ....86 E6
Castle Hill Ct SK10 .....86 F7
Castle Hill Farm **3**
  CW8 ....103 E8
Castle Ho ST7 ....195 C3
Castle Inn Rd CW12 ...179 C7
Castle Mews LL13 ....196 E8
Castle Mill La WA15 ....32 B5
Castle Park Arts Ctr
  WA6 ....74 A8
Castle Prim Sch ST7 ..195 D6
Castle Rd Kidsgrove ST7 .195 D7
  Runcorn WA7 ....23 D2
Castle Rise Prestbury SK10 86 F6
  Runcorn WA7 ....23 D2
Castle St Chester CH1 .237 B1
  Crewe CW1 ....190 C4
  Holt LL13 ....196 D8
  Macclesfield SK11 ......112 D8
  5 Nantwich CW5 .....204 E5
  Northwich CW8 ....103 F8
  Widnes WA8 ....13 D1
Castle View Prim Sch
  WA7 ....49 D8

Castle Way CH4 . . . . . . .162 A6
Castlecroft Rd CH4 . . . . .141 B5
Castlefields CH3 . . . . . . .166 C3
Castlefields Ave E WA7 . .24 A2
Castlefields Ave N WA7 . .23 F2
Castlefields Ave S WA7 . .24 A1
Castleford Dr SK10 . . . . . .86 E6
Castlegate SK10 . . . . .86 E6
Castlegate Mews SK10 . . .86 F6
Castlehill CH4 . . . . .162 C2
Castlemead Wlk CW9 . . . .103 E4
Castlemere Cl CH4 . . . . . .139 A3
Castlemere Dr CW1 . . . . .190 C7
Castleton Dr SK6 . . . . .37 F6
Castletown Cl SK10 . . . . . .87 C4
Castletown La CH3 . . . . . .197 D2
Castleview Rd ST7 . . . . .195 B3
Castleway WA15 . . . . .32 C7
Castner Ave WA7 . . . . .48 E7
Catalan Cl CW7 . . . . .127 A1
Catalyst Mus★ WA8 . . . . .23 A5
Catalyst Tade Pk WA8 . . .23 A6
Catchpenny La SK11 . . . .108 F3
Catford Cl WA8 . . . . .12 C2
Catfoss Cl WA2 . . . . .8 E1
Cathcart Gn CH3 . . . . . . .119 F5
Cathedral Church of Christ &
the Blessed Virgin Mary★
CH1 . . . . .237 B2
Catherine Ct/Llys Catrin
CH5 . . . . .139 B6
Catherine St
Chester CH1 . . . . .118 B2
Crewe CW2 . . . . .190 D2
Macclesfield SK11 . . . . .112 C8
Warrington WA5 . . . . . . .15 F7
Warrington WA5 . . . . . . .16 A7
Widnes WA8 . . . . .23 A7
Catherine Way WA12 . . . . .2 B2
Catholic High Sch The
CH4 . . . . .141 D6
Catterall Ave WA2 . . . . .8 D2
Caughall Rd CH2 . . . . .95 E2
Caunce Ave Golborne WA3 . .3 A7
Newton-le-W WA12 . . . . . .2 C1
Causeway Ave WA4 . . . . . .16 C3
Causeway Pk WA4 . . . . . . .16 C3
Cavalier Dr CH1 . . . . .117 E6
Cavan Dr WA11 . . . . .1 D7
Cavell Dr CH65 . . . . .70 A4
Cavendish Ave WA3 . . . . . .9 F5
Cavendish Cl
5 Macclesfield SK10 . . . .87 D3
Warrington WA5 . . . . . . .15 D7
Winsford CW7 . . . . .149 A8
Cavendish Cres ST7 . . . .193 D5
Cavendish Ct WA8 . . . . . . .12 F1
Cavendish Farm Rd WA7 .49 A5
Cavendish Gdns CH65 . . . .70 A4
Cavendish Mews SK9 . . . .60 A6
Cavendish Pl WA3 . . . . .9 F5
Cavendish Rd
Chester CH4 . . . . .141 B6
Crewe CW2 . . . . .189 C5
Hazel Grove SK7 . . . . . . .36 E8
Cavendish Sch WA7 . . . . .49 C5
Cavendish St **7** WA7 . . . .22 F2
Cavendish Way CW4 . . . .130 A3
Caversham Cl WA4 . . . . . .26 E6
Cawdor Dr CH3 . . . . .119 A2
Cawdor St Runcorn WA7 . . .22 F3
Warrington WA4 . . . . . . .26 C8
Cawfield Ave WA8 . . . . . . .12 D1
Cawley Ave WA3 . . . . .4 E4
Cawley La SK10 . . . . .62 E7
Cawley St
8 Macclesfield SK11 . . . .112 E7
Runcorn WA7 . . . . .23 A1
Cawood Cl CH66 . . . . .69 B5
Cawthorne Ave WA4 . . . . .17 A4
Caxton Cl
Ellesmere Port CH66 . . . .69 E4
Widnes WA8 . . . . .12 C3
Cecil Rd ST8 . . . . .179 C2
Cecil Rigby Cl 1 CW11 . .175 B6
Cecil St CH3 . . . . .119 A1
Cedab Rd CH65 . . . . .70 C6
Cedar Ave Alsager ST7 . . .193 D3
Connah's Quay CH5 . . . . .91 C1
Connah's Quay,Garden City
CH5 . . . . .116 A7
Ellesmere Port CH66 . . . .69 D6
Golborne WA3 . . . . .3 F7
Kidsgrove ST7 . . . . .194 D1
Runcorn WA7 . . . . .49 C7
Sutton WA7 . . . . .50 B4
Widnes WA8 . . . . .13 B2
Cedar Cl
Connah's Quay CH5 . . . .116 A7
Holmes Chapel CW4 . . . .130 D4
Lostock Gralam CW9 . . . .80 A3
Middlewich CW10 . . . . . .151 E6
Poynton SK12 . . . . .36 E3
Sandbach CW11 . . . . . . .175 C5
Cedar Cres Audley ST7 . .209 F1
Newton-le-W WA12 . . . . . .2 D2
Cedar Ct Alsager ST7 . . . .193 E4
Congleton CW12 . . . . . .178 F8
Culcheth WA3 . . . . .4 F1
Willaston CW5 . . . . .205 D6
Cedar Dr Barnton CW8 . . . .78 A4
Chester CH2 . . . . .119 B4
Haydock WA11 . . . . .1 E7

Cedar Gr continued
Macclesfield SK11 . . . . .112 D5
Nantwich CW5 . . . . .205 A5
Neston CH64 . . . . .66 F8
Warrington WA1 . . . . .17 A7
Warrington, Latchford WA4 .16 D3
Winsford CW7 . . . . .127 A1
Cedar Ho CH3 . . . . .142 B8
Cedar Lo SK7 . . . . .35 F7
Cedar Mews CH1 . . . . . . .117 E4
Cedar Pk CH3 . . . . .119 C2
Cedar Rd
Newcastle-u-Lyme ST5 . .210 D1
Partington M31 . . . . .11 E3
Warrington WA5 . . . . . . .14 F6
Weaverham CW8 . . . . . .102 C8
Cedar St WA12 . . . . .2 C2
Cedar Way CW2 . . . . .206 B7
Cedardale Dr CH66 . . . . . .94 F8
Cedardale Pk WA8 . . . . . . .13 E4
Cedarfield Rd WA13 . . . . . .18 F2
Cedars SK9 . . . . .59 F6
Cedars The Alsager ST7 . .193 F1
Mobberley WA16 . . . . . . .58 E2
8 Northwich CW9 . . . . .103 E6
Cedarway Bollington SK10 . .88 A7
Heswall CH60 . . . . .41 B5
Wilmslow SK9 . . . . .59 F5
Cedarways WA4 . . . . .26 D5
Cedarwood
Cuddington CW8 . . . . . . .101 D5
Poynton SK12 . . . . .36 E3
Cedarwood Ct CW6 . . . . .146 C3
Celandine Cl CH3 . . . . . . .142 A7
Celandine Way WA9 . . . . . .6 B7
Celyn Cres CH4 . . . . .140 D5
Cement Pl CH1 . . . . .237 B3
Cemetery Rd CW2 . . . . . .207 B5
Cemlyn Cl CH1 . . . . .117 E3
Centenary Ho WA7 . . . . . .49 C8
Centenary Pl CW12 . . . . .156 E3
Central Ave Alsager CW2 .192 F1
Ellesmere Port CH65 . . . .70 C4
Warrington WA2 . . . . . . .16 C8
Warrington,Latchford WA4 .16 B3
Haydock WA11 . . . . .1 B6
Heald Green SK8 . . . . . . .34 D8
Central Dr Barnton CW8 . . .78 A3
Central Expressway WA7 .49 D6
Central Gr CW9 . . . . .104 D6
Central Rd
Northwich CW9 . . . . . . .104 D7
Partington M31 . . . . .11 F3
Central St ST7 . . . . .195 B6
Central Trad Est CH4 . . . .140 E7
Central Way WA12 . . . . .2 E2
Centre Ct ST7 . . . . .193 E4
Centre Park Sq WA1 . . . . .16 A4
Centre Pk WA1 . . . . .16 A4
Centurion Cl WA3 . . . . .9 D4
Centurion Row WA7 . . . . . .23 F2
Century Rd ST5 . . . . .210 F2
Century Way SK10 . . . . . . .87 F2
Cestria Cl CW11 . . . . .174 D7
Chads Gn CW5 . . . . .206 A1
Chadwick Ave Croft WA3 . .9 B7
Warrington WA4 . . . . . . .16 E1
Chadwick Cl SK9 . . . . .34 C1
Chadwick Ct CW10 . . . . . .151 D7
Chadwick Fields Orch
CW10 . . . . .151 D6
Chadwick Pl WA3 . . . . .9 E5
Chadwick Rd
Middlewich CW10 . . . . . .151 C6
Runcorn WA7 . . . . .23 E3
Chadwick Terr SK11 . . . . .87 E1
Chadwicke Cl CW5 . . . . . .204 F4
Chaffinch Cl
Congleton CW12 . . . . . .156 E1
Warrington WA3 . . . . .9 F3
Chaffinch Way CW7 . . . . .149 D6
Chaigeley Sch WA4 . . . . . .17 E4
Chailey Rise CH3 . . . . . . .182 D1
Chain Maker's Row CH4 .140 E7
Chalfield Ave CH66 . . . . . .69 C5
Chalfield Cl
1 Ellesmere Port CH66 . . .69 C5
Wistaston CW2 . . . . .206 B7
Chalfont Cl WA4 . . . . .26 E6
Chalfont Cres CW2 . . . . . .207 B2
Chalfont Ct WA16 . . . . .57 C3
Chalgrave Cl WA8 . . . . . . .13 F3
Chalkwell Dr CH60 . . . . . . .41 C7
Challinor St CH3 . . . . .119 A1
Chamber Brook La WA6 . .75 D2
Chamberlain Ct CW1 . . . .191 C4
Chamberlain Dr SK9 . . . . .34 D1
Chambers St CW2 . . . . . .190 D2
Chance Hall La CW12,
ST7 . . . . .177 C3
Chancel La SK9 . . . . .60 B8
Chancellor Rd WA7 . . . . . .24 D5
Chancery La Alsager ST7 .193 B3
Bollington SK10 . . . . .88 B7
Chandler Way WA3 . . . . . . .3 E8
Chandlers Ct WA7 . . . . . . .22 E1
Chandos Cl CH4 . . . . .141 E6
Change La CH64 . . . . .68 B8
Channel The CH1 . . . . .95 B4
Chantler Ave WA4 . . . . . . .16 E4
Chantry Ave CW8 . . . . . . .103 B4
Chantry Cl SK12 . . . . .38 E5
Chantry Ct Chester CH1 . .117 E2
Crewe CW1 . . . . .190 D4
Macclesfield SK11 . . . . .112 D5
Chantry Fold SK12 . . . . . .38 E6
Chantry Rd SK12 . . . . .38 E6

Chantry The CW6 . . . . . .169 E2
Chantry Wlk CH60 . . . . . . .41 A6
Chapel Ave WA6 . . . . .75 C2
Chapel Bank ST7 . . . . . . .195 D6
Chapel Cl Audlem CW3 . . .229 F3
Cholmondeston CW7 . . . .170 F4
Comberbach CW9 . . . . . .78 D7
Ellesmere Port CH65 . . . .70 C7
Mount Pleasant ST7 . . . .195 B6
Saughall CH1 . . . . .94 A1
Waverton CH3 . . . . .143 A5
Chapel Cotts CH3 . . . . . .143 A5
Chapel Croft SK11 . . . . . . .84 B3
Chapel Cross Rd WA2 . . . . .9 A2
Chapel Ct Northwich CW9 .103 F7
Wilmslow SK9 . . . . .60 A6
Chapel Dr WA15 . . . . .32 C7
Chapel Gn CW6 . . . . .122 C5
Chapel House La CH64 . . .93 A7
Chapel La
Acton Bridge CW8 . . . . . .76 E4
Aldford CH3 . . . . .164 D5
Allostock WA16 . . . . .106 E3
Altrincham WA15 . . . . . . .32 C7
Appleton Thorn WA4 . . . .27 B4
Chester CH3 . . . . .119 A1
Crewe CW1 . . . . .173 D1
Dutton WA4 . . . . .77 B7
Hargrave CH3 . . . . .144 A1
Hollinfare WA3 . . . . .11 A2
Hollins Green WA3 . . . . . .10 F1
Holt LL13 . . . . .196 D8
Kelsall CW6 . . . . .122 E2
Kidsgrove ST7 . . . . .195 E4
Kingsley WA6 . . . . .75 C2
Ledsham CH66 . . . . .68 F1
Manley WA6,CH3 . . . . . . .98 F3
Mere WA16 . . . . .30 B4
Milton Green CH3 . . . . . .165 B4
Moulton CW9 . . . . .126 E8
Norton in Hales TF9 . . . .236 C2
Partington M31 . . . . .11 F2
Rainow SK10 . . . . .88 E5
Ravensmoor CW5 . . . . . .203 D2
Rode Heath ST7 . . . . . . .193 F7
Saighton CH3 . . . . .142 E1
Threapwood SY14 . . . . . .222 E8
Warrington WA4 . . . . . . .26 C8
Widnes WA8 . . . . .12 C4
Wilmslow SK9 . . . . .60 A6
Windyharbour SK11 . . . . .109 D2
Woodbank CH1 . . . . .93 B8
Chapel Lodge CH1 . . . . . .237 C3
Chapel Mews
Alsager ST7 . . . . .193 C3
Ellesmere Port CH65 . . . .70 B4
Elton CH2 . . . . .72 B3
1 Nantwich CW5 . . . . .204 E5
Chapel Mus Mow Cop★
ST7 . . . . .195 D7
Chapel Rd
Alderley Edge SK9 . . . . . .60 A1
Ollerton WA16 . . . . .82 F6
Warrington WA5 . . . . . . .14 E3
Whaley Bridge SK23 . . . .65 F5
Wilmslow SK9 . . . . .61 A8
Winsford CW7 . . . . .126 F1
Chapel Rise SY14 . . . . . . .213 B3
Chapel Row
Barbridge CW5 . . . . .187 D6
Nantwich CW5 . . . . .204 D5
Chapel St
7 Alderley Edge SK9 . . . .60 A1
Audley ST7 . . . . .209 E3
Bollington SK10 . . . . .88 B8
Chester CH3 . . . . .237 C3
Congleton CW12 . . . . . . .156 D2
Crewe CW2 . . . . .190 D3
Haydock WA11 . . . . .1 E6
Holt LL13 . . . . .196 D8
Kidsgrove ST7 . . . . .194 D2
Macclesfield SK11 . . . . .112 D6
Moulton CW9 . . . . .126 E8
Mount Pleasant ST7 . . . .195 B6
New Mills SK22 . . . . .39 B6
Newton-le-W WA12 . . . . . .2 B3
Northwich CW8 . . . . .103 E7
Sandbach CW11 . . . . . . .175 B6
Sandbach,Wheelock CW11 175 A3
Weaverham CW8 . . . . . . .77 C1
Whaley Bridge SK23 . . . .65 E8
Widnes WA8 . . . . .23 A7
Wincham CW9 . . . . .79 C3
Chapel Terr WA3 . . . . .4 B8
Chapel View
Bebington CH62 . . . . .44 A6
Helsby WA6 . . . . .73 B2
Chapel Wlk WA3 . . . . .4 B8
Chapel Wlks
Broomedge WA13 . . . . . .19 D1
Cheadle Hulme SK8 . . . . .35 B6
Chapel Yd WA3 . . . . .16 A6
Chapelfields WA6 . . . . .74 A8
Chapelmere Cl CW11 . . . .174 E7
Chapelmere Ct CW1 . . . . .190 C7
Chapman Cl WA8 . . . . .12 D4
Chapterhouse Cl CH65 . . . .70 E5
Charcoal Rd WA14 . . . . . . .20 F3
Charity La
Macclesfield SK11 . . . . .113 F8
Macclesfield Forest SK11 .114 B6
Charlcote Cres CW2 . . . . .206 C8
Charlecote Rd SK12 . . . . . .36 F4
Charles Ave
Davenham CW9 . . . . . . .103 F2
Warrington WA5 . . . . . . .14 F6
Charles Cres CH4 . . . . . . .237 C1

Charles Darwin Prim Sch
CW8 . . . . .103 E7
Charles Forbes Ct 8
WA1 . . . . .16 B5
Charles Price Gdns 8
CH65 . . . . .70 C6
Charles Rd CH2 . . . . .95 C1
Charles Sq CW11 . . . . . . .175 F2
Charles St Chester CH1 . .237 B3
Chester,Hoole Park CH2 . .118 F3
Crewe CW1 . . . . .190 C4
Irlam M44 . . . . .11 E6
Widnes WA8 . . . . .23 A8
Charleston Cl CH66 . . . . . .69 D3
Charlesworth Cl SK23 . . . .39 D3
Charlesworth Cres SK23 . .39 D3
Charlesworth Ct CW11 . . .175 C6
Charlesworth Pl 1
CW12 . . . . .156 F4
Charlesworth Rd SK23 . . . .39 D3
Charlesworth St CW1 . . . .190 D6
Charlock Wlk 6 M31 . . . .11 F3
Charlotte Cl CH1 . . . . .237 B3
Charlotte St Chester CH1 .118 B2
Macclesfield SK11 . . . . .112 D7
Charlotte St W 22 SK11 . .112 C8
Charlotte Wlk 2 WA8 . . . .23 B7
Charlton Cl WA7 . . . . .50 A7
Charlton Ct CH2 . . . . .119 A4
Charlton St
23 Macclesfield SK11 . . .112 C8
Warrington WA4 . . . . . . .16 F3
Charminster Cl WA5 . . . . .15 D5
Charmouth Cl WA12 . . . . . .2 B4
Charnock Ave WA12 . . . . . .1 C5
Charnock Rd WA3 . . . . .4 F3
Charnwood ST7 . . . . .195 B1
Charnwood Cl
Macclesfield SK10 . . . . . .87 A1
Warrington WA3 . . . . . . .10 B5
Charnwood Cres SK7 . . . .36 D8
Charon Way WA5 . . . . .7 B3
Charter Ave WA5 . . . . .16 A4
Charter Cres CH66 . . . . . .69 E3
Charter Rd SK10 . . . . .88 A7
Charter Way SK10 . . . . .87 F3
Charterhall Dr CH2 . . . . . .118 F2
Chartley Gr CW10 . . . . . . .128 D2
Chartwell Gr CW7 . . . . . . .149 C5
Chartwell Pk CW11 . . . . . .175 A4
Chase Dr CH66 . . . . .69 D3
Chase The Bebington CH63 43 C5
5 Heswall CH60 . . . . . .41 A8
Chase Way CH66 . . . . .69 D2
Chaser Ct CH1 . . . . .117 F3
Chasewater WA7 . . . . .24 F4
Chassagne Sq CW1 . . . . .189 F7
Chatburn Cl WA3 . . . . .4 F2
Chater Dr CW5 . . . . .204 F3
Chatfield Dr WA3 . . . . .9 E3
Chatham Cl WA4 . . . . .16 F3
Chatham St 9 SK11 . . . . .112 D8
Chatham Way CW1 . . . . . .191 C5
Chatsworth Ave
Culcheth WA3 . . . . .4 F4
Macclesfield SK11 . . . . .111 C6
Chatsworth Cl
Ellesmere Port CH66 . . . .69 C5
Northwich CW9 . . . . . . .104 C6
Wistaston CW2 . . . . .206 A7
Chatsworth Dr
Chester CH2 . . . . .119 A5
Congleton CW12 . . . . . .155 F3
Widnes WA8 . . . . .12 C5
Chatsworth Ho CH1 . . . . .118 B3
Chatsworth Rd
Hazel Grove SK7 . . . . . . .36 F8
High Lane SK6 . . . . .37 F6
Wilmslow SK9 . . . . .59 E4
Chatteris Pk WA7 . . . . .24 E2
Chatterton Dr WA7 . . . . . . .50 E8
Chatwell Gdns WA4 . . . . . .26 F5
Chaucer Cl CH1 . . . . .117 E6
Chaucer Gr CW11 . . . . . . .174 C5
Chaucer Pl WA4 . . . . .16 F4
Chaucer St WA7 . . . . .23 A1
Cheadle Hulme Coll SK8 . .35 B7
Cheadle Hulme Sta SK8 . .35 A8
Cheadle La WA16 . . . . .81 A1
Cheadle Wood SK8 . . . . . .34 E8
Checkley Dr ST8 . . . . .179 C1
Checkley La CW3,CW5 . . .221 E1
Checkley Rd ST5 . . . . .210 C5
Checkley Row CW5 . . . . . .232 C8
Cheddar Gr WA5 . . . . .6 F7
Chedlee Dr SK8 . . . . .34 E8
Chedworth Dr WA8 . . . . . .12 C4
Cheerbrook Rd CW5 . . . . .205 D4
Cheese Hill La WA6,CW8 101 B4
Chelford Ave WA3 . . . . .3 D8
Chelford CE Prim Sch
SK11 . . . . .84 A3
Chelford Cl Chester CH1 . .117 F1
Warrington WA4 . . . . . . .26 C4
Chelford Dr CW9 . . . . .103 F5
Chelford La WA16 . . . . .83 C1
Chelford Mews 2 CH3 . . .119 B1
Chelford Rd
Alderley Edge SK9 . . . . . .59 E1
Chelford SK10,SK11 . . . . .84 D1
Chelford, Marthall WA16,
SK11 . . . . .83 D4
Congleton CW12 . . . . . .155 E6
Goostrey CW4 . . . . .131 B7
Handforth SK9 . . . . .34 D5
Macclesfield SK10,SK11 .111 C8
Monks Heath SK10 . . . . . .85 B1
Nether Alderley SK9 . . . . .84 C7
Ollerton WA16 . . . . .82 D7

Chelford Rd continued
Prestbury SK10 . . . . .86 D5
Whisterfield SK11 . . . . . .109 F3
Chelford Rdbt SK11 . . . . . .84 B1
Chelford Sta SK11 . . . . . . .84 A2
Chell St CW1 . . . . .190 B5
Chells Hill CW11 . . . . .176 C1
Chelsea Cl ST8 . . . . .179 C1
Chelsea Gdns WA5 . . . . . .15 C4
Chelston Dr SK8 . . . . .34 C6
Cheltenham Cl
2 Macclesfield SK10 . . . .87 C4
Warrington WA5 . . . . . . .15 A8
Cheltenham Cres
Crewe CW1 . . . . .190 B7
Runcorn WA7 . . . . .49 B6
Cheltenham Dr WA12 . . . . .2 C5
Cheltenham Rd CH65 . . . . .70 D3
Chemical St WA12 . . . . . . .2 B3
Cheney Wlk CW2 . . . . . . .206 D8
Chepstow Cl
Biddulph ST8 . . . . .179 C1
Macclesfield SK10 . . . . . .87 C4
Warrington WA5 . . . . .7 E3
1 Winsford CW7 . . . . . .149 C7
Cherington Cl SK9 . . . . . . .34 F3
Cherington Cres SK11 . . . .112 B7
Cheriton Way CW2 . . . . . .206 A8
Cherrington Rd CW5 . . . . .204 E3
Cherry Blossom Rd WA7 . .49 F4
Cherry Brow Terr CH64 . . .67 F8
Cherry Cl
Newcastle-u-Lyme ST5 . .210 D1
Newton-le-W WA12 . . . . . .1 C4
Willaston CH64 . . . . .67 C8
Cherry Cnr WA13 . . . . .28 A7
Cherry Cres CW7 . . . . . . .149 C8
Cherry Dale Rd CH4 . . . . .139 A3
Cherry Gdns CH3 . . . . . . .119 A1
Cherry Gr
Ellesmere Port CH66 . . . .70 A1
Nantwich CW5 . . . . .204 D5
Cherry Grove Prim Sch
CH3 . . . . .119 A1
Cherry Grove Rd CH3 . . . .119 A1
Cherry La
Congleton CW12 . . . . . .179 E8
Cuddington CW8 . . . . . . .101 F2
Lawton Heath ST7 . . . . . .193 E6
Lymm WA13 . . . . .18 C1
Weaverham CW8 . . . . . .102 D8
Cherry Orch/Y Berllan
Geirios LL13 . . . . .196 D8
Cherry Rd CH3 . . . . .119 A1
Cherry Tree Ave
Barnton CW8 . . . . .78 A4
Lawton-gate ST7 . . . . . . .194 A5
Lymm WA13 . . . . .18 D2
Poynton SK12 . . . . .36 F3
Runcorn WA7 . . . . .49 C8
Warrington WA5 . . . . . . .14 F4
Cherry Tree Cl Elton CH2 . .72 B4
Hale L24 . . . . .21 E1
Haydock WA11 . . . . .1 A5
Wilmslow SK9 . . . . .60 E8
Cherry Tree Dr
Hazel Grove SK7 . . . . . . .37 A8
St Helens WA9 . . . . .1 A2
Cherry Tree Ho SK9 . . . . . .85 C8
Cherry Tree La
Rostherne WA14 . . . . . . .30 E6
Woore CW3 . . . . .232 C2
Cherry Tree Mews 3
CH60 . . . . .41 A8
Cherry Tree Prim Sch
WA13 . . . . .18 C2
Cherry Tree Rd
Audley ST7 . . . . .209 F1
Crewe CW1 . . . . .190 E6
Golborne WA3 . . . . .3 F8
Newcastle-u-Lyme ST5 . .210 E1
Cherry Tree Way CW12 . . .156 E2
Cherry Wlk
Cheadle Hulme SK8 . . . . .35 C8
Partington M31 . . . . .11 D2
Swan Green WA16 . . . . .106 D7
Cherryfields Rd SK11 . . . .111 F8
Cherrysutton WA8 . . . . . . .12 B3
Cherrysutton Mews WA8 . 12 B4
Cherrywood Cres CW8 . . . .78 B4
Cherwell Cl
Cheadle Hulme SK8 . . . . .35 A7
Warrington WA2 . . . . .8 D2
Cheryl Ct CW8 . . . . .102 A4
Cheryl Dr WA8 . . . . .13 D1
Chesford Grange WA1 . . . .17 F7
Chesham Cl SK9 . . . . .59 F4
Chesham Ct CH65 . . . . . . .70 D4
Chesham Rd SK9 . . . . .59 F4
Chesham St CH1 . . . . .237 C3
Cheshire Acad CW1 . . . . .190 E2
Cheshire Candle
Workshops★ CH3 . . . . .184 C6
Cheshire Cl WA12 . . . . .2 E3
Cheshire Farm★ CH3 . . . .166 D4
Cheshire Military Mus★
CH1 . . . . .237 A1
Cheshire Oaks Outlet Village
CH65 . . . . .70 E2
Cheshire Oaks Way CH65 .70 E2
Cheshire Pk WA6 . . . . .97 D5
Cheshire Rd M31 . . . . .11 D2
Cheshire Row WA16 . . . . .108 B8
Cheshire St CW3 . . . . .229 F4
Cheshire View
Bollington SK10 . . . . .88 B6
Chester CH4 . . . . .141 E7
Cheshyre Dr WA7 . . . . .23 F1

Cheshyre's La WA7 . . . . . .48 E7
Chessington Cl WA4 . . . .26 F6
Chester Aerospace Pk
  CH5 . . . . .139 B6
Chester Ave WA3 . . . . .3 D8
Chester Bsns Pk CH4 . . .141 B3
Chester Cl Handforth SK9 .34 E2
  Irlam M44 . . . . .11 D5
  Runcorn WA7 . . . . .24 A2
  Talke ST7 . . . . .210 E7
Chester Classic The
  CH1 . . . . .237 B3
Chester Heritage Ctr★
  CH1 . . . . .237 B1
Chester High Rd
  Neston CH64 . . . . .41 E4
  Willaston CH64 . . . . .67 D7
Chester La CW7 . . . . . . .125 D2
Chester New Rd WA4 . . . .25 F7
Chester Race Course★
  CH1 . . . . .237 A1
Chester Rd Acton CW5 . .204 A6
  Audley ST7 . . . . .209 D2
  Barbridge CW5 . . . . . . .187 D5
  Broughton CH4 . . . . . . .139 D5
  Churton CH3 . . . . .180 F6
  Connah's Quay CH6 . . . . .91 A3
  Cuddington CW8 . . . . . .101 D1
  Daresbury WA4 . . . . .25 B1
  Delamere CW6,CW8 . . . .123 C5
  Dunham-on-t-H CH2,WA6 . .97 D5
  Ellesmere Port, Whitby
   CH65,CH66 . . . . .70 A2
  Ellesmere Port,Great Sutton
   CH66 . . . . .69 D4
  Frodsham WA6 . . . . .74 A7
  Gatesheath CH3 . . . . . .165 E5
  Hartford CW8 . . . . .102 E3
  Hartford, Greenbank CW8 103 C6
  Helsby WA6 . . . . .73 C4
  Heswall CH60,CH64 . . . .41 C6
  Higher Walton WA4 . . . . .25 D5
  Holmes Chapel CW4 . . . .130 B2
  Hooton CH66 . . . . .44 A1
  Huntington CH3 . . . . . . .142 A6
  Kelsall CW6 . . . . .122 D5
  Macclesfield SK11 . . . . .112 B8
  Malpas SY14 . . . . .213 B4
  Mere WA16 . . . . .56 B6
  Middlewich CW10 . . . . . .128 B2
  Neston CH64 . . . . .66 E7
  Over Tabley WA16 . . . . . .56 A2
  Plumley WA16 . . . . .80 E5
  Poynton SK12 . . . . .36 B4
  Rostherne WA14,WA16 . . .30 C5
  Runcorn WA7 . . . . .50 E5
  Saltney CH4 . . . . .140 C6
  Sandycroft CH5 . . . . . . .116 A2
  Sutton WA7 . . . . .50 B4
  Talke ST7 . . . . .210 D7
  Warrington WA4 . . . . . . .16 A2
  Warrington,Grappenhall
   WA4 . . . . .17 B1
  Whitchurch SY13 . . . . . .225 D2
  Winsford CW7 . . . . .125 F2
  Woodford SK7 . . . . .35 E2
Chester Ret Pk CH1 . . . .118 A3
Chester Row WA12 . . . . . . .7 D8
Chester Sq CW1 . . . . . . .190 C4
Chester St Chester CH4 . .140 F7
  Crewe CW1 . . . . .190 C4
  Warrington WA2 . . . . . . .16 B6
  Widnes WA8 . . . . .13 B1
Chester Sta CH1 . . . . . .237 C3
Chester Toy & Doll Mus★
  CH1 . . . . .237 B2
Chester Trad Pk CH1 . . . .117 F2
Chester Way CW9 . . . . . .104 A8
Chester West Employment Pk
  CH1 . . . . .117 E2
Chester Zoo★ CH2 . . . . . .95 E1
Chester Zoological Gdns★
  CH2 . . . . .118 D8
Chester's Croft Pk SK8 . . .35 A5
Chesterbank Bsns Pk
  CH4 . . . . .140 D7
Chesterfield Cl CW7 . . . .125 F1
Chesterfield Rd CH62 . . . .43 D4
Chestergate SK10,SK11 . .112 D8
Chesterton Cl CW10 . . . .151 E5
Chesterton Ct CH2 . . . . .118 D4
Chesterton Dr
  Crewe CW2 . . . . .189 F1
  Winwick WA2 . . . . .8 A5
Chesterton Gr CW11 . . . .174 D5
Chestnut Ave
  4 Ellesmere Port CH66 . . .69 F1
  Irlam M44 . . . . .11 D5
  Macclesfield SK10 . . . . . .87 E2
  Rode Heath ST7 . . . . . . .193 F7
  Shavington CW2 . . . . . . .206 C5
  Warrington WA5 . . . . . . .14 F6
  Widnes WA8 . . . . .13 B2
Chestnut Cl Chester CH2 . .119 A3
  Cuddington CW8 . . . . . .101 F2
  Middlewich CW10 . . . . . .128 B2
  Tarporley CW6 . . . . .146 D2
  Wilmslow SK9 . . . . .60 E8
Chestnut Ct
  Tarporley CW6 . . . . .146 C2
  Widnes WA8 . . . . .12 D1
Chestnut Dr Alsager ST7 193 E2
  Congleton CW12 . . . . . .156 A4
  Holmes Chapel CW4 . . . .130 D3
  Poynton SK12 . . . . .36 F3
Chestnut Gr Barnton CW8 .78 B4
  Bebington CH62 . . . . . . .43 C8
  Crewe CW1 . . . . .190 E5

Chestnut Gr continued
  Golborne WA3 . . . . .3 F8
  Newcastle-u-Lyme ST5 . .210 E1
  Winsford CW7 . . . . .149 C8
Chestnut Grange CH4 . . .141 B7
Chestnut Ho 6 CW11 . . .175 B6
Chestnut La WA6 . . . . . . .73 E4
Chestnut Lodge Specl Sch
  WA8 . . . . .12 E1
Chestnut Mews WA16 . . .58 E1
Chestnut Wlk M31 . . . . . .11 D2
Chetham Ct WA2 . . . . .8 A3
Chetton Dr WA7 . . . . .50 E7
Chetwode Mews WA4 . . .52 C2
Chetwode St CW1 . . . . . .190 C5
Chetwood Dr WA8 . . . . . .12 F4
Cheveley Cl SK10 . . . . . . .87 C2
Chevin Gdns SK7 . . . . . . .36 A7
Cheviot Ave WA2 . . . . .8 A3
Cheviot Cl CH66 . . . . .69 A6
Cheviot Ct CW7 . . . . .149 C7
Cheviot Sq CW7 . . . . . . .149 B7
Chevron Cl CH1 . . . . .117 E4
Chevron Hey CH1 . . . . . . .117 E4
Cheyne Wlk CW5 . . . . . . .204 E3
Cheyney Rd CH1 . . . . .118 B3
Chicago Ave M90 . . . . .33 B7
Chichester Cl
  Grappenhall Heys WA4 . . .27 A7
  Runcorn WA7 . . . . .50 D6
Chichester Ct CH1 . . . . .237 A3
Chichester St CH1 . . . . .237 A3
Chidlow Cl Hough CW2 . .206 E2
  Widnes WA8 . . . . .23 A5
Child's La CW12 . . . . . . .177 C6
Childer Cres CH66 . . . . . .69 B7
Childer Gdns CH66 . . . . . .69 B7
Childer Thornton Prim Sch
  CH66 . . . . .69 B8
Childwall Ct CH66 . . . . . .69 B8
Childwall Gdns CH66 . . . .69 B8
Childwall Rd CH66 . . . . . .69 B8
Chilham Cl CW7 . . . . .149 C7
Chilham Pl SK11 . . . . . . .111 F6
Chillington Ave WA8 . . . . .22 D8
Chillingham Cl CW10 . . .128 D2
Chiltern Ave SK11 . . . . . .112 A7
Chiltern Cl Chester CH4 . .141 B5
  Chorlton CW2 . . . . .207 B1
  Cuddington CW8 . . . . . .102 A2
Chiltern Cres WA2 . . . . . . .8 A3
Chiltern Pl WA2 . . . . .8 A3
Chiltern Rd Culcheth WA3 . .4 E4
  St Helens WA9 . . . . .1 A3
  Warrington WA2 . . . . .8 A3
Chiltern Way CW7 . . . . . .149 B7
Chilton Dr CH66 . . . . .69 F2
Chilwell Cl WA8 . . . . .12 D4
Chilworth Cl CW2 . . . . . .206 C8
China La WA1 . . . . .16 C2
Chines The CW8 . . . . . . .101 D5
Chippindall Cl WA5 . . . . . .15 C5
Chipstead Cl CH4 . . . . . .103 A4
Chirk Cl CH2 . . . . .118 F6
Chirk Gdns CH65 . . . . . . .70 D3
Chirk Pl CW7 . . . . .126 A1
Chirton Cl WA11 . . . . .1 D7
Chisledon Cl WA11 . . . . . . .1 D7
Chislet Ct WA8 . . . . .12 E4
Chiswick Cl WA7 . . . . .50 D7
Chiswick Gdns WA4 . . . . .26 F6
Chollerton Cl WA16 . . . . . .29 C4
Cholmley Dr WA12 . . . . . . .1 F4
Cholmondeley Castle Gdns★
  SY14 . . . . .201 A4
Cholmondeley La SY14 . .200 E7
Cholmondeley Rd
  Ellesmere Port CH65 . . . .69 F4
  Hampton Heath SY14 . . .213 E7
  Runcorn WA7 . . . . .49 D4
  Wrenbury CW5 . . . . .216 C5
Cholmondeley St
  Macclesfield SK11 . . . . .112 D6
  Widnes WA8 . . . . .23 A4
Cholmondley Rise WA4 214 B4
Chorley Bank Council Hos
  CW5 . . . . .201 E1
Chorley Green La CW5,
  SY14 . . . . .201 E5
Chorley Hall Cl SK9 . . . . .59 F1
Chorley Hall La
  Alderley Edge SK9 . . . . . .60 A1
  Faddiley CW5 . . . . .202 C2
Chorley St
  Warrington WA2 . . . . . . .16 B6
  Warrington WA2 . . . . . . .16 C6
Chorley Stock La CW5 . . .202 A2
Chorley's La WA8 . . . . . . .13 E3
Chorleywood Cl SK10 . . . .87 B4
Chorlton Cl WA7 . . . . .24 D1
Chorlton La CW7 . . . . . . .207 B2
Chowley Oak La CH3 . . . .182 F6
Chrimes Dr CW8 . . . . . . .123 F6
Christ Church CE Prim Sch
  CH65 . . . . .70 B2
Christ Church CE Sch
  CW8 . . . . .76 B1
Christ The King RC Prim Sch
  CH62 . . . . .43 E7
Christchurch Ave CW2 . .190 A1
Christie Cl CH66 . . . . .44 A2
Christie St WA8 . . . . .13 D1
Christleton Ave
  Crewe CW2 . . . . .189 D5
  Northwich CW9 . . . . . . .104 A4
Christleton Ct WA7 . . . . . .24 C4
Christleton Dr CH66 . . . . .69 E6

Christleton High Sch
  CH3 . . . . .142 F7
Christleton Prim Sch
  CH3 . . . . .142 E8
Christleton Rd CH3 . . . . .119 A1
Christleton Sports Ctr
  CH3 . . . . .142 F8
Christleton Way 15 SK9 . .34 D5
Christopher Dr CH62 . . . . .44 A5
Church Ave SK9 . . . . .34 A2
Church Bank Audley ST7 209 D2
  Goostrey CW4 . . . . .107 F1
  Kelsall CW6 . . . . .122 D5
  Tattenhall CH3 . . . . .166 B2
Church Bk SK23 . . . . .65 D7
Church Cl Handforth SK9 . .34 D3
  Weaverham CW8 . . . . . . .77 D1
Church College Cl CH1 . .118 B3
Church Coppenhall Jun Sch
  CW1 . . . . .190 B6
Church Cotts Astle SK11 .109 B8
  Rainow SK10 . . . . .88 E5
  Sealand CH1 . . . . .116 E6
  Waverton CH3 . . . . .143 C3
Church Croft CH4 . . . . . .162 A6
Church Ct
  Ashton Hayes CH3 . . . . .121 F8
  Farndon CH3 . . . . .180 E2
Church Dr
  Newton-le-W WA12 . . . . . .2 C1
  Warrington WA2 . . . . .9 A1
Church End L24 . . . . .21 D1
Church Farm CW5 . . . . . .216 E4
Church Farm Ct
  Heswall CH60 . . . . .40 F7
  Willaston CH64 . . . . .67 F8
Church Fields TF9 . . . . . .236 C2
Church Gn WA13 . . . . .19 B8
Church Hall Cl CH1 . . . . .117 F4
Church Hill WA16 . . . . . . .57 A2
Church La
  Alderley Edge SK9 . . . . . .60 A2
  Aldford CH3 . . . . .163 F3
  Backford CH1 . . . . .95 B4
  Bebington CH62 . . . . . . .44 A4
  Bramhall SK7 . . . . .35 C2
  Chester CH2 . . . . .118 D7
  Congleton CW12 . . . . . .134 E1
  Culcheth WA3 . . . . .4 F3
  Ellesmere Port CH66 . . . .69 D3
  Farndon CH3 . . . . .180 E1
  Golborne WA3 . . . . .3 D7
  Guilden Sutton CH3 . . . .119 F5
  Hargrave CH3 . . . . .144 B1
  Henbury SK11 . . . . .111 C8
  Huxley CH3,CW6 . . . . . .167 C6
  Lawton-gate ST7 . . . . . .194 C4
  Mobberley WA16 . . . . . . .58 C5
  Mow Cop ST7 . . . . .195 E7
  Nantwich CW5 . . . . .204 E5
  Neston CH64 . . . . .66 E7
  New Mills SK22 . . . . .39 C8
  Rainow SK10 . . . . .88 E5
  Sandbach CW11 . . . . . . .175 E7
  Scholar Green ST7 . . . . .194 C7
  Smallwood CW11 . . . . . .176 E4
  Stoak CH2 . . . . .96 A7
  Sutton Lane Ends SK11 . .112 F3
  Warren SK11 . . . . .134 D8
  Warrington WA4 . . . . . . .17 B1
  Weaverham CW8 . . . . . . .77 D1
  Wistaston CW2 . . . . .205 E8
Church Lawton Prim Sch
  ST7 . . . . .194 A5
Church Mdw TF9 . . . . . . .236 C2
Church Mdws
  Little Leigh CW8 . . . . . . .77 D5
  Whitchurch SY13 . . . . . .226 A1
Church Mead CH3 . . . . . .181 A5
Church Meadow La CH60 40 F7
Church Meadow Wlk
  WA8 . . . . .22 B5
Church Mews
  Bollington SK10 . . . . .88 B8
  Higher Wincham CW9 . . .79 E5
  Knutsford WA16 . . . . .57 B2
  6 Macclesfield SK11 . . .112 D8
Church Par 5 CH65 . . . . .70 C6
Church Rd Alsager ST7 . .193 C4
  Ashton Hayes CH3 . . . . .121 F8
  Barnton CW8 . . . . .78 A2
  Broughton CH4 . . . . . . .139 C4
  Burwardsley CH3 . . . . . .184 A5
  Cheadle Hulme SK8 . . . . .35 B8
  Dodleston CH4 . . . . .162 B8
  Eccleston CH4 . . . . .141 E2
  Frodsham WA6 . . . . .74 C7
  Hale L24 . . . . .47 E8
  Handforth SK9 . . . . .34 D3
  Haydock WA11 . . . . .1 E7
  Little Leigh CW8 . . . . . . .77 D4
  Lymm WA13 . . . . .18 E2
  Mouldsworth CH3 . . . . . .98 F1
  New Mills SK22 . . . . .39 C7
  Northwich CW9 . . . . . . .104 A8
  Saughall CH1 . . . . .94 A1
  Shocklach CH3 . . . . .197 C1
  Thornton Hough CH63 . . .42 B6
  Tilston SY14 . . . . .198 B3
  Wilmslow SK9 . . . . .59 E4
  Worleston CW5 . . . . . . .188 D6
Church Rise CW8 . . . . . . .102 B2
Church Row CH6 . . . . . . .168 F1
Church St Audley ST7 . . .209 D2
  Audley,Wood Lane ST7 . .210 A1
  Bollington SK10 . . . . .88 B8
  Chester CH1 . . . . .237 B4
  Connah's Quay CH5 . . . . .91 D1

Church St continued
  Davenham CW9 . . . . . . .104 A3
  Ellesmere Port CH65 . . . .70 C6
  Farndon LL13 . . . . .180 E2
  Frodsham WA6 . . . . .74 B8
  Great Budworth CW9 . . . .79 A8
  Higher Wincham CW9 . . .79 E5
  Kelsall CW6 . . . . .122 D4
  Kidsgrove, Butt Lane ST7 .194 D1
  Kidsgrove, The Rookery
   ST7 . . . . .195 C4
  Macclesfield SK10,SK11 . .112 D8
  Malpas SY14 . . . . .213 B3
  Moulton CW9 . . . . .126 F8
  Mount Pleasant ST7 . . . .195 C6
  Newton-le-W WA12 . . . . . .2 E4
  Runcorn WA7 . . . . .23 A3
  Sandbach CW11 . . . . . . .175 C6
  Tarvin CH3 . . . . .121 C2
  Warrington WA1 . . . . . . .16 C5
  Weaverham CW8 . . . . . . .77 D1
  Widnes WA8 . . . . .23 A5
  Wilmslow SK9 . . . . .60 B7
  Winsford CW7 . . . . .126 E1
Church St N CW6 . . . . . . .122 C5
Church St W SK11 . . . . . .112 C8
Church Steadings CH3 . . .143 C3
Church Terr SK9 . . . . .34 D4
Church View
  Audlem CW3 . . . . .230 A4
  Handforth SK9 . . . . .34 A2
  Haslington CW1 . . . . . . .191 D5
  Kingsley WA6 . . . . .75 B2
  15 Knutsford WA16 . . . . .57 A2
  Lymm WA13 . . . . .19 B4
  New Mills SK22 . . . . .39 C8
Church View Terr SK11 . .112 F3
Church View Wlk CW2 . . .205 E8
Church Way Alvanley WA6 73 A1
  Blacon CH1 . . . . .117 C5
  Wybunbury CW5 . . . . . . .220 B8
Church Wlk
  Broughton CH4 . . . . . . .139 C5
  Crowton CW8 . . . . .76 C2
  2 Ellesmere Port CH65 . .70 C6
  Holmes Chapel CW4 . . . .130 C3
  Knutsford WA16 . . . . . . .57 A2
  Lower Peover WA16 . . . . .81 E1
  Malpas SY14 . . . . .213 B3
  Northwich CW9 . . . . . . .104 A8
  Wilmslow SK9 . . . . .59 F6
  Winwick WA2 . . . . .8 A6
Church Wlks
  Christleton CH3 . . . . . . .142 E8
  Norton in Hales TF9 . . . .236 C2
Churche's Ct 15 CW5 . . .204 E5
Churche's Mansion★
  CW5 . . . . .204 F5
Churchfield Rd WA6 . . . . .74 C8
Churchfields
  Audlem CW3 . . . . .230 A4
  Barnton CW8 . . . . .78 B3
  Croft WA3 . . . . .9 B7
  Cuddington CW8 . . . . . .102 B2
  Helsby WA6 . . . . .73 C4
  Knutsford WA16 . . . . .57 C2
  Widnes WA8 . . . . .13 B5
  Wybunbury CW5 . . . . . . .220 B8
Churchill Ave WA3 . . . . . . .5 B4
Churchill Cl CW12 . . . . . .156 A3
Churchill Dr CW6 . . . . . . .146 D1
Churchill Mans 10 WA7 . .23 A3
Churchill Parkway CW7 149 D8
Churchill Way
  Macclesfield SK11 . . . . .112 D8
  Neston CH64 . . . . .66 E8
Churchmere Dr CW1 . . . .190 C7
Churchside SK10 . . . . . . .112 D8
Churchside Wlk CH4 . . . .140 F7
Churchway WA16 . . . . .86 F2
Churchward Cl CH2 . . . . .118 D4
Churchway Rd L24 . . . . . .21 A2
Churchwood View WA13 .18 F3
Churchyard Side CW5 . . .204 E5
Churton Cl Hough CW2 . .206 E3
  3 Northwich CW9 . . . . .103 E4
Churton Rd Chester CH3 119 A2
  Farndon CH3 . . . . .180 E2
Churton St CH3 . . . . .119 A2
Cicely Mill La WA16 . . . . .30 D3
Cinder Cl CH3 . . . . .119 F5
Cinder Hill CW7 . . . . .125 F6
Cinder La Chelford SK11 . .83 E1
  Guilden Sutton CH3 . . . .119 F5
  Lostock Green CW9 . . . .105 A8
  Nantwich CW5 . . . . .188 C2
  Over Peover WA16 . . . . .108 C7
  Warrington WA4 . . . . . . .17 C1
Cinder Rock Way ST7 . . .195 C1
Cinder-Hill La ST7 . . . . . .194 F7
Cinnamon Brow CE Prim Sch
  WA2 . . . . .8 F2
Cinnamon La WA2 . . . . . . .8 F2
Cinnamon La N WA2 . . . . .8 F3
Cinnamon Pk WA2 . . . . . . .9 B3
Circle Ave CW5 . . . . .205 E5
Circle The Crewe CW2 . . .190 D1
  Mere WA16 . . . . .30 C1
Circuit The
  Alderley Edge SK9 . . . . . .60 B3
  Cheadle Hulme SK8 . . . . .35 A7
  Wilmslow SK9 . . . . .59 D6
Circular Dr CH4 . . . . .140 F4
City Apartments CH1 . . .237 C3
City Bank ST8 . . . . .179 C2
City Rd CH1 . . . . .237 C3
City Walls Rd CH1 . . . . . .237 A2

Civic Way
  Ellesmere Port CH65 . . . .70 B4
  Middlewich CW10 . . . . . .128 C1
Clair Ave CH5 . . . . .116 A3
Clamhunger La WA16 . . . .56 D7
Clamley Ct L24 . . . . .21 A3
Clamley Gdns L24 . . . . . . .21 E2
Clanfield Ave WA8 . . . . . . .12 C3
Clap Gate Cres WA8 . . . . .22 B5
Clap Gates Cres WA5 . . . .15 E7
Clap Gates Rd WA5 . . . . . .15 E7
Clare Ave Chester CH2 . . .119 A3
  Handforth SK9 . . . . .34 C3
Clare Dr Crewe CW2 . . . .189 F1
  Ellesmere Port CH65 . . . .70 B1
  Macclesfield SK10 . . . . . .87 C3
Clare Ho CH1 . . . . .117 E6
Clare Pl CW7 . . . . .149 C7
Clare St Kidsgrove ST7 . .195 E4
  Mount Pleasant ST7 . . . .195 C6
Claremont Ave WA8 . . . . .13 C4
Claremont Cl 15 CW9 . . .103 F3
Claremont Dr WA8 . . . . . .13 B4
Claremont Rd
  Cheadle Hulme SK8 . . . . .35 A8
  Crewe CW2 . . . . .190 B2
  Culcheth WA3 . . . . .4 D4
  Runcorn WA7 . . . . .23 B2
Clarence Ave
  Chester CH3 . . . . .119 B2
  Warrington WA5 . . . . . . .14 D6
  Widnes WA8 . . . . .13 A4
Clarence Ct
  Newton-le-W WA12 . . . . . .2 A4
  Wilmslow SK9 . . . . .60 A6
Clarence Gr CW1 . . . . . . .190 B5
Clarence Mill Bsns Pk
  SK10 . . . . .63 A1
Clarence Rd
  Bollington SK10 . . . . .63 A1
  Warrington WA4 . . . . . . .17 B2
Clarence St
  Newton-le-W WA12 . . . . . .1 F4
  Runcorn WA7 . . . . .22 F3
  Warrington WA1 . . . . . . .16 E7
Clarence Terr
  Bollington SK10 . . . . .63 A1
  7 Runcorn WA7 . . . . . . .23 A3
Clarendon Cl
  Chester CH4 . . . . .141 E6
  Runcorn WA7 . . . . .50 D7
Clarendon Cotts SK9 . . . .34 A3
Clarendon Ct WA2 . . . . . . .7 F4
Clarendon Dr SK10 . . . . . .88 A1
Clarendon Rd M44 . . . . . .11 F7
Clares Farm Cl WA1 . . . . .17 F7
Clarke Ave Culcheth WA3 . .5 A4
  Warrington WA4 . . . . . . .16 D2
Clarke Gdns 3 WA8 . . . . .23 B7
Clarke La Bollington SK10 .87 E5
  Langley SK11 . . . . .113 D3
Clarke Terr SK11 . . . . . . .112 D6
Clarks Terr WA7 . . . . .48 D8
Clary Mdw CW1 . . . . .78 E1
Clatterbridge Hospl
  CH63 . . . . .42 D8
Clatterbridge Rd CH63 . . .42 D8
Clatterwick La CW8 . . . . .77 D7
Claude St WA1 . . . . .16 C6
Claughton Ave CW2 . . . .190 C1
Claverton Cl WA7 . . . . . . .49 B6
Claverton Ct CH4 . . . . . .237 C1
Clay Heyes SK11 . . . . .84 A3
Clay La Bickerton SY14 . .200 B3
  Burtonwood WA5 . . . . . . .6 E5
  Handforth SK9 . . . . .34 C5
  Haslington CW1,CW11 . .191 D7
  Over Peover WA16 . . . . .108 B8
  Sandbach CW11,CW1 . . .174 B2
  Wilmslow SK9 . . . . .59 C4
  Winsford CW7 . . . . .125 B2
Claydon Gdns WA3 . . . . . .10 F1
Clayhill Gn CH66 . . . . .69 D7
Clayhill Gr WA3 . . . . .4 B8
Clayhill Light Ind Pk
  CH64 . . . . .41 F2
Claypit Rd CH4 . . . . .141 B5
Claypits La CH3 . . . . .142 F5
Clayton Ave
  Congleton CW12 . . . . . .157 A5
  Golborne WA3 . . . . .3 E8
Clayton Cl CW1 . . . . .190 A1
Clayton Cres Runcorn WA7 22 F1
  Widnes WA8 . . . . .12 F1
Clayton Dr SY13 . . . . . . .226 B1
Clayton Rd WA3 . . . . .9 F6
Clayton's Row CW5 . . . . .204 E7
Clayton-By-Pass CW12 .156 C3
Cleadon Way WA8 . . . . . .12 E4
Cleaver Mews SK11 . . . . .112 C5
Cleaver Rd CH1 . . . . .117 E4
Cledford Cres CW10 . . . .151 E6
Cledford Inf Sch CW10 . .151 C7
Cledford Jun Sch CW10 151 C7
Cledford La CW10 . . . . . .151 E7
Cledwen Rd/Ffordd Cledwen
  CH4 . . . . .139 D5
Cleethorpes Rd WA7 . . . . .50 C7
Cleeve Way SK8 . . . . .35 B6
Cleeves Cl WA1 . . . . .16 F6
Clegge St WA2 . . . . .16 B7
Clelland St WA4 . . . . .16 C3
Clement Dr CW1 . . . . . . .189 F7
Clemley Cl CW6 . . . . . . .122 D6
Clerewood Ave SK8 . . . . .34 B7

Clevedon Cl SK11 ....112 A7
Cleveland Dr CH66 ....69 A6
Cleveland Rd WA2 ....8 B3
Cleveland Way CW7 ...149 B2
Cleveleys Ave WA8 ....13 C2
Cleveleys Rd WA5 ....15 B4
Cleves Cl CH1 ....117 D6
Cliff La Acton Bridge CW8 .76 C4
 Lymm WA13 ....28 B6
 Macclesfield SK10 ....88 B1
 Warrington WA4 ....17 D1
Cliff Rd Acton Bridge CW8 .76 E4
 Wilmslow SK9 ....60 B8
Cliff Side SK9 ....60 B8
Cliff View WA6 ....74 A8
Cliffbrook Gr **2** SK9 ...34 D2
Cliffe Rd Crewe CW1 ...190 B7
 Neston CH64 ....66 F5
 Warrington WA4 ....26 C7
Cliffe St **3** WA8 ....13 C1
Clifford Dr CH4 ....140 F5
Clifford Gr CW1 ....191 C4
Clifford Pl **4** CW7 ...149 C8
Clifford Rd
 Macclesfield SK11 ......112 A8
 Poynton SK12 ....36 D3
 Warrington WA5 ....15 A4
 Wilmslow SK9 ....59 F6
Clifton Ave
 Bebington CH62 ....43 E3
 Crewe CW2 ....190 B3
 Culcheth WA3 ....4 D3
Clifton Cl WA1 ....17 C7
Clifton Cres WA6 ....49 C1
Clifton Ct WA7 ....49 B6
Clifton Dr Blacon CH1 ..117 E3
 Northwich CW9 ....104 A5
 Wilmslow SK9 ....59 E4
Clifton Gdns CH65 ....70 C3
Clifton La WA7 ....49 E3
Clifton Park Ave CH5 ....91 E1
Clifton Rd
 Runcorn,Clifton WA7 .....49 E3
 Runcorn,Heath WA7 ......49 B6
 Sandbach CW11 ....174 D7
Clifton St
 Alderley Edge SK9 ....60 A1
 Crewe CW2 ....190 B3
 Warrington WA4 ....16 C4
Cliftonmill Mdws WA3 ...2 F8
Cliftonville Rd WA1 .....17 D6
Clincton Cl WA8 ....22 A8
Clincton View WA8 ......22 A8
Clipsley Cres WA11 ......1 B7
Clipsley La WA11 ....1 C5
Clitheroe Rd CW8 ....77 E1
Clive Ave WA2 ....8 C1
Clive Back La CW7 ......150 D7
Clive La CW7 ....150 C8
Cliveden Rd CH4 ....140 F5
Clivegreen La CW10 ....150 E7
Clock Face Rd WA8 ....13 E8
Clocktower The CW4 ....130 D2
Cloister Way CH65 ....70 E5
Clones Way CW5 ....205 A4
Clonners Field CW5 .....205 A4
Close La Alsager ST7 ....192 F3
 Mow Cop ST7 ....195 D7
Close The Alsager ST7 ..193 A3
 Hartford CW8 ....103 D6
 Newton-le-W WA12 ......2 E1
 Saughall CH1 ....94 A1
 Tarporley CW6 ....146 C2
Closeburn Ave CH60 .....40 E6
Cloud The* CW12 ....158 A4
Cloud View CW12 ....157 A2
Cloudberry Wlk M31 ....11 F3
Clough Ave Handforth SK9 34 B2
 Warrington WA2 ....8 B2
Clough Bank SK10 ....87 F7
Clough Field Cl SK23 ....65 D8
Clough Hall Dr ST7 .....210 E6
Clough Hall Rd ST7 .....210 F8
Clough Hall Tech Sch
 ST7 ....194 F1
Clough La CW8 ....103 D6
Clough Rd CW7 ....126 E1
Clough The WA7 ....23 F1
Clough Wlk CW2 ....206 D8
Cloughside SK12 ....38 E6
Cloughwood Sch CW8 ...103 D5
Clovelly Ave WA5 ....14 E2
Clovelly Gr WA7 ....50 C5
Clover Ave WA6 ....74 D7
Clover Ct WA7 ....50 B5
Clover Dr Pickmere WA16 .79 F7
 Winsford CW7 ....126 D3
Clover La CH4 ....140 F5
Clover Pl CH4 ....140 F5
Cloverdale CW8 ....103 C7
Cloverdale Rd SK11 ....112 B5
Cloverfield Lymm WA13 ..18 F4
 Runcorn WA7 ....50 C7
Cloverfield Gdns CH66 ..69 D2
Cloverfields CW1 ....191 B4
Clowes Ave ST7 ....193 F2
Clowes St SK11 ....112 B8
Clumber Cl SK12 ....36 E3
Clumber Rd SK12 ....36 E3
Clutton CE Prim Sch
 CH3 ....182 D1
Clwyd Cl CH5 ....139 B6
Clwyd Way CH66 ....69 A6
Clyde Ave ST8 ....179 E1
Clyde Cres CW7 ....127 B1

Clyde Gr CW2 ....190 A3
Clydesdale CH65 ....70 B3
Clydesdale Ave CW2 ...190 B3
Clydesdale Rd WA4 .....26 D8
Coach Rd Broxton CH3 ..183 A3
 Edge Green SY14 ......199 D2
 Little Budworth CW6 ...147 D8
Coachway SK10 ....86 F7
Coalbrookdale Rd CH64 .41 F2
Coalpit La
 Clive Green CW10 ......150 F7
 Dunkirk CH1 ....94 E6
 Langley SK11 ....113 C5
 Mollington CH1 ....94 D4
Coalport Dr CW7 ....126 F3
Coare St SK10 ....87 D1
Coastguard La CH64 ....41 B1
Coatings By Pass Rd CH5 91 F2
Coatings Two CH5 ....91 E2
Cob Hall La WA6 ....98 D5
Cob Moor Rd ST7 ......195 A4
Cobal Ct WA6 ....74 B8
Cobbett's Way SK9 ......59 F4
Cobblers Cross La CW6 .146 E2
Cobblers La / Lon Y Cryddion
 LL12 ....161 B1
Cobbles The
 Chester CH4 ....141 D7
 Cuddington CW8 ....101 A3
 Lower Peover WA16 ......81 E1
Cobblestone Ct CH2 ...119 E8
Cobbs Inf Sch The WA4 .26 E8
Cobbs La Hough CW2 ...206 E2
 Warrington WA4 ....26 E8
Cobden St
 Newton-le-W WA12 ......2 D4
 Warrington WA2 ....16 B6
Cock Hall La SK11 .....113 D3
Cock La
 Great Budworth CW9 .....78 F8
 Sound CW5 ....217 F4
Cock Lane Ends WA8 ....22 B4
Cockedge La WA1 ....16 C5
Cockhedge Sh Ctr WA1 .16 B5
Cockhedge Way WA1 ...16 B5
Cocklade La L24 ....21 D1
Cockpit La CW8 ....102 B1
Cockshades farm CW5 .206 C2
Cocksheadhey Rd SK10 .63 C1
Cocksmoss La
 Congleton SK11 ....134 A3
 Marton SK11 ....133 D3
Cocoa Gdns **11** CW5 ..204 E5
Cocoa Yard The **10**
 CW5 ....204 E5
Coe La WA14 ....30 C7
Cogshall La Anderton CW9 78 C5
 Comberbach CW9 ....78 B7
Colchester Sq CH4 .....140 F5
Coldmoss Dr CW11 ....175 C4
Coldstream Cl WA2 ......8 E3
Coldstream Dr CH66 ....68 F5
Cole Ave WA12 ....2 C4
Colebrook Cl WA3 ......10 A4
Coleclough Pl WA3 ......4 F4
Coleg Glannau
 Dyfrdwy/Deeside Coll
 CH5 ....91 B1
Colehill Bank CW12 ....156 E2
Colehill Pl CH5 ....91 D1
Colemere Cl WA1 ....17 A8
Colemere Ct CH65 ......70 C7
 Sandbach CW11 ....174 C5
Coleridge Cl Blacon CH1 118 A5
Coleridge Gr WA8 ......12 E1
Coleridge Way CW1 ...190 F5
Colinwood Ave CH4 ....139 B3
Coliseum Way CH65 .....70 D2
Collar House Dr SK10 ...86 E6
College Cl
 Warrington WA1 ....16 D5
 Warrington, Fearnhead WA2 .9 B2
 Wilmslow SK9 ....59 F8
College Fields CW2 ....190 A1
College Gn CH4 ....141 D7
College La CW6 ....168 F1
College of Law (Christleton
 Hall) CH3 ....142 D8
College Rd ST7 ....193 B5
College View CH5 ....91 C1
Colley La CW11 ....175 D5
Colleys La CW5 ....205 B7
Collier St WA7 ....22 F3
Collier's Row WA7 ......48 E7
Colliers La CW9 ....54 D7
Colliery Green Cl CH64 .66 E5
Colliery Green Ct CH64 .66 E5
Colliery Green Dr CH64 .66 E5
Collin St WA5 ....15 F5
Collinbrook Ave CW2 ..190 B1
Collingham Gn CH66 ....69 B5
Collingtree Ave CW7 ...127 A3
Collingwood Cl
 Macclesfield SK10 ....87 B2
 Poynton SK12 ....37 A3
Collingwood Rd WA12 ...2 B3
Collins Green La WA5 ...1 E1
Collins St CW2 ....190 A3
Collinson Ct **2** WA6 ...74 B8
Colne Rd WA5 ....6 F6
Colorado Cl WA5 ....15 C7
Colshaw Dr SK9 ....34 E1
Colshaw Hall Cotts WA16 82 F1
Colshaw La SK11 ......109 E1
Colson Ct CH2 ....237 A4

Coltsfoot Cl CH3 ....142 B5
Columbine Cl
 Huntington CH3 ....142 A6
 Widnes WA8 ....12 B4
Columbine Way WA9 .....6 B7
Columbine Wlk **8** M31 .11 F3
Colville Ct WA2 ....8 A3
Colville Rd SK11 ....111 F8
Colwyn Cl
 Ellesmere Port CH65 .....70 D3
 Warrington WA5 ....7 E2
Colwyn Rd SK7 ....35 E6
Comber Way WA6 ....82 A8
Comberbach Dr CW5 ...205 A4
Comberbach Prim Sch
 CW9 ....78 C8
Combermere Pl CW1 ...190 B5
Comboy Dr CW9 ....104 C6
Combs Cl SK22 ....39 A8
Commercial Ave SK8 ....34 F5
Commercial Rd SK10 ...112 E8
Common Farm La SK11 ..83 E1
Common La Betley CW3 .221 F6
 Chelford SK11 ....83 E1
 Culcheth WA3 ....4 E4
 Duddon CW6 ....145 C7
 Hapsford WA6 ....72 D1
 Kelsall CW6 ....122 C3
 Lach Dennis CW9 ......105 E5
 Norbury SY13 ....215 C5
 Stretton WA4 ....52 E3
 Warrington WA4 ....16 E2
 Waverton CH3 ....143 B4
 Winsford CW7 ....126 B2
Common Rd WA12,WA5 ..1 E3
Common St WA12 ....1 E3
Common The WA7 ......49 F8
Commongate SK10 .....112 A8
Commonhall St CH1 ....237 A2
Commons Mill CW11 ...175 B7
Commons The CW11 ...175 B6
Commonside WA6 ....73 E1
Commonwealth Cl CW7 149 D6
Commonwealth Ho
 WA15 ....33 B8
Commonwood Rd LL13 .196 A8
Company's Cl WA7 .....48 F6
Compass Cl WA7 ....50 D5
Compton Cl WA11 ....1 C7
Compton Pl Chester CH4 141 A6
 Ellesmere Port CH65 .....70 D5
Concorde Pl WA2 ....8 D2
Concourse Way WA9 .....1 A2
Condliffe Cl CW11 .....175 C5
Conery Cl WA6 ....73 C4
Coney Gr WA7 ....50 B5
Congleton Bsns Ctr
 CW12 ....156 E3
Congleton Bsns Pk
 CW12 ....156 C4
Congleton Cl SK9 ....85 A8
Congleton Edge Rd
 CW12 ....179 B6
Congleton High Sch
 CW12 ....155 F3
Congleton La SK11 .....109 D5
Congleton Mus★ CW12 .156 E2
Congleton Rd
 Biddulph ST8 ....179 D2
 Broughton CH4 ....139 C4
 Kidsgrove ST7 ....194 D1
 Macclesfield SK11 ......112 B5
 Marton SK11 ....133 B5
 Mow Cop ST7 ....178 F1
 North Rode SK11 ......134 C6
 Sandbach CW11 ....175 B8
 Sandbach CW11 ....175 E8
 Scholar Green CW12,ST7 177 E3
 Siddington SK11 ....110 B5
 Smallwood CW11 ......177 A6
 Swettenham CW12 .....131 F4
 Warren SK11 ....111 E2
Congleton Rd N ST7 ...194 E6
Congleton Rd S ST7 ...194 D3
Congleton Ret Pk
 CW12 ....156 D4
Congleton Sta CW12 ...157 A1
Congleton War Meml Hospl
 CW12 ....156 F1
Conifer Cl CH66 ....95 A8
Conifer Gr Moore WA4 ..25 A7
 Warrington WA5 ....14 F7
Conifer Wlk M31 ....11 E3
Conifers The ST7 ....193 B3
Coningsby Dr CW7 .....126 E3
Coningsby Gdns **13** WA3 .3 E8
Coniston Ave
 Bebington CH63 ....43 C4
 Congleton CW12 ....155 F2
 Warrington WA5 ....14 C4
 Winsford CW7 ....126 C2
Coniston Cl
 Alderley Edge SK9 ....84 A7
 Hooton CH66 ....44 B2
 Nantwich CW5 ....205 A6
 Runcorn WA7 ....49 D6
Coniston Dr
 Frodsham WA6 ....74 D8
 Handforth SK9 ....34 C4
 Holmes Chapel CW4 ...130 A3
Coniston Rd Chester CH2 118 F5
 High Lane SK6 ....37 D8
 Neston CH64 ....66 E6
 Newton-le-W WA12 ......2 B4
Coniston Way SK11 ....111 F5
Connah's Quay High Sch
 CH5 ....91 C1
Connaught Ave WA1 ....16 E4

Connaught Cl SK9 ......60 C5
Connaught Dr WA12 .....2 C2
Conrad Cl CW1 ....190 E4
Conroy Way WA12 ....7 C8
Consort Cl SK10 ....87 E7
Constable Dr SK9 ....60 E8
Constables Cl WA7 ......24 A1
Constance Rd M31 ......11 F3
Constance Way WA8 ....23 A5
Convamore Rd SK7 .....35 D7
Conway Ave Irlam M44 ..11 F8
 Warrington WA5 ....7 F2
 Winsford CW7 ....149 C7
Conway Cl Crewe CW1 .190 E8
 Knutsford WA16 ....82 A8
 Saltney CH4 ....140 D5
 Warrington WA5 ....14 F6
Conway Cres SK10 ......87 F1
Conway Ct CH65 ....70 C3
Conway Dr WA12 ....2 E3
Conwy Ct WA7 ....24 A1
Coogee Ave WA5 ....14 E2
Cook Ave WA11 ....1 F7
Cook St CH65 ....70 C6
Cooke's La CW9 ....104 F6
Cookes Cl CH64 ....41 E5
Cookes Ct CH3 ....166 B1
Cookesmere La CW11 ..175 A8
Cooks La SY13 ....225 D7
Cooksmere La CW11 ...152 F1
Coole La
 Hack Green CW5 ......218 E3
 Newhall CW3 ....229 A5
Coombe Dr WA7 ....239 A5
Coombe Park Ct **1** CH66 69 C6
Coombe Pk CH66 ....69 C6
Coope Rd SK10 ....87 E6
Cooper Ave
 Newton-le-W WA12 ......1 F3
 Warrington WA2 ....8 B2
Cooper La WA11 ....1 C6
Cooper St
 Congleton CW12 ....156 E3
 Runcorn WA7 ....23 A3
 Widnes WA8 ....13 B1
Cooper Terr CW6 ......146 D1
Cooper's Croft CH3 ....142 A7
Cooper's Fold SK8 ......34 F6
Cooper's La CH5 ....91 D1
Cooperative St SK12 ....38 D6
Coopers Opening CW11 175 B7
Coopers Pl WA4 ....16 C1
Coopers La CW9 ....104 F6
Cop Ave SK11 ....112 F2
Cope Ave CW5 ....204 D4
Copeland Gr WA7 ......49 E5
Copeland Rd WA4 ......16 B2
Copes La CW5 ....204 C4
Copeswood Cl CH4 ....139 C3
Copgrove Wlk M22 .....33 E7
Coppenhall Gr CW2 ...190 A4
Coppenhall Heys CW2 .190 A4
Coppenhall High Sch
 CW1 ....190 E5
Coppenhall La CW2 ...189 D4
Copper Beech Cl CH4 ..139 C3
Copper St SK11 ....112 E6
Copper Wood CW1 .....101 E5
Copperfield Cl WA3 .....9 C5
Copperfield Rd
 Cheadle Hulme SK8 ....35 B5
 Poynton SK12 ....36 D2
Copperfields
 Poynton SK12 ....36 D2
 Tarporley CW6 ....146 D2
 Wilmslow SK9 ....60 D1
Copperhill Rd CW12 ...179 B7
Coppermine La SY14 ..184 B2
Copperwood WA7 ......24 C1
Coppice Ave SK12 ......38 A6
Coppice Cl High Lane SK12 38 A6
 Runcorn WA7 ....24 A1
 Willaston CW5 ....205 D6
Coppice Dr CW10 ......151 E6
Coppice Gn Elton CH2 ..72 C4
 Warrington WA5 ....7 A1
Coppice Gr WA16 ....57 A3
Coppice Ho Poynton SK12 .36 D2
 Talke ST7 ....210 C8
Coppice La SK12 ....38 A5
Coppice Rd
 Haslington CW11 ......192 A8
 Poynton SK12 ....37 B3
 Talke ST7 ....210 C8
 Willaston CW5 ....205 D6
Coppice Rise SK11 ....112 D5
Coppice The
 Altrincham WA15 ....32 B8
 Bramhall SK7 ....35 E6
 Cuddington CW8 ......101 D5
 Nantwich CW5 ....204 F3
 Sandbach CW11 ....174 E2
 Whaley Bridge SK23 .....65 F5
 Wincham CW9 ....79 C3
Coppice Way SK9 ....34 E3
Coppicemere Dr CW1 ..191 D2
Coppins Cl Chester CH3 119 A2
 Helsby WA6 ....73 B4
Coppins The
 Warrington WA2 ....8 C2
 Wilmslow SK9 ....59 E4
Copse The
 Altrincham WA15 ....32 D7
 High Lane SK6 ....37 E7
 Newton-le-W WA12 ......2 B4
 Runcorn WA7 ....50 A6
Copthorne Cl CW12 ...156 F2
Copthorne Dr CW3 ....229 F3
Copyhold CW8 ....102 D8

Corbet Ave WA2 ....16 B8
Corbet Dr TF9 ....235 A4
Corbet St WA2 ....16 B8
Corfe Way CW7 ....149 C7
Coriander Cl CW10 ....128 C3
Corks La SK12 ....38 C5
Cormorant Cl CW1 ....190 F4
Cormorant Dr WA7 .....22 E2
Cornbrook Rd SK11 ...112 C4
Corner Croft SK9 ....60 A4
Cornerhouse La WA8 ...12 D3
Corners The WA8 .....102 E7
Cornfield Cl
 Ellesmere Port CH66 ....69 F1
 Macclesfield SK10 ....87 C3
Cornforth Way WA8 ....12 F3
Cornhill Cl ST5 ....210 D1
Cornish Cl M22 ....33 D8
Cornishway M22 ....33 D8
Cornishway Ind Est M22 .33 D8
Cornubia Rd WA8 ......23 D7
Cornwall Ave WA7 ......23 A2
Cornwall Cl
 3 Congleton CW12 ....157 A1
 High Lane SK6 ....37 E7
 Macclesfield SK10 ....86 E1
 Runcorn WA7 ....23 F1
Cornwall Gr CW1 ......190 B5
Cornwall Rd Chester CH2 118 F7
 Heald Green SK8 ....34 B8
 Irlam M44 ....11 D5
 Widnes WA8 ....13 B8
Cornwall St Chester CH1 237 B4
 Warrington WA1 ....16 E7
Cornwell Cl SK9 ....60 D8
Coronation Ave
 Alsager ST7 ....193 A3
 Glazebury WA3 ....5 C7
 Warrington WA4 ....17 C2
 Winsford CW7 ....126 E1
Coronation Bldgs SK10 .88 A8
Coronation Cres
 Crewe CW1 ....190 E6
 Kidsgrove ST7 ....194 E1
 Sandbach CW11 ....175 A5
Coronation Dr
 Frodsham WA6 ....49 D1
 Haydock WA11 ....2 A7
 Newton-le-W WA12 ......2 E1
 Warrington WA5 ....14 F4
 Widnes WA8 ....22 C8
Coronation Gr CW8 .....78 A4
Coronation Ho WA7 ....49 C8
Coronation Rd
 Broughton CH4 ....139 B3
 Congleton CW12 ....156 F3
 Ellesmere Port CH65 ....70 C4
 Middlewich CW10 .....151 D6
 Runcorn, Higher Runcorn
  WA7 ....23 B1
 Runcorn, Preston Brook
  WA7 ....50 F6
Coronation Sq **18** WA16 .57 A2
Coronation St
 Chester CH4 ....140 F7
 Crewe CW1 ....190 D5
 Macclesfield SK11 ......112 D6
Coronation Terr CW6 ..146 D1
Coroner's La WA8 ......13 A4
Coronet Ave CW9 .....103 F3
Coronet Way WA8 ......22 B8
Correction Brow SK12 ..37 C6
Corridor Rd CH65 ......71 B6
Corwen Cl WA5 ....7 F1
Cossack Ave WA2 ....8 C1
Cote Lea Ct WA7 ....49 F6
Cotebrook Dr CH2 .....118 E7
Cotebrook Rd CW9 ....104 C8
Cotes Pl CH1 ....117 E3
Cotgreaves Ct CH4 ....141 B5
Cotswold Ave WA3 ......3 D6
Cotswold Cl Chester CH2 118 F6
 Cuddington CW8 ......102 A2
 Macclesfield SK10 ....86 E1
Cotswold Cl **7** CH3 ...119 A1
Cotswold Gr WA9 ....1 A3
Cotswold Pl WA2 ....8 B4
Cotswold Rd WA2 ....8 B3
Cotswold Way CW7 ....149 B7
Cottage Cl Bebington CH63 43 C5
 Neston CH64 ....66 F7
 Rudheath CW9 ....104 E8
Cottage Dr E CH60 .....40 F5
Cottage Dr W CH60 ....40 F5
Cottage Gr SK9 ....59 F5
Cottage La Heswall CH60 .40 F5
 Macclesfield SK10 ......112 F7
Cottage Lawns SK9 .....60 B2
Cottage Rd CH4 ....141 B5
Cottage St SK11 ....112 B8
Cottages The
 Lawton Heath End ST7 ..193 D6
 Sproston Green CW4 ...129 C2
Cottam Dr WA2 ....9 A3
Cotterdale Cl WA5 .....14 F7
Cotterill St CW2 ......190 D2
Cotterill Dr WA1 ....17 C7
Cotterill St CW2 ......190 D2
Cottesmore Dr CH60 ...41 D8
Cottesmore Gdns WA15 .32 C8
Cotton La
 Christleton CH3 ....120 D2
 Runcorn WA7 ....49 D8
 Sandbach CW11 ....175 A3
Cotton Mews CW3 .....230 A4
Cottons Bridge WA4 ....50 F5
Cottonwood Gr ST7 ...195 E4
Cottrell Rd WA15 ....32 D7

Coulton Rd WA8 ....13 F3
Council Hos Audlem CW3 229 E2
Congleton CW12 ....156 F4
Newhall CW5 ....228 B8
Council Houses CW5 ...216 B6
Countess Ave SK8 ....34 E5
Countess Cl 7 SK11 ....111 F7
Countess Ct CH1 ....118 B5
Countess of Chester Health Pk CH2 ....118 B6
Countess of Chester Hospl CH2 ....118 B6
Countess Rd SK11 .....111 F7
Countess Way CH2 .....118 C5
Counting House Rd SK12 38 E5
County Terr WA16 ......56 F1
Courier Row SK10 ....87 F7
Court 2 SK10 ....87 F1
Court Ho The 9 CH65 ....70 C6
Court No 4 6 SK10 ....112 C8
Court The CH64 ....66 F6
Courtney Gn SK9 ....34 D2
Courtney Rd CH4 ......140 E5
Courtyard The
Bostock Green CW10 ....127 D5
Congleton CW12 ....156 B3
Cuddington CW8 ....101 E2
Haughton CW6 ....186 F4
Newton-le-W WA12 ....2 E4
Smallwood CW11 ....177 A7
5 Warrington WA1 ....16 B5
Weaverham CW8 ....102 A8
Willaston CH64 ....67 F8
Cousens Way CH1 ......118 B4
Covell Rd SK12 ....36 D5
Coventry Ave CH66 ......94 E8
Coverdale Cl WA5 ....14 F7
Coverdale Fold CW11 ..174 D5
Covert Cl CW7 ....149 B8
Covert Gdns ST7 ......210 D8
Covert Rise CH3 ....166 A2
Covington Pl SK9 ....60 B6
Cow Hey La WA7 ....49 A5
Cow La Ashley WA15 .....31 F6
Bollington SK10 ....88 B7
Hargrave CH3 ....144 A2
Macclesfield SK11 ......112 D6
Norley WA6 ....101 A5
Rainow SK10 ....88 D4
Wilmslow SK9 ....60 C7
Winsford CW7 ....149 E8
Cowanway WA8 ....12 F5
Cowbrook La SK11 .....135 B6
Cowdell St WA2 ....16 B7
Cowfields CW5 ....204 E6
Cowhey Cl CH4 ....141 B5
Cowley Way CW1 ......190 E1
Cowper Cl CW2 ....206 A8
Cowthorne Dr CH3 .....143 A4
Crab La WA2 ....9 B3
Crab Tree Cl L24 ....21 E2
Crabmill Dr CW11 .....174 E7
Crabmill La Norley WA6 .100 E6
Warmingham CW11 .....173 E7
Crabtree Ave
Altrincham WA15 ....32 D7
Disley SK12 ....38 E5
Crabtree Cl WA12 ....2 E3
Crabtree Ct SK12 ....38 D6
Crabtree Fold WA7 ......50 C8
Crabtree Gr CW1 ......190 E6
Crabtree Green Ct CW8 101 C2
Crabtree Green Pk CW8 ....124 C8
Crabtree La WA13 ....29 A7
Crabwall Pl CH1 ....117 F5
Crackley Bank ST5 .....210 E1
Crackley Bank Prim Sch ST5 ....210 E1
Craddock Ct SY14 .....213 B3
Cradley WA8 ....12 C2
Cragside Way SK9 ....60 C6
Craig Cl SK11 ....112 B5
Craig Dr SK23 ....65 E6
Craig Gdns CH66 ....69 E7
Craig Rd Congleton CW12 156 F4
Macclesfield SK11 ......112 B5
Craig Wlk ST7 ....193 F2
Craigleigh Gr CH62 ......43 F4
Craigside ST8 ....179 C1
Craithie Rd CH3 ....119 A2
Crampton Dr WA15 ......32 C8
Cranage Cl WA7 ....49 D7
Cranage Ct 3 CW12 ....156 F3
Cranage La CW9 ....79 D1
Cranage Rd CW2 ....190 A3
Cranage Way 16 SK9 ....34 D5
Cranberry Dr ST5 ......210 D1
Cranberry Inf Sch ST7 .193 A3
Cranberry Jun Sch ST7 193 A3
Cranberry La ST7 ......193 A3
Cranberry Moss La ST7 193 A3
Cranberry Rd M31 ....11 F3
Cranborne Ave WA4 .....16 B1
Cranborne Rd CW1 ....190 D6
Crane Ho CH1 ....118 B1
Cranebrook Cl CW1 ....190 A8
Cranfield Dr ST7 ....193 A3
Cranford Ave
Knutsford WA16 ....56 F1
Macclesfield SK11 .....112 F7
Cranford Cl CH62 ....43 F4
Cranford Ct Chester CH4 141 A5
Warrington WA1 ....17 E8
Cranford Mews ST7 ....193 A3
Cranford Rd SK9 ....34 A1
Cranford Sq WA16 ....56 F1
Cranham Ave WA3 ....3 E7
Cranleigh Cl WA4 ....26 B7
Cranleigh Cres CH1 ....118 B4
Cranleigh Dr SK7 ....37 A8
Cranmere Cl CW9 ......104 A4
Cranshaw La WA8 ....13 B6
Cransley Sch CW9 ....53 E1
Cranswick Gn CH66 .....69 C5
Crantock Dr SK8 ....34 C8
Cranwell Ave WA3 ....4 F4
Crauford Rd CW12 .....157 A8
Craven Ave WA3 ....3 E7
Craven Ct WA2 ....7 F4
Crawford Ave WA8 ....12 B1
Crawford Pl WA7 ....49 B6
Crawford's Wlk CH2 ....118 F3
Crawley Ave WA2 ....8 A3
Crayford Ave CW12 ....157 A5
Cresanne Cl CW10 .....151 C7
Crescent Dr Helsby WA6 .73 B3
Whaley Bridge SK23 ......39 D2
Crescent Rd
Alderley Edge SK9 ....60 B2
Congleton CW12 ....156 C2
Cranage CW4 ....129 F6
Ellesmere Port CH65 .....70 D6
Rostherne WA16 ....30 B3
Crescent The
Chester CH2 ....118 D4
Congleton CW12 ....156 C2
Ellesmere Port CH65 .....69 F5
Hartford CW8 ....103 A5
Heswall,Gayton CH60 .....41 B6
Lymm WA13 ....18 F2
Macclesfield SK10 ....87 E1
Middlewich CW10 ......128 B1
Mottram St Andrew SK10 ..61 A1
Nantwich CW5 ....204 F6
New Mills SK22 ....39 B8
Northwich CW9 ....103 F6
Rostherne WA16 ....30 B3
Utkinton CW6 ....146 B7
Weaverham CW8 ....77 E1
Cressbrook Rd 2 WA4 ...16 C1
Cressington Gdns 7 CH65 ....70 C6
Cresswell Ave
New Mills SK22 ....39 C8
Newcastle-u-Lyme ST5 ..210 D1
Cresswell Cl WA5 ....7 D2
Cresswell St SK22 ....39 C8
Cresswellshawe Rd ST7 193 D4
Cresta Dr WA7 ....48 F6
Crestwood Cl CW2 .....206 B7
Crew Ave SK10 ....87 E1
Crewe Bsns Pk CW1 ....190 F2
Crewe Gates Farm Ind Est CW1 ....190 E2
Crewe Gates Ind Est CW1 ....207 A8
Crewe Green Ave CW1 .191 B4
Crewe Green Rd CW1 ..191 A3
Crewe Hall Ent Pk CW1 207 D8
Crewe Hill La CH3 .....197 A6
Crewe La CH3 ....180 F1
Crewe La S CH3 ....197 A7
Crewe Rd Alsager ST7 ..193 B3
Alsager ST7 ....193 F4
Crewe CW1 ....190 F2
Haslington CW1,CW11 ..191 D5
Hatherton CW5 ....219 F3
Nantwich CW2,CW5 .....205 D6
Sandbach CW11 ....175 A4
Shavington CW2 ....206 C6
Crewe St Chester CH1 ..237 C3
Crewe CW1 ....190 D4
Crewe Sta CW1 ....190 E2
Crewood Common Rd CW8 ....76 A3
Crib La CW6 ....168 A8
Criccieth Ct CH65 ....70 D2
Criftin Cl CH66 ....69 C2
Crimes La CH3,CW6 ....167 D4
Crisham Ave CW5 ......218 E8
Crispin Rd M22 ....33 E8
Critchley Rd L24 ....21 A3
Croasdale Dr WA7 ....49 E5
Crocus Gdns WA9 ....6 A7
Crocus St CW8 ....78 B3
Croesmere Dr CH66 .....69 D2
Croft Cl Altrincham WA15 .32 C6
Congleton CW12 ....156 F2
Utkinton CW6 ....146 B7
Waverton CH3 ....143 A5
Croft Cotts
Dunham-on-t-H WA6 .....97 E6
Ellesmere Port CH66 .....69 A8
Croft Ct CH65 ....70 E3
Croft Gdns WA4 ....27 A7
Croft Heath Gdns WA3 ...9 A8
Croft Ho WA3 ....9 A7
Croft La Dodleston CH4 .162 A7
Knutsford WA16 ....82 B8
Croft Prim Sch WA3 ......9 A8
Croft Rd SK9 ....59 E4
Croft St Golborne WA3 ....3 A8
Widnes WA8 ....23 A6
Croft The Chester CH2 ..118 D5
Norton in Hales TF9 ....236 B3
Runcorn WA7 ....23 F1
Croften Dr CH64 ....66 E5
Crofters Cl
6 Ellesmere Port CH66 ...69 E1
Pickmere WA16 ....80 A7
Wistaston CW2 ....206 B8
Crofters Ct
Holmes Chapel CW4 ....130 C3
Newcastle-u-Lyme ST5 ..210 D3
Crofters Gn SK9 ....59 F6
Crofters Heath CH66 ....69 E1
Crofters Lea CW8 ......103 D7
Crofters Pk CH5 ....116 A3
Crofters Way CH1 .....116 F8
Crofton Cl WA4 ....27 C5
Crofton Cotts WA6 .....100 B8
Crofton Gdns WA3 ....4 E3
Crofton Rd WA7 ....22 E1
Crofts The CH3 ....180 F1
Croftside WA1 ....17 F7
Croftside Way SK9 ......60 C6
Croftsway CH60 ....40 D8
Croftwood Cl 10 CW7 ..149 A8
Cromdale Way WA5 .....14 E6
Cromer Dr CW1 ....190 B8
Cromford Ct SK23 ....65 E6
Cromford Mews SK23 ...65 E5
Cromley Rd SK6 ....37 E6
Crompton Dr WA2 ....8 A6
Crompton Rd SK11 .....112 C7
Cromwell Ave WA5 ......15 D6
Cromwell Ave S WA5 ....15 D4
Cromwell Cl WA12 ....2 A4
Cromwell Ct Irlam M44 ..11 E7
6 Nantwich CW5 ....204 E5
2 Warrington WA1 ....16 A5
Cromwell Dr CW2 .....206 C4
Cromwell Rd
Bramhall SK7 ....35 D6
Ellesmere Port CH65 .....70 D5
Irlam M44 ....11 E7
Northwich CW8 ....103 E8
Cromwell St WA8 ....23 A6
Cronkinson Ave CW5 ..204 F4
Cronkinson Oak CW5 ..204 F4
Cronton CE Prim Sch WA8 ....12 C6
Cronton Farm Ct WA8 ..12 E4
Cronton La Cronton L35 ..12 B8
Widnes WA8 ....12 F5
Cronton Park Ave WA8 ..12 C6
Cronton Park Cl WA8 ...12 C6
Cronton Rd L35,WA8 ....12 C5
Cronulla Dr WA5 ....14 E7
Crook La CW7 ....127 A2
Crook St CH1 ....237 A2
Crooked La CH3,CW6 ..145 C4
Crookedyard Rd SK11 ..113 E7
Crookenden Cl CH2 ......95 C1
Crookenden Rd CH2 .....95 C1
Croppers Rd WA2 ....8 F3
Crosby Ave WA5 ....16 A8
Crosby Gr CH64 ....43 B1
Crosfield St WA1 ....16 A5
Cross Farm WA2 ....9 A2
Cross Gn CH2 ....118 E6
Cross Hey CH4 ....237 C1
Cross La Audley ST7 ....209 E5
Church Minshull CW1,CW5 172 C6
Congleton CW12 ....157 A1
Croft WA3 ....9 D7
Frodsham WA6 ....73 B8
Haslington CW11 ....191 F8
Middlewich CW10 ......151 D6
Neston CH64 ....66 E5
Newton-le-W WA12 ....2 B4
Sandbach CW11 ....175 D5
Smallwood CW11 ....176 F5
Swettenham CW12 ......131 F4
Warrington WA4 ....17 A3
Wilmslow SK9 ....60 F8
Cross La E M31 ....11 F3
Cross La W M31 ....11 F2
Cross Lane S WA3 ....9 E6
Cross Lanes Tarvin CH3 .121 E2
Tarvin, Old Moss CH3 ...144 C8
Cross o' th' Hill SY14 ...213 D4
Cross O' Th' Hill Rd SY14 ....214 A4
Cross Rd Haslington CW1 191 D4
Heald Green SK8 ....34 B7
Cross St Alsager ST7 ...193 C3
Barnton CW8 ....78 B3
Chester CH2 ....118 F2
Congleton CW12 ....156 D3
Crewe CW1 ....190 D3
Golborne WA3 ....3 A7
Haslington CW1 ....191 D4
Holt LL13 ....196 E8
Macclesfield SK11 ......112 E6
Marston CW9 ....79 C3
Neston CH64 ....66 E8
New Mills SK22 ....39 C8
Warrington WA2 ....16 B7
Widnes WA8 ....13 C1
Cross The Holt LL13 ....196 E8
Kingsley WA6 ....75 C2
Lymm WA13 ....18 E3
8 Neston CH64 ....66 E8
Cross Wood St 2 CW5 .204 D5
Crossall St SK11 ....112 C7
Crossdale Rd CH62 ......43 D5
Crossfield Ave
Culcheth WA3 ....4 F2
Lymm WA13 ....18 F3
Winsford CW7 ....149 D7
Crossfield Rd
Bollington SK10 ....87 E6
Handforth SK9 ....34 D4
Crossfields CH3 ....121 B2
Crossgates WA8 ....13 F3
Crossings The WA12 ......2 C3
Crosskeys Cl CW6 .....145 A6
Crossland Terr WA6 .....73 B2
Crosslands
Congleton CW12 ....157 A1
Haslington CW1 ....191 D4
Crossledge CW12 ......156 B3
Crossley Ave CH66 ......69 E6
Crossley Cres CH2 .....119 B5
Crossley Dr CH60 ....40 D8
Crossley Pk WA6 ....99 C7
Crossley St WA1 ....16 C5
Crossway Bramhall SK7 ..35 E5
Crewe CW1 ....190 D6
Widnes WA8 ....22 D8
Crossway The CH63 .....42 C4
Crossways ST8 ....179 E1
Crossways Rd ST7 .....194 A4
Crosthwaite Ave CH62 ...43 F4
Croston Cl
Alderley Edge SK9 ....60 C1
Widnes WA8 ....12 C3
Crotia Ave CW2 ....207 B5
Crouch La CW12 ....157 D4
Crouchley Hall Mews WA13 ....18 F1
Crouchley La WA13 ......18 F1
Croughton Ct CH66 ......69 F8
Croughton Rd
Ellesmere Port CH66 .....69 F8
Stoak CH2 ....96 A7
Stoak, Croughton CH2 ....95 F6
Crow La E WA12 ....2 C4
Crow La W WA12 ....2 A4
Crow Wood La WA8 ......13 D2
Crow Wood Pl WA8 ......13 D3
Crow's Nest Cotts CH3 .166 C6
Crowbrook Gr 7 SK9 ....34 D1
Crowder's La CW9 .....105 B4
Crowe Ave WA2 ....8 B2
Crowland Gdns SK8 .....35 B6
Crowley La CW9,WA16 ...28 A3
Crowmere Cl CW8 .....102 A2
Crown Ave WA8 ....22 B8
Crown Bank
3 Sandbach CW11 ......175 B6
Talke ST7 ....210 D6
Crown Bank Cres ST7 ..210 D6
Crown Bldgs WA6 ....73 B1
Crown Cotts CW8 ......124 A7
Crown Ctr The 24 SK11 .112 C8
Crown Ctyd CW3 ....229 F4
Crown Fields Cl WA12 ....2 B5
Crown Gate WA7 ....49 F7
Crown Gdns
Newton-le-W WA12 ....2 B4
Talke ST7 ....210 D6
Crown Gn WA13 ....19 B4
Crown La WA16 ....106 D8
Crown Mews CW3 ......229 F4
Crown Park Dr WA12 .....2 B5
Crown St
Newton-le-W WA12 ....2 A3
8 Northwich CW8 ......103 F8
3 Warrington WA1 ......16 B5
Crown St W SK11 ......112 C7
Crownest La CW9 ....78 E8
Crowton Cotts CW7 ....170 F4
Croxton Gn SY14 ....201 C6
Croxton La CW10 ......128 A4
Croxton Way CW8 .....103 A4
Croyde Cl M22 ....33 F7
Croyde Rd L24 ....21 A3
Crum Hill 2 CW9 ....104 A8
Cryers La Elton CH2 .....72 A2
Thornton-le-M CH2 ....96 F8
Cty High Sch Leftwich The CW9 ....104 A4
Cuckoo Clock Mus★ WA16 ....80 F8
Cuckoo La Acton CW5 ..203 E8
Neston CH64 ....67 C7
Cuckstoolpit Hill SK10 .112 E8
Cuddington La CW8 ...101 D4
Cuddington Prim Sch CW8 ....101 F2
Cuddington Sta CW8 ...102 A4
Cuddington Way 7 SK9 .34 D5
Cuerdley Gn WA5 ....14 A2
Cuerdley Rd WA5 ....14 C3
Cuerdon Dr WA4 ....17 D1
Culbin Cl WA3 ....10 A6
Culcheth Hall Barns WA3 .4 F4
Culcheth Hall Dr WA3 ....4 F4
Culcheth High Sch WA3 ...5 A3
Culcheth Prim Sch WA3 ...5 A3
Culford Cl WA7 ....24 D1
Culland St CW2 ....190 C2
Cullen Cl CH63 ....43 C4
Cullen Rd WA7 ....48 D7
Cumber Cl SK9 ....59 D4
Cumber Dr SK9 ....59 D4
Cumber La SK9 ....59 D4
Cumberland Ave
Irlam M44 ....11 C5
Nantwich CW5 ....204 F6
Cumberland Cl
Crewe CW1 ....190 D5
Talke ST7 ....210 E7
Cumberland Cres WA11 ..1 A6
Cumberland Dr
Altrincham WA14 ....31 B8
Bollington SK10 ....88 B8
Cumberland Gr CH66 ....69 C3
Cumberland Rd
Congleton CW12 ....156 A3
Partington M31 ....11 E2
Cumberland St
2 Macclesfield SK10 ....112 D8
Warrington WA4 ....16 C3
Cumbermere Dr CW11 .174 E7
Cumbers Dr CH64 ....67 A5
Cumbers La CH64 ....67 A5
Cumbrae Dr 4 CH65 ....70 C1
Cumbria Cl 2 CH66 .....69 E1
Cundiff Cl SK11 ....112 E6
Cunliffe Ave WA12 ....2 B5
Cunliffe Cl WA7 ....50 A7
Cunningham Cl WA5 .....14 F5
Cunningham Dr
Bebington CH63 ....43 C7
Heald Green M22 ....34 A8
Runcorn WA7 ....22 E1
Cunningham Ho WA7 ....48 E8
Cunningham Rd WA8 ....22 D8
Cuppin St CH1 ....237 A2
Curlender Way L24 ......21 E2
Curlew Cl Golborne WA3 ...3 D8
Macclesfield SK10 ....87 C5
Winsford CW7 ....149 C5
Curlew Gr WA3 ....9 E3
Curlew Rd ST7 ....195 E1
Currans Rd WA2 ....8 B2
Curzon Ave ST7 ....193 D5
Curzon Cl CH4 ....141 B8
Curzon Dr WA4 ....27 A7
Curzon Gr CW7 ....126 F1
Curzon Mews SK9 ....60 A5
Curzon Pk N CH4 ......141 B7
Curzon Pk S CH4 ......141 B7
Curzon Rd
Heald Green SK8 ....34 B7
Poynton SK12 ....36 E2
Curzon St Chester CH4 ..140 F7
4 Runcorn WA7 ....22 F1
Cwat Erwain CH4 ......140 E7
Cygnet Cl CH66 ....69 D4
Cygnet Ct WA1 ....16 A3
Cyman Cl CH1 ....117 D3
Cynthia Ave WA1 ....17 B7
Cynthia Rd WA7 ....22 F1
Cypress Ave
Ellesmere Port CH66 .....69 F1
Widnes WA8 ....13 B2
Cypress Cl WA1 ....17 E7
Cypress Gr WA7 ....49 C7
Cypress Mews CW8 ....102 E7
Cypress Way SK6 ....38 A7
Cyril Bell Cl WA13 ....18 F3
Cyril St WA2 ....16 B7

D

D'Arcy Cotts CH63 ......42 B6
Daffodil Cl WA8 ....13 E4
Daffodil Gdns WA9 ....6 A7
Dagfields Craft & Antiques Ctr★ CW5 ....220 A4
Dagnall Ave WA5 ....7 F2
Dahlia Cl WA9 ....6 A7
Daintry St SK11 ....112 E7
Daintry Terr SK10 ......112 E8
Dairy Bank CH2 ....72 B4
Dairy Farm Cl WA13 .....18 F4
Dairy House La SK7,SK8 .35 B4
Dairy House Rd SK7,SK8 .35 B5
Dairy House Small Holdings SK7 ....35 B4
Dairy House Way CW2 ..189 F2
Dairy La CW5 ....188 D6
Dairybrook Gr 7 SK9 ....34 E1
Dairyground Rd SK7 .....35 F7
Dairylands Rd ST7 .....193 F4
Daisy Ave WA12 ....2 C2
Daisy Bank CW5 ....204 D5
Daisy Bank Cres CW3 ..229 F5
Daisy Bank La CW9 ......78 C3
Daisy Bank Mill Cl WA3 ...4 E3
Daisy Bank Rd
Lymm WA13 ....18 C3
Warrington WA5 ....14 F4
Daisy Cl WA16 ....79 F6
Daisy Way SK6 ....37 F7
Daisybank Dr
Congleton CW12 ....156 D4
Sandbach CW11 ....175 C6
Dakota Dr WA5 ....15 C7
Dalby Cl WA3 ....10 B5
Dalby Ct CW9 ....104 E5
Dale Ave Bebington CH62 .43 D8
Bramhall SK7 ....35 F8
Ellesmere Port CH66 .....69 C6
Dale Cl Warrington WA5 ..15 D4
Widnes WA8 ....22 A8
Dale Cres CW12 ....156 F2
Dale Ct Heswall CH60 ....40 F8
Middlewich CW10 ......151 D7
Dale Dr Chester CH2 ...118 D8
Ellesmere Port CH65 .....69 F5
Dale Gdns CH65 ....70 B3
Dale Gr Congleton CW12 .157 A2
Irlam M44 ....11 E6
Dale Head Rd SK10 ......86 F4
Dale Hey CH66 ....43 E2
Dale House Fold SK12 ...37 A4
Dale La WA4 ....26 E7
Dale Pl CW12 ....156 F2
Dale Rd Bebington CH62 ..43 D6
Golborne WA3 ....3 A7
New Mills SK22 ....39 C7
Dale St Chester CH3 ...119 A1
Macclesfield SK10 ......112 E8
Runcorn WA7 ....23 A1
Dale The Neston CH64 ...66 E6
Tiverton CW6 ....168 C6
Warrington WA5 ....14 F5
Dale View Kidsgrove ST7 .195 C5
Newton-le-W WA12 ....2 E4
Dale's Sq CW9 ....103 F6

Dalecroft WA6 .....72 E1
Daleford Manor CW8 .125 B8
Daleford Manor Cvn Pk
CW8 ....125 A8
Dalefords La
　Cuddington CW8 .....102 A1
　Whitegate CW8 .....125 D7
Dales Green Rd ST7 ..195 C5
Dalesford Cl WN7 ....4 C8
Dalesford Cres SK10 .111 E8
Daleside CH2 ....118 D8
Dalesway CH60 ......40 E8
Dalewood Cl WA2 ....16 A6
Dalewood Cres CH2 ..72 A3
Dallam Com Prim Sch
WA5 ....7 F1
Dallam La WA2 ......16 A7
Dalmahoy Cl CW7 ....126 C2
Dalston Dr SK7 .....35 C5
Dalton Ave
　Warrington WA5 .....15 F7
　Warrington,Birchwood WA3 .9 E6
Dalton Bank WA1 ....16 C6
Dalton Cl CH1 ......117 E3
Dalton Ct Runcorn WA7 .23 E3
　Sandbach CW11 ......174 E7
Dalton St Runcorn WA7 .23 D2
　Warrington WA3 .....9 E5
Dalton Way CW8 .....128 D1
Dalwood Cl WA7 .....50 E7
Dam Head La WA3 ...11 A5
Dam La Hollinfare WA3 .11 A4
　Mobberley WA16 .....58 C3
　Warrington WA1 .....17 D7
　Winwick WA3 ....8 F7
Dame Hollow SK8 ....34 D7
Damery Ct SK7 .....35 E8
Damery Rd SK7 .....35 E8
Damhead La CH64 ...67 E7
Damian Dr WA12 ....2 A5
Dams La WA16 ......106 D5
Damson La WA16 ....58 C3
Damson Wlk M31 ....11 D3
Dan's Rd WA8 ....13 E2
Danby Cl Runcorn WA7 .49 D6
　Warrington WA5 .....15 E7
Dane Bank Ave
　Congleton CW12 .....156 E4
　Crewe CW2 ....190 A2
Dane Bank Dr SK12 ..38 D6
Dane Bank Rd
　Lymm WA13 ....18 E4
　Northwich CW9 .....104 B3
Dane Bank Rd E WA13 .18 E4
Dane Cl Alsager ST7 .193 A4
　Chester CH4 ....140 F5
　Sandbach CW11 ......174 E7
Dane Dr Biddulph ST8 .179 E1
　Wilmslow SK9 ......60 D6
Dane Gdns ST7 ......195 C2
Dane Gr CH2 ....119 F8
Dane Hill Cl SK12 ...38 D5
Dane Mill Bsns Ctr
CW12 ....156 C3
Dane Pl Crewe CW1 ..190 B6
　Winsford CW7 ......127 B1
Dane St Congleton CW12 156 C2
　Middlewich CW10 ....128 D2
　Northwich CW9 .....103 F8
Danefield Ct SK8 ....34 D8
Danefield Rd
　Holmes Chapel CW4 ..130 C4
　Northwich CW9 .....104 B7
Danes Sq SK11 ......112 D5
Danescroft WA8 .....12 B3
Daneside Bsns Pk
CW12 ....156 E4
Daneswell Rd L24 ....21 A2
Daniel Adamson Ave
M31 ....11 D3
Daniel Cl WA3 ......10 A4
Daniel Ct M31 ......11 F4
Daniell Way CH3 ....142 A7
Danily Cl SY14 ......213 B3
Dapplehealth Rd CW2 .190 A1
Darby Cl CH64 ......66 E4
Darent Rd WA11 ....1 B7
Daresbury Cl
　Holmes Chapel CW4 ..130 A3
　Wilmslow SK9 ......60 C8
Daresbury Ct WA8 ..13 E3
Daresbury Expressway
　Daresbury WA4 .....25 A3
　Runcorn WA7 ......23 C2
Daresbury La WA4 ..25 D2
Daresbury Pk WA4 ..51 B3
Daresbury Prim Sch
WA4 ....25 B2
Darian Ave M22 .....33 D8
Dario Gradi Dr CW2 .190 D1
Dark Ark La CH3,WA6 .99 B3
Dark La Henbury SK11 .111 B8
　Higher Whitley WA4 ..52 D6
　Kingsley WA6 ......75 B1
　Marston CW9 ....79 C6
　Tattenhall CH3 ......183 E7
　Warren SK11 ....111 C3
　Whitchurch SY13 ....227 B1
Darkie Mdw CW6 ....185 E8
Darland La LL12 .....162 C1
Darley Ave Crewe CW2 .190 A3
　Warrington WA2 .....8 A3
Darley Cl WA8 ......12 B3
Darley Rd SK7 ......36 F7
Darleydale Dr CH62 .43 F5

Darlington Ave CW1 .189 F5
Darlington Cres CH1 .94 A1
Darlington Ct **3** WA8 .23 A7
Darlington St CW10 .128 C1
Darnaway Cl WA3 ...10 B6
Darnhall Prim Sch CW7 149 D6
Darnhall School La
CW7 ....149 C6
Dart Cl Alsager ST7 .193 A4
　Biddulph ST8 ....179 D1
Dart Wlk CW7 ......127 B2
Dartnall Cl SK12 ....38 A6
Darwen Gdns WA2 ...8 E1
Darwin Gr SK7 .....35 E6
Darwin Rd CH1 .....117 C4
Darwin St CW8 .....103 E7
Daryl Rd CH60 .....41 A8
Dashwood Cl WA4 ..27 A7
Daten Ave WA3 .....9 E6
Daten Pk WA3 ......9 F6
Dauncey Cl CH2 .....95 C1
Davehall Ave SK9 ...60 A7
Daven Prim Sch CW12 .156 E2
Daven Rd CW12 .....156 F1
Davenham Ave WA1 .16 E8
Davenham CE Prim Sch
CW9 ....103 F2
Davenham Cres CW2 .190 A3
Davenham Ct CW9 ..104 A3
Davenham Mdws CW9 .103 E3
Davenham Rd
　Davenham CW9 .....104 E3
　Handforth SK9 ......34 D4
Davenham Rdbt CW9 .103 F3
Davenham Way CW10 .151 D5
Davenport Ave
　Crewe CW2 ....206 D8
　Nantwich CW5 ......204 E7
　Warrington WA4 ....16 F5
　Wilmslow SK9 ......59 E4
Davenport Cl CW11 .175 D8
Davenport La
　Brereton Green CW11 .154 C2
　Marton SK11 ....132 F5
　Mobberley WA16 .....58 D6
Davenport Park La
CW12 ....131 D2
Davenport Rd CH60 .40 E7
Davenport Row WA7 .49 D8
Davenport St
　Congleton CW12 .....156 C2
　Crewe CW1 ....190 C6
　Macclesfield SK10 ...112 E8
Davey La SK9 ......60 A2
Daveylands SK9 ....60 D7
David Lewis Sch SK9 .83 F6
David Rd WA13 .....18 C3
David St CW8 ......103 E7
David's Ave WA5 ...15 B5
Davidson Ave CW12 .157 A5
Davies Ave
　Heald Green SK8 ....34 B6
　Newton-le-W WA12 ..2 C4
　Warrington WA4 ....16 F4
Davies Cl WA8 .....23 A4
Davies St SK10 .....112 E8
Davies Way WA13 ..18 E3
Davis Cl ST7 ....193 E3
Davy Ave WA3 .....9 E5
Davy Rd WA7 ......23 E3
Dawlish Ave SK8 ....34 B7
Dawlish Cl Bramhall SK7 .35 E7
　Hollinfare WA3 .....11 B3
Dawn Cl CH64 ......67 A5
Dawn Gdns CH65 ...70 B4
Dawpool Cl CH2 ....118 D5
Dawpool Ct CH2 ....118 D5
Dawpool Dr CH62 ..43 C7
Dawson Cl CH2 .....118 D5
Dawson Dr CH2 ....237 A4
Dawson Rd
　Bollington SK10 .....88 A7
　Heald Green SK8 ....34 D8
　Macclesfield SK11 ...111 F7
Dawstone Ct CH60 ..40 F8
Dawstone Rd CH60 .41 A7
Dawstone Rise CH60 .40 F7
De Lacy Row WA7 ..24 A2
De Trafford Mews **9**
SK9 ....34 D2
Deacon Rd WA8 ....13 B1
Deacon Trad Est WA12 .2 A2
Deacons Cl WA3 ....9 A8
Deadman's La CW5 .205 B2
Deakin's Rd
　Winsford CW7 ......126 F4
　Winsford CW7 ......127 A4
Dean Bank CW6 ....168 C3
Dean Cl Bollington SK10 .88 A7
　Handforth SK9 ......34 C1
　Partington M31 .....11 F4
　Sandbach CW11 .....174 E8
Dean Cres WA2 .....8 B2
Dean Ct Bollington SK10 .88 B8
　Golborne WA3 ......3 A7
Dean Dr SK9 ....34 C2
Dean Hollow ST7 ...209 D2
Dean La CH3 ....36 E8
Dean Mdw WA12 ...2 C4
Dean Pk SY14 ......214 A5
Dean Rd Golborne WA3 .3 A7
　Handforth SK9 .....34 E3
　Irlam M44 ....11 E6
Dean Row **10** SK9 ..34 D1
Dean Row Jun Sch SK9 .34 E1
Dean Row SK9 .....61 A8

Dean St
　Middlewich CW10 ....128 C1
　Northwich CW9 .....104 C8
　Widnes WA8 ....23 B8
　Winsford CW7 ......126 D1
Dean Valley Com Prim Sch
SK10 ....87 E8
Dean View ST7 .....209 D1
Dean's La
　Barthomley CW2 ....208 C4
　Newcastle-u-Lyme ST5 .210 D2
Deane Ct WA5 .....205 B4
Deanery Cl WA4 ....118 C4
Deans Cl Chester CH2 .118 A4
　Tarvin CH3 ....121 B1
Deans La Sandbach CW11 174 E6
Deans Rd CH65 .....70 F3
Deans Way
　Higher Kinnerton CH4 .161 A2
　Tarvin CH3 ....121 C1
Deansfield Way CH2 .72 A3
Deansgate CH65 ....70 A5
Deansgreen Ct WA13 .29 A7
Deansway WA8 .....22 C8
Deanwater Cl WA3 ..9 A4
Deanwater Ct SK8 ..34 D7
Deanway SK9 ......34 C1
Deanway Tech Ctr SK9 .34 D3
Deanway Trad Est SK9 .34 D3
Dearnford Ave CH62 .43 D6
Dearnford Cl CH62 ..43 D6
Debra Cl CH66 .....69 C4
Debra Rd CH66 ....69 C4
Decade Cl ST5 .....210 F2
Dee Banks Chester CH3 .142 A8
　Huntington CH3 ....141 F7
Dee Banks Sch CH3 .142 A8
Dee Cl Biddulph ST8 .179 C1
　Sandbach CW11 .....174 E8
　Talke ST7 ....210 E7
Dee Cres CH3 ......180 C2
Dee Fords Ave CH3 ..119 A1
Dee Hills Pk CH3 ...237 C2
Dee La Chester CH1,CH3 .237 C2
　Holt LL13 ....196 D7
Dee Mdws LL13 ....196 D7
Dee Park Cl CH60 ..41 B6
Dee Park Rd CH60 .41 B5
Dee Pk LL13 ....196 D8
Dee Point Prim Sch
CH1 ....117 D3
Dee Rd CH2 ....96 F1
Dee Side CH60 .....40 C8
Dee Sq CW7 ....127 B2
Dee View CH3 .....180 E2
Dee View Cotts CH64 .41 D1
Dee View Ct CH64 ..66 E6
Dee View Rd
　Connah's Quay CH5 .91 E1
　Heswall CH60 ......40 F8
Dee Villas LL13 ....180 E1
Dee Way CW7 .....127 A2
Deefords CH3 ......118 F1
Deep Dale WA5 ....14 F6
Deepdale WA8 .....12 C3
Deer Park Ct WA7 ..49 F6
Deerwood Cl
　Ellesmere Port CH66 .69 D7
　Macclesfield SK10 ..86 F1
Deerwood Cres CH66 .69 D7
Deeside
　Ellesmere Port CH65 .70 B2
　Holt LL13 ....196 E6
Deeside Cl CH65 ...70 B2
Deeside Coll/Coleg Glannau
Dyfrdwy CH5 ......91 B1
Deeside Cres LL11 ..116 E5
Deeside Ct Chester CH3 .237 C2
　Neston CH64 ....41 B1
Deeside Ind Pk/Parc
Ddiwydiannol Glannau
Dyfrdwy CH5 ......92 C2
Deeside La CH1 ....116 D4
Deirdre Ave WA8 ..13 A1
Delafield Cl WA2 ...8 F3
Delaisy Way CW7 ..127 A1
Delamere Ave
　Bebington CH62 ....43 E4
　Ellesmere Port CH66 .69 E5
　Golborne WA3 .....3 E6
　Widnes WA8 ....12 C1
Delamere CE Prim Sch
CW6 ....123 C5
Delamere Cl Barnton CW8 78 A3
　Bebington CH62 ....43 E4
　Sandbach CW11 .....174 F8
Delamere Ct Alsager ST7 192 F4
　Bebington CH62 ....43 E4
Delamere Dr
　Ellesmere Port CH66 .69 E5
　Macclesfield SK10 ..87 F2
Delamere Forest Sch
WA6 ....100 C4
Delamere Forest Trail*
WA6 ....100 A4
Delamere Forest Visitor Ctr*
CW8 ....100 B2
Delamere Gn CH66 .69 E5
Delamere Gr CW8 ..123 D7
Delamere La CH3 ..99 B2
Delamere Park Way E
CW8 ....101 D5
Delamere Park Way W
CW8 ....101 D5
Delamere Rd
　Congleton CW12 ....155 F3
　Handforth SK9 .....34 E4

Delamere Rd continued
　Nantwich CW5 .....204 F3
　Norley WA6 ....100 B6
Delamere Rise CW7 .126 B1
Delamere St
　Chester CH1 ....237 A3
　Crewe CW1 ....190 C4
　Warrington WA5 ...15 E5
　Winsford CW7 ......126 B1
Delamere Sta CW8 ..100 D1
Delamere's Acre CH64 .68 A8
Delavor Cl CH60 ...40 E8
Delavor Rd CH60 ..40 E8
Delenty Dr WA3 ...9 E4
Delery Dr WA1 ....16 F8
Delfur Rd SK7 .....35 F7
Delhi Rd M44 ......11 F8
Dell Cl CH63 ......43 B6
Dell Dr WA2 ....9 A2
Dell La CH60 ......41 B7
Dell The Ashley WA14 .31 E8
　Cuddington CW8 ...101 D5
　Guilden Sutton CH3 .119 F5
　Kelsall CW6 ....122 D5
　Whaley Bridge SK23 .65 F5
Delmar Rd WA16 ..57 C1
Delph La Daresbury WA4 .25 A2
　Warrington,Houghton Gn
　WA2 ....8 A5
　Winwick WA2 ......8 A5
Delphfields Rd WA4 .26 C7
Delphield WA7 .....50 D8
Delphside ST7 .....209 F2
Delta Cres WA5 ....7 C2
Delta Ct CH4 ......140 B6
Delves Ave WA5 ...15 F7
Delves Broughton Ct
CW1 ....191 D5
Delves Cl CW2 .....206 B4
Delves Wlk CH3 ...142 B7
Delvine Dr CH2 ....118 D6
Demage Dr CH66 ..69 D3
Demage La Backford CH1 .94 F4
　Chester CH2 ....118 D8
Demage La S CH2 ..118 D7
Den La CW3,CW5 ..221 D4
Denbigh Cl
　Hazel Grove SK7 ...36 C8
　Helsby WA6 ....73 A1
Denbigh Cres CW10 .151 C7
Denbigh Ct CH65 ..70 D3
Denbigh Dr CW7 ..149 B7
Denbigh Gdns CH65 .70 C3
Denbigh St CH1 ...118 B3
Denbury Ave WA4 .16 F2
Dene Ave WA12 ...1 F4
Dene Dr CW7 ......149 D8
Denehurst Cl WA5 .14 F4
Denehurst Park Way
CW8 ....101 D5
Denesgate **1** CW7 .149 D8
Deneside Ave CW1 .190 C6
Deneway Bramhall SK7 .35 D7
　High Lane SK6 .....37 F8
Denewood Ct **3** SK9 .60 A6
Denford CH4 ......139 C4
Denford Pl ST7 ....193 D6
Denhall Cl CH2 ....118 E5
Denhall La CH64 ...67 A3
Denham Ave WA5 ..15 B5
Denham Dr SK7 ...35 D7
Denise Ave WA5 ...14 E5
Denison Rd SK7 ...36 E8
Dennett Cl WA1 ...17 E6
Dennis Dr CH4 ....141 B5
Dennis Rd WA8 ...23 C7
Dennis Round Ct ST7 .193 C3
Dennison Rd SK8 ..35 B8
Densham Ave WA2 .8 A2
Denston Cl CW2 ...190 B1
Denstone Dr CH4 ..141 A4
Dentith Dr CH1 ....117 E5
Denton Cl CW7 ....126 C1
Denton Dr CW9 ....79 C1
Denton Drive Ind Est
CW9 ....79 C2
Denton St WA8 ....13 C1
Denver Ave CW2 ..190 B3
Denver Rd WA4 ...17 A3
Denwall Ho **5** CH64 .66 E8
Depenbech Cl SY14 .213 B4
Depmore La WA6 ..75 A2
Derby Cl Irlam M44 .11 C5
　Newton-le-W WA12 ..2 B3
Derby Dr WA1 .....16 F7
Derby Knoll SK23 ..39 F1
Derby Rd Golborne WA3 .3 C8
　Talke ST7 ....210 D7
　4 Warrington WA4 .16 C1
　Widnes,Barrow's Green
　WA8 ....13 D4
　Widnes,Lunts Heath WA8 .13 B4
Derby Row W12 ...2 B3
Derby St Congleton CW12 156 C3
　Crewe CW1 ....190 B6
　Newton-le-W WA12 ..2 B3
Derbyshire Hill Rd WA9 .1 A2
Derbyshire Rd
　Partington M31 .....11 E2
　Poynton SK12 ......37 D5
Dereham Way WA7 .24 D3
Derek Ave WA2 ....8 E1
Derfel Cotts **4** WA6 .74 B8
Derrington Ave CW2 .190 C3
Derwent Ave CW7 ..127 B1
Derwent Cl Alsager ST7 .193 A4
　Culcheth WA3 ......5 A2

Derwent Cl continued
　Holmes Chapel CW4 ..130 A3
　Macclesfield SK11 ..112 A6
　Partington M31 .....11 F4
　Willaston CW5 .....205 D6
Derwent Cres ST7 ..195 C2
Derwent Dr Biddulph ST8 179 E1
　Bramhall SK7 ......35 C5
　Congleton CW12 ...156 F1
　Handforth SK9 .....34 C5
　Hooton CH66 ......44 B2
Derwent Rd Chester CH2 119 A5
　High Lane SK6 .....37 E8
　Warrington WA4 ...16 B2
　Widnes WA8 ....12 C1
Derwent Way
　Neston CH64 ......66 F7
　Alderley Edge SK9 .83 F7
Desoto Rd WA8 ....22 E5
Desoto Rd E WA8 ..22 F6
Desoto Rd W WA8 .22 F6
Deva Ave CH4 .....140 D6
Deva Bsns Pk CH5 .116 A8
Deva Cl SK12 ......36 B4
Deva Ct CH2 ....118 F2
Deva Hts CH3 ......141 F7
Deva La CH2 ....118 C6
Deva Link CH1 ....118 A3
Deva Rd CW2 ......189 D4
Deva Ret Pk CH1 ..118 A3
Deva Roman Experience
Mus* CH1 ....237 B2
Deva Stad (Chester City FC)
CH1 ....117 E1
Deva Terr CH3 .....237 C2
Devon Cl
　Macclesfield SK10 ..86 F2
　Middlewich CW10 ...128 C2
Devon Gr ST8 .....179 C1
Devon Pl
　Congleton CW12 ...156 E4
　Widnes WA8 ....13 B3
Devon Rd Chester CH2 .118 F5
　Irlam M44 ....11 D5
　Partington M31 .....11 E2
Devonshire Dr SK9 .60 B2
Devonshire Gdns WA12 .2 C2
Devonshire Pl CH4 .141 E7
Devonshire Rd
　Broughton CH4 ....139 C4
　Hazel Grove SK7 ...36 F8
　Warrington WA1 ...16 E8
Dewar Ct WA7 ....23 E3
Dewar St WA3 .....9 E5
Dewes St CW1 .....190 B5
Dewhurst Rd WA3 .9 D2
Dexter Way CW10 .128 D2
Dial Cl WA12,SK11 .158 B1
Dial Rd WA15 .....32 C8
Dial St WA1 ....16 C5
Diamond Ave **3** ST7 .195 B2
Dibbins Gn CH63 ..43 B7
Dibbinsdale Rd CH63 .43 B7
Dickens Cl
　Cheadle Hulme SK8 .35 B5
　Sandbach CW11 .....174 D6
Dickens La SK12 ...36 E2
Dickenson Ho CW10 .128 C1
Dickenson St WA2 .16 C7
Dickinson Cl WA11 .1 A6
Dickinson Way ST7 .193 A3
Dicklow Cob SK11 .132 A8
Dickson Cl WA8 ...23 B8
Dickson St **2** Widnes WA8 .23 B8
Dicksons Dr CH2 ..118 D4
Dierden St CW7 ...127 B1
Dierdens Terr CW10 .128 C1
Dig La Acton CW5 ..203 E4
　Frodsham WA6 ....74 A7
　Shavington CW5 ...206 B2
　Warrington WA2 ...9 B3
Diglake Cl ST7 .....210 C6
Diglake Cotts ST7 .210 A2
Diglake St ST7 .....209 F3
Diglee Rd SK23 ....39 C3
Dillors Croft CW1 .173 A1
Dimelow Ct SY14 ..213 A2
Dinas Cl CH1 ......117 D3
Dingle Ave
　Newton-le-W WA12 ..1 F2
　Row-of-trees SK9 ..59 D3
Dingle Bank
　Chester CH4 ....141 C7
　Sandbach CW11 ....175 C6
Dingle Bank WA13 .18 E3
Dingle Cl SK10 ....87 B3
Dingle La
　Bridgemere CW5 ...231 F6
　Kelsall CW6 ....122 C6
　Sandbach CW11 ....175 C6
　Warrington WA4 ...26 F6
Dingle Row CH66 ..126 E1
Dingle Prim Sch The
CW1 ....191 D6
Dingle The Barnton CW8 .78 B4
　Haslington CW1 ....191 D5
　Lymm WA13 ......18 E3
Dingle Way CW8 ..101 E5
Dingle Wlk **4** CW7 .126 D1
Dingleway WA4 ...26 E8
Dinglebrook Gr **5** SK9 .34 D1
Dinnington Ct WA8 .12 E3
Diploma Dr CW10 .128 C2
Dipping Brook Ave WA4 .26 F4
Disley Prim Sch SK12 .38 D6
Disley Sta SK12 ...38 D6

Distaff Rd SK12 .36 B4
District CE Prim Sch The WA12 .2 A4
Ditchfield La WA16 .29 D3
Ditchfield Pl WA8 .22 B8
Ditchfield Rd
Warrington WA5 .14 E3
Widnes WA8 .22 B8
Ditton CE Prim Sch WA8 12 A1
Ditton Prim Sch WA8 .12 E1
Ditton Rd WA8 .22 D6
Dixon Ave WA12 .2 C5
Dixon Cl WA11 .2 A8
Dixon Dr SK11 .84 B3
Dixon Rd CW12 .157 A5
Dixon St Irlam M44 .11 F8
Warrington WA1 .16 A5
Dixon's Hos CH3 .142 E8
Dobb Hedge Cl WA15 .32 C6
Dobell's Rd CW9 .103 F6
Dobers La WA6 .74 C4
Dobson Ct SY14 .213 B3
Dock Rd Northwich CW9 .103 F7
Widnes WA8 .22 F5
Dock Road Edwardian Pumping Station The★ CW9 .103 F7
Dock St
Ellesmere Port CH65 .70 C7
Widnes WA8 .23 A5
Dock Yard Rd CH65 .70 E6
Dodd's Green La CW5, SY13 .228 C4
Dodd's La SY13,SY14 .224 E7
Doddington Dr CW11 .175 C8
Doddington Rd CW2 .190 A3
Doddlespool Barns CW3 .221 F7
Dodds La CW12 .178 C6
Doddswood Dr 2 CW12 156 F4
Dodgsley Dr WA6 .75 C1
Dodleston CE Prim Sch CH4 .162 A7
Dodleston La CH4 .162 C3
Doe's Meadow Rd CH63 .43 B7
Doeford Cl WA3 .4 E5
Dog La
Brereton Green CW4, CW11 .153 E7
Kelsall CW6 .122 B5
Nantwich CW5 .204 E6
Tattenhall CH3 .182 D4
Threapwood SY14 .223 C7
Dogmore La CW6 .147 C4
Dolly La SK23 .39 F3
Dolmans La 10 WA1 .16 B5
Dolphin Cres CH66 .69 E2
Dolphin Ct CH4 .141 A7
Dombey Rd SK12 .36 D2
Domestic App M90 .33 C6
Domville Cl WA13 .18 E3
Don Wlk CH65 .70 A7
Donagh Cl SK10 .86 F2
Donkey La SK9 .60 A5
Donne Pl CH1 .117 F6
Donnington Way CH4 .140 F7
Dood's La WA4 .27 A5
Dooley's Grig SK11 .108 F1
Dooley's La SK9 .33 C2
Dorac Ave SK8 .34 C7
Dorchester Cl
Kidsgrove ST7 .195 A3
Wilmslow SK9 .60 D8
Dorchester Pk WA7 .24 E3
Dorchester Rd
Chester CH4 .140 F5
Warrington WA5 .15 C5
Dorchester Way
Burtonwood WA5 .6 F6
Macclesfield SK10 .87 C4
Doreen Ave CW12 .179 B8
Dorfold Cl CW11 .175 C7
Dorfold Dr CW5 .204 D5
Dorfold Hall★ CW5 .204 B5
Dorfold St CW1 .190 C4
Dorfold Way CH2 .118 E6
Doric Ave WA6 .74 D7
Dorin Park Sch CH2 .118 D6
Dormer Cl CH3 .143 A5
Dorney Cl WA4 .26 E6
Dornoch Ct CW4 .130 B2
Dorothea St WA2 .16 C7
Dorric Way CW1 .190 C7
Dorrington Cl WA7 .50 E8
Dorrit Cl SK12 .36 E2
Dorset Cl CW12 .156 E4
Dorset Ct WA7 .50 A6
Dorset Dr ST8 .179 C1
Dorset Pl Chester CH2 .119 A5
Kidsgrove ST7 .195 A2
Dorset Rd Chester CH2 .118 F7
Irlam M44 .11 D5
Dorset Way WA1 .17 B8
Dorset Wlk SK10 .86 F2
Douglas Ave WA9 .6 B6
Douglas Cl
Northwich CW8 .103 C5
Widnes WA8 .13 F3
Douglas La CW7 .171 A6
Douglas Pl CH4 .140 E6
Doulton Cl CW7 .126 F3
Doune Ct CH65 .70 D3
Dounrey Cl WA2 .9 A2
Dove Bank Prim Sch ST7 .195 A2
Dove Cl
Ellesmere Port CH66 .70 A8
Elton CH2 .72 C4
Dove Cl *continued*
Helsby WA6 .73 C5
Sandbach CW11 .175 A8
Warrington WA3 .9 F4
Dove Gr ST8 .179 D1
Dove Ho ST7 .195 C3
Dove Pl CW7 .127 B2
Dovecote Cl CW2 .206 B8
Dovecote Dr WA11 .1 C7
Dovecote Gn WA5 .7 A1
Dovedale Ave CH62 .43 E5
Dovedale Cl
Congleton CW12 .157 A4
High Lane SK6 .37 E7
Warrington WA2 .8 E3
Dovedale Ct WA8 .12 B3
Dover Cl WA7 .50 E6
Dover Ct CH65 .70 D2
Dover Dr
Ellesmere Port CH65 .70 D2
Winsford CW7 .149 B6
Dover Rd Chester CH4 .141 A6
Macclesfield SK10 .87 F2
Warrington WA4 .17 A3
Dover St WA7 .23 B3
Dovesmead Rd CH60 .41 C7
Doward St WA8 .13 C2
Downes Cl SK10 .87 A1
Downesway SK9 .59 F1
Downham Ave WA3 .4 F2
Downham Ct 1 CH60 .41 A8
Downham Dr CH60 .41 A8
Downham Pl CH1 .117 E4
Downham Road S CH60 .41 A8
Downing Cl SK11 .112 F3
Downs End WA16 .57 C1
Downs Rd WA7 .23 A1
Downs The CW8 .101 D5
Downsfield Rd CH4 .141 A6
Downside WA8 .12 B3
Downswood Ct CH2 .118 C4
Downswood Dr CH2 .118 C4
Downway La WA9 .1 A1
Dragon Yd WA8 .13 B4
Dragon's La
Middlewich CW11 .151 F1
Sandbach CW11 .152 B1
Dragons Wharf CW11 .152 C1
Drake Ave M44 .11 E6
Drake Cl WA5 .7 D1
Drake La CW5 .203 F4
Drake Rd CH64 .41 E1
Drakelow La CW10 .128 F8
Drakes Way SY14 .213 B5
Draxford Ct SK9 .60 B6
Draycott Dr ST5 .210 D2
Drayton Cl Runcorn WA7 .22 F1
13 Handforth SK9 .34 D1
Drayton Cres CW1 .190 F5
Drayton Dr SK8 .34 B7
Drenfell Rd ST7 .194 F7
Drill Field Rd CW9 .103 F8
Drillfield Ct 20 CW9 .103 F8
Drillfield Rd CW9 .104 A8
Drive A CH5 .93 A2
Drive B CH5 .93 A2
Drive C CH5 .93 A2
Drive D CH5 .93 A1
Drive The
Altrincham WA15 .32 D8
Bollington SK10 .87 F7
Broomedge WA13 .19 D1
Holmes Chapel CW4 .130 C2
Drome Rd CH5 .93 A2
Drovers Way CW11 .175 A5
Drumber La ST7 .195 B8
Drumber The CW7 .126 D1
Drumble Field SK11 .84 A3
Drummond Ave CH66 .69 C4
Drummond Ct WA8 .13 D2
Drummond Way SK10 .86 E1
Druridge Dr WA5 .14 F4
Drury Cl CW1 .190 F5
Drury La Knutsford WA16 .57 A2
Warmingham CW1 .173 D4
Dryden Cl CW2 .190 A1
Dryden Pl WA2 .8 C2
Dryersfield 5 CH3 .142 A8
Dryhurst Dr SK12 .38 D6
Dryhurst La SK12 .38 D6
Dublin Croft CH66 .69 E1
Duchess Pl CH2 .237 A4
Duchy Rd CW1 .207 A8
Duck La CH3 .121 F7
Duckworth Gr WA2 .9 A1
Duddon Cl Duddon CW6 .145 B6
3 Northwich CW9 .103 F4
Duddon Hook La CW6 .144 F6
Duddon Rd CW6 .145 B5
Duddon St Peter's CE Prim Sch CW6 .145 B6
Dudleston Rd CH66 .69 B6
Dudley Ave WA7 .23 D2
Dudley Cres CH65 .44 B3
Dudley Rd
Ellesmere Port CH65 .70 B5
Irlam M44 .11 D4
Dudley St WA2 .16 B7
Dudley Wlk 2 SK11 .111 F7
Dudlow Green Rd WA4 .26 E5
Dufton Wlk M22 .33 E8
Duke Ave
Cheadle Hulme SK8 .34 F6
Glazebury WA3 .5 C7
Duke Cl WA7 .22 F2
Duke St Alderley Edge SK9 .60 B2
Chester CH1 .237 B1
Congleton CW12 .156 D2
Duke St *continued*
Crewe CW2 .190 C3
Macclesfield SK11 .112 D7
Newton-le-W WA12 .2 B3
Duke's Cres CW11 .175 A7
Duke's Ct CH1 .237 B1
Dukes Ct 2 SK11 .112 D7
Dukes Way CW9 .103 E5
Dukes Wharf WA7 .50 E6
Dukesway CH2 .118 E7
Dulas Ct CH2 .118 E8
Dulverton Ave CH3 .119 C2
Dumbah La SK10 .87 D6
Dumbers SK11 .136 A2
Dumbill Ho ST7 .210 C8
Dunbar Cl
Connah's Quay CH5 .91 D1
Ellesmere Port CH66 .69 C5
Holmes Chapel CW4 .130 C2
Dunbar Ct CH66 .69 C5
Duncan Ave
Newton-le-W WA12 .2 C5
Runcorn WA7 .23 C1
Duncan St WA2 .16 C7
Duncansby Cres WA5 .14 E6
Duncansby Dr CH63 .43 C4
Dundalk Rd WA8 .22 E8
Dundee Cl WA2 .8 F4
Dundee Ct CH65 .70 E3
Dundonald Ave 5 WA4 .16 C1
Dundonald Rd SK8 .35 A7
Dundrennan Cl SK12 .36 D5
Dunge Valley Gdns★ SK23 .89 F8
Dunham Cl Alsager ST7 .193 C3
Bebington CH62 .43 F3
Sandbach CW11 .175 C6
Dunham Cres CW2 .206 B8
Dunham Ct WA6 .97 E6
Dunham Hill Prim Sch WA6 .97 E6
Dunham Ho WA14 .20 F3
Dunham Massey Hall★ WA14 .20 D3
Dunham Pk★ WA14 .20 D3
Dunham Rd
Altrincham,Bowgreen WA14 20 F1
Handforth SK9 .34 D5
Mossbrow WA13 .19 E7
Northwich CW9 .104 A4
Dunham Way CH2 .118 F6
Dunkirk ST7 .210 A6
Dunkirk Ave CW7 .149 D8
Dunkirk Dr CH65 .70 B1
Dunkirk La
Capenhurst CH1 .94 C7
Ellesmere Port CH65 .70 A1
Dunkirk Trad Est CH1 .94 D6
Dunley Cl WA3 .10 A5
Dunlin Ave WA12 .2 C4
Dunlin Cl Poynton SK12 .36 A4
Runcorn WA7 .49 F5
Warrington WA2 .8 E3
Dunlin Rise SK10 .87 B5
Dunlop St WA4 .16 B3
Dunmore Cl CW10 .151 C7
Dunmore Cres CH66 .69 B6
Dunmore Rd CH66 .69 B6
Dunmow Rd WA4 .17 C3
Dunn's Cotts CW1 .192 C1
Dunn's La CH3 .121 F7
Dunnillow Field CW5 .205 A4
Dunnock Cl WA2 .8 E3
Dunnock Gr WA3 .9 E4
Dunnocksfold Rd ST7 .193 A4
Dunnockswood ST7 .193 A4
Dunoon Cl CW4 .130 B2
Dunraven Rd CH64 .67 A7
Dunscar Cl WA3 .9 D5
Dunsford WA8 .12 B3
Dunsmore Cl WA11 .1 C7
Dunstan La CH64 .67 E3
Dunster Cl CW9 .104 A4
Dunster Gr CH60 .41 B7
Dunster Rd SK10 .87 F1
Dunwood Dr ST7 .193 D6
Dunwoody Way CW1, CW2 .190 B4
Durban Ave CH3 .142 D7
Durber Cl ST7 .209 D1
Durham Cl
Macclesfield SK10 .86 F2
Warrington WA1 .17 E7
Durham Ct CH65 .70 E3
Durham Dr CW7 .149 C6
Durham Gr M44 .11 C6
Durham Rd Blacon CH1 .117 F5
Widnes WA8 .13 B3
Durlston Cl WA8 .12 C2
Durrell Way WA3 .3 E8
Dutton Gn CH2 .70 F3
Dutton Hall Ct WA4 .76 E8
Dutton La CW8,WA6 .101 B6
Dutton Way Crewe CW1 .190 B6
Nantwich CW5 .204 E3
Dutton's La CW6 .122 C5
Duttons Bsns Ctr CW9 .103 F7
Duxford Ct WA2 .8 E1
Dyar Terr CW8 .78 D1
Dye House La SK22 .39 C8
Dyers Cl WA13 .19 A4
Dyers Ct SK10 .88 B8
Dyers La WA13 .19 A4
Dykin Cl WA8 .13 E3
Dykin Rd WA8 .13 E3
Dysart Bldgs CW5 .204 E5
Dyserth Rd CH1 .117 D3
Dystelegh Rd SK12 .38 D6

E

Eadie Gr CW1 .190 A7
Eaglais Way SK10 .86 F2
Eagland Pl CW12 .156 E4
Eagle Brow WA13 .18 D3
Eagle La CH66 .69 D7
Eagle Mount WA4 .16 C2
Eagle Park Dr WA2 .8 A1
Eagles Way WA7 .49 E6
Eaglesfield CW8 .103 C4
Ealing Cl WA7 .24 D1
Ealing Rd WA5 .15 B5
Eanleywood La WA7 .50 C7
Eardley Cres CW12 .156 E4
Eardley Ct CW1 .190 B5
Eardleyend Rd ST7 .209 E7
Eardswick Cl CH2 .237 B4
Eardswick La CW1 .172 D5
Eardswick Rd CW10 .151 C6
Earl Rd SK8,SK9 .34 E5
Earl St WA2 .16 B7
Earl's Port CH1 .118 B2
Earl's Villas CH1 .237 C3
Earle Cl WA12 .1 F3
Earle Cres CH64 .41 D1
Earle Dr CH64 .41 D1
Earle Rd WA8 .23 C7
Earle St Crewe CW1 .190 D4
Newton-le-W WA12 .2 A3
Earle's La CW6 .122 C5
Earles La CW9 .79 E6
Earlestown Sta WA12 .2 B3
Earls Gdns CH65 .70 B5
Earls Oak CH2 .118 D7
Earls Rd CW2 .206 B4
Earls Way
Northwich CW9 .103 E4
Runcorn WA7 .49 E6
Earlston Ct CH3 .237 C2
Earlsway Chester CH4 .141 A8
Macclesfield SK11 .111 F7
Earlswood Mews CW9 .103 F3
Easby Cl
Cheadle Hulme SK8 .35 B6
Poynton SK12 .36 D4
Runcorn WA7 .23 C2
Easenhall Cl WA8 .13 C5
East Ave Bollington SK10 .87 F7
Heald Green SK8 .34 D8
Northwich CW9 .104 D6
Warrington WA2 .16 C8
Warrington, Stockton Heath WA4 .16 D1
Warrington,Great Sankey WA5 .15 A4
Weston CW2 .207 C5
East Ct ST7 .193 E4
East Dam Wood Rd L24 .21 A2
East Dudley St CW7 .126 F1
East Gn CH5 .116 A6
East La Cuddington CW8 .102 A3
Runcorn WA7 .49 F7
East Lancashire Rd WA11, WA12,WA3 .2 C7
East Mains L24 .21 A3
East Millwood Rd L24 .21 A4
East Park Rd SK11 .112 B5
East Rd Halewood L24,L26 .21 A5
Middlewich CW10 .128 B1
Woodhouse Park M90 .33 C7
East St WA8 .13 D1
East Terr WA16 .56 F1
East View
10 Nantwich CW5 .204 E6
Warrington WA4 .17 B2
Eastbury Cl WA8 .13 C5
Eastcott Cl CW12 .155 F4
Eastdale WA15 .31 F8
Eastdale Rd WA1 .17 A7
Easter Ct WA5 .7 B2
Eastern Pathway CH4 .237 C1
Eastern Rd CW5 .205 F5
Eastfields Gr CH1 .117 A8
Eastford Rd WA4 .16 A1
Eastgate SK10 .112 E8
Eastgate Rd
Holmes Chapel CW4 .130 D3
Runcorn WA7 .24 E5
Eastgate Row N CH1 .237 B2
Eastgate Row S CH1 .237 B2
Eastgate St CH1 .237 B2
Eastgate Way WA7 .24 D4
Eastham Ctry Pk★ CH62 .44 A8
Eastham Ho CH62 .44 A4
Eastham Mews CH62 .44 A4
Eastham Rake CH62,CH64 43 D3
Eastham Rake Sta CH63 .43 D3
Eastham Village Rd CH62 .44 A5
Eastham Way 11 SK9 .34 D5
Eastward Ave SK9 .59 F6
Eastway
Ellesmere Port CH66 .69 D7
Widnes WA8 .12 D1
Eastwood WA7 .24 C2
Eastwood Ave WA12 .2 F3
Eastwood Ct CH5 .139 B7
Eastwood Rd WA5 .6 F7
Eaton Ave CH4 .141 D7
Eaton Bank CW12 .156 F4
Eaton Bank Ind Est CW12 .156 F4
Eaton Bank Sch CW12 .156 F5
Eaton Cl Broughton CH4 .139 C4
Poynton SK12 .37 A3
Sandbach CW11 .175 C7
Eaton Cres CW9 .103 E2
Eaton Ct
1 Northwich CW9 .103 E5
Wilmslow SK9 .60 A6
Eaton Dr Alderley Edge SK9 59 F2
Middlewich CW10 .151 B8
Eaton Gr CH4 .140 E6
Eaton La Davenham CW9 .103 E2
Eaton CW6 .147 A5
Goostrey CW4 .107 C1
Macclesfield SK11 .112 D5
Tarporley CW6 .168 E8
Eaton Mews CH4 .141 D7
Eaton Pl CW8 .102 F4
Eaton Prim Sch CW6 .147 B3
Eaton Rd Alsager ST7 .193 D4
Chester CH4 .141 E4
Tarporley CW6 .146 D1
Wettenhall CW7 .170 B8
Eaton St Crewe CW2 .190 C4
14 Runcorn WA7 .23 A2
Eaton View CW9 .126 E8
Eaton Way CW3 .230 A4
Eaves Brow Rd WA3 .9 B7
Eaves Knoll Rd SK22 .39 B8
Ebnal La SY14 .213 E4
Ebury Pl CH4 .141 D7
Eccles Cl SK23 .65 D8
Eccles Rd SK23 .65 F5
Eccleston Ave
Chester CH4 .141 D6
Ellesmere Port CH66 .69 E5
Eccleston CE Prim Sch CH4 .141 E2
Eccleston Cl WA3 .9 C5
Eccleston Ct 5 CW9 .103 E5
Eccleston Dr WA7 .23 C1
Eccleston Rd CH4 .161 A7
Eccleston Way 3 SK9 .34 D4
Ecclestone Ave CH62 .43 C8
Eccups La SK9 .59 C8
Echo Cl CH4 .140 E5
Ecton Ave SK10 .113 A7
Ecton Cl CW7 .127 A4
Edale Cl Bebington CH62 .43 E5
Heald Green SK8 .34 D7
Edale Dr CW6 .122 D5
Edburton Ct WA3 .3 A8
Eddisbury Cl SK11 .112 F7
Eddisbury Dr ST5 .210 D2
Eddisbury Hill CW6,CW8 123 D7
Eddisbury Hill Pk CW8 .123 D7
Eddisbury Rd CH66 .69 F1
Eddisbury Sq WA6 .74 B8
Eddisbury Terr SK11 .112 F7
Eddisbury Way CW9 .103 E3
Eddisford Dr WA3 .4 D4
Edelsten St WA5 .15 F5
Eden Ave
Fowley Common WA3 .5 C4
High Lane SK6 .37 E7
Winsford CW7 .126 F2
Eden Cl Biddulph ST8 .179 E1
5 Ellesmere Port CH66 .69 C5
Kidsgrove ST7 .195 B2
Wilmslow SK9 .59 E5
Eden Dr SK10 .87 F1
Eden Park Rd SK8 .34 E8
Edenbridge Cl CW2 .207 B2
Edenbridge Gdns WA4 .26 E3
Edendale WA8 .12 B2
Edenfield Cl WA16 .58 A3
Edenfield Rd WA16 .58 A4
Edenhall Cl CW4 .130 A3
Edgar Ct Chester CH4 .237 B1
25 Macclesfield SK11 .112 C8
Edgar Pl CH4 .237 B1
Edgars Dr WA2 .9 A2
Edge Gr CH2 .118 F2
Edge La SY14 .199 C1
Edge View La SK9 .59 B2
Edgecroft CH3 .166 A1
Edgehill Chase SK9 .60 E7
Edgerley La CH3 .181 B6
Edgerton Rd WA3 .3 F8
Edgeview Rd CW12 .179 B7
Edgeway Henbury SK11 .111 C8
Wilmslow SK9 .60 B5
Edgewell La CW6 .147 A3
Edgewood 8 CH3 .142 A8
Edgewood Dr
Bebington CH62 .43 D5
Wistaston CW2 .206 A7
Edgworth St WA2 .16 A6
Edinburgh Ct CH65 .70 D3
Edinburgh Dr SK10 .87 A1
Edinburgh Pl CW12 .156 F2
Edinburgh Rd
Congleton CW12 .156 F2
Widnes WA8 .22 A8
Wistaston CW2 .205 E8
Edinburgh Way CH4 .237 C1
Edison Rd WA7 .23 D3
Edith St WA7 .22 F3
Edleston Hall La CW5 .203 F2
Edleston Prim Sch CW2 190 C3
Edleston Rd CW2 .190 D3
Edlestone Gr 2 SK9 .34 E1
Edmund Wright Way CW5 .204 C5
Edna St CH2 .118 F3
Edward Gdns WA1 .17 F6
Edward Rd WA5 .14 D6
Edward St Audley ST7 .209 F3
Crewe CW2 .190 D2

Edward St continued
Ellesmere Port CH65 . . . . . . .70 C7
Haydock WA11 . . . . .1 A6
Macclesfield SK11 . . . . .112 F6
Northwich CW9 . . . . .104 C8
Widnes WA8 . . . . .13 D1
Edwards Ave CW2 . . . . . . .206 C5
Edwards Cl CW2 . . . . .206 C5
Edwards Ct SK7 . . . . .36 F8
Edwards Rd CH4 . . . . .141 A6
Edwards Way
Alsager ST7 . . . . .193 E4
Widnes WA8 . . . . .22 C8
Edwin St WA8 . . . . .13 C1
Egdon Cl WA8 . . . . .13 E2
Egerton WA16 . . . . .29 C5
Egerton Ave
Hartford CW8 . . . . .103 A4
Partington WA13 . . . . .19 C8
Warrington WA1 . . . . .16 F7
Egerton Ct CW6 . . . . .122 B5
Egerton Dr CH2 . . . . .118 D5
Egerton Mews 1 WA4 . . . .16 C1
Egerton Moss WA15 . . . . .31 E5
Egerton Prim Sch WA16 . .56 F2
Egerton Rd Blacon CH1 . . .117 E5
Handforth SK9 . . . . .34 B1
Lymm WA13 . . . . .18 C2
Egerton Sq 6 WA16 . . . . .57 A2
Egerton St Chester CH1 . .237 C3
Congleton CW12 . . . . .156 C2
Ellesmere Port CH65 . . . . . .70 C6
Runcorn WA7 . . . . .22 F3
Warrington, Howley WA1 . . . .16 D5
Warrington, Stockton Heath
WA4 . . . . .16 C1
Egerton Terr CW9 . . . . . . .105 D4
Egerton Wlk CH4 . . . . . . .162 A7
Eggbridge La CH3 . . . . . .143 A6
Egypt St
3 Warrington WA1 . . . . . . .16 A5
Widnes WA8 . . . . .22 F7
Eilison Ct CH1 . . . . .237 B3
Eisenhower Cl WA5 . . . . . .15 B5
Elaine Cl
Ellesmere Port CH66 . . . . . .69 C4
Widnes WA8 . . . . .13 C1
Elaine Price Ct 2 WA7 . . .22 F1
Elaine St WA1 . . . . .16 D7
Elanor Rd CW1 . . . . .174 D7
Elcombe Ave WA3 . . . . .3 E7
Elder Dr CH4 . . . . .140 E5
Elderberry Way SK9 . . . . .60 E8
Elderberry Wlk M31 . . . . . .11 E3
Eldon Rd SK10 . . . . .111 F8
Eldon St WA1 . . . . .16 C5
Eldon Terr CH64 . . . . .66 E7
Eleanor Cl CW1 . . . . .189 F5
Eleanor St
Ellesmere Port CH65 . . . . . .70 C6
5 Widnes WA8 . . . . .23 A7
Electra Way CW1 . . . . . . .191 A4
Electricity St CW2 . . . . . .190 C3
Elgar Ave CH62 . . . . .43 E5
Elgar Cl CH65 . . . . .69 F3
Elgin Ave
Holmes Chapel CW4 . . . . . .130 B2
Macclesfield SK10 . . . . .87 A2
Warrington WA4 . . . . .16 A2
Elgin Cl CH3 . . . . .119 B3
Eliot Cl CW1 . . . . .191 A4
Elizabeth Ave SK12 . . . . . .38 D5
Elizabeth Cl Kelsall CW6 . .122 D5
Sandbach CW11 . . . . .174 D7
Elizabeth Cres CH4 . . . . .237 C1
Elizabeth Ct Talke ST7 . . .210 D5
Widnes WA8 . . . . .23 B7
Elizabeth Dr WA1 . . . . .17 A8
Elizabeth Gaskell Ct
WA16 . . . . .56 F2
Elizabeth Ho 15 SK11 . . .112 E7
Elizabeth Rd Haydock WA11 .1 E7
Partington M31 . . . . .11 F4
Elizabeth St
Congleton CW12 . . . . .156 C2
Crewe CW1 . . . . .190 B5
Macclesfield SK11 . . . . . . .112 D7
Elizabeth Terr WA8 . . . . . .12 D1
Elizabethan Way CW9 . . .104 E6
Elk View SY14 . . . . .222 F5
Elkan Cl WA8 . . . . .13 E2
Elkan Rd WA8 . . . . .13 E2
Ella Gr WA16 . . . . .57 B2
Elland Dr CH66 . . . . .69 C5
Ellen Brook Rd M22 . . . . . .33 D8
Ellen St WA5 . . . . .15 F7
Ellerby Cl WA7 . . . . .50 E7
Ellerton Ave CH66 . . . . . . .69 C5
Ellerton Cl WA8 . . . . .12 D3
Ellesmere Ave
Broughton CH4 . . . . .139 D4
Chester CH2 . . . . .118 D5
Ellesmere Cl CW11 . . . . . .174 F8
Ellesmere Pl CW1 . . . . . . .190 B5
Ellesmere Port Hospl
CH65 . . . . .70 A2
Ellesmere Port RC High Sch
CH65 . . . . .70 A3
Ellesmere Port Sta CH65 .70 C6
Ellesmere Port Stadium The
CH65 . . . . .70 A4
Ellesmere Rd Culcheth WA3 .4 E3
Northwich CW9 . . . . .104 A4
Warrington WA4 . . . . .16 B1

Ellesmere St
Runcorn WA7 . . . . .23 B2
Warrington WA1 . . . . .16 C5
Ellesworth Cl WA5 . . . . . . .15 C8
Ellingham Way CW9 . . . . .103 E3
Elliot Ho CH1 . . . . .118 A5
Elliot St 9 WA8 . . . . .23 B8
Elliott Ave WA1 . . . . .16 E7
Ellis La WA6 . . . . .49 D1
Ellis St Crewe CW1 . . . . . .190 B6
Widnes WA8 . . . . .22 F7
Ellison St
Warrington, Howley WA1 . . . .16 C5
Warrington, Stockton Heath
WA4 . . . . .16 D1
Elloway Rd L24 . . . . .21 A3
Ellwood Cl L24 . . . . .21 E2
Ellwood Gn CW2 . . . . .206 E3
Widnes WA8 . . . . .13 B2
Elm Ave Newton-le-W WA12 .2 C2
Widnes WA8 . . . . .13 B2
Elm Beds Rd SK12 . . . . . . .37 C3
Elm Cl Crewe CW2 . . . . . .189 E2
2 Partington M31 . . . . .11 F3
Poynton SK12 . . . . .36 F3
Tarporley CW6 . . . . .146 D2
Elm Cres SK9 . . . . .60 B3
Elm Ct CW1 . . . . .190 D6
Elm Dr Crewe CW1 . . . . . .190 E6
Holmes Chapel CW4 . . . . . .130 D4
Macclesfield SK10 . . . . .87 D6
Elm Gn CH64 . . . . .67 F8
Elm Gr Alderley Edge SK9 . .60 A2
Alsager ST7 . . . . .193 E4
Ellesmere Port CH66 . . . . . .70 A1
Handforth SK9 . . . . .34 C3
Saltney CH4 . . . . .140 E5
Warrington WA1 . . . . .16 F7
Widnes WA8 . . . . .13 B1
Winsford CW7 . . . . .127 A1
Elm Ho 9 CW11 . . . . .175 B6
Elm Rd Congleton CW12 . .156 B3
Haydock WA11 . . . . .1 E7
High Lane SK6 . . . . .37 F7
Hollinfare WA3 . . . . .11 A2
Middlewich CW10 . . . . .151 D7
Runcorn WA7 . . . . .49 C8
Warrington WA5 . . . . .14 F4
Warrington, Winwick Quay
WA2 . . . . .8 B4
Weaverham CW8 . . . . .102 D7
Willaston CH64 . . . . .67 F8
Elm Ridge Dr WA15 . . . . .32 C8
Elm Rise Frodsham WA6 . . .74 C7
Prestbury SK10 . . . . .86 E6
Elm Sq CH4 . . . . .140 E5
Elm St Ellesmere Port CH65 70 C7
Northwich CW9 . . . . .79 B1
Elm Terr CW1 . . . . .190 E6
Elm Tree Ave Lymm WA13 .18 D2
Warrington WA1 . . . . .16 F8
Elm Tree Cotts CH3 . . . . .167 A7
Elm Tree Ct CW6 . . . . . . .147 A3
Elm Tree Dr ST7 . . . . .209 F1
Elm Tree La CW11 . . . . . .174 D8
Elm Tree Rd Golborne WA3 .3 F8
Lymm WA13 . . . . .18 D2
Elmfield Cl SK9 . . . . .60 B2
Elmfield Rd SK9 . . . . .60 B2
Elmore Cl
Holmes Chapel CW4 . . . . . .130 B3
Runcorn WA7 . . . . .24 D1
Elmridge Ct WA3 . . . . .3 F8
Elmridge Prim Sch
WA15 . . . . .32 C8
Elmridge Way CW8 . . . . . .78 D1
Elms The Golborne WA3 . . . .3 F7
Mobberley WA16 . . . . .58 E2
7 Northwich CW9 . . . . . . .103 E6
Runcorn WA7 . . . . .22 F1
Tallarn Green/Tallwrn Green
SY14 . . . . .222 F5
Elmsett Cl WA5 . . . . .14 E5
Elmstead Cres WA1 . . . . .189 F8
Elmstead Rd SK11 . . . . . . .84 A3
Elmsway Altrincham WA15 .32 B8
Bollington SK10 . . . . .88 A8
Bramhall SK7 . . . . .35 C7
High Lane SK6 . . . . .37 E6
Elmuir CH1 . . . . .117 E3
Elmwood Ave
Chester CH2 . . . . .118 F4
Warrington WA1 . . . . .16 E7
Elmwood Cl ST7 . . . . .194 A4
Elmwood Gr CW7 . . . . . . .149 F8
Elmwood Rd CW8 . . . . . . .78 B4
Elnor Ave SK23 . . . . .65 E5
Elnor La SK23 . . . . .65 F4
Elsby Rd ST7 . . . . .193 F2
Elston Ave WA12 . . . . .2 C5
Elstree Ave CH3 . . . . .119 B3
Elswick Ave SK7 . . . . .35 E7
Eltham Cl WA8 . . . . .13 E3
Eltham Wlk WA8 . . . . .13 E3
Elton Cl Bebington CH62 . . .43 E3
Golborne WA3 . . . . .3 E7
Handforth SK9 . . . . .34 E1
Warrington WA3 . . . . .9 C4
Elton Crossings Rd
CW11 . . . . .174 D6
Elton Dr SK7 . . . . .36 D8
Elton La Elton CH2 . . . . . . .72 E4
Haslington CW11,CW1 . . . .174 D1
Winterley CW11 . . . . .191 F8
Elton Lordship La WA6 . . .73 B7
Elton Prim Sch CH2 . . . . . .72 B4
Elton Rd CW11 . . . . .174 D5

Elvington Cl
Congleton CW12 . . . . .156 E2
Runcorn WA7 . . . . .49 F4
Elwood Way CW5 . . . . . . .205 B4
Elworth Ave WA8 . . . . .13 A5
Elworth CE Prim Sch
CW11 . . . . .174 E7
Elworth Ct
12 Congleton CW12 . . . . . .156 F3
Sandbach CW11 . . . . .174 D7
Elworth Hall Prim Sch
CW11 . . . . .174 E7
Elworth Rd CW11 . . . . . . .174 E6
Elworth St CW11 . . . . .175 A7
Elworth Way 6 SK9 . . . . . .34 D4
Elwyn Dr L26 . . . . .21 A8
Ely Cl CH66 . . . . .94 E8
Ely Pk WA7 . . . . .24 E2
Embassy Cl CH1 . . . . .117 C4
Emberton Pl CW3 . . . . . . .230 A5
Embleton Ct WA7 . . . . .49 D5
Embridge Cswy SK10,
SK17 . . . . .90 B5
Emerald Dr CW11 . . . . . . .175 C8
Emerald Rd M22 . . . . .33 F7
Emily St 7 WA8 . . . . .23 A7
Emmett St CW8 . . . . .78 A3
Empire Ct WA4 . . . . .16 A4
Empress Dr CW2 . . . . .190 B3
Emral Ct SY14 . . . . .211 A1
Emslie Ct CH64 . . . . .66 C7
Enderby Rd CH1 . . . . .237 A3
Endon Ave SK10 . . . . .88 A7
Endon Hall Mews SK10 . . .88 B5
Endsleigh Cl CH2 . . . . . . .118 E8
Endsleigh Gdns CH2 . . . . .118 E8
Enfield Cl CW2 . . . . .206 B3
Enfield Park Rd WA2 . . . . . .9 A3
Enfield Rd CH65 . . . . .70 B5
Engelsea Brook La CW2 208 A3
Engineer Pk CH5 . . . . .116 A4
Englefield Ave CH4 . . . . . .140 D6
Englefield Cl CW1 . . . . . . .190 A6
Englesea Brook Mus of
Primitive Methodism ★
CW2 . . . . .208 A4
Englesea Gr CW2 . . . . . . .190 B1
Ennerdale Chester CH2 . . .118 F5
Macclesfield SK11 . . . . . . .111 F5
Ennerdale Ave
Bebington CH62 . . . . .43 F4
Warrington WA2 . . . . .8 B3
Ennerdale Cl
Alderley Edge SK9 . . . . .83 F7
Winsford CW7 . . . . .126 D3
Ennerdale Dr
Congleton CW12 . . . . .156 B2
Frodsham WA6 . . . . .74 C8
Ennerdale Rd
Crewe CW2 . . . . .189 D3
Partington M31 . . . . .11 F3
Ennis Cl L24 . . . . .21 D2
Ensor Way SK22 . . . . .39 C7
Enterprise Ctr The
CW12 . . . . .156 E3
Enterprise Way WA3 . . . . . .4 A7
Enticott Rd M44 . . . . .11 C5
Enville St WA4 . . . . .16 C4
Epping Dr WA1 . . . . .17 D8
Epsom Ave SK8,SK9 . . . . . .34 E4
Epsom Ct CH1 . . . . .118 B2
Epsom Gdns WA4 . . . . .26 E8
Epworth Cl WA5 . . . . .6 F7
ERF Way CW10 . . . . .151 E8
Eric Ave WA1 . . . . .16 E8
Eric Fountain Rd CH65 . . . .44 D3
Eric St WA8 . . . . .13 C2
Erindale Cres WA6 . . . . . . .74 A6
Ermine Rd CH2 . . . . .237 C4
Ernest St CW2 . . . . .190 C1
Ernley Cl CW5 . . . . .204 D6
Errington Ave CH65 . . . . . .70 C6
Errwood Forest Walks ★
SK17 . . . . .90 E2
Erskine Rd M31 . . . . .11 F3
Erwood St WA2 . . . . .16 B6
Esk Dale Cl CW7 . . . . .126 C2
Esk Rd WA7 . . . . .127 A2
Eskdale CH65 . . . . .70 B3
Eskdale Ave
Bebington CH62 . . . . .43 E5
Bramhall SK7 . . . . .35 C5
Warrington WA2 . . . . .8 C3
Eskdale Cl WA7 . . . . .49 D5
Essex Cl CW12 . . . . .156 E5
Essex Dr Biddulph ST8 . . .179 D2
Kidsgrove ST7 . . . . .194 F2
Essex Gdns M44 . . . . .11 C4
Essex Rd CH2 . . . . .119 A5
Essex Wlk SK10 . . . . .86 F1
Esthers La CW8 . . . . .102 D8
Etchells Prim Sch SK8 . . . .34 C8
Ethelda Dr CH2 . . . . .119 A5
Etherow Cl CW11 . . . . . . .174 E7
Eton Dr CH63 . . . . .41 F6
Eton Rd CH65 . . . . .70 D4
Ettiley Ave CW11 . . . . . . .174 C5
Ettrick Pk CH3 . . . . .119 A2
Euclid Ave WA4 . . . . .17 B2
Europa Bvd WA5 . . . . .7 D3
Europa Way CH65 . . . . . . .70 C6
Eustace St WA2 . . . . .16 A6
Eva St CW11 . . . . .174 D8
Evans Bsns Ctr CH5 . . . . . .93 A1
Evans Cl WA11 . . . . .1 F7
Evans Pl WA4 . . . . .16 D3
Evans St CW1 . . . . .190 C6
Evansleigh Dr CH5 . . . . . .116 A3

Evelyn St WA5 . . . . .15 D4
Evelyn Street Prim Sch
WA5 . . . . .15 E4
Evenwood Cl WA7 . . . . . . .24 E4
Everdon Cl CW7 . . . . .126 F4
Everest Cl CH66 . . . . .69 F3
Everest Rd ST7 . . . . .195 C3
Everglade Cl SK11 . . . . . . .112 B5
Evergreen Way WA9 . . . . . .6 A7
Everite Rd WA8 . . . . .22 B7
Eversley WA8 . . . . .12 B2
Eversley Cl Frodsham WA6 74 C6
Warrington WA4 . . . . .26 F5
Eversley Ct CH2 . . . . .118 C4
Eversley Pk CH2 . . . . .118 C4
Evesham Cl
Macclesfield SK10 . . . . .87 E4
Warrington WA4 . . . . .26 C8
Evesham Dr SK9 . . . . .34 C2
Evington Ho 2 SK11 . . . . .112 B6
Ewart St CH4 . . . . .140 B7
Ewloe Ct CH65 . . . . .70 D2
Ewrin La SK10 . . . . .89 D5
Excalibur Ind Est ST7 . . . .193 E3
Excalibur Prim Sch ST7 193 E2
Exchange Cl 12 SK11 . . . .112 D8
Exchange St SK11 . . . . . . .112 C8
Exeter Cl SK8 . . . . .34 F8
Exeter Pl CH1 . . . . .117 F5
Exeter Rd CH65 . . . . .70 C5
Exeter Wlk SK7 . . . . .35 F7
Exit Rd W M90 . . . . .33 B7
Exmouth Cres WA7 . . . . . .50 E6
Exmouth Way WA5 . . . . . . .6 F6
Express Ind Est WA8 . . . . .22 A7
Exton Pk CH1 . . . . .237 A4
Eyam Rd SK7 . . . . .36 E8
Eyebrook Rd WA14 . . . . . . .20 F1
Eyre Pl CH65 . . . . .70 B6
Eyston Cl CW9 . . . . .103 E5

F

Facit Glen Ind Est CH4 . .140 F7
Factory La
Warrington WA1,WA5 . . . . . .15 F4
Widnes WA8 . . . . .13 B3
Factory Rd CH5 . . . . .116 A3
Fair Haven's Ct WA8 . . . . .23 B8
Fair Isle Cl CH65 . . . . .70 C1
Fair Mead WA16 . . . . .82 B8
Fair Oak Rd ST5 . . . . .210 D1
Fair View Cl CW8 . . . . .77 F3
Fairacre Dr CW10 . . . . . . .151 E6
Fairacres Rd SK6 . . . . .37 E8
Fairbourne Ave
Alderley Edge SK9 . . . . .60 B3
Wilmslow SK9 . . . . .59 F4
Fairbourne Cl
Warrington WA5 . . . . .7 E3
Wilmslow SK9 . . . . .59 F4
Fairbourne Dr SK9 . . . . . . .59 F4
Fairbrook CW2 . . . . .189 E2
Fairbrother Cres WA2 . . . . .8 D2
Fairburn Ave CW2 . . . . . . .189 F4
Fairburn Cl WA8 . . . . .13 E3
Fairclough Ave WA1 . . . . . .16 C4
Fairclough Cres WA11 . . . .1 A6
Fairclough St
Burtonwood WA5 . . . . .6 E6
Newton-le-W WA12 . . . . . . .2 B3
Fairfax Dr Nantwich CW5 204 D6
Runcorn WA7 . . . . .23 D2
Wilmslow SK9 . . . . .59 F4
Fairfield Ave
Bollington SK10 . . . . .88 A8
Ellesmere Port CH65 . . . . . .70 A2
Sandbach CW11 . . . . .175 B5
Fairfield Gdns WA4 . . . . . .16 E2
Fairfield High Sch WA8 . . .13 B3
Fairfield Inf Sch WA8 . . . . .13 B2
Fairfield Jun Sch WA8 . . . .13 B2
Fairfield Rd
Broughton CH4 . . . . .139 B4
Chester CH2 . . . . .119 A4
Irlam M44 . . . . .11 C5
Lymm WA13 . . . . .18 F3
Northwich CW9 . . . . .104 A4
Warrington WA4 . . . . .16 E2
Widnes WA8 . . . . .13 B2
Fairfield St WA1 . . . . .16 D6
Fairfields Audley ST7 . . . . .209 F2
Whitchurch SY13 . . . . .225 F1
Fairford Cl WA5 . . . . .15 B6
Fairford Rd CH4 . . . . .140 F6
Fairford Way SK9 . . . . .60 D7
Fairhaven CW2 . . . . .207 B1
Fairhaven Cl Bramhall SK7 35 E8
Macclesfield SK10 . . . . .87 B4
Warrington WA5 . . . . .14 E3
Fairhaven Dr CH63 . . . . . . .43 C5
Fairhaven Rd WA8 . . . . . . .13 C2
Fairhills Ind Est M44 . . . . .11 F8
Fairhills Rd M44 . . . . .11 F8
Fairholme Ave CH64 . . . . . .41 D1
Fairholme Cl CH1 . . . . .94 B1
Fairholme Pl 8 CH3 . . . . .119 A1
Fairholme Rd CW9 . . . . . .127 A8
Fairmeadow CH4 . . . . .162 D2
Fairoak Cl 12 CW7 . . . . . .149 A8
Fairoak Ct WA7 . . . . .50 F3
Fairoak La WA7 . . . . .50 F3
Fairview LL13 . . . . .196 E8
Fairview Ave
Alsager ST7 . . . . .193 D4

Fairview continued
Weston CW2 . . . . .207 B5
Fairview Rd
Ellesmere Port CH65 . . . . . .70 A2
Macclesfield SK11 . . . . . . .112 A6
Fairway Bramhall SK7 . . . . .35 D6
Sandycroft CH5 . . . . .116 A2
Fairway The ST7 . . . . .193 C4
Fairways Frodsham WA6 . . .74 D7
Warrington WA4 . . . . .26 D5
Fairways Dr
Ellesmere Port CH66 . . . . . .69 D7
Whitchurch SY13 . . . . .226 A1
Fairways The
Macclesfield SK10 . . . . .87 B4
Winsford CW7 . . . . .126 A2
Fairywell Cl SK9 . . . . .34 D1
Falcon Cl
Middlewich CW10 . . . . .151 D5
New Mills SK22 . . . . .39 D8
Winsford CW7 . . . . .149 D6
Falcon Dr CW1 . . . . .190 B8
Falcon Rd CH66 . . . . .69 F3
Falcondale Rd WA2 . . . . . . .8 B6
Falconers Gn WA5 . . . . .7 B2
Falcons Way WA7 . . . . .49 E6
Falkirk Ave WA8 . . . . .12 F3
Fallbroome Cl SK10 . . . . . .111 E8
Fallbroome High Sch
SK10 . . . . .86 E2
Fallbroome Rd SK10 . . . . .111 E8
Fallon Ct CW10 . . . . .151 C7
Fallowfield WA7 . . . . .23 D1
Fallowfield Cl CW7 . . . . . .125 F1
Fallowfield Ct CW1 . . . . . .190 A6
Fallowfield Gr WA2 . . . . . . .9 B1
Falmouth Cl SK10 . . . . . . .111 E8
Falmouth Dr WA5 . . . . .14 E3
Falmouth Pl WA7 . . . . .50 E6
Falmouth Rd
Congleton CW12 . . . . .178 E8
Crewe CW1 . . . . .190 A6
Falstone Cl WA3 . . . . .10 B6
Falstone Dr WA7 . . . . .50 E7
Fanner's La WA16 . . . . .28 D5
Fanny's Croft ST7 . . . . . . .193 D2
Fanshawe La SK11 . . . . . . .110 E5
Fanshawe Wlk CW2 . . . . . .206 C3
Faraday Rd
Ellesmere Port CH65 . . . . . .70 A4
Runcorn WA7 . . . . .23 D3
Faraday St WA3 . . . . .9 E5
Farams Rd ST7 . . . . .193 E7
Farbailey Cl CH4 . . . . .141 B5
Farfields Cl SK11 . . . . .111 E1
Farley Cl CW10 . . . . .151 B8
Farm Cl CW8 . . . . .77 D1
Farm Dr CH5 . . . . .91 C1
Farm Hollow ST7 . . . . .210 A2
Farm La High Lane SK12 . . .38 A6
Warrington WA4 . . . . .26 E8
Withington Green SK11 . . . .108 C1
Farm Rd Northwich CW9 . .104 E7
Oakmere CW8 . . . . .124 A8
Weaverham CW8 . . . . .77 D1
Farm Way WA12 . . . . .2 E1
Farm Wlk WA14 . . . . .20 E1
Farmdale Dr CH2 . . . . .72 A3
Farmer Cl CW2 . . . . .190 A4
Farmer's La WA5 . . . . .7 A6
Farmers Heath CH66 . . . . .69 D2
Farmfield Dr SK10 . . . . .87 C3
Farmfields Rise CW3 . . . . .232 C1
Farmfold SK9 . . . . .33 F3
Farmleigh Dr CW1 . . . . . .189 F8
Farmleigh Gdns WA5 . . . . .15 C6
Farmside CW5 . . . . .15 F7
Farmstead Way CH66 . . . . .69 E1
Farndale WA8 . . . . .13 A5
Farndale Cl
Warrington WA5 . . . . .14 F7
Wistaston CW2 . . . . .206 A6
Farndale Wlk SK11 . . . . . . .112 C6
Farndon Cl
Broughton CH4 . . . . .139 C4
Cuddington CW8 . . . . .102 A3
Farndon Prim Sch CH3 . . .180 E2
Farndon Rd CH66 . . . . .69 E6
Farne Cl CH65 . . . . .95 C8
Farnham Ave SK11 . . . . . . .112 A6
Farnham Cl
Cheadle Hulme SK8 . . . . . . .35 A7
Warrington WA4 . . . . .26 E7
Farnhill Cl WA7 . . . . .50 D8
Farnley Cl WA7 . . . . .24 D1
Farnworth CE Prim Sch
WA8 . . . . .13 A4
Farnworth Cl WA8 . . . . .13 A4
Farnworth Rd WA5 . . . . . . .14 C4
Farnworth St WA8 . . . . .13 B4
Farr Hall Dr CH60 . . . . .40 E7
Farr Hall Rd CH60 . . . . .40 F8
Farrant St WA8 . . . . .23 B8
Farrell Rd WA4 . . . . .26 C8
Farrell St WA1 . . . . .16 D5
Farriers Way CW7 . . . . . . .126 A1
Farringdon Rd WA2 . . . . . . .8 B6
Farthing La CW9 . . . . .79 B8
Farthings The WA13 . . . . . .18 D4
Farwood Cl SK10 . . . . .86 F2
Faulkner Dr CW10 . . . . . . .151 E6
Faulkner St CH2 . . . . .118 F3
Faulkner's La WA16 . . . . . .58 E2
Faulkners Cl CH4 . . . . .161 A7
Faulkners La CH3 . . . . . . .142 D8
Fawns Keep SK9 . . . . .60 D7
Fawns Leap CW8 . . . . .101 E5
Fearndown Way SK10 . . . . .87 C4

Fearnhead Cross WA2 ....8 F2
Fearnhead La WA2 ....9 A2
Fearnley Way WA12 ......2 C1
Feather La CH60 ....40 F8
Feather's La CH1 ......237 B2
Feilden Ct CH1 ....94 F1
Felix Rd CW8 ....103 E8
Felskirk Rd M22 ....33 C8
Fence Ave SK10 ....112 E8
Fence Ave Ind Est SK10 112 E8
Fence Ct SK10 ....112 E8
Fence La CW12 ....178 D4
Fenham Dr WA5 ....14 F4
Fennel St WA1 ....16 C5
Fenton Cl
Congleton CW12 ....157 A1
Widnes WA8 ....12 C3
Fenwick La WA7 ....49 D6
Fenwick Rd CH66 ....69 E2
Ferguson Ave CH66 ......69 E6
Ferguson Dr WA2 ....8 D1
Ferma La CH3 ....120 D6
Fern Ave WA12 ....2 D2
Fern Cl
Mount Pleasant ST7 .....195 C6
Warrington WA3 ....9 D4
Fern Cres CW12 ....157 A3
Fern Ct CW1 ....190 E3
Fern Lea Dr SK11 ....112 A8
Fern Rd CH65 ....70 B2
Fern Way CW8 ....77 C1
Fernbank Cl Crewe CW1 .190 F3
Warrington WA3 ....9 E4
Winsford CW7 ....127 B1
Fernbank Rise SK10 .....88 B8
Ferndale SK9 ....34 D3
Ferndale Ave CH2 ....72 A3
Ferndale Cl
Bold Heath WA8 ....13 E7
Sandbach CW11 ....175 C5
Warrington WA1 ....17 C7
Weston CW2 ....207 B5
Ferndale Cres SK11 .....111 E7
Ferndale Gdns ST7 ......195 E3
Fernhill Rd CH1 ....117 E6
Fernhurst WA7 ....49 D8
Fernilee Cott SK23 ......65 E1
Fernlea Ct CH1 ....116 F8
Fernlea Rd Heswall CH60 .41 A8
Marston CW9 ....79 B6
Fernleaf Cl ST7 ....193 F8
Fernleigh CW8 ....103 C7
Fernleigh Cl
Middlewich CW10 ....151 E6
Winsford CW7 ....126 A1
Fernway CW7 ....127 B1
Fernwood WA7 ....24 B1
Fernwood Gr SK9 ....60 C8
Fernyess La CH64 ....67 E7
Ferrous Way M44 ....11 F6
Ferry Cl CH5 ....116 A6
Ferry La Sealand CH1 ...117 C1
Warrington WA4 ....17 E4
Ferry Rd CH62 ....44 A6
Festival Ave
Buerton CW3 ....230 E3
Warrington WA2 ....8 D2
Festival Cres WA2 ....8 D2
Festival Dr SK10 ....85 F6
Festival Hill CW12 .....156 F2
Festival Rd CH65 ....69 F5
Festival Way WA7 ....49 C8
Ffordd Cledwen/Cledwen Rd
CH4 ....139 D5
Ffordd Smithfield/Smithfield Dr LL13 ....196 D8
Fiddler's Ferry Rd WA8 ..13 D1
Fiddlers Ferry Rd WA8 ..23 C8
Fiddlers La CH1 ....94 C1
Field Ave CW2 ....189 F1
Field Cl Bollington SK10 ..87 F7
Bramhall SK7 ....35 D4
Northwich CW8 ....103 C7
Tarvin CH3 ....121 B2
Field Hey La CH64 ....43 B1
Field La Crewe CW2 .....189 E2
Tarvin CH3 ....121 B2
Tattenhall CH3 ....166 B1
Warrington WA4 ....26 C6
Field Side Cl WA16 .....58 A4
Field View ST8 ....179 D1
Field View Dr SK11 .....112 E5
Field Way ST7 ....193 E4
Field Wlk M31 ....11 E3
Fieldbank Rd SK11 ......112 B8
Fieldfare CW7 ....150 A8
Fieldfare Cl Golborne WA3 .3 D8
Warrington WA3 ....9 F4
Fieldgate WA8 ....22 B6
Fieldhead Mews SK9 .....60 E8
Fieldhead Rd SK9 ....60 E8
Fieldhouse Row WA7 .....49 D7
Fielding Ave SK12 ....36 E2
Fields Cl ST7 ....193 E4
Fields Dr CW11 ....175 A5
Fields Rd Alsager ST7 ..193 E3
Congleton CW12 ....178 F8
Haslington CW1 ....191 D4
Fields The CW5 ....205 D5
Fields View SY13 ....228 D1
Fields View Cl CW5 .....220 B8
Fieldsend Dr WN7 ....4 C8
Fieldside CW6 ....145 B6
Fieldside Cl CW4 ....107 E1
Fieldside Ct CW4 ....139 B4
Fieldsway WA7 ....49 A6
Fieldview Dr WA2 ....8 C1
Fieldway Chester CH2 ...118 E4
Fieldway *continued*
Ellesmere Port CH66 ......69 B7
Frodsham WA6 ....74 C7
Saughall CH1 ....94 A2
Weaverham CW8 ....77 C1
Widnes WA8 ....13 E2
Fieldways WA13 ....18 C4
Fife Rd WA1 ....16 E7
Fifth Ave Kidsgrove ST7 ..194 E1
2 Runcorn WA7 ....49 F7
Fildes Cl WA5 ....15 C5
Filkin's La CH3 ....119 A1
Finch La L26 ....21 B7
Finchdale Gdns WA3 ......4 B8
Finchett Ct CH1 ....118 B3
Finchett Dr CH1 ....118 B3
Findlay Cl WA12 ....2 C2
Finger Post La WA6 .....101 A4
Finlan Rd WA8 ....22 F7
Finlay Ave WA5 ....14 E3
Finlow Hill La SK10 .....85 E6
Finney Cl SK9 ....34 C2
Finney Dr SK9 ....34 C2
Finney Gr WA11 ....1 E6
Finney La SK8 ....34 B8
Finney's La CW10 ....128 B2
Finningley Ct WA2 ....8 E1
Finsbury Cl WA5 ....15 C4
Finsbury Pk WA8 ....13 C5
Finsbury Way SK9 ....34 E2
Finsbury Wlk CW7 ....149 A8
Fir Ave Bramhall SK7 .....35 E8
Halewood L26 ....21 A8
Fir Cl Halewood L26 ......21 A8
Poynton SK12 ....36 F3
Tarporley CW6 ....146 D2
Fir Ct SK10 ....86 F1
Fir Gr Macclesfield SK11 .112 D5
Warrington WA1 ....16 F7
Weaverham CW8 ....102 E8
Fir La CW8 ....102 A2
Fir Rd SK7 ....35 E8
Fir St Irlam M44 ....11 D6
Widnes WA8 ....13 C2
Fir Tree Ave Chester CH4 141 B5
Golborne WA3 ....3 F8
Knutsford WA16 ....82 C8
Fir Tree Cl WA4 ....26 D1
Fir Tree Cotts CW2 .....208 C5
Fir Tree La
Burtonwood WA5 ....7 A7
Chester CH3 ....119 E2
Faddiley CW5 ....202 B3
Fir Tree Wlk WA3 ....3 F8
Fir Trees Holiday Pk
CH1 ....117 C2
Fir Way CH60 ....41 B5
Firbank CH2 ....72 C3
Firbank Cl WA7 ....24 D1
Firbeck Cl
Broughton CH4 ....139 B3
Congleton CW12 ....155 F3
Firbeck Gdns CW2 ....189 D4
Firdale Rd CW8 ....103 D7
Firecrest Ct WA1 ....16 A3
Firemans Sq CH1 ....237 A3
Firman Cl WA5 ....15 B8
Firs La WA4 ....26 B6
Firs Pottery The★ CW5 .217 C1
Firs Sch CH2 ....118 E5
Firs The SK9 ....60 A5
Firs View WA6 ....73 D4
First Ave
Connah's Quay CH5 ......93 A2
Crewe CW1 ....190 F2
Kidsgrove ST7 ....194 E1
Poynton SK12 ....36 D1
Sandbach CW11 ....175 A5
First Dig La CW5 ....219 C8
First Wood St CW5 ......204 D5
Firth Fields CW9 ....103 F2
Firthfields Cl CW9 .....103 F2
Firtree Ave WA1 ....17 A8
Firtree Cl Barnton CW8 ...78 B4
Winsford CW7 ....127 B1
Firtree Gr CH66 ....95 A8
Firwood Rd ST8 ....179 E1
Firwood Wlk CW2 ....190 C1
Fisher Ave WA2 ....8 B2
Fisher Rd CH1 ....117 E4
Fisher St WA7 ....23 B3
Fisherfield Dr WA3 ......10 A6
Fishermans Cl CW11 .....191 F7
Fishers Gn CW6 ....146 B5
Fishers La CW5 ....203 C8
Fishpool Rd CW8 ....123 F3
Fishwicks Ind Est WA11 ....1 F8
Fistral Ave SK8 ....34 C8
Fitton St CW9 ....80 A2
Fitton's Cl CW5 ....217 F5
Fitz Cl SK10 ....87 D3
Fitz Cres SK10 ....87 D3
Fitzherbert St WA2 ......16 C7
Fitzwalter Rd WA1 ....17 D7
Fitzwilliam Ave SK11 ...112 F3
Fitzwilliam Wlk WA7 .....24 A2
Five Ashes Rd CH4 ......141 B5
Five Ways CH64 ....41 F3
Fiveashes Cotts SK10 ....88 B5
Fivelanes End WA6 ....74 C6
Fiveways Par SK7 ....36 E8
Fiveways Pk CH64 ....41 F3
Flacca Ct CH3 ....166 B1
Flag La Crewe CW1,CW2 .190 C4
Neston CH64 ....66 F7
Flag La N CH2 ....118 E8
Flag La S CH2 ....118 E8
Flander Cl WA8 ....12 C2
Flash La Antrobus CW9 ...53 F5
Bollington SK10 ....87 D7
Flashes La CH64 ....67 B5
Flat La Kelsall CW6 ....122 C4
Sandbach CW11 ....175 B6
Flatt La CH65 ....70 B5
Flatts La SK23 ....64 F4
Flavian Cl CW10 ....128 C2
Flavian Ct WA7 ....23 E2
Flaxley Cl WA3 ....10 A5
Flaxmere Dr CH3 ....142 B8
Flaxyards CW6 ....146 F2
Fleet La WA9 ....1 A2
Fleet St CH65 ....70 A5
Fleetwood Cl WA5 ....15 B4
Fleetwood Dr WA12 ....2 B4
Fleetwood Wlk WA7 ....50 C6
Fleming Dr WA2 ....8 A6
Fleming St CH65 ....70 C6
Flers Ave WA4 ....16 C3
Fletcher Ct WA16 ....56 F1
Fletcher Dr SK12 ....37 F6
Fletcher Gr CW9 ....104 C6
Fletcher St Crewe CW1 ..190 B5
Warrington WA4 ....16 B3
Fletcher's Bldgs
Chester CH1 ....237 B2
6 Runcorn WA7 ....23 F1
Fletcher's Row 5 WA7 ...23 F1
Fletchers La WA13 ....18 F4
Fletsand Rd SK9 ....60 D6
Flexible House Havannah Bsns Ctr 6 CW12 .....156 F4
Flint Cl CH64 ....66 E6
Flint Ct CH65 ....70 D2
Flint Dr CH64 ....66 E6
Flint Gr M44 ....11 C6
Flint Mdw CH64 ....66 E7
Flint St SK10 ....112 E8
Flittogate La WA16 ......80 E8
Flixton Dr CW2 ....190 A2
Florence St WA4 ....16 D3
Florida Cl WA5 ....15 C7
Flour Mill Way CW1 ....191 A3
Flowcrete Bsns Pk
CW11 ....152 C1
Flower St CW8 ....103 E7
Flowers La CW1 ....172 E1
Flowerscroft CW5 ....205 A4
Fluin La WA6 ....74 C8
Flying Fields Dr SK11 ..112 A5
Foden Ave ST7 ....194 A3
Foden La
Alderley Edge SK9 ....59 C1
Bramhall SK7 ....35 D3
Foden St SK10 ....87 D1
Foden Wlk 7 SK9 ....34 D2
Fodens Terr CW11 ....175 A6
Fog Cotts CW3 ....221 E4
Fogg's La CW9,WA4 ....53 A6
Fol Hollow CW12 ....156 B1
Fold La Biddulph ST8 ...179 E4
Bosley SK11 ....135 D2
Fold The SK10 ....87 A8
Folds La SK23 ....65 F3
Folds The CH63 ....42 A6
Foley Wlk M22 ....33 E8
Folkestone Cl SK10 ......87 B2
Folkestone Way WA7 ......50 C7
Folly La WA5 ....15 F7
Forbes Cl WA3 ....9 E3
Forbes Pk SK7 ....35 D7
Ford Cl CW1 ....190 B5
Ford Ct CW7 ....149 C6
Ford La Crewe CW1 ......190 B6
Tattenhall CH3 ....166 F4
Ford St WA1 ....16 D6
Ford's La SK7 ....35 D6
Fordington Rd WA5 ....15 B5
Fords La ST7 ....195 D6
Fordsham Manor House Prim Sch WA6 ....49 C1
Fordsham Weaver Vale Prim Sch WA6 ....49 C2
Fordton Leisure Ctr WA2 .8 A3
Foregate St CH1 ....237 B2
Foreland Cl WA5 ....14 C7
Forest Ave CW4 ....107 C1
Forest Cl
Cuddington CW8 ....101 F3
Rainow SK10 ....88 E5
Forest Dr Broughton CH4 139 C3
Langley SK11 ....113 C4
Forest Gate Com Prim Sch
M31 ....11 D3
Forest Gate La CW6 .....122 E7
Forest Gdns M31 ....11 D3
Forest Ho SK10 ....87 F2
Forest La WA6 ....100 C6
Forest Pl 3 CW9 ....79 A1
Forest Rd
Cuddington CW8 ....101 F2
Delamere CW6 ....124 B1
Ellesmere Port CH66 ......69 E7
Heswall CH60 ....41 A8
Macclesfield SK11 ......113 E6
Tarporley CW6 ....146 D3
Winsford CW7 ....149 B8
Forest Road Pk CW8 .....101 E2
Forest St Chester CH1 ..237 C2
Weaverham CW8 ....102 C8
Forest Wlk 5 WA7 ....49 F7
Forester Ave WA16 ....57 C2
Foresters Cl WA6 ....101 A6
Forge Cl Cronton WA8 ....12 C5
Warren SK11 ....111 D2
Forge Fields CW11 ......174 F3
Forge La Congleton CW12 156 B3
Forge La *continued*
Norton in Hales TF9 .....236 C1
Forge Mill La CW10 .....151 C1
Forge Rd
Ellesmere Port CH66 ......69 C6
Warrington WA5 ....14 F5
Whaley Bridge SK23 ......65 E7
Forge Sh Ctr The WA4 ...16 C1
Forge St CW1 ....190 D4
Forge Way CH4 ....140 F4
Formby Cl WA5 ....14 F4
Formby Dr SK8 ....34 B8
Forrest Way WA5 ....15 D3
Forshaw St WA2 ....16 C7
Forshaw's La WA5 ....6 E8
Forster Ave CW8 ....102 E8
Forster St WA2 ....16 B7
Forsythia Wlk 2 M31 ....11 E2
Forty Acre La CW4,
CW12 ....131 D6
Forum The CH1 ....237 A2
Forwood Rd CH62 ....43 D8
Fossa Cl CW10 ....128 C2
Foster Rd CW12 ....157 A5
Foster St WA8 ....13 B1
Fothergill Grange SK8 ...35 A8
Fothergill St WA1 ....16 D7
Fotheringay Ct 3 CH65 ...70 D2
Foulkes Ave CW1 ....189 F6
Foundry Bank CW12 ......156 E3
Foundry Ct SK22 ....39 C7
Foundry La
Sandbach CW11 ....174 D7
Scholar Green ST7 ......194 F7
Widnes WA8 ....22 C5
Foundry St
Bollington SK10 ....88 B8
Newton-le-W WA12 ....2 B3
Warrington WA2 ....16 B6
Fountain Cl SK12 ....36 D4
Fountain Ct
Biddulph ST8 ....179 D1
Davenham CW9 ....103 F2
2 Winsford CW7 ....126 D1
Fountain Ho SK10 ....112 E8
Fountain La
Davenham CW9 ....103 F2
Frodsham WA6 ....74 A8
Fountain Pl SK12 ....36 D4
Fountain Sq SK12 ....38 C6
Fountain St
Congleton CW12 ....156 D2
Macclesfield SK11 ......112 E8
Fountains Ave WA11 ....1 F7
Fountains Cl
Middlewich CW10 ....128 B1
Runcorn WA7 ....50 C5
Fountains Rd SK7,SK8 ....35 C6
Fountains Wlk WA3 ....4 B8
Four Lane Ends
Alvanley WA6 ....74 B1
Warrington WA3 ....9 D3
Four Lanes Ct 2 CW7 ...149 B8
Four Lanes End
Betley CW2 ....207 F2
Thornton Hough CH63 .....42 D5
Fourlanes End CW11 .....176 E4
Fourseasons Cl CW2 .....206 B8
Fourth Ave
Connah's Quay CH5 ......92 E2
Crewe CW1 ....190 F1
Kidsgrove ST7 ....194 F1
1 Runcorn WA7 ....49 F7
Fourways CW2 ....207 B5
Fourways Tech Pk
CW11 ....176 E4
Fowey Cl SK10 ....86 D1
Fowler Rd CH1 ....117 D4
Fowler St SK10 ....87 D1
Fowlers Bench La CH3 .184 C5
Fowley Common La WA3 ..5 C5
Fox Bank Cl WA8 ....12 F4
Fox Bench Cl SK7 ....35 C6
Fox Cover CH3 ....119 F5
Fox Cover Rd CH60 ....41 D7
Fox Covert WA7 ....50 C7
Fox Covert La
Hoole Bank CH2 ....119 B8
Picton CH2 ....96 A1
Fox Covert Way CW1 .....173 A1
Fox Gdns Lymm WA13 .....18 C4
Talke ST7 ....210 D8
Fox Gr WA16 ....57 C1
Fox Hill CW6 ....122 D4
Fox La Clutton CH3 .....182 D1
Waverton CH3 ....143 B5
Fox Lea CH1 ....117 A8
Fox St Congleton CW12 ..156 F3
Runcorn WA7 ....23 A1
Warrington WA5 ....15 E5
Fox Wood Sch WA3 ....9 E3
Fox's Dr CH5 ....116 A6
Foxall Way CH66 ....69 D2
Foxcote WA8 ....12 B2
Foxcote Cl CH1 ....117 D5
Foxcovert La WA16 ......106 E7
Foxdale Ct WA4 ....26 C7
Foxendale Cl CW8 ....103 D7
Foxes Covert CW11 ......154 B1
Foxes Fold CW8 ....78 E1
Foxes Hey CW8 ....101 D5
Foxes Hollow CW1 ....190 E7
Foxes Wlk CH3 ....142 A7
Foxfield Cl WA2 ....8 E3
Foxfield La CW7 ....126 A1
Foxglove Cl
Bollington SK10 ....88 C8
2 Golborne WA3 ....3 D8
Foxglove Cl *continued*
Huntington CH3 ....142 A6
Wistaston CW2 ....206 B7
Foxglove Ct WA6 ....74 C8
Foxglove Dell WA6 ....73 D2
Foxglove Way CH64 ......66 E5
Foxglove Wlk M31 ....11 F2
Foxhill Ct CW6 ....146 E1
Foxhill Gr WA6 ....73 D4
Foxhills Cl WA4 ....26 D3
Foxhunter Cl CH3 ....121 F7
Foxlea CW9 ....78 C7
Foxley Cl WA13 ....19 A2
Foxley Hall Mews WA13 .19 A1
Foxley Heath WA8 ....22 E8
Foxwist Cl CH2 ....237 B4
Foxwist Gn CW8 ....125 E6
Foxwood Dr WA16 ....108 A8
Frances St Crewe CW2 ..190 D2
Irlam M44 ....11 E5
Macclesfield SK11 ......112 B8
Francesca Ct CH1 ....237 B2
Francis Cl WA8 ....22 C8
Francis Ct CH1 ....237 C3
Francis La Holt LL13 ...196 B6
Holt LL13 ....196 D7
Francis Rd Frodsham WA6 49 C1
Irlam M44 ....11 F8
Warrington WA4 ....16 B1
Francis St CH1 ....237 C3
Frank Bott Ave CW1 .....190 A7
Frank Perkins Way M44 ...11 F7
Frank St WA8 ....13 C1
Frank Webb Ave CW1 ....190 A6
Franklin Cl
Macclesfield SK11 ......112 B5
Warrington WA5 ....15 C8
Franklyn Ave CW2 ....190 B3
Fraser Ct CH4 ....141 D7
Fraser Rd WA5 ....14 D6
Frawley Ave WA12 ....2 C5
Freckleton Cl WA5 ....15 B4
Frederick St
Warrington WA4 ....16 E3
Widnes WA8 ....23 B8
Frederick Terr WA8 ......22 A4
Fredric Pl WA7 ....23 B3
Free Green La WA16 .....107 A8
Freedom Dr ST7 ....195 E3
French La CW5 ....218 C5
French Lane End CW5 ...218 E5
French St WA8 ....13 D1
Freshfield SK8 ....34 B8
Freshfield Dr SK10 ....87 C3
Freshfields
Comberbach CW9 ....78 C7
Knutsford WA16 ....56 E3
Wistaston CW2 ....206 A7
Freshfields Dr WA2 ....9 C1
Freshmeadow La WA6 ....73 B2
Freshwater Cl WA5 ......14 D7
Freshwater Dr CW2 ......221 C8
Friar's Cl SK9 ....59 E8
Friars Ave WA5 ....14 E5
Friars Cl Rainow SK10 ...88 D5
Wistaston CW2 ....205 F8
Friars Ct 12 WA1 ....16 B5
Friars Gate Chester CH1 .237 B2
Warrington WA1 ....16 B4
Friars La WA1 ....16 B4
Friars Way SK10 ....86 F2
Frida Cres CW9 ....103 E6
Friends La WA5 ....14 D6
Friesian Gdns ST5 ......210 C2
Frith Ave CW8 ....123 D8
Frith La CW5 ....216 C4
Frith Terr SK11 ....112 D4
Frobisher Ct WA5 ....15 D8
Frobisher Rd CH64 ....66 E8
Froda Ave WA6 ....74 B7
Frodsham Bsns Ctr WA6 .49 C1
Frodsham CE Prim Sch
WA6 ....74 C7
Frodsham Rd WA6 ....73 D1
Frodsham Sch WA6 ....74 B8
Frodsham Sq CH1 ....237 B3
Frodsham St CH1 ....237 B3
Frodsham Sta WA6 ....74 B8
Frodsham Way SK9 ....34 E4
Frog La Holt LL13 ......196 D8
Milton Green CH3 ......165 E2
Pickmere WA16 ....55 B1
Worthenbury LL13,SY14 ..211 B1
Worthenbury SY14 ......211 C2
Froghall La
High Legh WA16 ....29 D7
High Legh WA16 ....29 E6
Warrington WA2,WA5 .....15 F5
Frome Ct CH65 ....70 B7
Front St CW11 ....175 C6
Frosts Mews CH65 ....70 B6
Fryer Rd CW9 ....80 A3
Fryer St 16 WA7 ....23 A3
Fuchsia Cl CH66 ....69 F1
Fulbeck WA8 ....12 C2
Fulbeck Cl CW2 ....206 B8
Fulbrook Dr SK8 ....35 A6
Fuller Dr CW2 ....206 B7
Fullerton Rd CW8 ....103 A4
Fulmar Cl SK12 ....36 A4
Fulmards Cl SK9 ....60 C7
Fulshaw Ave SK9 ....60 A6
Fulshaw Cross SK9 ....60 A5
Fulshaw Ct SK9 ....60 A5
Fulshaw Pk SK9 ....60 A5

Fulshaw Pk S SK9 60 A4
Fulton Gr CW9 103 F2
Fulwood Gdns CH66 69 C6
Fulwood Mews CH66 69 C6
Fulwood Rd
Ellesmere Port CH66 69 C5
Golborne WA3 3 E7
Furber St CW1 190 C5
Furne Rd CH1 117 E4
Furness Cl
Holmes Chapel CW4 130 A3
Poynton SK12 36 D4
Winsford CW7 149 B8
Furness Ct WA7 24 F4
Furness Lodge Cl SK23 39 D4
Furness Rd SK8 35 C6
Furness Vale Bsns Ctr SK23 39 D4
Furness Vale Prim Sch SK23 39 D3
Furness Vale Sta SK23 39 D4
Furnival St CW2 190 C2
Furnivall St CW11 175 B7
Furrocks Cl CH64 66 F5
Furrocks La CH64 66 F5
Furrocks Way CH64 66 F5
Furrows The CH66 94 E8
Fylde Ave SK8 34 C8
Fytton Cl SK11 111 D1

G

Gable Ave SK9 60 A7
Gable Ct 5 CW5 204 E6
Gable St WA12 2 B3
Gables Cl WA2 8 F3
Gables The ST7 193 C3
Gabriel Bank CW8 76 A1
Gadbrook Bsns Ctr CW9 104 D5
Gadbrook Pk CW9 104 D5
Gadbrook Rd CW9 104 D6
Gail Cl SK9 60 B2
Gainford Cl WA8 12 C3
Gainsborough Cl SK9 60 D8
Gainsborough Ct WA8 12 B1
Gainsborough Inf Sch CW2 190 B3
Gainsborough Jun Sch CW2 190 B2
Gainsborough Rd
Crewe CW2 190 B3
Warrington WA4 16 B2
Gairloch Cl WA2 8 F4
Gaisgill Ct WA8 12 C1
Gala Cl CH4 139 C3
Galbraith Cl CW12 156 C2
Gale Ave WA5 7 F1
Galion Way WA8 12 F3
Galleys Bank ST7 195 B3
Gallimore Ho ST7 210 D8
Galloway Cl
Holmes Chapel CW4 130 C2
Middlewich CW10 128 E2
Gallowsclough La WA6 100 F4
Galway Ave WA8 12 E3
Galway Gr CW2 206 B4
Game St CW11 175 A3
Gamul Pl CH1 237 B1
Ganton Cl WA8 13 B4
Garden Cl SK10 87 E1
Garden Ct CH1 237 A3
Garden La Chester CH1 237 A3
Harthill CH3 183 E3
Garden Rd WA16 56 F3
Garden St Bollington SK10 87 F8
Congleton CW12 156 C3
Macclesfield SK10 87 E1
Garden Terr
Chester CH1 237 A3
Chester,Boughton CH2 118 F2
Garden Villas SK8 34 B7
Garden Wlk M31 11 E3
Gardens The Holt LL13 180 E1
Sandbach CW11 175 B6
Gardiner Ave WA11 1 C6
Garfit St CW10 128 C2
Garner St WA2 16 C7
Garnett Ave WA4 17 A4
Garnett Cl CW5 204 F4
Garnetts La WA8 22 A3
Garrett Field WA3 9 D5
Garrigill Cl WA8 13 C5
Garsdale Cl WA5 14 F7
Garside Ave WA3 3 D7
Garth Dr CH2 118 C5
Garth Hts SK9 60 C7
Garth Rd CH65 71 A5
Garton Dr WA3 3 E8
Garven Pl WA1 16 A5
Garwood Cl WA5 15 C8
Gas Rd SK11 112 D8
Gas Works Ind Est ST7 194 E2
Gaskell Ave
Knutsford WA16 56 F2
Warrington WA4 17 A3
Gaskell St WA4 16 C1
Gatcombe Mews 1 SK9 60 A6
Gate Warth St WA5 15 D4
Gateacre Ct CH66 69 F8
Gatefield St CW1 190 C4
Gateley Cl WA4 17 E3
Gatesheath Dr CH2 118 E7
Gatesheath La CH3 165 F5
Gatewarth Ind Est WA5 15 D3
Gateway Crewe CW1 190 F2
Newcastle-u-Lyme ST5 210 D2
Gathurst Ct WA8 22 D8
Gauntley Bird of Prey Ctr★ SK10 85 B2
Gauntons Bank SY13 215 E3
Gaunts Way WA7 49 E6
Gavin Rd WA8 22 B7
Gaw End La SK11 112 C2
Gawer Pk CH2 118 C4
Gawsworth Ave CW2 189 F3
Gawsworth Cl
Alsager ST7 193 C3
Bramhall SK7 35 E6
Holmes Chapel CW4 130 B3
Northwich CW9 104 A4
Poynton SK12 36 F2
Gawsworth Ct WA3 9 F5
Gawsworth Dr CW11 175 C7
Gawsworth Hall★ SK11 134 E8
Gawsworth Prim Sch SK11 111 D2
Gawsworth Rd
Ellesmere Port CH66 69 E5
Macclesfield SK11 111 D5
Gawsworth Way SK9 34 E4
Gayhurst Ave WA2 8 F2
Gaymoore Cl CH2 237 A4
Gaynor Ave WA11 1 F7
Gayton Cl CH2 118 E5
Gayton Farm Rd CH60 41 A5
Gayton La CH60 41 B6
Gayton Mill Cl CH60 41 B7
Gayton Parkway CH60 41 C5
Gayton Prim Sch CH60 41 A6
Gayton Rd CH60 41 A6
Gemini Bsns Pk WA5 7 E3
Gemmull Cl CW3 229 F4
General St WA1 16 C5
Genesis Ctr The WA3 9 E5
Geneva Rd CW7 126 C1
Geo Hampson's Bldgs WA3 5 C8
George Bates Cl ST7 193 C3
George Ho CW5 204 E7
George Kenyon Mews CH4 140 E6
George Rd WA5 15 C4
George St
Alderley Edge SK9 60 A1
Audley ST7 209 D1
Barnton CW8 78 B3
Chester CH1 237 A3
Ellesmere Port CH65 70 C7
Knutsford WA16 57 A2
Macclesfield SK11 112 D7
Newton-le-W WA12 2 A4
Sandbach CW11 174 E8
Whaley Bridge SK23 65 E7
Winsford CW7 126 E1
George St W SK11 112 C8
George VI Ave CW10 151 D6
George VI Cl CW10 151 D6
George's Cl SK12 36 E3
George's La CW9 54 D1
George's Prec WA5 14 D6
George's Rd E SK12 36 E3
George's Rd W SK12 36 E3
George's Wlk CW11 175 B6
Georges Cres WA4 17 B2
Georges Ct 13 SK10 112 C8
Georges Way ST7 209 F2
Georgia Pl WA5 15 C7
Gerard Dr CW5 204 C4
Gerosa Ave WA2 8 B8
Gerrard Ave
Ellesmere Port CH66 69 C4
Warrington WA5 15 F7
Gerrard Dr CW8 77 D1
Gerrard Rd WA3 9 A7
Gerrard St WA8 23 B8
Gerrards Ave CH3 119 A1
Giantswood La
Congleton CW12 156 C6
Marton CW12 132 F1
Gibb Hill CW9 53 D1
Gibbon Dr CW9 80 B3
Gibson Cl CW5 204 D6
Gibson Cres CW11 174 D6
Gibson Ct Trad Est CH65 70 C8
Gibson St
Warrington, Howley WA1 16 C5
Warrington, Stockton Heath WA4 16 D1
Gig La WA1 17 E8
Gigg La Moore WA4 25 B5
Warrington WA4 17 E3
Gilbert Cl 2 ST7 195 A2
Gilbert Cl WA3 4 F3
Gilchrist Ave SK11 111 E7
Gilchrist Rd M44 11 F6
Gilderdale Cl WA3 10 B5
Gillan Cl WA7 50 C5
Gillbent Rd SK8 35 A7
Gillow Cl CW1 190 A8
Giltbrook Cl WA8 12 F3
Gilwell Cl WA4 17 C2
Gingerbread La CW5 205 A5
Gipsy Cnr SY13 224 E2
Girton Cl CH65 70 D4
Girton Rd CH65 70 D4
Girvin Dr CH64 66 F6
Gladewood Cl 1 SK9 60 C8
Gladstone Ave CH1 118 B2
Gladstone Rd
Broughton CH4 139 B3
Chester CH1 118 B3
Gladstone Rd *continued*
Neston CH64 66 E8
Gladstone St Crewe CW1 190 C4
Northwich CW8 103 E7
Warrington WA2 16 A6
8 Widnes WA8 23 B8
Willaston CW5 205 D6
Winsford CW7 149 D8
Gladstone Way WA12 2 B4
Glaisdale Cl CW2 206 A6
Glamis Cl Chester CH3 119 A2
Wistaston CW2 205 E8
Glan Aber Dr CH4 140 F7
Glan Aber Pk CH4 141 A7
Glanaber Ct CH4 141 A7
Glandon Dr SK8 35 C8
Glastonbury Ave
Cheadle Hulme SK8 35 C6
Chester CH2 118 F7
Golborne WA3 4 C8
Glastonbury Cl WA7 24 F3
Glastonbury Dr
Middlewich CW10 128 B1
Poynton SK12 36 D5
Glastonbury Mews WA4 16 E2
Glazebrook La WA3 11 B5
Glazebrook St WA1 16 D6
Glazebrook Sta WA3 11 B5
Glazebury CE Prim Sch WA3 5 C7
Glaziers La WA3 4 D2
Gleadmere WA8 12 C2
Gleaner Cl WA7 22 F3
Gleave Ave SK10 88 B8
Gleave Rd Burtonwood WA5 6 F6
Weaverham CW8 77 D1
Glebe Ave WA4 17 C1
Glebe Cl CW5 220 A8
Glebe Farm Mews CH2 71 E2
Glebe Green Dr CW7 149 C6
Glebe La WA8 13 B5
Glebe Mdws CH2 96 F1
Glebe Rd CW8 102 A4
Glebe St ST7 194 D2
Glebe The WA7 23 E1
Glebecroft Ave CH2 72 A3
Glebeland WA3 4 E2
Glebelands Rd WA16 57 A1
Glebeway Rd CH65 70 F5
Glegg St SK11 112 E7
Gleggs Cl CH3 142 B7
Glen Cl WA3 11 B2
Glen Rd CH66 69 C4
Glen The Blacon CH1 117 E5
Runcorn WA7 49 F5
Glenathol Rd CH66 69 C4
Glenbourne Pk SK7 35 D5
Glenburn Ave CH62 43 E4
Glencoe Cl CW4 130 C2
Glencoe Rd CH66 69 C4
Glencourse Rd WA8 13 A5
Glendale Ave Elton CH2 72 A3
Sandycroft CH5 116 A3
Glendale Bsns Pk CH5 116 A3
Glendale Cl Buerton CW3 230 F4
Crewe CW2 189 D3
Glendale Pk CH5 116 A3
Glendene Ave SK7 35 D5
Glendyke Rd CH66 69 C4
Gleneagles Cl
Bramhall SK7 36 A7
Chester CH3 119 B3
Golborne WA3 3 F7
Wilmslow SK9 60 D8
Gleneagles Dr
Haydock WA11 1 A5
Holmes Chapel CW4 130 B2
Macclesfield SK10 87 C4
Widnes WA8 13 B5
Winsford CW7 126 C2
Gleneagles Rd CH66 69 C4
Glenesk Rd CH66 69 C4
Glenfield Dr SK12 36 D3
Glenholme Rd SK7 35 D7
Glenmaye Rd CH66 69 C4
Glenn Pl WA8 12 E1
Glenorchy Cl CW4 130 C2
Glenside Cl CH1 117 D5
Glenside Dr SK9 60 C6
Glenton Pk CH64 66 F6
Glenville Cl WA7 49 B6
Glenwood WA7 24 C1
Glenwood Cl 3 CH66 69 C6
Glenwood Gdns CH66 69 C6
Glenwood Rd CH66 69 C6
Gleyve WA16 29 C5
Gloucester Ave WA3 3 B8
Gloucester Cl
Ellesmere Port CH66 94 E8
Macclesfield SK10 87 E4
Warrington WA1 17 D7
Gloucester Rd
Heald Green SK8 34 C7
Kidsgrove ST7 195 A3
Knutsford WA16 81 F8
Poynton SK12 36 D4
Widnes WA8 13 B3
Gloucester St CH1 237 B4
Glover Rd WA3 9 C4
Glover St Crewe CW1 190 A5
Newton-le-W WA12 2 C3
Glovers Loom CH3 142 B7
Gloverstone Ct CH1 237 B1
Glyn Ave CH62 43 E7
Glyn Garth CH1 117 D3
Goathland Way SK11 112 D6
Goddard Rd WA7 23 E3
Goddard St CW1 190 B5
Godfrey St WA2 16 D7
Godscroft La WA6 73 E6
Godshill Cl WA5 14 D7
Godstall La CH1 237 B2
Godstow WA7 24 E4
Godward Rd SK22 39 B8
Golborne Dale Rd WA3, WA12 3 A5
Golborne Jun & Inf Sch WA3 3 A8
Golborne La WA16 28 F3
Golborne Rd Golborne WA3 3 C8
Winwick WA12,WA2 8 A7
Golborne St
Newton-le-W WA12 2 E4
Warrington WA1 16 A5
Gold Triangle Complex WA8 22 C5
Goldcliffe Cl WA5 7 D3
Goldcrest Cl Runcorn WA7 49 F5
Winsford CW7 149 C5
Golden Sq WA1 16 B5
Goldfinch Cl CW12 156 E1
Goldfinch Dr ST7 193 B3
Goldfinch La WA3 9 E4
Goldfinch Rd ST7 195 F1
Goldford La SY14 199 F6
Goldsmith Dr CW11 174 D6
Golftyn Dr CH5 91 C1
Golftyn La CH5 91 C1
Gongar La
Ashton Hayes CH3 121 E8
Mouldsworth CH3 98 E1
Gonsley Cl CH2 237 B4
Gonville Ave SK11 112 F3
Gooch Dr WA12 2 D2
Goodall St SK11 112 E7
Goodall's Cnr CW2 206 C3
Goodrington Rd SK9 34 E3
Goodwin Cres CW2 206 C4
Goodwood Cl
Barnton CW8 78 B3
Chester CH1 118 B2
Goodwood Gr CH66 69 D3
Goodwood Rise CW10 128 A2
Goose La WA4 26 A2
Gooseberry La
Kelsall CW6 122 E3
Runcorn WA7 24 D1
Goosebrook Cl CW9 78 D8
Goosebrook La WA4,CW9 52 F2
Goosetrey Cl SK9 34 E1
Goostrey Com Prim Sch CW4 130 F8
Goostrey Com Prim Sch (The Annexe) CW4 107 F1
Goostrey Ct 4 CW12 156 F3
Goostrey La
Goostrey CW4 130 B8
Holmes Chapel CW4 131 A6
Goostrey Sta CW4 131 A8
Goostry La WA16 108 A7
Gordale Cl
Congleton CW12 157 A5
Northwich CW8 103 D8
Warrington WA5 14 F7
Winnington CW8 78 D1
Gordon Ave
Bebington CH62 43 E7
Haydock WA11 1 F7
Warrington WA1 17 B7
Gordon La CH1 95 B5
Gore La SK9 59 C3
Gorran Haven WA7 50 C5
Gorse Bank Rd WA15 32 C7
Gorse Cl WA6 101 A6
Gorse Covert CW9 79 C3
Gorse Covert Prim Sch WA3 10 B5
Gorse Covert Rd WA3 10 B6
Gorse La CW12 178 D5
Gorse Sq M31 11 D3
Gorse Stacks CH1 237 B3
Gorse The WA14 31 B8
Gorse Way CH3 142 A5
Gorsefield CH3 166 A1
Gorsefield Ave CH62 43 D5
Gorsefield Cl CH62 43 D5
Gorsefield Hey SK9 60 E8
Gorselands SK8 35 B5
Gorsewood Prim Sch WA7 50 D7
Gorsewood Rd WA7 50 D6
Gorsey Bank Cres CW5 220 A8
Gorsey Bank Prim Sch SK9 59 F7
Gorsey La
Partington WA13 20 B7
St Helens WA5,WA9 6 C5
Warrington WA1,WA2 16 D7
Widnes WA8 13 E1
Gorsey Rd SK9 59 F8
Gorseywell La WA7 50 F6
Gorsley Cl CW10 151 C6
Gorstage La CW8 102 C7
Gorsthills Com Prim Sch CH66 69 C3
Gorston Wlk M22 33 C8
Gorstons La CH64 67 A6
Gorsty Hill Cl CW2 207 F2
Gosberryhole La CW12 158 A2
Gosforth Ct WA7 49 E7
Gosforth Pl CH2 118 F3
Gosling Cl WA4 26 A1
Gosling Rd WA3 9 B7
Gosling Way CW12 156 A3
Gosport Cl WA2 8 F1
Goss St CH1 237 A2
Gough Ave WA2 8 B2
Gough's La WA16 82 C7
Goulden St Crewe CW1 190 A5
Warrington WA5 15 E6
Goulders Ct WA7 50 B5
Gowy Cl Alsager ST7 192 F3
Handforth SK9 34 E1
Sandbach CW11 174 E8
Gowy Cres CH3 121 B2
Gowy Ct Alpraham CW6 169 E2
Ellesmere Port CH66 69 E8
Gowy Rd CH2 96 F1
Gowy Wlk CW7 127 A3
Goyt Pl SK23 65 E7
Goyt Rd Disley SK12 38 D5
New Mills SK22 39 C6
Whaley Bridge SK23 65 E6
Goyt Valley Ind Est SK23 39 D4
Goyt View SK22 39 B6
Goyt's La SK17 90 F2
Grace Ave WA2 16 B8
Grace Cl CW1 191 C4
Grace Rd CH65 70 C7
Gradbach Mill★ SK17 138 A1
Grafton Mews CH2 237 B4
Grafton Rd CH65 70 C7
Grafton St
Newton-le-W WA12 2 B3
Warrington WA5 15 E6
Graham Ave CH66 69 D5
Graham Cl WA8 12 C1
Graham Cres M44 11 C3
Graham Dr Disley SK12 38 C6
Halewood L26 21 A8
Graham Rd Blacon CH1 117 F3
Widnes WA8 22 C8
Grainger's Rd CW9 103 F5
Grammar School Ct WA4 16 F3
Grammar School Rd
Lymm WA13 18 F2
Warrington WA4 16 F3
Grampian Way
Bebington CH62 43 E4
Neston CH64 66 E5
Winsford CW7 149 A7
Granary Mill WA7 50 F6
Granby Cl WA7 50 C5
Granby Rd
Cheadle Hulme SK8 35 B8
Warrington WA4 26 B8
Grand Junction Ret Pk CW1 190 D3
Grandford La CW5 217 D2
Grange Ave Barnton CW8 78 A3
Warrington WA4 16 E4
Grange Cl Crewe CW1 190 E3
Golborne WA3 3 C6
Sandbach CW11 174 F7
Grange Com Prim Sch CW7 126 B1
Grange Comp Sch WA7 23 C1
Grange Cres CH66 44 A1
Grange Ct Biddulph ST8 179 D2
13 Knutsford WA16 57 A2
Winsford CW7 126 B2
Grange Dr Hartford CW8 103 A6
Thornton Hough CH63 42 A7
Warrington WA5 15 A4
Widnes WA8 12 D1
Grange Farm Cl WA5 15 D6
Grange Green Manor WA4 25 E7
Grange Inf Sch The WA7 23 C1
Grange Jun Sch The
Hartford CW8 103 A6
Runcorn WA7 23 C1
Grange La Tilston SY14 198 E3
Weaverham CW8 102 A7
Whitegate CW8 125 F7
Winsford CW7 126 B4
Grange Lea CW10 128 B1
Grange Park Ave
Runcorn WA7 23 C2
Wilmslow SK9 60 A8
Grange Park Dr ST8 179 E3
Grange Pl M44 11 E5
Grange Rd Barnton CW8 78 A3
Biddulph ST8 179 E3
Chester CH2 118 D4
Chester,Vicars Cross CH3 119 C2
Cuddington CW8 101 F3
Ellesmere Port CH65 70 C4
Haydock WA11,WA12 1 D5
Macclesfield SK11 112 C6
Mouldsworth CH3 99 B1
Northwich,Rudheath CW9 104 D6
Runcorn WA7 23 C2
Grange Rd N WA7 23 C2
Grange Rd W CH3 119 C2
Grange Sch The CW8 103 B6
Grange The
Hartford CW8 103 B5
Macclesfield SK11 112 A6
Grange Valley WA11 1 D6
Grange Valley Prim Sch WA11 1 D5
Grange Villas CH3 142 F6
Grange Way CW11 174 F7
Grangebrook Dr CW7 126 C3
Grangefields ST8 179 E4
Grangelands SK10 86 F2
Grangemoor WA7 49 D8
Grangeside CH2 118 D7
Grangeway Handforth SK9 34 D4
Runcorn WA7 49 C8
Grangeway Ct WA7 49 C8
Grangewood Dr SK11 83 F3
Granston Cl WA5 7 E2

Grant Cl WA5 7 D1
Grant Rd WA5 15 B6
Grantham Ave
Warrington WA4 26 B8
Warrington,Bruche WA1 16 E7
Grantham Cl CW9 104 C7
Granville Dr CH66 69 B7
Granville Rd
Chester CH1 118 B3
Northwich CW9 104 A5
Wilmslow SK9 59 F5
Granville Sq CW7 149 E8
Granville St
15 Runcorn WA7 23 A3
Warrington WA1 16 D6
Winsford CW7 149 E8
Grapes St 9 SK11 112 D7
Grappenhall Hall Sch WA4 17 B1
Grappenhall Heys Com Prim Sch WA4 27 A7
Grappenhall La WA4 27 E6
Grappenhall Rd
Ellesmere Port CH65 69 F3
Warrington WA4 16 D1
Grappenhall St Wilfrid's CE Prim Sch WA4 17 B1
Grasmere SK11 112 A6
Grasmere Ave
Congleton CW12 155 F2
Crewe CW2 189 F5
Warrington WA2 8 E3
Grasmere Cl CW7 126 D2
Grasmere Cres
Bramhall SK7 35 E8
High Lane SK6 37 E8
Grasmere Dr
Holmes Chapel CW4 130 A3
Runcorn WA7 49 D5
Grasmere Rd
Alderley Edge SK9 60 A1
Chester CH2 118 F5
Ellesmere Port CH65 70 C2
Frodsham WA6 74 C8
Lymm WA13 18 F4
Neston CH64 66 E6
Partington M31 11 E3
Grason Ave SK9 34 C1
Grassfield Way WA16 82 A8
Grassmoor Cl CH62 43 E8
Grassy Green La ST7 209 E1
Gratrix Rd CH62 43 D8
Gravel La SK9 59 E5
Gravenhunger La CW3 232 D1
Graveyard La WA16 58 F5
Gray Ave WA11 1 D6
Gray's Cl ST7 195 B7
Graylag Cl WA7 49 F5
Graymarsh Dr SK12 36 E2
Greasby Dr CH66 69 E4
Great Ashfield WA8 12 D3
Great Budworth CE Prim Sch CW9 79 B8
Great Delph WA11 1 D7
Great King St SK11 112 C8
Great Oak Rd ST7 209 F4
Great Queen St SK11 112 C8
Great Riding WA7 50 C7
Great Sankey High Sch WA5 14 E7
Great Sankey Prim Sch WA5 15 A5
Greater Grace Sch CH1 95 B4
Greaves La SY14 222 E6
Greaves La E SY14 222 E7
Greaves Rd SK9 59 E7
Grebe Cl Knutsford WA16 57 B3
Poynton SK12 36 B4
Greeba Ave WA4 16 B3
Greek St WA7 22 F3
Green Acre Cl WA16 82 B8
Green Ave
Alpraham CW6 169 D4
Barnton CW8 78 A3
Davenham CW9 103 F3
Green Bank
Adderley TF9 235 A5
Chester CH4 141 E6
Green Bridge Cl WA7 24 A2
Green Coppice WA7 50 C8
Green Dr Alsager ST7 193 D4
Handforth SK9 34 D2
Green Farm CW4 163 B2
Green Hall Mews SK9 60 B6
Green Jones Brow WA5 6 F6
Green La Acton CW5 204 B3
Alderley Edge SK9 59 F1
Audlem CW3 229 F2
Barbridge CW5 187 A7
Bollington SK10 63 B1
Burtonwood WA5 6 E7
Chester CH4 140 E4
Chester,Vicars Cross CH3 119 B3
Davenham CW9 103 F3
Disley SK12 38 D4
Ellesmere Port CH65 70 C4
Ellesmere Port,Great Sutton CH66 69 C4
Higher Kinnerton CH4 161 B6
Higher Wincham CW9 79 F4
Irlam M44 11 E5
Kelsall CW6 122 D4
Knutsford WA16 56 D4
Lindow End SK9 84 F8
Over Peover WA16 83 D1
Picton CH2 96 C3
Plumley WA16 80 E6
Poynton SK12 37 C4
Green La *continued*
Sandbach CW11 173 F7
Saughall CH1 117 C7
Shocklach SY14 211 C7
Tattenhall CH3 182 F5
Tilston SY14 212 B8
Warrington,Dudlow's Green WA4 26 F5
Warrington,Paddington WA1 17 A8
Widnes WA8 12 E1
Willaston CW5 205 E5
Wilmslow SK9 60 B7
Winwick WA2 8 A7
Green Lake La CH3 163 F3
Green Lane Cl WA2 8 A7
Green Lane Com Specl Sch WA1 17 B8
Green Lane E
Connah's Quay CH5 93 C1
Sealand CH5 116 D7
Green Lane Est
Connah's Quay CH5 93 C1
Sealand CH5 116 C8
Green Lane W CH5 93 B3
Green Lawns Dr CH66 94 F8
Green Mdws Golborne WA3 3 E5
Macclesfield SK11 111 F6
Green Oaks Path WA8 23 C8
Green Oaks Way WA8 23 C8
Green Pk CW8 102 E7
Green Rd M31 11 E3
Green St
5 Alderley Edge SK9 60 A1
Holt LL13 180 E1
Knutsford WA16 57 A2
Macclesfield SK10 112 E7
Sandbach CW11 175 B6
Warrington WA5 15 E5
Warrington WA5 15 F5
Green The
Cheadle Hulme SK8 34 F8
Congleton CW12 156 C2
Ellesmere Port CH65 70 B2
Hale L24 21 D1
Handforth SK9 34 E3
Hartford CW8 103 B5
Harthill CH3 183 E3
Higher Kinnerton CH4 161 B7
Lawton-gate ST7 194 A4
Middlewich CW10 151 D6
Nantwich CW5 204 D8
Neston CH64 66 D8
Neston, Little Neston CH64 66 F6
Partington M31 11 F4
4 Runcorn WA7 23 F1
Tarvin CH3 121 F2
Thornton Hough CH63 42 C4
Wrenbury CW5 216 E4
Green View WA13 19 B5
Green Villa Pk SK9 59 E4
Green Wlk
Cuddington CW8 102 B4
Partington M31 11 E3
Greenacre SK8 34 C7
Greenacre Dr CH63 43 C7
Greenacre Rd CH4 140 F4
Greenacres Crewe CW1 190 D6
Duddon CW6 145 A6
Frodsham WA6 74 C6
Sandbach CW11 175 A7
Greenacres Cl WA3 4 B8
Greenacres Ct CH2 95 F1
Greenacres Rd CW12 155 F2
Greenacres The WA13 19 A4
Greenall Ave WA5 14 D4
Greenall Rd CW9 104 B8
Greenall's Ave WA4 16 C2
Greenbank CH4 141 E6
Greenbank Ave CH66 69 C7
Greenbank Cl CW5 205 D6
Greenbank Dr SK10 88 A8
Greenbank Gdns WA4 16 F2
Greenbank La CW8 103 D6
Greenbank Pk CW11 175 A2
Greenbank Rd
Chester CH2 119 A4
Warrington WA4 16 F2
Greenbank Residential Sch CW8 103 D6
Greenbank St WA4 16 C2
Greenbank Sta CW8 103 D6
Greenbridge Rd WA7 24 B2
Greencourts Bsns Pk M22 34 A8
Greendale Dr
Middlewich CW10 151 B7
Newcastle-u-Lyme ST5 210 D1
Greendale Gdns CW1 190 E5
Greendale La SK10 86 D8
Greenfield Ave CH4 161 A7
Greenfield Cl SK22 39 A8
Greenfield Cres
Chester CH2 119 B5
Waverton CH3 143 B6
Greenfield Farm Ind Est CW12 156 B3
Greenfield Gdns CH2 72 B3
Greenfield La
Chester CH2 119 B5
Frodsham WA6 49 B1
Greenfield Rd
Bollington SK10 88 A7
Broughton CH4 139 C4
Congleton CW12 156 B3
Ellesmere Port CH66 69 B7
Waverton CH3 143 B6
Greenfield Way CW8 102 A4
Greenfields Chester CH2 95 F1
Winsford CW7 127 B1
Greenfields Ave
Bebington CH62 43 C7
Shavington CW2 206 B4
Warrington WA4 26 D8
Greenfields Cl
Neston CH64 66 F5
Newton-le-W WA12 2 C4
Warrington WA1 17 C7
Greenfields Cres CH62 43 C7
Greenfields Croft CH64 66 E5
Greenfields Dr
Alsager ST7 193 E3
Neston CH64 66 F5
Greenfields La
Malpas SY14 213 B4
Rowton CH3 142 F5
Greenfields Lodge CH3 120 D6
Greenfields Prim Sch CW7 126 A1
Greengate WA15 32 D7
Greengate Rd ST7 193 F5
Greengates Cres CH64 66 E5
Greenhaven Ct CW5 219 E5
Greenhill La WA4 52 A5
Greenhill Wlk SK12 38 D6
Greenhills Cl SK11 112 E7
Greenhouse Farm Rd WA7 50 B6
Greenhythe Rd SK8 34 C6
Greenland Cl CW6 146 D1
Greenlands CH3 166 B3
Greenlands Cl 3 SK8 34 E8
Greenlaw Cl CW9 104 A5
Greenlea Cl CH65 70 B2
Greenoaks Ctr WA8 23 B8
Greenoaks Farm Ind Est WA8 23 C8
Greenock Mews WA8 12 E3
Greenore Dr L24 21 D2
Greens The WA15 32 D7
Greenshall La SK12 38 F5
Greenshank Cl WA12 2 C4
Greenside Ave WA6 74 D7
Greenside Ct CW9 105 D5
Greenside Dr CW9 105 A8
Greensway CH4 141 A7
Greenway Alsager ST7 193 B5
Bramhall SK7 35 D6
Congleton CW12 156 B3
Crewe CW1 190 D7
Farndon CH3 180 F1
Neston CH64 41 B2
Saughall CH1 94 A1
Tilston SY14 198 C3
Warrington WA4 26 D7
Warrington,Great Sankey WA5 14 E7
Warrington,Paddington WA1 16 F7
Wilmslow SK9 60 B6
Greenway Cl Helsby WA6 73 B3
Rode Heath ST7 193 F8
Greenway Dr CW9 104 C7
Greenway Rd
Biddulph ST8 179 E2
Heald Green SK8 34 C6
Runcorn WA7 23 A1
Speke L24 21 A3
Widnes WA8 13 B1
Greenway St CH4 237 B1
Greenway Wlk CW9 104 C7
Greenways ST7 209 F2
Greenways Ct CH62 43 C6
Greenwell Rd WA11 1 C6
Greenwich Ave WA8 13 D4
Greenwood Ave
Chester CH4 141 D7
Congleton CW12 156 F3
Greenwood Cl CW8 77 D1
Greenwood Cres WA2 8 E2
Greenwood Ct WA3 4 F1
Greenwood Dr
Newton-le-W WA12 2 D2
Runcorn WA7 24 F4
Wilmslow SK9 60 D8
Greenwood Rd WA13 18 F2
Greenwood Terr WA16 58 A4
Greenwood The CW6 168 D8
Greg Ave SK10 87 E8
Greg Mews SK9 34 B2
Gregory Cl WA5 15 C7
Gregorys Row WA3 4 A8
Gregson Rd WA8 13 C1
Grenfell Cl CH64 41 C1
Grenfell Ct CH64 66 C8
Grenfell Pk CH64 41 C1
Grenfell St 11 WA8 23 B8
Grenville Cl CW1 191 C5
Grenville Cres CH63 43 C7
Grenville Rd CH64 41 F1
Gresford Ave CH2 237 C4
Gresford Cl WA5 7 E1
Gresley Way ST7 209 F2
Gresty Bldgs 3 CW5 204 E6
Gresty Green Rd CW2 206 D7
Gresty La CW2 206 B7
Gresty Rd CW2 190 D1
Gresty Road Football Gd (Crewe Alexandra FC) CW2 190 D2
Gresty Terr CW1 190 E4
Greta Ave SK8 34 C6
Greville Dr CW7 127 A1
Grey Friars CH1 237 A2
Grey St WA1 16 C6
Greyfriars Cl WA2 9 A3
Greyfriars Rd WA2 9 A3
Greyhound Park Rd CH1 118 A3
Greyhound Pk CH1 118 A3
Greyhound Rd SK10 86 B5
Greymist Ave WA1 17 C7
Greys Ct WA1 9 C1
Greystoke Dr SK9 60 A2
Greystoke Rd SK10 87 F2
Greystone Pk CW1 190 D4
Greystone Rd WA5 14 F4
Greystones CH66 69 D4
Greystones Rd CH3 119 C1
Grice St WA4 16 C1
Griffin Cl Blacon CH1 117 F6
New Mills SK22 39 D6
Norton in Hales TF9 236 C2
Griffin La SK8 34 D7
Griffin Mews WA8 13 B3
Griffith Ave WA3 9 E5
Griffiths Dr CW9 104 D6
Griffiths Rd
Lostock Gralam CW9 79 F1
Northwich CW9 104 E8
Griffiths St WA4 16 F4
Grig Pl ST7 193 C5
Grimsditch La WA4 52 B5
Grimshaw Ave SK10 88 A7
Grimshaw La SK10 88 A7
Grindley Bank CH2 119 F8
Grindley Gdns CH65 70 C2
Grindley Gn SY13 228 B3
Grisedale Ave WA2 8 B3
Grisedale Cl WA7 49 E5
Grisedale Rd CH62 43 F8
Grisedale Way SK11 112 A5
Gritstone Dr SK10 112 A8
Grizedale WA8 12 B2
Grizedale Cl CW2 189 D2
Groarke Dr WA5 14 D5
Groby Rd CW1 190 E8
Grocotts Row 12 CW5 204 E5
Grosvenor Ave
Alsager ST7 193 D5
3 Golborne WA3 3 D8
Hartford CW8 103 A4
Warrington WA1 16 F7
Grosvenor Cl
Warrington WA5 15 C5
Wilmslow SK9 60 A4
Grosvenor Cotts CH4 141 D7
Grosvenor Ct
Chester CH1 237 C2
Winsford CW7 149 C7
Grosvenor Ctr SK11 112 D8
Grosvenor Dr SK12 36 D3
Grosvenor Gdns WA12 2 C2
Grosvenor Grange WA1 9 B1
Grosvenor Mus★ CH1 237 A1
Grosvenor Nuffield Hospl CH4 141 C6
Grosvenor Pk Rd CH1 237 C2
Grosvenor Pk Terr CH1, CH3 237 C2
Grosvenor Pl CH1 237 B1
Grosvenor Rd
Chester CH4 141 C7
Congleton CW12 156 A3
Haydock WA11 1 B7
Tarvin CH3 121 A2
Widnes WA8 13 B5
Grosvenor Sh Ctr The CH1 237 B2
Grosvenor St
Chester CH1 237 A2
Crewe CW1 190 B5
3 Macclesfield SK10 112 C8
Runcorn WA7 23 B3
Winsford CW7 149 E8
Grotsworth La SY14 214 E8
Grotto La WA16 108 B7
Grounds St WA2 16 B7
Grove Arc 8 SK9 60 B7
Grove Ave Chester CH3 119 B3
Kidsgrove ST7 194 E1
Lawton-gate ST7 194 A4
Lostock Gralam CW9 80 A3
Lymm WA13 18 C3
Wilmslow SK9 60 B7
Grove Cl CW7 149 B8
Grove Cres CW3 232 C1
Grove Ct Alsager ST7 193 E4
Lymm WA13 18 C3
Grove Gdns CH3 119 E2
Grove Ho SK8 35 A5
Grove La SK8 35 A6
Grove Park Ave ST7 194 A4
Grove Pk WA16 57 A1
Grove Rd CH1 94 E4
Grove Rise WA13 18 E3
Grove St New Mills SK22 39 B7
Runcorn WA7 22 F3
Warrington WA4 16 C4
Wilmslow SK9 60 B7
Grove Terr WA6 73 C4
Grove The
Cheadle Hulme SK8 35 A6
Knutsford WA16 57 C4
Lawton-gate ST7 194 A4
Lymm WA13 18 E3
Tarporley CW6 146 C2
Warrington WA5 14 F4
Whitchurch SY13 225 F1
Grove Way SK9 60 B7
Grovemount CW9 103 F2
Groves The Chester CH1 237 B2
Ellesmere Port CH66 95 A8
Grovewood Mews SK11 112 C6
Grub La CW6 122 C5
Grundy Cl WA8 12 F3
Grundy St WA3 3 A7
Guardian St WA5 15 F6
Guardian Street Ind Est WA5 15 F6
Guernsey Cl
Congleton CW12 157 A2
Middlewich CW10 128 D2
Warrington WA4 26 D8
Guernsey Dr CH65 70 C1
Guernsey Ho CH2 119 B5
Guernsey Rd WA8 13 E3
Guest St WA8 23 A7
Guests Slack WA6 100 B8
Guilden Gn CH3 119 E4
Guilden Sutton CE Prim Sch CH3 119 E5
Guilden Sutton La CH3 119 D5
Guildford Ave SK8 35 A6
Guildford Cl
1 Chester CH4 140 F6
Warrington WA2 9 A1
Guillemot Cl CW1 190 F5
Gull Cl SK12 36 B3
Gullane Cl SK10 87 B4
Gullet The CW5 204 E5
Gullivers World Theme Pk★ WA5 7 E1
Gulls Way CH60 40 E7
Gunco La
Macclesfield SK11 112 E6
Prestbury SK10 87 C8
Gunn Gr CH64 66 F8
Gutterscroft CW1 191 D5
Gutticar Rd WA8 12 B1
Guy La CH3 143 D5
Gwyneth Morley Ct SK9 34 D3
Gypsy La CH1 94 F2

H

Hack Green Secret Nuclear Bunker★ CW5 218 D4
Hacked Way La SK11 113 F6
Haddon Cl
Alderley Edge SK9 59 F2
High Lane SK6 37 E6
Holmes Chapel CW4 130 B3
Macclesfield SK11 112 B5
Wistaston CW2 206 B7
Haddon Dr WA8 12 C3
Haddon Ho 4 CH64 66 E8
Haddon La CH64 67 C4
Haddon Rd Burton CH64 67 D2
Heald Green SK8 34 C7
Hadfield Cl WA8 13 E2
Hadfield St CW9 79 B1
Hadleigh Cl WA5 14 E5
Hadley Ave CH62 43 C8
Hadlow La CH64 67 F7
Hadlow Rd CH64 67 F6
Hadlow Terr CH64 67 F7
Hadrian Dr CH1 117 E6
Hadrian Way
Cuddington CW8 102 B2
Middlewich CW10 128 C2
Hadyn Jones Dr CW5 204 F4
Hafod Cl Blacon CH1 117 D3
Connah's Quay CH5 91 C1
Hag Bank La SK12 38 D7
Hague Bar Prim Sch SK22 38 E8
Hague Bar Rd Disley SK22 38 F8
New Mills SK22 39 A7
Hague Fold Rd SK22 38 F8
Haig Ave Irlam M44 11 C4
Warrington WA5 15 A5
Haig Ct WA16 57 C4
Haig Rd Knutsford WA16 57 C4
Widnes WA8 13 A1
Hale Ave SK12 36 D2
Hale Bank Terr WA8 22 A4
Hale CE Prim Sch L24 21 E1
Hale Ct WA8 22 A4
Hale Gate Rd Hale WA8 21 F3
Widnes WA8 22 A3
Hale Gr WA5 15 A6
Hale Rd Altrincham WA15 32 D8
Hale L24 21 B2
Widnes WA8 22 C7
Widnes,Ditton WA8 22 C8
Hale Road Ind Est WA8 22 B4
Hale St WA2 16 B7
Hale View WA7 48 E8
Hale View Rd WA6 73 C4
Halebank CE Prim Sch WA8 22 A5
Halebank Rd WA8 21 F5
Halewood Lane Ends L26 21 A8
Haley Rd N WA5 6 E6
Haley Rd S WA5 6 E5
Half St SK11 112 D6
Halfacre La WA4 17 F2
Halghton La LL13 222 B2
Halifax Cl WA2 8 D2
Halkett Cl CH4 140 E5
Halkyn Rd CH2 237 C4
Hall Acres La SK8 34 E8
Hall Ave WA8 12 A1
Hall Bank WA16 58 C4
Hall Bank N WA16 58 C4
Hall Bank S WA16 58 C4

Hall Cl SK10 . . . . .87 D4
Hall Dr Alsager ST7 . . . .193 C3
 Marston CW9 . . . . .79 B6
 Warrington WA4 . . . . . . .26 D6
 Willaston CW5 . . . . .205 C6
Hall Farm CH62 . . . . .44 A4
Hall Farm Cl SK23 . . . . . .65 D8
Hall Gr SK10 . . . . .87 D3
Hall Hill SK10 . . . . .87 E7
Hall La
 Appleton Thorn WA4 . . . . .27 B8
 Audlem CW3 . . . . .230 C7
 Brown Knowl CH3 . . . . . .199 C7
 Cronton L35 . . . . .12 C7
 Daresbury WA4 . . . . .25 D2
 Haughton CW6 . . . . . . .186 D5
 Kelsall CW6 . . . . .122 D6
 Little Leigh CW9 . . . . .77 F8
 Lostock Gralam CW9 . . . . .79 F3
 Mobberley WA16 . . . . . . .58 D4
 Newton-le-W WA5 . . . . .7 B8
 Ollerton WA16 . . . . .83 B5
 Partington M31 . . . . .11 F4
 Pickmere WA16 . . . . .55 B1
 Sandbach CW11 . . . . . . .174 B5
 Shotwick CH1 . . . . .93 B5
 St Helens WA9 . . . . .6 A4
 Stretton WA4 . . . . .52 D8
 Sutton Lane Ends SK11 . . .112 F3
 Utkinton CW6 . . . . .146 C6
 Winsford CW7 . . . . .149 B3
Hall La The CW6 . . . . . . .147 D2
Hall Moss La SK7 . . . . . . .35 C4
Hall Nook WA5 . . . . .14 F3
Hall O'shaw St CW1 . . . . .190 E4
Hall Rd Handforth SK9 . . . .34 E3
 Haydock WA11 . . . . .1 E7
 Warrington WA1 . . . . . . .17 C7
 Wilmslow SK9 . . . . .60 A7
Hall St Audley ST7 . . . . . .209 D2
 Macclesfield SK10 . . . . . .112 C8
 New Mills SK22 . . . . .39 B8
 Warrington WA1 . . . . . . .16 C5
Hall Terr WA5 . . . . .14 E7
Hall View CH3 . . . . .166 B1
Hall View Cl CW8 . . . . . . .102 A7
Hall Wood Ave WA11 . . . . . .1 E8
Halla-Way WA4 . . . . .16 E3
Hallams Dr CW5 . . . . . . .205 B4
Hallastone Rd WA6 . . . . . .73 C4
Hallcroft M31 . . . . .11 F4
Hallcroft Pl WA4 . . . . .17 A2
Hallefield Cres **5** SK11 . .112 E7
Hallefield Dr **4** SK11 . . .112 E7
Hallefield Rd SK10,SK11 . .112 E7
Hallfield Dr CH2 . . . . .72 B3
Hallfield Pk CH66 . . . . . . .69 D4
Hallfields Rd Tarvin CH3 . .121 C2
 Warrington WA2 . . . . .8 D1
Hallgreen La CW12 . . . . .155 D8
Halliday Cl WA3 . . . . .9 F3
Halliwel Jones Stad
 (Warrington Wolves RLFC)
 The WA2 . . . . .16 A6
Halliwell's Brow WA16 . . . .29 B3
Hallows Ave WA2 . . . . . . .16 D8
Hallows Cl CW6 . . . . . . .122 C4
Hallows Dr CW6 . . . . . . .122 C4
Hallowsgate Ct CW6 . . . .122 C4
Halls Rd Biddulph ST8 . . . .179 C1
 Mow Cop ST7 . . . . .195 C7
Hallsgreen La CH2 . . . . . . .96 F7
Hallshaw Ave CW1 . . . . . .190 E5
Hallside Pk WA16 . . . . . . .57 C1
Hallwood Cl WA7 . . . . . . .49 B6
Hallwood Dr CH66 . . . . . .68 D4
Hallwood Link Rd WA7 . . . .49 F6
Hallwood Park Ave WA7 . . .49 E6
Hallwood Park Prim Sch
 WA7 . . . . .49 E6
Hallwood Rd SK9 . . . . . . .34 D2
Halsall Ave WA2 . . . . .16 D8
Halsall Cl WA7 . . . . .50 C5
Halstone Ave SK9 . . . . . . .59 E4
Halton Brook Ave WA7 . . . .23 D1
Halton Brow WA7 . . . . . . .23 E1
Halton Castle ★ WA7 . . . . .23 F1
Halton Coll WA8 . . . . .23 A8
Halton Coll Runcorn Campus
 WA7 . . . . .22 E3
Halton Cres CH66 . . . . . . .69 F2
Halton Ct WA7 . . . . .23 D2
Halton Dr CW7 . . . . .189 D5
Halton General Hospl
 WA7 . . . . .49 F7
Halton High Sch WA7 . . . . .50 C6
Halton Lea S Ctr WA7 . . . . .49 E8
Halton Link Rd WA7 . . . . . .49 E8
Halton Lodge Ave WA7 . . . .49 D7
Halton Lodge Prim Sch
 WA7 . . . . .49 D8
Halton Rd Chester CH2 . . .118 F6
 Ellesmere Port CH66 . . . . .69 E2
 Runcorn WA7 . . . . .23 D2
 Warrington WA5 . . . . . . .14 F6
Halton St WA11 . . . . .1 E6
Halton Station Rd WA7 . . . .49 F3
Halton View Rd WA8 . . . . .13 C1
Halton Way CH66 . . . . . . .69 F2
Hamble Dr WA5 . . . . .14 F3
Hamble Way SK10 . . . . . . .86 E1
Hambleton Cl CH66 . . . . . .69 A6
Hambleton Cl WA8 . . . . . .12 C3
Hambleton Rd SK8 . . . . . .34 C8

Hambleton Way CW7 . . . .149 A7
Hambletts Hollow WA6 . . .100 F6
 Sandycroft CH5 . . . . . . .116 A3
Hamilton Cl
 Haslington CW1 . . . . . . .191 C4
 Macclesfield SK10 . . . . . .113 A8
 Neston CH64 . . . . .41 B2
Hamilton Ct CH64 . . . . . . .66 F8
Hamilton Pl CH1 . . . . . . .237 A2
Hamilton Rd CH5 . . . . . . .91 D1
Hamilton St CH2 . . . . . . .118 F3
Hamlin Cl WA7 . . . . .49 A6
Hammond Sch CH2 . . . . .119 B7
Hammond St CW2 . . . . . .190 D3
Hamnett Ct WA3 . . . . .9 E3
Hampshire Cl CW12 . . . . .156 D4
Hampshire Rd M31 . . . . . .11 D2
Hampshire Wlk SK10 . . . . .86 F2
Hampson Ave WA3 . . . . . . .4 F3
Hampson Cres SK9 . . . . . .34 C4
Hampstead Ct **7** CW7 . . .149 A8
Hampton Cl Neston CH64 . .66 E6
 Widnes WA8 . . . . .13 C1
Hampton Cres
 Neston CH64 . . . . .66 E6
 No Man's Heath SY14 . . . .214 A5
Hampton Ct WA7 . . . . .24 C4
Hampton Dr Cronton WA8 . .12 C5
 Warrington WA3 . . . . .15 C4
Hampton Gdns CH65 . . . . .70 A5
Hampton Heath Ind Est
 SY14 . . . . .213 D7
Hampton Rd
 Chester CH4 . . . . .140 F6
 Irlam M44 . . . . .11 D4
Hamson Dr SK10 . . . . .63 B1
Hamsterley Cl WA3 . . . . . .10 B6
Hanbury Cl CW2 . . . . . . .206 B7
Hancock Ct WA4 . . . . .16 C4
Hancock Rd CW12 . . . . . .156 F4
Hand St SK11 . . . . .112 B8
Handa Dr CH65 . . . . .95 B8
Handbridge CH4 . . . . . . .237 B1
Handford Ave CH62 . . . . . .43 F5
Handford Rd CH2 . . . . . . .118 F6
Handforth Cl WA4 . . . . . . .17 C3
Handforth La WA7 . . . . . . .49 D6
Handforth Rd
 Crewe CW2 . . . . .189 E3
 Handforth SK9 . . . . .34 E1
Handforth Sta SK9 . . . . . . .34 D3
Handley Hill CW7 . . . . . . .149 C8
Handley Hill Prim Sch
 CW7 . . . . .149 C8
Handley St WA7 . . . . .22 F3
Hangman's La CW9 . . . . . .105 C7
Hankelow Cl
 Chester CH2 . . . . .237 B4
 Middlewich CW10 . . . . . .151 C6
Hankey St **2** WA7 . . . . . .22 F2
Hankins Heys La CW3 . . . .231 A1
Hankinson Cl M31 . . . . . . .11 E2
Hanley Cl Disley SK12 . . . . .38 D5
 Widnes WA8 . . . . .12 C1
Hanley Rd WA8 . . . . .12 C1
Hannah's Wlk **2** CW10 . .151 C8
Hanns Hall Farm CH64 . . . .67 D8
Hanns Hall Rd CH64 . . . . . .67 D8
Hanover Ct WA7 . . . . .50 A6
Hanover Dr **2** CW7 . . . . .149 D6
Hanover Ho **6** CW7 . . . .103 C5
Hanover St WA1 . . . . .16 A4
Hapsdale View WA6 . . . . . .72 E1
Hapsford Cl WA3 . . . . .9 C4
Hapsford La
 Dunham-on-t-H WA6 . . . . .97 E3
 Elton CH2 . . . . .72 D4
Hapsford Mews WA6 . . . . .72 E4
Harbbour Cl CH2 . . . . . . .118 E7
Harbord St WA1 . . . . .16 C4
Harbour Cl WA7 . . . . .50 D6
Harbour La CH66 . . . . . . .111 C1
Harburn Wlk M22 . . . . . . .33 E8
Harcourt Cl WA3 . . . . .9 E3
Harden Pk SK9 . . . . .60 A3
Harding Ave
 Tattenhall CH3 . . . . .166 C2
 Warrington WA2 . . . . .8 E1
Harding Rd Chester CH2 . . .118 B8
 Nantwich CW5 . . . . .204 C4
Hardings Mdw ST7 . . . . . .194 F2
Hardings Row ST7 . . . . . .195 D7
Hardingswood Rd ST7 . . . .194 E2
Hardknott Rd CH62 . . . . . .43 E8
Hardwick Cl SK6 . . . . .37 F6
Hardwick Dr SK11 . . . . . .112 B5
Hardwick Grange WA1 . . . .17 E8
Hardwick Rd WA7 . . . . . . .23 D3
Hardwicke Ct CW7 . . . . . .190 E4
Hardwicke Rd SK12 . . . . . .36 F4
Hardy Cl
 Ellesmere Port CH66 . . . . .69 F3
 Wistaston CW2 . . . . .205 F8
Hardy Dr SK7 . . . . .35 D7
Hardy Rd WA13 . . . . .18 C2
Hardy St WA2 . . . . .16 B6
Hare Hill Gdn ★ SK10 . . . . .86 B6
Hare La CH3 . . . . .119 D3
Hare's La WA6 . . . . .73 F7
Harebell Cl CH3 . . . . .142 A6
Harebell Gr ST7 . . . . .195 F1
Harecastle Ave ST7 . . . . . .194 E1
Harecastle Ct ST7 . . . . . . .210 E6
Harefield Dr SK9 . . . . .60 B5
Harefield Rd SK9 . . . . .34 E4
Harewood Ave CH66 . . . . . .69 C4

Harewood Cl
 Northwich CW8 . . . . .103 F4
 Winsford CW7 . . . . .126 A1
Harewood Way SK11 . . . . .112 B5
Harfield Gdns CH66 . . . . . .69 C5
Harford Cl WA5 . . . . .14 F4
Hargrave Ave CW2 . . . . . .189 F3
Hargrave Dr CH66 . . . . . . .69 E5
Hargrave La
 Bebington CH64 . . . . .43 A4
 Thornton Hough CH63,CH64 .42 F5
Hargreave Ho **7** CH64 . . .66 E8
Hargreaves Ct WA8 . . . . . .13 D1
Hargreaves Ho **5** WA8 . . .13 D1
Hargreaves Rd CW9 . . . . .104 C8
Harington Cl CW2 . . . . . . .118 C8
Harlech Cl WA5 . . . . .7 E2
Harlech Cl CH66 . . . . .70 D3
Harlech Gr **3** WA7 . . . . . .23 F1
Harlech Way CH65 . . . . . . .70 D3
Harlow Cl WA4 . . . . .17 C3
Harlyn Ave SK7 . . . . .35 F7
Harlyn Gdns WA5 . . . . . . .14 D3
Harn The CH66 . . . . .69 C3
Harold Rd WA11 . . . . .1 F7
Haroldgate SY13 . . . . .225 F1
Harper Cl CH66 . . . . .69 D4
Harper Gr CW12 . . . . .156 E4
Harpers Rd WA2 . . . . .9 B2
Harpur Cl SK11 . . . . .112 D6
Harpur Cres ST7 . . . . .193 B5
Harrier Rd WA2 . . . . .8 F2
Harriet St M44 . . . . .11 E5
Harrington Dr SK11 . . . . .111 D1
Harris Cl CW1 . . . . .173 B1
Harris Rd CW9 . . . . .80 A2
Harris St WA8 . . . . .13 C1
Harriseahead La ST7 . . . . .195 D4
Harrison Dr
 Goostrey CW4 . . . . .107 B1
 Haydock WA11 . . . . .1 A6
Harrison Gr CH5 . . . . . . .116 A3
Harrison Sq WA5 . . . . .7 F1
Harrison St WA8 . . . . .22 D3
Harrison Way WA12 . . . . . . .2 C4
Harrisons Pl **4** WA8 . . . .103 E8
Harrisons Terr CH66 . . . . . .69 C6
Harrogate Cl
 Bebington CH62 . . . . .43 D4
 Warrington WA5 . . . . .7 A1
Harrogate Rd CH62 . . . . . .43 D4
Harrop La SK10 . . . . .62 E5
Harrop Rd Bollington SK10 . .88 C8
 Runcorn WA7 . . . . .23 B1
Harrow Cl Crewe CW2 . . . .190 A1
 Warrington WA4 . . . . .26 E6
Harrow Dr WA7 . . . . .23 E2
Harrow Gr CH62 . . . . .43 E8
Harrow Rd CH65 . . . . .70 D4
Harrow Way CW9 . . . . . . .103 E3
Hart Ave SK9 . . . . .59 F5
Hartford Bsns Ctr CW8 . . .102 F4
Hartford Cl CW11 . . . . . . .175 C7
Hartford Dr CH65 . . . . .69 F4
Hartford High Sch CW8 . . .103 B4
Hartford Manor Com Prim
 Sch CW8 . . . . .103 C5
Hartford Mews **3** CW8 . .119 B1
Hartford Prim Sch CW8 . . .103 B4
Hartford Rd CW9 . . . . . . .103 F2
Hartford Sta CW8 . . . . . . .103 A4
Hartford Way CH1 . . . . . . .118 A2
Harthill Cl CW9 . . . . .103 E5
Harthill La CH3 . . . . .183 E4
Harthill Prim Sch CH3 . . . .183 E3
Harthill Rd Blacon CH1 . . . .117 E6
 Burwardsley CH3 . . . . . . .184 A6
Hartington Dr SK7 . . . . . . .36 E8
Hartington Rd
 Bramhall SK7 . . . . .35 E6
 Heald Green SK8 . . . . . . .34 D8
 High Lane SK12,SK6 . . . . .37 F7
Hartington St CH4 . . . . . .141 E7
Hartland Cl Poynton SK12 . .36 D5
 Widnes WA8 . . . . .13 A5
Hartley Cl WA13 . . . . .18 F3
Hartley Gdns CW12 . . . . . .179 B8
Hartley Gn SK10 . . . . .87 F8
Harton Cl WA8 . . . . .12 E3
Hartswood Cl WA4 . . . . . . .26 E3
Hartwell Gr CW7 . . . . .126 F4
Harty Rd WA11 . . . . .1 A5
Harvard Cl WA7 . . . . .24 D2
Harvard Ct WA2 . . . . .8 A3
Harvest Cl CW9 . . . . .126 F8
Harvest Rd SK10 . . . . .87 C3
Harvey Ave
 Nantwich CW5 . . . . .205 A6
 Newton-le-W WA12 . . . . . . .1 F3
Harvey Cl WA2 . . . . .8 B3
Harvey Rd CW12 . . . . . . .157 A5
Harwood Gdns WA4 . . . . . .17 A2
Haryngton Ave WA5 . . . . . .15 F7
Haseley Cl SK12 . . . . .36 E5
Haslemere Ave WA15 . . . . .32 C6
Haslemere Dr WA5 . . . . . . .14 D4
Haslemere Way CW1 . . . . .190 B6
Haslin Cres CH3 . . . . .142 D7
Haslington Cl ST5 . . . . . . .210 D1
Haslington Gr L26 . . . . . . .21 A6
Haslington Prim Sch
 CW1 . . . . .191 D4
Hassall Rd Alsager ST7 . . . .193 B5
 Haslington CW11 . . . . . . .192 B7
 Sandbach CW11 . . . . . . .175 C4
 Winterley CW11 . . . . . . .191 F8
Hassall Way **7** SK9 . . . . .34 E5
Hassals La CH2 . . . . .96 F3

Hastings Ave WA2 . . . . .8 B4
Hastings Rd CW5 . . . . . . .204 F5
Hasty La Altrincham WA15 . .32 E8
 Woodhouse Park WA15 . . . .32 F8
Hatch Mere ★ WA6 . . . . . .100 C4
Hatchery Cl WA4 . . . . .27 B4
Hatchings The WA13 . . . . .18 E2
Hatchmere Cl
 Sandbach CW11 . . . . . . .174 F7
 Warrington WA5 . . . . .15 E5
Hatchmere Dr CH3 . . . . . .142 B8
Hatchmere Pk WA6 . . . . . .100 C5
Hatfield Cl CW4 . . . . .130 B3
Hatfield Gdns WA4 . . . . . . .26 E4
Hathaway Cl SK8 . . . . .34 B7
Hathaway Dr SK11 . . . . . .112 C5
Hatherton Cl
 Newcastle-u-Lyme ST5 . . .210 D2
 5 Northwich CW9 . . . . .103 F4
Hatherton Gr L26 . . . . . . .21 A6
Hatherton Way CH2 . . . . . .237 B4
Hatley La WA6 . . . . .73 F7
Hatter St CW12 . . . . .156 E3
Hatton Ave CH62 . . . . .43 E3
Hatton Bldgs CH2 . . . . . . .237 C4
Hatton Brow Terr SK11 . . . .112 F4
Hatton La Hartford CW8 . . .103 D6
 Stretton WA4 . . . . .26 E1
Hatton Rd CH1 . . . . .117 E6
Hatton St SK11 . . . . .112 C7
Haughton Cl SK10 . . . . . . .86 F1
Havannah La
 Congleton CW12 . . . . . . .156 F6
 St Helens WA9 . . . . .1 B3
Havannah Prim Sch
 CW12 . . . . .157 A6
Havannah St CW12 . . . . . .156 F6
Haven The Crewe CW1 . . . .190 D7
 Sandbach CW11 . . . . . . .174 E2
Havergal St **3** WA7 . . . . . .22 F1
Haverhill Cl CW2 . . . . .207 C3
Haverty Prec WA12 . . . . . . .2 B1
Havisham Cl WA3 . . . . .9 D5
Hawarde Cl WA12 . . . . .2 C4
Hawarden Airport CH4,
 CH5 . . . . .139 D7
Hawarden Gdns CH65 . . . .70 D2
Hawarden Ind Pk CH5 . . . .139 B6
Hawarden Pk CH5 . . . . . . .139 B6
Haweswater Ave
 Crewe CW1 . . . . .173 B1
 Haydock WA11 . . . . .1 A6
Haweswater Cl WA7 . . . . . .50 A5
Haweswater Dr CW7 . . . . .126 D2
Hawick Cl CH66 . . . . .69 A5
Hawk Rd SK22 . . . . .39 D8
Hawk St WA11 . . . . .175 B6
Hawker Cl CH4 . . . . .139 C4
Hawkins La SK10 . . . . .88 D4
Hawkins Rd CH64 . . . . .41 F1
Hawkins View CH3 . . . . . .120 E6
Hawks Ct WA7 . . . . .49 E6
Hawks Way CH60 . . . . .40 E8
Hawksey Dr CW5 . . . . . . .204 F4
Hawkshaw Cl WA3 . . . . . . .9 C4
Hawkshead Cl WA7 . . . . . .50 A4
Hawkshead Rd WA5 . . . . . .6 F6
Hawkshead Way CW7 . . . .126 D2
Hawkstone Gr WA6 . . . . . .73 C4
Hawley Dr WA15 . . . . .32 B8
Hawley La WA15 . . . . .32 B8
Hawley's Cl WA5 . . . . .7 F1
Hawley's La WA2,WA5 . . . .8 A1
Hawley's Lane Trad Pk
 WA2 . . . . .8 A1
Haworth Ave CW12 . . . . . .157 A5
Haworth Cl SK11 . . . . . . .112 B5
Hawthorn Ave
 3 Nantwich CW5 . . . . .204 F5
 Newton-le-W WA12 . . . . . . .2 D3
 Runcorn WA7 . . . . .23 A1
 1 Widnes WA8 . . . . . . .13 B2
 Wilmslow SK9 . . . . .60 A7
Hawthorn Bank SK22 . . . . .39 B6
Hawthorn Cl
 Holmes Chapel CW4 . . . .130 D3
 Winsford CW7 . . . . .126 C3
Hawthorn Cotts CH60 . . . . .40 F8
Hawthorn Dr M44 . . . . . . .11 D5
Hawthorn Gdns ST7 . . . . . .210 D8
Hawthorn Gn **2** SK9 . . . . .60 A7
Hawthorn Gr
 Bramhall SK7 . . . . .35 C6
 Crewe CW1 . . . . .190 D7
 Warrington WA4 . . . . . . .16 D1
 Wilmslow SK9 . . . . .60 B7
Hawthorn La
 Congleton CW12 . . . . . . .155 C6
 Crewe CW2 . . . . .189 F2
 Wilmslow SK9 . . . . .60 A7
Hawthorn Pk **1** SK9 . . . . .60 A7
Hawthorn Rd
 Bollington SK10 . . . . .87 F8
 Chester CH4 . . . . .141 A6
 Christleton CH3 . . . . .142 E7
 Ellesmere Port CH66 . . . . .69 D6
 Lymm WA13 . . . . .18 D3
 Neston CH64 . . . . .41 C1
 Newcastle-u-Lyme ST5 . . .210 E1
 Plumley WA16 . . . . .80 F3
 Weaverham CW8 . . . . . . .102 C8
Hawthorn Rise SK10 . . . . . .86 E6
Hawthorn St WA3 . . . . .60 A6
Hawthorn Terr SK9 . . . . . . .60 A6
Hawthorn View
 Connah's Quay CH5 . . . . .116 A7
 Lindow End WA16 . . . . . . .59 B2
 4 Wilmslow SK9 . . . . . .60 A7

Hawthorn Villas CW4 . . . . .130 C3
Hawthorn Way SK10 . . . . . .87 E2
Hawthorn Wlk
 3 Partington M31 . . . . .11 E3
 Wilmslow SK9 . . . . .60 A7
 Wincham CW9 . . . . .79 C3
Hawthorne Ave
 Audley ST7 . . . . .209 F1
 Fowley Common WA3 . . . . .5 A6
 Warrington WA5 . . . . .15 A6
 Warrington,Woolston WA1 . .17 A8
Hawthorne Bsns Pk WA5 . .16 A8
Hawthorne Cl
 Congleton CW12 . . . . . . .156 A4
 Haydock WA11 . . . . .1 A5
Hawthorne Ct ST7 . . . . . .193 E4
Hawthorne Dr
 Sandbach CW11 . . . . . . .175 D6
 Willaston CH64 . . . . .43 B1
Hawthorne Gr
 Barnton CW8 . . . . .77 F4
 Poynton SK12 . . . . .37 C4
 Warrington WA3 . . . . .4 B2
 Winsford CW7 . . . . .127 A1
Hawthorne La CH62 . . . . . .43 D8
Hawthorne Rd
 Frodsham WA6 . . . . .49 B1
 Warrington WA4 . . . . . . .26 C8
Hawthorne St WA5 . . . . . . .16 A8
Hawthorns The
 Bunbury CW6 . . . . .185 E8
 Ellesmere Port CH66 . . . . .69 F7
 Haslington CW1 . . . . . . .191 D5
 Northwich CW8 . . . . .103 C7
 Tarporley CW6 . . . . .146 D1
Haycroft SK8 . . . . .34 E8
Haycroft Cl CH66 . . . . .69 D2
Haydan Mews WA6 . . . . . . .73 E6
Haydn Jones Dr CW5 . . . . .204 F3
Haydock Cl Chester CH1 . . .118 B2
 Macclesfield SK10 . . . . . . .87 C3
Haydock English Martyrs' RC
 Prim Sch WA11 . . . . .1 C1
Haydock High Sch WA11 . . .1 C1
Haydock La WA11 . . . . .1 C2
Haydock La Ind Est WA11 . .1 C1
Haydock Park Racecourse
 WA3 . . . . .2 E3
Haydock St
 Newton-le-W WA12 . . . . . . .2 A3
 Warrington WA2 . . . . . . .16 B5
Haye's Rd M44 . . . . .11 E5
Hayes Cl CW5 . . . . .204 E2
Hayes Cres WA6 . . . . .49 C1
Hayes Dr CW8 . . . . .78 C3
Hayes Pk CH1 . . . . .237 A4
Hayfield Cl SK10 . . . . .87 B3
Hayfield Rd
 New Mills SK22 . . . . .39 D8
 Warrington WA16 . . . . . . .17 C2
Hayfields WA16 . . . . .57 C3
Hayfields Gr CW3 . . . . . . .229 F1
Hayhead Cl ST7 . . . . .195 B2
Hayhurst Ave CW10 . . . . .151 C6
Hayhurst Cl CW9 . . . . . . .103 F8
Hayle Cl CW1 . . . . .190 B6
Hayling Cl CW1 . . . . .190 B6
Haymakers Cl CH4 . . . . . .140 F4
Haymakers Way CH1 . . . . .117 A8
Haymoor Green Rd
 CW5 . . . . .205 E3
Hayscastle Cl WA5 . . . . . . .7 F3
Hayside Wlk SY14 . . . . . . .213 A1
Hayton St WA16 . . . . .56 F7
Haywood Cres WA7 . . . . . .24 D7
Hazel Ave
 Macclesfield SK11 . . . . . .112 A5
 Runcorn WA7 . . . . .48 C6
Hazel Cl
 1 Ellesmere Port CH66 . .69 F7
 Kidsgrove ST7 . . . . .195 B1
Hazel Dr Heald Green M22 . .34 A3
 Lymm WA13 . . . . .18 F2
 Poynton SK12 . . . . .36 F7
 Weaverham CW8 . . . . . . .102 D2
 Winsford CW7 . . . . .149 C5
Hazel Gr Alsager ST7 . . . . .194 A4
 Crewe CW1 . . . . .190 C7
 Golborne WA3 . . . . .3 B8
 Warrington WA1 . . . . . . .17 A4
Hazel Grove High Sch
 SK7 . . . . .36 C6
Hazel Rd CH4 . . . . .140 F6
Hazel St WA1 . . . . .16 D6
Hazel Wlk M31 . . . . .11 E5
Hazelbadge Cl SK12 . . . . . .36 C6
Hazelbadge Rd SK12 . . . . .36 C6
Hazelbank CH65 . . . . .69 F6
Hazelborough Cl WA3 . . . . .10 B6
Hazelcroft SK9 . . . . .85 A4
Hazelcroft Gdns SK9 . . . . .85 A4
Hazeldean Ct **17** SK9 . . . .34 E6
Hazelhurst Dr SK10 . . . . . .88 A4
Hazelmere Cl CW8 . . . . . .103 C4
Hazelshaw La CW11 . . . . .154 B8
Hazelwood Cl WA8 . . . . . . .22 A4
Hazelwood Mews WA4 . . . .17 C3
Hazelwood Rd
 Barnton CW8 . . . . .78 B4
 Wilmslow SK9 . . . . .60 D7
Hazlehurst Rd WA6 . . . . . .74 D7
Hazlemere Ave SK11 . . . . .112 A4
Headland Cl WA3 . . . . .3 E8
Headlands The CH1,CH3 . .237 C4
Headworth Cl CW9 . . . . . .103 F6
Heald Ct SK9 . . . . .60 A4
Heald Green Ho M22 . . . . .34 A4

Heald Green Sta M22 ...34 A8
Heald St WA12 ...1 F3
Healey Cl CW1 ...190 A8
Heapy St SK11 ...112 E6
Hearn's La CW5 ...202 E5
Heath Ave
  Ellesmere Port CH65 ...70 A1
  Rode Heath ST7 ...193 F7
  Sandbach CW11 ...175 E6
Heath Bank CH3 ...119 D5
Heath Bsns & Technical Pk
  The WA7 ...49 A7
Heath Cl Chester CH3 ...142 B8
  Sandbach CW11 ...175 D6
  Tarvin CH3 ...121 B1
Heath Ct Alsager ST7 ...193 F6
  Ellesmere Port CH66 ...69 B6
Heath Dr Knutsford WA16 ...56 F2
  Runcorn WA7 ...49 A7
  Tarvin CH3 ...121 B1
Heath End Rd ST7 ...193 B5
Heath Gn CW6 ...146 C4
Heath Gr CH66 ...69 B7
Heath La Chester CH3 ...142 A8
  Culcheth WA3 ...4 A1
  Ellesmere Port,Little Sutton CH66 ...69 B7
  Golborne WA3 ...3 D6
  Golborne,Kenyon WA3 ...3 F2
  Great Barrow CH3 ...120 E6
  Great Budworth CW9 ...54 A1
  High Legh WA16 ...28 D5
  Little Leigh WA4,CW8 ...77 B7
  Marbury SY13 ...226 E6
  Stoak CH2 ...95 E7
  Stoak CH2 ...95 F7
  Swan Green WA16 ...106 F6
  Willaston CH64,CH66 ...68 D7
Heath Park Gr WA7 ...48 F8
Heath Rd Bollington SK10 ...87 C6
  Chester CH2 ...118 E7
  Congleton CW12 ...156 A2
  Runcorn WA7 ...23 B2
  Sandbach CW11 ...175 D6
  Warrington WA5 ...14 F5
  Weaverham CW8 ...77 C1
  Widnes WA8 ...12 D2
Heath Rd S WA7 ...48 F6
Heath Road Cres WA7 ...49 B8
Heath Sch The WA7 ...49 B7
Heath St Crewe CW1 ...190 D4
  Golborne WA3 ...3 A8
  Warrington WA4 ...26 C8
Heath Terr Chester CH2 ...118 E4
  Smallwood CW11 ...154 B1
Heath View Alsager ST7 ...193 E6
  Weston CW2 ...207 B5
Heath Way CW6 ...168 D8
Heathbank Rd SK8 ...34 F8
Heathbrook CW9 ...104 E7
Heathcote Cl CH2 ...118 C4
Heathcote Gdns CW9 ...104 D7
Heathcote St ST7 ...195 A2
Heather Ave M44 ...11 D6
Heather Brae WA12 ...2 A4
Heather Cl
  Ellesmere Port CH66 ...69 E3
  Macclesfield SK11 ...112 C4
  Runcorn WA7 ...49 E4
  Warrington WA3 ...9 D5
Heather Ct CH3 ...142 A8
Heather Falls SK22 ...39 B8
Heather Wlk M31 ...11 E3
Heatherfield Ct SK9 ...60 E8
Heathergate Pl CW2 ...206 B8
Heatherside ST7 ...195 C6
Heatherways CW6 ...146 C3
Heathfield SK9 ...60 A5
Heathfield Ave CW1 ...190 C4
Heathfield Cl
  Congleton CW12 ...155 F3
  Nantwich CW5 ...204 F6
Heathfield Ct
  Ellesmere Port CH65 ...70 B5
  Ellesmere Port CH66 ...95 A8
Heathfield Dr ST5 ...210 D1
Heathfield Pk
  Warrington WA4 ...17 A2
  Widnes WA8 ...12 D3
Heathfield Rd
  Audlem CW3 ...230 A5
  Ellesmere Port CH65 ...70 B5
Heathfields Cl CH2 ...237 B4
Heathgate Ave L24 ...21 A2
Heathlands Ho WA16 ...56 F2
Heathlands Rd CH66 ...69 B7
Heathmoor Ave WA3 ...3 D6
Heaths La CW6 ...123 D2
Heathside CW5 ...204 F6
Heathview CW1 ...191 D3
Heathview WA8 ...22 A5
Heathview Rd WA8 ...22 A5
Heathway CH60 ...41 B7
Heathwood ST7 ...193 F7
Heathwood Dr ST7 ...193 B5
Heathwood Gr WA1 ...17 B7
Heatley Cl WA13 ...19 A4
Heatley La CW5 ...217 F3
Heatley Way 5 SK9 ...34 D4
Heaton Cl CW10 ...151 C6
Heaton Ct WA3 ...9 F6
Heaton Sq CW7 ...149 C8
Heaward Cl CW2 ...206 B4
Hebden Ave WA3 ...5 B5
Hebden Green Com Sch
  CW7 ...149 A7

Hebden Green Specl Sch
  Grounds CW9 ...149 A7
Heber Wlk CW9 ...104 A8
Heber's Cl SY14 ...213 C5
Hedge Hey WA7 ...24 A1
Hedge Row SK10 ...63 E1
Hedgerow Dr CW9 ...79 C3
Hedgerows The WA11 ...1 F7
Hedingham Cl 7 SK10 ...111 F8
Hefferston Grange Dr
  CW8 ...102 A7
Hefferston Rise CW8 ...102 A7
Heights The WA6 ...73 C4
Helena Cl WA16 ...57 C2
Hellath Wen CW5 ...204 E2
Hellyar-Brook Rd ST7 ...193 B4
Helmdon Cl CW7 ...127 A3
Helmsdale Cl CW1 ...190 B6
Helmsdale La CW1 ...15 C6
Helmsley Cl WA5 ...15 E7
Helsby Ave CH62 ...43 F3
Helsby High Sch WA6 ...73 D5
Helsby Hillside Prim Sch
  WA6 ...73 D4
Helsby Pk WA6 ...73 C5
Helsby Rd WA6 ...73 C1
Helsby St WA1 ...16 D6
Helsby Sta WA6 ...73 B4
Helsby Way 4 SK9 ...34 D4
Helston Cl Bramhall SK7 ...35 F7
  Runcorn WA7 ...50 B5
  Warrington WA5 ...14 E5
Helston Gr SK8 ...34 C8
Helton Cl WA4 ...130 A3
Hemingford Cl CH66 ...69 D2
Hemlegh Vale WA6 ...73 B2
Hemming St WA6 ...78 D1
Hemmingshaw La CW11 ...176 B8
Hemswell Cl CW7 ...149 E8
Hemsworth Ave CH66 ...69 C5
Henbury Cl CW10 ...151 C7
Henbury Gdns WA4 ...26 E3
Henbury High Sch SK10 ...111 E8
Henbury La SK8 ...34 F6
Henbury Pl WA7 ...49 B6
Henbury Rd SK9 ...34 D4
Henbury Rise SK11 ...111 C8
Henderson Cl WA5 ...14 D6
Henderson Rd
  2 Widnes WA8 ...13 A1
  Widnes,Lower House WA8 ...22 F8
Henderson St SK11 ...112 C7
Hendon Cl CW1 ...190 F5
Henley Ave M44 ...11 E6
Henley Cl
  Macclesfield SK10 ...87 B4
  Neston CH64 ...66 E6
  Warrington WA4 ...26 E6
Henley Ct WA7 ...23 D2
Henley Dr CW7 ...126 E3
Henley Rd Chester CH4 ...140 F6
  Chorlton CW2 ...207 B1
  Neston CH64 ...66 E6
Henrietta St CW12 ...156 C3
Henry Pl CH1 ...237 B3
Henry St Crewe CW1 ...190 D5
  Haslington CW1 ...191 D4
  2 Lymm WA13 ...18 E3
  Tarporley CW6 ...146 C2
  Warrington WA1 ...16 A5
Henry Wood Ct CW4 ...140 C6
Henshall Ave WA4 ...16 F4
Henshall Dr CW11 ...175 D8
Henshall Hall Dr ST7 ...157 B1
Henshall La WA14 ...20 C6
Henshall Rd SK10 ...87 F7
Henshall St CH1 ...237 A4
Henshaw La SK11 ...110 E2
Hepherd St WA5 ...15 D4
Hepley Rd SK12 ...37 A3
Herald Dr CW1 ...190 E3
Herald Pk CW1 ...190 E3
Heralds Cl WA8 ...22 C8
Heralds Gn WA5 ...7 A2
Herbert St Burtonwood WA5 ...6 E6
  Congleton CW12 ...156 F3
  Crewe CW1 ...191 A5
  Lostock Gralam CW9 ...80 A2
Herbert Swindells Cl
  CW2 ...190 D1
Herberts La CH60 ...40 F8
Herdman St CW2 ...190 D2
Hereford Ave
  Ellesmere Port CH66 ...94 E8
  Golborne WA3 ...3 B8
Hereford Cl
  Macclesfield SK10 ...86 F1
  Warrington WA1 ...17 D7
Hereford Dr SK9 ...34 E3
Hereford Pl CH1 ...118 A5
Hereford Way CW10 ...128 E2
Hereward Rd CH3 ...119 B1
Heritage Ct CH1 ...237 B3
Hermitage Ct
  Holmes Chapel CW4 ...130 D3
  Saughall CH1 ...117 A8
Hermitage Dr CW4 ...130 D3
Hermitage Green La WA2,
  WA12 ...8 A8
Hermitage La CW4 ...130 C7
Hermitage Prim Sch
  CW4 ...130 D4
Hermitage Rd CH1 ...117 B7
Hermitage The CH60 ...40 F7
Heron Cl Broughton CH4 ...139 C4
  Farndon CH3 ...180 F1
  Knutsford WA16 ...57 B3

Heron Cl continued
  Runcorn WA7 ...50 D8
  Winsford WA7 ...149 D5
Heron Cres CW1 ...190 F5
Heron Ct Neston CH64 ...66 C7
  Northwich CW9 ...79 C2
Heron Dr SK12 ...36 A3
Herons Way Chester CH4 ...141 B2
  Runcorn WA7 ...24 F4
Herrick Ct CW2 ...206 D8
Hertford Apartments WA2 ...9 A3
Hertford Cl
  Congleton CW12 ...156 E4
  Warrington WA1 ...17 E7
Hertford Gr M44 ...11 C6
Hesketh Cl WA5 ...14 F4
Hesketh Croft CW1 ...190 A8
Hesketh Dr CW9 ...80 A3
Hesketh Grange Cotts
  CH63 ...42 A7
Hesketh Meadow La WA3 ...3 F8
Hesketh Rd L24 ...21 E2
Hesketh St WA5 ...15 D4
Hesketh St N WA5 ...15 D4
Hesnall Cl WA3 ...5 C8
Hessle Dr CH60 ...40 F7
Heswall Ave WA3 ...4 C4
Heswall Rd CH66 ...69 D4
Heswall St Peter's CE Prim
  Sch CH60 ...40 F8
Heswall Sta CH60 ...41 D8
Hetherson Green La
  SY14 ...214 D8
Hewetson Cres SK11 ...111 E7
Hewitt Dr CW7 ...150 D3
Hewitt Gr CW9 ...79 F5
Hewitt St Chester CH2 ...118 F3
  Crewe CW2 ...190 D2
  Northwich CW9 ...79 D2
  Warrington WA4 ...16 C3
Hexham Ct CH1 ...118 B2
Hexham Way 4 SK10 ...87 C4
Hey Lock Cl WA12 ...7 C8
Hey Shoot La WA3 ...5 C5
Hey Wood Cl WA12 ...7 C8
Heybridge La WA7 ...87 B6
Heydon Cl CW12 ...156 C3
Heyes Ave WA11 ...1 D5
Heyes Dr WA13 ...18 C2
Heyes Farm Rd SK11 ...111 E8
Heyes Ho SK11 ...111 E8
Heyes La
  Alderley Edge SK9 ...60 B3
  Warrington WA4 ...26 E8
Heyes Pk CW8 ...102 F4
Heyes Rd WA8 ...22 C8
Heyeswood La CW8 ...103 A4
Heyfield Park Rd CH66 ...69 B7
Heygarth Prim Sch CH62 ...43 E5
Heygarth Rd CH62 ...43 E5
Heys Ave CH62 ...43 D8
Heys The Bebington CH62 ...43 F5
  Runcorn WA7 ...23 E1
Heysbank Rd SK12 ...38 D5
Heysham Cl WA7 ...50 D6
Heysoms Ave CW8 ...103 D7
Heysoms Cl CW8 ...103 D7
Heythrop Dr CH60 ...41 D8
Heywood Cl SK9 ...60 B2
Heywood Gn CW2 ...206 C8
Heywood La CW3,SY13 ...234 C7
Heywood Rd
  Alderley Edge SK9 ...60 B2
  Ellesmere Port CH66 ...69 D5
Heywood St CW12 ...156 C2
Heywoods Ridge CW3 ...229 E3
Heywoods The CH2 ...118 C4
Hibbert St New Mills SK22 ...39 B6
  6 Widnes WA8 ...23 B8
Hibel Rd SK10 ...87 D1
Hickhurst La CW6 ...147 D3
Hickmore Heys CH3 ...119 F5
Hickory Cl WA1 ...17 E7
Hickson St CW8 ...78 B3
Hidcote Cl CW2 ...206 B8
Hield Brow CW9 ...79 C4
Hield Gr CW9 ...79 C8
Hield La CW9 ...79 C8
Higginbotham Gn SK11 ...112 E6
Higginson Cl CW12 ...179 C8
High Bank Cl M44 ...11 D6
High Bent Ave SK8 ...35 A6
High Carr Bsns Pk ST5 ...210 F2
High Carr Network Ctr
  ST5 ...210 F2
High Cross La CH3 ...182 D1
High Ct SK10 ...88 B8
High Elm Dr WA15 ...32 C8
High Elm Rd WA15 ...32 D7
High Elms SK8 ...35 B5
High Field WA14 ...20 B2
High Gates Cl WA5 ...15 E4
High Gates Lodge WA5 ...15 E7
High Hill Rd SK22 ...39 C8
High Lane Prim Sch SK6 ...37 F8
High Lea Rd SK22 ...39 A8
High Legh Prim Sch
  WA16 ...29 C5
High Legh Rd WA13 ...29 C8
High Lowe Ave CW12 ...157 A4
High Mdw 2 SK8 ...34 E8
High Mount CH60 ...40 F8
High St Audley ST7 ...210 A1
  Bollington SK10 ...88 B8
  Congleton CW12 ...156 D2
  Crewe CW2 ...190 D3
  Duddon CW6 ...145 D4

High St continued
  Farndon CH3 ...180 E2
  Frodsham WA6 ...49 B1
  Golborne WA3 ...3 A8
  Great Budworth CW9 ...79 A7
  Hale L24 ...21 D1
  Kidsgrove, Harriseahead
    ST7 ...195 E5
  Kidsgrove, Newchapel ST7 ...195 E2
  Kidsgrove, The Rookery
    ST7 ...195 C4
  Macclesfield SK11 ...112 D6
  Malpas SY14 ...213 B3
  Mow Cop ST7 ...195 D7
  Nantwich CW5 ...204 E5
  Neston CH64 ...66 E7
  New Mills SK22 ...39 C8
  Newton-le-W WA12 ...2 D4
  Norley WA6 ...100 F5
  Northwich CW9 ...103 F8
  Runcorn WA7 ...23 A2
  Saltney CH4 ...140 E7
  Sandbach CW11 ...175 B6
  Talke ST7 ...210 D6
  Tarporley CW6 ...146 C2
  Tarvin CH3 ...121 B2
  Tattenhall CH3 ...166 B1
  Warrington WA1 ...16 C5
  Weaverham CW8 ...77 C1
  Winsford CW7 ...126 D1
High View Helsby WA6 ...73 C4
  Mount Pleasant ST7 ...195 B5
High Warren Cl WA4 ...26 C5
Higham Ave WA5 ...7 F1
Highbank Cl CW8 ...78 B3
Highbank Rd
  Kingsley WA6 ...75 C2
  Northwich CW8 ...103 D7
Highcliffe Ave CW1 ...118 B4
Highcroft Ave CW12 ...156 F2
Higher Ash Rd ST7 ...210 D8
Higher Ashton WA8 ...12 F3
Higher Carden La SY14 ...198 D6
Higher Downs WA16 ...57 C2
Higher Fence Rd SK10 ...87 F1
Higher Ferry CH1 ...140 B8
Higher Heyes Dr WA6 ...75 C1
Higher Knutsford Rd
  WA4 ...16 F2
Higher La Bollington SK10 ...88 B6
  Disley SK12 ...38 E1
  Dutton WA4 ...51 D4
  Kettleshulme SK23 ...64 E6
  Lymm WA13 ...19 B1
Higher Rd L26,WA8 ...21 C5
Higher Works Cotts
  SK11 ...158 C6
Higherland 6 ST7 ...195 A2
Highfield Elton CH2 ...72 B4
  Prestbury SK10 ...87 A5
Highfield Ave
  Audlem CW3 ...230 A4
  Golborne WA3 ...2 F8
  Kidsgrove ST7 ...195 B2
  Lostock Gralam CW9 ...80 A3
  Warrington WA5 ...15 A5
  Warrington,Dudlow's Green
    WA4 ...26 D4
Highfield Cl CH64 ...66 E8
Highfield Com Prim Sch
  CH1 ...117 F4
Highfield Cres
  Handforth SK9 ...34 C1
  Widnes WA8 ...13 A2
Highfield Dr Lymm WA13 ...18 C2
  Macclesfield SK10 ...87 A1
  Nantwich CW5 ...205 A6
Highfield Est SK9 ...34 C1
Highfield La
  Coddington CH3 ...181 E4
  Golborne WA3 ...3 C5
  Winwick WA2 ...8 C7
Highfield Parkway SK7 ...35 D4
Highfield Pl 1 CW8 ...103 E8
Highfield Rd Blacon CH1 ...117 D6
  Bollington SK10 ...88 A8
  Cheadle Hulme SK8 ...34 F8
  Congleton CW12 ...156 E2
  Ellesmere Port CH65 ...70 C5
  Ellesmere Port,Little Sutton
    CH66 ...69 B6
  Lymm WA13 ...18 C2
  Macclesfield SK11 ...112 C7
  Neston CH64 ...66 E8
  Northwich CW8 ...103 F7
  Poynton SK12 ...36 A4
  Widnes WA8 ...13 A2
Highfield Rd N 11 CH65 ...70 C6
Highfield Sch L26 ...21 A7
Highfield Terr SK22 ...39 D8
Highfields SY13 ...224 A2
Highfields Com Prim Sch
  CW5 ...204 F6
Highgate Cl Crewe CW1 ...190 A8
  Runcorn WA7 ...24 D1
Highgrove Mews 2 SK9 ...60 A6
Highland Way WA16 ...82 A7
Highlands Rd WA7 ...48 F8
Highlands The CW6 ...185 E8
Highmarsh Cres WA12 ...2 B4
Hightown Crewe CW1 ...190 C4
  Middlewich CW10 ...128 C1
  Sandbach CW11 ...175 B6
Hightree Dr SK11 ...111 C8
Highwood Rd WA4 ...26 C5
Hignett Ave WA9 ...1 B2
Hilary Ave SK8 ...34 D8
Hilary Cl Chester CH3 ...119 B1

Hilary Cl continued
  Warrington WA5 ...14 D6
  Widnes WA8 ...13 E3
Hilbre Ave CH66 ...40 E6
Hilbre Bank CW6 ...169 E4
Hilbre Dr CH65 ...70 C1
Hilden Pl WA2 ...16 D8
Hilden Rd WA2 ...8 E1
Hill Cl CH64 ...67 B5
Hill Cliffe Rd WA4 ...26 B8
Hill Cotts CH3 ...164 A4
Hill Croft CW11 ...191 F8
Hill Ct CH4 ...67 B5
Hill Dr Handforth SK9 ...34 C8
  Whaley Bridge SK23 ...65 D8
Hill Fields Cl CW12 ...156 D4
Hill La Brown Knowl CH3 ...199 C8
  Peckforton CW6 ...184 E6
Hill Rd CH4 ...141 E2
Hill Rd N WA6 ...73 D3
Hill Rd S WA6 ...73 C3
Hill Side Cl SK12 ...38 E6
Hill St Crewe CW1 ...190 D4
  Macclesfield SK11 ...112 D6
  Runcorn WA7 ...23 A2
  Sandbach CW11 ...174 D7
  Warrington WA1 ...16 B5
  Winsford CW7 ...126 F1
Hill Terr ST7 ...209 D2
Hill The Knutsford WA16 ...32 A8
  Sandbach CW11 ...175 D5
Hill Top Altrincham WA15 ...32 A8
  Barnton CW8 ...78 B2
Hill Top Ave
  Cheadle Hulme SK8 ...35 B8
  Wilmslow SK9 ...60 B8
  Winsford CW7 ...126 C1
Hill Top La Heswall CH60 ...41 B8
  Neston CH64 ...67 B5
Hill Top Rd
  Acton Bridge CW8 ...76 F2
  Dutton WA4 ...51 C1
  Runcorn WA7 ...50 F6
  Warrington, Stockton Heath
    WA4 ...16 F2
  Warrington,Woolston WA1 ...17 C7
Hill Top Rise SK23 ...65 D8
Hill View Bollington SK10 ...87 F7
  Whaley Bridge SK23 ...65 C8
  Widnes WA8 ...12 F5
Hill View Ave WA6 ...73 A1
Hill View Prim Sch WA7 ...49 E4
Hillary Ave CW12 ...157 A2
Hillary Dr CW3 ...230 A4
Hillary Rd Bebington CH62 ...43 E5
  Kidsgrove ST7 ...195 B3
Hillberry Cres WA4 ...16 B3
Hillbre Way 1 SK9 ...34 D4
Hillbrook Rd SK7 ...35 D6
Hillcourt Rd SK6 ...37 F7
Hillcrest WA7 ...23 D1
Hillcrest Ave CW4 ...130 B3
Hillcrest Dr CH66 ...69 A6
Hillcrest Rd
  Bollington SK10 ...87 F7
  Ellesmere Port CH66 ...69 B6
  Kelsall CW6 ...122 E6
  Warren SK11 ...112 A4
Hillesden Rise CW12 ...156 F2
Hillfield Frodsham WA6 ...74 B7
  Runcorn WA7 ...50 D8
Hillfield Gdns CW5 ...204 E4
Hillfield Pl CW5 ...204 E4
Hillfield Rd CH66 ...69 D7
Hillfield View CW5 ...204 E4
Hillfields
  Congleton CW12 ...156 D3
  Congleton CW12 ...156 D4
Hillfoot Cres WA4 ...26 B7
Hillfoot La WA6 ...74 E3
Hilliards Ct CH4 ...141 B3
Hillingden Ave L26 ...21 A7
Hillock La WA1 ...17 C8
Hillsboro Ave WA6 ...74 C7
Hillsdown Way CH66 ...69 C2
Hillside Broomedge WA13 ...19 E1
  Northwich CW8 ...103 C7
Hillside Ave
  Newton-le-W WA12 ...1 F2
  Runcorn WA7 ...48 E8
Hillside Cl Bramhall SK7 ...36 A7
  Helsby WA6 ...73 D4
  Kidsgrove ST7 ...195 D7
Hillside Ct SK10 ...88 A1
Hillside Dr Crewe CW1 ...190 E5
  Ellesmere Port CH66 ...69 B6
  Macclesfield SK10 ...88 A1
Hillside Gr WA5 ...14 F4
Hillside Ho 7 CW8 ...103 C5
Hillside La CW9 ...126 F2
Hillside Rd Blacon CH1 ...117 E4
  Frodsham WA6 ...74 C7
  Heswall CH60 ...41 A7
  Kelsall CW6 ...122 D4
  Knutsford WA16 ...57 C2
  Warrington WA4 ...26 D3
Hillside View SK22 ...39 A8
Hilltop WA7 ...50 C7
Hilltop Com Prim Sch
  ST7 ...210 D7
Hilltop Pk WA16 ...79 F7
Hilltop Rd
  Guilden Sutton CH3 ...119 F5
  Lymm WA13 ...18 C2
Hillview Cl WA6 ...74 C7

Hillview Rise CW8 78 E1
Hilton Ave WA5 15 B5
Hilton Cl
9 Macclesfield SK11 111 F7
Middlewich CW10 151 B8
Hilton Dr M44 11 C5
Hilton Gr SK12 36 D4
Hilton Rd Disley SK12 38 B7
Poynton SK12 37 C5
Hinchley Cl CW8 103 A5
Hinckley Ct CW12 156 A3
Hind Heath La CW11 174 F4
Hind Heath Rd CW11 174 E4
Hinde St CW5 204 D4
Hinderton Dr CH60 40 F6
Hinderton Gn CH64 66 F8
Hinderton La CH64 67 A8
Hinderton Rd CH64 66 F8
Hinderton Sch CH65 69 F3
Hindle Ave WA5 7 F1
Hindley Cres CW8 78 A3
Hinton Cres WA4 26 E8
Hinton Rd Crewe CW2 206 D8
Runcorn WA7 23 A1
Hirsch Cl CW5 205 A4
Hitch Lowes SK11 84 A3
Hitchen's Cl WA7 50 D7
Hitchens La SY14 184 D1
Hob Hey La WA3 4 D3
Hob La Churton CH3 180 F5
Dunham-on-t-H WA6 97 C6
Hobart Cl SK7 35 F4
Hobart Way CH1 117 D4
Hobb La WA4 25 C5
Hobbs Cl CW1 191 D4
Hobbs Hill La WA16 28 E1
Hobby Ct WA7 49 E6
Hobcroft La WA16 58 A7
Hobson St SK11 112 D6
Hockenhull Ave CH3 121 B2
Hockenhull Cres CH3 121 B2
Hockenhull La
Tarvin CH3 121 B1
Tarvin CH3 121 B2
Hocker La
Adder's Moss SK10 85 F4
Nether Alderley SK10 85 C4
Hockerley Ave SK23 65 D8
Hockerley Cl SK23 65 D8
Hockerley La SK23 65 D8
Hockerley New Rd SK23 65 D8
Hockley Cl SK12 37 A3
Hockley Paddock SK12 36 F3
Hockley Rd SK12 37 A3
Hodge La Hartford CW8 103 A6
Weaverham CW8 102 D5
Hodgehill La SK11 132 E5
Hodgkin Cl CW5 204 F4
Hodgkinson Ave WA5 7 F1
Hoghton Rd L24 21 E2
Hogshead La CW8 124 C7
Holbeck WA7 50 C7
Holbein Cl CH4 141 E6
Holborn Ct WA8 12 F3
Holbrook Cl WA5 14 E5
Holbury Cl CW1 190 B8
Holcombe Ave WA3 3 C8
Holcombe Dr SK10 87 B3
Holcot Ct CW7 127 A4
Holcroft La WA3 5 D2
Holdings La CW3 232 F4
Hole House La CW8 77 E4
Holehouse La
Langley SK11 113 C4
Scholar Green ST7 194 D8
Whiteley Green SK10 62 D2
Holes La WA1 17 B7
Holford Ave
Lostock Gralam CW9 80 A3
Warrington WA5 15 F8
Holford Cres WA16 57 B1
Holford Moss WA7 24 D3
Holford St CW12 156 D3
Holford Way WA12 2 F3
Holgrave Cl WA16 29 C4
Holkam Cl CW9 103 F5
Holker Cl SK12 36 F4
Holkham Cl WA8 12 F1
Holkham The CH3 119 B1
Holland Cl CW11 175 C5
Holland Ct SK12 36 E3
Holland Rd SK7 35 E7
Holland St Crewe CW1 190 B6
5 Macclesfield SK11 112 C7
Hollands La CW6 122 C5
Hollands Pl SK11 112 F7
Hollands Rd CW9 103 F7
Hollies La SK9 60 F7
Hollies The Moulton CW9 126 E8
1 Northwich CW9 103 E6
Runcorn WA7 49 D8
Shavington CW2 206 B4
Hollin Green La CW5 202 E6
Hollin La Langley SK11 113 A1
Newhall CW5 228 D8
Styal SK9 33 F5
Sutton Lane Ends SK11 136 C6
Hollin Rd SK10 88 A7
Hollingford Pl WA16 82 A8
Hollingreen La CW5 229 B7
Hollinhey Prim Sch
SK11 112 F3
Hollins Cres ST7 194 E1
Hollins Dr WA2 8 A6
Hollins Grange ST7 210 D8
Hollins Green St Helens CE Prim Sch WA3 11 B2
Hollins Hill CW6 146 F8
Hollins La Antrobus CW9 53 F4
Marbury SY13 226 E7
Winwick WA2 7 E6
Hollins Park Hospl WA2 7 F6
Hollins Rd SK11 112 F6
Hollins Terr SK11 112 F6
Hollins Way WA8 22 B5
Hollinshead Cl ST7 194 F7
Hollinwood Cl ST7 210 E8
Hollinwood Rd
Disley SK12 38 D6
Talke ST7 210 E8
Hollow Dr WA4 16 E1
Hollow La Kingsley WA6 75 B3
Knutsford WA16 57 B1
Hollow Oak La CW8 101 D4
Hollow The ST7 195 B5
Holloway WA7 22 F1
Hollowmoor Heath CH3 121 A6
Hollowood Rd SY14 213 B5
Holly Ave WA12 2 D3
Holly Bank Frodsham WA6 74 C8
Helsby WA6 73 D2
Lymm WA13 18 D2
Holly Bank Rd SK9 34 B1
Holly Bush La WA3 10 C2
Holly Cl
Connah's Quay CH5 91 C1
Hale L24 21 D2
Mickle Trafford CH2 119 F8
Holly Cotts Marton CW12 132 C1
Wilmslow SK9 59 E8
Holly Croft CW12 154 F6
Holly Ct Helsby WA6 73 C5
Middlewich CW10 128 B2
Holly Dr CW7 149 D8
Holly Farm Ct WA8 12 E4
Holly Gr Over Tabley WA16 56 A3
Warrington WA1 17 A7
Holly Heath Cl CW11 175 C5
Holly Hedge La WA4 25 D6
Holly House Est CW10 129 C6
Holly La Alsager ST7 193 E3
Kidsgrove ST7 195 F5
Styal SK9 33 E5
Holly Mount CW2 206 E5
Holly Rd Bramhall SK7 35 E5
Chester CH4 140 F5
Ellesmere Port CH65 70 C5
Golborne WA3 3 C8
Haydock WA11 1 A6
High Lane SK6 37 F7
Lymm WA13 19 B5
Macclesfield SK11 112 B7
Newcastle-u-Lyme ST5 210 D1
Poynton SK12 36 E3
Warrington WA5 14 E5
Weaverham CW8 102 C8
Holly Rd N SK9 60 B6
Holly Rd S SK9 60 B5
Holly Terr Tilston SY14 198 C3
Warrington WA5 14 F5
Holly Tree Dr
Biddulph ST8 179 C2
Swan Green WA16 106 D7
Holly Wlk Northwich CW8 103 C7
Partington M31 11 D3
Hollybank Audlem CW3 229 E3
Moore WA4 25 B5
Hollybank Cl CW8 78 D1
Hollybank Ct WA8 12 F1
Hollybank Rd WA7 49 F8
Hollybush Cres CW5 205 D5
Hollyfield Rd CH65 70 B5
Hollyfields CW11 191 F8
Hollyhurst Rd SY13 227 B7
Hollythorn Ave SK8 35 C7
Hollytree Rd WA16 80 F3
Holm Dr CH2 72 C3
Holm Oak Way CH66 94 F8
Holme St CH3 120 F2
Holmefield Dr SK8 35 B8
Holmes Chapel Bsns Pk
CW4 130 D3
Holmes Chapel Comp Sch
CW4 130 A2
Holmes Chapel Prim Sch
CW4 130 B3
Holmes Chapel Rd
Allostock WA16 106 B3
Brereton Green CW4, CW12 154 D8
Congleton CW12 155 C4
Knutsford WA16 82 C3
Lach Dennis CW9 105 E4
Middlewich CW10 128 E2
Sandbach CW11 153 E1
Sproston Green CW4, CW10 129 B2
Withington Green SK11 109 A7
Holmes Chapel Sta
CW4 130 D2
Holmes Ct WA3 9 C4
Holmesville Ave CW12 156 B3
Holmeswood Cl SK9 60 C8
Holmfield Ave WA7 23 C2
Holmfield Dr CH66 69 D3
Holmlea Dr CW1 190 F3
Holmlee Way SK10 86 D6
Holmsfield Rd WA1 16 D5
Holmshaw La CW1 192 B3
Holmwood Dr CH65 70 B2
Holt Hey CH64 67 A5
Holt La WA7 49 F8
Holt St CW1 190 B4
Holt's Com Prim Sch
LL13 196 D8
Holt's La SK9 33 F3
Holtridge La SY13 215 E6
Holy Family RC Prim Sch
WA8 12 D5
Holy Spirit RC Prim Sch
WA9 1 A3
Holy Spirit RC Prim Sch The
WA7 49 D7
Holyhead Cl WA5 7 D3
Holyrood Ave WA8 13 A4
Holyrood Dr CW2 205 E8
Holyrood Way CH3 119 B2
Holywell Cl CH64 41 B1
Holywell La CH3 182 D2
Home Cl CH3 142 E7
Home Farm Ave SK10 86 F1
Home Farm Pk CW5 172 A8
Home Pk CH1 94 F1
Homecrofts CH64 66 E5
Homedee Ho CH1 237 A3
Homeshire Ho ST7 193 D3
Homestead Ave WA11 1 E6
Homestead Ct CW9 104 D7
Homestead Rd SK12 38 C6
Homesteads The CW5 172 A6
Homeway WA6 73 B2
Homewood Cres CW8 103 B5
Honey Fields CW6 146 C1
Honey Suckle Cl CH66 94 F8
Honeysuckle Cl
Broughton CH4 139 C3
Widnes WA8 13 B4
Honford Ct SK9 34 D3
Hong Kong Ave M90 33 A8
Honister Ave WA2 8 C2
Honister Gr WA7 49 E5
Honiton Way
Middlewich CW10 128 D2
Warrington WA5 14 E4
Hoo Green La WA16 29 E1
Hood La WA5 15 C4
Hood La N WA5 15 C6
Hood Rd WA8 12 F1
Hoofield La CH3 145 A1
Hook La CW6 145 A6
Hooker St CW8 103 E7
Hookstone Dr CH66 69 C6
Hoole CE Prim Sch CH2 119 A3
Hoole Gdns CH2 119 B3
Hoole Ho CH2 119 B4
Hoole La CH2 119 A3
Hoole Pk CH2 118 F2
Hoole Rd CH2 118 F3
Hoole Way CH1 237 B3
Hooleyhey La SK10,SK11 89 D4
Hoolpool La WA6 72 F5
Hooton Gn CH66 44 B2
Hooton La CH66 44 B1
Hooton Rd CH64,CH66 43 D1
Hooton Sta CH66 43 D1
Hooton Way
14 Handforth SK9 34 D5
Hooton CH66 44 A2
Hope Ave SK9 34 C3
Hope Croft CH66 69 F2
Hope Farm Prec CH66 69 F2
Hope Farm Rd CH66 69 E2
Hope Green Way SK10 36 D2
Hope La Midway SK10 36 D1
Wardsend SK10 36 E1
Hope Rd CH4 139 B3
Hope St Audley ST7 209 F3
Chester CH4 140 F7
Crewe CW2 190 D2
Macclesfield SK10 112 E8
Newton-le-W WA12 2 B3
Northwich CW8 103 E7
Sandbach CW11 175 B6
Hope St W SK10 112 C8
Hopefield Rd WA13 19 B4
Hopkins Cl CW12 156 B3
Hopkinson Ct CH1 118 B1
Hopwood Cl 5 WA3 3 F8
Hopwood St WA1 16 C6
Horace Black Gdns CH65 70 C6
Horace Lawton Ct 2
CW12 156 D3
Horbury Gdns CH66 69 C5
Horn's Mill Prim Sch
WA6 73 A1
Hornbeam Ave CH66 69 F1
Hornbeam Cl
Chester CH2 119 B3
Runcorn WA7 24 C1
Hornbeam Dr CW8 102 E4
Hornbeam Rd L26 21 A7
Hornby Dr
Congleton CW12 156 A3
Nantwich CW5 205 A5
Hornby La WA2 8 A6
Horncastle Cl 4 WA3 3 F8
Horridge Ave WA12 2 C5
Horrocks La WA1 16 B5
Horrocks Rd CH2 118 E5
Horsemarket St WA1 16 B5
Horseshoe Cl WA6 75 B2
Horseshoe Cres WA2 8 E3
Horseshoe Dr SK11 112 B7
Horseshoe La SK9 60 A2
Horsley La CW6 167 E1
Horstone Cres CH66 69 F2
Horstone Gdns CH66 70 A2
Horstone Rd CH66 69 F2
Horton Way CW5 205 A4
Horwood Ho SK9 60 B2
Hoscar Ct WA8 22 D7
Hospital La CW5 203 E2
Hospital of St John
Almhouses CH1 237 A3
Hospital St Crewe CW1 190 D6
Nantwich CW5 204 E5
Hospital Way WA7 49 F7
Hotel Rd M90 33 C7
Hotel St WA12 2 B3
Hothershall Ct CW1 173 B1
Hough Cl SK10 88 D5
Hough Cotts CW2 206 E3
Hough Gn Ashley WA15 31 E5
Chester CH4 141 B7
Hough Green Rd WA8 12 B3
Hough Green Sta WA8 12 A2
Hough La
Alderley Edge SK9 60 D3
Barnton CW8,CW9 78 B4
Comberbach CW9 78 A7
Norley WA6 100 F5
Hough's La WA4 26 A6
Hougher Wall Rd ST7 209 D1
Houghley Cl SK10 87 C2
Houghton Cl
Chester CH2 118 F3
Newton-le-W WA12 2 B3
9 Northwich CW9 103 F4
Widnes WA8 13 D2
Houghton Croft WA8 12 C5
Houghton St
Newton-le-W WA12 2 B3
Warrington WA2 16 B6
Widnes WA8 13 D2
Houndings La CW11 175 B4
Hourd Way CH66 94 E8
Housesteads Dr CH2 118 F3
Housman Cl CH1 118 A5
Hove Cl CW1 190 B8
Hove The WA7 50 D6
Hovis Mill SK11 112 E7
Howard Ave
Bebington CH62 43 D8
Lymm WA13 19 B4
Howard Ct Neston CH64 41 F1
Runcorn WA7 24 C4
Howard Rd Culcheth WA3 5 A2
Saltney CH4 140 D6
Howard St CW1 191 A5
Howards Way CH64 67 A6
Howarth Ct 4 WA7 23 B2
Howbeck Cres CW5 220 A8
Howbeck Wlk CW2 206 D8
Howe Rd CH4 141 B7
Howe St SK10 87 F1
Howells Ave CH66 69 D3
Howey Hill CW12 156 D1
Howey La
Congleton CW12 156 D2
Frodsham WA6 74 B7
Howey Rise WA6 74 B7
Howgill Cl CH66 68 F6
Howley La WA1 16 E5
Howley Quay Ind Est
WA1 16 D5
Howson Rd WA2 8 C3
Howty Cl SK9 34 D1
Hoylake Cl WA7 50 C6
Hoyle St WA5 15 F7
Hubert Dr CW10 151 C8
Hubert Worthington Ho 8
SK9 60 A1
Hudson Cl WA5 15 D8
Hudson Gr 9 WA3 3 E8
Hugh St CH4 141 D7
Hughes Ave WA2 8 D2
Hughes Dr CW2 189 F4
Hughes Pl WA2 8 D2
Hughes St WA4 16 C3
Hulley Pl SK10 87 F1
Hulley Rd SK10 87 F2
Hullock's Pool Rd ST7 209 E5
Hulme Hall Ave SK8 35 B8
Hulme Hall Cres SK8 35 A8
Hulme hall Gram Sch
SK8 35 A8
Hulme Hall La WA16 106 B4
Hulme Hall Rd SK8 35 A8
Hulme La WA16 106 C7
Hulme Sq SK11 112 D5
Hulme St CW1 189 F5
Hulse La CW9 105 D6
Hulseheath La WA16 30 A3
Hulton Cl CW12 157 B1
Humber Cl WA8 13 F3
Humber Dr ST8 179 E1
Humber Rd
Ellesmere Port CH66 69 F2
Warrington WA2 8 E2
Humble Bee Bank Cotts
CW5 187 C8
Hume St WA1 16 D6
Humphrey's Cl WA7 50 D7
Hungerford Ave CW1 190 E4
Hungerford Pl
Barthomley CW2 208 D5
Sandbach CW11 175 A5
Hungerford Prim Sch
CW1 190 E5
Hungerford Rd CW1 190 F4
Hungerford Terr CW1 190 F4
Hungerford Villas CW1 190 F4
Hunsterson Rd
Bridgemere CW5 231 D8
Hatherton CW5 220 B3
Hunt Cl WA5 15 B8
Hunt Rd WA11 1 E6
Hunter Ave
Shavington CW2 206 D7
Hunter Ave *continued*
Warrington WA2 8 B3
Hunter St CH1 237 A3
Hunter's Cres CH3 121 C1
Hunter's Dr CH3 121 C1
Hunter's View SK9 34 C3
Hunters Cl SK9 34 F1
Hunters Ct Helsby WA6 73 D4
Runcorn WA7 49 E6
Hunters Field CW8 103 D7
Hunters Hill Kingsley WA6 75 C1
Weaverham CW8 77 C1
Hunters Lodge SK9 34 F1
Hunters Mews SK9 60 C7
Hunters Pointe CW12 155 C6
Hunters Pool La SK10 86 C8
Hunters Rise CW7 126 C1
Hunters Way Neston CH64 66 C8
Talke ST7 210 D8
Hunters Wlk CH1 237 A2
Huntersfield CW2 206 B3
Hunting Lodge Mews
CW8 102 A4
Huntington Com Prim Sch
CH3 142 A5
Huntley St WA5 15 C4
Huntly Chase SK9 60 C7
Hunts Cl CH3 119 B1
Hunts Field Cl WA13 18 D2
Hunts La WA4 16 F2
Huntsbank Bsns Pk
CW2 205 E7
Huntsbank Dr ST5 210 D1
Huntsman Dr M44 11 F7
Hurdsfield Cl CW10 151 C7
Hurdsfield Com Prim Sch
SK10 87 F2
Hurdsfield Gn SK10 87 E2
Hurdsfield Ind Est SK10 87 E3
Hurdsfield Rd SK10 87 E1
Hurford Ave CH65 69 F3
Hurlbote Cl SK9 34 D5
Hurleston Bldgs CW5 204 E6
Hurlestone Cl CH2 96 F1
Hurley Cl WA5 15 C5
Hurn Cl CW1 190 B8
Hurst Ave SK8 35 C6
Hurst Cl ST7 210 D6
Hurst Ct CW6 185 E8
Hurst La Bollington SK10 88 A8
Glazebury WA3 5 C7
Hurst Lea Ct SK9 60 A2
Hurst Lea Rd SK22 39 C7
Hurst Mews WA6 75 C2
Hurst Mill La WA3 5 C8
Hurst Rd ST8 179 F4
Hurst St WA8 23 A4
Hurst The WA6 75 C2
Hursthead Inf Sch SK8 35 C6
Hursthead Jun Sch SK8 35 C7
Hursthead Rd SK8 35 B7
Hurstwood CH3 143 A4
Hush Ho CH1 237 A2
Huskisson Way WA12 2 B4
Hutchins' Cl CW10 151 E6
Hutchinson St WA8 22 F6
Huttfield Rd L24 21 A4
Hutton Cl WA3 4 E5
Hutton Dr CW12 157 A2
Huxley CE Prim Sch
CH3 167 A7
Huxley Cl Bramhall SK7 35 E7
Macclesfield SK10 87 B
Huxley Ct CH66 69 F
Huxley Dr SK7 35 E
Huxley La CW6 168 B
Huxley St CW8 103 E
Hyacinth Cl WA11 1 F
Hyacinth Wlk 9 M31 11 E
Hyde Bank Ct SK22 39 C
Hyde Bank Rd SK22 39 C
Hyde Cl
Ellesmere Port CH65 69 F
Runcorn WA7 49 D
Hydrangea Way WA9 6 A
Hylton Ct CH65 70 E
Hylton Dr SK8 35 C
Hythe Ave CW1 190 B

I

Ian Rd ST7 195 D
Iberis Gdns WA9 6 A
Ibis Ct WA1 16 A
Ikey La CW5 202 F
Ikins Dr ST7 209 F
Ilex Ave WA2 8 B
Imperial Ave CH1 117 C
Imperial Mews
Crewe CW2 190 D
Ellesmere Port CH65 70 B
Ince & Elton Sta CH2 72 B
Ince Ave CH62 43 E
Ince Dr CH3 180 F
Ince La Elton CH2 72 B
Wimbolds Trafford CH2 96 F
Ince Orchards CH2 72 B
Indigo Rd CH65 70 F
Ingersley Ct SK10 88 B
Ingersley Rd SK10 88 C
Ingersley Vale SK10 88 B
Ingham Ave WA12 2 C
Ingham Cl CH3 119 A
Ingham Rd WA8 12 F
Inglegreen CH60 41 E
Inglenook Rd WA5 14 F

Ingleton Cl
  Holmes Chapel CW4 . . . . . .130 A3
  Newton-le-W WA12 . . . . .2 B4
Ingleton Gr WA7 . . . . .49 D5
Inglewood Ave CW10 . . . . .151 D5
Inglewood Cl
  Partington M31 . . . . .11 F4
  Warrington WA3 . . . . .10 B6
Inglewood Cvn Pk M31 . . . .11 F4
Inman Ave WA9 . . . . .1 B2
Inner Gosling Cl WA4 . . . .25 F1
Innisfree Cl 4 CH66 . . . . . .69 C5
Innovation Ho CW7 . . . . . .149 A7
Insall Rd WA2 . . . . .8 F2
Int Peace Ctr WA5 . . . . . . .15 D5
Intack La WA1 . . . . .28 B3
Intake Cl CH64 . . . . .68 A8
International App M90 . . . .33 C7
Inveresk Rd SY14 . . . . . . .198 C3
Inward CH65 . . . . .70 B7
Ion Path CW7 . . . . .127 C1
Irby Cl CH66 . . . . .69 E4
Ireland Blackburne Ho
  WA1 . . . . .16 E7
Ireland Rd Hale L24 . . . . . . .21 E1
  Haydock WA11 . . . . .1 C6
Ireland St Warrington WA2 16 B8
  Widnes WA8 . . . . .13 D2
Iris Cl WA8 . . . . .12 C2
Iris Wlk 7 M31 . . . . .11 E2
Irlam & Cadishead Com High
  Sch M44 . . . . .11 E7
Irlam Ind Est M44 . . . . .11 E7
Irlam Sta M44 . . . . .11 E7
Ironbridge Dr CW4 . . . . . .130 C2
Irons La CH3 . . . . .120 F7
Irvin Dr M22 . . . . .34 A8
Irving's Cres CH4 . . . . . . .140 E6
Irwell La WA7 . . . . .23 B3
Irwell Rd WA4 . . . . .16 B2
Irwell Rise SK10 . . . . .87 F7
Irwell St WA8 . . . . .23 A4
Irwin Dr SK9 . . . . .34 C5
Isabella Ct CH4 . . . . .140 E6
Isherwood Cl WA2 . . . . .8 F3
Isis Cl CW12 . . . . .156 F1
Islay Cl CH65 . . . . .70 C1
Iveagh Cl WA4 . . . . .50 A7
  Cronton WA8 . . . . .12 C6
Iver Cl Chester CH2 . . . . . .118 E7
Iver Rd CH2 . . . . .118 E7
Ivy Ave WA12 . . . . .2 C2
Ivy Bank Prim Sch SK11 112 A5
Ivy Cotts SY13 . . . . .225 A8
Ivy Ct CH4 . . . . .162 D2
Ivy Dr CW8 . . . . .102 A2
Ivy Farm Cl L21 . . . . .21 D1
Ivy Farm Dr CH64 . . . . .66 F6
Ivy Farm Gdns WA3 . . . . . . .4 D4
Ivy Farm La CH3 . . . . .183 C1
Ivy Gdns CW12 . . . . .156 C2
Ivy Ho Macclesfield SK11 112 A7
  Nether Alderley SK9 . . . . . . .84 C7
Ivy House Rd ST8 . . . . . . .179 C2
Ivy La Alsager ST7 . . . . . . .193 E2
  Macclesfield SK11 . . . . .112 A6
Ivy Meade Cl 10 SK11 . . . .111 F7
Ivy Meade Rd SK11 . . . . . .111 F6
Ivy Mews CH2 . . . . .119 A5
Ivy Rd Golborne WA3 . . . . . . .3 B8
  Macclesfield SK11 . . . . .112 A7
  Poynton SK12 . . . . .36 C3
  Warrington WA1 . . . . .17 E7
Ivy St WA7 . . . . .23 A1
Ivy Wlk M31 . . . . .11 D3
Ivychurch Mews WA7 . . . .23 D2

J

Jack La
  Moulton CW9,CW10 . . . . . .127 A7
  Weston CW2 . . . . .207 D6
Jackie Stewart Bsns Ctr
  CW6 . . . . .147 D6
Jackson Ave Culcheth WA3 .4 E3
  Nantwich CW5 . . . . .204 F6
  Warrington WA1 . . . . .16 F6
Jackson Ct CH5 . . . . .139 B7
Jackson Ho CW12 . . . . . . .156 D2
Jackson La SK10 . . . . .88 B7
Jackson Rd CW12 . . . . . . .156 E5
Jackson St
  Burtonwood WA5 . . . . .6 E6
  Haydock WA11 . . . . .1 A7
  Macclesfield SK11 . . . . .112 D6
Jackson's La SK7 . . . . .36 C8
Jacksons Cl SK10 . . . . .88 B7
Jacksons Edge Rd SK12 . .38 B6
Jacobs Way WA16 . . . . .79 F7
Jamage Rd ST7 . . . . .210 D5
James Atkinson Way
  CW1 . . . . .189 F7
James Ave CH66 . . . . .69 C3
James Cl WA8 . . . . .23 A4
James Hall St CW5 . . . . . .204 E6
James Pl CH2 . . . . .118 F2
James Rd WA11 . . . . .1 F7
James St Chester CH1 . . . .237 B3
  Macclesfield SK11 . . . . .112 D6
  Northwich CW9 . . . . .104 C8
  6 Warrington WA1 . . . . . . .16 B5
Jamieson Cl Alsager ST7 193 E4
  Chester CH3 . . . . .119 A2
Jan Palach Ave CW5 . . . .204 F4
Jane Maddock Cotts
  ST7 . . . . .193 B3
Jankyns Croft SK12 . . . . . .38 E5

Japonica Gdns WA9 . . . . . . .6 A7
Jarman SK11 . . . . .112 F4
Jasmin Way ST7 . . . . .195 D2
Jasmine Cres ST7 . . . . . . .195 D2
Jasmine Gdns WA9 . . . . .6 A7
Jasmine Gr WA8 . . . . .22 D8
Jasmine Wlk M31 . . . . .11 F2
Jay Cl WA3 . . . . .10 A4
Jays Cl WA1 . . . . .50 E7
Jedburgh Ave CH66 . . . . . .69 A6
Jellicoe Ave M44 . . . . .11 E6
Jennet's La WA3 . . . . .5 C8
Jenny La SK7 . . . . .35 E4
Jensen Ct WA7 . . . . .23 C3
Jersey Ave CH65 . . . . .70 C1
Jersey La CW12 . . . . .157 A2
Jersey Way CW10 . . . . . . .128 C2
Jervis Cl WA2 . . . . .9 A3
Jesmond Cres CW2 . . . . . .190 B2
Jesmond Gr SK8 . . . . .35 B8
Jesmond Rd CH1 . . . . .118 B2
Jessop Way CW1 . . . . .191 C4
JH Godwin Prim Sch
  CH1 . . . . .117 D4
Jockey St WA2 . . . . .16 B7
Jodrell Bank Obsy★
  CW4 . . . . .108 C3
Jodrell Bank Visitor Ctr★
  SK11 . . . . .108 D3
Jodrell Cl
  Holmes Chapel CW4 . . . . . .130 A3
  Macclesfield SK11 . . . . .112 E7
Jodrell Mdw SK23 . . . . .65 E8
Jodrell Rd SK23 . . . . .65 D8
Jodrell St
  Macclesfield SK11 . . . . .112 E7
  New Mills SK22 . . . . .39 B7
John Brunner Cres
  CW9 . . . . .103 E6
John Fryer Ave WA4 . . . . .80 A5
John Gresty Dr CW5 . . . . .205 D6
John Lloyd Ct M44 . . . . . . .11 F8
John May Ct SK10 . . . . . . .87 B2
John Middleton Cl L24 . . .21 E2
John Morris Ho 1 WA1 .16 C5
John Nicholas Cres
  CH65 . . . . .70 C6
John Rd WA13 . . . . .18 C3
John St Bollington SK10 . . .88 B8
  Congleton CW12 . . . . .156 C2
  Crewe CW1 . . . . .190 C5
  Ellesmere Port CH65 . . . . . . .70 B6
  Golborne WA3 . . . . .3 A8
  Irlam M44 . . . . .11 E5
  Macclesfield SK11 . . . . .112 D6
  1 Northwich CW9 . . . . . . .104 A8
  Utkinton CW6 . . . . .146 B7
  Warrington WA2 . . . . .16 B6
  Winsford CW7 . . . . .126 C1
John Street Com Prim Sch
  CH65 . . . . .70 B6
Johns Ave Haydock WA11 . . .1 C7
  Runcorn WA7 . . . . .48 F8
Johns Cl SK10 . . . . .88 D5
Johnson Ave WA12 . . . . .2 B5
Johnson Cl CW12 . . . . .157 B1
Johnson St SK23 . . . . .65 E8
Johnson's La WA8 . . . . .13 C1
Johnsons Cl CH4 . . . . .141 B5
Jonathan's Way CH1 . . . .117 C5
Jones's La CW10 . . . . .152 D6
Jonson Rd CH64 . . . . .66 E8
Jordangate SK10 . . . . .112 D8
Joseph Cres ST7 . . . . .193 F2
Joseph Groome Twrs 10
  CH65 . . . . .70 C6
Joseph St WA8 . . . . .13 C2
Joy La WA5 . . . . .6 E4
Joyce Ave CW7 . . . . .126 C2
Jubilee Almshouses
  CW5 . . . . .204 E6
Jubilee Ave Crewe CW2 . .190 B3
  Warrington WA5 . . . . .14 E4
  Warrington,Padgate WA1 . . .16 F8
Jubilee Cres WA11 . . . . .1 F7
Jubilee Ct
  2 Handforth SK9 . . . . .34 E5
  Holmes Chapel CW4 . . . . . .130 A3
Jubilee Gdns
  Nantwich CW5 . . . . .204 E4
  New Mills SK22 . . . . .39 C7
Jubilee Gn CH65 . . . . .70 C4
Jubilee Gr WA13 . . . . .18 C4
Jubilee Rd CW12 . . . . .156 E2
Jubilee St SK22 . . . . .39 C7
Jubilee Terr CW5 . . . . .204 E4
Jubilee Villas CW1 . . . . . .175 C2
Jubilee Way Widnes WA8 .12 E1
  5 Winsford CW7 . . . . . . .126 D1
Jubits La WA8 . . . . .13 A8
Juddfield St WA11 . . . . .1 A7
Julian Way WA4 . . . . .12 F4
July Cotts CH4 . . . . .141 E2
Jumper La SK10 . . . . .88 F7
Junction Eight Bsns Ctr
  CH65 . . . . .70 A7
Junction La WA12 . . . . .2 B3
June Ave CH62 . . . . .43 E8
Juniper Cl ST5 . . . . .210 E1
Juniper Ct CH2 . . . . .119 B4
Juniper Dr CH66 . . . . .69 E1
Juniper Gr CH66 . . . . .69 F1
Juniper La WA3 . . . . .18 A7
Juniper Rise SK10 . . . . .86 E1
Jupiter Dr CH1 . . . . .117 E2
Jurby Ct WA2 . . . . .9 A3
Justice St SK10 . . . . .87 D1

K

Kansas Pl WA5 . . . . .15 B7
Karen Cl WA5 . . . . .7 A6
Karen Way CH66 . . . . .69 D3
Kay La WA13 . . . . .29 B8
Kaye Ave WA3 . . . . .4 F3
Keats Cl
  Ellesmere Port CH66 . . . . . . .94 E8
  Widnes WA8 . . . . .22 F8
Keats Dr Macclesfield SK10 86 F1
  Rode Heath ST7 . . . . .193 E8
  Wistaston CW2 . . . . .206 A8
Keats Gr WA2 . . . . .8 C2
Keats La WA9 . . . . .80 A5
Keats Terr CH1 . . . . .118 A5
Keble St WA8 . . . . .23 B7
Keckwick La WA4 . . . . .25 A3
Keel Hey CH64 . . . . .43 B1
Keele Cres SK11 . . . . .112 B6
Keeper's La CW8 . . . . .102 E8
Keeper's Rd WA4 . . . . .27 A7
Keepers Cl WA16 . . . . .57 D3
Keepers La CW9 . . . . .53 D4
Keepers Wlk WA7 . . . . .23 F2
Keith Ave WA5 . . . . .14 E6
Keith Dr CH63 . . . . .43 D5
Kelburn Ct WA3 . . . . .9 F6
Kelmscott Cl CH66 . . . . . . .69 D2
Kelsall Ave CH62 . . . . .43 F3
Kelsall Cl Macclesfield SK11 112 E7
  Warrington WA3 . . . . .9 C3
  Widnes WA8 . . . . .12 D1
Kelsall Com Prim Sch
  CW6 . . . . .122 C4
Kelsall Rd CH3 . . . . .121 C4
Kelsall St CW12 . . . . .156 E3
Kelsall Way Audley ST7 . .209 D1
  6 Handforth SK9 . . . . .34 D5
Kelsborrow Cl CW9 . . . . . .103 E3
Kelsborrow Way CW6 . . . .122 D4
Kelso Way SK10 . . . . .87 C4
Kelstern Cl 2 CW9 . . . . . .104 B8
Kelsterton Ct CH5 . . . . .91 C1
Kelsterton La CH5 . . . . .91 B1
Kelsterton Rd
  Connah's Quay CH5,CH6 . . . .91 C2
  Flint/Y Fflint CH6 . . . . .91 A3
Kelvin Cl WA3 . . . . .9 D6
Kelvin Gr CH2 . . . . .118 E4
Kelvin St WA3 . . . . .9 F5
Kemberton Dr WA8 . . . . . . .13 A5
Kemble Cl CW2 . . . . .206 B8
Kemmel Ave WA4 . . . . .16 C3
Kempsell Way L26 . . . . .21 A7
Kempsell Wlk L26 . . . . .21 A7
Kempton Ave CW1 . . . . . .190 C7
Kempton Cl Chester CH1 118 B2
  Newton-le-W WA12 . . . . .2 D5
  Runcorn WA7 . . . . .49 C6
Kempton Way SK10 . . . . . .87 C4
Kendal Ave WA2 . . . . .8 C2
Kendal Cl Chester CH2 . . .119 A6
  Ellesmere Port CH66 . . . . . . .69 D2
  Macclesfield SK11 . . . . .111 E6
Kendal Ct CW12 . . . . .156 F1
Kendal Dr Bramhall SK7 . . .35 C5
  Ellesmere Port CH66 . . . . . . .69 E2
Kendal Rd
  Macclesfield SK11 . . . . .111 F6
  Widnes WA8 . . . . .12 C1
Kendal Rise WA7 . . . . .49 D5
Kendal Way CW2 . . . . .207 C1
Kendrick Cl CW8 . . . . .77 D1
Kendrick St WA1 . . . . .16 A5
Kenilworth Ave
  Handforth SK9 . . . . .34 D3
  Knutsford WA16 . . . . .57 C2
  Runcorn WA7 . . . . .49 B8
Kenilworth Cl
  Macclesfield SK11 . . . . .111 F6
  Wistaston CW2 . . . . .206 A7
Kenilworth Ct CH65 . . . . . .70 E2
Kenilworth Dr
  Hazel Grove SK7 . . . . .36 D8
  Warrington WA1 . . . . .16 F8
Kenilworth Gdns WA12 . . .2 C1
Kenilworth Gn SK11 . . . . .111 F6
Kenilworth Ho CH1 . . . . . .237 C3
Kenilworth Rd
  Golborne WA3 . . . . .3 E7
  Macclesfield SK11 . . . . .111 F6
  Neston CH64 . . . . .66 E5
Kenley Ave WA8 . . . . .12 D5
Kenmare Bank CW9 . . . . .104 A5
Kenmore Gr M44 . . . . .11 D6
Kennedy Ave SK10 . . . . . . .86 F2
Kennedy Cl CH2 . . . . .119 A5
Kennel La
  Cuddington CW8 . . . . .102 A1
  Little Budworth CW8 . . . . . .124 E7
Kennelwood Rd CW9 . . . . .78 C7
Kennerley Cl 3 SK9 . . . . . .60 A7
Kennerley's La SK9 . . . . . . .60 A7
Kennet Cl SK9 . . . . .34 D2
Kennet Dr CW12 . . . . .156 F1
Kennet Rd WA11 . . . . .1 C6
Kennet Way 10 SK11 . . . .111 F8
Kenneth Rd WA8 . . . . .22 C8
Kennington Pk WA8 . . . . . .12 E4
Kenrick Cl CW3 . . . . .232 C1
Kensington Ave WA4 . . . . .17 C2
Kensington Cl
  Chester CH4 . . . . .141 A6
  Widnes WA8 . . . . .13 D4
Kensington Ct
  Alsager ST7 . . . . .192 F3

Kensington Ct continued
  Wilmslow SK9 . . . . .60 A6
  Winsford CW7 . . . . .149 C7
Kensington Dr
  Congleton CW12 . . . . .156 F6
  Willaston CW5 . . . . .205 D4
Kensington Gn CH4 . . . . . .140 F6
Kensington Pl 9 CW5 . . .204 E6
Kensington Rd
  Chester CH4 . . . . .141 A6
  Ellesmere Port CH66 . . . . . . .70 A5
Kensington Way CW9 . . . .103 E3
Kent Ave WA15 . . . . .87 E6
Kent Cl CH63 . . . . .43 B8
Kent Dr CW12 . . . . .156 D4
Kent Gdns CH2 . . . . .118 F5
Kent Gr WA7 . . . . .23 B1
Kent Ho ST7 . . . . .210 D6
Kent Rd Chester CH2 . . . . .118 F5
  Irlam M44 . . . . .11 C5
  Partington M31 . . . . .11 E2
  Warrington WA5 . . . . .15 C4
Kent St Warrington WA4 . . .16 C4
  Widnes WA8 . . . . .13 B1
Kent Way WA12 . . . . .2 C1
Kent Wlk SK10 . . . . .86 F1
Kent's Green La CW1,
  CW11 . . . . .191 E7
Kent's La CW1 . . . . .173 C1
Kentmere Ave CW7 . . . . . .126 D2
Kentmere Pl WA2 . . . . .8 A3
Kenton Rd L26 . . . . .21 A7
Kentridge Dr CH66 . . . . . . .69 D3
Kentwell St SK10 . . . . .87 C3
Kenview Cl WA8 . . . . .22 A4
Kenwick Cl CH66 . . . . .69 C3
Kenwood Ave CW9 . . . . . . .35 D5
Kenyon Ct WA8 . . . . .23 A6
Kenyon La Culcheth WA3 . . .4 A4
  Golborne WA3 . . . . .3 F5
  Golborne,Kenyon WA3 . . . . . .3 F3
Kenyon's La S WA11 . . . . . .1 F7
Kenyons La N WA11 . . . . . . .1 F8
Kerfoot Bsns Pk WA2 . . . .16 A8
Kerfoot St WA2 . . . . .16 A7
Keristal Ave CH3 . . . . .142 A7
Kerridge Cl CW10 . . . . . . .151 B8
Kerridge Rd SK10 . . . . .88 B3
Kerry Croft CH66 . . . . .69 E1
Kershaw Ave SK11 . . . . . . .112 B8
Kershaw St WA8 . . . . .12 D1
Kershaw Way WA12 . . . . . . .2 C5
Kestrel Ave WA16 . . . . .57 B3
Kestrel Cl
  Congleton CW12 . . . . .156 E1
  Middlewich CW10 . . . . .151 D6
  Winsford CW7 . . . . .149 D5
Kestrel Dr CW1 . . . . .190 B8
Kestrel La WA3 . . . . .9 E4
Kestrel Rd Heswall CH60 . .41 C7
  Northwich CW8 . . . . .103 C7
Kestrels Way WA7 . . . . .49 F6
Keswick Ave
  Bebington CH63 . . . . .43 C4
  Macclesfield SK11 . . . . .111 F6
  Warrington WA2 . . . . .8 C2
Keswick Cl Chester CH2 . .119 A6
  Crewe CW2 . . . . .189 E3
  Irlam M44 . . . . .11 D4
  Macclesfield SK11 . . . . .111 F6
  Widnes WA8 . . . . .12 C1
Keswick Cres WA2 . . . . .8 C2
Keswick Ct CW12 . . . . .156 A2
Keswick Dr Bramhall SK7 . .35 C5
  Frodsham WA6 . . . . .74 D8
Keswick Gdns CH63 . . . . . .43 C5
Keswick Rd SK6 . . . . .37 E8
Ketlan Ct CH4 . . . . .140 E7
Kettell Ave CW1 . . . . .190 A6
Kettle La CW3 . . . . .230 C2
Kettleshulme St James CE
  Prim Sch SK23 . . . . .64 F4
Kettleshulme Way SK12 . .37 A3
Kettleshulme Wlk 4 SK9 34 E1
Kew Gardens Cl WA8 . . . .13 D4
Keyes Cl WA3 . . . . .9 F4
Keyes Gdn WA3 . . . . .9 F4
Keysbrook CH3 . . . . .166 C2
Keysbrook Ave CH3 . . . . . .166 C2
Kidderton Cl CW5 . . . . . . .202 E7
Kidderton La CW5 . . . . . . .202 E7
Kidsgrove Sta ST7 . . . . . .194 F1
Kidston Dr CW1 . . . . .189 F7
Kilbuck La WA11 . . . . .2 A5
Kilburn Ave CH62 . . . . .43 E6
Kilburn Cl SK8 . . . . .34 B7
Kildare Cl L24 . . . . .21 D2
Kildonan Rd WA4 . . . . .17 A2
Kilford Cl WA5 . . . . .7 E2
Killingworth La WA3 . . . . .10 B5
Kilmorey Park Rd CH2 . . .118 F3
Kilmorey Pk Cl CH2 . . . . .118 F4
Kilmorey Pk Ave CH2 . . . .237 C4
Kiln Croft La SK9 . . . . .34 E4
Kiln La CW5 . . . . .220 B8
Kilncroft WA7 . . . . .50 B5
Kilsby Dr WA8 . . . . .13 E2
Kilshaw Rd WA5 . . . . .6 F6
Kilsyth Cl WA2 . . . . .8 F4
Kimberley Dr WA4 . . . . . . .16 C1
Kimberley St WA5 . . . . .15 E5
Kimberley Terr CH2 . . . . . .118 F2
Kinder Dr CW2 . . . . .189 D3
Kinder View SK22 . . . . .39 C7
Kinderton Cl WA16 . . . . . . .29 C4

Ing – Kin 261

Kinderton Mobile Home Pk
  CW10 . . . . .152 A7
Kinderton St CW10 . . . . . .128 D1
King Arthur's Wlk WA7 . .24 A1
King Charles Ct CH1 . . . .237 A4
King Edward Bldgs 4
  CH3 . . . . .119 A1
King Edward Cl CW9 . . . .103 F5
King Edward Rd
  Knutsford WA16 . . . . .57 A2
  3 Macclesfield SK10 . . . . .112 D8
King Edward St
  Macclesfield SK10 . . . . .112 D8
  Middlewich CW10 . . . . .128 C2
  Warrington WA1 . . . . .16 E7
King George Ave CW9 . . .104 B8
King George Cres WA1 . . .16 E7
King George Rd WA11 . . . . .2 A7
King Ho ST7 . . . . .210 D5
King James Ct WA7 . . . . . .49 E6
King Pl CW5 . . . . .204 E6
King St Audley ST7 . . . . . .209 D1
  Chester CH1 . . . . .237 A3
  Congleton CW12 . . . . .156 F4
  Ellesmere Port CH65 . . . . . . .70 C6
  Hartford CW8 . . . . .103 C5
  Kidsgrove ST7 . . . . .195 A2
  Knutsford WA16 . . . . .57 A2
  Macclesfield SK10 . . . . .112 E8
  Middlewich CW10 . . . . .128 B5
  Newton-le-W WA12 . . . . .2 C2
  Northwich CW9 . . . . .104 F6
  Runcorn WA7 . . . . .23 A3
  Sandbach CW11 . . . . .174 E8
  Talke ST7 . . . . .210 D5
King Street Trad Est
  CW10 . . . . .128 C2
King's Bldgs CH1 . . . . . . .237 A3
King's Cres CW10 . . . . . . .128 C2
King's Cres E CH3 . . . . . . .119 A1
King's Cres W CH3 . . . . . .119 A1
King's Ct CH1 . . . . .237 A3
King's Gate CW8 . . . . .102 A2
King's La
  Allostock CW10,WA16 . . . . .106 C1
  Nantwich CW5 . . . . .204 D5
King's Rd SK9 . . . . .59 E8
King's Sch The
  Chester CH4 . . . . .141 B4
  Macclesfield SK10 . . . . .112 E8
  Macclesfield SK10 . . . . .87 C1
Kingfisher Cl
  Congleton CW12 . . . . .156 E1
  Farndon CH3 . . . . .180 F1
  Nantwich CW5 . . . . .204 E8
  Runcorn WA7 . . . . .49 F5
  Warrington WA3 . . . . .9 F4
Kingfisher Ct
  Chester CH2 . . . . .237 A4
  Northwich CW9 . . . . .79 C2
Kingfisher Dr 5 SK7 . . . . .149 D6
Kingfisher Gr CW9 . . . . . . .79 F5
Kingham Cl 3 WA8 . . . . . .13 D1
Kings Cl Chester CH4 . . . .140 F5
  Wilmslow SK9 . . . . .60 A6
Kings Croft CH5 . . . . .91 C1
Kings Ct Nantwich CW5 . .204 D5
  Runcorn WA7 . . . . .24 D4
Kings Dr Helsby WA6 . . . . .73 B3
  Wistaston CW2 . . . . .205 E8
Kings Grove Sch CW2 . . .190 A3
Kings La CW5 . . . . .147 D4
Kings Lea Ho CH3 . . . . . . .142 A8
Kings Mdw Hough CW2 . .206 E2
Kings Mews CH66 . . . . .69 C7
Kings Rd
  Connah's Quay CH5 . . . . . . .91 D1
  Ellesmere Port CH66 . . . . . . .69 C7
  Golborne WA3 . . . . .3 A7
  Irlam M44 . . . . .11 E6
  Warrington WA2 . . . . .9 A2
Kings Wood Wlk CW6 . . .122 D5
Kingsbury Cl WA4 . . . . . . .26 D3
Kingsbury Dr 15 SK9 . . . . .34 D1
Kingsbury Rd WA8 . . . . . . .13 D4
Kingsdale Rd WA5 . . . . . . .14 F7
Kingsdown Ct CW2 . . . . . .207 C1
Kingsfield Ct CH4 . . . . . . .141 C3
Kingshead Cl WA7 . . . . . . .24 A2
Kingsland Grange WA1 . . .9 D1
Kingslawn Cl CW9 . . . . . .103 F5
Kingsley Ave
  Bebington CH62 . . . . .43 E3
  Handforth SK9 . . . . .34 C2
Kingsley Cl
  Northwich CW8 . . . . .103 C5
  Talke ST7 . . . . .210 D6
Kingsley Com Prim Sch
  WA6 . . . . .74 F2
Kingsley Cres WA7 . . . . . . .23 A1
Kingsley Ct CW11 . . . . . . .174 D8
Kingsley Dr
  Northwich CW9 . . . . .104 A6
  Warrington WA4 . . . . .26 C2
Kingsley Gdns CH3 . . . . . .142 B8
Kingsley Gn WA6 . . . . .74 E2
Kingsley Rd Chester CH3 142 B8
  Congleton CW12 . . . . .157 A3
  Crowton CW8 . . . . .76 B1
  Ellesmere Port CH65 . . . . . . .70 C5
  Frodsham WA6 . . . . .74 E2
  Haslington CW1 . . . . .191 C4
  Runcorn WA7 . . . . .23 A1

Kingsley Rd *continued*
Talke ST7 ....210 D6
Kingsley Wlk CW7 .....126 B2
Kingsmead Chester CH2 .118 C8
Northwich CW9 ....103 F5
Kingsmead Crossroads 10
CW9 ....103 F4
Kingsmead Ct WA3 ......9 A8
Kingsmead Prim Sch
CW9 ....103 E5
Kingsmead Sq CW9 ....103 E4
Kingston Ave
Macclesfield SK11 ....112 F7
Warrington WA5 ....14 E6
Kingston Cl WA7 ....23 E2
Kingston Ct
14 Handforth SK9 ......34 E1
Saughall CH1 ....94 B2
Kingston Pl ST8 ......179 E2
Kingston Rd SK9 ....34 D5
Kingstreet SK7 ....35 B1
Kingsway Bollington SK10 .87 E7
Chester CH2 ....118 F5
Crewe CW2 ....190 B2
Frodsham WA6 ....74 B8
Heswall CH60 ....41 C6
Newton-le-W WA12 ......2 C2
Northwich CW9 ....104 B8
Widnes WA8 ....13 A1
Winsford CW7 ....126 F1
Kingsway High Sch CH2 118 F5
Kingsway Ho WA4 ......16 F4
Kingsway N WA1 ....16 F6
Kingsway S WA1,WA4 ...16 F4
Kingsway W CH2 ......118 E4
Kingswood ST7 ....195 B1
Kingswood Ave
Chorlton CW2 ....207 B3
Saughall CH1 ....94 C1
Kingswood Cres CW10 .151 E5
Kingswood Ct 7 SK9 ...60 B7
Kingswood La CH1 .....94 C1
Kingswood Rd WA5 ......7 A2
Kinloch Cl Crewe CW1 .190 B6
Halewood L26 ....21 A7
Kinnerley Rd CH65 .....70 A3
Kinnersley Ave ST7 ..210 F8
Kinnersley St 1 ST7 ..195 A2
Kinnerton Cl CH4 ....140 E5
Kinnerton Hts CH4 ...161 A7
Kinnerton La CH4 ....161 A6
Kinnerton Rd CH4 ....162 A7
Kinnington Way CH1 ...94 F7
Kinnock Pk WA5 ....6 E6
Kinross Cl WA2 ....8 F4
Kinsale Dr WA3 ....9 C4
Kinsey Rd CH65 ....70 D1
Kinsey St CW12 ......156 E2
Kinsey's La CH2 ......71 F6
Kintore Cl Bebington CH63 43 C4
Winsford CW7 ....127 A3
Kintore Dr WA5 ....14 D6
Kintyre Cl CH65 ......70 C1
Kipling Ave WA12 ......8 C1
Kipling Cres WA8 .....22 F8
Kipling Rd CH1 ......117 F5
Kipling Way CW1 .....190 F4
Kirby Cl CH2 ....118 D5
Kirkacre Ave WA12 .....7 C8
Kirkby Rd WA3 ....4 F3
Kirkcaldy Ave WA5 ...14 D6
Kirkfell Dr SK6 ......37 E8
Kirkham Ave WA3 ......3 E6
Kirkham Cl WA5 ......15 B4
Kirkham Rd
Heald Green SK8 ......34 C8
Widnes WA8 ....13 C4
Kirkstall Cl
Macclesfield SK10 ....87 B2
Poynton SK12 ....36 D4
Kirkstead Rd SK8 .....35 C6
Kirkstead Way WA3 .....3 A8
Kirkstone Ave WA2 .....8 C2
Kirkstone Cres CW12 .156 A1
Kirkwall Dr WA5 ......15 A3
Kirkwood Cl CH3 .....119 A2
Kishfield La SK23 ....65 A6
Kitchen St CH1 ......118 B1
Kitchener Ave M44 ....11 C4
Kite Gr ST7 ....195 D3
Kitfield Ave CW10 ...151 D7
Kitt's Moss La SK7 ...35 D6
Knap The CH60 ....41 A6
Knebworth Ct CW12 ..179 B8
Knight Rd WA5 ......6 F6
Knight St SK11 ......112 E7
Knight's Cl SK11 ....112 E7
Knight's Grange (Sports
Complex) CW7 ....126 B3
Knights La CW6 ......123 E1
Knights Mdw CW2 ....126 C3
Knights Way CW2 ....206 A2
Knightsbridge Ave
4 Northwich CW9 ....103 E3
Warrington WA4 ......17 C2
Knightsbridge Cl
14 Handforth SK9 .....34 D1
Widnes WA8 ....13 D4
Knightsbridge Ct
Chester CH4 ....237 C2
Warrington WA1 ......16 A5
Knightwake Rd SK22 ..39 A8
Knole Ave SK12 ......36 F4
Knoll St SK22 ....39 B8

Knoll The WA7 ....49 F7
Knott's Hos WN7 ....4 B8
Knottingley Dr CH66 ..69 C5
Knotty La CW12 ......179 F8
Knowe The CH64 ......68 A8
Knowl Hey Rd L26 ....21 A6
Knowl La CH3 ....180 E5
Knowl The CH3 ......180 F5
Knowle Cl CH66 ......69 E3
Knowle Gn SK9 ....34 C3
Knowle Pk SK9 ....34 C3
Knowles Ind Est SK23 .39 D3
Knowles St 3 WA8 ....13 C2
Knowsley Ave WA3 .....3 B8
Knowsley Ct CH2 ....118 F4
Knowsley Expressway
L35,WA8 ....21 F8
Knowsley La ST7 ....194 F4
Knowsley Rd
Chester CH2 ....118 F4
Hazel Grove SK7 .....36 F8
Macclesfield SK11 ...112 C5
Knutsford & Dist Hospl
WA16 ....56 F1
Knutsford High Sch (Lower
Sch) WA16 ....56 F1
Knutsford High Sch (Upper
Sch) WA16 ....56 F1
Knutsford Old Rd WA4 .17 A2
Knutsford Rd
Alsager ST7 ....193 F6
Antrobus CW9 ....53 D4
Chelford SK11 ....84 A3
Grappenhall WA4 ......17 C1
Great Budworth CW9 ..54 A2
Holmes Chapel CW4 ..130 B5
Mobberley WA16 ......57 E4
Row-of-trees SK9,WA16 .59 D3
Warrington WA4 ......16 D3
Knutsford Road Wlk 12
SK11 ....112 E7
Knutsford Sta WA16 ...57 A1
Knutsford View WA15 .32 C8
Knutsford Way 1 CH1 117 F2
Kohima Cres CH3 ....142 B5
Kronsbec Ave CH66 ...69 D6
KUS Ind Est CH5 ....139 A6
Kynaston Dr CH4 ....140 C7

L

Laburnam Cl ST7 ....210 E8
Laburnum Ave
Crewe CW2 ....189 F7
2 Nantwich CW5 ....204 F5
Warrington WA1 ......17 C7
Laburnum Cl CW12 ...156 A4
Laburnum Ct WA13 ....19 B4
Laburnum Farm Cl CH64 67 A5
Laburnum Gr
Crewe CW1 ....190 D6
Ellesmere Port CH66 ..95 A8
Runcorn WA7 ....49 C7
Saltney CH4 ....140 E6
Weaverham CW8 ......102 D8
Laburnum La
Altrincham WA15 .....31 E8
Warrington WA5 ......14 C5
Laburnum Rd
Davenham CW9 ....103 F3
Golborne WA3 ....3 F7
Irlam M44 ....11 D5
Macclesfield SK11 ...112 E5
Northwich CW9 ......104 C6
Laburnum Way LL13 ..180 D1
Lacey Ave SK9 ....34 B1
Lacey Cl SK9 ....34 B1
Lacey Ct 1 Handforth SK9 .34 B1
Widnes WA8 ....23 B7
Lacey Gn SK9 ....34 B1
Lacey Gr SK9 ....34 C1
Lacey Green Prim Sch
SK9 ....34 B1
Lacey St WA8 ....23 A7
Lache Hall Cres CH4 .140 F4
Lache La
Chester,Roughill CH4 .140 E3
Chester,Westminster Park
CH4 ....141 B5
Roughhill CH4 ......140 D1
Lache Park Ave CH4 .141 A6
Lache Prim Sch CH4 .141 A5
Lacy Ct CW12 ....156 F2
Ladies Mile WA16 ....56 F2
Ladies Wlk CH64 .....66 E8
Lady Acre Cl WA13 ...18 D2
Lady Helen Wlk CW5 .204 E6
Lady La Croft WA3 ....9 C8
Culcheth WA3 ....4 C1
Mobberley WA16 ......58 C7
Lady Richeld Cl WA7 ..24 D3
Ladybarn Ave WA3 .....2 F7
Ladybarn Cres SK7 ...35 F6
Ladybarn Manor SK7 .35 E8
Ladybower Gr 6 SK9 .34 D2
Ladybrook Prim Sch SK7 35 F7
Ladycroft Cl WA1 ....17 E7
Ladyfield St SK9 .....60 A8
Ladyfield Terr SK9 ...60 C7
Ladypit Rd SK23 .....39 E4
Ladypool L24 ....21 C2
Ladys Cl SK12 ....36 E4
Ladythorn Cres SK7 ..35 F6
Ladythorn Gr SK7 ....35 F6
Ladythorn Rd SK7 ....35 E6

Ladywood Rd WA5 .....7 D1
Lagos Gr CW7 ....126 E2
Laidon Cl CW2 ......206 A7
Laira Ct WA2 ....16 C7
Laira St WA2 ....16 C7
Lake House Cl CW8 ...77 D1
Lake La WA4 ....52 F5
Lake View Alsager ST7 .193 C2
Congleton CW12 .....156 B2
Whaley Bridge SK23 ..39 D4
Lakelands CH5 ......112 F7
Lakemore Ctry Pk★
CW1 ....174 C1
Lakeside Bosley SK11 .158 D8
Chester CH4 ....141 B2
Lakeside Cl Chester CH2 .118 F7
Widnes WA8 ....22 A8
Lakeside Cvn Pk CW7 .149 F7
Warrington WA5 .....16 A3
Lakeside Dr Poynton SK12 .36 E5
Lakeside Rd WA13 ....18 D2
Lakeside View
Moulton CW7 ....126 F7
Nantwich CW5 ......204 E3
Lakewood CH4 ......141 B2
Laleston Cl WA8 .....22 E8
Lamb Cottage Cvn Pk
CW8 ....125 C7
Lamb La WA14 ....31 D4
Lamb St ST7 ....195 A2
Lambert Cres CW5 ..204 C6
Lambert Way CW8 ...103 A4
Lambert's La CW12 ..156 E1
Lambourn Ave WA8 ...12 C5
Lambourn Cl SK12 ...36 D4
Lambourn Dr CW1 ...173 B1
Lambourne Cl
Ellesmere Port CH66 ..94 F8
Woodhouse Park M22 ..33 D8
Lambourne Gr
Middlewich CW10 ....128 C1
St Helens WA9 ....1 A4
Lambs House Sch CW12 156 F4
Lambs La Warrington WA1 .17 A7
Warrington,Padgate WA1 .17 A8
Lambsickle Cl WA7 ...48 F6
Lambsickle La WA7 ...49 A6
Lamerton Cl WA5 .....14 D4
Lamerton Way SK9 ...34 E2
Lampeter Cl WA5 ......7 E2
Lampits La CH3 .....120 E6
Lamport Cl WA8 .....13 E3
Lanark Gdns WA8 ....12 E3
Lanark Wlk SK10 ....86 F2
Lancashire Rd M31 ...11 E2
Lancaster Ave
Golborne WA3 ....3 C8
Runcorn WA7 ....48 E8
Widnes WA8 ....12 A2
Lancaster Cl
Hazel Grove SK7 .....36 D8
Newton-le-W WA12 .....1 F4
Warrington WA2 ....8 F2
Winsford CW7 ....149 D6
Lancaster Ct 3 WA4 ..16 E1
Lancaster Dr CH3 ...119 B2
Lancaster Fields WA1 191 A2
Lancaster Gdns CH65 .70 D3
Lancaster Pk CH4 ...139 A3
Lancaster Rd
Handforth SK9 ....34 E1
Irlam M44 ....11 D5
Widnes WA8 ....13 B3
Lancaster St WA5 ....15 E5
Lanceley Ct SY14 ...213 B3
Lancelyn Dr SK9 .....60 D8
Lancer Ct WA7 ....23 E3
Lancers Croft CH66 ..69 E1
Lancing Ave WA3 ......8 A4
Lancing Rd CH65 ....70 C4
Land Cut La WA3 ......9 D3
Land La SK9 ....60 C6
Lander Cl WA5 ....15 D7
Landor Cl WA3 ....3 E7
Landscape Dene WA6 ..73 D4
Landseer Ave
Neston CH64 ....66 F7
Warrington WA4 ......16 B2
Landseer Dr SK10 ...111 E8
Landswood Pk CW8 ..103 B4
Lane Ends WA8 ......21 D5
Lane Head Ave WA3 ...3 F8
Lane The SY13,SY14 ..223 C3
Lanehead Rd SK23 ...65 C5
Laneside Rd SK22 ....39 E7
Langcliffe Cl WA3 ....4 E3
Langdale Ave WA13 ..18 F4
Langdale Cl High Lane SK6 37 E8
Macclesfield SK11 ...111 F5
Warrington WA8 ....8 A7
Widnes WA8 ....22 C8
Winsford CW7 ....126 D2
Langdale Ct CW12 ...156 A1
Langdale Rd Bramhall SK7 35 C5
Crewe CW2 ....189 D2
Partington M31 ......11 E3
Runcorn WA7 ....23 B1
Langdale Way WA6 ...49 C1
Langden Cl WA3 ....4 D4
Langdon Ho CH4 ....141 A7
Langfield WA3 ....3 A8
Langfield Gr CH62 ...43 D5
Langford L24 ....21 C2
Langford CH3 ....121 C2
Langford Rd CW9 ....80 A3
Langford St 21 SK11 .112 C8
Langford Way WA1 ...27 D4
Langland Cl WA5 ......7 E2

Langley Ave WA12 .....2 C1
Langley Cl
Newcastle-u-Lyme ST5 .210 D2
Sandbach CW11 .....175 C8
Langley Ct CH65 .....70 E3
Langley Dr Chester CW2 .190 A2
Handforth SK9 ....34 E3
Langley Gn WA1 .....17 D7
Langley Hall Cl SK11 113 B4
Langley Hall Cotts SK11 113 B4
Langley Rd Langley SK11 113 B3
Northwich CW9 .....104 A6
Langport Dr CH3 ...119 C2
Langton Cl
Newton-le-W WA12 .....2 A4
Widnes WA8 ....12 B3
Langton Gn WA1 ......17 D7
Langwell WA3 ....10 A5
Lanreath Cl SK10 ....86 D1
Lansdown Cl WA5 ....35 C7
Lansdown Rd CH4 ...139 B4
Lansdowne Culcheth WA3 ..4 E2
Frodsham WA6 ....74 D6
Lansdowne Gr CH4 .141 A3
Lansdowne Rd
Connah's Quay CH5 ...91 D1
Crewe CW1 ....190 F5
Great Barrow CH3 ...120 D3
Lansdowne St SK10 ..87 E1
Lapwing Cl Golborne WA3 ..3 D8
Newton-le-W WA12 .....2 C3
Packmoor ST7 ......195 E1
Winsford CW7 ....149 C5
Lapwing Gr WA7 .....50 A6
Lapwing La Moore WA4 ..25 A4
Whisterfield SK11 ...109 C4
Whisterfield SK11 ...109 C6
Lapwing Rd ST7 ....195 D3
Lapwing Rise CH60 ...40 F6
Larch Ave Hough CW2 .206 F5
Macclesfield SK11 ...112 A5
Newton-le-W WA12 .....2 C2
Warrington WA5 .....14 E5
Widnes WA8 ....13 B2
Larch Cl Golborne WA3 ..3 F6
Poynton SK12 ....36 F3
Runcorn WA7 ....49 C7
Weaverham CW8 ....102 D7
Larch Rd Crewe CW2 .189 E2
Haydock WA11 ....1 E7
Partington M31 ......11 E3
Runcorn WA7 ....49 C7
Larch Rise SK10 ....86 D6
Larch Way CH4 ......140 E6
Larchdale Cl CH66 ...94 F8
Larches The WA16 ...58 E2
Larchfields CH1 .....117 A8
Larchtree Cl CW8 ....78 B4
Larchway Bramhall SK7 .35 C7
High Lane SK6 ....37 F7
Larchways WA4 ......26 D5
Larchwood Dr SK9 ...60 E8
Lark Ave ST7 ....195 D3
Lark Hall Cl SK10 ...113 A7
Lark Hall Cres SK10 .113 A8
Lark Hall Rd SK10 ..113 A7
Lark Hill Cotts SK22 .39 A8
Larkfield WA1 ....195 B1
Larkfield Ave WA1 ...17 A7
Larkspur Cl Chester CH4 .140 F4
Nantwich CW5 ......204 E8
Larkstoke Cl WA4 ....26 E6
Larksway CH60 ......41 B8
Larkwood Way SK10 ..87 E5
Larne Ct WA8 ....12 E2
Larne Dr CH4 ......139 C4
Laskey La WA4 ....17 F4
Laskey Lane farm WA4 .17 E4
Latchford CE Prim Sch
WA4 ....16 B4
Latchford Rd CH60 ...41 B6
Latchford St WA4 ....17 A3
Latham Ave Helsby WA6 ..73 B1
Newton-le-W WA12 .....2 C4
Runcorn WA7 ....23 C1
Latham Ho WA12 ......2 B4
Latham St CW11 ....175 A5
Lathom Ave WA2 ......16 B8
Lathom St M44 ....11 F8
Lathom Way SK10 ....87 F2
Latimer Dr CW2 ....190 A4
Launceston Cl
Runcorn WA7 ....50 C6
Winsford CW7 ....149 D1
Launceston Dr
Bramhall SK7 ....35 F7
Warrington WA4 .....14 E3
Laura St CW2 ....190 D1
Laurel Ave
Newton-le-W WA12 .....2 D3
Warrington WA1 .....17 D7
Laurel Bank
Warrington WA4 .....17 C1
Widnes WA8 ....13 A3
Winsford CW7 ....149 D8
Laurel Cl Barnton CW8 ..78 A4
Middlewich CW10 ...128 B2
Sandbach CW11 .....175 C5
Laurel Dr Crewe CW2 .189 F2
Ellesmere Port CH65 ..70 B2
Kidsgrove ST7 ......195 E4
Willaston CH64 ....43 B1
Laurel Gr Chester CH2 .119 A3
Golborne WA3 ....3 D8
Laurel Pk CW6 ......145 A6
Laurel Way SK8 ......35 C8

Laurel Wlk M31 ......11 E2
Laurels Farm Ct CW2 .72 B3
Laurels The SK6 .....37 F8
Laurelwood Dr 4 CH66 .69 E1
Laureston Ave CW1 ..190 F4
Lavender Cl WA7 .....23 C1
Lavender Dr CW9 ...104 C8
Lavender Gdns WA9 ...6 A7
Lavender Wlk M31 ...11 E2
Lavenham Cl
Hazel Grove SK10 ....36 E8
Macclesfield SK10 ....87 C2
Lavister Cl 6 CW9 ..103 F4
Lavister Wlks LL12 ..162 C1
Law St CH2 ....118 F3
Lawford Cl CW1 ....189 F8
Lawford Dr CH60 ....41 C8
Lawn Ave WA1 ....16 F8
Lawn Dr CH2 ....118 D7
Lawns Ave CH63 .....43 B6
Lawns The SK9 ......59 E4
Lawnsdale CW8 .....101 D5
Lawnswood Gr CH2 ..72 B3
Lawrence Ave
Middlewich CW10 ....128 C1
Moulton CW9 ....126 E8
Lawrence Ave E CW10 .128 C1
Lawrence Cl
Cranage CW4 ....130 A5
3 Sandbach CW11 ..174 D6
Lawrence Ho SK12 ...36 D2
Lawrence Pl SK12 ...36 D2
Lawrence St Crewe CW1 190 C4
Sandycroft CH5 .....116 A3
Laws Gdns CH3 .....142 A8
Lawson Cl WA1 ......17 E7
Lawton Ave Bramhall SK7 .35 E8
Lawton-gate ST7 ....194 D3
Lawton Cl WA3 ....4 E3
Lawton Coppice ST7 .194 E4
Lawton Hall ST7 ....194 E4
Lawton Heath Rd ST7 .193 F5
Lawton Rd ST7 .....193 E4
Lawton St
Congleton CW12 ....156 E2
Crewe CW2 ....190 C3
Kidsgrove ST7 ......195 C4
Lawton Way CW11 ...174 E7
Lawtongate Est ST7 .194 A5
Laxey Ave WA1 ......17 D6
Laxton Cl CH66 ......94 F8
Laxton Way CW10 ...128 C2
Layland Ave WA3 ......4 E4
Layton Cl WA3 ....9 E3
Lea Ave Crewe CW1 .190 F4
Goostrey CW4 ....107 C1
Lea Bank Cl SK11 ...112 A8
Lea Cl CW11 ....175 C5
Lea Cross Gr WA8 ...12 C3
Lea Dr Nantwich CW5 .204 C4
Wimboldsley CW10 ..151 A4
Lea Hall Pk CH1 .....95 A3
Lea Homes CW5 ....217 B7
Lea La CH3 ....164 C3
Lea St SK22 ....39 B8
Lea Way ST7 ....193 D3
Lea's Pas CW10 ......128 B1
Leacroft Rd WA3 .....10 A7
Leadbeaters Cl SK11 .112 F7
Leadbeaters Rd SK11 .112 F7
Leadgate La CH3 ....144 F2
Leadsmithy St CW10 .128 C1
Leaf Gr CW7 ....126 B1
Leaf La CW7 ....127 A2
Leaf Lane Inf Sch CW7 127 A2
Leafield Dr SK8 .....34 F6
Leafield Rd SK12 ....38 C6
Leafy Way CW8 .....102 D7
Leahurst Cl CH2 ....118 F4
Leamington Ave WA12 ..2 C1
Leamington Cl
Neston CH64 ....66 E6
Warrington WA5 .....15 A8
Leamington Rd
Congleton CW12 ....155 F3
Macclesfield SK10 ...86 F1
Lear Dr CW2 ....205 F8
Leas Cl 3 CH66 ......69 C5
Leaside WA7 ....23 D1
Leaside Rd CH1 ....117 E6
Leaside Way SK9 ....60 C6
Leatham Cl WA3 ......9 E3
Leathers La L26 .....21 A7
Leawood Cl CW8 ...103 A6
Ledbury Dr CW2 ...206 A7
Ledge Ley SK8 ......34 E8
Ledger Rd WA11 ......1 A5
Ledley St SK10 ......87 F7
Ledsham Cl WA3 ......9 C3
Ledsham Hall La CH66 .68 E4
Ledsham La CH66 ...68 E4
Ledsham Park Dr CH66 .69 A6
Ledsham Rd CH66 ...69 B6
Ledsham Village CH66 .68 F2
Ledston Cl WA7 .....24 D1
Ledward Cl CW7 ....127 A1
Ledyard Cl WA5 .....15 D7
Lee La WA16 ....56 F1
Lee Ct Runcorn WA7 ..23 D2
Warrington WA2 ......8 C2
Lee Dr CW8 ....103 E7
Lee Green La CW5 ..150 A1
Lee Rd WA5 ....15 B6
Lee St CH1 ....237 C3
Leech Rd SY14 .....213 B3
Leek Old Rd SK11 ..112 E2
Leek Rd CW12 ......179 A8

Leen La CH1 . . . . 237 B2
Lees La
  Ellesmere Port CH65 . . . . . 70 E4
  Mottram St Andrew SK10 . . 61 B7
  Neston CH64 . . . . 67 A7
Lees Mill SK22 . . . . 39 C7
Lees Rd SK7 . . . . 35 D5
Leftwich Com Prim Sch
  CW9 . . . . 104 A4
Leftwich Warehouse
  CW9 . . . . 103 F7
Legh Cl SK12 . . . . 36 E6
Legh Ct Golborne WA3 . . . . 3 A8
  Knutsford WA16 . . . . 57 D4
Legh Gdns WA16 . . . . 57 B1
Legh Ho **2** WA16 . . . . . . 57 B1
Legh Rd Adlington SK10 . . . 62 C5
  Haydock WA11 . . . . 1 B6
  High Lane SK12 . . . . 38 A6
  Knutsford WA16 . . . . 82 B8
  Prestbury SK10 . . . . 87 A8
Legh St Golborne WA3 . . . . 3 A8
  3 Lymm WA13 . . . . 18 E3
  Newton-le-W WA12 . . . . . . 2 A3
  Warrington WA1 . . . . 16 A5
Legh Vale Prim Sch WA11 . . 1 B6
Leicester Ave ST7 . . . . . . 193 D5
Leicester St
  Northwich CW9 . . . . 79 A1
  Warrington WA5 . . . . 15 F5
Leigh Ave Knutsford WA16 . 57 C3
  Widnes WA8 . . . . 13 A1
Leigh Green Cl **4** WA3 . . . 22 C8
Leigh La CW8 . . . . 77 C5
Leigh Rd Congleton CW12 . 157 B5
  Wilmslow SK9 . . . . 59 D5
Leigh St SK11 . . . . 112 E7
Leigh Way CW8 . . . . 77 C5
Leigh's Brow CW8 . . . . . . 77 F3
Leighton Chase CH2 . . . . 237 A4
Leighton Ct CH64 . . . . . . 66 D8
Leighton Dr WN7 . . . . 4 B8
Leighton Hospl WN7 . . . . 172 E1
Leighton Pk CH64 . . . . . . 66 D8
Leighton Prim Sch CW1 189 F8
Leighton Rd CH64 . . . . . . 41 D4
Leighton St CW1 . . . . . . 190 B5
Leighton View CW1 . . . . 190 B4
Leightons The CH64 . . . . . 66 C8
Leinster Gdns WA7 . . . . . . 22 F3
Leinster St WA7 . . . . 22 F3
Leiria Way WA7 . . . . 23 B2
Lenham Wlk M22 . . . . 33 D8
Lenthall Ave CW12 . . . . . 178 F8
Leon Cl WA5 . . . . 14 D7
Leonard St Chester CH1 . . 118 B3
  Runcorn WA7 . . . . 48 D7
  Warrington WA2 . . . . 16 C7
  Warrington, Stockton Heath
    WA4 . . . . 16 C1
Leslie Rd CW7 . . . . 149 A7
Lessingham Rd WA8 . . . . . 12 F3
Lester St ST7 . . . . 193 D4
Leven Ave CW7 . . . . 126 F2
Leven Wlk CH66 . . . . 70 A7
Levens Way **1** WA8 . . . . 22 C8
Leveret Rd L24 . . . . 21 A3
Levisham Gdns WA5 . . . . . 15 E7
Lewin St CW10 . . . . 128 C1
Lewis Ave WA5 . . . . 7 F2
Lewis Cl
  Ellesmere Port CH65 . . . . . 95 C8
  Nantwich CW5 . . . . 205 A5
Lewis Cres WA8 . . . . 23 A7
Lewis Gr WA8 . . . . 12 D1
Lewis St CW1 . . . . 190 C3
Lexden St WA5 . . . . 15 E6
Lexington Wlk WA5 . . . . . . 15 C7
Leycester Cl WA16 . . . . . . 82 C8
Leycester Dr WA16 . . . . . . 57 F7
Leycester Rd WA16 . . . . . 82 B8
Leyfield Ct CH4 . . . . 140 F5
Leygate View SK22 . . . . . . 39 B8
Leyland Gr
  Haslington CW1 . . . . 191 C4
  Haydock WA11 . . . . 1 B6
Leyland Wlk CW7 . . . . . . 149 C6
Leyton Cl WA7 . . . . 49 B6
Libris Ct **2** WA16 . . . . . . 57 A1
Libris Ho **1** WA16 . . . . . 57 A1
Libris Pl **3** WA16 . . . . . . 57 A1
Libson Cl WA2 . . . . 9 A3
Lichfield Ave
  Golborne WA3 . . . . 3 D8
  Grappenhall Heys WA4 . . . 27 A7
Lichfield Cl WA16 . . . . . . 57 D2
Lichfield Ct CW7 . . . . . . 149 D7
Lichfield Dr CH66 . . . . . . 94 E8
Lichfield Rd Blacon CH1 . . 117 F5
  Talke ST7 . . . . 210 D7
Lichfield St CW10 . . . . . . 128 D2
Lidgetts La SK13 . . . . 88 C3
Liebig St WA8 . . . . 23 B8
Lift La CW9 . . . . 78 D3
Light Alders La SK12 . . . . . 38 A6
Light Oaks Rd WA3 . . . . . . 5 C6
Lightburn St **5** WA7 . . . . 22 F1
Lightfoot Cl CH60 . . . . . . 41 B7
Lightfoot La Eaton CW6 . . 147 A4
  Heswall CH60 . . . . 41 B7
Lightfoot St CH2 . . . . . . 118 F2
Lighthouse Rd L24 . . . . . . 47 C7
Lightley Cl CW11 . . . . . . 175 A4
Lightwood Green Ave
  CW3 . . . . 229 A2
Lightwood Rd ST5 . . . . . . 210 D1

Lilac Ave Knutsford WA16 . . 56 E1
  Warrington WA5 . . . . 15 A5
  Widnes WA8 . . . . 13 B2
Lilac Cl Kelsall CW6 . . . . . 122 E2
  Newcastle-u-Lyme ST5 . . . 210 D1
Lilac Cres WA7 . . . . 49 C8
Lilac Ct CW12 . . . . 156 E2
Lilac Dr CW8 . . . . 103 D6
Lilac Gr
  Ellesmere Port CH66 . . . . . 95 A8
  Warrington WA4 . . . . 16 E1
Lilac Wlk M31 . . . . 11 E3
Lilford Ave WA5 . . . . 15 F8
Lilford Dr WA5 . . . . 14 F6
Lilford Sq SK11 . . . . 112 D5
Lilford St WA5 . . . . 15 F7
Lillyfield CH60 . . . . 40 F6
Lily Ave WA12 . . . . 2 D2
Lily La CW10 . . . . 129 B6
Lilybrook Dr WA16 . . . . . . 57 B1
Limbrick Rd ST7 . . . . 209 A1
Lime Ave Frodsham WA6 . . 74 C8
  Northwich CW9 . . . . 103 F5
  Weaverham CW8 . . . . . . 102 D8
  3 Widnes WA8 . . . . 13 B2
Lime Cl Hollinfare WA3 . . . 11 A2
  Middlewich CW10 . . . . . . 128 B2
  Sandbach CW11 . . . . 175 A7
  Tarporley CW6 . . . . 146 D2
Lime Ct CW9 . . . . 103 F5
Lime Gr Alsager ST7 . . . . 193 E2
  Chester CH2 . . . . 119 A3
  Elton CH2 . . . . 72 A3
  Golborne WA3 . . . . 3 E4
  Macclesfield SK10 . . . . . . 112 E8
  Saltney CH4 . . . . 140 D6
  Shavington CW2 . . . . . . 206 A3
  Winsford CW7 . . . . 127 A1
Lime Kiln La ST7 . . . . 194 C1
Lime St Congleton CW12 . . 156 D2
  Crewe CW1 . . . . 190 C6
  Ellesmere Port CH65 . . . . . 70 C7
Lime Tree Ave
  Congleton CW12 . . . . . . 156 B3
  Crewe CW1 . . . . 190 C6
Lime Tree Cl CH66 . . . . . . 95 A8
Lime Tree Dr CH3 . . . . . . 180 F1
Lime Tree Gr CH60 . . . . . . 41 C8
Lime Tree La WA16 . . . . . . 29 D6
Lime Wlk
  6 Handforth SK9 . . . . . 34 D1
  Partington M31 . . . . 11 D3
Limefield Ave WA13 . . . . . 18 F2
Limehurst Gr CH62 . . . . . . 43 D6
Limekiln La WA5 . . . . 6 E3
Limekiln Row WA7 . . . . . . 50 A8
Limerick Cl WA8 . . . . 12 E3
Limes Cl CW1 . . . . 191 C4
Limes La WA4 . . . . 52 D6
Limes The Culcheth WA3 . . . 4 D4
  Golborne WA3 . . . . 3 D8
  Middlewich CW10 . . . . . . 128 B1
Limetree Ave
  Warrington WA1 . . . . 17 A8
  Warrington, Stockton Heath
    WA4 . . . . 16 E1
Limeways WA4 . . . . 26 E5
Limewood Cres CW8 . . . . . 78 B4
Limewood Gr CW8 . . . . . . 78 B4
Linacre La WA8 . . . . 12 E5
Lincoln Ave
  Heald Green SK8 . . . . 34 B7
  Irlam M44 . . . . 11 C4
Lincoln Cl Golborne WN7 . . . 4 C4
  Macclesfield SK10 . . . . . . 86 F2
  Rainow SK10 . . . . 88 E5
  Runcorn WA7 . . . . 49 C6
  Warrington WA1 . . . . 17 E6
Lincoln Ct WA6 . . . . 73 B3
Lincoln Dr CH2 . . . . 119 A5
Lincoln Pl SK10 . . . . 86 F2
Lincoln Rd Blacon CH1 . . . 117 F5
  Ellesmere Port CH66 . . . . . 69 D3
  Handforth SK9 . . . . 34 E1
  Kidsgrove ST7 . . . . 194 F2
Lincoln Sq WA8 . . . . 13 A2
Lincoln St CW1 . . . . 190 B5
Lincoln Wlk SK10 . . . . 86 F2
Lincombe Hey SK10 . . . . . 87 C8
Lincombe Rd M22 . . . . 33 D8
Lindale Cl CW12 . . . . 157 A5
Linden Cl
  Congleton CW12 . . . . . . 179 A8
  Ellesmere Port CH66 . . . . . 94 F8
  Lymm WA13 . . . . 19 A4
  Warrington WA1 . . . . 17 D7
Linden Ct
  Macclesfield SK10 . . . . . . 87 B2
  Sandbach CW11 . . . . 174 F3
  Widnes WA8 . . . . 12 F4
Linden Dr Biddulph ST8 . . 179 C1
  Crewe CW1 . . . . 190 F4
  Helsby WA6 . . . . 73 B1
  Mickle Trafford CH2 . . . . . 96 F1
Linden Gr Biddulph ST8 . . 179 C1
  Bramhall SK7 . . . . 35 D4
  Chester CH2 . . . . 119 A4
  Saltney CH4 . . . . 140 D6
Linden Way High Lane SK6 . 38 A7
  Widnes WA8 . . . . 12 F4
Lindens The CW10 . . . . . . 128 B2
Lindfield Cl WA4 . . . . 25 A5
Lindfield Est N SK9 . . . . . . 60 A6
Lindfield Est S SK9 . . . . . . 59 F6
Lindfields CH4 . . . . 140 F6
Lindi Ave WA4 . . . . 17 C2

Lindisfarne Ave
  Ellesmere Port CH65 . . . . . 70 C2
  Golborne WA3 . . . . 4 C8
Lindisfarne Cl CW10 . . . . 128 B1
Lindisfarne Ct WA8 . . . . . . 12 F6
Lindisfarne Dr SK12 . . . . . 36 D4
Lindley Ave WA4 . . . . 16 F4
Lindop Cl WA16 . . . . 57 C2
Lindow Com Prim Sch
  SK9 . . . . 59 D3
Lindow Court Pk WA16 . . . 59 B5
Lindow Ct SK9 . . . . 59 E8
Lindow Fold Dr SK9 . . . . . 59 D5
Lindow La SK9 . . . . 59 E6
Lindow Par SK9 . . . . 59 F6
Lindrick Cl SK10 . . . . 87 C4
Lindrum Ave SK11 . . . . . . 112 D2
Lindsay Way ST7 . . . . 193 A4
Lindsay Wlk CW8 . . . . . . 102 A4
Lindsworth Cl WA5 . . . . . . 15 C6
Linear View WA12 . . . . 2 C1
Linen Hall Pl CH1 . . . . . . 237 A2
Lines Rd M44 . . . . 11 F8
Lingdale Wlk SK11 . . . . . . 112 D5
Lingfield Cl SK10 . . . . 87 C4
Lingfield Dr CW1 . . . . 190 C7
Lingfield Ho WA7 . . . . 48 E8
Lingfield Rd WA7 . . . . 22 E1
Lingley Green Ave WA5 . . . 14 D8
Lingley Mere Bsns Pk
  WA5 . . . . 14 D8
Lingley Rd WA5 . . . . 14 D6
Linglongs Ave SK23 . . . . . 65 C5
Linglongs Rd SK23 . . . . . . 65 C5
Lingmell Gdns CW4 . . . . . 129 F3
Lingwell Ave SK11 . . . . . . 112 D2
Lingwood Rd WA5 . . . . . . 14 F6
Link The SK9 . . . . 34 D3
Link Wlk M31 . . . . 11 D2
Links Ave CH66 . . . . 69 C7
Links Cl CH63 . . . . 43 B6
Links Rd SK9 . . . . 59 E4
Links View CH66 . . . . 69 C7
Linkside Way WA2 . . . . 8 F2
Linkside Way CH66 . . . . . . 94 F8
Linksway Chester CH2 . . . 118 C7
  Congleton CW12 . . . . . . 178 E8
Linksway Cl CW12 . . . . . . 178 F8
Linkway WA7 . . . . 49 C8
Linley Gr ST7 . . . . 193 F3
Linley La ST7 . . . . 194 A2
Linley Rd Alsager ST7 . . . . 193 F2
  Cheadle Hulme SK8 . . . . . 35 B8
  Talke ST7 . . . . 210 D8
Linley Trad Est ST7 . . . . . 194 C1
Linnards La SY9,WA16 . . . . 80 B5
Linnet Cl Crewe CW1 . . . . 190 A4
  Newton-le-W WA12 . . . . . . 2 C3
  Warrington WA2 . . . . 8 D3
  Winsford CW7 . . . . 150 B8
Linnet Gr
  Macclesfield SK10 . . . . . . 87 A1
  Warrington WA3 . . . . 9 E4
Linnets Pk WA7 . . . . 23 C3
Linnets Way CH60 . . . . . . 40 E8
Linnett Gr ST7 . . . . 195 E1
Linton Ct WA7 . . . . 127 A3
Linum Gdns WA9 . . . . 6 B7
Linwood CW7 . . . . 150 B8
Linwood Cl WA7 . . . . 50 C5
Lion Salt Works Mus ★
  CW9 . . . . 79 C3
Lion St CW12 . . . . 156 D2
Liskeard Cl WA7 . . . . 50 B6
Liskeard Dr SK7 . . . . 35 F7
Lismore Wlk M22 . . . . 33 E8
Lister Cl CW10 . . . . 151 D6
Lister Rd WA7 . . . . 23 C3
Little Abbey Gateway
  CH1 . . . . 237 A3
Little Aston Cl SK10 . . . . . 87 C4
Little Bollington CE Prim Sch
  WA14 . . . . 20 B2
Little Budworth Ctry Pk★
  CW6 . . . . 147 C8
Little Delph WA11 . . . . 1 C7
Little Gn CH66 . . . . 69 D3
Little Heath Cl WA3 . . . . . 230 A5
Little Heath La WA14 . . . . . 20 D5
Little Heath Rd
  Chester CH3 . . . . 119 E1
  Christleton CH3 . . . . 142 E8
Little La CW7 . . . . 41 C1
Little Leigh Prim Sch
  CW8 . . . . 77 D5
Little Meadow Cl SK10 . . . 87 B2
Little Moreton Hall★
  CW12 . . . . 177 E2
Little Moss Cl ST7 . . . . . . 194 E5
Little Moss La ST7 . . . . . . 194 E5
Little Roodee CH5 . . . . . . 139 B7
Little Row **6** ST7 . . . . . . 195 B2
Little St Congleton CW12 . 156 D2
  4 Macclesfield SK10 . . . 112 D8
Little St John St **1** 237 B2
Little Stanney La CH2 . . . . 95 F8
Little Sutton CE Prim Sch
  CH66 . . . . 69 A4
Little Sutton Sta CH66 . . . 69 C6
Little Wissage CH66 . . . . . 69 C7
Littlebourne WA7 . . . . 50 E7
Littlecote Gdns WA4 . . . . . 26 D4
Littledale Rd WA5 . . . . . . 14 F7
Littledales La CW8 . . . . . 102 E4
Littlegate WA7 . . . . 49 E8
Littler Grange Ct CW7 . . . 126 A1
Littler La CW7 . . . . 125 F1
Littler Rd WA11 . . . . 1 A5

Littlestone Cl WA8 . . . . . . 13 A4
Littleton Cl
  1 Northwich CW9 . . . . 103 F4
  Warrington WA5 . . . . 15 D4
Littleton La CH3 . . . . 119 E2
Littondale Cl CW12 . . . . . 157 A5
Liverpool Pl WA8 . . . . 12 C1
Liverpool Rd
  Backford CH1,CH2 . . . . . . 95 B4
  Chester CH2 . . . . 118 C6
  Haydock WA11 . . . . 1 B8
  Irlam,Cadishead M44 . . . . 11 D4
  Kidsgrove ST7 . . . . 195 A1
  Neston CH64 . . . . 41 F1
  Newcastle-u-Lyme ST5 . . . 210 D2
  Warrington WA5,WA1 . . . . 15 F5
  Warrington,Great Sankey
    WA5 . . . . 14 E6
  Warrington,Penketh WA5 . . 14 B4
  Widnes WA8 . . . . 12 C1
Liverpool Rd E ST7 . . . . . 194 E2
Liverpool Rd W ST7 . . . . . 194 B4
Liverpool Row WA12 . . . . . 7 D8
Liverpool St CW9 . . . . . . 104 C8
Livingstone Cl
  Macclesfield SK10 . . . . . . 111 F8
  Warrington WA5 . . . . 15 D7
Livingstone Rd CH65 . . . . . 70 C7
Livingstone Way CW7 . . . . 151 D6
Liz Kaye Ho SK11 . . . . . . 112 E7
Llandaff Cl CH66 . . . . 69 E1
Llandovery Cl CW7 . . . . . 149 B7
Lloyd Cl CH3 . . . . 180 E2
Lloyd Cres WA12 . . . . 1 F3
Lloyd Dr CH65 . . . . 70 D1
Lloyd Pl CH1 . . . . 117 E4
Llyndir La LL12 . . . . 162 B1
Llys Cadnant/Cadnant Ct
  CH4 . . . . 139 D5
Llys Caer CH4 . . . . 139 A3
Llys Catrin/Catherine Ct
  CH5 . . . . 139 B6
Llys Derwen CH4 . . . . 161 A8
Llys Maes Y Ffynnon /
  Springfield Ct CH4 . . . . . 161 A8
Llys Rhuddlan/Rhuddlan Ct
  5 CH4 . . . . 140 F6
Llys Sant Iago/St James Ct
  CH5 . . . . 91 D1
Loachbrook Ave CW12 . . . 156 A2
Lobelia Gr WA7 . . . . 49 F4
Lobelia Wlk **6** M31 . . . . . 11 E3
Loch St **5** Runcorn WA7 . . 23 A2
  14 Runcorn WA7 . . . . . 23 A3
Lochinvar Ave CH66 . . . . . 68 F6
Lochleven Rd CW2 . . . . . 206 A7
Lochmaben Cl CW4 . . . . . 130 B2
Lock La M31 . . . . 11 E3
Lock Rd Bebington CH62 . . 44 A8
  Warrington WA1 . . . . 16 F6
Locker Ave WA2 . . . . 8 B2
Lockerbie Cl
  Holmes Chapel CW4 . . . . 130 C2
  Warrington WA2 . . . . 8 E3
Lockett Rd WA8 . . . . 13 B3
Lockett St WA4 . . . . 16 F3
Lockgate E WA7 . . . . 24 C2
Lockgate W WA7 . . . . 24 C2
Locking Stumps Com Prim
  Sch WA3 . . . . 9 D4
Locking Stumps La WA3 . . . 9 B4
Lockitt St CW2 . . . . 190 D3
Locks The WA4 . . . . 17 B3
Lockton La WA5 . . . . 15 E3
Lockwood View WA7 . . . . . 50 F5
Lodge Brow SK10 . . . . 63 A1
Lodge Cl WA3 . . . . 19 B4
Lodge Dr Culcheth WA3 . . . 4 F3
  Moulton CW9 . . . . 126 F7
  Winsford CW7 . . . . 127 A1
Lodge Gdns CH2 . . . . 118 D6
Lodge Hollow WA6 . . . . . . 73 B4
Lodge La Antrobus CW9 . . . 54 A6
  Dutton WA4 . . . . 76 C8
  Hatherton CW5 . . . . 220 A4
  Haydock WA11,WA12,WA2 . . 2 B8
  Lostock Gralam CW9 . . . . 80 A2
  Middlewich CW10 . . . . . . 128 E2
  Runcorn WA7 . . . . 49 E8
  Saughall CH1 . . . . 94 A2
  Warrington WA5 . . . . 15 F7
  Widnes WA8 . . . . 12 B4
Lodge Rd Alsager ST7 . . . . 193 C4
  Knutsford WA16 . . . . 57 C3
  Sandbach CW11 . . . . 174 E5
  Talke ST7 . . . . 210 D6
  Widnes WA8 . . . . 22 B8
Lodgebury Ct SY14 . . . . . 211 C2
Lodgefields Com Prim Sch
  CW2 . . . . 189 E4
Lodgefields Dr CW2 . . . . . 189 E4
Lodmore La SY13 . . . . . . 233 C6
Lofthouse Gate WA8 . . . . . 12 F4
Lomas Sq SK11 . . . . 112 D5
Lomax Rd CW5 . . . . 205 D6
Lomond Gr CH66 . . . . 69 A5
Lon Y Cryddion / Cobblers La
  LL12 . . . . 161 B1
Lon yr Orsaf / Station App
  CH1 . . . . 116 F7
Lon yr Ywen / Yew Tree Ave
  CH1 . . . . 116 F7
London Rd Adlington SK10 . 62 C5
  Alderley Edge SK9 . . . . . . 60 A1
  Allostock CW4 . . . . 106 F3
  Bridgemere CW5,CW3 . . . 232 A5
  Davenham CW9 . . . . 104 A1

London Rd *continued*
  Frodsham WA6 . . . . 74 B8
  Hatherton CW5 . . . . 220 D4
  Holmes Chapel CW4 . . . . 130 C2
  Macclesfield SK11 . . . . . . 112 D3
  Midway SK10,SK12 . . . . . 36 C1
  Nantwich CW5 . . . . 204 F5
  Northwich CW9 . . . . 103 F7
  Northwich CW9 . . . . 104 A5
  Sandbach CW11 . . . . 174 D8
  Stapeley CW5 . . . . 205 B3
  Warrington WA4 . . . . 26 D5
  Woore CW3 . . . . 232 C1
London Rd N SK12 . . . . . . 36 E5
London Rd S SK12 . . . . . . 36 D3
London Road Terr SK11 112 D5
London Row WA12 . . . . 7 D8
Loney St SK11 . . . . 112 C7
Long Acre
  Cuddington CW8 . . . . 101 D4
  Weaverham CW8 . . . . 77 C1
Long Acres Rd CH64 . . . . . 41 E2
Long Barn La
  Warrington WA2 . . . . 9 B2
  Warrington,Woolston WA1 . 17 D8
Long Croft La SK8 . . . . . . 34 E8
Long Gn CH23 . . . . 97 C3
Long Hill SK23 . . . . 65 F2
Long La Alpraham CW6 . . . 169 E4
  Bickerton SY14 . . . . 199 F4
  Bollington SY10 . . . . 63 B2
  Burland CW5 . . . . 203 A8
  Chester CH2 . . . . 118 F7
  Hargrave CH3 . . . . 143 D2
  Haughton CW6 . . . . 186 D4
  Huxley CH3 . . . . 166 C8
  Kidsgrove ST7 . . . . 195 E4
  Middlewich CW10 . . . . . . 151 C7
  Saughall CH1 . . . . 94 B2
  Swan Green WA16 . . . . . . 107 D7
  Swettenham CW12 . . . . . 131 F5
  Tilston SY14 . . . . 198 B3
  Warrington WA2 . . . . 8 B1
  Wettenhall CW6,CW7 . . . 170 C6
  Whaley Bridge SK23 . . . . . 65 F3
Long La S CW10 . . . . 151 D7
Long Lane Com Prim Sch
  WA2 . . . . 8 B1
Long Looms CH3 . . . . 120 D6
Long Marl Dr SK9 . . . . 34 F4
Long Mdw CH60 . . . . 40 F6
Long Row ST7 . . . . 195 A1
Long Shoot CW4 . . . . 130 D8
Long Shoot Rd SK11 . . . . 108 E1
Long Spinney WA7 . . . . . . 50 C8
Long Valley Rd ST8 . . . . . 179 C2
Long Wlk M31 . . . . 11 D3
Longacre St SK10 . . . . . . 112 C8
Longacres Rd WA15 . . . . . 32 D7
Longbarn Bvd WA2 . . . . 9 C2
Longbarn Com Prim Sch
  WA2 . . . . 9 B1
Longbenton Way WA7 . . . . 24 B4
Longburgh Cl CH2 . . . . . . 118 F3
Longbutt La WA13 . . . . . . 19 A2
Longbutts La SK11 . . . . . . 111 E2
Longclough Rd ST5 . . . . . 210 D2
Longdale Dr CH1 . . . . 117 C5
Longden Ct SK7 . . . . 35 E5
Longden La CW11 . . . . . . 113 A6
Longden St SK10 . . . . 112 E8
Longdin St WA4 . . . . 16 F3
Longdown Rd CW12 . . . . . 155 F4
Longfield Ave
  Chester CH2 . . . . 118 E7
  Heald Green SK8 . . . . 34 C7
Longfield Gdns M44 . . . . . 11 D4
Longfield Rd WA2 . . . . 8 C1
Longfield Dr WA8 . . . . 12 E2
Longford St
  4 Crewe CW2 . . . . 190 D2
  Warrington WA2 . . . . 16 B7
Longhill La CW3 . . . . 230 E5
Longhorn Cl CW10 . . . . . . 128 D2
Longlands Dr SK22 . . . . . . 39 B8
Longlands Rd SK22 . . . . . . 39 B8
Longley Ave CW6 . . . . 122 D6
Longlooms Rd CH65 . . . . . 70 C3
Longmeade Gdns SK9 . . . . 60 C6
Longmeadow
  Cheadle Hulme SK8 . . . . . 35 C7
  Weaverham CW8 . . . . 102 C8
Longmoss Cl CW10 . . . . . 151 B8
Longmynd Rise CW7 . . . . 149 B8
Longnor Rd
  Hazel Grove SK7 . . . . 36 E7
  Heald Green SK8 . . . . 34 D8
Longridge WA16 . . . . 57 D3
Longridge Trad Est
  WA16 . . . . 57 D3
Longsdon Cl ST5 . . . . 210 C1
Longshaw St
  Warrington,Bewsey WA5 . . 15 F8
  Warrington,Dallam WA5 . . . 7 F1
Longsides Rd WA15 . . . . . 32 C7
Longsight La SK8 . . . . 34 F6
Longster Cl WA6 . . . . 73 B2
Longstone La CW6 . . . . . . 124 E3
Longton Ave WA3 . . . . 9 C7
Longview Ave ST7 . . . . . . 193 E4
Longwood Cl CW10 . . . . . 151 C2
Longwood Rd WA4 . . . . . . 26 C5
Lonsdale Cl
  Warrington WA5 . . . . 14 F8
  3 Widnes WA8 . . . . 22 C8

Lonsdale Ct CH4 ....140 F4
Looe Cl WA8 ....12 E2
Looms The CH64 ....41 B2
Loont The CW7 ....149 C7
Lord Nelson St WA1 ......16 C5
Lord St Bollington SK10 ...88 B8
Chester CH3 ....118 F2
Crewe CW2 ....190 D3
Croft WA3 ....9 A8
Macclesfield SK11 ......112 D6
Macclesfield SK11 ......112 D7
Newton-le-W WA12 ....2 A3
Runcorn WA7 ....22 F3
Warrington WA4 ....16 B4
Lord's St M44 ....11 C5
Lords La WA3 ....9 C4
Lords Mill Rd CW2 ......206 B4
Lordship La WA6 ....73 B7
Lordshire Pl ST7 ....195 F2
Lorne St CH1 ....237 A3
Lorraine St ST7 ....195 F1
Lostock Ave Poynton SK12 36 B4
Warrington WA5 ....15 F8
Lostock Cl ☑ CW9 ....103 E5
Lostock Ct SK9 ....34 D4
Lostock Gn CW9 ....80 A1
Lostock Gralam CE Prim Sch
CW9 ....80 A2
Lostock Gralam Sta CW9 80 A2
Lostock Hall Prim Sch
SK12 ....36 B3
Lostock Hall Rd SK12 ....36 B3
Lostock Hollow CW9 ......80 A2
Lostock Rd SK12 ....36 D2
Lostock Way SK9 ....34 D4
Lotus Gdns WA9 ....6 A7
Louise St CH1 ....237 A3
Loushers La WA4 ....16 D2
Lovage Cl WA2 ....9 C1
Lovat Dr WA16 ....82 B7
Lovatt Ct WA13 ....19 B4
Love La
Hassall Green CW11 ....176 C3
Nantwich CW5 ....204 E5
Love Lane (Overton Heath
Lane) SY14 ....213 A4
Love St CH1 ....237 A3
Lovel Terr WA8 ....22 B5
Lovell Ct WA4 ....130 C3
Lovely La WA5 ....15 E6
Low Hill WA6 ....97 D5
Low Leighton Rd SK22 ...39 D8
Low Mdw SK23 ....65 D8
Low St ST7 ....193 E8
Lowcross La SY14 ....198 D3
Lowe Ave
Congleton CW12 ....156 E2
Warrington WA4 ....16 F4
Lowe Cres CW9 ....53 C4
Lowe Dr WA16 ....57 B2
Lowe St Golborne WA3 ....3 A8
Macclesfield SK11 .....112 D7
Lower Appleton Rd WA8 .13 D1
Lower Ash Rd ST7 ......194 E1
Lower Beech Cotts SK10 87 D2
Lower Bridge St CH1 ...237 B1
Lower Brook St CH5 .....91 D1
Lower Church St WA8 ....23 A5
Lower Cl L26 ....21 A8
Lower Darwin St CW9 ..103 E6
Lower Exchange St
SK11 ....112 D8
Lower Farm Mews CW4 147 B3
Lower Greenshall La
SK12 ....38 F6
Lower Hague SK22 ....38 E8
Lower Haigh St ☑ CW7 149 C8
Lower Hall La CH3 .....182 D2
Lower Hall Mews CH3 ..182 C3
Lower Hall Rd SY13 ....215 D4
Lower Heath CW12 .....156 E4
Lower Heath Ave CW12 156 E4
Lower Heath Terr CW12 156 E4
Lower High St ST7 .....195 D7
Lower House La WA8 .....22 F8
Lower La Aldford CH3 ..164 A2
Eaton CW6 ....147 A3
Lower Macclesfield Rd
SK23 ....65 E6
Lower Meadow Dr
CW12 ....156 C2
Lower Meadow Rd SK9 ..34 E4
Lower Mersey St CH65 ..70 C7
Lower Park Cres SK12 ...36 C6
Lower Park Prim Sch
SK12 ....36 C4
Lower Park Rd
Chester CH4 ....237 C2
Poynton SK12 ....36 B5
Lower Park St CW12 ...156 E3
Lower Peover CE Prim Sch
WA16 ....81 E1
Lower Rake La WA6 ......73 B4
Lower Rd L26,WA8 ....21 C7
Lower Robin Hood La
WA6 ....73 B3
Lower Rock St SK22 .....39 C7
Lower Sandy La ST7 ....199 C7
Lower Wash La WA4 .....16 E3
Lowerfield Rd
Chester CH4 ....141 A5
Macclesfield SK10 ......87 E1
Lowerhouse SK10 ....87 E8
Lowerlea SK12 ....38 C6

Lowes La SK11 ....111 F2
Loweswater Cl WA2 ....8 B3
Loweswater Cres WA11 ...1 A6
Lowfield Gdns WA3 ....5 C7
Lowfields Ave CH62 .....43 E3
Lowfields Cl CH62 ......43 E3
Lowland Way WA16 ....82 A8
Lowlands Rd ☑ WA7 .....22 F2
Lownorth Rd M22 ....33 E8
Lowood SK9 ....60 B2
Lowry Cl WA5 ....15 D6
Lowther Ave WA3 ....4 F4
Lowther St SK10 ....88 C8
Lowton Bsns Pk WA3 .....4 A7
Lowton Com Sports Coll
WA3 ....4 B8
Lowton Gdns WA3 ....3 B5
Lowton Jun & Inf Sch
WA3 ....4 A7
Lowton Rd WA3 ....3 C8
Lowton St Mary's CE Prim
Sch WA3 ....4 A8
Lowton West Prim Sch
WA3 ....3 D8
Loxdale Dr CH65 ....69 F4
Loxley Cl
Macclesfield SK11 .....112 B7
Warrington WA5 ....15 A8
Loyola Hey L35 ....12 E8
Lucerne Cl CH3 ....142 B6
Ludford CI ST5 ....210 D2
Ludford St CW1 ....190 C5
Ludlow Ave CW1 ....190 F3
Ludlow Cl
Macclesfield SK10 ......87 E2
Warrington,Paddington
WA1 ....17 B8
Winsford CW7 ....149 B7
Ludlow Cres WA7 ....49 B8
Ludlow Dr CH65 ....70 E3
Ludlow Rd CH1 ....118 A5
Ludwell Ct CW4 ....141 B6
Lugsdale Rd WA8 ....23 B7
Lulworth Cl CW7 ....149 B7
Lumb Brook Mews ☑
WA4 ....16 E1
Lumb Brook Rd
Appleton Thorn WA4 .....27 A5
Warrington WA4 ....26 F8
Lumb Cl SK7 ....35 E6
Lumb Ho SK7 ....35 E6
Lumb La SK7 ....35 E6
Lumber La WA5 ....6 F8
Lumley Pl CH1 ....237 B2
Macclesfield SK11 .....111 F7
Lumley Wlk L24 ....21 A1
Lumpy St CW12 ....156 C3
Lundy Dr CH65 ....95 C8
Lune Cl ☑ CW12 ....157 A1
Lune Way WA8 ....12 C1
Lunehurst ☑ WA3 ....3 E8
Lunt Ave CW2 ....190 C2
Lunt's Heath Rd WA8 ...13 B5
Lunts Heath Prim Sch
WA8 ....13 B5
Lunts Moss ST7 ....194 C6
Luntswood Gr WA12 ......2 A4
Lupin Dr Haydock WA11 ..1 F6
Huntington CH3 ....142 B6
Lupus Way CH66 ....69 F3
Luscombe Cl L26 ....21 A8
Luther Gr WA9 ....1 B2
Luton Rd CH65 ....70 A5
Luton St WA8 ....23 A7
Lutyens Cl SK10 ......111 F8
Lyceum Cl CW1 ....190 A8
Lyceum Way CW1 ......190 A8
Lychgate WA4 ....25 F7
Lycroft Cl WA7 ....49 B6
Lydbury Cl WA5 ....7 D2
Lydden Rd CH65 ....70 B7
Lydgate Cl CW2 ....205 F8
Lydiat La SK9 ....60 A1
Lydiate La Runcorn WA7 .48 D7
Willaston CH64 ....42 E1
Lydiate The CH60 ......40 F7
Lydney Ave SK8 ....34 C7
Lydstep Ct WA5 ....7 E2
Lydyett La CW8 ....78 B3
LyMCote Dr CW8 ....103 A4
Lyme Ave Handforth SK9 .34 B1
Macclesfield SK11 .....112 D5
Lyme Com Prim Sch WA12 1 F4
Lyme Gr WA13 ....18 C2
Lyme Green Bsns Pk
SK11 ....112 C3
Lyme Green Settlement
SK11 ....112 D2
Lyme Lea Cl SK8 ....35 B8
Lyme Park Ctry Pk★
SK12 ....38 B2
Lyme Pk★ SK12 ....38 B1
Lyme Rd High Lane SK12 .38 A6
Poynton SK12 ....37 C3
Lyme St Haydock WA11 ...1 E6
Newton-le-W WA12 ....1 F4
Lyme View SK11 ....112 D2
Lymewood Dr Disley SK12 38 C6
Wilmslow SK9 ....60 E8
Lymm Brook ☑ WA13 ....18 E3
Lymm Hall WA13 ....18 E4
Lymm High Sch WA13 ...19 B3
Lymm Rd
Little Bollington WA14 ..20 B1
Warrington WA4 ....17 F4
Lymmhay La WA13 ....18 E4
Lymmington Ave WA13 ..18 C3

Lynalls Cl CW12 ....155 F3
Lynbrook Rd CW1 ......190 F4
Lyncastle Rd WA4 ......27 D4
Lyncastle Way WA4 .....27 D4
Lyncombe CI SK8 ....35 B6
Lyncroft CI CW1 ......190 F3
Lyndale Ave
Bebington CH62 ....43 E4
Warrington WA2 ....16 D8
Warrington, Fearnhead WA2 8 F2
Lyndale Cl CW7 ....127 A3
Lyndale Sch The CH62 ..43 F5
Lyndhurst Cl SK9 ......59 D5
Lyndon Gr WA7 ....49 B8
Lyneal Ave CH66 ....69 C3
Lyngard Cl SK9 ....34 E1
Lynham Ave WA5 ....15 B5
Lynn Ave ST7 ....210 C8
Lynn Cl WA7 ....49 C7
Lynn Gr SK11 ....112 C6
Lynndene CH66 ....69 D7
Lynside Wlk M22 ....33 E8
Lynthorpe Ave M44 ....11 D6
Lynton Ave M44 ....11 E6
Lynton CI Chester CH4 .140 F6
Heswall CH60 ....41 B6
Knutsford WA16 ....57 C1
Warrington WA5 ....14 E4
Lynton Cres WA8 ....12 E2
Lynton Dr SK6 ....37 E8
Lynton Gdns WA4 ....26 D4
Lynton Gr CW1 ....191 D5
Lynton La SK9 ....60 A2
Lynton Mews SK9 ....60 A2
Lynton Park Rd SK8 ....34 F8
Lynton Pl Alsager ST7 .193 D4
Broughton CH4 ....139 B4
Lynton Way CW2 ....206 A8
Lynwood Altrincham WA15 32 A8
Wilmslow SK9 ....60 A6
Lynwood Ave
Golborne WA3 ....3 E6
Warrington WA4 ....26 C7
Lynwood Rd CH1 ......117 F5
Lyon Ct WA4 ....16 F3
Lyon St Chester CH1 ..237 B3
Crewe CW1 ....190 D4
Macclesfield SK11 .....112 C7
Lyon's La WA4 ....26 E6
Lyons Rd WA5 ....15 A4
Lyster Cl WA3 ....9 F3
Lytham Cl WA5 ....15 B3
Lytham Dr Bramhall SK7 .36 A7
Winsford CW7 ....126 C2
Lytham Rd M44 ....13 C2
Lytherton Ave M44 ....11 D4
Lythgoes La WA2 ....16 B6

M

Mableden Cl SK8 ....34 D8
Mablins La CW1 ....190 B8
Mablins Lane Com Prim Sch
CW1 ....190 B8
Macarthur Rd WA5 .....15 B6
Macbeth Ho ST7 ......210 C8
Macclesfield Coll SK11 .112 B6
Macclesfield District General
Hospl SK10 ....112 B8
Macclesfield Forest Walks★
SK11 ....114 A3
Macclesfield Heritage Ctr★
SK11 ....112 B8
Macclesfield Prep Sch
SK11 ....112 B8
Macclesfield Rd
Alderley Edge SK9 ......85 D7
Congleton CW12 ....156 F6
Eaton CW12 ....134 B2
Hazel Grove SK7 ....36 F8
Holmes Chapel CW4 ...130 E4
Kettleshulme SK23,SK10 64 D3
Prestbury SK10 ....86 F4
Rainow SK10 ....89 B7
Whaley Bridge SK23 ....65 D6
Wilmslow SK9 ....60 D6
Macclesfield Sta SK11 .112 D8
Macdermott Rd WA8 ....22 F5
Macdonald Rd M44 .....11 E8
Macon Ct CW1 ....190 E3
Macon Ind Pk CW1 ....190 E3
Macon Way CW1 ....190 E3
Maddock St ST7 ......209 D1
Maddocks Hill WA6 ...100 F5
Madeley Cl
Altrincham WA14 ....31 E4
Broughton CH4 ....139 C4
Madeley St CW2 ......190 C1
Madeline McKenna Ct
WA8 ....12 C3
Madron Ave SK10 ......86 D3
Maelor Cl CH63 ....43 C6
Maes-y-Coed CH4 ....140 E6
Mag La WA13,WA16 .....28 F6
Magdala Pl CW9 ......104 C8
Magdalen Ct CW2 .....190 A1
Magecroft CW1 ....173 B1
Magenta Ave M44 .....11 E6
Maggoty La SK11 .....111 D3
Magnolia Cl
☑ Ellesmere Port CH66 .69 F1
☑ Partington M31 ......11 E2
Warrington WA1 ....17 E7
Magnolia Dr WA7 ......49 F4
Magnolia Rise SK10 ...86 E6
Magpie Cres ☑ ST7 ...195 B2

Maiden Est CW5 ....228 C8
Maiden Gdns CH65 .....70 D3
Maidenhills CW10 .....128 D1
Maidstone CI SK10 .....87 B2
Maidwell Cl CW7 .....127 A4
Main Cl WA11 ....1 A6
Main La WA3 ....3 F3
Main Rd Betley CW2,CW3 221 F8
Broughton CH4 ....139 B4
Goostrey CW4 ....107 E1
Higher Kinnerton CH4 .161 A8
Langley SK11 ....113 C4
Moulton CW9 ....126 F8
Norton in Hales TF9 ...236 C1
Shavington CW2 ....206 B4
Weston CW2 ....207 C6
Worleston CW5 ....188 F5
Wybunbury CW5 ....220 B8
Main St Frodsham WA6 ..74 B8
Great Barrow CH3 .....120 E5
Runcorn WA7 ....49 F8
Maintree Cres L24 ......21 A4
Mainwaring Cl CW5 ...205 A4
Mainwaring Dr
Saltney CH4 ....140 C7
Wilmslow SK9 ....60 D8
Mainwaring Rd
Bebington CH62 ....43 D8
Over Peover WA16 .....108 A8
Mairesfield Ave WA4 ...17 B2
Maisterson Ct ☑ CW5 .204 E5
Maitland Way CW1 ....117 D4
Maitland-Wood Cl CW9 104 D7
Major Cross St ☑ WA8 .23 A7
Makepeace CI CH3 ....119 C3
Makerfield Dr WA12 ....2 A5
Malaga Ave M90 ....33 B7
Malahide Ct WA8 ......12 E2
Malam Dr CW9 ....104 D6
Malbank CW5 ....204 E6
Malbank Rd CW2 .....189 E4
Malbank Sch CW5 ....204 C6
Malcolm Ave WA2 ....8 D1
Malcolm Cres CH63 ...43 C6
Malcolm St WA7 ....23 B2
Malham Cl WA5 ....14 E8
Malhamdale Rd CW2 ..157 A5
Malin Cl L24 ....21 D2
Maliston Rd WA5 ....15 B5
Mallaig Cl CW4 ....130 C2
Mallard Cl Knutsford WA16 57 B3
Runcorn WA7 ....49 F5
Warrington WA2 ....8 D3
Mallard Cres SK12 .....36 A4
Mallard Ct Chester CH2 118 F7
Crewe CW1 ....191 A2
Heald Green SK8 ......34 B8
Mallard La WA3 ....9 F3
Mallard Way Crewe CW1 191 A2
Winsford CW7 ....149 D6
Mallory Ct
Congleton CW12 ......155 F3
Mobberley WA16 ....58 A4
Mallory Rd CH65 ......70 A4
Mallory Wlk CH4 .....162 A7
Mallow Cl CH3 ....142 A6
Mallow Wlk M31 ....11 F2
Mallowdale Cl CH62 ...43 F5
Malmesbury Cl
Middlewich CW10 .....128 D1
Poynton SK12 ....36 D4
Malmesbury Pk WA7 ...24 E2
Malmesbury Rd SK8 ...35 B6
Malory Cl WA1 ....190 F5
Malpas Alport Prim Sch
SY14 ....213 B4
Malpas Cl Handforth SK9 34 E1
Northwich CW9 ....104 B7
Malpas Dr WA5 ....15 C4
Malpas Rd
Ellesmere Port CH65 ...69 F4
Northwich CW9 ....104 C7
Runcorn WA7 ....49 C7
Malpas Way WA5 ....15 C4
Malt Kiln Rd WA16 .....80 F4
Malt St WA16 ....57 A2
Malta Rd CH2 ....95 B1
Maltmans Rd WA13 ....18 D3
Malton Ave WA3 ....3 E7
Malton Cl WA8 ....12 C5
Malton Dr SK7 ....36 D7
Malvern Ave CH65 .....70 D3
Malvern Cl
Congleton CW12 ......155 F3
Shavington CW2 ....206 B4
Warrington WA5 ....15 A8
Malvern Dr SK10 ....87 E4
Malvern Rd Blacon CH1 118 A5
Haydock WA9 ....1 A4
Knutsford WA16 ....81 F8
Malvern Way CW7 .....149 B7
Manchester Airport Sta
M90 ....33 B7
Manchester Bridge
CW1 ....190 E4
Manchester Bsns Pk
M22 ....33 D8
Manchester Int Airport
M90 ....33 A7
Manchester Int Office Ctr
M22 ....34 A7
Manchester Met Univ
(Alsager Campus) ST7 193 A4
Manchester Met Univ, Crewe
& Alsager Faculty, (Crewe
Campus) CW1 ....190 D1
Manchester New Rd M31 11 D4

Manchester Rd
Congleton CW12 ......156 E5
Handforth SK9 ....34 C2
Hollinfare WA3 ....11 A2
Hollinfare,Hollins Green
WA3 ....11 B3
Knutsford WA16 ....56 F5
Macclesfield SK10 .....87 D4
Partington M31 ....11 F4
Warrington WA3 ....18 D7
Warrington,Bruche WA1 .16 F7
Warrington,Woolston WA1 17 C7
Wincham CW9 ....79 D1
Manchester Row WA12 ..7 D8
Mancroft Cl WA1 ......17 E7
Mandarin Ct WA1 ......16 A3
Manifold Cl CW11 ....174 E8
Manifold Dr SK6 ....37 F6
Manley Cl Antrobus CW9 53 C4
Holmes Chapel CW4 ..130 A3
Northwich CW9 ....104 A5
Manley Gdns WA5 ......15 F5
Manley Gr SK7 ....35 E6
Manley La
Dunham-on-t-H WA6 ....97 F5
Manley WA6 ....98 C4
Manley Mere★ WA6 ....98 B5
Manley Rd Frodsham WA6 74 B3
Manley WA6 ....98 E7
Warren WA16 ....112 A5
Manley View CH2 ......72 C3
Manley Village Sch WA6 99 A5
Manna Dr CH2 ....72 C3
Manners La CH60 ......40 E6
Manning St CW2 .....190 D1
Mannings La CH2 .....119 B6
Mannings La S CH2 ...119 A5
Manor Ave Crewe CW2 190 A1
Golborne WA3 ....3 C8
Goostrey CW4 ....107 F1
Marston CW9 ....79 B6
Newton-le-W WA12 ......1 F4
Manor Bsns Pk CW4 ..130 D3
Manor Cl Broughton CH5 139 C7
Cheadle Hulme SK8 ....35 C8
Congleton CW12 ......157 A1
Great Barrow CH3 ....120 E6
Lymm WA13 ....18 E2
Neston CH64 ....66 C7
Warrington WA1 ....17 D7
Wilmslow SK9 ....59 F8
Manor Cres
Broughton CH4 ....139 C8
Knutsford WA16 ....57 B1
Macclesfield SK10 .....87 D3
Middlewich CW10 .....151 C7
Manor Ct Crewe CW2 .190 B1
Golborne WA3 ....3 C8
Knutsford WA16 ....57 B1
☑ Nantwich CW5 .....204 E6
Ravensmoor CW5 .....204 B4
Manor Dr Barnton CW8 .78 B2
Chester CH3 ....119 C1
Northwich,Rudheath CW9 104 C7
Manor Farm Barns WA7 24 D4
Manor Farm Cl CH2 ...119 F8
Manor Farm Cres CH1 .94 B8
Manor Farm Ct
Broughton CH5 ....139 B7
☑ Frodsham WA6 ......49 C1
Manor Farm Rd WA7 ...24 D4
Manor Fell WA7 ....50 B7
Manor Fields CW10 ...151 C7
Manor Gdns
Nantwich CW5 ....204 E6
Wilmslow SK9 ....60 D7
Manor Gr CW8 ....103 C6
Manor Ho Bebington CH62 43 D8
Ellesmere Port CH66 ...69 D2
Row-of-trees SK9 ......59 D3
Manor Ind Est WA4 ....16 B8
Manor La Broughton CH5 139 B7
Davenham CW9 ....104 D2
Ellesmere Port CH66 ...69 D3
Holmes Chapel CW4 ..130 D3
☑ Middlewich CW10 ..151 C8
Ollerton WA16 ....82 E6
Manor Park Ave WA7 ..24 C4
Manor Park Dr CH66 ...69 D2
Manor Park N WA16 ...57 C2
Manor Park Prim Sch
WA16 ....57 C2
Manor Park Rd CW12 .134 D2
Manor Park S WA16 ....57 C1
Manor Pk Broughton CH5 139 B7
Great Barrow CH3 ....120 E6
Manor Pl WA8 ....12 E5
Manor Rd Bebington CH62 43 E6
Chester CH4 ....141 B6
Cuddington CW8 ......101 F2
Frodsham WA6 ....49 C1
Haydock WA11 ....1 F7
Heswall CH60 ....41 F8
Lymm WA13 ....18 E2
Mow Cop ST7 ....195 D7
Nantwich CW5 ....204 E6
Runcorn WA7 ....23 D2
Sandbach CW11 ....175 D6
Sealand CH5 ....116 A6
Thornton Hough CH63 ..42 A7
Whaley Bridge SK23 ...65 E5
Widnes WA8 ....12 B1
Wilmslow SK9 ....59 E8
Manor Rd N CW5 .....204 E7
Manor Sq CW7 ....149 A8
Manor St CW8 ....103 C6
Manor Terr SK11 .....113 B3
Manor Way Crewe CW2 .190 C1

Manor Way *continued*
Sandbach CW11 . . . .**175** E6
Manora Rd CW9 . . . . .**104** A8
Manorfield Cl CH1 . . . . . .**69** A1
Manorial Rd CH64 . . . . .**66** C8
Manorial Rd S CH64 . . . .**66** C7
Manse Field Rd WA6 . . .**75** B1
Manse Gdns WA12 . . . . . .**2** D4
Mansell Cl WA8 . . . .**13** C5
Mansfield Apartments
WA2 . . . .**9** A3
Mansfield Cl WA3 . . . . . .**10** A4
Mansfield Prim Sch
CH65 . . . .**69** F3
Mansfield Rd CH65 . . . . .**70** A2
Mansion Ct 5 CW5 . . . .**204** F5
Mansion Dr WA16 . . . . . .**57** B2
Manston Rd WA5 . . . .**14** D3
Manuel Perez Rd WA5 . . .**15** B6
Manx Rd WA4 . . . .**16** B3
Maori Dr WA6 . . . .**74** A8
Maple Ave Alsager ST7 . .**193** E2
Disley SK12 . . . .**39** A6
Ellesmere Port CH66 . . . . .**69** D6
Golborne WA3 . . . .**3** F7
Haydock WA11 . . . .**1** B7
Macclesfield SK11 . . . . . .**112** D5
Newcastle-u-Lyme ST5 . . .**210** E1
Newton-le-W WA12 . . . .**2** D2
Poynton SK12 . . . .**36** F3
Runcorn WA7 . . . .**49** C8
Sutton WA7 . . . .**50** A4
Talke ST7 . . . .**210** D8
5 Widnes WA8 . . . .**13** B1
Maple Cl
Brereton Green CW11 . . . .**153** F5
Congleton CW12 . . . .**155** F4
Holmes Chapel CW4 . . . . .**130** D4
Sandbach CW11 . . . .**175** C6
Maple Cres WA5 . . . .**14** A5
Maple Ct CW7 . . . .**127** A3
Maple Gr Barnton CW8 . . .**78** B4
Bebington CH62 . . . .**43** C8
Chester CH2 . . . .**119** B4
Crewe CW1 . . . .**190** E6
Ellesmere Port CH66 . . . . .**95** A8
Northwich, Greenbank
CW8 . . . .**103** C7
Saltney CH4 . . . .**140** D5
Warrington WA4 . . . .**16** D3
Winsford CW7 . . . .**127** A1
Maple La CW8 . . . .**101** F2
Maple Pl ST7 . . . .**193** F7
Maple Rd
Alderley Edge SK9 . . . .**60** B3
Bramhall SK7 . . . .**35** E6
Partington M31 . . . .**11** E3
Warrington WA1 . . . .**17** E7
Winwick WA2 . . . .**8** B6
Maples SK9 . . . .**59** F6
Maples The
Mobberley WA16 . . . .**58** E1
Winsford CW7 . . . .**127** A3
Mapleton Dr WA7 . . . . . .**49** F3
Maplewood SK11 . . . . . .**112** D5
Maplewood Cl WA8 . . . . .**22** A7
Maplewood Gr CH1 . . . .**117** B8
Maplewood Rd SK9 . . . . .**60** E8
Mapplewell Cres WA5 . . .**15** A6
Marble Arch 4 WA16 . . .**57** A2
Marbury Gdns CH65 . . . . .**69** F6
Marbury House Farm
WA4 . . . .**52** E5
Marbury La CW9 . . . .**78** E5
Marbury Park Ctry Pk★
CW9 . . . .**78** E5
Marbury Rd Chester CH3 **119** C2
Comberbach CW9 . . . .**78** D6
Handforth SK9 . . . .**34** B1
Norbury SY13 . . . .**215** B3
Marbury St WA4 . . . .**16** C3
March St CW1 . . . .**190** E4
Marchwiel Rd CH65 . . . . .**70** D4
Marcien Way WA3 . . . . . .**12** F3
Marcliff Gr WA16 . . . .**57** A1
Marcross Cl WA5 . . . .**7** E1
Mardale Ave WA2 . . . .**8** C3
Mardale Cl CW12 . . . . . .**157** B5
Mardale Cres WA13 . . . . .**18** F3
Mardale Ct CW4 . . . .**130** A2
Mardon Cl WA16 . . . .**57** D3
Marfields Prim Sch
CW12 . . . .**156** C2
Marford Cl CW9 . . . .**103** C6
Marfords Ave CH63 . . . . .**43** C7
Margaret Ave WA1 . . . . . .**17** B7
Margaret Ct WA8 . . . .**23** B7
Margaret's La CH66 . . . . .**69** A7
Margery Ave ST7 . . . . . .**194** E7
Marian Ave WA12 . . . .**1** F3
Marian Dr CH3 . . . .**142** B8
Marian Rd WA11 . . . .**1** E7
Marie Cl CW5 . . . .**216** F4
Marie Dr WA4 . . . .**17** D2
Marigold Cl SK11 . . . . . .**111** F8
Marigold Way WA9 . . . .**6** A7
Marina Ave WA5 . . . .**15** C4
Marina Cl SK9 . . . .**34** D5
Marina Dr Chester CH2 . .**118** E7
Ellesmere Port CH65 . . . . .**70** B5
Warrington WA2 . . . .**8** C1
Marina Flats CH3 . . . . . .**142** E7
Marina Gr WA7 . . . .**23** B1
Marina La WA7 . . . .**50** E7
Marina Village WA7 . . . . .**50** E7
Marina Wlk CH65 . . . .**70** B5
Marine App CW8 . . . . . .**103** F8
Marine Ave M31 . . . .**11** D3

Marine Dr CH60 . . . .**40** D6
Mariner Cl WA7 . . . .**50** D6
Marion Dr WA7 . . . .**48** F6
Maritime WA12 . . . .**2** C5
Mark Ave CH66 . . . .**69** C4
Mark Cl CH2 . . . .**118** F2
Market Cl CW1 . . . .**190** D5
Market Ct CW6 . . . .**146** C2
Market Ctr CW1 . . . .**190** D4
Market Gate WA1 . . . .**16** B5
Market Pl Bollington SK10 .**88** B8
Hampton Heath SY14 . . . .**213** D7
Macclesfield SK10,SK11 . .**112** D8
Winsford CW7 . . . .**126** F1
Market Sq Chester CH1 . .**237** B2
Congleton CW12 . . . .**156** D2
Crewe CW1 . . . .**190** D4
4 Market St
Congleton CW12 . . . .**156** D3
Crewe CW1 . . . .**190** D4
Crewe CW1 . . . .**190** D4
Disley SK12 . . . .**38** D6
Kidsgrove ST7 . . . .**195** A1
Nantwich CW5 . . . .**204** E5
New Mills SK22 . . . .**39** B8
9 Northwich CW9 . . . . . .**103** F8
Whaley Bridge SK23 . . . . . .**65** E8
Widnes WA8 . . . .**23** A7
Market Way 7 CW9 . . . .**103** F8
Marl Cl CH3 . . . .**102** A4
Marl Croft CH3 . . . .**142** B7
Marl Edge SK10 . . . .**87** A5
Marl Heys CH2 . . . .**118** E7
Marlborough Ave
Alderley Edge SK9 . . . .**60** B3
Winsford CW7 . . . .**126** C3
Marlborough Cl
Knutsford WA16 . . . .**57** C4
Macclesfield SK10 . . . .**87** D4
Wistaston CW2 . . . .**205** E8
Marlborough Cres
Warrington WA4 . . . .**16** F2
Widnes WA8 . . . .**13** A5
Marlborough Ct
1 Chester CH3 . . . .**119** B2
3 Macclesfield SK11 . . . .**112** D7
Marlborough Dr
Helsby WA6 . . . .**73** B2
Macclesfield SK10 . . . .**87** D4
Marlborough Ho 8
SK11 . . . .**111** F8
Marlborough Prim Sch The
SK10 . . . .**87** D4
Marlborough Rd CH65 . . .**70** D3
Marlborough Way WA11 . . .**1** E8
Marlborough Wlk CH65 . . .**70** C3
Marleston Ct CH4 . . . . . .**140** C4
Marley Ave CW1 . . . .**190** B7
Marley Gn SY13 . . . .**227** C8
Marley Rd SK12 . . . .**36** E2
Marley Way CH4 . . . .**140** E7
Marlfield Rd
Altrincham WA15 . . . .**32** D7
Warrington WA4 . . . .**17** A2
Marline Ave CH63 . . . . . .**43** C6
Marling Cl WA6 . . . .**74** D6
Marling Pk WA8 . . . .**12** B1
Marlow Ave CH2 . . . .**118** F7
Marlow Cl
Sandbach CW11 . . . .**174** D5
Warrington WA3 . . . .**9** C5
Marlow Dr
Altrincham WA14 . . . .**20** F2
Handforth SK9 . . . .**34** C5
Marlowe Cl Blacon CH1 . .**118** A5
Widnes WA8 . . . .**12** F1
Wistaston CW2 . . . .**206** A8
Marlowe Ct SK11 . . . . . .**112** C5
Marlowe Dr CW5 . . . . . .**204** F3
Marlowe Rd
1 Neston CH64 . . . .**66** E8
Northwich CW9 . . . .**104** C6
Marlston Ave CH4 . . . . . .**141** A4
Marlston Pl WA7 . . . .**49** B6
Marlwood Pl CH4 . . . . . .**139** A3
Maroon Rd M22 . . . .**33** F7
Marple Cres CW2 . . . . . .**189** E2
Marple Rd CW9 . . . .**104** C8
Marquis Dr SK8 . . . .**34** C7
Marriott Rd CW11 . . . . . .**174** F3
Marron Ave WA2 . . . .**8** A2
Marryat Cl WA12 . . . .**8** A6
Marsden Ave WA4 . . . . . .**17** A4
Marsden Ct WA8 . . . .**12** E1
Marsden Terr 3 SK11 . . .**112** C7
Marsh Ave ST7 . . . .**195** E2
Marsh Cl ST7 . . . .**193** A3
Marsh Gr ST8 . . . .**179** C3
Marsh Green Cl ST8 . . . .**179** D2
Marsh Green Rd CW11 . .**174** E8
Marsh Hall Pad WA8 . . . .**13** B4
Marsh House La WA1,
WA2 . . . .**16** C7
Marsh La Alsager ST7 . . .**193** A3
Ashley WA16 . . . .**31** A4
Barton CH3,SY14 . . . .**181** E3
Churton CH3 . . . .**181** B5
Dutton WA4 . . . .**51** E3
Elton CH2 . . . .**72** B4
Frodsham WA6 . . . .**74** A8
Holmes Chapel CW4 . . . . .**130** E2
Ince CH2 . . . .**72** D6
Mere WA16 . . . .**30** F3
Nantwich CW5 . . . .**204** C5
New Mills SK22,SK23 . . . . .**39** D6
Norley CW8,WA6 . . . .**101** B7

Marsh La *continued*
Ravensmoor CW5 . . . .**203** F2
Runcorn WA7 . . . .**23** F3
Warrington WA4 . . . .**16** E3
Warrington,Penketh WA5 . .**14** C2
Marsh Lane Trad Est
SK22 . . . .**39** D7
Marsh Rd WA4 . . . .**27** B4
Marsh St Warrington WA1 .**16** C4
Widnes WA8 . . . .**23** A6
Marshall Ave WA5 . . . .**7** F2
Marshall Gr CW12 . . . . . .**179** B8
Marshall La CW8 . . . . . .**103** D6
Marshall Rd WA1 . . . .**17** A4
Marshalls Ct 2 CW8 . . . .**103** C5
Marshfield Ave CW2 . . . .**189** D4
Marshfield Bank CW2 . . .**189** D4
Marshfield La ST8 . . . . . .**179** C2
Marshgate WA8 . . . .**22** B6
Marshgate Pl WA6 . . . . . .**49** D2
Marshgreen Rd ST8 . . . . .**179** D3
Marshlands Rd CH64 . . . .**66** E5
Marshway Dr WA12 . . . . . .**2** B5
Marson St WA2 . . . .**16** A6
Marston Cl CH62 . . . .**43** E3
Marston Gdns CH65 . . . . .**69** F6
Marston La CW9 . . . .**79** C6
Marten Ave CH63 . . . .**43** C7
Marthall La WA16 . . . . . .**83** B7
Marthall Way 8 SK9 . . . .**34** E5
Martham Cl WA4 . . . .**17** A3
Martin Ave
Newton-le-W WA12 . . . .**2** C5
Warrington WA3 . . . .**9** E7
Martin Cl Chester CH2 . . .**118** C8
Runcorn WA7 . . . .**50** A7
Martin Rd Chester CH2 . . .**118** C8
Frodsham WA6 . . . .**74** B8
Martin's La CH3 . . . .**143** F3
Martindale Gr WA7 . . . . . .**49** D5
Martins Mill CW12 . . . . . .**179** C8
Martinscroft Gn WA1 . . . .**17** F7
Martinsfields CW8 . . . . . .**77** A5
Martland Ave WA3 . . . .**3** E7
Martlet Ave SK12 . . . .**38** C6
Marton & District CE Prim
Sch SK11 . . . .**133** C5
Marton Cl
Congleton CW12 . . . .**156** E5
Culcheth WA3 . . . .**4** E4
Hough CW2 . . . .**206** A3
Macclesfield SK10 . . . .**86** F1
Marton Hall La SK11 . . . .**133** B3
Marton La Marton SK11 . .**133** D7
Warren SK11 . . . .**111** B1
Marton Rd CH4 . . . .**139** C3
Marton Way 5 SK9 . . . . .**34** E5
Martree Ct CW9 . . . .**174** D8
Mary St Crewe CW1 . . . . .**190** E5
Widnes WA8 . . . .**23** D7
Maryfield Cl WA3 . . . .**3** A7
Maryhill Cl ST7 . . . .**195** A3
Maryhill High Sch ST7 . . .**195** A3
Maryhill Prim Sch ST7 . . .**195** A3
Maryhill Rd WA7 . . . .**49** A8
Maryland Cl WA5 . . . .**15** C7
Marys Gate CW2 . . . .**205** E8
Maryville Cl 3 CH65 . . . . .**70** C6
Masefield Ave WA8 . . . . . .**22** F8
Masefield Dr Blacon CH1 .**117** E6
Crewe CW1 . . . .**190** F4
Winwick WA2 . . . .**8** A5
Masefield Way CW11 . . . .**174** D5
Maskery Pl CW12 . . . . . .**156** E4
Mason Ave
Warrington WA1 . . . .**16** E8
Widnes WA8 . . . .**13** B4
Mason Cl CH66 . . . .**69** D2
Mason St Chester CH2 . . .**237** A3
Runcorn WA7 . . . .**23** C3
Warrington WA1 . . . .**16** C5
Mason's Row CW6 . . . . .**169** E2
Masons La SK10 . . . .**87** F1
Massey Ave
Hartford CW8 . . . .**103** A4
Lymm WA13 . . . .**18** B2
Warrington WA5 . . . .**7** F2
Winsford CW7 . . . .**126** F1
Massey Brook La WA13 . . .**18** B2
Massey Cl CW5 . . . .**205** A4
Massey Hall Sch WA4 . . . .**17** F2
Massey St 6 SK9 . . . .**60** A1
Masseyfield Rd WA7 . . . . .**50** B5
Masters Cl WA16 . . . .**56** F1
Mates La SY14 . . . .**213** B6
Mather Ave Golborne WA3 . .**3** E6
Runcorn WA7 . . . .**48** D7
Mather Ct CW10 . . . .**151** C4
Mather Dr
Comberbach CW9 . . . .**78** C8
Northwich CW9 . . . .**104** D7
Mathers Cl WA2 . . . .**9** A4
Matheison Rd WA8 . . . . . .**22** C5
Matlock Cl WA5 . . . .**15** A8
Matlock Dr SK7 . . . .**36** E8
Matlock Rd SK8 . . . .**34** C7
Matterdale Cl WA6 . . . . . .**74** D7
Matthew Cl CH2 . . . .**118** F2
Matthews Pl CW12 . . . . .**157** A2
Matthews St WA1 . . . .**16** D7
Matty's La WA6 . . . .**74** A7
Mavor Cl CW1 . . . .**190** B4
Maw Green Cl CW1 . . . . .**190** F7
Maw Green Rd CW1 . . . .**190** F7
Maw La CW1 . . . .**191** C7
Mawdsley Ave WA1 . . . . . .**17** E7

Mawdsley Cl ST7 . . . . . .**193** A3
Mawson Cl WA5 . . . .**15** D8
Maxfield Cl SK11 . . . .**111** F8
Maxwell Cl CH65 . . . .**70** A2
Maxwell Rd CW12 . . . . . .**179** A8
Maxwell St Crewe CW2 . .**190** C3
Warrington WA3 . . . .**9** E5
May Ave SK8 . . . .**35** B6
May Rd Cheadle Hulme SK8 **35** B6
Heswall CH60 . . . .**41** A8
May Wlk 2 M31 . . . .**11** E3
Mayberry Gr WA2 . . . .**9** A1
Maybrook Pl WA4 . . . .**16** F3
Maydor Ave CH4 . . . .**140** C7
Mayfair Cl Poynton SK12 . .**36** E4
Warrington WA5 . . . .**14** D7
Mayfair Ct CH4 . . . .**162** E5
Mayfair Dr CW9 . . . .**103** F3
Mayfair Gr WA8 . . . .**12** D1
Mayfield Ave
Macclesfield SK11 . . . . . .**112** C5
Widnes WA8 . . . .**12** B1
Mayfield Cl CW4 . . . .**130** D3
Mayfield Ct WA8 . . . .**13** A2
Mayfield Dr
Bebington CH62 . . . .**44** B6
Cuddington CW8 . . . .**102** A4
Golborne WN7 . . . .**4** C8
Winsford CW7 . . . .**127** A3
Mayfield Gdns CH64 . . . . .**41** E1
Mayfield Gr
Cuddington CW8 . . . .**102** A4
Wilmslow SK9 . . . .**59** E5
Mayfield Mews CW1 . . . .**189** F6
Mayfield Rd Blacon CH1 . .**117** D5
Bramhall SK7 . . . .**35** E4
Mobberley WA16 . . . .**57** F4
Northwich CW9 . . . .**104** C8
Warrington WA4 . . . .**17** A2
Mayfield Terr SK11 . . . . .**112** C5
Mayfield View WA13 . . . . .**18** F2
Mayflower Rd CW5 . . . . .**204** E3
Mayity Cl WA12 . . . .**2** A3
Maythorn Ave WA3 . . . .**9** A7
Maytree Ave CH3 . . . . . .**119** B2
Maywood SK9 . . . .**59** E4
Mc Clellan Pl WA8 . . . . . .**13** B1
McCarthy Cl WA3 . . . .**10** A3
McGarva Way CH65 . . . . .**70** C4
McGowan Ho ST7 . . . . . .**210** D8
McKee Ave WA2 . . . .**8** B2
Mckellin Cl ST7 . . . .**209** E2
Mckinley Way WA8 . . . . . .**12** F3
McLaren St CW1 . . . .**190** C7
McMinnis Ave WA9 . . . .**1** B2
McNeill Ave CW1 . . . .**190** A5
Mead Ave ST7 . . . .**194** E7
Mead Cl WA16 . . . .**56** F1
Mead Rd WA1 . . . .**17** A8
Meade The SK9 . . . .**60** C8
Meadow Ave
Congleton CW12 . . . .**156** C1
Goostrey CW4 . . . .**107** C1
Warrington WA4 . . . .**16** B2
Weston CW2 . . . .**207** B5
Meadow Bank
Adderley TF9 . . . .**235** A4
Kelsall CW6 . . . .**122** C4
Meadow Bank Cvn Pk
WA4 . . . .**25** C6
Meadow Brow SK9 . . . . . .**60** A2
Meadow Cl
Cuddington CW8 . . . .**102** A4
Farndon CH3 . . . .**180** F1
Goostrey CW4 . . . .**107** E1
Helsby WA6 . . . .**73** B3
High Lane SK6 . . . .**37** F8
Neston CH64 . . . .**66** E6
Newton-le-W WA12 . . . .**1** F3
Shavington CW2 . . . .**206** D5
Tarvin CH3 . . . .**121** B2
Whaley Bridge SK23 . . . . . .**65** D8
Widnes WA8 . . . .**12** D3
Willaston CH64 . . . .**67** F8
Wilmslow SK9 . . . .**59** E4
Winsford CW7 . . . .**126** C3
Meadow Cotts 5 CW12 **156** D3
Meadow Croft
Alsager ST7 . . . .**193** E2
Willaston CH64 . . . .**67** E8
Meadow Ct
Frodsham WA6 . . . .**49** C1
Mollington CH1 . . . .**94** F1
No Man's Heath SY14 . . . .**214** A5
Packmoor ST7 . . . .**195** E2
Meadow Dr Barnton CW8 . .**78** A3
Knutsford WA16 . . . .**81** F8
Prestbury SK10 . . . .**87** B7
Wistaston CW2 . . . .**205** F7
Meadow Gate CW9 . . . . . .**79** F5
Meadow Gr
Northwich CW9 . . . .**104** B5
Winsford CW7 . . . .**126** A5
Meadow Home Pk CW7 **126** D6
Meadow House Pk
CW6 . . . .**185** D5
Meadow La
Comberbach CW9 . . . .**78** C7
Disley SK12 . . . .**38** D6
Ellesmere Port CH65 . . . . .**70** D6
Huntington CH3 . . . .**142** A5
Moulton CW9 . . . .**126** F8
Partington WA14 . . . .**20** A4
Warrington WA2 . . . .**9** A2
Willaston CH64 . . . .**67** F8
Meadow Lane Ind Pk
CH65 . . . .**70** D5
Meadow Mill Ct CW12 . .**156** E3

Man – Mel 265

Meadow Prim Sch CH66 .**69** E2
Meadow Rd
Broughton CH4 . . . .**139** B4
Weaverham CW8 . . . .**102** E7
Meadow Rise
Clutton CH3 . . . .**182** D2
Winsford CW7 . . . .**126** A1
Meadow Row WA7 . . . . . .**24** A1
Meadow St
New Mills SK22 . . . .**39** B8
3 Northwich CW9 . . . . . .**104** A8
Meadow The CW4 . . . . . .**130** D8
Meadow View
Chester CH3 . . . .**118** F1
Elton CH2 . . . .**72** A3
Lymm WA13 . . . .**18** D4
Middlewich CW10 . . . .**128** B2
Sealand CH5 . . . .**116** A6
Meadow View Dr WA6 . . . .**74** A7
Meadow Way
Lawton-gate ST7 . . . .**194** A5
Macclesfield SK10 . . . .**87** E2
Wilmslow SK9 . . . .**59** E4
Meadow Wlk
Partington M31 . . . .**11** E3
4 Runcorn WA7 . . . .**49** C7
Meadowbank Gdns WA3 . .**5** C7
Meadowcroft
Higher Kinnerton CH4 . . . .**161** A7
Saughall CH1 . . . .**94** B1
Meadowfield
Tarporley CW6 . . . .**146** C1
Whaley Bridge SK23 . . . . . .**65** D8
Meadowfield Rd CH4 . . . .**141** A5
Meadowgate Cl CW11 . . .**174** D5
Meadowgate Farm WA7 . .**49** F2
Meadows La
Chester CH4 . . . .**237** C1
Saughall CH1 . . . .**117** A8
Tilston SY14 . . . .**212** B6
Meadows Pl CH4 . . . .**141** E7
Meadows Rd
Cheadle Hulme SK8 . . . . . .**34** F8
Kidsgrove ST7 . . . .**194** F1
Meadows The
Ashton Hayes CH3 . . . . . .**121** E7
Congleton CW12 . . . .**156** E3
Irlam M44 . . . .**11** E6
Neston CH64 . . . .**66** F6
Meadowside Disley SK12 . .**39** A6
Fourlane-ends SK10 . . . . . .**63** B8
Northwich CW8 . . . .**103** D7
Whaley Bridge SK23 . . . . . .**65** D8
Meadowside Ave ST7 . . . .**209** D2
Meadowside La ST7 . . . . .**195** B7
Meadowside Mews CH1 .**118** B4
Meadowside Rd CH62 . . . .**43** D8
Meadowsway CH2 . . . . . .**118** C8
Meadowsweet Rd WA16 . .**57** F3
Meadowvale Cl CW5 . . . .**204** E7
Meads Rd ST7 . . . .**193** D4
Meadscroft Dr SK9 . . . . . .**59** F1
Meadway Bramhall SK7 . . .**35** E5
Ellesmere Port CH66 . . . . .**69** B7
Golborne WA3 . . . .**3** D7
Heswall CH60 . . . .**40** F6
High Lane SK6 . . . .**37** F8
Poynton SK12 . . . .**36** B4
Prestbury SK10 . . . .**87** A5
Meakin Cl CW12 . . . .**157** B1
Meal St SK22 . . . .**39** C8
Mealors New Cotts CH64 .**67** A4
Mealors Weint CH64 . . . . .**41** B5
Meddings Cl SK9 . . . .**85** A8
Medina Ave CW7 . . . .**126** F2
Medina Way ST7 . . . .**195** B2
Medlar Cl CH4 . . . .**140** F5
Medway Cl Golborne WN7 . .**4** C8
Handforth SK9 . . . .**34** D2
Warrington WA2 . . . .**8** E2
Medway Dr ST8 . . . .**179** D1
Medway Rd WA3 . . . .**5** A2
Mee St SK11 . . . .**112** E5
Meeanee Dr CW5 . . . . . .**204** E5
Meeting House La WA6 . . .**74** E2
Meeting La WA5 . . . .**14** E5
Meg La Langley SK11 . . . .**113** D1
Macclesfield SK10 . . . . . .**111** E8
Megacre ST7 . . . .**210** A1
Megs La CW9 . . . .**53** B4
Meir Ho ST7 . . . .**193** C3
Melbourne Ave M90 . . . . .**33** A8
Melbourne Gr CW1 . . . . .**191** C5
Melbourne Rd
Blacon CH1 . . . .**117** D4
Bramhall SK7 . . . .**35** A3
Melbury Cl WA3 . . . .**9** F6
Melbury Rd SK8 . . . .**35** B6
Melchett Cres CW9 . . . . .**104** D7
Melford Cl CW2 . . . .**206** C8
Melford Ct Lymm WA13 . . .**18** C4
Warrington WA1 . . . .**17** D8
Melford Dr
Macclesfield SK10 . . . .**87** C2
Runcorn WA7 . . . .**23** C1
Meliden Gr WA6 . . . .**73** B1
Melkridge Cl CH2 . . . . . .**119** A3
Melksham Cl SK11 . . . . . .**112** A7
Mellard St ST7 . . . .**209** D1
Mellock Cl CH64 . . . .**66** F6
Mellock La CH64 . . . .**66** F5
Mellor Cl WA7 . . . .**24** D1
Mellor Cres WA16 . . . .**56** E1

Mellor St Crewe CW1 ....190 D5
  Packmoor ST7 ....195 F2
Mellors Bank ST7 ......195 D6
Melrose Ave
  Burtonwood WA5 ....6 F7
  Chester CH3 ....119 B2
  Warrington WA4 ....26 D8
Melrose Cres SK12 ......37 D5
Melrose Ct 15 SK9 ....34 E1
Melrose Dr Crewe CW1 ...190 B8
  Ellesmere Port CH66 ......94 F8
Melton Ave WA4 ....26 B8
Melton Cl CW12 ....155 F3
Melton Dr CW12 ....155 F3
Melton Rd WA7 ....49 C7
Melverly Dr CH1 ......117 C4
Melville Cl
  Warrington WA2 ....16 B7
  2 Widnes WA8 ....13 D1
Melville Rd M44 ....11 C5
Mendell Cl CH62 ....43 E8
Mendell Prim Sch CH62 .43 E8
Mendip Ave WA2 ....8 B3
Mendip Cl
  Ellesmere Port CH66 ......69 E3
  Heald Green SK8 ....34 E7
  Winsford CW7 ....149 B8
Menin Ave WA4 ....16 C3
Menlow Cl WA4 ....17 C1
Mentmore Gdns WA4 ....26 F5
Meols Cl
  Ellesmere Port CH66 ......69 E4
  Hale L24 ....21 E2
Mercer Cl SY14 ....213 B3
Mercer Rd WA11 ....1 D6
Mercer St Burtonwood WA5 .6 E6
  Newton-le-W WA12 ....2 D4
Mercer Way Chester CH4 140 F6
  Nantwich CW5 ....204 E7
Mercer Wlk CH65 ....70 C4
Merchants Ct CW1 .....190 C7
Mercian Cl CW2 ....206 B4
Mercury Ct CW1 ....117 E2
Mere Ave CH63 ....43 B6
Mere Bank CW9 ....127 A8
Mere Brook Wlk CW2 ..190 C1
Mere Cl
  Ellesmere Port CH66 ....69 D2
  Haslington CW1 ....191 D4
  Pickmere WA16 ....80 A7
Mere Cres CW8 ....123 F6
Mere Ct Alsager ST7 ....193 D4
  Chelford SK11 ....83 F3
  5 Knutsford WA16 ......57 A2
  Weston CW2 ....207 B5
Mere Hall WA16 ....56 A8
Mere Home Farm WA16 .56 B8
Mere La Cuddington CW8 102 A2
  Pickmere WA16 ....79 F7
Mere Rd Marston CW9 ...79 B6
  Newton-le-W WA12 ....2 F4
  Warrington WA2 ....9 A2
  Weston CW2 ....207 B5
Mere St CW1 ....191 D4
Mere View Gdns WA4 ....26 E5
Merebank Rd CW2 ......190 B1
Merebrook Rd SK11 ....111 F8
Merecroft 1 CH3 ....119 A1
Meredith Ave WA4 ......17 B2
Meredith St CW1 ......190 C5
Merehaven Cl WA16 .....80 A7
Mereheath La WA16 .....56 E5
Mereheath Pk WA16 .....56 F3
Merelake Rd ST7 ......210 B8
Meremore Dr ST5 .....210 D2
Mereside Ave CW12 ...156 B3
Mereside Cl SK10 ......87 A1
Mereside Gdns SK23 ....65 D6
Mereside Rd WA16 .....30 C2
Merevale Cl WA7 ....49 E6
Merewood Cl WA2 ....8 D3
Mereworth Dr CW9 ....103 F5
Meridian Ho CW7 ......127 B3
Meriton Rd SK9 ....34 D4
Merlin Ave WA16 ....57 B3
Merlin Cl Runcorn WA7 ..24 A1
  Winsford CW7 ....150 A8
Merlin Way Crewe CW1 .190 A8
  Kidsgrove ST7 ....195 D3
Merrick Cl WA2 ....8 E3
Merridale The WA15 ....32 A8
Merriden Rd SK10 ......87 B2
Merrill's Ave CW2 .....189 E5
Merriman Ave WA16 ....57 C3
Merrivale Rd CW2 .....206 B8
Merrydale Cl SK10 ......86 F1
Merryman's La SK9 .....84 B7
Mersey Pl CW7 ....127 B1
Mersey Rd Runcorn WA7 .23 A3
  Widnes WA8 ....23 A4
Mersey St St Helens WA9 .1 A3
  Warrington WA1 ....16 B5
Mersey View WA7 ......48 D7
Mersey View Rd WA8 ...22 B4
Mersey Wlk WA4 ....16 F5
Merseyton Rd CH65 ....70 B8
Merseyton Road Workshops
  CH65 ....70 C7
Mersham Ct WA8 ....12 F4
Merton Ave SK7 ....36 F8
Merton Cl CH64 ....66 E5
Merton Dr CH4 ....141 A4
Merton House Sch CH2 118 C4
Merton Rd Bebington CH65 44 B3
  Ellesmere Port CH66 .....69 F3

Merton Rd continued
  Poynton SK12 ....36 B4
Mertoun Rd WA4 ....16 B1
Mervyn Rd CW8 ....77 E1
Merwood Ave SK8 ......34 D8
Messuage La CW12 ....132 E4
Meteor Cres WA2 ....8 D2
Mevagissey Rd WA7 ....50 C5
Mevril Rd SK23 ....65 E5
Mevril Springs Way SK23 65 E5
Mews The Barnton CW8 ..78 B2
  Burtonwood WA5 ....6 E6
  Holmes Chapel CW4 ...130 C3
  New Mills SK22 ....39 D8
  Styal SK9 ....33 D4
  Tarporley SK8 ....168 C8
  Willaston CH64 ....68 A8
Meynell Cl CW2 ....190 A1
Meynell Pl CH1 ....118 A5
Micawber Rd SK12 ......36 E2
Mickle Trafford Village Sch
  CH2 ....119 E8
Micklegate
  Mickle Trafford CH2 ....119 E8
  Runcorn WA7 ....50 D7
Micklewright Ave CW1 .190 D5
Mickley Hall La CW5 ...218 A4
Mid Cheshire Coll (London
  Road Studios) CW9 ...103 F6
Mid Cheshire Coll (Verdin
  Ctr) CW7 ....126 D1
Mid-Cheshire Coll (Hartford
  Campus) CW8 ....103 C6
Middle La Aldford CH3 .163 F3
  Congleton CW12 ......157 D4
  Kingsley WA6 ....74 F2
Middle Wlk
  Frodsham WA6 ....74 B7
  Knutsford WA16 ....57 B2
Middlecroft CH3 ......119 E5
Middlehills SK11 ......113 A6
Middlehurst Ave WA4 ..102 E8
Middlehurst Rd WA4 ....17 A2
Middlewich High Sch
  CW10 ....151 C8
Middlewich Prim Sch
  CW10 ....151 B8
Middlewich Rd
  Allostock WA16 ....106 D5
  Church Minshull CW1,
    CW10 ....172 C5
  Cranage CW4,CW10 ...129 E6
  Crewe CW1 ....189 D6
  Crewe CW5 ....189 B1
  Delamere CW6,CW8 ...123 D5
  Holmes Chapel CW4 ...130 B3
  Knutsford WA16 ....82 A3
  Lower Peover WA16 .....81 F2
  Nantwich CW5 ....204 D1
  Northwich CW9 ....104 D7
  Sandbach CW11 ....174 E7
  Winsford CW7,CW10 ...127 E1
Middlewich Road Ind Est
  CW10 ....129 A6
Middlewich St CW1 ....190 D6
Middlewood WA3 ....3 E8
Middlewood Rd
  Hazel Grove SK7,SK12 ...37 C7
  High Lane SK6 ....37 D7
  Poynton SK12 ....37 B4
Middlewood Sta SK12 ...37 D6
Middlewood View SK6 ...37 D7
Midfield Cl ST8 ....179 C2
Midhurst Cl SK8 ....34 F8
Midland St WA8 ....13 B1
Midland Terr SK22 ......39 C7
Midland Way WA1,WA5 ..16 B5
Midlothian Ho CH1 ....237 C3
Midpoint 18 Motorway Ind
  Est CW10 ....128 C1
Midway SK8 ....35 B5
Milborne Cl CH2 ......118 E5
Mildenhall Cl WA5 .....15 B6
Mile Bank Rd SY13 ....226 D3
Miles Cl WA3 ....9 F3
Milford Gdns WA4 ......26 D4
Milk St WA5 ....14 E7
Mill Bank CH64 ....67 A5
Mill Bridge Cl CW1 ....190 F3
Mill Brow WA8 ....13 C1
Mill Cl Chester CH2 ...118 D6
  Knutsford WA16 ....57 D4
  Warrington WA2 ....8 E4
Mill Cotts Bollington SK10 .88 B8
  Christleton CH3 ....142 D8
  Willaston CH64 ....42 F1
Mill Cross CH3 ....143 B5
Mill Ct CH65 ....69 F6
Mill Farm Cl WA2 ....8 E3
Mill Farm Est CW5 ....217 A3
Mill Field Cl CH3 .....180 F2
Mill Gn Congleton CW12 .156 D3
  Willaston CH64 ....67 F8
Mill Gr Bulkeley SY14 .184 E2
  Kidsgrove ST7 ....194 D1
Mill Green La WA3 .....13 E5
Mill Green Sch WA12 .....2 E3
Mill Hill Ave SK12 ......36 D7
Mill Hill Dr WA16 .....175 A5
Mill Hill La WA16 .....175 A4
Mill Hill Hollow SK12 ...36 D7
Mill Ho CW5 ....204 D5
Mill La Adlington SK10 ..62 B6
  Alsager CW11 ....192 E8
  Altrincham WA15 ......32 A8
  Audlem, Little Heath CW3 230 A4
  Audlem, Swanbach CW3 .229 E2

Mill La continued
  Barthomley CW2 ......208 C7
  Blakenhall CW5 ......221 B4
  Bold Heath WA8 ....13 D6
  Bollington SK10 ....88 C8
  Brereton Green CW4 ...153 E8
  Bulkeley SY14 ....184 E2
  Burton CH64 ....67 C1
  Chester CH2 ....118 D6
  Christleton CH3 ......120 D2
  Congleton CW12 ......179 C8
  Cronton WA8 ....12 D6
  Cuddington CW8 ......101 F4
  Duddon CW6 ....145 A7
  Eaton CW6 ....147 B2
  Ellesmere Port CH66 ....69 E5
  Frodsham WA6 ....49 E2
  Goostrey CW4 ....107 E2
  Great Barrow CH3 ....120 E5
  Hazel Grove SK7 ......36 F8
  Heswall CH60 ....41 B8
  Higher Walton WA4 .....25 E7
  Holmes Chapel CW4 ...154 A8
  Huxley CH3 ....144 C1
  Kelsall CW6 ....122 C1
  Kingsley WA6 ....75 E3
  Lindow End SK9 ....84 A7
  Little Budworth CW6 ..148 A8
  Lymm WA13 ....19 C4
  Macclesfield SK11 ....112 D7
  Marton CW12 ....132 F2
  Middlewich CW10 .....128 D1
  Middlewich,Stud Green
    CW11 ....152 C1
  Mobberley WA16 ....58 B4
  Mottram St Andrew SK10 .61 C5
  Neston CH64 ....67 C5
  Newton-le-W WA12 ......2 E3
  Over Peover WA16,SK11 .108 D8
  Prestbury SK10 ....61 F6
  Sandbach CW11 ....174 C8
  Sandbach,Wheelock CW11 175 B2
  Siddington SK11 ......109 F6
  Smallwood CW11 .....176 D7
  Tarvin CH3 ....121 C4
  The Bank ST7 ....195 A4
  Warrington WA2 ....7 F4
  Warrington,Houghton Gn
    WA2 ....8 E4
  Warrington,Stockton Heath
    WA4 ....16 E1
  Weston CW2 ....207 B6
  Whitegate CW7,CW8 ...126 B6
  Willaston CH64 ....42 F1
Mill Lane Cotts CH3 ...120 E5
Mill Mdw WA2 ....2 E3
Mill Park Dr CH62 ......43 E3
Mill Pool La CW5 ......187 C6
Mill Rd Macclesfield SK11 112 D6
  Wilmslow SK9 ....60 B7
Mill Rise ST7 ....195 A1
Mill Row CW11 ....175 C6
Mill St Chester CH4 ...237 B1
  Congleton CW12 ......156 D3
  Congleton, Buglawton
    CW12 ....156 F4
  Crewe CW2 ....190 D3
  Golborne WA3 ....3 A8
  Macclesfield SK11 ....112 D7
  Nantwich CW5 ....204 E5
  Neston CH64 ....66 D8
  Wilmslow SK9 ....60 B7
Mill Stream Cl CW4 ...107 C1
Mill The ST7 ....195 C5
Mill View Cl SY14 ....184 E2
Mill View Prim Sch CH2 118 E6
Mill Way CW5 ....204 F2
Mill Wharf CH3 ....143 B5
Millar Cres WA8 ....23 A7
Millbank WA13 ....18 E3
Millbank SK11 ....84 A3
Millbank Cotts CH3 ...166 C2
Millbank Ct WA6 ....74 A8
Millbank Dr SK10 ......86 F1
Millbeck Cl CW2 ......207 B5
Millbridge Gdns WA12 ...2 E3
Millbrook Cl
  Fowley Common WA3 .....5 C5
  Winsford CW7 ....148 F8
Millbrook Ct CW10 ....128 D1
Millbrook End CH3 ....166 A2
Millbrook Fold SK7 .....36 F8
Millbrook Gr 1 SK9 ....34 D1
Millbuck Way CW11 ...174 C6
Millcroft Neston CH64 ...41 E1
  Sandbach,Wheelock CW11 191 F8
Milldale Rd WN7 ....4 B8
Millend La ST7 ....209 C5
Millenium Ct CH64 ......41 E2
Millenium Way ST5 ....210 F2
Miller St WA4 ....16 C4
Millers Cl CH3 ....143 A4
Millers Croft 8 SK10 ..112 C8
Millers Ct 7 SK10 ....112 C8
Millers La WA13 ....19 B5
Millers Mdw SK10 .....88 E5
Millers View ST7 .....195 A1
Millers Wharf ST7 ....193 E7
Millersdale Cl CH62 ....43 F5
Millersdale Gr WA7 ....49 D6
Milley La WA16 ....80 C7
Millfield CH64 ....41 E1
Millfield Bsns Ctr WA11 ..1 E8
Millfield La Haydock WA11 ..1 F8
  Saighton CH3 ....142 F1
  Tarporley CW6 ....146 C2
Millfield Rd WA8 ....13 C2
Millfield Terr CH66 .....69 C7

Millfields CW5 ....204 D4
Millfields Prim Sch
  Bebington CH62 ....43 E4
  Nantwich CW5 ....204 C5
Millgate CW8 ....101 F4
Millhouse Ave WA4 .....16 D1
Millhouse La WA3 ......9 A6
Millingford Ind Est WA3 ..3 A8
Millington Cl
  Runcorn WA7 ....49 C6
  Widnes WA8 ....22 F8
Millington Hall La WA14 .30 B5
Millington La
  Rostherne WA14 ....30 B6
  Weaverham CW8 ......102 B6
Millmead ST7 ....193 F7
Millport Cl WA2 ....9 A2
Millrace Dr CW2 ......206 B8
Mills Way CW1 ....173 B1
Millstone Cl SK12 ......36 F5
Millstone La CW5 .....204 F5
Millstone Pas SK11 ...112 E6
Millway Altrincham WA15 .32 C7
  Waverton CH3 ....143 B5
Millway Rd L24 ....21 A4
Millwood Cl 4 SK8 .....34 E8
Millwood Ct L24 ....21 A4
Millyard The CH4 .....162 C1
Milne Cl CW2 ....189 F1
Milner Cop CH60 ....41 A8
Milner Rd Heswall CH60 .41 A8
  Northwich CW8 ....103 C6
Milner St WA5 ....15 F5
Milnthorpe Rd WA5 .....6 E6
Milton Ave Irlam M44 ...11 E6
  Newton-le-W WA12 ......2 B3
  Widnes WA8 ....22 F8
Milton Cl
  Higher Wincham CW9 ...80 A5
  Middlewich CW10 .....151 D5
Milton Cres ST7 ......210 C8
Milton Dr Poynton SK12 ..36 D4
  Wistaston CW2 ......206 A8
Milton Gr Helsby WA6 ...73 A1
  Warrington WA4 ......16 D3
Milton Rd Blacon CH1 ..117 F6
  Ellesmere Port CH65 ....70 D4
  Golborne WA3 ....3 A8
  Widnes WA8 ....23 A8
Milton Rough CW8 .....76 E2
Milton St Chester CH1 ..237 B3
  Widnes WA8 ....23 A5
Milton Way CW11 .....174 D6
Milvain Dr WA2 ....8 C1
Milverton Dr SK7 ......35 B5
Mimosa Cl CH2 ....72 C4
Mine Way WA11 ....1 F7
Miners Way Speke L24 ...21 A3
  Widnes WA8 ....23 A7
Minerva Ave CH1 ......117 E2
Minerva Cl WA4 ....16 D2
Minerva Ct CH1 ......117 E2
Minn-End-La SK11 ....159 B6
Minor Ave SK11 ....112 D3
Minshull La CW5,CW7 .171 D4
Minshull New Rd CW1 .189 F7
Minshull St WA16 ......57 A2
Minster Cl CW7 ......149 D5
Minster Ct Runcorn WA7 ..48 E8
  Wistaston CW2 ......205 E8
Minster Dr WA14 ....31 A8
Minton Cl CW12 ......157 B1
Minton Way WA8 ....13 B5
Mirfield Cl WA3 ....3 D7
Mirion St CW1 ....190 D4
Mission Mews CH2 ....118 F2
Misty Cl WA8 ....12 C2
Mitchell Ave
  Burtonwood WA5 ....6 E5
  Kidsgrove ST7 ....194 D1
Mitchell Dr ST7 ......194 D1
Mitchell Fold SK10 .....63 D8
Mitchell St Golborne WA3 ..3 A8
  Warrington WA4 ......26 C8
Mithril Cl WA8 ....13 E3
Mitton Cl WA3 ....4 E5
Moat Ho 18 CW8 ......103 F8
Moat La Audley ST7 ...209 B3
  Hollins Green WA3 .....10 E2
Mobberley CE Prim Sch
  WA16 ....58 C5
Mobberley Cl WA4 .....17 D4
Mobberley Rd
  Ashley WA14,WA15,WA16 .31 E3
  Knutsford WA16 ....57 B6
  Wilmslow SK9 ....33 D1
Mobberley Sta WA16 ...57 F7
Modyn CH2 ....118 C4
Moelfre Dr SK8 ....35 C7
Moggie La SK10 ....36 F1
Mold Rd CH4 ....139 A3
Mollington Ct CH1 .....94 F2
Mollington Rd M22 .....33 E8
Molly Pitcher Way WA5 .15 B5
Molly Potts Cl WA16 ...82 B8
Molyneux Ave WA5 .....15 F8
Monarch Cl Crewe CW2 .189 F4
  Irlam M44 ....11 E6
Monarch Dr CW9 .....103 E5
Monck Dr CW5 ....204 D6
Mond Rd WA8 ....23 A8
Mond St CW8 ....78 B3
Monica Dr WA8 ....13 A5

Monk St CW1 ....190 A5
Monk's Heath Crossroads
  SK10 ....85 A1
Monk's La CW3 ....230 C5
Monks Coppenhall Prim Sch
  CW1 ....190 E7
Monks Gr CH65 ....70 B6
Monks Heath Hall Wrkshps
  SK10 ....85 B1
Monks La Acton CW5 ..203 F7
  Crewe CW1 ....189 F5
  Nantwich CW5 ....204 E5
Monks Orch CW5 .....204 F5
Monks St WA16 ....15 E6
Monks Way CW8 ......103 B4
Monkswood Cl WA5 .....7 E2
Monmouth Cl WA1 .....17 E2
Monroe Cl WA1 ....17 B8
Monsall Cl SK11 ......112 F7
Monsall Dr SK11 .....112 F7
Montana Cl WA5 ....15 C7
Montclare Cres WA4 ...16 F1
Montcliffe Cl WA3 ......9 C5
Montgomery Cl WA16 ..57 C4
Montgomery Rd WA8 ...22 D8
Montgomery Way CW7 .149 B7
Montmorency Rd WA16 .57 D3
Montpelier Ave WA7 ...48 F6
Montrose Cl
  Macclesfield SK10 .....87 A1
  Shavington CW2 .....206 B3
  Warrington WA2 ....8 F7
Montrose Ct Chester CH4 140 F7
  Holmes Chapel CW4 ...130 C3
Monument Rd ST7 ....210 D6
Monument View ST7 ..209 F2
Moody St CW12 ......156 D2
Moor Cl ST8 ....179 E1
Moor Cres CH4 ......139 D1
Moor Ho WA6 ....74 B8
Moor La Bramhall SK7 ..35 E3
  Elton WA6 ....72 E1
  Frodsham WA6 ....74 B8
  Heswall CH60 ....40 F8
  Higher Kinnerton CH4 ..161 D8
  Lower Kinnerton CH4 ..161 C6
  Sandycroft CH5 ......116 A2
  Waverton CH3 ....143 A5
  Widnes WA8 ....22 F7
  Widnes WA8 ....23 A7
  Wilmslow SK9 ....59 D5
Moor La S WA8 ....22 F7
Moor Lane Bsns Ctr WA8 22 F7
Moor St CW12 ....156 E2
Moor-Park Way CW9 ..103 F4
Moorcroft La WA16 ....80 F3
Moorcroft Ave CH3 ...119 B1
Moorcroft Cres CH3 ..119 C4
Moorcroft Mews CH4 .140 D6
Moordale Rd WA16 ....57 B2
Moorditch La
  Frodsham WA6 ....48 D1
  Frodsham WA6 ....49 A1
Moore Ave St Helens WA9 .1 B3
  Warrington WA4 ......17 D3
Moore Cl WA8 ....13 D2
Moore Dr WA11 ....1 F6
Moore Gr WA13 ....19 B5
Moore La WA4 ....25 C7
Moore Prim Sch WA4 ...25 A5
Moorfield Cres WA3 .....4 A7
Moorfield Dr Neston CH64 41 C1
  Wilmslow SK9 ....59 E5
Moorfield Prim Sch WA8 13 D3
Moorfield Rd WA8 .....13 D3
Moorfields CW5 ......205 E6
Moorhead La CW11 ...154 D3
Moorhill Rd SK11 ....112 C4
Moorhouse Ave ST7 ..193 E4
Moorhouse Cl CH2 ...118 D5
Mooring Cl WA7 ....50 D6
Moorings Cl CW12 ...156 E1
Moorings CH64 ....41 E6
Moorings The
  Christleton CH3 ......142 E7
  Disley SK12 ....38 E6
  Heswall CH60 ....40 C8
  Middlewich CW10 .....128 C1
Moorland Cl CH60 .....41 A7
Moorland Dr
  Cheadle Hulme SK8 ....34 F8
  Runcorn WA7 ....50 E7
Moorland Pk CH60 .....41 A7
Moorland Rd
  Biddulph ST8 ....179 D1
  Ellesmere Port CH66 ...69 D1
  Kidsgrove ST7 ....195 D7
Moorlands Ave CW8 ..102 A4
Moorlands Cl SK10 .....87 C3
Moorlands Dr CW5 ...206 A1
Moorlands Pk CW8 ...102 A4
Moors La CW7 ....149 B8
Moorsbrook Gr 9 SK9 ..34 E1
Moorsfield Ave CW3 ..229 F3
Moorside WA16 ....57 A2
Moorside Ave CH64 ....66 C8
Moorside Ct WA8 ......22 F7
Moorside La Neston CH64 66 D8
  Pott Shrigley SK10 ....63 E4
Moorson Ave ST7 ....194 F8
Moorview Gdns ST7 ..195 E6
Moorway CH60 ....41 B8
Moran Cl SK9 ....34 E2
Moran Cres SK11 .....112 B7
Moran Dr WA5 ....15 A6
Moran Rd SK11 ......112 B7
Morcott La L24 ....21 D2
Moresby Cl WA7 ....50 E7

Moreton Ave SK7 . . . . .35 E5
Moreton Cl CW11 . . . . . .175 C7
Moreton Dr Alsager ST7 . .193 C3
  Handforth SK9 . . . . .34 E3
  Holmes Chapel CW4 . . . .130 B3
  Poynton SK12 . . . . .36 F4
Moreton Pl ST7 . . . . .194 E6
Moreton Rd CW2 . . . . . . .189 F3
Moreton St WA1 . . . . .78 C1
Moreton Terr WA6 . . . . . . .74 A8
Moreville Cl CW9 . . . . . .103 E3
Morgan Ave WA2 . . . . .8 C2
Morgan Cl Blacon CH1 . . .117 F6
  Crewe CW2 . . . . .190 A4
Morgans Way WA3 . . . . . . .4 A8
Morland Ave
  Bebington CH62 . . . . .43 D6
  Neston CH64 . . . . .66 F7
Morley Cl CH2 . . . . .119 F8
Morley Dr CW12 . . . . . . .157 A1
Morley Green Rd SK9 . . . .33 C1
Morley Rd Runcorn WA7 . . .23 A1
  Warrington WA4 . . . . .16 A1
Morley St WA1 . . . . .16 D6
Mornant Ave CW8 . . . . . .103 A3
Mornington Ave CH65 . . . .70 C5
Mornington Cl CW11 . . . .174 D7
Morphany La WA4 . . . . . . .51 E6
Morris Ave WA4 . . . . .16 F4
Morris Cl WA11 . . . . .1 A5
Morris Dr CW8 . . . . .77 D1
Morris Pk CW8 . . . . .103 B4
Morrison Cl WA5 . . . . .15 C8
Mort Ave WA4 . . . . .17 A5
Mortimer Ave WA2 . . . . . .16 B8
Mortimer Dr CW11 . . . . .175 C5
Mortlake Cl WA8 . . . . .12 C1
Mortlake Cres CH3 . . . . .119 A1
Morton Ave WA6 . . . . .73 B1
Morton Cl WA5 . . . . .15 C8
Morton Dr SK11 . . . . . . .112 F3
Morton Gdns CH1 . . . . . .117 E4
Morton Rd Blacon CH1 . . .117 E4
  Runcorn WA7 . . . . .50 D8
Morval Cres WA7 . . . . .23 D1
Morven Cl WA2 . . . . .8 E3
Mosedale Gr WA7 . . . . . . .49 E5
Moseley Ave WA4 . . . . . . .17 A3
Moses Ct CH1 . . . . .237 C3
Moss Bank Bramhall SK7 . .35 C5
  Chester CH2 . . . . .118 C4
  Winsford CW7 . . . . .126 C1
Moss Bank Rd WA8 . . . . . .23 D7
Moss Bower Rd SK11 . . . .112 C4
Moss Brow SK10 . . . . .87 E7
Moss Brow La WA16 . . . . .28 D4
Moss Cl Warrington WA4 . . .16 E2
  Willaston CH64 . . . . .68 A8
Moss Croft CW1 . . . . . . .190 A4
Moss Dr Manley WA6 . . . . .98 F4
  Middlewich CW10 . . . . . .151 D6
Moss End La CW11 . . . . .176 E8
Moss Farm Barns CW8 . .102 D4
Moss Farm Recn Ctr
  CW8 . . . . .103 B8
Moss Fields Alsager ST7 . .193 A3
  Crewe CW1 . . . . .173 A1
Moss Gate WA3 . . . . .10 A5
Moss Gr Lymm WA13 . . . . .19 B4
  Newcastle-u-Lyme ST5 . . .210 D3
  Saltney CH4 . . . . .140 D6
Moss Green Way WA9 . . . . .1 A1
Moss Hall La CW6 . . . . . .147 C4
Moss Hey Prim Sch SK7 . .35 C5
Moss La Alderley Edge SK9 .60 B1
  Bollington SK10 . . . . .87 E8
  Bramhall SK7 . . . . .35 D5
  Brereton Green CW12 . . .154 F5
  Byley CW10 . . . . .129 B7
  Congleton CW12 . . . . . . .156 E6
  Crewe CW1 . . . . .173 A2
  Cuddington CW8 . . . . . . .102 A3
  Fowley Common WA3 . . . . .5 D5
  Golborne WA3 . . . . .3 A1
  Harthill CH3,SY14 . . . . . .183 F1
  High Legh WA16 . . . . .29 E6
  High Legh, Sink Moss WA16 28 D4
  Hollins Green WA3 . . . . . .10 E5
  Irlam M44 . . . . .11 D5
  Lawton-gate ST7 . . . . . .194 F4
  Lostock Green CW9 . . . . .105 D8
  Macclesfield SK11 . . . . .112 C4
  Manley WA6 . . . . .99 A4
  Mere WA16 . . . . .56 C5
  Mobberley WA16 . . . . . . .58 F4
  Moore WA4 . . . . .25 A6
  Mottram St Andrew SK10 . .61 A2
  Norbury SY13 . . . . .215 C5
  Norley WA6 . . . . .101 B5
  Northwich CW8 . . . . .103 D7
  Over Peover WA16 . . . . . .83 C3
  Partington M31 . . . . .11 F3
  Partington WA13 . . . . .11 F1
  Partington WA13 . . . . .20 B8
  Sandbach CW11 . . . . . . .174 C7
  Siddington SK11 . . . . . . .109 E2
  St Helens,Moss Nook WA9 . .1 A1
  Styal SK9 . . . . .33 E6
  Tarporley CW6 . . . . .146 B2
  Warmingham CW1 . . . . .173 C3
  Warrington WA3 . . . . .9 E1
Moss Lane Bsns Ctr
  CW11 . . . . .174 D6
Moss Lane Ind Est
  CW11 . . . . .174 D7
Moss Mere CW11 . . . . . .176 F7
Moss Pl ST7 . . . . .195 B3

Moss Rd Alderley Edge SK9 60 C2
  Congleton CW12 . . . . . . .178 F7
  Irlam M44 . . . . .11 C7
  Northwich CW8 . . . . .103 D8
  Warrington WA4 . . . . .17 A3
Moss Rose SK9 . . . . .60 B2
Moss Rose Football Gnd
  SK11 . . . . .112 D4
Moss Side La
  Antrobus CW9 . . . . .53 D7
  Hollinfare WA3 . . . . .11 A2
  Hollins Green WA3 . . . . . .10 F3
  Moore WA4 . . . . .24 F7
Moss Side Rd M44 . . . . . . .11 E6
Moss Sq Crewe CW1 . . . .190 D4
  Macclesfield SK11 . . . . .112 D4
Moss St Weaverham CW8 . .77 D1
  Widnes WA8 . . . . .23 D7
Moss Terr Warren SK11 . . .112 A5
  Wilmslow SK9 . . . . .60 F8
  Winnington CW8 . . . . . . .78 D1
Moss The CW9 . . . . .78 D7
Moss View Rd SK11 . . . . .112 A4
Moss Way ST7 . . . . .193 A3
Mossdale Cl Crewe CW2 . .189 E4
  Warrington WA5 . . . . .15 A7
Mossfield Cres 4 ST7 . . .195 B2
Mossford Ave CW1 . . . . .190 B7
Mosshall La WA4 . . . . .26 F1
Mosslands Cl CH66 . . . . . .69 E2
Mossley Ave CH62 . . . . . . .43 D8
Mossley CE Prim Sch
  CW12 . . . . .179 B8
Mossley Ct CW12 . . . . . .178 F8
Mossley Garth Cl 4
  CW12 . . . . .157 A1
Mossvale CH66 . . . . .69 D8
Mossways Pk SK9 . . . . . . .59 C7
Mosswood Rd SK9 . . . . . . .34 E1
Moston Ct 5 CW2 . . . . . .156 F3
Moston Gr WA13 . . . . .18 D3
Moston Rd Chester CH2 . .118 D8
  Sandbach CW11 . . . . . . .174 D6
Moston Way CH66 . . . . . . .69 F3
Mostyn Ave CH60 . . . . . . .40 C8
Mostyn Gdns CH64 . . . . . .41 B1
Mostyn House Sch CH64 . .66 C8
Mostyn Pl CH1 . . . . .117 E6
Mostyn Sq CH64 . . . . .41 B1
Mote Hill Ct WA1 . . . . .16 D6
Motherwell Cl WA8 . . . . . .12 E3
Mottershead Cl 1 WA8 . . .23 A8
Mottershead Rd WA8 . . . . .23 A8
Mottram Cl
  Middlewich CW10 . . . . . .151 B7
  Warrington WA3 . . . . .17 B3
Mottram Dr CW5 . . . . . . .205 A4
Mottram Rd SK9 . . . . .60 D1
Mottram St Andrew Prim Sch
  SK10 . . . . .61 B1
Mottram Way SK10 . . . . . .87 E2
Moughland La WA7 . . . . . .49 A8
Moulders La WA1 . . . . .16 B4
Mouldsworth Cl 2 CW9 103 D4
Mouldsworth Motor Mus★
  CH3 . . . . .98 E1
Mouldsworth Sta CH3 . . . .99 A2
Moulton Cl
  Knutsford WA16 . . . . .57 C1
  Northwich CW9 . . . . .103 E4
  Runcorn WA7 . . . . .49 F4
Moulton Sch CW9 . . . . . .126 F8
Mount Ave CH60 . . . . .40 F8
Mount Barns CH2 . . . . . . .95 C6
Mount Cl CW5 . . . . .204 F6
Mount Ct 3 CH60 . . . . . . .40 F8
Mount Dr CW5 . . . . .204 F6
Mount Farm Way CH66 . . .69 C2
Mount Mews CH60 . . . . . .40 F8
Mount Pl CH2 . . . . .118 F2
Mount Pleasant
  Audlem CW3 . . . . .230 B4
  Congleton CW12 . . . . . . .156 E2
  Crewe CW1 . . . . .190 B6
  Elton CH2 . . . . .72 A4
  Haslington CW1 . . . . . . .191 D4
  Kidsgrove ST7 . . . . .195 A1
  Macclesfield SK10 . . . . . .87 B1
  Rainow SK10 . . . . .88 D3
  Widnes WA8 . . . . .13 B2
  Wilmslow SK9 . . . . .60 B8
Mount Pleasant Ave WA9 . .1 B3
Mount Pleasant Dr
  CW7 . . . . .149 A7
Mount Pleasant Rd
  Davenham CW9 . . . . . . .103 F2
  The Bank ST7 . . . . .195 B7
Mount Pleasant Residential
  Pk CW4 . . . . .130 D8
Mount Pleasent CH4 . . . .140 F7
Mount Rd Kidsgrove ST7 . .195 B2
  Runcorn WA7 . . . . .49 F8
Mount St WA8 . . . . .13 B1
Mount Terr SK11 . . . . . . .112 F7
Mount The
  Altrincham,Hale WA15 . . . .32 C8
  Chester CH3 . . . . .118 F1
  Congleton CW12 . . . . . . .156 A2
  Great Budworth CW9 . . . . .79 A7
  Heswall CH60 . . . . .40 F8
  Kidsgrove ST7 . . . . .195 A1
  Scholar Green ST7 . . . . .194 E7
Mount Way CH3 . . . . .143 A4
Mountain View
  Helsby WA6 . . . . .73 B3
  Saltney CH4 . . . . .140 E6
Mountbatten Ct CW2 . . . .190 A3

Mountbatten Way
  CW12 . . . . .156 E3
Mountfield Rd SK7 . . . . . . .35 E5
Mourne Cl CH66 . . . . .69 A6
Mow Cop Rd ST7 . . . . . . .195 D6
Mow La
  Mount Pleasant ST7 . . . .195 A5
  Mow Cop ST7 . . . . .179 A5
Mowcroft La WA5 . . . . .14 B3
Mowpen Brow WA16 . . . . .29 B6
Moxon Ave WA4 . . . . .16 F5
Moyles Cl WA8 . . . . .12 D2
Mudhouse La CH64 . . . . . .67 F2
Mudhurst La SK12 . . . . . . .38 E3
Muir Rd CH1 . . . . .117 E3
Muirfield Cl
  Northwich CW9 . . . . .104 A5
  Warrington WA2 . . . . .9 A3
  Wilmslow SK9 . . . . .60 D8
Muirfield Dr
  Macclesfield SK10 . . . . . .87 D4
  Winsford CW7 . . . . .126 C2
Muirfield Mews CW7 . . . .126 C2
Mulberry Ave WA3 . . . . . . .3 F7
Mulberry Cl Elton CH2 . . . .72 C3
  Heald Green SK8 . . . . . . .34 C7
  Warrington WA1 . . . . .17 E7
Mulberry Ct
  Macclesfield SK11 . . . . .112 D4
  Warrington WA4 . . . . .16 D1
Mulberry Dr SK10 . . . . . . .87 E1
Mulberry Gdns CW11 . . . .174 D7
Mulberry Rd CW2 . . . . . .189 E2
Mulberry Rise CW8 . . . . .103 C7
Mulcaster Ct CW1 . . . . . .191 D5
Mull Cl CH65 . . . . .70 C1
Mullein Cl WA3 . . . . .3 D8
Mullen Cl WA5 . . . . .7 F1
Mullins Ave WA12 . . . . .2 C5
Mullion Cl WA7 . . . . .50 B6
Mullion Gr WA2 . . . . .9 A1
Mulsford Ct LL13 . . . . . . .222 A8
Mulsford La LL13,SY14 . . .222 B8
Murdishaw Ave WA7 . . . . .50 F5
Murdishaw West Com Prim
  Sch WA7 . . . . .50 D6
Muriel Cl WA5 . . . . .14 D6
Murray Cl SK10 . . . . .87 A1
Murrayfield WA3 . . . . .87 A5
Murrayfield Dr CW5 . . . . .205 D5
Museum St WA1 . . . . .16 A4
Music Hall Pass CH1 . . . .237 B2
Mustard La WA3 . . . . .4 B1
Myddleton La WA2 . . . . . . .8 C6
Myrica Gr CH2 . . . . .119 B3
Myrtle Ave Haydock WA11 . .1 A7
  Higher Kinnerton CH4 . . .161 A7
  Newton-le-W WA12 . . . . . .2 C2
Myrtle Gr Warrington WA4 . 16 D3
  Widnes WA8 . . . . .22 D8
Myrtle Rd M31 . . . . .11 D3
Myrtle St Crewe CW2 . . . .190 C3
Mythorne Ave M44 . . . . . .11 C3
Mytton Dr CW5 . . . . .204 D6

N

Nab Cl SK10 . . . . .63 C1
Nab La SK10 . . . . .63 C1
Nabbs Cl ST7 . . . . .195 B2
Nabbswood Rd ST7 . . . . .195 B2
Nairn Ave CW4 . . . . .130 B2
Nairn Cl Bebington CH63 . .43 D4
  Warrington WA2 . . . . .9 B3
Nancy View SK10 . . . . .88 B8
Nansen Cl WA5 . . . . .15 C7
Nansmoss La SK9 . . . . . . .33 D1
Nant Peris CH1 . . . . .117 D3
Nantwich Mus★ CW5 . . . .204 E5
Nantwich Rd Audley ST7 . .209 B1
  Barbridge CW5 . . . . .187 B8
  Betley ST7 . . . . .208 E1
  Broxton CH3 . . . . .183 C1
  Crewe CW2 . . . . .190 C2
  Ellesmere Port CH66 . . . . .69 F3
  Middlewich CW10 . . . . . .151 A4
  Sound CW5 . . . . .217 B5
  Tarporley CW6 . . . . .168 D7
  Wimboldsley CW10 . . . . .150 F5
  Wistaston CW2,CW5 . . . .189 C2
  Woore CW3 . . . . .232 B1
  Wrenbury CW5 . . . . .201 E2
Nantwich Sta CW5 . . . . . .204 E4
Nantwich Way 6 SK9 . . . . .34 E5
Naomi Cl CH1 . . . . .117 D5
Napier Gdns 3 ST7 . . . . .195 A2
Napier Rd CW2 . . . . .118 C8
Napier St WA1 . . . . .16 C5
Napley Dr TF9 . . . . .236 D1
Napley Rd TF9 . . . . .236 D1
Nares Cl WA5 . . . . .7 C1
Narrow La
  Crewe Green CW1 . . . . . .191 C3
  Wardsend SK10 . . . . .37 A1
Naseby Rd CW12 . . . . . . .156 A3
Nat La CW7 . . . . .126 F2
Nat Lane Ret Pk CW7 . . . .126 F2
Nathan Dr WA11 . . . . .1 E6
Nathans Mdw CW12 . . . . .179 C7
Naughton La WA8 . . . . . . .12 D3
Naughton Rd 3 WA8 . . . . .23 A8
Navan Ct CW1 . . . . .190 B5
Navigation Cl WA7 . . . . . . .50 D6
Navigation Ho 17 CW9 . . .103 F8
Navigation Rd CW8 . . . . .103 F7
Navigation St WA1 . . . . . . .16 D5

Naylor Ave WA3 . . . . .3 B8
Naylor Cres
  Ellesmere Port CH66 . . . . .69 F7
  Nantwich CW5 . . . . .205 A4
Naylor Ct
  Ellesmere Port CH66 . . . . .69 E6
  12 Northwich CW9 . . . . .103 F8
Naylor Rd WA8 . . . . .13 D1
Naylor St WA1 . . . . .16 B5
Neal Ave SK8 . . . . .34 A8
Neath Cl SK12 . . . . .36 D5
Needham Cl M44 . . . . .11 E6
Needham Dr
  Cranage CW4 . . . . .130 A5
  Hartford CW8 . . . . .103 A4
Needhams Bank CW11 . . .174 C6
Needhams Wharf Cl
  SK10 . . . . .88 A1
Neil St WA8 . . . . .13 C2
Neills Rd WA5 . . . . .6 B6
Nelson Ave SK12 . . . . .37 A3
Nelson Bldgs ST7 . . . . . .195 A1
Nelson Cl SK12 . . . . .37 A3
Nelson Dr M44 . . . . .11 E6
Nelson Gr ST7 . . . . .193 F2
Nelson Ind Est ST7 . . . . .194 C1
Nelson Rd
  Ellesmere Port CH65 . . . . .70 C7
  Warrington,Birchwood WA3 . .9 D4
Nelson St Chester CH1 . . .237 C3
  Congleton CW12 . . . . . . .156 D2
  Crewe CW2 . . . . .190 C2
  Macclesfield SK11 . . . . .112 D7
  Newton-le-W WA12 . . . . . .2 A3
  6 Runcorn WA7 . . . . .23 A2
  Widnes WA8 . . . . .23 A6
Nemos Cl WA6 . . . . .73 C2
Neptune Cl WA7 . . . . .50 D7
Nesfield Ct CW11 . . . . . .191 F7
Nesfield Dr CW11 . . . . . .191 F7
Ness Acre La CH64 . . . . . .67 E8
Ness Botanic Gdns★
  CH64 . . . . .67 A3
Ness Ho CH64 . . . . .66 D8
Nessina Gr CW2 . . . . . . .205 E8
Neston Dr CH2 . . . . .118 E5
Neston Gn CH66 . . . . .69 D4
Neston High Sch CH64 . . .41 F1
Neston Prim Sch CH64 . . .66 E7
Neston Rd
  Heswall CH63,CH64 . . . . .41 F5
  Neston CH64 . . . . .67 B3
  Willaston CH64 . . . . .67 F8
Neston Road Cotts CH63 . 42 A6
Neston Sta CH64 . . . . .66 E8
Neston Way SK9 . . . . .34 D3
Nether Alderley Mill★
  SK10 . . . . .85 A5
Nether Alderley Prim Sch
  SK10 . . . . .85 A6
Nether Fold SK10 . . . . . . .87 A8
Nether Lea CW4 . . . . .130 C4
Netherfield WA8 . . . . .22 E8
Netherfields SK9 . . . . .85 A8
Netherley Rd WA8 . . . . . . .12 A2
Netherpool Rd CH66 . . . . .69 F8
Netherton Dr WA6 . . . . . . .74 A7
Netherton Farm Cotts
  WA6 . . . . .74 A7
Neumann St CW9 . . . . . .104 B8
Nevada Cl WA5 . . . . .15 C4
Neville Ave St Helens WA9 . .1 B1
  Warrington WA2 . . . . .8 D1
Neville Cres WA5 . . . . .15 A3
Neville Dr CH3 . . . . .119 B1
Neville Rd Bebington CH62 43 E8
  Chester CH3 . . . . .119 B1
Neville St Crewe CW2 . . . .190 B1
  Newton-le-W WA12 . . . . . .2 A3
Nevin Cl SK7 . . . . .36 A7
Nevin Rd CH1 . . . . .117 D3
Nevis Dr CW2 . . . . .189 D3
New Albert Terr WA7 . . . . .23 B3
New Bank Pl WA8 . . . . . . .12 B1
New Bank Rd WA8 . . . . . . .12 B1
New Barnet WA8 . . . . .12 E2
New Bridge Rd CH65,CH2 70 F3
New Chester Rd
  Bebington,Eastham CH62 . .43 E7
  Hooton CH62,CH66 . . . . .44 A2
New Cotts
  Hampton Heath SY14 . . . .213 A7
  Manley WA6 . . . . .99 C7
New Crane Bank CH1 . . . .118 B1
New Crane St CH1 . . . . . .118 B1
New Cut Ind Est WA1 . . . . .17 C7
New Cut La WA1 . . . . .17 B7
New Farm Cotts M44 . . . . .11 A7
New Farm Ct
  Great Barrow CH3 . . . . . .120 E5
  Malpas SY14 . . . . .213 A5
New Grosvenor Rd CH65 . .70 B2
New Hall Ave SK8 . . . . . . .34 B7
New Hall La Culcheth WA3 . .5 A4
  Culcheth,Wigshaw WA3 . . . .4 E1
New Hall St SK10 . . . . .87 D1
New Hampshire Cl WA5 . . .15 B7
New Hey La CH64 . . . . . . .68 A6
New Heyes CH64 . . . . .41 E1
New Home Farm Cotts
  CH64 . . . . .93 A7
New Horwich Rd SK23 . . . .65 E7
New Hos CW5 . . . . .187 D6
New Houses 143 B7
New Inn Cotts WA16 . . . . .108 C8
New Inn La WA11 . . . . . . .176 A2
New King St Audley ST7 . .209 C1
  Middlewich CW10 . . . . . .128 C2

New La
  Appleton Thorn WA4 . . . . .27 B5
  Churton CH3 . . . . .180 F6
  Croft WA3 . . . . .9 B7
  Harthill CH3 . . . . .183 F3
  Winsford CW7 . . . . .149 F4
New Lane End WA3 . . . . . . .4 A2
New Manchester Rd
  WA1 . . . . .17 A7
New Manor Rd WA4 . . . . . .51 B6
New Market Wlk 11 WA1 . 16 B5
New Mills Central Sta
  SK22 . . . . .39 B7
New Mills Newtown Sta
  SK22 . . . . .39 B6
New Mills Prim Sch SK22 39 B8
New Mills Sch & Sixth Form
  Ctr SK22 . . . . .39 C8
New Moss Rd M44 . . . . . . .11 D6
New Pale Rd WA6 . . . . . . .99 C6
New Park Ct SK22 . . . . . . .39 D7
New Platt La CW4 . . . . . . .107 B1
New Rd Anderton CW9 . . . .78 D4
  Antrobus CW9 . . . . .27 D1
  Astbury CW12 . . . . .178 B4
  Audley ST7 . . . . .209 E3
  Duddon CW6 . . . . .145 B6
  Ellesmere Port CH66 . . . . .69 A8
  Lymm WA13 . . . . .18 E3
  Marton CW12 . . . . .132 D1
  Mere WA16 . . . . .30 E3
  Mossend CW11 . . . . .154 F2
  Prestbury SK10 . . . . .87 A7
  Warrington WA4 . . . . .16 C4
  Whaley Bridge SK23 . . . . .65 E6
  Whaley Bridge,Bridgemont
   SK23 . . . . .39 F1
  Winsford CW7 . . . . .126 E2
New Russia Hall Craft Ctr★
  CH3 . . . . .165 C5
New School La CH66 . . . . .44 B1
New St Congleton CW12 . .156 E2
  Haslington CW1 . . . . . . .191 C5
  Neston CH64 . . . . .66 E5
  New Mills SK22 . . . . .39 D7
  10 Runcorn WA7 . . . . . . .23 A2
  Sandbach CW11 . . . . . . .174 D7
  Widnes WA8 . . . . .23 B8
  Wilmslow SK9 . . . . .59 E5
New Street Cotts CW12 . .157 A6
New Warrington Rd CW9 79 C2
New York Cotts WA16 . . . . .29 F2
Newall Ave CW11 . . . . . . .175 A5
Newall Cl CH3 . . . . .166 B1
Newall Cres CW7 . . . . . . .127 A1
Newbiggin Way 10
  SK10 . . . . .112 C8
Newbold Ct 9 CW12 . . . .156 F3
Newbold Way CW5 . . . . . .204 E3
Newborough Cl WA5 . . . . . .7 E2
Newbridge Cl
  Runcorn WA7 . . . . .50 C6
  Warrington WA5 . . . . .7 D2
Newbridge Rd CH65 . . . . . .70 F4
Newburgh Cl WA7 . . . . . . .24 D1
Newbury Ave
  Crewe CW1 . . . . .190 C7
  5 Winsford CW7 . . . . . . .149 A8
Newbury Cl
  Cheadle Hulme SK8 . . . . .35 A6
  Widnes WA8 . . . . .13 A3
Newbury Ct SK9 . . . . .60 A6
Newbury Rd Chester CH4 .140 F6
  Heald Green SK8 . . . . . . .34 C7
Newby Ct CW12 . . . . .156 A1
Newcastle Rd
  Astbury CW12 . . . . .178 A4
  Brereton Green CW11 . . .153 F4
  Congleton CW12 . . . . . . .156 A2
  Hassall Green CW11 . . . .176 A3
  Nantwich CW5 . . . . .205 B4
  Shavington CW2,CW5 . . .206 C3
  Smallwood CW11 . . . . . .176 D6
  Talke ST7 . . . . .210 E7
  Willaston CW5 . . . . .205 E4
  Woore CW3 . . . . .232 E1
Newcastle Rd N CW11 . . .153 E5
Newcastle Rd S CW11 . . .153 F5
Newcastle Road Cvn Pk
  CW11 . . . . .175 E5
Newcastle St WA1 . . . . . . .190 A5
Newchapel Obsy★ ST7 . . .195 C3
Newchapel Rd ST7 . . . . . .195 C3
Newchurch Com Prim Sch
  WA3 . . . . .4 F2
Newchurch La WA3 . . . . . . .4 F2
Newcombe Ave WA2 . . . . .16 E8
Newcroft CH1 . . . . .94 B2
Newdigate St
  Crewe CW1 . . . . .190 C4
  Crewe CW1 . . . . .190 C5
Newfield Ct WA13 . . . . . . .19 A5
Newfield Dr CW1 . . . . . . .190 E5
Newfield Rd WA13 . . . . . . .18 D3
Newfield St CW11 . . . . . .175 B7
Newfield Terr WA6 . . . . . . .73 B2
Newgate 1 SK11 . . . . . . .112 D7
Newgate Rd SK9 . . . . .59 D7
Newgate St CH1 . . . . .237 B2
Newgate Wlk CH1 . . . . . .237 B2
Newhall Ct CH2 . . . . .118 E6
Newhall Rd CH2 . . . . .118 F6
Newham Cl SK11 . . . . . . .112 F3
Newhaven Rd WA2 . . . . . . .8 B4

Newland Cl WA8 ......12 C3
Newland Mews WA3 ......4 E5
Newland Way CW5 ...205 B4
Newlands Ave
  Bramhall SK7 ......35 F8
  Cheadle Hulme SK8 ......35 A7
Newlands Cl
  Cheadle Hulme SK8 ......35 A7
  Frodsham WA6 ......74 C6
Newlands Dr Golborne WA3 3 D8
  Wilmslow SK9 ......59 E5
Newlands Rd
  Macclesfield SK10 ......111 E7
  Warrington WA4 ......16 F2
Newlyn Ave
  Congleton CW12 ......178 F8
  Macclesfield SK10 ......86 D1
Newlyn Cl WA7 ......50 B6
Newlyn Gdns WA5 ......14 D3
Newman Cl CW12 ......156 B3
Newman St WA4 ......16 F3
Newman's La CW5 ......219 D8
Newmarket Cl **1** SK10 ...87 C4
Newmoore La WA7 ......24 F4
Newnham Dr CH65 ......70 C4
Newport Gr ST5 ......210 E2
Newquay Cl WA7 ......50 B6
Newquay Ct CW12 ......178 E8
Newquay Dr Bramhall SK7 ...35 F7
  Macclesfield SK10 ......111 D8
Newry Ct CH2 ......118 D4
Newry Pk CH2 ......118 D4
Newry Pk E CH2 ......118 D4
Newsham Cl WA4 ......12 B4
Newsholme Cl WA3 ......4 F3
Newspaper Ho WA5 ......14 D3
Newstead Cl SK12 ......36 D5
Newstead Rd WA8 ......21 F6
Newtech Sq CH5 ......92 F2
Newton Ave WA3 ......9 E5
Newton Bank
  Middlewich CW10 ......128 B1
  Preston on t H WA4 ......51 B8
Newton Bank Sch WA12 ...2 E4
Newton Comm Hospl
  WA12 ......2 B2
Newton Cotts CH3 ......166 C4
Newton Gr WA2 ......8 F3
Newton Hall CH2 ......118 F5
Newton Hall Ct CH2 ......118 F5
Newton Hall Dr CH2 ......118 F5
Newton Hall La WA16 ...58 E5
Newton Hall Mews **1**
   ......151 C8
Newton Heath CW10 ...128 B1
Newton Ho CH2 ......118 F5
Newton Hollow WA6 ......74 D1
Newton La Chester CH2 ...118 F4
  Daresbury WA4 ......51 C8
  Daresbury WA4 ......51 E7
  Golborne WA12 ......2 E6
  Tattenhall CH3 ......166 D4
Newton Park Dr WA12 ...2 F3
Newton Park View CH2 ...118 D4
Newton Pl CW12 ......156 F2
Newton Prim Sch CH2 ...118 E4
Newton Rd
  Ellesmere Port CH65 ...70 C5
  Golborne,Lowton Common
    WA3,WN7 ......4 A8
  Golborne,Town of Lowton
    WA12,WA3 ......3 D5
  Handforth SK9 ......34 A1
  St Helens WA9 ......1 A3
  Winwick WA2 ......8 A5
Newton St Crewe CW1 ...190 D5
  Macclesfield SK11 ......112 C4
Newton-le-Willows Com
  High Sch WA12 ......2 E3
Newton-le-Willows Prim Sch
  WA12 ......2 D3
Newton-le-Willows Sta
  WA12 ......2 E3
Newtons Cres CW11 ...191 F7
Newtons Gr CW11 ...191 E7
Newtons La CW11 ...191 E7
Newtown Kidsgrove ST7 ...195 F2
  Neston CH64 ......66 F7
Newtown Cl CH1 ......237 B3
Newtown Prim Sch SK22 39 B6
Nicholas Ave CW9 ......104 C6
Nicholas Ct CH1 ......237 A2
Nicholas Dr
  Weaverham CW8 ......77 D1
  Widnes WA8 ......22 C8
Nicholas St CH1 ......237 A2
Nicholas St Mews CH1 ...237 A2
Nicholls St WA4 ......17 B2
Nicholson Ave SK10 ......87 E1
Nicholson Cl SK10 ......87 E1
Nicholson Dr WA1 ......15 F5
Nickleby Rd SK12 ......36 E3
Nickleford Hall Dr WA8 ...12 F6
Nickolson Cl CH2 ......119 F8
Nicol Ave WA1 ......17 F8
Nidderdale Cl CW12 ......157 A5
Niddries Ct CW9 ......126 F7
Niddries La CW9 ......126 F7
Nield Ct CW9 ......118 D7
Nigel Gresley Cl CW1 ...191 A4
Nigel Rd CH60 ......41 C8
Nigel Wlk WA7 ......24 A2
Nightingale Cl
  Farndon CH3 ......180 F1
  Handforth SK9 ......34 B1

Nightingale Cl *continued*
  Middlewich CW10 ......151 D6
  Runcorn WA7 ......49 F5
  Warrington WA3 ......9 F4
Nightingale Ct **4** CW7 ...149 D6
Nightingale Way ST7 ...193 B3
Nile St CW2 ......190 C2
Nine Hos The CH3 ......166 B1
Nixon Dr CW7 ......126 B2
Nixon Rd CW8 ......101 F3
Nixon St Crewe CW1 ...189 F5
  Macclesfield SK11 ......112 B8
Nixon's Row CW5 ......204 C5
No 1 Road N CW2 ......192 F1
No 1 Road S CW2 ......192 F1
No 156 CH1 ......237 C2
No 2 Road N CW2 ......192 F1
No 2 Road S CW2 ......192 F1
Noahs Ark La WA16 ......58 F1
Noble Cl WA3 ......9 E3
Nook La Antrobus CW9 ...53 E6
  Golborne WA3 ......3 B8
  Warrington WA4 ......17 A3
  Warrington, Fearnhead WA3 .9 E2
Nook The Backford CH1 ...95 B4
  Bramhall SK7 ......35 D5
  Chester CH2 ......118 C4
  Guilden Sutton CH3 ......119 C4
  Saltney CH4 ......140 E6
Noon Ct WA12 ......2 B1
Noonsun Farm WA16 ......58 E1
Nora St WA1 ......16 C5
Norbreck Ave CW2 ......190 B2
Norbreck Cl WA5 ......15 A4
Norbury Ave WA2 ......16 D8
Norbury Cl Hough CW2 ...206 E3
  Knutsford WA16 ......57 C3
  Widnes WA8 ......13 E1
Norbury Dr
  Congleton CW12 ......156 E4
  Middlewich CW10 ......151 B8
Norbury Hollow Rd SK7 ...37 B8
Norbury St
  Macclesfield SK11 ......112 C7
  Northwich CW9 ......104 B8
Norbury Town La SY13 ...215 C3
Norbury Way **9** SK9 ......34 D5
Norcott Ave WA4 ......16 D2
Norcott Dr WA5 ......6 F6
Norden Cl WA3 ......9 C5
Norfolk Cl M44 ......11 C5
Norfolk Dr WA5 ......14 E6
Norfolk Gr ST8 ......179 C1
Norfolk Ho ST7 ......210 D6
Norfolk House Prep Sch
  CW11 ......175 B7
Norfolk Pl WA8 ......22 C8
Norfolk Rd Chester CH2 ...118 F4
  Congleton CW12 ......156 E4
  Ellesmere Port CH65 ...70 C5
  Kidsgrove ST7 ......194 F2
Norfolk St WA7 ......23 B3
Norfolk Wlk SK10 ......86 F2
Norgrove Cl WA7 ......50 E8
Norland St WA8 ......13 D1
Norland's La L35,WA8 ...12 F7
Norlands Pk WA8 ......12 F6
Norleane Cres WA7 ......49 B8
Norley Ave
  Bebington CH62 ......43 E3
  Ellesmere Port CH65 ...69 F6
Norley CE Prim Sch
  WA6 ......100 F5
Norley Cl WA5 ......15 C6
Norley Dr CH3 ......119 C1
Norley La CW8 ......101 A8
Norley Pl CW9 ......103 E5
Norley Rd
  Cuddington CW8,WA6 ...101 E4
  Kingsley WA6 ......75 A1
  Norley WA6 ......100 D7
Norman Ave Haydock WA11 2 A7
  Newton-le-W WA12 ......2 E3
Norman Cl CH66 ......94 F8
Norman Dr CW7 ......149 C6
Norman Ho **3** CW8 ......103 C5
Norman Rd WA2 ......23 A1
Norman St WA2 ......16 B6
Norman Way WA1 ......117 E5
Norman's La WA4 ......52 F4
Normanby Cl WA5 ......15 E7
Normandy Ave **2** CW7 ...149 D8
Normandy Rd M31 ......95 C1
Normans Cotts **1** CH64 ...66 F7
Norreys Ave WA5 ......15 F8
Norris Rd CH1 ......117 E5
Norris St WA2 ......16 D8
North Ave WA2 ......16 B8
North Brook Rd CW6 ...146 B7
North Cheshire Hospl
  WA4 ......26 D2
North Crofts CW5 ......204 E5
North Downs WA16 ......57 D2
North Dr Heswall CH60 ...41 A7
  High Legh WA16 ......29 C4
  Northwich CW9 ......104 C4
North Florida Rd WA11 ...1 D8
North Gn CH5 ......116 A6
North Par CH64 ......41 B2
North Park Brook Rd WA5 7 E1
North Rd Altrincham WA15 32 A8
  Bebington CH65 ......44 E3
  Connah's Quay CH5 ......91 F2
  Ellesmere Port CH65 ...70 B8
  Halewood L26 ......21 A5
North St Chester CH3 ...119 A1
  Congleton CW12 ......156 D3
  Crewe CW1 ......190 C7

North St *continued*
  Haydock WA11 ......1 E6
  Mount Pleasant ST7 ...195 B6
  Newton-le-W WA12 ......1 F4
  Saltney CH4 ......140 B7
  Sandycroft CH5 ......116 A3
North Stafford St CW1 190 D4
North View Crewe CW1 ...190 A6
  Ellesmere Port CH66 ...69 C7
  Middlewich CW10 ......128 B2
  Warrington WA5 ......14 E7
North Way
  Holmes Chapel CW4 ...130 C3
  Shavington CW2 ......206 D5
Northbank Ind Pk M44 ...11 F6
Northbank Wlk CW2 ......206 C8
Northbury Rd CH66 ......69 E1
Northcote Rd SK7 ......35 F7
Northdale Rd WA1 ......17 A8
Northern La WA8 ......12 A3
Northern Pathway CH4 237 C1
Northern Rise CH66 ......69 C4
Northfield Dr
  Biddulph ST8 ......179 E2
  Wilmslow SK9 ......60 D8
Northfield Pl CW2 ......206 C5
Northfields WA16 ......57 C3
Northgate CW6 ......146 B7
Northgate Ave
  Chester CH2 ......237 B4
  Macclesfield SK10 ......87 C1
Northgate Row CH1 ......237 B2
Northgate St CH1 ......237 A3
Northlands CW3 ......232 C1
Northmead WA16 ......57 C3
Northolt CW2 ......8 E1
Northumberland Rd M31 11 E2
Northward Rd SK9 ......59 F6
Northway Chester CH4 ...141 A7
  Lymm WA13 ......18 D4
  Runcorn WA7 ......49 F8
  Warrington WA2 ......8 E1
  Widnes WA8 ......12 D1
  Winnington WA8 ......78 D1
Northwich Rd
  Allostock CW4,WA16 ...106 E1
  Antrobus WA4 ......53 B2
  Dutton WA4 ......51 B2
  Great Budworth CW9 ...78 F8
  Knutsford WA16 ......56 D1
  Runcorn, Brookvale WA7 ...50 C5
  Weaverham CW8 ......102 E7
Northwich Ret Pk CW9 ...79 C1
Northwich Sta CW9 ...104 B8
Northwood Ave
  Middlewich CW10 ......151 E5
  Newton-le-W WA12 ......2 F3
Northwood La WA16 ......28 F1
Northwood Rd WA7 ......23 E2
Norton Ave Saltney CH4 ...140 D6
  Warrington WA5 ......14 E5
Norton Cotts WA7 ......50 E7
Norton Gate WA7 ......50 C8
Norton Hill WA7 ......24 C2
Norton La Runcorn WA7 ...50 B8
  Runcorn, Norton WA7 ...24 D1
  Runcorn, Town Park WA7 ...50 A8
Norton Priory Mus ★
  WA7 ......24 D1
Norton Priory Walled Gdn ★
  WA7 ......24 D1
Norton Rd CH3 ......119 C2
Norton St SK10 ......112 C8
Norton Station Rd WA7 ...50 D8
Norton View WA7 ......50 A8
Norton Village WA7 ......24 D1
Norton Way CW11 ......174 D7
Norton's La CH3 ......98 B2
Norton-in-Hales CE Prim Sch
  TF9 ......236 C2
Nortons La CW6 ......122 F7
Nortonwood La WA7 ......24 C1
Norville CH66 ......69 D7
Norwich Ave WA3 ......3 D8
Norwich Dr CH66 ......94 B8
Norwood Ave
  Bramhall SK7 ......35 D5
  Golborne WA3 ......3 F7
  High Lane SK6 ......37 D7
Norwood Dr CH4 ......141 B6
Nottingham Cl WA1 ......17 C6
Nun House Cl CW7 ......127 B2
Nun House Dr CW7 ......127 B2
Nuns Rd CH1 ......237 A1
Nunsmere Cl CW7 ......127 B1
Nursery Ave WA15 ......31 E8
Nursery Cl Crewe CW2 ...190 A2
  Kidsgrove ST7 ......194 D1
  Shavington CW2 ......206 C3
  Widnes WA8 ......13 D3
Nursery Dr Biddulph ST8 179 C2
  Poynton SK12 ......36 D4
Nursery Gr M31 ......11 F4
Nursery La
  Congleton CW12 ......156 E2
  Nether Alderley SK10 ...84 D5
  Siddington SK11 ......110 A3
  Wilmslow SK9 ......59 F5
Nursery Pk WA6 ......100 B7
Nursery Rd Barnton CW8 ...78 B3
  Bollington SK10 ......87 E7
Nursery The 103 C6
Nutfield Ave CW1 ......190 B7
Nuthurst Gdns **4** CW5 ...204 F5
Nuttall Ave WA3 ......9 C4
Nuttall St M44 ......11 E6

O

O'Connell Cl WA11 ......1 C6
O'leary St WA2 ......16 C7
Oak Ave Alsager ST7 ...193 E2
  Disley SK12 ......39 A6
  Golborne WA3 ......3 B8
  Haydock WA11 ......1 E7
  Irlam M44 ......11 D5
  Macclesfield SK11 ......112 A5
  Newton-le-W WA12 ......2 D3
  Wilmslow SK9 ......59 F5
  Winsford CW7 ......149 D7
Oak Bank Alderley Edge SK9 ...60 A2
Oak Bank Cl CW5 ......205 E4
Oak Bank Dr SK10 ......63 B1
Oak Bank La CH2 ......119 C6
Oak Brow Cotts SK9 ......33 C4
Oak Cl SK9 ......59 F6
Oak Cotts Styal SK9 ......33 E4
  Wrenbury CW5 ......216 F4
Oak Dr Cheadle Hulme SK7 35 C7
  Higher Kinnerton CH4 ...161 A7
  Middlewich CW10 ......151 D7
  Runcorn WA7 ......49 C7
  Scholar Green ST7 ......194 E6
Oak Farm CW6 ......186 C5
Oak Gr
  Ellesmere Port CH65 ...70 A3
  Nantwich CW5 ......204 E3
  Poynton SK12 ......36 D4
Oak Grove Sch SK8 ......34 C7
Oak Ho **7** CW11 ......175 B6
Oak House La CW7 ......149 B8
Oak La Astbury CW12 ...178 B4
  Cuddington CW8 ......101 F2
  Kerridge SK10 ......88 A6
  Marton SK11 ......133 C5
  Wilmslow SK9 ......59 F6
Oak Lea Ave SK9 ......60 A5
Oak Lo SK7 ......35 F7
Oak Mdw CW8 ......102 E7
Oak Mews WA3 ......34 C1
Oak Rd Chelford SK11 ...84 A3
  Chester CH4 ......140 F5
  Hooton CH66 ......43 E1
  Lymm WA13 ......18 C3
  Morley Green WA16 ...59 B5
  Mottram St Andrew SK10 ...86 B7
  Partington M31 ......11 D2
  Warrington WA5 ......14 F3
Oak St Crewe CW2 ......190 D3
  Croft WA3 ......9 A8
  Ellesmere Port CH65 ...70 C7
  Northwich WA9 ......79 A1
  Rode Heath ST7 ......193 E8
  Sandbach CW11 ......174 D8
Oak Tree Cl CW1 ......190 F5
Oak Tree Ct CW6 ......122 E2
Oak Tree Dr CW1 ......190 F5
Oak Tree Gate CW3 ......229 F3
Oak Tree La CW10 ......129 E7
Oak View Knutsford WA16 ...57 C1
  Marton SK11 ......133 C5
  Speke L24 ......21 A3
Oak Villas CW5 ......216 F4
Oak Wood Rd WA16 ......29 F2
Oakdale Ave
  Frodsham WA6 ......74 D6
  Warrington WA4 ......16 D1
Oakdale Cl
  Broughton CH4 ......139 B3
  Chorlton CW2 ......207 B3
Oakdene Ave
  Ellesmere Port CH66 ...69 C5
  Heald Green SK8 ......34 C7
  Warrington WA1 ......17 C7
Oakdene Cl CH2 ......43 D5
Oakdene Way CW6 ......168 D8
Oakenbank La SK10 ......88 D7
Oakenclough Cl SK9 ......34 D2
Oakenclough Prim Sch
  SK9 ......34 D1
Oakes Cnr CW5 ......219 E3
Oakfield Ave
  Chester CH2 ......118 E8
  Knutsford WA16 ......57 C3
  Wrenbury CW5 ......216 F3
Oakfield Cl
  Alderley Edge SK9 ......60 B3
  Bramhall SK7 ......35 E4
  Wrenbury CW5 ......216 F3
Oakfield Com Prim Sch
  WA8 ......22 B8
Oakfield Dr Chester CH2 118 E8
  Widnes WA8 ......22 A8
Oakfield Rd
  Alderley Edge SK9 ......60 B2
  Bebington CH62 ......43 C8
  Blacon CH1 ......117 D4
  Ellesmere Port CH66 ...68 E8
  Plumley WA16 ......80 F3
  Poynton SK12 ......36 F4
Oakfield Rise CW4 ......130 B3
Oakfield Terr CH66 ......68 E8
Oakfold SK10 ......88 A6
Oakhill Cl SK10 ......87 B4
Oakhurst Chase SK9 ......60 A2
Oakhurst Dr CW2 ......206 B7
Oakland Ave CW1 ......191 C4
Oakland Ct SK12 ......36 D4
Oakland St
  Warrington WA1 ......16 E7
  Widnes WA8 ......23 A4
Oaklands CH3 ......119 F4
Oaklands Ave CH3 ......166 B2
Oaklands Cl SK9 ......34 E1

Oaklands Com Inf Sch
  SK9 ......34 E1
Oaklands Cres CH3 ...166 B2
Oaklands Dr WA13 ......18 D2
Oaklands Rd Golborne WA3 .3 F7
  Ollerton WA16 ......82 F6
Oaklands Sch CW7 ......149 B7
Oaklea Ave CH2 ......118 F4
Oakleaf Lodge SK11 ...112 D5
Oakleigh WA16 ......82 C7
Oakleigh Cl CW12 ......155 F3
Oakleigh Ho SK10 ......88 B8
Oakleigh Rd SK8 ......34 E8
Oakleigh Rise CW8 ......78 E1
Oakley Cl CW11 ......175 A8
Oakley Ct CH65 ......70 C4
Oakley St CW1 ......190 C5
Oakmere Barns CW8 ...124 A7
Oakmere Cl CW11 ......174 F7
Oakmere Dr Chester CH3 142 B8
  Ellesmere Port CH66 ...69 F1
  Warrington WA5 ......14 F3
Oakmere Hall CW8 ......101 E1
Oakmere Pl CW1 ......190 B5
Oakmere Rd
  Handforth SK9 ......34 D5
  Winsford CW7 ......149 B8
Oakmere St **8** WA7 ......23 A2
Oakmoore WA7 ......24 F4
Oaks Com Prim Sch The
  CH65 ......70 D3
Oaks Dr The CH2 ......118 D7
Oaks Pl WA8 ......23 A2
Oaks The
  Alderley Edge SK9 ......60 A2
  Bebington CH62 ......43 C8
  Goostrey CW4 ......130 D8
  Mobberley WA16 ......58 E1
   5 Northwich CW9 ......103 E6
Oaksway CH60 ......41 C6
Oakthorn Gr WA11 ......1 C6
Oaktree Cl Barnton CW8 ...78 B4
  Tarporley CW6 ......146 D2
Oaktree Ct CH2 ......119 A3
Oaktree La ST7 ......210 D5
Oakways WA4 ......26 D5
Oakwood WA16 ......56 F3
Oakwood Ave
  Warrington WA1 ......16 E7
  Wilmslow SK9 ......59 F6
Oakwood Avenue Com Prim
  Sch WA1 ......16 D7
Oakwood Cl CH66 ......69 D1
Oakwood Cres
  Crewe CW2 ......189 E4
  Sandbach CW11 ......175 E6
Oakwood Ct WA14 ......31 B8
Oakwood Dr SK10 ......87 C6
Oakwood Gate WA3 ......9 D4
Oakwood Ho
  Alderley Edge SK9 ......85 B8
  Barnton CW8 ......78 A2
Oakwood La
  Altrincham WA14 ......31 B8
  Barnton CW8 ......78 A2
  Sandbach CW11 ......174 B8
Oakwood Pk CH62 ......43 D5
Oakwood Rd Disley SK12 ...38 D6
  Rode Heath ST7 ......193 F8
Oakworth Cl CW12 ......156 C3
Oat Market **3** CW5 ......204 E5
Oathills SY14 ......213 B5
Oathills Cl CW6 ......146 D1
Oathills Dr CW6 ......146 D1
Oathills Lea CW6 ......146 D1
Oatlands SK9 ......85 B8
Oban Dr CH60 ......41 A8
Oban Gr WA2 ......9 A3
Obelisk Way CW12 ......156 C3
Oddfellows Pas CW10 ...128 B1
Odeon Bldg CH1 ......237 A3
Offley Ave CW11 ......175 B7
Offley Inf Sch CW11 ...175 B7
Offley Jun Sch CW11 ...175 B7
Offley Rd CW11 ......175 B7
Ogden Rd SK7 ......35 D5
Oglet La L24 ......46 E8
Oil Sites Rd CH65 ......71 C5
Okell St WA7 ......23 A2
Old Alder La WA2,WA5 ...7 D7
Old Applecroft CW11 ...174 C5
Old Boston WA11 ......2 A7
Old Boston Trad Est WA11 2 B8
Old Brickworks Ind Est
  SK10 ......63 E4
Old Butt La ST7 ......194 D2
Old Cherry La WA13 ......28 A7
Old Chester Ct CW5 ...187 D6
Old Chester Rd
  Barbridge CW5 ......187 D6
  Ellesmere Port CH66 ...69 D4
  Helsby WA6 ......73 C4
  Higher Walton WA4 ......25 F7
Old Church Cl CH65 ......70 C7
Old Coach Rd
  Brown Knowl SY14,CH3 ...199 B6
  Kelsall CW6 ......122 D5
  Runcorn WA7 ......22 F3
Old Constabulary The **1**
  CW5 ......204 D5
Old Court Ho The **8**
  WA16 ......57 A2
Old Creamery The CW5 217 A3
Old Farm Cl
  Macclesfield SK10 ......87 A2
  Willaston CH64 ......68 A8
Old Farm Cotts CH1 ...116 E3
Old Farm Mews SK8 ...35 C4

Old – Par 269

Old Foundary Est WA8 23 B7
Old Gate Cl CW10 151 B7
Old Gorse Cl CW2 189 E3
Old Hall Cl WA4 26 A8
Old Hall Cres SK9 34 E3
Old Hall Ct
Ashton Hayes CH3 121 F7
Malpas SY14 213 B3
Old Hall Dr
Ellesmere Port CH65 70 B4
Whaley Bridge SK23 65 E4
Old Hall Gdns CH2 237 C4
Old Hall La Elton CH2 72 B3
Over Tabley WA16 55 E4
Woodford SK7 35 D1
Old Hall Pk CH3 119 F5
Old Hall Pl CH1 237 A2
Old Hall Rd
Northwich CW9 104 A5
Warrington WA5 15 D7
Old Hall St SK10 87 D1
Old Hey Wlk WA12 2 C1
Old Higher Rd WA8 21 D5
Old Hutte La L26 21 A6
Old Knutsford Rd ST7 194 A6
Old La Acton Bridge CW8 76 F3
Antrobus CW9 53 C3
Davenham CW9 104 D2
Heswall CH60 41 D8
Pulford CH4 162 E2
Old Liverpool Rd WA5 15 E4
Old Man of Mow★ ST7 195 D8
Old Market Pl 7 WA16 57 A2
Old Marsh Farm Ho
CH5 116 A8
Old Mill Cl Heswall CH60 41 B7
Lymm WA13 19 C6
Old Mill Ct CH2 118 D6
Old Mill La
Hazel Grove SK7 37 A8
Higher Whitley WA4 52 F3
Macclesfield SK11 112 E6
Old Mill Pl CH3 166 B1
Old Mill Rd CW11 175 C6
Old Mill The CH66 69 C7
Old Moss La
Fowley Common WA3 5 E6
Tarvin CH3 144 D7
Old Newcastle Rd CW5 205 D4
Old Orch SK9 60 A7
Old Orchard The
Antrobus CW9 53 C4
Cuddington CW8 101 F4
Old Paddock The CW4 130 F8
Old Pale Cotts CW8 123 C7
Old Park Rd CW1 207 D8
Old Pearl La CH3 119 B1
Old Pewterspear La WA4 26 E4
Old Pump Ho The CH66 68 E8
Old Quay Cl CH64 66 C7
Old Quay La CH64 66 D7
Old Quay St WA7 23 B3
Old Rd Anderton CW9 78 D3
Audley ST7 209 E3
Handforth SK9 34 D3
Warrington WA4 16 B4
Whaley Bridge SK23 65 F3
Whaley Bridge, New Horwich
SK23 65 E6
Whaley Bridge,Furness Vale
SK23 39 D4
Wilmslow SK9 60 B8
Old School Cl
Barnton CW8 78 B2
Farndon CH3 180 E2
Kidsgrove ST7 195 A1
Neston CH64 66 F5
Old School Ho The
CW1 190 A5
Old School House La WA2 8 A7
Old School La SK8 35 A8
Old Seals Way CH1 118 A3
Old Smithy La WA13 18 C2
Old Stack Yd CH3 120 E6
Old Tannery CW5 204 F6
Old Upton La WA8 12 E4
Old Vicarage Gdn CW3 230 A3
Old Vicarage La CW8 103 C5
Old Vicarage Rd CH64 68 A8
Old Wargrave Rd WA12 2 C3
Old Warrington Rd CW9 79 A2
Old Whint Rd WA11 1 A6
Old Woman's La CH3 142 D7
Old Wrexham Rd CH4 141 C7
Oldcastle La SY14 222 E8
Olde George The CH1 237 B3
Oldfield Brow Prim Sch
WA14 20 F5
Oldfield Cres CH4 140 F5
Oldfield Dr Chester CH3 119 C2
Mobberley WA16 58 A4
Oldfield La WA14 20 F4
Oldfield Prim Sch CH3 119 C3
Oldfield Rd
Ellesmere Port CH65 70 B5
Lymm WA13 18 C4
Sandbach CW11 174 F3
Oldgate WA8 22 C7
Oldhall St SY14 213 B3
Oldham St Bollington SK10 88 B8
Warrington WA4 16 D3
Oldham's Rise SK10 87 D3
Oldhams Hill CW8 78 F1
Oldhill Cl ST7 210 E5
Olive Dr CH64 66 F8
Olive Gr ST5 210 D1
Olive Rd CH64 66 E8
Oliver Cl SK10 87 F7
Oliver Ho CH66 69 D4
Oliver La CH66 69 D4
Oliver St WA2 16 B6
Ollersett Ave SK22 39 D8
Ollersett Dr SK22 39 D8
Ollersett Ho SK22 39 D8
Ollershaw La CW9 79 C4
Ollerton Cl WA4 17 B3
Ollerton Pk WA5 6 E7
Ollerton Rd SK9 34 E5
Ollier St 1 WA8 23 A7
Omega Bvd WA5 6 D1
On The Air', The
Broadcasting Mus & Vintage
Sound Shop★ CH1 237 B2
One Oak La SK9 60 F7
Onslow Rd CH1 117 D4
Onston La CW8 101 E8
Openshaw La M44 11 E6
Orange Gr WA2 8 E2
Orchard Ave
Acton Bridge CW8 76 E4
Lymm WA13 18 F3
Partington M31 11 F4
Whaley Bridge SK23 65 D7
Orchard Brow WA3 11 A2
Orchard Cl Barnton CW8 78 B3
Bunbury CW6 185 F8
Cheadle Hulme SK8 35 C7
Chester CH2 118 D5
Ellesmere Port CH66 69 F1
Frodsham WA6 74 A6
Goostrey CW4 107 E1
Higher Wincham CW9 80 A6
Macclesfield SK11 112 B6
Middlewich CW10 151 D7
Poynton SK12 36 E3
Weaverham CW8 77 D1
Wilmslow SK9 59 F5
Winsford CW7 149 D7
Orchard Cotts CW6 146 D1
Orchard Cres
Kidsgrove ST7 194 D1
Nantwich CW5 204 E3
Nether Alderley SK10 84 F6
Orchard Croft CH3 119 E5
Orchard Ct Alsager ST7 193 E4
3 Chester CH3 119 A1
Frodsham WA6 74 A8
Haslington CW1 191 D4
Orchard Dene CW8 101 D5
Orchard Dr Handforth SK9 34 E2
Little Leigh CW8 77 D5
Neston CH64 66 E5
Orchard Gdns
Congleton CW12 156 A3
Tarporley CW6 168 D8
Weaverham CW8 77 B1
Orchard Gn SK9 60 B1
Orchard Gr CH3 180 F1
Orchard Haven CH66 69 E1
Orchard Ho SK10 86 E1
Orchard La CH66 69 A8
Orchard Park La CH2 72 B4
Orchard Pk CH2 72 B4
Orchard Pl Helsby WA6 73 C4
Poynton SK12 36 D4
Orchard Rd
Ellesmere Port CH65 70 B2
Lymm WA13 19 B5
Whaley Bridge SK23 65 D7
Orchard Rise CW9 126 E8
Orchard St Chester CH1 237 A3
Crewe CW1 190 C5
Northwich CW9 104 B8
Warrington WA1 16 C5
Warrington, Fearnhead WA2 9 A2
Warrington,Stockton Heath
WA4 26 C8
Willaston CW5 205 D6
Orchard The
Alderley Edge SK9 85 B8
Chester CH3 142 A8
Disley SK12 38 D6
Helsby WA6 73 B2
Orchard Way
Congleton CW12 156 A3
Kelsall CW6 122 D5
Widnes WA8 12 A3
Orchard Wlk Neston CH64 66 E8
3 Runcorn WA7 49 F7
Orchards The Holt LL13 196 D8
Pickmere WA16 79 F7
Saltney CH4 140 D6
Shavington CW2 206 C4
Orchid Cl Huntington CH3 142 A6
Irlam M44 11 E8
Orchid Way WA9 6 B7
Orchil Cl CH66 69 A6
Ordnance Ave
Warrington WA3 9 F4
Warrington,Birchwood WA3 10 A5
Ordsall Cl CW11 174 F3
Orford Ave Disley SK12 38 D6
Warrington WA1,WA2 16 C7
Orford Cl Golborne WA3 3 A7
Hale L24 21 E2
High Lane SK6 37 E7
Orford Gn WA2 8 D1
Orford La WA2 16 B7
Orford Rd WA2 16 E8
Orford St WA1 16 B5
Organsdale Cotts CW6 123 B5
Oriel Ho CH2 118 C4
Orion Bvd WA5 6 E1
Orkney Cl
3 Ellesmere Port CH65 70 C1
Widnes WA8 13 E3
Orme Cl Macclesfield SK10 87 D3
Prestbury SK10 87 A8
Orme Cres SK10 87 D3
Orme St SK9 60 A1
Ormerod Cl CW11 175 C5
Ormesby Gr CH63 43 B6
Ormond Cl WA8 12 C2
Ormonde Rd CH2 118 C4
Ormonde St CH1 237 C3
Orrell Cl WA5 15 A6
Orton Cl CW7 127 A4
Orwell Cl SK9 34 D2
Osborne Ave WA2 8 D1
Osborne Cl CW11 174 D5
Osborne Gr CW2 206 C5
Osborne Ho SK9 60 A6
Osborne Rd Golborne WA3 3 E7
Warrington WA4 16 B1
Osbourne Cl
Bebington CH62 43 E7
Wilmslow SK9 60 D6
Osier Cl CH2 72 C3
Osmere Cl SY13 226 B1
Osnath Wks WA2 16 B6
Osprey Ave CW7 149 D5
Osprey Cl
Middlewich CW10 151 D5
Runcorn WA7 49 F5
Warrington WA2 8 E3
Osprey Ct CH2 237 A4
Osprey Dr SK9 60 C8
Osprey View ST7 195 D3
Ossett Cl WA7 50 D8
Ossmere Cl CW11 174 F8
Ostler's La WA16 58 E7
Oteley Ave CH62 43 D8
Otters Bank 2 CW7 126 A1
Ottersbank Mews CW8 123 F3
Oughtrington Com Prim Sch
WA13 19 B4
Oughtrington Cres WA13 19 B4
Oughtrington La WA13 19 A2
Oughtrington View WA13 19 B4
Oulton Ave CH2 118 E7
Oulton Ct WA4 17 B2
Oulton Dr CW12 155 F3
Oulton Mill La CW6 147 B7
Oulton Pl CH1 237 B3
Our Lady Mother of the
Saviour RC Prim Sch
WA7 50 A6
Our Lady of Lourdes RC Prim
Sch M31 11 E3
Our Lady of Perpetual
Succour RC Prim Sch
WA8 22 A8
Our Lady's RC Inf & Jun Sch
CH65 70 A3
Our Lady's RC Prim Sch
WA4 16 E3
Ousel Nest CW8 101 D4
Out La CH3 184 C6
Outwood Dr SK8 34 A8
Outwood La M90 33 C7
Outwood La W M90 33 B8
Outwood Prim Sch SK8 34 D7
Outwood Rd SK8 34 B7
Oval The
Ellesmere Port CH65 70 C3
Heald Green SK8 34 B8
Oven La SK11 114 D5
Ovenhouse La SK10 87 E7
Over Hall Com Prim Sch
CW7 149 B7
Over Hall Dr CW7 149 C7
Over Pl WA16 82 C8
Over Rd
Church Minshull CW5 172 A7
Winsford CW7 149 F1
Over St John's CE Prim Sch
CW7 126 A1
Overdale La CW8 101 D1
Overdale Rd
New Mills SK12 38 F6
Willaston CH64 43 A1
Overdene Rd CW7 149 D8
Overfields WA16 57 D3
Overhill Dr SK9 60 E7
Overhill La SK9 60 E7
Overhill Rd SK9 60 D7
Overleigh Ct CH4 141 D7
Overleigh Rd CH4 141 C7
Overleigh St Mary's CE Prim
Sch CH4 141 D6
Overleigh Terr CH4 141 C7
Overpool Gdns CH66 69 F3
Overpool Rd CH65,CH66 69 F5
Overpool Sta CH66 69 E6
Oversley Ford Cvn Site
SK9 33 B3
Overton Cl
Congleton CW12 156 C3
Middlewich CW10 151 B8
Overton Dr WA6 74 C6
Overton Heath La SY14 212 F5
Overton Rd ST8 179 F6
Overton Way 2 SK9 34 D5
Overway CW7 126 E1
Overwood Ave CH1 94 E1
Overwood La
Blacon CH1 117 C4
Mollington CH1 94 E1
Ovington Cl WA7 49 F4
Owen Cl CH1 117 E6
Owen St Crewe CW2 190 C2
Northwich CW9 104 B8
Warrington WA2 16 A7
Owl Ind Est The CH5 116 B6
Owley Wood Rd CW8 77 E1
Owlhurst The SK10 88 B8
Owlsfield WA12 2 E3
Ox-Hey Cres ST8 179 D1
Ox-Hey Dr ST8 179 D1
Oxborough Cl WA8 12 F4
Oxenham Rd WA2 8 A3
Oxford Cl CH66 94 E8
Oxford Ct WA1 16 D6
Oxford Dr Halewood L26 21 A8
Heswall CH63 41 F6
Oxford Gr M44 11 C6
Oxford Rd Chester CH4 140 F6
Macclesfield SK11 112 B7
Runcorn WA7 49 A8
Oxford St Crewe CW1 190 B5
Newton-le-W WA12 2 B3
Warrington WA4 16 C4
Widnes WA8 23 B7
Oxhey Fst Sch ST8 179 E1
Oxheys WA7 50 C8
Oxmead Cl WA2 9 B1
Oxmoor Cl WA7 50 A5
Oxney Cl SK11 111 F8
Oxton Cl WA8 12 C4
Oxton Gn CH66 69 D4

P

Packmoor Prim Sch
ST7 195 F1
Packsaddle Pk SK10 86 E5
Padarn Cl CH4 140 D5
Paddington Bank WA1 16 F6
Paddock Brow SK10 87 A5
Paddock Chase SK12 36 F6
Paddock Cl SK23 64 F4
Paddock Dr CH64 41 D2
Paddock La Audlem CW3 230 B2
Kettleshulme SK23 64 F4
Lymm WA13 19 C7
Partington WA14 20 B5
Whaley Bridge SK23 65 F5
Paddock Rd CH4 141 E1
Paddock Rise WA7 49 E4
Paddock Row CH1 237 B2
Paddock The
Chester CH4 141 B7
Ellesmere Port CH66 69 D3
Elton CH2 72 A3
Handforth SK9 34 D4
Hartford CW8 103 C3
Hassall Green CW11 175 F2
Helsby WA6 73 C2
Heswall CH60 41 C8
Lymm WA13 19 C4
Sandbach CW11 175 B7
Tarporley CW6 146 D1
Whaley Bridge SK23 65 F6
Willaston CW5 205 D4
Paddock View CW10 128 C2
Paddock Way CH4 161 A7
Paddock Wlk CW8 101 D5
Paddockhill La WA16 59 A3
Paddocks Gn CW12 178 F8
Paddocks The
Prestbury SK10 87 A5
Whitegate CW8 125 B6
Padgate Bsns Ctr WA1 17 B8
Padgate CE Prim Sch
WA2 9 A1
Padgate Com High Sch
WA2 8 F1
Padgate La
Warrington WA1 16 D7
Warrington,Padgate WA1 16 F8
Padgate Sta WA1 9 A1
Padgbury Cl CW12 156 A1
Padgbury La CW12 156 A1
Padge La CH3 183 C2
Padmore Cl CW1 190 A7
Padston Dr ST7 193 B3
Padstow Cl Crewe CW1 190 C8
Macclesfield SK10 111 E8
Warrington WA5 14 E3
Padstow Dr SK7 35 F7
Padstow Sq WA7 50 B5
Padworth Pl CW1 173 B1
Page Gr CW2 206 B3
Page La WA8 13 C1
Paignton Cl WA5 14 E4
Painswick Rd CH66 69 E2
Paisley Ave CH62 43 E4
Palace Fields Ave WA7 50 A6
Palace Fields Local Ctr
WA7 50 A6
Palace Hey CH64 67 A5
Palacefields Prim Sch
WA7 50 A6
Palatine Cl CH1 117 D6
Palatine Ind Est WA4 16 C3
Palgrave Cl CH1 118 A5
Palin Dr WA5 14 F6
Pall Mall CW5 204 E5
Palliser Cl WA3 10 A3
Palm Gr CH66 70 A1
Palma Ave M90 33 B8
Palmer Cl CW9 103 F5
Palmer Cres WA5 15 D8
Palmer Rd CW11 175 C5
Palmerston Cl CW1 191 C5
Palmerston Rd SK11 112 A7
Palmerston St SK10 88 B8
Palmerston Way ST8 179 D1
Palmerstone Cl CH1 118 B4
Palmyra Sq N WA1 16 A5
Palmyra Sq S WA1 16 A5
Pangbourne Cl WA4 26 E6
Panton Pl CH2 118 F3
Panton Rd CH2 118 F3
Parade Rd M90 33 C7
Parade The
1 Alderley Edge SK9 60 A1
Blacon CH1 117 E5
Culcheth WA3 4 E3
Neston CH64 41 B1
Paradise CH4 237 B1
Paradise La CW5 171 E7
Paradise Mill & Silk Mus★
SK11 112 D7
Paradise St SK11 112 C7
Paragon Cl WA8 13 B5
Parbold Ct WA8 22 D8
Parc Ddiwydiannol Glannau
Dyfrdwy/Deeside Ind Pk
CH5 92 E2
Parc Ddiwydiannol Y
Ffin/Borders Ind Pk The
CH4 140 C7
Parchments The WA12 2 D4
Parish Cl ST7 193 B4
Park Ave Bramhall SK7 35 D5
Haydock WA11 1 A6
Poynton SK12 36 E4
Saltney CH4 140 E6
Saughall CH1 94 A2
Talke ST7 210 E8
Tattenhall CH3 166 B2
Warrington WA4 16 D3
Weaverham CW8 77 D1
Whaley Bridge SK23 39 D3
Widnes WA8 13 B1
Wilmslow SK9 60 C8
Winsford CW7 127 A3
Park Ave N WA12 2 C2
Park Ave S WA12 2 C2
Park Bank CW12 156 F2
Park Brook Rd SK11 112 A8
Park Bvd WA1 16 B4
Park Cl CH3 121 B2
Park Cres
Cuddington CW8 101 F4
Handforth SK9 34 B1
Warrington WA4 26 D6
Whaley Bridge SK23 39 D3
Park Ct Chester CH1 237 C2
Frodsham WA6 74 A8
Runcorn WA7 49 A8
1 Warrington WA1 16 A5
Park Dr Chester CH2 119 A4
Ellesmere Port CH65 70 B3
Wistaston CW2 205 F8
Park Dr S CH2 119 A4
Park Est CW2 206 D5
Park Gn SK11 112 D7
Park Gr SK11 112 C6
Park House Dr
Prestbury SK10 87 A8
Sandbach CW11 175 C8
Park House La SK10 87 A8
Park House Mews
CW11 175 D8
Park La Audley ST7 209 B4
Congleton CW12 156 F2
Frodsham WA6 74 B8
Hargrave CH3 144 E3
Hartford CW8 103 B4
Hatherton CW5 219 E4
Higher Walton WA4 25 F5
Little Bollington WA14 20 B2
Littleton CH3 119 F3
Macclesfield SK11 112 C6
Macclesfield SK11 112 D7
Moulton CW9 126 F7
Pickmere CW9,WA16 79 E8
Poynton SK12 36 F3
Pulford CH4 162 E5
Sandbach CW11 174 F6
Park Lane Sch SK11 112 B6
Park Mills Cl CW5 205 D5
Park Mount Cl SK11 112 A6
Park Mount Dr SK11 112 A6
Park Prim Sch CH3 166 B2
Park Prim Sch The WA7 24 A1
Park Rd
Bebington,Eastham CH62 43 F6
Congleton CW12 156 E3
Congleton, North Rode
CW12 134 F2
Ellesmere Port CH65 70 C4
Golborne WA3 3 A7
Haslington CW1 191 D5
Heswall CH60 41 B8
High Lane SK12 37 F6
Little Budworth CW6 124 F1
Lymm WA13 29 D8
Middlewich CW10 128 C1
Nantwich CW5 204 E3
New Mills SK22 39 C7
Partington,Warburton
WA13 19 C8
Runcorn WA7 49 A8
Sandbach CW11 174 D8
Tarporley CW6 146 D2
Thornton-le-M CH2 71 E1
Warrington WA5 14 E6
Warrington, Orford WA2 8 D1
Whaley Bridge SK23 65 D6
Widnes WA8 13 B1
Willaston CH64 68 B8
Willaston(nr Nantwich)
CW5 205 C5

Park Rd continued
Wilmslow SK9 ....59 F7
Winnington CW8 ....78 D1
Park Rd N WA12 ....2 E4
Park Rd S WA12 ....2 D2
Park Rd W CH4 ....141 A7
Park Road Com Prim Sch
WA5 ....14 E6
Park St Bollington SK10 ..88 B8
Chester CH1 ....237 B2
Congleton CW12 ....156 E2
Haydock WA11 ....1 A6
Macclesfield SK11 ....112 D7
Neston CH64 ....66 E8
Northwich CW8 ......103 E2
Park The Christleton CH3 .142 E8
Warrington WA5 ....14 D3
Park Vale SK11 ....112 C6
Park View Audlem CW3 .230 C8
Bebington CH62 ....43 C8
Congleton CW12 ....156 E3
Hazel Grove SK7 ......37 B8
Little Bollington WA14 ..20 B2
Nantwich CW5 ......204 F6
Newton-le-W WA12 .....2 E3
Warrington WA2 ....8 E3
Park View Ct SK12 .....36 E4
Park View Rd ST7 ....195 B3
Park W CH60 ....40 E7
Park Way CH1 ....94 A2
Park Wlk CH4 ....141 A7
Parkdale Ind Est WA1 ..16 C4
Parkdale Rd WA1 ......17 A7
Parker Ave CW8 ......103 A6
Parker Dr CH3 ....180 E1
Parker Dr S CH3 .....180 F1
Parker St
Macclesfield SK11 ....112 E7
Runcorn WA7 ....23 B3
Warrington WA1 ....16 A5
Parker Way CW12 ....156 A3
Parker's Bldgs CH1 ...237 C3
Parker's Rd CW1 .....190 A8
Parker's Row CH3 ....180 F6
Parkers Ct WA7 ....49 E6
Parkett Heyes Rd SK11 .111 E7
Parkfield CW1 ....173 A1
Parkfield Ave WA4 .....17 A4
Parkfield Dr
Ellesmere Port CH65 ...70 A3
Helsby WA6 ....73 B3
Nantwich CW5 ......204 E4
Parkfield Rd
Broughton CH4 ......139 C3
Knutsford WA16 ......82 B8
Northwich CW9 ......104 C8
Parkfields La WA2 ......8 F2
Parkgate WA16 ....57 C3
Parkgate Ave WA16 ...108 B8
Parkgate Ct CH1 .....118 B4
Parkgate Ho CH64 .....41 B2
Parkgate La Heswall CH64 41 F5
Knutsford WA16 ......57 C3
Parkgate Prim Sch CH64 41 C1
Parkgate Rd Blacon CH1 118 A6
Macclesfield SK11 ....112 C4
Neston CH64 ....66 D8
Puddington CH66 .....68 C2
Saughall CH1 ....94 C3
Warrington WA4 ......16 D1
Woodbank CH1 ....93 E7
Parkgate Trad Est WA16 .57 C4
Parkgate Way
Handforth SK9 ....34 D4
Runcorn WA7 ....50 D7
Parkhill Ct WA16 ......57 B1
Parkhouse Ind Est ST5 .210 F1
Parkhouse Rd E ST5 ..210 F1
Parkhouse Rd W ST5 ..210 E1
Parkland Cl WA4 ......27 B4
Parkland Dr CH2 ......72 B3
Parklands
Ellesmere Port CH66 ...69 D6
Kidsgrove ST7 ....195 B1
Widnes WA8 ....12 C3
Parklands Com Prim Sch
CH66 ....69 D5
Parklands Dr CH60 ....41 C6
Parklands Gdns CH66 ..69 D6
Parklands The CW12 ..157 A2
Parklands View CH66 ..69 D5
Parklands Way SK12 ...36 E4
Parklea CH66 ....69 D6
Parkleigh CW12 ......156 E2
Parkroyal Com Sch
SK11 ....112 C7
Parkside Bsns Pk WA3 ..3 A8
Parkside Cl High Lane SK6 37 D8
Neston CH64 ....66 D8
Parkside Ct WA8 ......13 A2
Parkside Rd WA12,WA2 ..3 B2
Parkstone Dr CW1 ....190 B8
Parksway WA1 ....17 D7
Parkview CH60 ....40 F8
Parkview Pk
Broomedge WA13 .....19 D1
Lymm WA13 ....29 D8
Parkway
Connah's Quay CH5 ...92 E1
Holmes Chapel CW4 ..130 C3
Wilmslow SK9 ....60 B6
Parkway Bsns Ctr CH5 .92 E1
Parkwood Cl
Bebington CH62 ....43 E8
Lymm WA13 ....18 D2

Parliament St 4 CW8 ..103 E7
Parliament Way CH66 ..94 F8
Parlington Cl WA8 .....22 C7
Parnell Sq CW12 .....157 A2
Parr Gr WA11 ....1 A6
Parr St Macclesfield SK11 112 C8
Warrington WA1 ......16 C4
1 Widnes WA8 ....13 C1
Parrs Wood View WA4 ..17 A1
Parry Dr WA4 ....17 E3
Parson St CW12 ......156 C2
Parsonage Gn Hale L24 .21 E1
9 Wilmslow SK9 .....60 B7
Parsonage Rd WA8 ....23 A4
Parsonage St SK11 ...112 D7
Parsonage Way WA5 ...15 A5
Parsons La CH2 ......118 B7
Partington Prim Sch
M31 ....11 F3
Partington Sh Ctr M31 .11 F3
Partridge Cl
Congleton CW12 ....156 E1
Warrington WA3 ....9 E4
Winsford CW7 ......149 D5
Partridge Way CW9 ....79 F5
Parvey La SK11 ......112 C6
Pasture Cl Kelsall CW6 .122 C4
Macclesfield SK10 ....87 C3
Pasture Dr WA3 ....9 B7
Pasture La WA2 ....9 B1
Pastures The WA9 ......6 A7
Patch La SK7 ....35 D5
Patmos Cl WA16 .....105 F8
Patrivale Cl WA1 ......16 F6
Patten La WA1 ....16 B5
Patterdale Ave WA2 ....8 C2
Patterdale Cl CW2 ....189 D3
Patterdale Rd M31 ....11 E3
Patterson Cl WA3 ......9 E3
Patterson St WA12 .....2 B3
Patton Dr WA5 ....15 B6
Paul Cl WA5 ....14 D6
Paul St WA2 ....16 A6
Paulden Rd CW9 ....80 A2
Pavement La WA16 ....57 F3
Pavilion Way
Congleton CW12 ....156 C3
Macclesfield SK10 ....86 F1
Pavilions The
Chester CH4 ....141 B3
Davenham CW9 ......103 E2
Paxford Pl SK9 ....60 A5
Payne Cl WA5 ....15 D6
Paythorne Cl WA3 ......4 F3
Peace Dr WA5 ....15 D5
Peach Field CH3 .....142 B7
Peach Gr WA11 ....1 E7
Peach La CW5 ....189 A1
Peach Tree Cl L24 .....21 E2
Peacock Ave
Warrington WA1 ......16 E6
Winsford CW7 ......149 C5
Peacock Dr SK8 ......34 B6
Peacock Hay Rd ST7 ..210 F4
Peacock La WA16 .....29 E6
Peacock Way 5 SK9 ...34 D5
Peak Rd SK22 ....39 D8
Pear Tree Ave
Crewe CW1 ....190 B7
Runcorn WA7 ....49 C7
Pear Tree Cl
Frodsham WA6 ....49 D1
Hale L24 ....21 E1
Weaverham CW8 ......77 C1
Winsford CW7 ......149 D7
Pear Tree Dr CW9 .....80 A6
Pear Tree Farm Cotts
CW9 ....104 F4
Pear Tree Field CW5 ..205 A4
Pear Tree La
Acton Bridge CW8 ....76 E4
Whitchurch SY13 ....225 D1
Pear Tree Prim Sch
CW5 ....205 A4
Pear Tree Rd ST7 ....209 F1
Pear Tree Way
Chester CH2 ....118 F6
5 Ellesmere Port CH66 .69 E1
Pearl La Chester CH3 ..119 C1
Littleton CH3 ....119 D1
Pearl St SK10 ....87 A7
Pearle St SK10 ....87 D1
Pearlings The CH3 ....119 B1
Pearson Ave WA4 .....16 D2
Pearson St 9 SK11 ...112 E7
Peartree La CW11 ....175 E6
Peartree La SY14 ....222 D1
Peartree Pl WA4 ......16 C4
Pearwood Cl CW6 ....146 D1
Peasley Cl WA2 ....9 B1
Pebble Brook Prim Sch
CW2 ....190 C1
Peck Mill La WA6 .....98 A2
Peckfield Cl WA7 .....50 A5
Peckforton Cl CW11 ..174 E7
Peckforton Dr
Ellesmere Port CH66 ...69 E3
Runcorn WA7 ....49 F4
Peckforton Hall Farm
CW6 ....185 A6
Peckforton Hall La CW6 185 B6
Peckforton Rd CW6 ..168 A2
Peckforton Way
Chester CH2 ....118 F6
2 Northwich CW8 ....103 E7
Peckmill Wlk 11 SK9 ..34 E1
Peckmill Cl SK9 ......34 E1
Peckmill Rdbt CW9 ..127 B8

Pedley Hill
Booth Green SK10 ....62 F7
Rainow SK10 ....88 E4
Pedley House La WA16 .58 E1
Pedley La Chelford WA16 .83 D8
Congleton CW12 ....157 F4
Pedley St CW2 ......190 D2
Peebles Cl
Ellesmere Port CH66 ...68 F6
Holmes Chapel CW4 ..130 B2
Peel Cl CH3 ....121 E7
Peel Cres CH3 ....121 E7
Peel Ct 4 ST7 ....195 A2
Peel Dr CW12 ....178 B7
Peel Hall La CH3 ....121 E7
Peel Hollow ST7 ....209 A2
Peel House La WA8 ...13 B2
Peel La CW12 ....178 D7
Peel Sq CW1 ....190 B5
Peel St Crewe CW1 ...190 B5
Macclesfield SK11 ....112 D6
Newton-le-W WA12 .....2 A3
Warrington WA7 ......22 F3
Peel Terr CH1 ....237 C3
Peerswood Ct CH64 ...66 E5
Peewit Cl WA7 ......149 D5
Peggie's La SK10 .....62 D2
Pelham Cl CW1 ......191 C5
Pelham Rd WA4 ......17 C3
Pelican Cl CW1 .....191 A5
Pemberton Cl CH64 ...68 A8
Pemberton Rd CH1 ..237 A3
Pembridge Ct CH65 ...70 E3
Pembridge Gdns CH65 .70 E3
Pembroke Apartments
WA2 ....9 A3
Pembroke Cl CH4 ....141 E6
Pembroke Ct WA7 ....24 D5
Pembroke Dr CH65 ...70 A3
Pembroke Gdns WA4 ..26 D4
Pembroke Gr M44 ....11 C6
Pembroke Rd SK11 ...111 F7
Pembroke Way CW7 ..149 B7
Penare WA7 ....50 C6
Penbrook Cl CW2 ....189 D3
Penda Way CW11 ....175 B6
Pendine Cl WA5 ....7 C2
Pendle Cl Crewe CW1 .191 A5
Ellesmere Port CH66 ...68 F6
Pendle Gdns WA3 .....4 E2
Pendlebury St WA4 ...17 A3
Pendleton Ct WA7 ....24 C5
Penfold Cl CH1 ....94 B8
Penfold Hey CH2 ....118 D7
Penfold Way CH4 ....162 A7
Penfolds WA7 ....23 D1
Penhale Mews SK7 ...35 F7
Peninsula Ho WA2 ....16 C7
Penistone Dr CH66 ...69 B5
Penketh Ave WA5 ....15 F8
Penketh Bsns Pk WA5 .15 B4
Penketh Com Prim Sch
WA5 ....14 D4
Penketh Ct
1 Runcorn WA7 ......23 B2
Warrington WA5 .....14 D4
Penketh High Sch WA5 .15 A5
Penketh Rd WA5 .....15 A4
Penketh South Com Prim Sch
WA5 ....14 E3
Penketh's La 19 WA7 ..23 A3
Penkford La WA5 ......1 D1
Penkford St WA12 .....1 E3
Penkford Tech Specl Sch
WA12 ....1 E2
Penkmans La WA6 ....74 C6
Penlington Ct CW5 ..204 F6
Penmann Cres L26 ....21 A7
Penmark Cl WA5 ......7 D2
Penmon Cl CH1 .....117 D3
Penn Bridge SK11 ...158 E6
Penn Gdns CH65 .....70 B5
Penn House La SK7 ...35 E8
Penn La WA7 ....22 F1
Pennant Cl WA3 ......10 A3
Pennine Ct SK10 ......87 E2
Pennine Rd WA2 ......8 E2
Pennine Way
Biddulph ST8 ....179 E1
Winsford CW7 ......149 B8
Pennine Wlk CH66 ...69 B6
Pennington Cl WA6 ...49 D2
Pennington Dr WA12 ..2 E3
Pennington Gn CH66 ..69 C3
Pennington La WA5,WA9 .1 D2
Penningtons La SK11 ..111 F5
Pennsylvania La CH3 .184 C6
Penny Bank CH4 .....139 A3
Penny Lane Collins Green WA5 1 D1
Cronton L35,WA8 .....12 B6
Haydock WA11 ....2 B7
Rainow SK10 ....88 D3
Penny's La
Northwich CW9 ......104 F7
Rudheath CW9 ......105 B5
Pennyfields Rd ST7 ..195 D2
Pennymoor Dr CW10 .128 D2
Pennypleck La CW9 ...28 A2
Penrhyn Cres
Hazel Grove SK7 .....36 C8
Runcorn WA7 ....49 B7
Penrhyn Rd CW8 ....103 E8
Penrith Ave
Macclesfield SK11 ....111 F5
Warrington WA2 ......8 C2
Penrith Cl Frodsham WA6 .49 D1
Partington M31 ....11 E3
Penrith Ct CW12 ....156 A2
Penrose Gdns WA5 ...14 D3

Penry Ave M44 ....11 E6
Penryn Cl WA5 ....14 E3
Pensarn Gdns WA5 ....7 D2
Pensby Ave CH2 .....118 D5
Pensby Dr CH66 ......69 D4
Pensby Rd CH60 ......40 F8
Penshaw Ct WA7 .....49 E7
Pentland Ave WA2 .....8 B3
Pentland Cl Chester CH3 119 A1
Winsford CW7 ......149 B8
Pentland Pl WA2 ......8 B3
Pentre Cl CH3 ....121 F7
Pentre La CH3 ....121 F7
Penzance Cl SK10 ...111 E8
Peony Gdns WA9 ......6 B7
Peover Hall & Gdns★
WA16 ....107 E8
Peover Cl Chelford SK11 108 F8
Congleton CW12 ....157 F6
Peover Prim Sch WA16 108 E8
Peover Rd SK9 ....34 E5
Pepper Ct SK9 ....60 A6
Pepper St
Appleton Thorn WA4 ..27 B3
Ashley SK11 ....31 F1
Chelford SK11 ....83 E2
Chester CH1 ....237 B2
Christleton CH3 .....142 D8
Hale L24 ....21 D1
Henbury SK11 ......111 B8
Lymm WA13 ....18 F3
Middlewich CW10 ...128 C1
Nantwich CW5 ......204 E5
Peppers The WA13 ...18 F3
Percival Cl CH2 .....118 C8
Percival La WA7 ......22 E2
Percival Rd Chester CH2 118 C8
Ellesmere Port CH65 ...70 B6
Percy James St ST7 ..193 E4
Percy Rd CH4 ....141 D7
Percy St Northwich CW9 104 A8
Warrington WA5 .....15 E5
Percyvale St SK10 ...112 E8
Peregrine Cl WA7 ...149 D5
Perimeter Rd CH2 ....72 D5
Perrin Ave WA7 ......48 E8
Perrins Rd WA5 ....6 F6
Perry Fields CW1 ....173 B1
Perry St WA7 ....23 B2
Perth Cl Bramhall SK7 .35 F5
Holmes Chapel CW4 ..130 B2
Warrington WA2 ......8 F4
Peter Destapleigh Way
CW5 ....205 A3
Peter Ellson Cl CW2 .190 D1
Peter House Rd WA7 .112 F3
Peter Pl CW1 ....190 B5
Peter Salem Dr WA5 ..15 B6
Peter St Golborne WA3 ..3 A8
Macclesfield SK11 ....112 C7
Northwich CW9 ......79 B1
Peter St W 1 SK11 ...112 C7
Peterborough Cl
Ellesmere Port CH66 ...94 F7
Macclesfield SK10 ....87 A2
Peters Cl SK10 ....87 A7
Petersfield Gdns WA3 ..4 F8
Petersgate WA7 ......50 D7
Petersham Dr WA4 ...26 E5
Peterstone Cl WA5 ....7 D2
Petham Ct WA8 ......12 E4
Petrel Ave SK12 ......36 B4
Petrel Mews SK12 ....39 A6
Peveril Cl WA4 ......26 D8
Peveril Dr SK7 ....36 F8
Peveril Gdns SK12 ...39 A6
Peveril Mews SK12 ...39 A6
Peveril Wlk 3 SK11 ..111 F7
Pewit La CW5 ....231 C7
Pewithall Prim Sch WA7 .49 B7
Pewterspear Green Rd
WA4 ....26 E3
Pewterspear La WA4 ..26 E4
Pex Hill Ct WA8 ......12 E5
Pexall Rd SK11 ......134 C3
Pexhill Dr SK10 .....111 E7
Pexhill Rd SK11 .....111 C5
Pheasant Cl WA3 ......9 F4
Pheasant Dr CW9 .....79 F5
Pheasant Field L24 ...21 C2
Pheasant Way CW7 ..149 D5
Pheasant Wlk WA16 ..29 C4
Philip Rd WA8 ....22 B8
Philip St CH5 ....116 A2
Philips Dr WA5 ....14 E7
Philips La CH66 ......69 C4
Phillip St CH2 ......118 F3
Phillips Rd CH1 .....117 D3
Phillips Way CH60 ....40 E8
Phipps' La WA5 ....6 E7
Phoenix Ave WA5 .....7 F2
Phoenix Cl ST7 .....195 C2
Phoenix St CH5 .....116 A3
Phythian Cres WA5 ...14 F4
Pichael Nook WA5 ....14 A4
Pickenham Cl SK11 ..111 F6
Pickering Cres WA4 ...17 D3
Pickering St CW12 ..237 C4
Pickering Way CW5 ..204 F4

Pickering's Pasture (Nature
Reserve)★ WA8 ......22 B3
Pickerings Cl WA7 ....49 C6
Pickerings Lock Cvn PK
CW8 ....76 A5
Pickerings O The Boat
CW8 ....76 B5
Pickerings Rd WA8 ...22 B5
Pickford St SK11 ....112 D7
Pickmere Cl CW11 ...174 F7
Pickmere Ct Crewe CW1 190 C5
10 Handforth SK9 ....34 D5
Pickmere Dr
Bebington CH62 ....43 F3
Bebington CH62 ....43 F4
Chester CH3 ....142 B8
Runcorn WA7 ....50 C5
Pickmere La
Higher Wincham CW9 ..79 F6
Pickmere WA16 ....55 D2
Pickmere Rd SK9 .....34 D5
Pickmere St WA5 .....15 E5
Pickwick Cl CW11 ...175 C8
Pickwick Pl ST7 ....194 D2
Pickwick Rd SK12 ....36 D3
Picow Farm Rd WA7 ..22 E1
Picow St 1 WA7 .....22 F1
Picton Ave
Ellesmere Port CH65 ...70 C5
Runcorn WA7 ....23 B2
Picton Cl Bebington CH62 43 E3
2 Northwich CW9 ....103 F4
Warrington WA3 ......9 C4
Picton Dr Handforth SK9 34 E2
Winsford CW7 ......126 B2
Picton Gorse La CH2 .119 B7
Picton La CH2 ....96 C4
Picton Sq CW4 ......130 C3
Piele Rd WA11 ....1 E8
Pierce St SK11 ......112 C8
Pierpoint La CH1 ....237 B2
Pierpoint St WA5 .....15 F7
Pigot Pl WA4 ....16 F5
Pike La WA6 ....75 A3
Pike Rd SK10 ....89 B6
Pike St WA4 ....16 D1
Pike The CW5 ....204 E3
Pikemere Prim Sch ST7 193 B5
Pikemere Rd ST7 ....193 B5
Pikenall La CW8 ......76 D3
Pilgrim Cl WA2 ....8 A4
Pilgrims Way WA7 ....24 D2
Pillar Box La CW11 ..153 B3
Pillmoss La WA4 .....52 B8
Pillory St CW5 ......204 E5
Pimblett Rd WA11 ....1 E7
Pimblett St WA3 ......3 A7
Pimlico Rd WA7 .....22 E2
Pine Ave
Newton-le-W WA12 .....2 D2
4 Widnes WA8 ....13 B2
Pine Cl Haydock WA11 ..1 C6
Macclesfield SK10 ....87 F1
Talke ST7 ....210 D7
Pine Ct ST7 ....193 E4
Pine Gdns CH2 ......118 C6
Pine Gr Chester CH2 .119 B4
Ellesmere Port CH66 ...70 A1
Golborne WA3 ....3 C8
Sandbach CW11 .....175 C6
Warrington WA1 ......17 A7
Winsford CW7 ......127 A1
Pine Lo SK7 ....35 F7
Pine Lodge SK12 .....36 D3
Pine Rd Bramhall SK7 .35 F8
Heswall CH60 ....41 C8
Macclesfield SK10 ....87 F1
Poynton SK12 ....36 F3
Runcorn WA7 ....49 C8
Pine Tree Cl CH4 ....139 C3
Pine Trees WA16 .....57 F8
Pine Wlk Nantwich CW5 204 F4
1 Partington M31 ....11 E3
Pineapple Pk CW7 ...127 B2
Pinedale Cl CH66 .....95 A8
Pinehey CH64 ....41 D1
Pinehurst SK10 ......86 E6
Pinellas WA7 ....23 B3
Pines The
Mobberley WA16 .....58 E1
6 Northwich CW9 ...103 E6
Pinetree Cl Barnton CW8 78 B4
Winsford CW7 ......127 A1
Pineways WA4 ....26 C5
Pinewood Ave WA1 ...16 E7
Pinewood Cl CH2 .....72 C3
Pinewood Ct CW2 ...206 B7
Pinewood Dr CH60 ...41 B8
Pinewood Gr ST5 ....210 D1
Pinewood Rd
Burtonwood WA5 .....6 F7
Wilmslow SK9 ....60 E8
Winsford CW7 ......126 B1
Pinfold Cl WA15 .....32 B2
Pinfold Craft Ctr★ CW5 188 B3
Pinfold Ct CH4 ......141 E6
Pinfold La
Alpraham CW6 ......169 D5
Chelford WA16 ....83 D6
Chester CH4 ....141 D6
Chester CH4 ....141 E7
Little Budworth CW6 .147 E7
Middlewich CW10 ...128 B1
Plumley WA16 ....81 B4
Woodhouse Park M90,
WA15 ....32 F6
Pinfold St 18 SK11 ..112 C8
Pinfold The LL13 ....196 D8

Pinfold Way CW8 ......77 D1
Pingard's La CW5 ......101 C6
Pingate Dr SK8 ......35 A6
Pingate La SK8 ......35 A6
Pingate La S SK8 ......35 A6
Pingot Croft CH3 ......142 B7
Pingot Rd SK22 ......39 D8
Pinmill Brow WA6 ......74 B7
Pinmill Cl WA6 ......74 C7
Pinners Brow WA2 ......16 B6
Pinners Brow Ret Pk WA2 ......16 B6
Pinners Fold WA7 ......24 B1
Pinsley Green Rd CW5 ......216 E2
Pinsley View CW5 ......216 E4
Pintail Pl CW7 ......149 D6
Pinwood Ct SK9 ......34 E1
Piper's Cl CH60 ......40 D8
Piper's End CH60 ......40 D8
Piper's La CH60 ......40 D8
Pipers Ash CW7 ......126 A1
Pipers Ct CH2 ......119 B4
Pipers La Chester CH2 ......119 B4
  Puddington CH64 ......93 A8
Pipers The Golborne WA3 ......3 F8
  Heswall CH60 ......40 D8
Pipit Ave WA12 ......2 C3
Pipit La WA3 ......9 E3
Pippin Cl CW10 ......151 C7
Pippits Row WA7 ......49 E4
Pirie Cl CW12 ......157 A4
Pirie Rd CW12 ......157 A4
Pit La Hough CW2 ......206 E2
  Talke ST7 ......210 C6
  Widnes WA8 ......13 A4
Pitcher La CW11 ......177 A8
Pitt La SK11 ......132 B8
Pitt St Macclesfield SK11 ......112 D6
  Warrington WA5 ......15 F7
  Widnes WA8 ......23 A5
Pitts Cl CH3 ......121 C2
Pitts Heath La WA7 ......24 E3
Pitville Terr WA8 ......22 C7
Plaistow Ct WA7 ......49 E7
Plane Gr ST5 ......210 E1
Plane Tree Dr CW1 ......190 E6
Plane Tree Gr WA1 ......2 A7
Plane Tree Rd M31 ......11 D3
Plant La CW11 ......174 B7
Plant St WA1 ......175 A7
Plantagenet Cl [3] CW7 ......149 D6
Plantation Cl WA7 ......24 A1
Plantation Dr CH66 ......69 E7
Plas Dinas CH1 ......117 D3
Plas Newton La CH2 ......118 F5
Plas Newydd CH4 ......161 B6
Platt Ave CW11 ......175 A7
Platt's La CH3 ......164 E5
Platts La Christleton CH3 ......143 D8
  Duddon CH3,CW6 ......144 E7
  Tarvin CH3 ......121 B2
  Tarvin, Broom Bank CH3 ......144 B8
  Tattenhall CH3 ......183 F7
Platts St WA11 ......1 A6
Pleasance Way WA12 ......2 D4
Pleasant St
  Macclesfield SK10 ......87 F1
  Northwich CW9 ......103 E2
Pleasant View SK10 ......111 C8
Pleasant Way SK8 ......35 C6
Pleck Rd CH65 ......70 A2
Plemstall Cl CH2 ......119 F8
Plemstall La CH2 ......97 A1
Plemstall Way CH2 ......96 F1
Plemston Ct CH66 ......69 F8
Plex The ST7 ......193 D4
Plinston Ave WA4 ......16 F4
Plough Croft ST3 ......193 A3
Plough Inn Pk The CW8 ......125 E5
Plough La CH3 ......143 B7
Ploughmans Cl CH66 ......94 E8
Ploughmans Way
  Ellesmere Port CH66 ......94 E8
  Macclesfield SK10 ......87 B3
Plover Ave CW7 ......149 D5
Plover Cl Farndon CH3 ......180 F1
  Newton-le-W WA12 ......2 C3
Plover Dr WA7 ......50 D8
Plover Way WA3 ......3 E8
Plovers La WA6 ......73 C5
Plum Terr CH1 ......237 A3
Plumbs Fold WA8 ......78 A2
Plumley Cl Chester CH3 ......119 C1
  [16] Macclesfield SK11 ......112 E7
Plumley Gdns WA8 ......12 A1
Plumley Moor Rd WA16 ......81 C2
Plumley Rd SK9 ......34 E5
Plumley Sta WA16 ......81 A3
Plumpstons La WA8 ......49 B1
Plumpton Cross [6] WA8 ......13 B2
Plumtre Ave WA5 ......15 F8
Plymouth Cl WA7 ......50 E6
Plymouth Dr SK7 ......35 F7
Plymyard Ave CH62 ......43 D5
Plymyard Cl CH62 ......43 D5
Poachers' La WA4 ......16 F3
Pochard Ave CW7 ......149 D6
Pochard Dr SK12 ......36 A4
Pochard Rise WA7 ......50 D8
Pochin Way CW10 ......128 E1
Pocket Nook La WA3 ......4 B7
Pocklington Ct WA2 ......8 F1
Polden Cl CH66 ......69 A6
Pole La CW9 ......53 E2
Pole Lane Ends CW9 ......53 C4
Poleacre Dr WA8 ......12 C2
Pollard Ave WA6 ......74 D7

Pollard Dr CW5 ......205 B4
Polperro Cl
  Macclesfield SK10 ......86 D1
  Warrington WA5 ......14 E3
Pond Cotts CH2 ......72 A3
Pond St WA3 ......4 A8
Pond View Cl CH60 ......41 C8
Pond Wlk WA9 ......1 A1
Pool Bank Bsns Pk CH3 ......121 C3
Pool Bank Cotts CH3 ......121 C3
Pool End Cl SK10 ......87 D4
Pool End Rd SK10 ......87 D4
Pool Hall Ind Est CH65, CH66 ......70 A8
Pool House Rd SK12 ......37 D5
Pool La Cuddington CW8 ......102 B2
  Haslington CW11 ......192 A7
  Ince CH2 ......71 F4
  Lymm WA13 ......18 B4
  Runcorn WA7 ......23 B3
  Tarvin CH3 ......121 C4
  Warrington WA4 ......16 A1
Pool Meadows Rd CW1 ......191 B4
Pool Rd WA3 ......11 A3
Pool Side ST7 ......194 E6
Pool St Macclesfield SK11 ......112 E6
  Widnes WA8 ......23 B7
Pool View CW11 ......191 F7
Poole Ave WA2 ......8 B2
Poole Cres WA2 ......8 B2
Poole Hall La CH66 ......69 E8
Poole Hall Rd CH66 ......69 E8
Poole Hill Rd CW5 ......188 A2
Poole La CW7 ......71 E2
Poole Old Hall La CW5 ......188 D4
Poolford La CW4 ......129 C2
Pools La CW11 ......177 A6
Pools Platt La CW9 ......53 E6
Poolside Ct ST7 ......193 E4
Poolside Rd WA7 ......23 B1
Pooltown Rd CH65 ......69 F5
Poplar Ave Culcheth WA3 ......4 F3
  Moulton CW9 ......126 E4
  Newton-le-W WA12 ......2 D3
  Runcorn WA7 ......49 C7
  Warrington WA5 ......14 E3
  Wilmslow SK9 ......59 F5
Poplar Cl
  Congleton CW12 ......156 A4
  Cuddington CW8 ......102 A3
  Ellesmere Port CH65 ......70 B4
  Runcorn WA7 ......49 C7
  Winsford CW7 ......149 B8
Poplar Dr Alsager ST7 ......193 E2
  Kidsgrove ST7 ......195 A1
  Middlewich CW10 ......151 D7
Poplar Gr Bollington SK10 ......88 A8
  Crewe CW1 ......190 E5
  Elton CH2 ......72 A3
  Haydock WA11 ......1 C6
  Irlam M44 ......11 D6
Poplar La TF9 ......236 F5
Poplar Rd Chester CH4 ......140 F5
  Haydock WA11 ......1 C6
  Macclesfield SK11 ......112 D6
  Weaverham CW8 ......102 D8
Poplar View WA4 ......25 A7
Poplar Way SK6 ......38 A7
Poplar Weint [2] CH64 ......66 E8
Poplar Wlk M31 ......11 D3
Poplars Ave
  Warrington,Hulme WA2 ......8 C3
  Warrington,Winwick Quay WA2 ......8 D2
Poplars Pl WA2 ......8 D2
Poplars The
  Golborne,Wash End WN7 ......4 C8
  Lymm WA13 ......18 D4
  Wistaston CW2 ......205 F7
Poppyfields ST7 ......193 B3
Porlock Cl Heswall CH60 ......41 B6
  Warrington WA5 ......14 E4
Port Arcs The CH65 ......70 C5
Porter Ave WA12 ......2 C5
Porter Dr CW9 ......104 C6
Porter St WA7 ......23 C2
Porter Way CW9 ......104 C6
Porters Croft CH3 ......119 F5
Portford Cl SK10 ......86 F1
Porthcawl Cl WA8 ......12 C2
Porthleven Rd WA7 ......50 B5
Portland Dr
  Biddulph ST8 ......179 D2
  Scholar Green ST7 ......194 E6
Portland Gr CW1 ......191 D5
Portland Pl WA6 ......73 C4
Portland St
  Newton-le-W WA12 ......1 F4
  Runcorn WA7 ......23 A3
Portland Wlk [4] SK11 ......111 F7
Portloe Rd SK8 ......34 B7
Portman Pl [3] CW7 ......149 A8
Portmarnock Cl SK10 ......87 B3
Portola Cl WA4 ......17 C2
Portree Ave CH63 ......43 D5
Portree Dr CW4 ......130 B2
Portrush Cl
  Macclesfield SK10 ......87 C4
  Widnes WA8 ......12 C2
Portside WA7 ......50 E7
Portside Bsns Pk CH65 ......70 B8
Portsmouth Pl WA4 ......50 E6
Portway M22 ......33 D8
Post Office La
  Betley CW2 ......207 F1
  Hampton Heath SY14 ......213 D3
  Norley WA6 ......100 E5
  Runcorn WA7 ......48 D7

Post Office Pl [1] CW9 ......79 A1
Postles St ST7 ......193 F6
Pott Shrigley Church Sch SK10 ......63 C3
Potter Cl CW5 ......205 D4
Potters Barn The* CW11 ......176 A1
Potters End ST8 ......179 C1
Potters La WA8 ......21 F5
Poulton Cres WA1 ......17 D8
Poulton Dr WA8 ......22 D8
Poulton Hall Rd CH63 ......43 A7
Poulton Rd CH63 ......43 A8
Pound Rd CH66 ......69 C7
Povey Rd WA2 ......8 D1
Powell Ave WA3 ......9 E4
Powell St WA4 ......16 F3
Powell's Orch CH4 ......141 C7
Powey La CH1 ......94 B5
Pownall Ave CW5 ......205 A6
Pownall Ct SK9 ......59 E8
Pownall Green Prim Sch SK7 ......35 E7
Pownall Hall Sch SK9 ......59 F8
Pownall Rd SK9 ......59 F8
Pownall Sq SK11 ......112 C8
Pownall St SK10 ......87 D1
Powy Dr ST7 ......195 B2
Powys Ct CH1 ......237 A3
Powys St WA5 ......15 F5
Poynton Cl WA4 ......17 B3
Poynton High Sch SK12 ......36 F2
Poynton Ind Est SK12 ......36 D1
Poynton St [15] SK10 ......112 C8
Poynton Sta SK12 ......36 C8
Pratchitts Row CW5 ......204 E5
Precinct The CW2 ......189 F2
Preece Cl WA8 ......12 D4
Preece Ct CW5 ......190 B5
Preesall Ave SK8 ......34 B8
Prenton Pl CH4 ......141 E7
Prescot Rd WA8 ......12 D2
Prescot St CH2 ......118 F3
Prescott Rd SK9 ......34 B1
Prescott St WA4 ......16 E3
Prestbury CE Prim Sch SK10 ......86 F7
Prestbury Cl [8] Northwich CW9 ......103 F4
  Widnes WA8 ......22 E8
Prestbury Ct SK10 ......86 F6
Prestbury Dr WA4 ......17 D4
Prestbury La SK10 ......87 B7
Prestbury Pk SK10 ......86 E6
Prestbury Rd
  Adder's Moss SK10 ......85 F6
  Macclesfield SK10 ......87 B1
  Nether Alderley SK10 ......86 A5
  Wilmslow SK9 ......60 E5
Prestbury Sta SK10 ......87 A7
Preston Ave M44 ......11 F7
Preston St W SK11 ......112 B6
Prestwich Ave WA3 ......4 E3
Prestwich Cl
  Macclesfield SK10 ......87 C5
  Widnes WA8 ......12 F3
  Winsford CW7 ......126 C2
Prestwood Ct WA3 ......10 A7
Pretoria St CH4 ......141 D7
Price Ave CW11 ......175 A5
Price Dr CW11 ......175 A5
Price Gr WA9 ......1 A2
Pride Cl WA12 ......2 E2
Priest La SK10 ......61 B1
Priestfield Rd CH65 ......70 C5
Priestley Bsns Ctr WA5 ......15 F5
Priestley Coll WA4 ......16 C3
Priestley St WA5 ......15 F5
Priestly Ct [13] CW5 ......204 E5
Priestner Dr WA6 ......73 B4
Priestway La CH64 ......67 E1
Priesty Ct CW12 ......156 D2
Priesty Fields CW12 ......156 D2
Primary Cl M44 ......11 D5
Primitive St ST7 ......195 C4
Primrose Ave
  Haslington CW1 ......191 C5
  Macclesfield SK11 ......112 B5
Primrose Chase CW4 ......130 D8
Primrose Cl
  Huntington CH3 ......142 A6
  Runcorn WA7 ......50 A8
  Warrington WA2 ......8 D2
  Widnes WA8 ......12 E1
Primrose Gr WA11 ......1 E7
Primrose Hill
  Crewe CW2 ......189 E5
  Cuddington CW8 ......101 F4
  Kelsall CW6 ......122 C6
Primrose La WA6 ......73 B1
Primula Cl WA9 ......6 A7
Primula Dr WA3 ......3 D8
Prince Albert St CW1 ......190 D4
Prince Edward St CW5 ......204 E6
Prince Henry Sq [4] WA1 ......16 B5
Prince Rd SK12 ......37 C5
Prince William Ave CH5 ......116 B3
Prince's St WA8 ......23 A8
Princes Ave
  Bebington CH62 ......43 E6
  Chester CH1 ......237 C3
  Northwich CW9 ......104 B8
Princes Cl WA7 ......23 F1
Princes Ct CW5 ......204 E7
Princes Pk CW8 ......78 A2
Princes Pl WA8 ......12 E1
Princes Rd CH65 ......70 B6
Princes St WA12 ......2 B3

Princes Way SK11 ......111 F7
Princess Ave Audley ST7 ......209 D1
  Haydock WA11 ......2 A7
  Warrington,Great Sankey WA5 ......14 E7
  Warrington,Padgate WA1 ......17 A3
Princess Cl CW2 ......205 F8
Princess Cres
  Middlewich CW10 ......151 D6
  Warrington WA1 ......16 F6
Princess Ct ST7 ......210 E1
Princess Dr
  Bollington SK10 ......87 E7
  Nantwich CW5 ......205 A6
  Sandbach CW11 ......175 A7
  Wistaston CW2 ......205 E8
Princess Gr CW2 ......205 F8
Princess Rd
  Allostock WA16 ......106 E3
  Lymm WA13 ......18 C3
  Wilmslow SK9 ......59 F5
Princess St
  Bollington SK10 ......87 E7
  Chester CH1 ......237 A2
  Congleton CW12 ......156 D3
  Crewe CW1 ......190 C6
  Knutsford WA16 ......57 A2
  Northwich CW9 ......79 E2
  [13] Runcorn WA7 ......23 A3
  Talke ST7 ......210 D5
  Warrington WA5 ......15 D4
  Winsford CW7 ......127 A2
Princess Wlk SK7 ......36 A7
Princeway WA6 ......74 B8
Prior Cl CW2 ......189 F1
Priory Ave CW9 ......103 F4
Priory Cl Chester CH2 ......118 C4
  Congleton CW12 ......179 B7
  Crewe CW1 ......190 B8
Priory Ct SK10 ......86 F1
Priory Dr SK10 ......86 F2
Priory La SK10 ......86 F2
Priory Pl Chester CH1 ......237 B2
  Kidsgrove ST7 ......195 B3
Priory Rd Altrincham WA14 ......31 B8
  Runcorn WA7 ......24 C2
  Wilmslow SK9 ......59 E8
Priory St Altrincham WA14 ......31 C8
  Northwich CW9 ......104 A3
  Warrington WA4 ......16 B3
Priory The Neston CH64 ......41 E1
  Winwick WA2 ......8 A7
Priory Way CW8 ......103 B8
Priscilla St CW1 ......190 E4
Pritchard Dr CW9 ......103 E2
Private Wlk CH3 ......142 A8
Probert Cl CW2 ......190 A4
Proctors Cl WA8 ......13 D2
Proctors La CW11 ......174 E5
Proffits La WA6 ......73 E4
Promenade Cvn Pk WA4 ......25 E7
Promised Land La CH3 ......142 E5
Prospect Ave M44 ......11 E6
Prospect Dr
  Altrincham WA15 ......32 D8
  Davenham CW9 ......103 E2
Prospect La WA3 ......10 C3
Prospect Rd M44 ......11 E6
Prospect Row WA7 ......48 F7
Prospect St CW12 ......156 C2
Prosperity Way CW10 ......128 D1
Prosser Rd CH2 ......95 C1
Protector Way M44 ......11 F8
Provan Way CH1 ......117 D5
Provident St WA9 ......1 A3
Prunus Rd CW1 ......190 E6
Pryors The CH3 ......121 C3
Ptarmigan Pl CW7 ......149 D5
Public Hall St [18] WA7 ......23 A3
Pudding La CW6 ......168 A7
Puddington La CH64 ......92 E8
Puddle Bank La CW12 ......178 F5
Puffin Ave SK12 ......36 B4
Puffin Cl CH65 ......95 C8
Pulford Cl
  Northwich CW9 ......103 E4
  Runcorn WA7 ......49 E6
Pulford Ct CH4 ......162 D2
Pulford La CH4 ......162 A6
Pulford Rd Blacon CH1 ......117 D5
  Ellesmere Port CH65 ......69 C4
  Winsford CW7 ......126 C1
Pullman Cl CH60 ......41 D8
Pullman Dr CW9 ......104 C8
Pump Ct ST7 ......209 D2
Pump La Churton CH3 ......181 A5
  Runcorn WA7 ......49 F8
  Tattenhall CH3 ......182 C6
Pumptree Mews SK11 ......111 F7
Purdy Cl WA3 ......7 D1
Puritan Bldgs WA7 ......23 C2
Purley Dr M44 ......11 C5
Purser Rd SY14 ......211 E4
Puss Bank Sch SK10 ......112 F8
Putney Ct WA7 ......49 F7
Pye Cl WA11 ......2 B8
Pye Rd CH60 ......41 A8
Pyecroft Cl WA5 ......14 D6
Pyecroft Rd WA5 ......14 D6
Pyecroft St CH4 ......141 D7
Pym's La CW1 ......189 E6
Pyrus Ave CW1 ......190 E6
Pyrus Gr WA6 ......73 C4
Pytcheley Hollow WA6 ......100 F6

Q

Quad The CH1 ......117 E2
Quadrant Cl WA7 ......50 D6
Quadrant The
  Chester CH1 ......117 E2
  Warrington WA3 ......9 F5
Quail Cl WA2 ......8 D3
Quaintways CW8 ......103 C4
Quakers Coppice CW1 ......191 A2
Quakers Way LL13 ......180 E1
Quantock Cl
  Ellesmere Port CH66 ......69 A6
  Winsford CW7 ......149 A7
Quarry Ave WA3 ......180 F1
Quarry Bank CW6 ......146 C8
Quarry Bank Cotts CW6 ......184 F5
Quarry Bank Mill* SK9 ......33 F2
Quarry Bank Rd SK9 ......33 F3
Quarry Bank Rise CW7 ......149 B8
Quarry Cl Chester CH3 ......141 C7
  Runcorn WA7 ......49 F8
Quarry Ct Farndon CH3 ......180 D1
  Widnes WA8 ......12 C1
Quarry Hill CH3 ......180 F1
Quarry La
  Christleton CH3 ......142 E7
  Kelsall CW6 ......122 D5
  Warrington WA4 ......26 C6
Quarry Rd Neston CH64 ......42 C1
  New Mills SK22 ......39 D7
Quarry Terr ST7 ......195 A1
Quarrybank CW6 ......184 F6
Quay Fold WA5 ......15 F4
Quay Pl WA7 ......50 E7
Quay Side WA6 ......49 D1
Quay The WA6 ......49 D2
Quayle Cl WA11 ......1 C6
Quayside
  Congleton CW12 ......156 E1
  Neston CH64 ......66 E5
Quayside Mews WA13 ......18 F3
Quayside Way SK11 ......112 E7
Queastybirch La WA4 ......26 A1
Quebec Rd WA2 ......16 D7
Queen Anne Ct SK9 ......60 C6
Queen Annes Ct [5] SK11 ......112 B6
Queen Elizabeth Ho CW9 ......79 A1
Queen St Audley ST7 ......209 C1
  Bollington SK10 ......88 B8
  Bunbury CW6 ......185 E8
  Chester CH1 ......237 B2
  Congleton CW12 ......156 C2
  Congleton, Buglawton CW12 ......156 F4
  Crewe CW1 ......190 E5
  Ellesmere Port CH65 ......70 C7
  Golborne WA3 ......3 B8
  Kidsgrove ST7 ......195 A2
  Knutsford WA16 ......56 F2
  Macclesfield SK10 ......112 D8
  Middlewich CW10 ......128 C1
  Nantwich CW5 ......204 E5
  Newton-le-W WA12 ......2 B3
  Northwich CW9 ......103 F7
  [8] Runcorn WA7 ......23 A3
  Shavington CW2 ......206 C4
Queen Victoria St [14] SK11 ......112 D8
Queen's Ave CH1 ......237 C3
Queen's Ave CH5 ......91 D1
Queen's Ave Glazebury WA3 ......5 C7
  Macclesfield SK10 ......87 E2
  Sandycroft CH5 ......116 A3
  Widnes WA8 ......22 B8
Queen's Cl
  Macclesfield SK10 ......87 E2
  Runcorn WA7 ......22 F1
Queen's Cres CW1 ......172 E2
Queen's Dr Chester CH4 ......237 C1
  Middlewich CW10 ......151 D7
  Nantwich CW5 ......204 D4
  Sandbach CW11 ......175 A8
Queen's Par [1] CW7 ......126 D1
Queen's Park Dr CW7 ......189 F3
Queen's Park Gdns CW2 ......189 E4
Queen's Park Ho CH4 ......237 B1
Queen's Park Rd CH4 ......237 B1
Queen's Park View CH4 ......237 B1
Queen's Rd Chester CH1 ......237 C3
  Runcorn WA7 ......22 F1
  Wilmslow SK9 ......60 A6
Queen's Sch (Lower) CH2 ......118 C4
Queen's Sch The CH1 ......237 A2
Queen's Way CH4 ......139 B4
Queens Ave
  Ellesmere Port CH65 ......70 A3
  Warrington WA1 ......16 E7
Queens Cl SK10 ......87 E6
Queens Cres
  Chester CH2 ......118 E7
  Warrington WA1 ......17 A8
Queens Ct CW7 ......126 D1
Queens Dr Golborne WA3 ......3 C8
  Helsby WA6 ......73 B3
  Heswall CH60 ......40 E8
  Newton-le-W WA12 ......2 C5
  Warrington WA4 ......17 A2

Queens Gdns
Ellesmere Port CH65 .....70 B5
Talke ST7 ....210 D5
Queens Park High Sch
CH4 ....237 B1
Queens Pl CH1 ......237 B3
Queens Rd Chester CH3 .119 B3
Ellesmere Port CH66 ....69 C7
Haydock WA11 ....2 A7
Queens Terr SK9 ......34 D3
Queensbury Cl
16 Handforth SK9 .....34 C1
Wilmslow SK9 ....60 D8
Queensbury Way WA8 ..12 E3
Queensgate Bramhall SK7 .35 E5
Northwich CW8 ....103 E8
Queensgate Prim Sch
SK7 ....35 E4
Queensway Alsager ST7 .193 B5
Chester CH2 ....118 F5
Crewe CW1 ....190 C4
Frodsham WA6 ....74 B8
Heald Green SK8 ......34 C8
Heswall CH60 ....41 C6
Knutsford WA16 ....56 E3
Partington M31 ....11 F4
Poynton SK12 ....36 D3
Runcorn WA7 ....22 F3
Widnes WA8 ....22 F6
Winsford CW7 ....149 D8
Queensway Trad Est
WA8 ....23 A5
Quill Ct M44 ....11 E6
Quillet The CH64 .....66 F7
Quinn St WA8 ....23 B7
Quinta Prim Sch The
CW12 ....156 A2
Quinta Rd CW12 ......156 A3

R

Raby Ave CH63 ....43 B6
Raby Cl Bebington CH63 .43 A7
Heswall CH60 ....40 F7
Widnes WA8 ....13 E2
Raby Ct CH65 ....70 D3
Raby Dr CH63 ....43 A6
Raby Gdns CH64 ....66 E8
Raby Hall Rd CH63 ....43 A6
Raby Mere Rd CH63 ...42 D5
Raby Park Cl CH64 ....66 E8
Raby Park Rd CH64 ....41 F1
Raby Rd Neston CH64 ..66 E8
Thornton Hough CH63 ..42 B5
Race The SK9 ....34 D2
Racecourse La CW6 ...124 A1
Racecourse Pk SK9 ....59 F6
Racecourse Rd SK9 ....59 E6
Racefield Cl WA13 ....18 F3
Racefield Rd WA16 ....56 F2
Radbroke Cl CW11 ....175 D8
Radcliffe Ave WA3 .....4 E3
Radcliffe Ct CH3 .....121 C3
Radcliffe Rd
Sandbach CW11 ....174 F3
Sutton Lane Ends SK11 .135 D7
Raddel La WA4 ....52 C5
Raddle Wharf CH65 ....70 C7
Raddon Pl WA4 ....16 E1
Radford Cl WA8 ....22 C7
Radlett Cl WA5 ....14 E3
Radley Dr CH63 ....41 F6
Radley La WA2 ....8 E4
Radnor Cl
Congleton CW12 ......156 B3
Sandbach CW11 ......174 E7
Widnes WA8 ....12 D2
Radnor Dr Chester CH4 .141 A4
Widnes WA8 ....12 D2
Radnor Park Ind Ctr
CW12 ....156 A4
Radnor Park Trad Est
CW12 ....156 A4
Radnor St WA5 ....15 E6
Radway Gn CH66 ......69 E5
Radway Green Bsns & Tech
Ctr CW2 ....192 F1
Radway Green Rd
Alsager CW2 ....208 E8
Barthomley CW2 .....208 D6
Raeburn Ave
Bebington CH62 ......43 E6
Neston CH64 ....66 F7
Raeburn Prim Sch CH62 .43 D6
Raglan Cl WA3 ....9 F6
Raglan Rd SK10 ....87 F2
Ragley Cl SK12 ....36 F4
Railbrook Ct CW2 ....190 D2
Railton Ave CW1 .....190 A7
Railway Age Mus The★
CW1 ....190 D3
Railway Cotts
Congleton CW12 ......157 A1
Hollinfare WA3 ....11 B5
Hooton CH66 ....43 D1
Wimboldsley CW10 ...150 F1
Railway St Crewe CW2 .190 D2
Newton-le-W WA12 .....2 B3
Railway Terr Disley SK12 .38 D6
Sandycroft CH5 ......116 B3
Railway View WA5 .....1 D1
Rainbow Cl WA8 ......12 C3
Rainbow St CW1 .....190 D4
Rainford Cl ST7 .....195 F1
Rainow Cl CW10 .....151 B7

Rainow Dr SK12 ....37 A2
Rainow Prim Sch SK10 .88 D4
Rainow Rd SK10 ....88 B2
Rainow View SK10 .....63 C1
Rainow Way 10 SK9 ....34 E1
Rajar Cotts WA16 .....57 F4
Rake House Mews WA6 .73 B4
Rake La Backford CH2 ..95 D6
Broughton CH5 ......139 A8
Christleton CH3 ......143 A7
Dunham-on-t-H WA6 ...97 B7
Dunham-on-t-H WA6 ...97 E7
Eccleston CH4 ....141 C1
Helsby WA6 ....73 C4
Helsby, Helsby Marsh WA6 .73 A5
Rake The Bebington CH62 .43 C8
Burton CH64 ....67 D1
Rake Way CH1 ....94 A1
Raleigh Cl WA5 ....7 D1
Raleigh Rd CH64 ......41 F1
Ramp Rd E M90 ....33 C7
Ramp Rd S M90 ....33 C7
Ramp Rd W M90 ....33 B7
Rampit Cl WA11 ....1 F7
Ramsay Cl WA3 ....9 E3
Ramsbottom St CW1 ..190 B5
Ramsbrook La L24,WA8 .21 C3
Ramsdale Rd SK7 .....35 E8
Ramsden Ct CH4 .....140 F4
Ramsey Cl WA8 ....13 E3
Ramsey Rd CH65 ......70 C1
Ramsfield Rd L24 .....21 A4
Randal Cres SK23 .....65 E5
Randall Cl WA12 ......2 B4
Randle Bennett Cl
CW11 ....174 E7
Randle Mdw CH66 .....69 F1
Randle Meadow Ct CH66 .69 F2
Randle's View CW12 ..179 C8
Range Ct SK10 ....87 E1
Rangemoor Cl WA3 ...10 A6
Rannoch Ct CH66 .....69 F3
Ranulph Ct WA6 ......74 C7
Ranwonath Ct CH2 ...237 B4
Ranworth Dr WA3 ......3 E7
Ranworth Rd WA5 ....14 E6
Rappax Rd WA15 ......32 A8
Raquets Ct The CW10 .127 C4
Rathbone Pk CW6 ....146 D2
Rathlin Cl WA3 ....13 E3
Rathmell Cl WA3 ......4 E3
Rathvale Dr M22 ......33 C8
Raven Cl CW11 ....175 A8
Raven Cotts TF9 .....235 A5
Raven's La ST7 ......209 F3
Ravenbank Com Prim Sch
WA13 ....18 F3
Ravendale Cl CW7 ...149 E8
Ravenfield Dr WA8 ...12 C3
Ravenho La SK10 ......88 D4
Ravenhurst Ct WA3 ....9 F5
Ravenoak Park Rd SK8 .35 B8
Ravenoak Rd SK8 .....35 B8
Ravens Cl ST7 ....209 E3
Ravens Cnr WA5 .....203 E2
Ravens La CW5 ......203 E5
Ravenscar Cres M22 ..33 D8
Ravenscliffe Rd ST7 .195 A1
Ravenscroft WA4 .....130 A3
Ravenscroft Ct CW11 .175 C7
Ravenscroft Rd CW2 .189 E3
Ravensdale Cl WA2 ....8 D3
Ravensfield CW8 .....101 D4
Ravensholme Ct CH3 .166 A2
Ravensholme La CH3 .166 A2
Ravensmead Com Prim Sch
ST7 ....209 E3
Ravenswood CW8 ....103 B4
Ravenswood Dr SK8 ..35 B8
Ravenswood Rd SK9 ..59 E4
Ravenwood Dr WA15 ..32 D7
Rawcliffe Cl WA8 .....12 F4
Rawdon Cl WA7 ....50 A7
Rawlings Cl WA3 ......9 F3
Rawlinson Cres L26 ..21 B8
Rawson Rd CH1 ......117 E3
Ray Ave CW5 ....204 F7
Rayleigh Ave CW4 ...127 A8
Rayleigh Way SK10 ...86 E1
Raymond Ave WA4 ....16 D2
Raymond St CH1 .....237 A3
Raymond Way CH64 ...67 A7
Rays Brow CW8 ....78 B2
Reade's La CW12 ....179 D8
Readesdale Ave CW2 .189 F2
Reading Room La SY14,
CH3 ....199 D8
Rean Mdw CH3 ......166 B2
Reaper Cl WA5 ....11 D6
Reaseheath Coll CW5 .188 D1
Reay St WA8 ....13 C2
Record Bsns Pk WA2 ..16 A8
Rectory Ave WA3 ......3 C8
Rectory Cl Farndon CH3 .180 E1
Heswall CH60 ....40 F7
8 Nantwich CW5 .....204 E5
Winwick WA2 ....8 A6
Wistaston CW2 ......205 E8
Rectory Gdns Lymm WA13 .18 F3
Talke ST7 ....210 D6
Rectory La Adderley TF9 .235 B5
Capenhurst CH1 ....94 A8
Heswall CH60 ....40 E7
Lymm WA13 ....18 F3
Winwick WA2 ....8 A6
Rectory View ST7 ....210 D6
Red Bank Ave WA12 ...2 F1
Red Brow La WA7,WA4 .50 F8

Red Cow Yd 10 WA16 ..57 A2
Red Gables WA4 ......27 B3
Red Ho SK10 ....87 E1
Red House La WA14 ...20 C8
Red La Disley SK12 ...38 C5
Frodsham WA6 ....74 C7
Huxley CH3 ....166 D6
Lower Whitley WA4 ....52 C1
Sandbach CW11 ......174 C6
Warrington WA4 ......26 C7
Red Lion Cl ST7 .....210 D7
Red Lion La
Ellesmere Port CH66 ..69 C7
Nantwich CW5 ....204 D5
Red Lodge SK12 ......38 A6
Red Pike CH66 ....69 D8
Red Row SK12 ....37 B8
Red Stone Hill WA6 ..73 C4
Redacre SK12 ....36 F6
Redacre Cl WA4 ......51 A3
Redbourne Dr
Chorlton CW2 ....207 D1
Widnes WA8 ....12 B4
Redbrook Cl CH62 ....43 D6
Redbrook Gr 2 SK9 ..34 D1
Redbrook Rd M31 ....11 E2
Redbrook Way SK10 ..62 C5
Redcar Dr CH62 ......43 D5
Reddish Ave CW12 ...156 F4
Reddish Cres WA13 ...18 F4
Reddish La Lymm WA13 .19 A3
Whaley Bridge SK23 ..65 D6
Reddish Rd SK23 .....65 D6
Reddy La
Little Bollington WA14 .20 B1
Rostherne WA14 ......30 B8
Redesdale Cl WA2 .....8 E2
Redesmere Cl
Macclesfield SK10 ....87 A1
Northwich CW9 ......104 A5
Sandbach CW11 ......174 F7
Redesmere Dr SK9 ...60 A1
Redesmere La SK11 ..110 B3
Redesmere Rd SK9 ...34 D5
Redfern Ave CW12 ...156 F4
Redgate CW8 ....103 D7
Redhill Mews CH65 ...70 B6
Redhill Rd Chester CH4 .140 F6
Kelsall CW6 ....122 C5
Redhouse La SK12 ....38 E7
Redhouses SK11 .....113 D3
Redland Cl CH4 ......141 B4
Redland Ho CH4 .....141 B7
Redmain Gr WA3 ......3 E8
Redmayne Cl WA12 ....2 B4
Redmere Dr CH60 ....41 D8
Redmoor La Disley SK12 .39 A4
New Mills SK22 ......39 B6
Redpoll La WA3 ....9 E4
Redrock Cres ST7 ...195 C1
Redruth Ave SK8 .....86 E1
Redruth Cl WA7 ......50 C6
Redshank Ave CW7 ..149 C5
Redshank Cl WA12 ....2 C4
Redshank Dr SK10 ....87 C5
Redshank La WA3 .....9 E4
Redshaw Cl WA10 ...151 C6
Redstart Cl 7 WA3 ...3 E8
Redstone Dr 3 CW7 .126 A1
Redtail Cl WA7 ....22 F3
Redvales Ct WA3 ......9 C4
Redvers Ave CH66 ...44 A2
Redway La SK10 ......88 B7
Redwing Cl ST7 .....195 F1
Redwood Cl Barnton CW8 .78 B4
Holt LL13 ....196 D8
Saltney CH4 ....140 E6
Warrington WA1 ......17 E7
Redwood Cl SK10 ....87 E5
Redwood Dr Crewe CW1 .189 F7
Ellesmere Port CH66 ..69 F1
Elton CH2 ....72 C4
Reece Cl CH2 ....119 E8
Reed La CW9 ....53 C6
Reedgate La CW9 .....27 F1
Reedsmere Cl WA4 ...16 E2
Reedsmere Wlk CW9 ..78 D8
Reeman Ct SK9 ....34 B2
Rees Cres CW4 ......130 C3
Reeve St WA3 ....4 B8
Reeves Rd CH3 ......142 B8
Regal Cl
Ellesmere Port CH66 ..69 E3
Northwich CW9 ......103 E4
Regal Cres WA8 ......22 B8
Regency Cl ST7 .....210 D5
Regency Ct Chester CH2 .119 E8
Winsford CW7 ....149 C7
Regency Gdns SK8 ...34 E8
Regency Hospl SK11 .112 E8
Regency Pk SK9 ......59 F5
Regency Way CW9 ...103 E4
Regent & Foundry Ct 19
SK11 ....112 C8
Regent Ave Haydock WA11 .1 B7
Macclesfield SK11 ...112 B6
Warrington WA1 ......17 A8
Regent Bank SK9 .....59 F5
Regent Cl Bramhall SK7 .35 D4
Shavington CW2 .....206 B3
Wilmslow SK9 ....59 F5
Regent Ct WA15 ......32 C8
Regent Rd WA8 ....13 B1
Regent St
Ellesmere Port CH65 ..70 A5
Moulton CW9 ....126 F8
Newton-le-W WA12 ....2 A3
12 Runcorn WA7 .....23 A3

Regent St continued
Warrington WA4 ......16 A5
Regents Cl CH3 .....119 B2
Regents Gate CW5 ...205 A5
Regents The SK9 .....60 C8
Regents Theological Coll
CW5 ....205 A5
Regents Way 4 CW7 .149 A8
Reginald Mitchell Prim Sch
The ST7 ....194 D1
Registry CW9 ....103 E4
Reid Ave WA5 ....15 F8
Reid Ct CH66 ....69 C7
Reid St CW1 ....190 C6
Reins Croft CH64 .....41 E1
Rembury Pl WA4 .....51 A3
Remer St CW1 ......190 D7
Renaissance Ct CW1 .191 A4
Renaissance Way CW1 .191 A3
Rendel Cl WA12 ....2 D2
Rendlesham Cl WA3 ..10 B6
Renfrew Ave CH62 ...43 E5
Renfrew Cl SK10 ....86 F2
Renown Cl WA3 ....9 D4
Renshaw Rd CW9 .....79 D2
Rensherds Pl WA16 ..29 C5
Renton Ave WA7 .....23 D2
Repton Ave WA16 ....29 C4
Repton Dr CW1 .....191 D5
Repton Rd CH65 .....70 D4
Reservoir Rd SK23 ...65 D6
Reservoir Terr CH2 ..118 F2
Retreat The CW1 ....190 C6
Revesby Cl WA8 ......12 D2
Rex Bldgs SK9 ....60 B6
Reynold's La CW11 ..175 F6
Reynolds Ave
St Helens WA9 ....1 B1
Warrington WA3 ....9 E5
Reynolds Mews SK9 ..60 E8
Reynolds St WA4 ....16 F3
Rhoden St CW1 .....191 A6
Rhodes Cl CW1 .....191 D4
Rhodes St WA2 ......16 C7
Rhodesway CH60 .....41 B7
Rhona Cl CW3 ....43 C4
Rhona Dr WA5 ....14 E6
Rhone Ct CH3 ....142 A8
Rhuddlan Ct CH65 ...70 D2
Rhuddlan Ct/Llys Rhuddlan
5 CH4 ....140 F6
Rhuddlan Rd CH1 ...117 D3
Rhum Cl CH65 ....70 C1
Rhyl St WA8 ....22 F7
Ribble Ave CW7 .....127 B1
Ribble Cl Culcheth WA3 ..4 F2
Widnes WA8 ....13 F3
Ribble Dr ST8 ......179 E1
Ribble Pl CW7 ......127 B1
Ribblesdale CH65 ....70 B3
Ribblesdale Ave CW12 .157 A5
Ribblesdale Cl CH62 .43 F5
Ribchester Gdns WA3 ..5 A3
Richard Cl WA7 ......24 A2
Richard Evans Com Prim Sch
WA11 ....1 A6
Richard Moon St CW1 .190 B4
Richard Reynolds Ct M44 .11 E6
Richard St Crewe CW1 .190 B5
Northwich CW9 ......104 A5
Richards Croft CH3 ..142 A7
Richards Gr CW12 ...156 A3
Richardson Cl
4 Sandbach CW11 ...174 D6
Shavington CW2 .....206 D5
Richardson St WA2 ..16 C8
Richbell Cl M44 ......11 F7
Richmond Ave
Handforth SK9 ....34 D4
Haydock WA11 ....1 B7
Runcorn WA7 ....23 E2
Warrington WA4 ......17 A4
Warrington, Grappenhall
WA4 ....17 C3
Richmond Cl
Chorlton CW2 ....207 D1
Culcheth WA3 ....4 E4
Lymm WA13 ....19 B4
Sandbach CW11 .....174 E7
Richmond Cres CH3 .119 C2
Richmond Ct
Chester CH3 ....118 F2
Ellesmere Port CH65 ..70 D3
Richmond Dr Lymm WA13 .19 B4
Northwich CW9 ......104 A4
Richmond Gdns WA12 ..2 C2
Richmond Gn SK7 ....35 F6
Richmond Hill
1 Knutsford WA16 ...57 B1
Macclesfield SK11 ...112 E6
Richmond Mews CH2 .118 F2
Richmond Pl SK11 ...112 E6
Richmond Rd CW1 ...190 E5
Richmond St
Warrington WA4 ......17 A3
Widnes WA8 ....13 C1
Richmond Village CW5 .205 A5
Rickaby Cl CH63 .....43 C8
Ridding La WA7 ......50 B5
Riddings Ct CW8 ....103 B4
Riddings La
Hartford CW8 ....103 B4
Wybunbury CW5 .....220 A8
Riddings The CH65 ...70 B4
Ridge Ave WA15 ......32 D6
Ridge Hill Langley SK11 .113 B2
Utkinton CW6 ....146 B5
Ridge Pk SK7 ....35 D6

Ridge The CW8 ......123 D7
Ridge View SK11 ....112 C5
Ridgeborne Cl WA5 ...7 D2
Ridgeway Golborne WA3 ..3 E7
Wilmslow SK9 ....60 F7
Ridgeway Cl CH66 ...69 C2
Ridgeway Ho CH3 ...121 C3
Ridgeway The
Alvanley WA6 ....74 A1
Cronton WA8 ....12 C6
Heswall CH60 ....41 B7
Runcorn WA7 ....50 D6
Tarvin CH3 ....121 C3
Ridgewell Ave 4 WA3 ..3 A8
Ridgmont Rd SK7 ....35 E5
Ridgway Gdns WA13 ..18 D3
Ridgway St Crewe CW1 .190 D5
Warrington WA2 ......16 D8
Ridgway The SK12 ...38 C6
Ridings Com Inf Sch The
CH1 ....94 A1
Ridings The
Saughall CH1 ....117 B8
Wilmslow SK9 ....59 D4
Ridley Cl CW2 ......206 E2
Ridley Dr WA5 ....15 C4
Ridley Hill Farm CW6 .185 C3
Ridley Rd SK10 ......87 E8
Ridley Wood Rd LL13 .196 A3
Ridsdale 2 WA8 .....22 C8
Rigby Ave CW1 .....190 A7
Rigby Rd ST7 ....195 B3
Rigby St WA3 ....3 A8
Rigby's Row CW5 ...204 E5
Rigg St CW1 ....190 B5
Riley Bank Mews WA6 .74 B1
Riley Cl CW11 ......174 E5
Riley Dr WA7 ....49 A8
Rileys Way ST7 .....209 F2
Rilshaw La CW7 .....150 B8
Rilston Ave WA3 ......4 D3
Rimington Cl WA3 ....4 E3
Rimsdale Cl CW2 ...206 A7
Ring Rd Chester CH2,CH3 .119 C3
Connah's Quay CH5 ..91 E2
Ring-o-Bells La SK12 .38 D6
Ringsfield Rd L24 ....21 A2
Ringstead Cl SK9 ....34 D1
Ringstead Dr 9 SK9 ..34 D1
Ringstone Way SK23 ..65 D8
Ringway
Ellesmere Port CH66 ..69 E4
Neston CH64 ....41 E1
Waverton CH3 ....143 B5
Ringway Cl SK10 .....87 B4
Ringway Rd Runcorn WA7 .23 D2
Woodhouse Park M22,M90 .33 D7
Ringway Rd W M22,M90 .33 D8
Ringway Trad Est M22 .33 E8
Ringwood Cl WA3 ....10 B5
Ripley Ave SK8 ......35 B5
Ripley Cl SK7 ....36 E8
Ripley St WA5 ....15 E6
Ripon Ave
Ellesmere Port CH66 ..69 C5
Golborne WA3 ....3 D8
Ripon Cl Macclesfield SK10 .87 C3
Newton-le-W WA12 ....2 C5
Ripon Dr CW2 ....206 A7
Ripon Row WA7 ......49 D6
Rise The SK23 ....65 C6
Riseley St SK10 ....112 C8
Rising Sun Cl SK11 ..112 A5
Rising Sun Rd SK11 ..112 A4
Risley Moss Local Nature
Reserve Visitor Ctr★
WA3 ....10 B4
Risley Rd WA3 ....9 F6
Rivacre Brow CH66 ...69 E5
Rivacre Bsns Ctr CH66 .69 E5
Rivacre Rd CH62,CH65,
CH66 ....44 C2
Rivacre Valley Ctry Pk★
CH66 ....69 D8
Rivacre Valley Prim Sch
CH66 ....69 E7
River La Chester CH4 .141 C7
Farndon CH3 ....180 E2
Partington M31 ......11 F4
Saltney CH4 ....140 F4
River Rd
Connah's Quay CH5 ..91 F1
Warrington WA1 ......16 B3
Warrington WA4 ......16 C2
River St Congleton CW12 .156 D3
Macclesfield SK11 ...112 E6
Wilmslow SK9 ....60 B8
River View CW7 .....126 E1
River Wlk 8 WA7 ....49 F7
Riverbank Cl
Bollington SK10 ......87 F8
Heswall CH60 ....40 F6
Nantwich CW5 ......204 E8
Riverbank Rd CH60 ...40 E6
Riverdane Rd CW12 .156 F4
Rivermead Ave WA15 .32 C7
Riversdale Frodsham WA6 .49 C1
Warrington WA1 ......16 E6
Riversdale Rd WA7 ...49 F7
Rivershill Gdns WA15 .32 D6
Riverside Nantwich CW5 .204 D5
Northwich CW9 ......104 B5
Riverside Bsns Pk SK9 .60 B7
Riverside Cres CW4 .130 C4
Riverside Ct
Huntington CH3 .....141 F7
Langley SK11 ....113 C4

Riverside Dr SK10 ....87 A5
Riverside Gr CW2 ....189 D3
Riverside Pk CW9 ....103 E6
Riverside Ret Pk WA1 ...16 C4
Riverside Trad Est
 Northwich CW8 ....103 F7
 Warrington WA5 ....14 D1
Riverside Wlk CH64 ......66 D5
Riversmead CH3 ....142 A6
Riverview Rd CH64 ....66 F5
Rivington CI WA1 ....17 E8
Rivington Gr M44 ....11 D6
Rivington Rd
 Ellesmere Port CH65 ....70 C5
 Runcorn WA7 ....50 F3
Rixton Ave WA5 ....15 F8
Rixton Clay Pits Nature
 Reserve★ WA3 ....10 E2
Rixton Park Homes WA3 .10 F2
Roaches The SK11 ......112 B5
Road Beta CW10 ....151 D8
Road Five CW7 ....127 C2
Road Four CW7 ....127 B2
Road One Weston CW1 .207 D8
 Winsford CW7 ....127 B3
Road Three CW7 ....127 D1
Road Two Weston CW1 ..207 C8
 Winsford CW7 ....127 C8
Roadside CW3 ....3 C8
Roan Ct SK11 ....112 F7
Roan House Way SK11 ..112 F7
Roan Mews SK11 ....112 F7
Roan Way SK9 ....85 B8
Rob La WA12 ....2 C5
Robert Moffat WA16 ......29 C5
Robert St Northwich CW9 103 E6
 Runcorn WA7 ....23 C2
 Warrington WA5 ....15 F6
 Widnes WA8 ....13 B1
Robert's Terr CH1 ....118 B1
Roberts Ave WA11 ....1 A5
Roberts Ct WA7 ....49 F6
Roberts Dr CW9 ....104 D6
Roberts Fold WA3 ....9 D4
Roberts Rd CW9 ....80 A2
Robin CI Chelford SK11 ...84 A2
 Rainow SK10 ....88 E5
 Runcorn WA7 ....50 D7
 Sandbach CW11 ....175 A8
Robin Cres SK11 ....112 D2
Robin Hood Ave SK11 ..112 D5
Robin Hood La WA6 ....73 B2
Robin La Chelford SK11 ..84 A3
 Sutton Lane Ends SK11 .112 D2
Robin's La SK7 ....35 D7
Robins CI SK7 ....35 E7
Robins Croft CH66 ....69 F2
Robins La WA3 ....4 D2
Robins Way SK10 ....88 A7
Robinsbay Rd M22 ....33 E8
Robinsons Croft CH3 ....142 B7
Robson St WA1 ....16 D6
Robson Way **3** WA3 .....3 F8
Roby Gr WA5 ....15 A6
Roche Gdns SK8 ....35 B6
Rochester CI Golborne WA3 3 A8
 Warrington WA5 ....15 C5
Rochester Cres CW1 ....190 F6
Rochester Dr CH65 ....70 D3
Rochester Ho SK10 ....86 F1
Rock Bank SK23 ....65 E6
Rock Cotts CH5 ....91 D1
Rock Dr WA6 ....49 C1
Rock Farm CH64 ....67 A6
Rock Farm Dr CH64 ....67 A6
Rock Farm Gr CH64 ....67 A6
Rock La Burwardsley CH3 184 C6
 Chester CH2 ....237 A4
 Widnes WA8 ....12 F4
Rock Mill La SK22 ....39 B7
Rock Rd
 Connah's Quay CH5 ......91 E1
 Warrington WA4 ....16 E4
Rock St SK22 ....39 C7
Rock The WA6 ....73 C2
Rock Villas LL13 ....180 E1
Rockfield CI WA8 ....12 D2
Rockfield Dr WA6 ....73 C2
Rockfield Mews WA4 .....16 F2
Rockford Lodge WA16 ....57 C1
Rockingham CI WA3 ......10 C6
Rocklands La CH63 ....42 C8
Rocklee Gdns CH64 ......67 A6
Rockliffe La CH6 ....91 A3
Rocksavage Expressway
 WA7 ....49 D5
Rockside ST7 ....195 C6
Rockwood Ave CW2 ......190 A3
Rockwood CI CW2 ....190 A3
Rocky La Heswall CH60 ...40 F8
 Tattenhall CH3 ....182 F7
Rocky La S CH60 ....41 A8
Roddy La WA6 ....75 E2
Rode Ct **7** CW12 ....156 F3
Rode Hall★ ST7 ....194 B7
Rode Heath Prim Sch
 ST7 ....193 F7
Rode St CW6 ....146 A3
Rode The ST7 ....193 D6
Rodeheath CI SK9 ....60 D7
Rodehouse CI ST7 ......193 F7
Rodepool CI SK9 ....34 D2
Rodgers CI WA6 ....49 B1
Rodney St SK11 ....112 D7
Roe Pk CW12 ....178 E1
Roe St Congleton CW12 .156 E2
 Macclesfield SK11 ......112 D7

Roebourne Rise CH1 ....117 D4
Roebuck St CW1 ....190 C5
Roeburn Way WA5 ....14 D3
Roedean Wlk CW1 ....190 D6
Roehampton Dr WA7 .....49 E7
Roehurst La CW7 ....126 D2
Roemarsh Ct WA7 ....49 E6
Roewood La
 Higher Hurdsfield SK10 ..88 A1
 Macclesfield SK10 ......113 B8
Roften Ind Est CH66 .....43 D1
Rokeby Ct WA7 ....24 D5
Rokeden WA12 ....2 D4
Roland Ave WA7 ....22 F1
Rolands Wlk WA7 ....23 F2
Rolleston St WA2 ....16 A6
Rolls Ave CW1 ....190 A6
Rolt Cres CW1 ....151 C7
Roman CI
 Newton-le-W WA12 ....2 C2
 Runcorn WA7 ....23 E2
Roman Ct CH64 ....66 F7
Roman Dr CH1 ....117 D6
Roman Rd WA4 ....16 C1
Roman Way WA11 ....174 E7
Romanes St CW8 ....103 E7
Romiley Rd CH66 ....69 E6
Romney CI Neston CH64 ..66 E7
 Widnes WA8 ....13 E2
Romney Croft CH64 ......66 F7
Romney Way CH64 ....66 F7
Romsey Dr SK8 ....35 C6
Rona Ave CH65 ....70 C1
Ronald Dr WA2 ....9 B2
Ronaldshay WA8 ....13 E2
Ronaldsway Halewood L26 21 A8
 Heswall CH60 ....40 F6
Ronan Rd WA8 ....22 E5
Rood Hill CW12 ....156 D3
Rood La CW12 ....156 E4
Rook St CW2 ....190 C2
Rookery CI
 1 Nantwich CW5 ......204 F5
 Sandbach CW11 ....174 C5
Rookery Ct CW11 ....174 C5
Rookery Dr
 Nantwich CW5 ....204 E4
 Tattenhall CH3 ....166 B2
Rookery Farm Rd CW6 ..169 A6
Rookery Gdns CW9 .....103 E3
Rookery Rd
 Kidsgrove ST7 ....195 C3
 Tilston SY14 ....198 B3
Rookery Rise CW7 ......150 A8
Rookery The
 Broughton CH4 ....139 B3
 Newton-le-W WA12 ....2 D4
Rookerypool CI SK9 ......34 D2
Rooks Way CH60 ....40 E8
Roome St WA2 ....16 C7
Rope Bank Ave CW2 ....206 A7
Rope La Shavington CW2 206 A5
 Wistaston CW2 ....205 F2
Rope Wlk CW12 ....156 D3
Ropewalk The CH64 ......66 C8
Ropeworks The CH1 ....118 B2
Rosam Ct WA7 ....49 E6
Roscoe Ave
 Newton-le-W WA12 ....2 E3
 Warrington WA2 ....16 D8
Roscoe Cres WA7 ....48 E7
Roscoe Rd M44 ....11 F8
Roscoes Yd **3** WA16 ...57 A2
Roscommon Way WA8 ...12 E3
Roscote CI CH60 ....40 F7
Roscote The CH60 ....40 F7
Rose Ave WA11 ....1 E6
Rose Bank Bollington SK10 87 F7
 Lymm WA13 ....18 E3
Rose CI WA7 ....50 D5
Rose Cnr CH3 ....166 A1
Rose Cotts CW12 ....154 F6
Rose Cres WA8 ....22 F7
Rose Farm CW6 ....146 B7
Rose Farm Ct CW9 ....79 E4
Rose Farm Mews WA6 ...73 B4
Rose Gdns CH64 ....66 F6
Rose Lea CI WA8 ....13 A4
Rose St WA8 ....22 F7
Rose Terr CW1 ....190 C5
Rose View Ave WA8 ......13 A4
Rose Wlk **4** M31 ....11 E3
Rosebank CI CW7 ....149 E8
Rosebank Mews CW8 ..129 E5
Rosebank Rd M44 ....11 C4
Rosebank Sch CW8 ....78 A3
Rosebank Wlk CW8 ....78 A4
Rosebery Way CW1 .....191 C4
Rosecroft CH62 ....43 C6
Rosedale Ave
 Golborne WA3 ....3 C7
 Warrington WA1 ....17 C7
Rosedene CI CH2 ....118 E8
Roseheath Dr L26 ....21 A6
Rosehill Ave WA9 ....6 B5
Rosehill Rd CW2 ....190 B1
Roselands Ct LL12 ......162 C1
Rosemary Ave
 Runcorn WA7 ....49 F4
 Warrington WA4 ....16 E2
Rosemary CI
 Broughton CH4 ....139 C3
 Warrington WA5 ....15 C6
Rosemary Dr WA12 ....2 F3
Rosemary La LL1 ....161 D1
Rosemary Row CH3 .....166 A1
Rosemary Wlk M31 ....11 F2
Rosemere Dr CH1 ....94 F7

Rosemoor Gdns WA4 .....26 F5
Rosemount CW10 ....128 C1
Rosemount Cotts WA2 ....8 B8
Rosetree Mdw CW9 ....80 A2
Rosevale Rd ST5 ....210 F1
Roseville Dr CW12 ....179 B8
Roseway SK11 ....112 D5
Rosewood Ave
 Chester CH2 ....118 D5
 Frodsham WA6 ....74 D7
 Warrington WA1 ....16 E7
Rosewood CI CW1 ......190 E6
Rosewood Dr CW7 ......126 A1
Rosewood Gr
 Saughall CH1 ....117 B8
 Widnes WA8 ....22 B8
Rosewood Ho CW12 ....156 A3
Ross CI WA5 ....15 D7
Ross Dr CH66 ....69 C5
Ross Rd CH65 ....70 A6
Ross St WA8 ....13 B1
Rossall CI L24 ....21 E2
Rossall Ct SK7 ....35 E6
Rossall Dr SK7 ....35 E6
Rossall Gr CH66 ....69 D6
Rossall Rd
 Warrington WA5 ....15 B4
 Widnes WA8 ....13 D2
Rossbank Rd CH65 ....70 A7
Rosscliffe Rd CH65 ......70 A6
Rossenclough Rd SK9 ...34 D1
Rossendale Dr WA3 ......10 A6
Rossendale Rd SK8 ......34 C8
Rossett Ave WA7 ....33 D8
Rossett Bsns Village
 LL12 ....162 B1
Rossett CI
 Northwich CW9 ....103 A4
 Warrington WA5 ....7 A1
Rossett Pk LL12 ....162 C1
Rossett Rd LL13 ....180 A1
Rossfield Rd CH65 ....70 A6
Rossfield Rd N CH65 ....70 B7
Rosslyn CI CH5 ....116 A2
Rosslyn La CW8 ....102 A3
Rosslyn Rd CH3 ....119 B3
Rossmill La WA15 ....32 B7
Rossmore Bsns Pk CH65 70 B7
Rossmore Gdns CH66 ...69 D6
Rossmore Ind Est CH65 .70 A6
Rossmore Rd E CH65 ...69 F7
Rossmore Rd W CH65 ...69 D7
Rossmore Sch CH66 .....69 C7
Rossmore Terraced Factories
 CH65 ....70 A6
Rossmount Rd CH65 .....70 A6
Rosswood Rd CH65 ......70 A6
Rostherne Ave
 Ellesmere Port CH66 ....69 E4
 Golborne WA3 ....3 D8
 High Lane SK6 ....37 E8
Rostherne Cres WA5 ....15 D4
Rostherne Cres WA8 ....12 D2
Rostherne La WA16 ......30 E4
Rostherne Rd SK9 ....59 F4
Rostherne Way CW11 ..174 F7
Rosyth CI WA7 ....8 F3
Rothay Dr WA5 ....14 D3
Rothbury CI WA7 ....49 D6
Rother Dr CH65 ....70 A7
Rotherhead Dr SK11 ...112 B5
Rotherwood Rd SK9 .....59 D6
Rothesay CI WA7 ....23 F7
Rothesay Dr CH62 ....43 E4
Rothesay Rd CH4 ......141 A7
Rough Bank CW12 ......179 E8
Rough Heys La SK11 ...111 A8
Roughlea Ave WA3 ....4 D4
Roughley Ave WA5 ....15 D4
Roughlyn Cres CH4 ....140 E1
Roughwood La
 Alsager CW11,ST7 .....193 B7
 Hassall Green CW11 ...176 A1
Round Gdns WA8 ....88 A8
Round Hill Mdw CH3 ...142 B7
Round Mdw SK10 ....88 E5
Round Thorn WA3 ....9 A8
Round Way SK22 ....39 D8
Roundabout The WA8 ...12 D6
Roundhey SK8 ....34 C8
Roundway SK7 ....35 D6
Roundy La SK10 ....62 E9
Routledge St WA8 ....13 B1
Row The
 3 Winsford CW7 ......126 D1
 Wrenbury CW5 ....217 B5
Rowan Ave WA3 ....3 F7
Rowan CI Alsager ST7 ..193 D3
 Delamere CW8 ....123 D7
 Lawton Heath End ST7 .193 D6
 Middlewich CW10 ....151 E6
 Runcorn WA7 ....49 C7
 Sandbach CW11 ....174 F7
 Warrington WA5 ....14 F6
 Winsford CW7 ....126 D3
Rowan Ct SK9 ....60 B7
Rowan Dr SK8 ....35 C8
Rowan Gr CH5 ....91 C1
Rowan Lo SK7 ....35 F7
Rowan Pk CH3 ....142 E7
Rowan Pl CH2 ....119 B4
Rowan Rd CW8 ....102 D8
Rowan Rise CW8 ....78 A3
Rowan Tree Rd WA16 ...59 C5
Rowan Way SK10 ....87 B1
Rowan Wlk M31 ....11 E3

Rowans The
 Broughton CH4 ....139 B3
 4 Northwich CW9 ....103 E6
Rowanside SK10 ....86 E6
Rowanside Dr SK9 ....60 E8
Rowcliffe Ave CH4 ......141 A4
Rowena Ct CH2 ....118 F3
Rowland CI WA2 ....9 A3
Rowlands View CW6 ....146 B7
Rowley Bank La WA16 ...29 E1
Rowley Rd SK7 ....36 E8
Rowley Way WA16 ....82 B7
Rowson Dr M44 ....11 D6
Rowswood Farm WA4 ....25 E5
Rowthorn CI WA8 ....22 E8
Rowton Bridge Rd CH3 142 E7
Rowton CI **7** CW9 ....103 F4
Rowton La CH3 ....142 F6
Rowton Rd CW2 ....189 D4
Roxborough CI WA5 ......7 A6
Roxburgh CI SK10 ....87 A1
Roxburgh Rd CH66 ......68 F6
Roxby Way WA16 ....82 A6
Roxholme Wlk M22 ....33 C8
Royal Arc **3** CW1 .....190 C4
Royal Ave WA8 ....12 A1
Royal Gdns
 Altrincham WA14 ....20 F2
 Northwich CW9 ....103 E3
Royal La CW6 ....147 A3
Royal Mdws SK10 ....87 A1
Royal Mews CW9 ....104 D5
Royal Pl WA8 ....22 B8
Royal Rd WA8 ....12 A1
Royal Sch CW8 ....52 D5
Royal Schools for The Deaf &
 Communication Disorders
 SK8 ....34 D6
Royal Sh Arc The **9**
 CH64 ....66 E8
Royce CI CW1 ....190 A7
Royce CI WA16 ....56 F2
Royden Ave Irlam M44 ...11 F8
 Runcorn WA7 ....49 A8
Royds CI CW8 ....103 B4
Royds Ct CW11 ....174 D5
Roylance Dr CW10 .....151 C8
Royle St Congleton CW12 156 D3
 Northwich CW9 ....104 B8
Royle's Pl CW8 ....103 D6
Royleen Dr WA6 ....74 D6
Royles Sq **2** SK9 ......60 A1
Royston Ave WA1 ....17 A7
Royston CI
 Ellesmere Port CH66 ....69 F3
 2 Golborne WA3 ....3 E8
Rozel Cres WA5 ....15 B5
Rubin Dr CW1 ....189 F7
Rudd Ave WA9 ....1 B2
Rudheath CI CW2 ....189 D5
Rudheath Com High Sch
 CW9 ....104 D7
Rudheath Com Prim Sch
 CW9 ....104 D6
Rudheath La WA7 ....24 D3
Rudheath Way CW9 ....104 E5
Rudloe Ct WA2 ....8 F1
Rudstone CI CH66 ....69 B5
Rudyard CI SK10 ....112 B6
Rue De Bohars CW6 ...168 D8
Rufford CI Widnes WA8 ..12 C2
 Wistaston CW2 ....206 B8
Rufford Ct WA1 ....17 E8
Rufus Ct CH1 ....237 A3
Rugby CI SK10 ....87 E4
Rugby Dr SK10 ....87 E4
Rugby Ho SK10 ....87 D3
Rugby Rd CH65 ....70 D3
Rugby Wlk CH65 ....70 D3
Ruislip Ct WA2 ....8 F1
Runcorn All Saints CE Prim
 Sch WA7 ....23 A3
Runcorn Docks Rd WA7 .22 E2
Runcorn East Sta WA7 ..50 D7
Runcorn Rd Barnton CW8 .78 B2
 Higher Walton WA4 ......25 D5
 Little Leigh CW8 ....77 D5
Runcorn Spur Rd WA7 ..23 B1
Runcorn Sta WA7 ....22 F2
Runger La M90,WA15 ...32 F8
Runnell The CH64 ....41 D4
Runnymede WA8 ....13 C1
Runnymede Ct **2** WA8 .13 C1
Runnymede Dr WA11 .....1 A6
Runnymede Gdns **5**
 WA8 ....13 C2
Runnymede Wlk **3** WA8 13 C2
Rupert Row WA7 ....50 A8
Ruscoe Ave CW1 ....174 E6
Ruscolm CI WA5 ....14 D7
Rush Gdns WA13 ....19 A4
Rushes Mdw WA13 ....19 B5
Rushey CI WA15 ....32 D7
Rushfield Cres WA7 ......50 D6
Rushfield Rd
 Cheadle Hulme SK8 ......35 A6
 Chester CH4 ....141 B5
Rushgreen Rd WA13 .....19 A4
Rushmere CI SK10 ....62 F2
Rushmere La CH3 ......163 F3
Rushmore Gr WA1 ....17 A7
Rusholme CI L26 ....21 A6
Rushside Rd SK8 ....35 A6
Rushton Ave WA12 ....2 B4
Rushton CE Prim Sch
 SK11 ....159 B2
Rushton CI
 Burtonwood WA5 ....6 F7

Rushton CI continued
 Northwich CW9 ....104 C7
 Widnes WA8 ....12 F3
Rushton Dr Chester CH2 .118 E7
 Hough CW2 ....206 E2
 Middlewich CW10 ....151 C7
Rushton Fold SK10 ....61 A2
Rushton La CW6 ....147 D6
Rushton Rd SK8 ....35 A6
Rushy View WA12 ....2 A4
Ruskin Ave
 Newton-le-W WA12 ....2 C4
 Warrington WA2 ....8 C2
Ruskin CI WA16 ....57 A2
Ruskin Dr CH65 ....70 D3
Ruskin Rd
 Congleton CW12 ....156 C2
 Crewe CW2 ....190 C2
Ruskin Sports Coll & Com
 High Sch WA2 ....190 C2
Ruskin Way WA16 ....57 A3
Russel Ct WA8 ....13 B4
Russell Ave Alsager ST7 193 D5
 High Lane SK6 ....37 E7
Russell CI CW12 ....179 A8
Russell Dr CW1 ....191 C5
Russell Rd Runcorn WA7 .48 E8
 Winsford CW7 ....149 C8
Russell St CH1,CH3 ....237 C3
Russet CI CW10 ....128 B2
Russet Rd CW8 ....102 D8
Russett Sch & Cheshire MSI
 Unit The CW8 ....102 E8
Rutherford Dr WA16 .....82 C7
Ruthin CI WA5 ....7 E3
Ruthin Ct CH65 ....70 D3
Ruthin Wlk WA6 ....73 A1
Rutland Ave Golborne WA3 .3 D7
 Halewood L26 ....21 A8
 Warrington WA4 ....26 B8
Rutland CI
 Congleton CW12 ....156 E4
 Sandbach CW11 ....174 C5
Rutland Dr
 Middlewich CW10 ....151 C7
 Weaverham CW8 ....77 C1
Rutland Pl CH2 ....119 A5
Rutland Rd
 Hazel Grove SK7 ....36 E8
 Irlam M44 ....11 D5
 Kidsgrove ST7 ....195 A2
 Macclesfield SK11 ......112 D4
 Partington M31 ....11 E2
Rutland St **1** WA7 .....22 F2
Rutter Ave WA5 ....7 F2
Ryburn CI CW2 ....207 B3
Ryburn Rd SK11 ....112 A5
Rydal Ave High Lane SK6 .37 E8
 Warrington WA4 ....16 A2
Rydal CI
 Ellesmere Port CH65 ....70 C2
 Holmes Chapel CW4 ...130 B2
 Neston CH64 ....66 F6
 Winsford CW7 ....126 D3
Rydal Ct CW12 ....156 A2
Rydal Dr WA15 ....32 D8
Rydal Gr Chester CH4 ..141 A6
 Helsby WA6 ....73 B1
 Runcorn WA7 ....49 B8
Rydal Mews CW8 ....34 C1
Rydal Pl SK11 ....112 A6
Rydal St WA12 ....2 C3
Rydal Way Alsager ST7 .193 C5
 Widnes WA8 ....12 C1
Ryde CI CW1 ....190 B8
Ryder Rd Warrington WA1 .17 C7
 Widnes WA8 ....13 B4
Ryders St CW8 ....103 E8
Rye CI ST7 ....193 B3
Ryebank Ave CW1 ......190 B7
Ryebank Way SK10 ......87 C3
Ryecroft CH2 ....72 B3
Ryecroft CI CW10 ......151 B7
Ryecroft La
 Duddon CH3,CW6 ......144 C6
 Mobberley WA16 ....57 E4
Ryecroft Rd CH60 ....41 C7
Ryedale Way CW12 .....179 C8
Ryehills ST7 ....209 E1
Rylands CI SY14 ....213 B4
Rylands St
 Warrington WA1 ....16 B5
 5 Widnes WA8 ....23 B8
Ryle St SK11 ....112 D6
Ryle's Park Rd SK11 ...112 C6
Ryles CI SK11 ....112 C5
Ryles Cres SK11 ....112 C5
Ryles Ho SK11 ....112 C5
Ryleys Farm SK9 ....59 F1
Ryleys La SK9 ....59 F1
Ryleys Sch The SK9 .....59 F1

S

Sabre CI WA7 ....50 D7
Sack La CW9 ....54 F6
Sacred Heart RC Prim Sch
 WA5 ....15 E5
Saddleback Dr SK10 .....86 F7
Saddlers Rise WA7 ....50 C8
Sade Ct CW1 ....190 B5
Sadler CI CW7 ....126 D1
Sadler Rd CW7 ....126 D1

Sadler St WA8 . . . . .13 C1
Sadler's Cl CW4 . . . . . .130 B3
Sadlers La CW6 . . . . . .124 A1
Sadlers Wells CW6 . . . .185 E8
Saffron Cl Warrington WA3 . .3 E8
Warrington WA2 . . . . .9 B1
Saffron Wlk M31 . . . . . . .11 F2
Sagars Rd Handforth SK9 . .34 C3
Styal SK9 . . . . .34 B4
Sage Cl WA2 . . . . .9 C2
Saighton CE Prim Sch
CH3 . . . . .142 E1
Saighton La CH3 . . . . . .142 F2
SS Peter & Paul RC High Sch
WA8 . . . . .12 F2
St Aelred's RC Tech Coll
WA12 . . . . .2 D4
St Aidans Dr WA8 . . . . . .12 F6
St Alban Rd WA5 . . . . . . .14 E5
St Alban's RC Prim Sch
Macclesfield SK10 . . . . . . .86 F1
Warrington WA5 . . . . . . .15 F6
St Albans Cl WA11 . . . . . .2 A7
St Albans Dr CW5 . . . . .204 F3
St Albans Pl SK22 . . . . . .39 C7
St Albans St SK22 . . . . . .39 C8
St Ambrose Coll WA15 . . .32 B8
St Ambrose RC Prim Sch
L24 . . . . .21 A1
St Ambrose Rd WA8 . . . . .13 C1
St Andrew's Ave CW2 . .190 C1
St Andrew's CE Prim Sch
WA2 . . . . .8 C3
St Andrew's Gdns ST7 . .193 E2
St Andrew's Rd
Ellesmere Port CH65 . . . . .70 C4
Macclesfield SK11 . . . . . .112 B7
St Andrews Cl
Northwich CW9 . . . . .104 E7
Warrington WA2 . . . . .9 A4
St Andrews Ct
Crewe CW2 . . . . .190 C1
Ellesmere Port CH65 . . . . .70 C4
Macclesfield SK11 . . . . . .112 B7
St Andrews Dr
Holmes Chapel CW4 . . . . .130 B2
Kidsgrove ST7 . . . . .195 C3
St Andrews Wlk
Mickle Trafford CH2 . . . . . .96 F1
New Mills SK22 . . . . .39 D8
St Ann's Rd CW10 . . . . .151 C8
St Ann's Rd S SK8 . . . . . .34 C8
St Ann's Sq SK8 . . . . . . .34 C8
St Anne St CH1 . . . . . . .237 B3
St Anne's Ave CW10 . . . .151 D8
St Anne's Fulshaw CE Prim
Sch SK9 . . . . .59 F6
St Anne's La CW5 . . . . .204 D5
St Anne's RC Prim Sch
CW5 . . . . .204 E3
St Anne's Rd WA8 . . . . . .13 B2
St Annes CH1 . . . . .237 B3
St Annes Ave WA4 . . . . . .17 B2
St Annes Ave E WA4 . . . .17 B2
St Anthony Pl WA2 . . . . . .8 B6
St Anthony's RC Prim Sch
CH4 . . . . .140 E6
St Asaph Dr WA5 . . . . . . .7 E3
St Asaph Rd CH66 . . . . . .94 E8
St Augustine's Ave WA4 . .16 F4
St Augustine's RC Prim Sch
Runcorn WA7 . . . . .24 A2
Warrington WA4 . . . . . . .16 F4
St Austell Ave SK10 . . . . .86 E1
St Austell Cl
Macclesfield SK10 . . . . . . .86 E1
Runcorn WA7 . . . . .50 B6
Warrington WA5 . . . . . . .14 E3
St Austell Dr SK8 . . . . . . .34 B8
St Austins La WA1 . . . . . .16 B4
St Barnabas CE Prim Sch
Macclesfield SK11 . . . . . .112 D6
Warrington WA5 . . . . . . .15 F5
St Barnabas Ct SK11 . . . .112 D6
St Barnabas Pl WA5 . . . . .15 E6
St Bartholomews Ct
CH5 . . . . .116 E6
St Basil's RC Prim Sch
WA8 . . . . .12 A2
St Bede's Ave CW8 . . . . . .77 D1
St Bede's RC Inf Sch
WA8 . . . . .13 A1
St Bede's RC Jun Sch
WA8 . . . . .13 A1
St Bede's RC Prim Sch
CW8 . . . . .102 F7
St Benedict's RC Prim Sch
Handforth SK9 . . . . .34 E3
Warrington WA2 . . . . . . .16 D7
St Benedicts Cl WA2 . . . . .16 B7
St Bernard's RC Prim Sch
CH65 . . . . .70 D3
St Berteline's CE Prim Sch
WA7 . . . . .50 C8
St Brannocks Rd SK8 . . . .35 B7
St Brides Cl WA5 . . . . . . .14 E3
St Bridget's RC Prim Sch
WA2 . . . . .8 E3
St Bridgets Cl WA2 . . . . . .8 F3
St Bridgets Ct CH4 . . . . .141 B6
St Catherine Dr CW8 . . . .103 A4
St Catherine's RC Prim Sch
WA3 . . . . .3 E7
St Chad's CE Prim Sch
Newcastle-u-Lyme ST5 . .210 D2

St Chad's CE Prim Sch
continued
Winsford CW7 . . . . .149 E8
St Chad's Fields CW7 . . .149 C5
St Chad's RC High Sch
WA7 . . . . .49 D7
St Chad's Rd CH1 . . . . . .117 F4
St Chads Cl CW5 . . . . . .220 A8
St Chads Way TF9 . . . . .236 C2
St Christophers Cl CH2 . 118 D8
St Clair St CW2 . . . . . . .190 D1
St Clare's RC Prim Sch
CH4 . . . . .141 A5
St Clement's RC Prim Sch
WA7 . . . . .49 A8
St David Rd CH62 . . . . . .44 A6
St David's High Sch
CH4 . . . . .140 C6
St David's Terr CH4 . . . .140 C6
St Davids Dr
Ellesmere Port CH66 . . . . .94 F8
Warrington WA5 . . . . .7 E2
St Davids' Ret Pk CH4 . . .140 D7
St Edward's RC Prim Sch
Macclesfield SK11 . . . . . .112 C5
Runcorn WA7 . . . . .23 B3
St Edwards Cl SK11 . . . . .112 D6
St Elmo Pk SK12 . . . . . . .37 C4
St Elphin's (Fairfield) CE
Prim Sch WA1 . . . . .16 D6
St Elphins Cl WA1 . . . . . .16 C5
St Gabriel's RC Prim Sch
ST7 . . . . .193 D2
St Gabriels Ct ST7 . . . . .193 D2
St George's CE Prim Sch
SK22 . . . . .39 C8
St George's Cl WA16 . . . .82 C8
St George's Cres
Chester CH4 . . . . .237 C1
Waverton CH3 . . . . .143 A5
St George's Ct WA8 . . . . .22 D8
St George's Pl SK11 . . . .112 D7
St George's Rd CW7 . . . .149 C8
St George's St SK11 . . . .112 D6
St George's Way
Northwich CW9 . . . . .103 F5
Thornton Hough CH63 . . . .42 A7
St Georges Ave CH66 . . . .94 F8
St Georges Cl WA4 . . . . .26 E3
St Georges Rd SK22 . . . . .39 C8
St Gerard's RC Prim Sch
WA8 . . . . .23 B7
St Gregory's RC High Sch
WA5 . . . . .15 D5
St Gregory's RC Prim Sch
SK10 . . . . .87 B3
St Helens Cl WA3 . . . . . . .11 B3
St Helens Coll Newton
Campus WA12 . . . . .2 B4
St Helens Rd Golborne WN7 4 B8
Northwich CW9 . . . . . . .104 A8
St Hilda's Dr WA6 . . . . . .49 C1
St Ives Cl SK10 . . . . .86 E1
St Ives Pk CH5 . . . . .116 A3
St Ives Way CH5 . . . . . .116 A3
St James Ave
Chester CH2 . . . . .118 F7
Congleton CW12 . . . . . . .156 C2
Warren SK11 . . . . .111 E2
St James Cl Audlem CW3 230 A4
Frodsham WA6 . . . . .49 C1
St James Ct Audley ST7 . .209 D2
Cheadle Hulme SK8 . . . . . .34 F6
Chester CH2 . . . . .118 F3
St James Ct/Llys Sant Iago
CH5 . . . . .91 D1
St James St CH1 . . . . . .237 B3
St James Terr CW7 . . . .149 A8
St James Wlk CW8 . . . .103 E7
St James' CE Prim Sch
WA11 . . . . .1 E6
St James' Ct
Biddulph ST8 . . . . .179 E3
Warrington WA4 . . . . . . .16 B3
St James' Dr SK9 . . . . . .60 A4
St James' RC High Sch
SK8 . . . . .34 F6
St James' Sq SK22 . . . . .39 C8
St James' Way SK8 . . . . .34 F6
St John Ave WA4 . . . . . . .16 B2
St John Fisher RC Prim Sch
WA8 . . . . .13 D1
St John St Chester CH1 . .237 B2
Newton-le-W WA12 . . . . . .2 A3
St John The Evangelist CE
Prim Sch SK11 . . . . . . .112 A7
St John The Evangelist RC
Prim Sch (Annexe)
ST7 . . . . .194 F1
St John's Ave
Knutsford WA16 . . . . . . .56 F1
Lostock Gralam CW9 . . . . .79 F3
St John's Brow WA7 . . . .23 B3
St John's CE Prim Sch
Bollington SK10 . . . . .88 A7
Kingsley WA6 . . . . .75 C2
Sandbach CW11 . . . . . . .175 E6
St John's Cl CW9 . . . . . .104 E8
St John's Ct
Knutsford WA16 . . . . . . .57 C2
Warrington WA1 . . . . . . .16 F7
St John's Rd
Bebington CH62 . . . . .44 A5
Chester CH4 . . . . .237 C1
Congleton CW12 . . . . . . .157 A5
Knutsford WA16 . . . . . . .57 A1
Macclesfield SK11 . . . .112 C7
Wilmslow SK9 . . . . .59 E3

St John's Rear Rd CH4 . .237 C1
St John's St WA7 . . . . . .23 B3
St John's Way
Cuddington CW8 . . . . . . .102 B2
Sandbach CW11 . . . . . . .175 E6
St John's Wood ST7 . . . .194 F1
St John's Wood Com Sch
WA16 . . . . .57 D2
St Johns Ct Chester CH1 . 237 B2
Winsford CW7 . . . . .126 B1
St Johns Dr CW7 . . . . . .149 A8
St Joseph's Cl WA5 . . . . .14 C2
St Joseph's RC Prim Sch
Warrington WA5 . . . . . . .14 C5
Winsford CW7 . . . . .149 B8
St Josephs Way CW5 . . .205 A5
St Katherines Way WA1 . .16 D5
St Kilda Cl CH65 . . . . . . .70 C1
St Lawrence Ct CW5 . . . .204 F6
St Lawrence Rd WA6 . . . .74 B8
St Leonard's Way CW3 . .232 C1
St Lewis RC Prim Sch
WA3 . . . . .4 B1
St Luke's Ave WA8 . . . . . .13 B4
St Luke's CE Prim Sch
WA3 . . . . .3 E7
St Luke's Cres WA8 . . . . .13 B4
St Luke's Ho SK10 . . . . .111 F8
St Luke's RC Prim Sch
WA6 . . . . .74 C8
St Luke's Way WA6 . . . . .49 B1
St Lukes Cl CW4 . . . . . .130 D3
St Margaret's Ave WA2 . . .8 D1
St Margaret's CE Prim Sch
WA2 . . . . .8 C1
St Mark's CE Prim Sch
CW9 . . . . .53 C4
St Mark's RC Prim Sch
L26 . . . . .21 A8
St Mark's St WA11 . . . . . .1 A6
St Marks Cres CH66 . . . . .94 F8
St Marks Rd CH4 . . . . . .140 F6
St Martin's Rd ST7 . . . . .210 E6
St Martin's Way CH1 . . . .237 A3
St Martins Dr CH66 . . . . .69 D2
St Martins La WA7 . . . . . .50 D7
St Martins RC Prim Sch
WA7 . . . . .50 D7
St Mary of the Angels RC
Prim Sch CH66 . . . . . . .69 D6
St Mary's Ave CW8 . . . . .77 D1
St Mary's CE Inf Sch
CH2 . . . . .118 E7
St Mary's CE Prim Sch
Bebington CH62 . . . . .44 A5
Bosley SK11 . . . . .158 A5
Irlam M44 . . . . .11 C5
Runcorn WA7 . . . . .50 A8
St Mary's Cl Alsager ST7 193 C5
Hale L24 . . . . .21 E2
Warrington WA4 . . . . . . .26 C6
St Mary's Ct CW12 . . . . .156 A2
St Mary's Ct WA3 . . . . . .4 B8
St Mary's Dr CW8 . . . . . .126 A8
St Mary's Hill CH1 . . . . .237 B1
St Mary's RC Inf Sch
WA12 . . . . .2 C4
St Mary's RC Jun Sch
WA12 . . . . .2 B3
Congleton CW12 . . . . . . .156 D3
Crewe CW2 . . . . .190 A1
Middlewich CW10 . . . . . . .151 C8
New Mills SK22 . . . . .39 B8
St Mary's Rd Disley SK12 . 38 D5
Dodleston CH4 . . . . .162 A7
Nantwich CW5 . . . . .204 E2
New Mills SK22 . . . . .39 B7
Runcorn WA8 . . . . .23 F1
Warrington WA5 . . . . . . .14 F5
Widnes WA8 . . . . .23 A4
St Mary's St Crewe CW1 . 190 C4
Warrington WA4 . . . . . . .16 D3
St Mary's Way CH4 . . . .139 C5
St Marys Cl CW5 . . . . . .204 A7
St Matthews CE Prim Sch
WA4 . . . . .26 E2
St Matthews Cl
Haslington CW1 . . . . . . .191 D4
Warrington WA4 . . . . . . .26 D7
St Mawes Cl WA8 . . . . . .12 E2
St Mawes Cl SK10 . . . . . .86 E1
St Mawgan Ct WA2 . . . . . .8 F7
St Michael's Ave SK7 . . . .35 E8
St Michael's Cl
Little Leigh CW8 . . . . .77 D5
Widnes WA8 . . . . .22 C7
St Michael's Cotts
CW12 . . . . .156 B7
St Michael's Ind Est WA8 22 C7
St Michael's RC Prim Sch
WA8 . . . . .22 C7
St Michael's Rd WA8 . . . .22 C7
St Michael's Sq CH1 . . . .237 B2
St Michael's View CW1 . .190 B5
St Michael's Way CW10 128 C1
St Michaels Terr
SK11 . . . . .112 D8
St Monica's RC Prim Sch
WA4 . . . . .26 D7
St Monicas Cl WA4 . . . . . .26 D7
St Nicholas Ct CW5 . . . .204 F5
St Nicholas RC High Sch
CW8 . . . . .103 D6
St Nicholas Rd WA3 . . . . .4 A8
St Olave St CH1 . . . . . . .237 B1
St Oswald's CE Prim Sch
CH1 . . . . .94 F2

St Oswald's Cres CW11 .153 F5
St Oswald's RC Prim Sch
WA1 . . . . .16 F8
St Oswald's Worleston CE
Prim Sch CW5 . . . . . . .188 E6
St Oswalds CH1 . . . . . . .237 B3
St Oswalds Cl
Malpas SY14 . . . . .213 B3
Winwick WA2 . . . . .8 B6
St Oswalds Way CH1,
CH2 . . . . .237 B3
St Paul of the Cross RC Prim
Sch WA5 . . . . .6 E6
St Paul's Cl CW1 . . . . . .190 C4
St Paul's Ct
Macclesfield SK11 . . . .112 E7
Warrington WA2 . . . . . . .16 A6
St Paul's Inf Sch CH3 . . .237 A2
St Paul's Pl CW9 . . . . . .79 A1
St Paul's RC Prim Sch
SK12 . . . . .36 E2
St Paul's Rd
Macclesfield SK11 . . . .112 E7
Widnes WA8 . . . . .23 A7
St Paul's St CW1 . . . . . .190 C4
St Pauls Gdns CH66 . . . . .69 B7
St Peter's Ave WA16 . . . .56 F1
St Peter's CE Prim Sch
WA12 . . . . .2 E4
St Peter's Cl Heswall CH60 40 F7
Lymm WA13 . . . . .19 A4
St Peter's Ct WA2 . . . . . .16 C6
St Peter's Dr CW6 . . . . .147 F7
St Peter's Ho SK11 . . . . .112 E6
St Peter's RC Prim Sch
WA1 . . . . .17 C7
St Peter's Rise CW11 . . .174 E7
St Peter's Way WA2 . . . . .16 B6
St Peters Rd CW12 . . . . .156 E1
St Peters Way CH2 . . . . .119 F8
St Philip (Westbrook) CE
Prim Sch WA5 . . . . .7 B1
St Saviour's CE Prim Sch
ST7 . . . . .194 D1
St Saviour's RC Inf Sch
CH66 . . . . .69 E3
St Saviour's RC Jun Sch
CH66 . . . . .69 E3
St Saviour's St ST7 . . . .194 D1
St Stephen Rd WA5 . . . . .14 F5
St Stephen's Ave WA2 . . .8 B3
St Stephen's RC Prim Sch
WA2 . . . . .8 B3
St Stephens Cl CH60 . . . .41 C6
St Stephens Ct
Congleton CW12 . . . .156 F3
Sandbach CW11 . . . . . . .174 D7
St Teresa's RC Prim Sch
M44 . . . . .11 E8
St Theresa's RC Prim Sch
CH1 . . . . .117 F5
St Thomas CE Prim Sch
ST7 . . . . .195 A1
St Thomas Ct WA8 . . . . .12 E1
St Thomas More RC High Sch
CW2 . . . . .190 A2
St Thomas of Canterbury
Blue Coat CE Jun Sch
CH1 . . . . .237 A4
St Thomas St ST7 . . . . .195 E7
St Thomas' View CH65 . . .70 B4
St Thomas's CE Prim Sch
WA4 . . . . .16 D1
St Thomas's Pathway
CH1 . . . . .237 B2
St Vincent Dr CW8 . . . . .102 F3
St Vincent Rd WA5 . . . . .14 F5
St Vincent's RC Prim Sch
Knutsford WA16 . . . . . . .57 C1
Warrington WA5 . . . . . . .14 F3
St Wenefredes Gn SY13 214 F1
St Werburgh St CH1 . . . .237 B2
St Werburgh's & St
Columba's RC Prim Sch
CH2 . . . . .118 F2
St Wilfrid's Dr WA4 . . . . .17 C1
St Wilfrid's RC Prim Sch
CW8 . . . . .103 D5
St Wilfrids Cl CW9 . . . . .104 A3
St Winefride's RC Prim Sch
CH64 . . . . .66 F7
Salander Cres CW2 . . . .206 A7
Salerno Rd CH2 . . . . . . .95 B1
Salesbrook La CW5 . . . .228 C7
Salford CW3 . . . . .230 A4
Salford Pl CW12 . . . . . .156 E3
Salisbury Ave
Crewe CW2 . . . . .190 C1
Saltney CH4 . . . . .140 E6
Salisbury Cl Crewe CW2 .190 C1
Ellesmere Port CH66 . . . . .94 F8
Salisbury Pl SK10 . . . . . .87 E4
Salisbury Rd WA11 . . . . . .1 E8
Salisbury St Chester CH1 118 B3
Golborne WA3 . . . . .3 A8
Runcorn WA7 . . . . .23 A1
Warrington WA1 . . . . . . .16 D6
Widnes WA8 . . . . .23 B8
Salkeld St CW9 . . . . . . .104 B8
Salop Pl ST7 . . . . .195 A3
Salop Wlk SK10 . . . . . . .86 F2
Salt Line Way CW11 . . . .174 D6
Salt Mdws CW5 . . . . . . .204 C5
Salt Mus The CW9 . . . . .103 F7
Saltash Cl WA7 . . . . .50 B6
Salter's La
Bickerton SY14 . . . . .199 F8
Broxton CH3,SY14 . . . . . .183 E1

Salter's La continued
Hoole Bank CH2 . . . . . . .119 C8
Salters Ford CW8 . . . . . .77 F3
Salters La
Lower Withington SK11 . . .132 B8
Windyharbour SK11 . . . . .109 D1
Saltersbrook Gr SK9 . .34 E1
Saltersford Cnr CW4 . . . .130 E3
Saltersgate CH66 . . . . . .69 F2
Saltney Bsns Ctr CH4 . . .140 F7
Saltney Ferry Prim Sch
CH4 . . . . .140 B6
Saltney Ferry Rd CH4 . . .140 B7
Saltney Terr CH4 . . . . . .140 B7
Salton Gdns WA5 . . . . . .15 E7
Saltwood Dr WA7 . . . . . .50 C5
Saltworks Cl WA6 . . . . . .49 D2
Samian Cl WA10 . . . . . .128 C2
Samphire Gdns WA9 . . . . .6 B7
Samuel St Chester CH1 . .237 C3
Crewe CW1 . . . . .190 B5
Macclesfield SK11 . . . . . .112 D7
Packmoor ST7 . . . . .195 F1
Warrington WA5 . . . . . . .15 E4
Sanbec Gdns WA8 . . . . . .12 D5
Sand La SK10 . . . . .84 F5
Sandalwood WA7 . . . . . .24 C1
Sandalwood Cl WA2 . . . . .8 D2
Sandbach Com Prim Sch
CW11 . . . . .175 A6
Sandbach Crosses*
CW11 . . . . .175 B6
Sandbach Dr CW9 . . . . .103 E6
Sandbach High Sch & Sixth
Form Coll CW11 . . . . . .175 A7
Sandbach Rd
Congleton CW12 . . . . . . .156 A3
Rode Heath ST7 . . . . . . .193 E7
Sandbach Rd N ST7 . . . .193 C4
Sandbach Rd S ST7 . . . .193 D3
Sandbach Sch CW11 . . . .175 A6
Sandbach Sta CW11 . . . .174 D8
Sanderling Rd WA12 . . . . .2 C4
Sanders Hey Cl WA7 . . . .50 B5
Sanders Sq SK11 . . . . . .112 D5
Sanderson Cl
Crewe CW2 . . . . .206 C8
Warrington WA5 . . . . . . .14 D6
Sandfield Ave CW5 . . . . .216 F3
Sandfield Cl WA3 . . . . .3 E4
Sandfield Cres WA3 . . . . .5 C7
Sandfield Ct
Frodsham WA6 . . . . .74 B8
Wrenbury CW5 . . . . .216 F4
Sandfield Hall WA3 . . . . . .3 A4
Sandfield La
Acton Bridge CW8 . . . . . . .76 E1
Hartford CW8 . . . . .103 C4
Sandfield Pk CH60 . . . . . .40 D8
Sandfield Terr CW8 . . . . .76 F1
Sandfields WA6 . . . . .74 B8
Sandford Cres CW2 . . . .207 D2
Sandford Rd CW5 . . . . . .204 F7
Sandgate Rd SK10 . . . . . .87 C4
Sandham Gr CH60 . . . . . .41 D7
Sandham Rd L24 . . . . . . .21 A4
Sandheys CH64 . . . . .41 C1
Sandhill Terr WA4 . . . . . .16 E1
Sandhole Cotts CW7 .149 B8
Sandhole La
Chelford WA16 . . . . .83 D4
Crowton CW8 . . . . .101 B7
Sandhurst Ave CW2 . . . .190 A1
Sandhurst Dr SK9 . . . .60 C8
Sandhurst Rd L26 . . . . . . .21 A4
Sandhurst St WA4 . . . . . .16 F3
Sandiford Rd CW4 . . . . .130 C3
Sandiford Sq CW9 . . . . .104 A8
Sandileigh Ave WA16 . . . .56 F2
Sandington Dr CW8 . . . . .101 F2
Sandiway Bebington CH63 .43 C6
Knutsford WA16 . . . . . . .57 B2
Sandiway Ave WA8 . . . . .12 A1
Sandiway Cl CW8 . . . . . .102 A2
Sandiway La CW9 . . . . . .53 A2
Sandiway Pk CW8 . . . . . .102 E4
Sandiway Prim Sch
CW8 . . . . .102 B3
Sandiway Rd
Crewe CW1 . . . . .190 A7
Handforth SK9 . . . . .34 C8
Sandle Bridge La WA16,
SK9 . . . . .83 E3
Sandle Bridge Rise WA16 83 F6
Sandon Cres CH64 . . . . . .66 E5
Sandon Park Gdns CW2 189 D4
Sandon Pl WA8 . . . . .13 D1
Sandon Rd CH2 . . . . . . .118 E4
Sandon St CW1 . . . . . . .190 D4
Sandown Cl Culcheth WA3 . .4 F4
Middlewich CW10 . . . . . . .151 C8
Runcorn WA7 . . . . .49 C6
Wilmslow SK9 . . . . .60 D8
Sandown Cres CW8 . . . . .102 A3
Sandown Dr WA15 . . . . . .32 D6
Sandown Pl SK11 . . . . . .111 F7
Sandown Rd CW1 . . . . . .190 C7
Sandown Terr CH3 . . . . .118 F1
Sandpiper Cl WA12 . . . . .2 C4
Sandpiper Ct
Chester CH4 . . . . .141 B6
Kidsgrove ST7 . . . . .195 C2
Sandpiper Way CH4 . . . .141 B6
Sandra Dr WA12 . . . . . . .2 E3
Sandringham Ave
Chester CH3 . . . . .119 A2
Helsby WA6 . . . . .73 B4

Sandringham Cl
Altrincham WA14 ....20 F1
Northwich CW9 ....103 E4
Winsford CW7 ....126 C3
Sandford Ct
Golborne WA3 ....3 E7
5 Wilmslow SK9 ....60 A6
Sandringham Dr
Poynton SK12 ....36 D3
Warrington WA5 ....15 C4
Wistaston CW2 ....205 E8
Sandringham Gdns 2
CH65 ....70 D2
Sandringham Rd
Congleton CW12 ....156 F4
Macclesfield SK10 ....87 F1
Widnes WA8 ....13 A6
Sandringham Way 4
SK9 ....60 A6
Sandrock Rd CH3 ....142 E7
Sands Rd ST7 ....195 E6
Sandsdown Cl ST8 ...179 C1
Sandside Rd ST7 .....193 B3
Sandstone Mews WA8 ..12 E4
Sandstone Wlk CH60 ...41 A7
Sandwich Dr WA8 ......87 C4
Sandwood Ave CH4 ...139 B3
Sandy Brow La WA3 .....3 E2
Sandy Cl SK10 ....87 F7
Sandy La Allostock CW4 .106 E1
Astbury CW12 ....177 E6
Aston CW5 ....217 C2
Bold Heath WA8 ....14 B6
Brown Knowl CH3 ......199 C7
Bulkeley SY14 ....184 C1
Chester CH3 ....119 A1
Congleton CW12 ....155 D3
Congleton, Astbury Marsh
CW12 ....156 B2
Croft WA3 ....9 A8
Cronton WA8 ....12 D5
Culcheth WA3 ....4 A1
Golborne WA3 ....2 F8
Golborne,Lowton Common
WA3 ....4 A8
Goostrey CW4 ....107 D1
Haslington CW11 ......192 B7
Hatherton CW5 ....219 F5
Helsby WA6 ....73 B2
Higher Kinnerton CH4 ...161 A6
Huntington CH3 ....141 F8
Knutsford WA16 ....82 D3
Lymm WA13 ....19 B4
Macclesfield SK10 ....86 C2
Neston CH64 ....67 A7
Runcorn WA7 ....48 E7
Runcorn, Preston Brook
WA7 ....50 F6
Saighton CH3 ....142 C3
Saltney CH4 ....140 D6
Sandbach CW11 ....174 D5
Swan Green WA16 .....106 E6
Swettenham CW12 .....131 F3
Tarvin CH3 ....121 C4
Threapwood SY14 .....222 E8
Warrington, Longford WA2 ..8 C2
Warrington,Penketh WA5 ..15 A4
Warrington,Stockton Heath
WA4 ....26 D8
Weaverham CW8 ....77 C2
Whitegate CW8 ....125 D6
Wilmslow SK9 ....59 E8
Sandy La W WA2 ....8 B3
Sandy Moor La WA7 ....24 D3
Sandy Rd ST8 ....179 C2
Sandy Way CW7 ......149 B8
Sandybank CW8 ....78 D1
Sandyfield Ct ST8 ....179 C1
Sandyhill Pl 1 CW7 ...149 D6
Sandyhill Rd CW7 ....149 D6
Sandylands Cres ST7 ..193 F5
Sandylands Pk CW7 ...205 D7
Sandylane Mews CW7 ..156 C5
Sandymere Ct CW7 ....126 B1
Sandymoor La WA7 ....24 D3
Sankey Bridges Ind Est
WA5 ....15 C4
Sankey For Penketh Sta
WA5 ....14 F6
Sankey St Golborne WA3 ..3 A8
Newton-le-W WA12 ....2 A3
Warrington WA1 ....16 A5
Widnes WA8 ....23 A6
Sankey Valley Ind Est
WA12 ....2 A2
Sankey Valley Pk★
Newton-le-W WA5 ....1 E3
★ Warrington WA5 ......15 D5
Sankey Valley St James CE
Prim Sch WA5 ....15 C6
Sankey Way WA5 ....15 D5
Sanky La WA4 ....25 F1
Santon Dr WA3 ....3 E8
Sapling La CW6 ......146 F3
Sark Ave CH65 ....95 B8
Sark Ho CW2 ....219 B4
Sarl Williams Ct CH1 ..237 A3
Sarn Bank Rd SY14 ...222 E6
Sarn Rd SY14 ....222 D8
Sarra La CH3 ....184 B5
Sarsfield Ave 1 WA3 ...3 D8
Sarus Ct WA7 ....24 B4
Saughall Cl CW9 .....103 E4
Saughall Hey CH1 ......94 A1
Saughall Rd Blacon CH1 .117 E5
Blacon,Abbot's Meads
CH1 ....118 A4
Saunders St CW1 .....190 B4

Saundersfoot Cl WA5 ....7 E2
Saunderton Cl WA11 ....1 C7
Saville Ave WA5 ....15 F7
Saville St SK11 ....112 E7
Savoy Rd CW1 ....207 B8
Sawley Cl Culcheth WA3 ..5 A2
Runcorn WA7 ....50 E7
Sawley Dr SK8 ....35 C6
Sawpit St WA13,WA14 ...20 A1
Sawyer Dr ST8 ....179 C1
Saxon Cl WA4 ....26 B5
Saxon Crossway CW7 ..126 B1
Saxon Rd WA7 ....23 C2
Saxon Terr 4 WA8 .....13 B1
Saxon Way Blacon CH1 ..117 E6
Ellesmere Port CH66 .....94 F8
Sandbach CW11 ....175 C6
Saxons La Hartford CW9 .103 E6
Northwich CW8 ....103 D1
Sayce St WA8 ....13 B1
Scafell Ave WA2 ....8 C3
Scafell Cl Bebington CH62 .43 D3
High Lane SK6 ....37 E8
Scaife Rd CW5 ....204 F5
Scaliot Cl SK22 ....39 B8
Scar La SY14 ....198 F1
Sceptre Cl WA12 ....2 A3
Scholar Green Prim Sch
ST7 ....194 E6
Scholar's Ct 3 CH64 ...66 E8
Scholars Cl
Macclesfield SK10 ......111 D8
Saltney CH4 ....140 F4
Scholars Green La WA13 .18 F2
School Ave CH64 ....66 F6
School Bank Norley WA6 .101 A6
Wybunbury CW5 ....220 B8
School Brow WA1 ....16 C6
School Cl Audley ST7 ...210 A1
Knutsford WA16 ....56 F1
Marbury SY13 ....226 E8
Poynton SK12 ....36 F3
School Cotts
Bradwall Green CW11 ..153 B4
Wimboldsley CW10 ....150 F4
School Cres CW1 ......190 E4
School Dr CW8 ....78 A3
School Field Cl CW3 ...230 F4
School Gn CH3 ....182 C1
School Hill CH60 ....40 F1
School Hos SK11 ....109 A1
School House Cotts
CH66 ....69 B6
School La Aldford CH3 .163 F7
Antrobus CW9 ....53 C3
Astbury CW12 ....178 B8
Audlem CW3 ....230 A4
Bold Heath WA8 ....13 E7
Brereton Green CW11 ..153 F5
Bunbury CW6 ....168 E1
Burwardsley CH3 .....184 B6
Cuddington CW8 ......102 A2
Eaton (nr Congleton)
CW12 ....156 E8
Ellesmere Port CH66 ....69 A8
Elton CH2 ....72 B3
Frodsham WA6 ....74 C7
Great Budworth CW9 ....79 B8
Guilden Sutton CH3 ...119 E5
Hartford CW8 ....103 C4
Henbury SK11 ....111 B6
Higher Whitley WA4 .....52 E6
Hollinfare WA3 ....11 A2
Hooton CH66 ....43 F1
Irlam M44 ....11 D5
Lostock Gralam CW9 ....80 A2
Manley WA6 ....99 A5
Marton SK11 ....133 C5
Mickle Trafford CH2 ...119 E8
Moulton CW9 ....126 F8
4 Nantwich CW5 .....204 E6
Neston CH64 ....42 B2
Neston, Little Neston CH64 .66 F6
Neston,Parkgate CH64 ...41 B1
Nether Alderley SK10 ....86 A6
Norbury SY13 ....215 E2
Norley WA6 ....100 D5
Ollerton WA16 ....83 B4
Onneley CW3 ....232 F3
Partington WA14 ....20 D5
Poynton SK12 ....36 F4
Runcorn WA7 ....49 F8
Sandbach CW11 ......174 D7
Sandbach Heath CW11 .175 E6
Smallwood CW11 .....176 F5
Warmingham CW11 ...173 D1
Warrington WA3 ....10 D5
School Mews SK7 ....35 E7
School Rd
Ellesmere Port CH65 .....70 B5
Handforth SK9 ....34 D4
Northwich,Higher Shurlach
CW9 ....104 D6
Warrington WA2 ....8 C1
Winsford,Meadowbank
CW7 ....126 E5
Winsford,Wharton CW7 .127 A2
School Rd N CW9 .....104 E6
School Rd S CW9 .....104 E6
School St Chester CH2 .118 F3
Golborne WA3 ....3 A8
Haslington CW1 ....191 D5
Newton-le-W WA12 ....2 B3
Warrington WA4 ....16 B4
School Terr WA3 ....3 A8
School Way
Northwich CW9 ....104 A8
Widnes WA8 ....13 D3

Schoolfold La SK10 .....63 A7
Schooner Cl WA7 ......50 D6
Scilly Cl CH65 ....70 C1
Scope Ho CW1 ....190 E1
Scotch Hall La CW9 ....53 A3
Scotia Wlk 1 WA3 ......3 F8
Scotland Rd WA1 ....16 B5
Scott Ave Crewe CW1 ..190 F4
Widnes WA8 ....22 F8
Scott Cl
Macclesfield SK10 ......113 A7
Rode Heath ST7 ....193 E8
2 Sandbach CW11 ...174 D6
Scott Rd SK10 ....87 A7
Scott St WA2 ....16 C6
Scott Wlk WA12 ....2 C1
Scotton Ave CH66 ......69 B5
Scroggins La M31 ......11 F4
Sea Bank CW10 ....128 D1
Sea La WA7 ....23 D2
Sea View CH64 ....66 E4
Seabank Rd CH60 ......40 E6
Seabury St WA4 ....17 A3
Seacombe Dr CH66 .....69 E3
Seafield Ave CH60 .....40 E6
Seaford Cl WA7 ....24 D1
Seaford Pl WA2 ....8 A4
Seagrave Cl CW9 ......103 F5
Seagull Cl CW1 ....190 F5
Seahill Rd CH1 ....116 F8
Seal Rd SK7 ....36 A7
Sealand Cl WA2 ....8 E1
Sealand Ind Est CH1 ...117 F2
Sealand Rd Blacon CH1 .117 C3
Chester CH1 ....118 A2
Chester CH1,CH5 .....116 D6
Sealand Trad Pk CH1 ..117 F2
Sealand Way 2 SK9 ....34 D4
Seathwaite Cl WA7 .....49 C5
Seaton Cl WA7 ....190 B8
Seaton Pk CW7 ....24 E3
Seaton St CW7 ....127 D1
Seaview Ave CH62 ......44 B6
Seaville St CH3 ....237 C3
Secker Ave WA4 ....16 D2
Secker Cl WA4 ....16 D2
Second Ave
Connah's Quay CH5 .....92 F3
Crewe CW1 ....190 F2
Kidsgrove ST7 ....194 E1
Poynton SK12 ....36 D1
Runcorn WA7 ....49 F8
Sandbach CW11 ......175 A5
Second Dig La CW5 ...219 C8
Second Wood St CW5 ..204 D5
Sedbergh Cl WA4 ......130 A3
Sedbergh Gr WA7 ......49 E5
Seddon St CW10 ......128 C2
Sedgefield Cl 3 SK10 ...86 F2
Sedgefield Rd CH1 ....118 B2
Sedgeford Cl SK9 ......34 D1
Sedgemere Ave CW1 ...190 A8
Sedgewick Cres WA5 ....6 E6
Sedum Cl CH3 ....142 A6
Sefton Ave
Congleton CW12 ......157 A1
Widnes WA8 ....13 A3
Sefton Dr SK9 ....34 C2
Sefton Rd CH2 ....119 A4
Sefton St WA1 ....16 D5
Selby Cl Poynton SK12 ..36 D5
Runcorn WA7 ....24 F4
Selby Gdns SK8 ....35 C6
Selby Gn CH66 ....69 B5
Selby St WA5 ....15 E5
Selkirk Ave
Bebington CH62 ....43 E4
Warrington WA4 ....17 A3
Selkirk Cl
Ellesmere Port CH66 ....68 F5
Macclesfield SK10 ......86 F2
Selkirk Dr Chester CH4 .141 A7
Holmes Chapel CW4 ...130 B2
Selkirk Rd CH4 ....141 A7
Seller St CH1 ....237 C3
Selsdon Ct CH4 ....141 C7
Selsey Cl CW1 ....190 B8
Selworthy Dr
Crewe CW1 ....190 B7
Warrington WA4 ....17 D3
Selwyn Cl
Newton-le-W WA12 ......2 B5
Widnes WA8 ....13 E3
Selwyn Dr
Cheadle Hulme SK8 .....35 C7
Sutton Lane Ends SK11 .112 F3
Semper Cl CW12 ......157 A4
Seneschal Ct WA7 .....49 E6
Senna La CW9 ....78 C8
Sennen Cl WA7 ....50 C5
Sens Cl CH1 ....237 A2
Sephton Ave WA3 ....4 E3
Serin Cl WA12 ....2 C3
Serpentine The CH4 ...141 B7
Servite Cl CH65 ....69 F6
Servite Pl CH64 ....66 E7
Sett Cl SK22 ....39 B8
Seven Row CH64 ....66 E5
Seven Sisters La WA16 .82 E5
Sevenoaks Cl SK10 .....87 B2
Severn Cl Biddulph ST8 .179 E1
Congleton CW12 ......156 F1
Macclesfield SK10 ......86 F2
Warrington WA2 ....8 E2
Severn Dr SK7 ....35 C6
Severn Rd WA3 ....4 F2

Severn Wlk CW7 ......127 A2
Severnvale CH65 ....70 B3
Sewell St 7 WA7 ....23 B2
Sextant Cl WA7 ....50 D6
Sexton Ave WA9 ....1 D7
Seymour Chase WA16 ...82 A8
Seymour Dr WA7 ....24 C4
Seymour Dr
Ellesmere Port CH66 ....69 E6
Warrington WA1 ....17 A8
Seymour Ho 16 SK9 ....34 E1
Seymour Rd SK8 ....35 A8
Sgt York Loop WA5 .....15 B6
Shackleton Cl WA5 .....15 D8
Shade Terr SK6 ....37 F7
Shadewood Cres WA4 ...17 B2
Shadewood Rd SK11 ...112 A6
Shadowmoss Rd M22 ....33 E8
Shady Brook La CW8 ....77 C1
Shady Gr ST7 ....193 D4
Shaftesbury Ave
Chester CH3 ....119 C2
Warrington WA5 ....14 E2
Shaftesbury Way WA5 ....6 F7
Shaftway Cl WA11 ....1 F7
Shakerley Ave CW12 ...156 F3
Shakespeare Cl CW7 ...104 C7
Shakespeare Dr CW1 ...191 A4
Shakespeare Gr WA2 ....8 C2
Shakespeare Rd
Neston CH64 ....41 E1
Widnes WA8 ....13 A1
Shalcombe Cl L26 ......21 A7
Shallacres CH65 ....69 F7
Shallcross Ave SK23 ...65 E5
Shallcross Cres SK23 ..65 E5
Shallcross Mill Cotts
SK23 ....65 E5
Shallcross Mill Rd SK23 .65 E5
Shallcross Rd SK23 .....65 E5
Shambles The WA16 ....57 B1
Shanklin Cl WA5 ....14 C6
Shannon Cl Chester CH4 .140 E5
Willaston CW5 ....205 D6
Shannon Gr WA8 ....12 E2
Shargate Cl SK9 ....34 C1
Sharnbrook Dr CW2 ...189 D4
Sharon Park Cl WA4 ....17 C1
Sharp St Warrington WA2 .16 C6
Widnes WA8 ....23 A8
Sharpley St 11 SK10 ...112 C8
Sharston Cres WA16 ....57 B1
Shavington Ave CH2 ...118 F4
Shavington High Sch
CW2 ....206 A5
Shavington Home Farm
TF9 ....234 B3
Shavington Prim Sch
CW2 ....206 C4
Shavington Way CW9 ..103 F4
Shaw Cl
Ellesmere Port CH66 ....69 E4
Ellesmere Port,Great Sutton
CH66 ....69 F4
Shaw Dr WA16 ....57 C3
Shaw Entry L35,WA8 ...12 A7
Shaw Heath View WA16 .57 C2
Shaw St Culcheth WA3 ...5 A3
Haydock WA11 ....1 E6
Macclesfield SK11 .....112 C8
Runcorn WA7 ....22 F2
Shaw's Ave WA2 ....16 C8
Shawbury Gr WA1 ....17 A8
Shawell Ct WA8 ....13 E2
Shaws Fold SK9 ....33 F3
Shaws La Winsford CW7 .126 F4
Winsford CW7 ....127 A3
Shay La
Ashton Hayes CH3 .....121 F7
Hampton Heath SY14 ..200 A1
Tarvin CH3 ....121 E3
Shay's La CW6 ....124 E4
Sheaf Cl CH3 ....121 C2
Shearbrook La CW4 ....107 E1
Sheardhall Ave SK12 ...38 E5
Sheath St CW9 ....104 A8
Sheepfield Cl CH66 .....69 C7
Sheerwater Cl WA1 .....16 F7
Sheffield Cl WA5 ....15 C5
Sheffield Row WA12 .....7 D8
Sheilings The WA3 ....3 F8
Shelagh Ave WA8 ......13 A1
Shelbourne Mews 2
SK10 ....111 F8
Shelburne Dr CW1 ....191 C5
Sheldon Ave
Chester CH3 ....119 B2
Congleton CW12 ......157 A1
Sheldon Cl M31 ....11 F3
Sheldon Pl SK10 ....88 B7
Sheldon Rd
Hazel Grove SK7 ....36 E8
Poynton SK12 ....37 C2
Sheldrake Gr CH64 .....66 E5
Shell Green Est WA8 ....23 E8
Shellbrook Gr 3 SK9 ...34 D1
Shelley Ave CW9 ....80 A5
Shelley Cl Crewe CW1 ..190 F4
Middlewich CW10 .....151 C6
Rode Heath ST7 ......193 E8
Shelley Ct 5 CW11 ....174 D6
Shelley Dr CW2 ....189 F1
Shelley Gr WA4 ....16 F1
Shelley Rd Blacon CH1 .117 F6
Widnes WA8 ....13 A1
Shellow La CW12,SK11 .134 C5
Shellway Rd CH2 ....71 A3

Shelton Cl WA8 ....13 F3
Shenhurst Cl SK9 ......59 E4
Shepcroft La WA4 ......26 C3
Shepherd's La CH2 ....118 D5
Shepherds Fold Dr
CW7 ....126 F3
Shepherds Row WA7 ....23 F2
Shepherds View CW8 ...78 B2
Shepley Cl SK7 ....36 D8
Sheppard Cl 1 CW1 ...190 D5
Sheppenhall Gr CW5 ...217 C1
Sheppenhall La CW5,
SY13 ....228 D5
Shepperton Cl WA4 .....26 E6
Shepsides Cl CH66 .....69 C3
Shepton Rd CH66 ......69 E2
Sheraton Rd CH3 ......143 B5
Sherborne Cl WA7 ......24 F3
Sherborne Rd CW1 ....190 D6
Sherbourne Ave CH4 ..141 B5
Sherbourne Cl SK8 .....35 B6
Sherbourne Rd
Ellesmere Port CH65 ....70 D3
Macclesfield SK11 .....111 F7
Sherbourne Way WA5 ....6 F6
Sherbrook Rise SK9 ....60 C6
Sherbrooke Rd SK12 ...38 D6
Sheri Dr WA12 ....2 E2
Sheridan Ave WA3 ......3 D7
Sheridan Cl CW1 .....173 B1
Sheridan Pl WA2 ....8 A5
Sheridan Way WA7 .....24 D2
Sheringham Cl CH4 ...140 E5
Sheringham Dr CW1 ...190 B8
Sheringham Rd WA5 ....14 E6
Sherlock Ave WA11 ......1 E7
Sherratt Cl
Congleton CW12 ......156 E2
Nantwich CW5 ....204 F4
Sherrington's La CH3 ..199 D8
Sherwin St CW2 ....190 C1
Sherwood Cl WA8 ......12 C1
Sherwood Cres WA5 .....6 E6
Sherwood Gr WA6 ....73 A3
Sherwood Rd
Blacon CH1 ....117 E5
Macclesfield SK11 .....112 D5
Shetland Cl
Warrington WA2 ....8 E4
Widnes WA8 ....13 E3
Shetland Dr
Bebington CH62 ....43 E8
Ellesmere Port CH65 ....70 C1
Shevington Cl WA8 .....13 E3
Shevington Wlk WA8 ...13 E3
Shiggins Cl WA5 ....15 D6
Shilton Cl CW10 ......151 E5
Ship St WA6 ....49 C1
Shipbrook Rd
Chester CH2 ....118 F6
Davenham CW9 ....104 C3
Northwich CW9 ....104 C6
Shipgate St CH1 ......237 B1
Shipgate The CH1 .....237 B1
Shipton Cl
Warrington WA5 ....15 B8
Widnes WA8 ....12 D3
Shirley Ave SK8 ....34 C6
Shirley Dr WA4 ....17 A2
Shirleys Cl SK10 ....87 A6
Shirleys Dr SK10 ....87 A6
Shocklach Oviatt CE Prim
Sch SY14 ....211 C7
Shocklach Rd CH2 .....118 F6
Shones Croft CH64 .....67 A5
Shop La Congleton CW12 .156 E1
Little Budworth CW6 ..124 F2
Shopping Precinct The
CH2 ....72 B3
Shoreham Dr WA5 ......15 A3
Shores Green Dr CW9 ...79 F5
Shores La CW5 ....203 D7
Short Cl WA12 ....1 E3
Short St Haydock WA11 ..1 E6
11 Macclesfield SK11 .112 D8
Newton-le-W WA12 ......1 E3
Widnes WA8 ....23 A6
Shorthorn Cl CW10 ...128 D2
Shorwell Cl WA5 ....14 C7
Shotwick La CH1 ....93 D6
Shotwick Rd CH5 ....92 F3
Shrewbridge Cres CW5 .204 E4
Shrewbridge Rd CW5 ..204 D4
Shrewsbury Dr ST5 ....210 E2
Shrewsbury Gdns SK8 ..35 C6
Shrewsbury Rd 4 CH65 .70 C5
Shrewsbury St WA4 ....16 D3
Shrewsbury Way CH4 ..140 F4
Shrigley Cl SK9 ....34 D1
Shrigley Rd
Pott Shrigley SK10 .....63 B5
Poynton SK10,SK12 ....37 C2
Shrigley Rd N SK12 ....37 D3
Shrigley Rise SK10 .....63 C1
Shropshire Cl
Middlewich CW10 .....151 C8
Warrington WA1 ....17 E6
Shropshire La SY13 ...227 E2
Shropshire Rd CH2 .....70 F3
Shropshire St CW3 ....229 F4
Shuldham St WA16 .....29 C4
Shurlach Rd CW9 .....104 D6
Shutley La CW8 ....77 D6
Shutlingsloe Way SK10 .112 A8

Sibbersfield La CH3 ....180 F4
Sibell St CH1 ....237 C3
Siddall St **7** CW9 ....104 B8
Siddals Ct CW5 ....204 C5
Siddeley Cl CH4 ....139 C4
Siddeley Dr WA12 ....1 F4
Siddington Ave CW9 ....104 A4
Siddington Rd
  Handforth SK9 ....34 D5
  Poynton SK12 ....36 F2
Siddorn St CW7 ....126 E1
Side End La SK23 ....64 F3
Side La CW6 ....144 E6
Sidings The SK23 ....65 F8
Sidlaw Cl CH66 ....69 A6
Sidmouth Cl WA5 ....14 E4
Sidmouth Gr SK8 ....34 F7
Sidney Rd CH64 ....41 F1
Siemens Rd M44 ....11 E5
Sienna Cl M44 ....11 E6
Signal Ct CH2 ....118 F2
Silk Hill SK23 ....65 F8
Silk Mill
  Macclesfield SK11 ....112 D6
  Poynton SK12 ....36 C4
Silk Mill St WA16 ....57 A2
Silk Rd The
  Bollington SK10 ....87 C4
  Macclesfield SK10 ....112 E8
Silk St CW12 ....156 C2
Silkstone Cres CW7 ......50 B7
Silsden Ave WA3 ....4 B8
Silvan Ct SK10 ....87 B1
Silver Ave WA11 ....1 A5
Silver La Croft WA3 ......9 C7
  Warrington WA3 ....10 C6
  Warrington,Risley WA3 ..9 F7
Silver St Bollington SK10 ..88 B8
  Congleton CW12 ......156 E2
  Warrington WA2 ....16 B6
Silver Terr CW11 ......175 D6
Silverbirch Croft CH4 ..139 B3
Silverbirch Way CH66 ....94 F8
Silverdale CW8 ....103 D7
Silverdale Cl
  Chorlton CW2 ....207 C2
  Frodsham WA6 ....74 C7
  High Lane SK6 ....37 E8
Silverdale Dr SK9 ....60 A4
Silverdale Rd
  Newton-le-W WA12 ......2 B4
  Warrington WA4 ....16 B2
Silvergate Ct CW12 ....178 E8
Silvermine Cl **8** ST7 ..195 B2
Silvermuir CH1 ....117 E3
Silverne Dr CH65 ....70 A2
Silverwood ST7 ....195 B1
Simkin Ave WA4 ....16 F4
Simmonds Cl CW9 ......103 E3
Simms Cross Prim Sch
  WA8 ....23 A8
Simons La WA6 ....74 B5
Simonside WA8 ....12 C2
Simonstone Rd CH4 ....139 D4
Simonswood Cl CW10 ..151 B8
Simpson Cl CH2 ....95 C1
Simpson Ct CW1 ......173 B1
Simpson La SK10 ....63 D7
Simpson Rd CH2 ....95 C1
Simpson St SK9 ....59 F6
Simpson's Ct **17** SK11 ..112 C8
Simpsons Way CH4 ....139 B3
Sinclair Ave Alsager ST7 193 B3
  Warrington WA2 ....8 B2
  Widnes WA8 ....23 A8
Sinderland La
  Partington WA13 ....20 B8
  Partington WA14 ....20 E8
Singapore Ave M90 ......33 A8
Singleton Ave CW1 ....190 C6
Singleton Rd CH65 ......69 F4
Sir John Deane's Coll
  CW9 ....103 F6
Sir Thomas Boteler CE High
  Sch WA4 ....16 E3
Siskin Cl WA12 ....2 C3
Six Acre Gdns WA4 ......25 A5
Six Acre La WA4 ....25 A5
Sixth Ave CH5 ....92 E1
Skeath Cl CW11 ......175 E6
Skellern St ST7 ......194 D2
Skellorn Green La
  Skellorn Green SK10 ....62 F8
  Wardsend SK10 ....36 F1
Skiddaw Cl WA7 ....50 A4
Skip's La CH3 ....142 F7
Skipton Cl
  Hazel Grove SK7 ....36 C8
  2 Runcorn WA7 ......23 F1
Skipton Dr CH66 ....69 C5
Skye Cl
  Ellesmere Port CH65 ....70 C1
  Widnes WA8 ....13 E3
Skylark Cl CW1 ......189 F7
Slack St SK11 ....112 E6
Slacken La ST7 ......194 D2
Slade La Mobberley WA16 ..58 A7
  Nether Alderley SK10 ....85 E5
Slade St **5** CW9 ....104 B8
Slag La Golborne WA3 ....3 D8
  Haydock WA11 ....1 B7
Slater St
  Macclesfield SK11 ....112 C6
  Warrington WA4 ....16 D3
Slicks Bsns Ctr CW8 ....78 C2

Slindon Cl ST5 ....210 D1
Slutchers La WA1 ....16 A3
Small Ave WA2 ....8 C2
Small Cres WA2 ....8 C2
Small La WA16 ....58 A8
Smallbrook Wlk CW2 ..206 C8
Smallman Rd CW2 ......190 C1
Smallwood CE Prim Sch
  CW11 ....176 F5
Smallwood Cl
  4 Middlewich CW10 ..151 C8
  Newcastle-u-Lyme ST5 ..210 A1
Smallwood Ct **1** CW12 156 F3
Smallwood Forge
  CW11 ....176 D5
Smethwick La CW11,
  CW12 ....154 E4
Smith Cl ST7 ....193 B4
Smith Cres WA2 ....16 D8
Smith Dr WA2 ....16 D8
Smith Gr CW1 ....190 A6
Smith La Ashley WA16 ....31 E1
  Mobberley WA16 ....57 F6
  Rainow SK10 ....89 A5
Smith Rd WA8 ....22 F7
Smith St
  Macclesfield SK11 ....112 D6
  Warrington WA1 ....16 B5
Smith's La CW8 ....77 C1
Smith's Terr SK11 ....112 E6
Smithfield Dr/Fford
  Smithfield LL13 ......196 D8
Smithfield Gn LL13 ....196 D8
Smithfield La CW11 ....175 C6
Smithfield St LL13 ....196 D8
Smithfields CH3 ......166 C2
Smithills Cl WA3 ....9 D5
Smiths Lawn SK9 ....60 A6
Smithy Bank Acton CW5 204 A6
  Winsford CW7 ....149 A3
Smithy Brow
  Bollington SK10 ....88 C8
  Winwick WA3 ....8 F7
Smithy Cl Cronton WA8 ..12 C5
  Neston CH64 ....67 A4
  Saughall CH1 ....94 A1
Smithy Cotts SY14 ....213 A2
Smithy Ct
  Christleton CH3 ......142 E7
  5 Ellesmere Port CH66 ..69 C6
Smithy Gn
  Cheadle Hulme SK8 ....35 A8
  Gatesheath CH3 ......165 E5
Smithy Gr CW11 ......176 A2
Smithy Hill CH63 ....42 A6
Smithy La Alsager CW2 208 D7
  Altrincham WA14 ....20 D3
  Barthomley CW2 ......208 C6
  Biddulph ST8 ....179 D2
  Bosley SK11 ....158 E6
  Broxton CH3 ....183 D1
  Congleton CW12 ......156 C7
  Crewe CW1 ....189 E8
  Croft WA3 ....9 A7
  Cronton WA8 ....12 C5
  Cuddington CW8 ......102 A5
  Ellesmere Port CH66 ....69 C6
  Great Budworth CW9 ....79 A8
  Helsby WA6 ....73 C5
  Kingsley WA6 ....75 B2
  Little Leigh WA6 ....77 B6
  Lostock Gralam CW9 ....80 A2
  Malpas SY14 ....213 A2
  Mottram St Andrew SK10 ..61 A2
  Mouldsworth CH3 ......98 F2
  Partington M31 ....11 F3
  Rainow SK10 ....88 E5
  Utkinton CW6 ....146 C6
  Weston CW2 ....207 C5
  Willaston CH64 ....68 A7
Smithy Pathway CH4 ..140 F4
Smithy The CH2 ......118 E8
Smithy Wlk CW11 ....176 A2
Smokehall La CW7,CW9 126 F6
Smokehall Lane Ind Est
  CW7 ....127 A5
Smokey La SY13 ......224 A1
Smokies Way ST8 ....179 C1
Smyth Rd WA8 ....13 D2
Snab La Neston CH64 ....66 F4
  Norbury SY13 ....215 B5
Snabwood Cl CH64 ......66 E5
Snaefell Rise WA4 ......26 C7
Snape Hollow CW2 ....207 F4
Snape La CW2 ....207 E4
Snape Rd Crewe CW2 ..206 D8
  Macclesfield SK10 ......87 F1
Snapebrook Gr **6** SK9 ..34 E1
Snelson La Chelford SK11 108 E7
  Chelford,Marthall WA16,
  SK9 ....83 D3
Snipe Cl SK12 ....36 A4
Snow Hill SK11 ....112 E6
Snowberry Cl WA8 ......13 F4
Snowberry Wlk M31 ....11 E3
Snowdon Cl
  Ellesmere Port CH66 ....69 A6
  Warrington WA5 ....14 E6
Snowdon Cres CH4 ....141 A5
Snowdon Dr CW2 ......189 D3
Snowdon St CW8 ....77 F3
Snowdonia Way CW7 ..149 B7
Snowdrop Cl WA7 ......49 F4
Solly Cres CW9 ....156 A2
Solvay Rd CW8 ....78 D1
Solway Cl WA2 ....8 F4
Solway Ct CW1 ....191 A4
Solway Gr WA7 ....49 D5

Somerford Ave CW2 ....190 A3
Somerford Cl CW11 ....175 C8
Somerford Ct **2** CW12 156 F3
Somerford Rd CH4 ....139 C4
Somerford Way **3** SK9 ..34 E5
Somerford Wlk WA8 ....13 E3
Somerley Cl CW1 ......190 B8
Somerset Ave ST7 ....194 F2
Somerset Cl
  Congleton CW12 ......156 D4
  Irlam M44 ....11 D6
Somerset Rd CH2 ......118 F5
Somerset St CH1 ......237 B4
Somerset Way WA1 ......17 B8
Somerton Cl **5** SK11 ..111 F7
Somerton Rd SK11 ....111 F7
Somerville Cl
  Bebington CH63 ....43 B6
  High Legh WA16 ....29 C4
  Neston CH64 ....66 E5
Somerville Cres CH65 ..70 C4
Somerville Rd WA8 ......22 D8
Somerville St CW2 ....190 B2
Soot Hill CW8,CW9 ......78 C3
Sorbus Cl CH2 ....72 C3
Sorbus Dr CW1 ....190 E6
Sorby Rd M44 ....11 F7
Sorrel Cl Huntington CH3 142 A6
  Warrington WA2 ....9 C2
Soss Moss Hospl (Mary
  Dendy Unit) SK10 ......84 C6
Sossmoss La SK10 ......84 D6
Sound & District Prim Sch
  CW5 ....217 F5
Sound La
  Ravensmoor CW5 ......203 E1
  Sound CW5 ....217 D7
Souter's La CH1 ......237 B2
South Acre Dr
  Handforth SK9 ....34 D3
  Macclesfield SK11 ....113 A7
South Ave Chester CH2 237 C4
  Haslington CW1 ......191 D4
  Warrington WA2 ....16 B8
  Warrington, Stockton Heath
  WA4 ....16 C1
South Bank CH2 ......118 C4
South Bank Cl SK9 ......60 B2
South Bank Gr CW12 ..156 F2
South Bank Terr WA7 ..22 F3
South Cheshire Coll
  CW2 ....190 B2
  CW1 ....172 E1
South Cl Tarporley CW6 146 C2
  Wilmslow SK9 ....59 F6
South Crescent Rd CH4 237 C1
South Croft CW5 ......185 D6
South Crofts CW5 ....204 F5
South Dale WA5 ....14 F5
South Downs WA16 ......57 C1
South Downs Dr WA14 ..31 D8
South Dr Heswall CH60 ..41 A7
  Northwich CW9 ......104 D6
  Plumley WA16 ....80 F3
  Wilmslow SK9 ....60 B6
South Gn CH5 ....116 A6
South Gr **9** SK9 ....60 A1
South La
  Warrington WA5,WA8 ..14 E5
  Widnes WA8 ....13 F4
South Lane Entry WA8 ..13 F5
South Lodge CW6 ....168 D8
South Mead SK12 ......36 B5
South Meadway SK6 ....37 F7
South Oak La SK9 ......59 F5
South Par WA7 ....48 D7
South Park Dr SK12 ....36 E5
South Park Rd SK11 ..112 C7
South Pier Rd CH65 ....70 D7
South Rd
  Altrincham,Ashley Heath
  WA14 ....31 B8
  Ellesmere Port CH65 ....70 C3
  Halewood L24 ....21 A4
  Runcorn WA7 ....48 D7
  Stanlow CH65 ....70 F4
South St Alderley Edge SK9 60 A1
  Chester CH3 ....119 A1
  Congleton CW12 ......156 D3
  Crewe CW2 ....190 D2
  Mount Pleasant ST7 ..195 B6
  3 Widnes WA8 ....23 B8
South Terr **12** SK9 ......60 A1
South View Chester CH4 141 D7
  Christleton CH3 ......142 F7
  Lower Withington SK11 132 A8
  New Mills SK22 ....39 B8
South View Ave SK11 ..111 D2
South View Cotts SK11 193 F4
South View La CW7 ....170 F2
South View Rd CH1 ....118 B2
South Way CH1 ....117 F4
South West Ave SK10 ..87 F6
South Wirral High Sch
  CH62 ....43 D4
Southampton Way WA7 ..50 E6
Southbank CW9 ....79 A7
Southbank Ave CW2 ..206 C5
Southdale Rd WA1 ......17 A7
Southdown Cl SK10 ....87 D4
Southdown Cres SK8 ....34 F8
Southern St WA4 ......16 C1
Southey Cl
  8 Sandbach CW11 ....174 D6
  Widnes WA8 ....22 F8
Southfield SK10 ....87 A4
Southfield Cl SK9 ......34 C3

Southfield Rd CH66 ......69 C7
Southfields WA16 ....57 C3
Southfields Ave WA5 ....14 F6
Southfields Cl CW5 ....220 A8
Southlands CW4 ......130 C2
Southlands Ave WA5 ....14 F3
Southlands St WA7 ......48 F8
Southlands Mews **7**
  WA7 ....22 F1
Southlands Rd CW12 ..157 A1
Southlands View CW4 107 E1
Southlawn SK9 ....60 A5
Southport St WA9 ....1 A3
Southward Rd WA11 ......2 A7
Southwark Pl CW7 ....149 A8
Southway
  Middlewich CW10 ....128 C1
  Runcorn WA7 ....49 F7
  Widnes WA8 ....22 D8
Southway Ave WA4 ......26 D7
Southwell St WA3 ....3 C8
Southwold Cres WA5 ....14 E5
Southwood Ave WA7 ....24 C2
Southworth Ave WA5 ....15 F4
Southworth La WA2,WA3 ..8 E7
Southworth Rd WA12 ....3 B1
Sovereign Cl Golborne WA3 3 E7
  Northwich CW9 ......104 F6
  Runcorn WA7 ....50 D7
Sovereign Ct WA3 ....9 C4
Sovereign Way CH1 ....117 C2
Sowcar Way SK10 ....88 C8
Spark Hall Cl WA4 ......26 E1
Spark La Runcorn WA7 ..23 F1
  Smallwood CW11 ....154 C2
Sparks Cl CH3 ....142 B7
Sparrow La WA16 ....57 B1
Sparrowbutts Gr ST7 ..195 C2
Sparrowhawk Cl WA7 ....50 A7
Spath La SK8 ....34 F5
Spath La E SK8 ....35 B5
Spath Wlk SK8 ....35 B5
Spawell Cl WA3 ....3 E1
Speakman Ave WA12 ....2 C5
Speakman St WA7 ......22 F3
Speed's Way CH3 ......180 E2
Speedwell Cl
  11 Golborne WA3 ......3 E8
  Heswall CH60 ....41 C8
  Huntington CH3 ......142 A5
Speedwell Dr CH60 ....41 C8
Speedwell Rd ST5 ....210 F1
Speke Bvd L24,L26,WA8 ..21 B5
Speke Ho L24 ....21 A2
Speke Rd WA8 ....22 C6
Spencer Brook SK10 ....86 F6
Spencer Cl Alsager ST7 192 F4
  Wistaston CW2 ....206 A8
Spencer Mews SK10 ....86 F6
Spencer St Barnton CW8 ..78 B3
  Northwich CW8 ......103 E7
Spenlow Cl SK12 ....36 E1
Spennymoor Ct WA7 ....49 E7
Spenser Cl WA8 ....12 F1
Spenser Rd CH64 ......41 E1
Spey Cl Middlewich CW10 128 C1
  Winsford CW7 ....126 F1
Spey Dr ST7 ....195 C2
Spike Island (Nature
  Reserve)* WA8 ....23 A5
Spindle St CW12 ......156 E2
Spink La WA16 ....80 A6
Spinnaker Cl WA7 ......50 D5
Spinner Cres CW9 ......78 D7
Spinners La SK12 ....36 C4
Spinners Way SK10 ....87 F7
Spinney Ave
  Goostrey CW4 ....107 F1
  Widnes WA8 ....12 A1
Spinney Cl Handforth SK9 34 C3
  Winsford CW7 ....150 A8
Spinney Dr
  Ellesmere Port CH66 ....69 D2
  Weston CW2 ....207 B5
Spinney End CH3 ......166 A1
Spinney Gdns WA4 ......27 B4
Spinney La WA16 ....56 E3
Spinney Mead SK10 ....87 E2
Spinney The
  Cuddington CW8 ......101 D5
  Heswall CH60 ....41 C5
  Lawton-gate ST7 ......194 E4
  Neston CH64 ....41 D1
  Norley WA6 ....100 E5
  Sandbach CW11 ......175 C6
  Willaston CW5 ......205 D6
Spinney Wlk WA7 ....24 A1
Spires Gdns WA2 ....8 A7
Spital Wlk CH2 ....118 F2
Spodegreen La WA14 ....30 C8
Spout La WA16 ....58 B4
Spragg St CW12 ......156 E3
Spring Ave **2** CH66 ....69 C6
Spring Bank ST7 ......195 A7
Spring Bank Rd SK22 ....39 C8
Spring Cl ST7 ....193 E8
Spring Ct **2** WA2 ......23 B2
Spring Gdns Crewe CW1 190 D5
  Ellesmere Port CH66 ....69 C6
  Macclesfield SK10 ......87 D1
  Mobberley WA16 ....58 A1
  Nantwich CW5 ....204 F5
Spring Hill CW6 ......168 C8
Spring La
  Coddington CH3 ......181 E6
  Croft WA3 ....9 B6
  Lymm WA13 ....19 F3
Spring Mdw CW8 ....78 E1

Spring Mount SK22 ......39 C8
Spring Rd SK12 ....36 F2
Spring St
  Congleton CW12 ......156 E2
  Widnes WA8 ....23 A6
  Wilmslow SK9 ....60 A7
Springbank SK10 ....87 F7
Springbank Cl WA7 ......49 B6
Springbank Cres CW7 ..77 F3
Springbank Gdns WA13 ..19 B5
Springbourne WA6 ......74 D6
Springburn Gdns WA1 ..17 F7
Springcroft CH64 ......41 C1
Springe La CW5 ......203 B5
Springfield Ave
  Golborne WA3 ....2 F8
  Helsby WA6 ....73 B3
  Lymm WA13 ....19 B5
  Malpas SY14 ....213 C3
  Warrington, Grappenhall
  WA4 ....17 B3
  Warrington,Padgate WA1 ..17 A8
Springfield Cl CH4 ....161 A2
Springfield Cres CW8 ..77 F3
Springfield Ct / Llys Maes Y
  Ffynnon CH4 ....161 A4
Springfield Dr Talke ST7 210 E8
  Wilmslow SK9 ....59 D5
  Wistaston CW2 ....205 F7
Springfield Ho **5** SK9 ..60 A7
Springfield Pk WA11 ......1 C7
Springfield Rd
  Macclesfield SK11 ....111 F8
  Malpas SY14 ....213 B3
  Mobberley WA16 ....57 F4
  Widnes WA8 ....22 A8
Springfield Sch CW1 ..191 A3
Springfield St WA1 ......16 A5
Springfields
  Cuddington CW8 ......101 D4
  Helsby WA6 ....73 B3
  Knutsford WA16 ....57 C3
  Mickle Trafford CH2 ..119 E8
  Prestbury SK10 ....87 A7
Springfields Dr CW12 ..156 D3
Springhead Prim Sch
  ST7 ....210 D6
Springhill SK10 ....88 A1
Springhill Ave CH62 ....43 D6
Springholm Dr WA4 ....26 D3
Springmount WA3 ....3 E7
Springvale Ind Est
  CW11 ....174 D6
Springwell Cl CW2 ....206 C8
Springwood Ave WA16 ..57 C3
Springwood Cl
  Blacon CH1 ....117 C4
  Macclesfield SK10 ......87 D5
Springwood Way SK10 ..87 D5
Sprink La CW12 ......157 D5
Sproston Way CW9 ....103 E4
Spruce Ave CW8 ......102 B3
Spruce Cl Golborne WA3 ..3 F7
  Warrington WA1 ....17 E7
Spruce Gr ST7 ....193 F7
Spuley La SK10 ....63 D2
Spunhill Ave CH66 ......69 D2
Spurling Rd WA5 ....6 F5
Spurston Ct WA16 ......29 C4
Spurstow Mews SK8 ....35 B8
Square St SK11 ....112 E6
Square The
  Altrincham WA15 ......32 C8
  Audlem CW3 ....229 F4
  Christleton CH3 ......142 E8
  Holmes Chapel CW4 ..130 C3
  Ince CH2 ....71 F5
  6 Lymm WA13 ....18 E3
  Woore CW3 ....232 C1
Squires Ave WA8 ....23 A8
Squires Cl WA11 ....1 B6
Squirrel Cl CW8 ......103 C7
Squirrel's Jump SK9 ....60 C1
Squirrels Chase SK10 ..86 F5
St Michael's Row CH1 ..237 B2
Stable La
  Mouldsworth CH3 ......99 A3
  Utkinton CW6 ....123 F1
Stables The
  Bostock Green CW10 ..127 D5
  Guilden Sutton CH3 ..119 F5
Stablings The SK9 ......60 A5
Stadium Way CH1 ......118 B3
Stadmorslow La ST7 ..195 F4
Staffin Ave CH65 ....95 B8
Stafford Cl SK10 ....86 F2
Stafford Gdns CH65 ....70 B5
Stafford Rd WA4 ....16 C2
Stafford St Audlem CW3 230 A4
  Crewe CW1 ....190 C5
Stafford Wlk SK10 ......86 F2
Stage La WA13 ....19 C4
Stainer Cl WA12 ....2 B5
Staines Cl WA4 ....26 E5
Stainforth Cl WA3 ....4 D4
Stainmore Cl WA3 ......10 B6
Staithes Rd M22 ....33 D8
Stalbridge Rd CW2 ....190 C2
Stallard Way CW10 ....151 C8
Stalmine Ave SK8 ......34 B8
Stamford Ave CW2 ....190 C3
Stamford Cl SK11 ......112 C4
Stamford Ct Chester CH3 119 C2
  Lymm WA13 ....18 F3
  Macclesfield SK11 ....112 C5
Stamford La CH3 ......120 A1
Stamford Pl SK9 ....60 B7

Stamford Rd
Alderley Edge SK9 ....60 B1
Blacon CH1 ....117 E6
Handforth SK9 ....34 A1
Little Bollington WA14 .....20 B2
Macclesfield SK11 .....112 C4
Stamford St CH65 ......70 A5
Stamp Ave CW1 ....190 D6
Stamp Cl CW1 ....190 D6
Standford Dr CW9 .....104 A5
Standish Ct WA8 ....22 D8
Stanford Cl CW9 ......103 F5
Stanhope Ave CW1 .....190 E3
Stanhope Cl SK9 ....60 D8
Stanier Cl CW1 ....191 A4
Stanlaw Rd CH65 ....70 C4
Stanley & Brocklehurst Ct 5
SK10 ....112 C8
Stanley Ave
Warrington WA5 ....14 D7
Warrington, Stockton Heath
WA4 ....16 F2
Stanley Bank Rd WA11 ....1 A7
Stanley Cl Hartford CW8 .103 A4
Widnes WA8 ....13 C2
Stanley Ct ST7 ....193 C4
Stanley Dr
Heald Green SK9 ....34 D6
Newcastle-u-Lyme ST5 ...210 C1
Stanley Gr CW9 ....79 E2
Stanley Green Ind Est
SK8 ....34 E5
Stanley Green Ret Pk
SK8 ....34 F6
Stanley Hall La SK12 .....38 C6
Stanley La CH62 ....43 F4
Stanley Park Ct CH4 ....140 E5
Stanley Park Dr CH4 ....140 E5
Stanley Pl Chester CH1 ..237 A2
Warrington WA4 ....16 F2
Stanley Place Mews
CH1 ....237 A2
Stanley Rd Biddulph ST8 .179 C2
Ellesmere Port CH65 ......70 C7
Handforth SK8,SK9 ......34 E6
Knutsford WA16 ....56 F2
Stanley Rd Ind Est WA16 57 A1
Stanley St Chester CH1 ..237 A2
1 Crewe CW1 ....190 C4
7 Macclesfield SK11 ....112 D8
Newton-le-W WA12 ....2 A3
Northwich CW9 ....104 C8
Runcorn WA7 ....23 B3
Warrington WA1 ....16 B4
Stanley Villas 6 WA7 ....22 F1
Stanlow & Thornton Sta
CH2 ....71 D5
Stanlow Abbey Bsns Ctr
CH65 ....70 D2
Stanmore Rd WA7 ....23 D2
Stannage La CH3 ....180 F5
Stanner Cl WA5 ....7 D2
Stannerhouse La CW11 .175 E4
Stanney Cl
Bebington CH62 ....43 E3
Neston CH64 ....66 E7
Stanney Grange Sports
Complex The CH65 .....70 E3
Stanney High Sch CH65 .70 C2
Stanney La
Ellesmere Port CH65 ......70 C3
Stoak CH2 ....70 E1
Stanney Mill Ind Est CH2 70 F3
Stanney Mill La CH2 .....70 F2
Stanney Mill Rd CH2 .....70 F2
Stanney Ten Ind Est CH2 .70 F1
Stanney Woods Ave
CH65 ....70 C1
Stanney Woods Ctry Pk*
CH65 ....70 B1
Stanneybrook Cl WA6 ..101 A6
Stanneylands Cl SK9 ....34 C2
Stanneylands Dr SK9 ....34 B2
Stanneylands Rd SK9 ....34 B2
Stansfield Ave WA1 ......16 F6
Stansfield Dr WA4 ....27 A7
Stanstead Ave WA5 ......14 F3
Stanthorne Ave CW2 ...190 A3
Stanton Cl WA11 ....1 C6
Stanton Ct CH64 ....66 E8
Stanton Dr CH2 ....118 D5
Stanton Rd WA4 ....17 D3
Stanyer Ct CW5 ....205 A4
Stapeley Broad Lane CE Prim
Sch CW5 ....205 A1
Stapeley Cl CW9 ....103 E4
Stapeley Ct CW1 ....190 B5
Stapeley Gdns L26 ....21 A6
Stapeley Terr CW5 .....205 A4
Stapeley Water Gdns*
CW5 ....205 A3
Stapleford Ct CH66 ......69 F8
Stapleton Ave WA2 ....16 D8
Stapleton Ct WA6 ....74 C8
Stapleton Rd SK10 ....87 B2
Stapleton Way WA8 ......22 B5
Stapley Cl WA7 ....22 F1
Star La Lymm WA13 ......18 C4
Macclesfield SK11 ......112 D4
Starbeck Dr CH66 ....69 B5
Starkey Gr WA4 ....16 F4
Starling Cl Farndon CH3 .180 F1
Kidsgrove ST7 ....195 D3
Runcorn WA7 ....50 D7
Start La SK23 ....65 B7
Statham Ave Lymm WA13 .18 D3
Warrington WA2 ....8 C2
Statham Cl WA13 ....18 D3
Statham Com Prim Sch
WA13 ....18 C4
Statham Dr WA13 ....18 D3
Statham La WA13 ....18 B5
Statham St SK11 ....112 D7
Station App / Lon yr Orsaf
CH1 ....116 F7
Station Ave
Ellesmere Port CH66 ......69 C7
Helsby WA6 ....73 B4
Station Cl CH64 ....66 F7
Station Cotts CH1 ......116 F7
Station Gn CH66 ....69 C7
Station Hill CW8 ....76 F2
Station La
Dunham-on-t-H CH3 ......97 D3
Guilden Sutton CH2,CH3 ..119 F7
Rushton Spencer SK11 ...159 B2
Station Rd Adderley TF9 .235 A5
Alpraham CW6 ....169 E2
Alsager ST7 ....193 D3
Astbury ST7,CW12 ......178 B1
Backford CH1 ....95 A3
Biddulph ST8 ....179 C1
Bosley CW12 ....135 A2
Burton CH64 ....67 B1
Chelford SK11 ....84 A2
Chester CH1 ....237 C4
Crowton CW8 ....76 D2
Delamere CW8 ....123 D8
Ellesmere Port CH65 ......70 C6
Ellesmere Port,Little Sutton
CH66 ....69 C6
Elton CH2 ....72 A5
Goostrey CW4 ....131 A8
Handforth SK9 ....34 D3
Haydock WA11 ....1 C6
Heswall CH60 ....40 F6
Holmes Chapel CW4 .....130 D2
Irlam M44 ....11 E7
Kidsgrove ST7 ....194 F1
Kidsgrove, Newchapel ST7 195 E2
Lostock Gralam CW9 ......80 A2
Mobberley WA16 ....57 F7
Mouldsworth CH3 ....99 A2
Mow Cop ST7 ....195 C8
Nantwich CW5 ....204 E5
Neston CH64 ....66 F7
Neston, Parkgate CH64 ....66 C8
New Mills SK22 ....39 B7
Northwich CW9 ....79 B1
Partington WA14 ....20 B5
Runcorn WA7 ....22 F2
Sandbach CW11 ....174 D7
Sandycroft CH5 ....116 A2
Scholar Green ST7 ......194 F7
Styal SK9 ....34 A4
Sutton WA7 ....50 B4
Warrington WA4 ....16 E2
Warrington, Fearnhead WA2 .9 A2
Warrington,Great Sankey
WA5 ....14 F6
Warrington,Penketh WA5 ..14 E3
Weaverham CW8 ....77 A1
Whaley Bridge SK23 ......39 D4
Wilmslow SK9 ....60 B7
Winsford CW7 ....127 A1
Worleston CW5 ....188 E6
Wrenbury CW5 ....216 F3
Station Rd N WA2 ....9 A1
Station Rd S WA2 ....9 A1
Station St SK10 ....87 D1
Station Terr WA7 ....50 B4
Station View
Chester CH2 ....118 F2
Hampton Heath SY14 ....213 D7
Nantwich CW5 ....204 E4
Sandbach CW11 ....174 D8
Station Yard Trad Est
CW4 ....130 D3
Staveley Dr CW7 ....126 D2
Steadings Rise WA16 ....56 D6
Steadings The CH3 .....120 A4
Steam Mill St CH1,CH3 .237 C3
Stearns Cl CH1 ....118 A5
Stearns Ho CH1 ....118 A5
Steel St WA1 ....16 D7
Steele Rd CW10 ....151 D5
Steele St CH1 ....237 B2
Steeple Ct CH64 ....66 E7
Steeple St SK10 ....87 E1
Stein Ave WA3 ....3 E8
Stenhills Cres WA7 ......23 C2
Stephen St WA1 ....16 D6
Stephen's Gr WA6 ....73 B2
Stephens Gdns CH66 .....69 B6
Stephens Terr CH66 .....69 B6
Stephens Way ST7 ......209 F2
Stephenson Dr CW1 ....191 A4
Stephenson Rd WA12 .....2 D2
Stephenson Wlk CW7 ...149 A8
Sterling Cl
Congleton CW12 ....156 C3
Northwich CW9 ....103 F5
Sterne Cl CW11 ....174 D6
Stetchworth Rd WA4 .....16 B1
Steven Ct CH3 ....237 C3
Stevenage Cl SK11 .....112 B7
Stevenage Dr SK11 .....112 B7
Stevens Rd CH60 ....41 C7
Stevens St SK9 ....60 A1
Steventon WA7 ....24 E4
Steward's Ave WA8 ......22 F8
Stewart St CW2 ....190 A3
Stile End CH2 ....119 F8
Stiles The CW8 ....101 D5
Stiperstones Cl CH66 ....69 A6
Stirling Cl Chester CH3 ..119 A2
Stirling Cl *continued*
Macclesfield SK10 ....86 F2
Warrington WA1 ....17 E7
Winsford CW7 ....127 A3
Stirling Ct
Ellesmere Port CH65 ......70 D3
Holmes Chapel CW4 .....130 B2
Stirrup Cl WA2 ....9 A3
Stoak Lodge CH65 ....70 C4
Stock La CW2,CW5 .....206 B2
Stockdale Dr WA5 ....14 E7
Stockham Cl WA7 ....50 A8
Stockham La WA7 ....50 B7
Stockley Farm* CW9 ....54 E7
Stockley La WA4 ....52 F7
Stockport Rd WA4 ....17 E3
Stocks Ave 5 CH3 ......119 A1
Stocks Hill CW7 ....149 F7
Stocks La Chester CH3 ..119 A1
Ollerton WA16 ....82 E1
Rainow SK10 ....88 E5
Warrington WA5 ....14 D5
Stockswell Rd WA8 ......12 A3
Stockton Heath Prim Sch
WA4 ....16 C1
Stockton La WA4 ....16 F1
Stockton Rd SK9 ....59 F4
Stockton View WA4 .....16 B2
Stockwell Farm Ct WA8 .12 E4
Stoke Abbot Cl SK7 .....35 E7
Stoke Cl CH62 ....43 E3
Stoke Gdns CH65 ....70 C4
Stoke Hall La CW5 .....187 E6
Stoke Wlk CH65 ....70 C4
Stokes St WA3 ....9 E5
Stokesay Ct CH65 ....70 E3
Stone Bank Rd ST7 .....195 B1
Stone Barn La WA7 ......49 F6
Stone Chair La ST7 .....194 E7
Stone Cotts CW12 ......157 E2
Stone Croft CH3 ....142 B7
Stone Cross Dr WA8 .....12 E5
Stone Cross La N WA3 ....3 C7
Stone Cross La S WA3 ....3 C6
Stone Cross Pk WA3 ......3 B7
Stone Heyes La CW8,CW9 77 F5
Stone House La CW6 ...184 E4
Stone Mead Ave WA15 ...32 C7
Stone Pit La WA3 ....3 F2
Stone Pl CH2 ....118 F3
Stoneacre Gdns WA4 ....26 E4
Stonebank Dr CH64 ......67 A6
Stonebridge Rd CW5 ...204 E3
Stonechat Cl
10 Golborne WA3 ....3 E8
Runcorn WA7 ....49 E5
Stonecrop Cl
Runcorn WA7 ....49 F4
Warrington WA3 ....9 C4
Stonehaven Dr WA2 ....9 A3
Stoneheads SK23 ....65 D8
Stoneheads Rise SK23 ...65 D8
Stonehill Cl WA4 ....26 D4
Stonehills Ct WA7 ....23 C2
Stonehills La WA7 ....23 C2
Stonehouse Gn 6
CW12 ....156 D3
Stonelea WA7 ....24 B2
Stoneleigh Cl SK10 ......87 C2
Stoneleigh Ct WA4 ......17 D1
Stoneleigh Gdns WA4 ....17 D1
Stoneley Ave CW1 ......190 D7
Stoneley Rd CW1 ....190 D8
Stones Manor La CW8 ..103 C5
Stoneway Ct 1 CH60 .....40 F8
Stoney Holt WA7 ....50 C8
Stoney La Delamere CW6 123 C6
Wilmslow SK9 ....59 F5
Stoneyfold La SK11 ....113 A6
Stoneyfold La CW8 .....101 C2
Stoneyland Dr SK22 .....39 B8
Stony La CW12 ....156 C1
Stonyhurst Cres WA3 .....4 D5
Stopsley Cl CW12 ......155 F4
Store St SK10 ....88 B8
Stores Rd M90 ....33 A6
Stour Ct CH65 ....70 B7
Stradbroke Cl WA3 ....4 A7
Straight Length WA6 .....73 E7
Straight Mile CH4 ......162 F5
Straker Ave CH65 ....69 F6
Stratford Gdns CH1 .....117 E4
Stratford Rd Blacon CH1 .117 E4
Neston CH64 ....66 D6
Stratford Sq SK8 ....34 C7
Stratford Way SK11 ....112 C5
Strathaven Ave CW2 ...205 E8
Strathearn Rd CH60 ......40 F7
Strathmore Cl CW4 .....130 B2
Stratton Cl WA7 ....50 B6
Stratton Pk WA8 ....12 F5
Stratton Rd WA5 ....15 B5
Strawberry Cl WA3 ....9 C4
Strawberry Dr CH66 .....95 A8
Strawberry Fields CH3 .142 B7
Strawberry Gn CH66 .....95 A8
Strawberry La
Acton Bridge CW8 ....76 F3
Mollington CH1 ....94 D4
Wilmslow SK9 ....59 E6
Street Forest Walks The*
SK17 ....90 E4
Street Hey La CH64 ......43 B1
Street La
Lower Whitley WA4 ......52 C3
Rode Heath ST7 ....176 F2
Skellorn Green SK10 .....62 D8
Street The
Mickle Trafford CH2 .....119 D8
Whaley Bridge SK10,SK17 .90 C5
Streethead Cott WA14 ...20 F1
Stretton Ave WA3 ....3 E7
Stretton Cl CH62 ....43 E3
Stretton Hall Mews WA4 .52 E8
Stretton Mill* SY14 ....198 A7
Stretton Rd WA4 ....26 E2
Stretton Way 3 SK9 .....34 D5
Stretton Wlk CW9 ......103 F4
Strickland Cl WA4 ....27 A7
Strines Rd SK6 ....38 D8
Stringer Ave CW11 .....175 C5
Stringer Cres WA4 ......16 E4
Stringer's La LL12,CH4 ..161 B4
Stroma Ave CH65 ....95 B8
Stromness Cl WA2 ....9 B3
Stuart Cl Chester CH3 ...119 C3
Winsford CW7 ....149 C5
Stuart Ct SK10 ....87 B2
Stuart Dr WA4 ....16 F2
Stuart Pl CH1 ....237 B3
Stuart Rd WA7 ....24 C4
Stubbs La
Lostock Gralam CW9 ......80 A2
Mobberley WA16 ....58 E4
Stubbs Pl CH1 ....117 E3
Stubbs Terr 17 SK11 ....112 E7
Stubby La SK10 ....84 E2
Sturgess St WA12 ....1 F3
Styal Cl 4 CW9 ....103 F4
Styal Cross SK9 ....33 E4
Styal Ctry Pk* SK9 .....33 E3
Styal Gn SK9 ....33 F3
Styal Prim Sch SK9 .....33 E3
Styal Rd Wilmslow SK9 ....60 B8
Woodhouse Park M22 .....33 F7
Styal Sta SK9 ....34 A4
Styal View SK9 ....34 B2
Styperson Way SK12 .....36 E3
Sudbrook Cl WA3 ....3 E8
Sudbury Dr SK8 ....34 C8
Sudbury Rd SK7 ....36 E8
Sudlow La
Knutsford WA16 ....56 D1
Plumley WA16 ....81 C7
Suez St Newton-le-W WA12 .2 B3
Warrington WA1 ....16 B5
Suffolk Ave CH65 ....69 F5
Suffolk Cl
Congleton CW12 ....156 D4
Macclesfield SK10 ....86 F1
Warrington WA1 ....17 E6
Suffolk Dr SK9 ....34 C1
Suffolk Ho CH1 ....237 C3
Suffolk Pl WA8 ....22 C7
Suffolk St WA7 ....22 F3
Sugar La Bollington SK10 .63 A3
Manley WA6 ....98 E5
Rainow SK10 ....88 D5
Sugar Pit La WA16 ......56 E3
Sugar St SK11 ....159 C2
Sulby Ave WA4 ....16 B3
Sulgrave Ave SK12 ......36 F4
Summer Cl WA7 ....23 F1
Summer La
Daresbury WA4 ....51 D7
Runcorn WA7 ....23 F1
Summercroft Cl WA3 ......3 A7
Summerfield ST7 ....195 B1
Summerfield Ave WA5 .....7 F2
Summerfield Cl CH4 ....139 A3
Summerfield Dr CW9 ...126 F8
Summerfield Ho CH3 ....119 F5
Summerfield Pl SK9 .....60 A5
Summerfield Rd
Guilden Sutton CH3 .....119 F5
Mobberley WA16 ....57 F4
Summerfields WA16 ......57 C3
Summerfields Ctr 11
SK9 ....34 D1
Summerhill Dr ST5 .....210 D1
Summerhill Rd SK10 .....86 F4
Summerlea SK8 ....35 B8
Summerlea Cl SK10 ......87 D1
Summers Cl WA16 ....82 A7
Summers Way WA16 ......82 A7
Summertrees Rd CH66 ....69 E3
Summerville Gdns WA4 ..16 F1
Summit Cl WA4 ....26 E1
Sumner Rd CH1 ....117 E4
Sumner St WA11 ....1 A6
Sumpter Pathway CH2 ..118 F3
Sunart Cl CW2 ....206 B6
Sunbank La WA15 ....32 E6
Sunbeam Cl WA7 ....22 F3
Sunbeam St WA12 ....2 C3
Sunbury Cl SK9 ....34 E2
Sunbury Cres 3 CH4 ....140 F6
Sunbury Gdns WA4 ......26 E7
Suncroft Cl WA1 ....17 E7
Suncroft Rd CH60 ....41 C7
Sundale Dr CW2 ....189 D4
Sunderland St SK11 ....112 D7
Sundial Ho WA3 ....4 F3
Sundown Cl SK22 ....39 A8
Sunfield Cl CH66 ....69 D3
Sunflower Cl WA9 ....6 A7
Sunningdale Ave WA8 ....12 B1
Sunningdale Cl
Burtonwood WA5 ....6 F6
Northwich CW9 ....104 E7
Winsford CW7 ....126 A2
Sunningdale Dr
Bebington CH63 ....43 B6
Bramhall SK7 ....36 A7
Sunningdale Rd
Cheadle Hulme SK8 ......35 A7
Macclesfield SK11 ......112 A6
Sunningdale Way CH64 ..66 E4
Sunninghey Ct SK9 ......59 F2
Sunny Bank
Macclesfield SK11 ......112 D5
Wilmslow SK9 ....59 D4
Wilmslow,Fulshaw Park SK9 60 B6
Sunny Bank Cl SK11 ...112 D5
Sunny Bank Cotts
Ashton Hayes CH3 ......121 E7
Warrington WA8 ....14 A4
Sunny Bank Rd WA14 ....31 C8
Sunny Lea Mews SK9 ....60 A6
Sunnybank Cl WA12 ....2 C4
Sunnybank Rd CW1,CW2 189 E5
Sunnymill Dr CW11 ....175 A6
Sunnyside Alsager ST7 ..193 A4
4 Ellesmere Port CH65 ...70 C6
Malpas SY14 ....212 F2
Warrington WA5 ....14 E6
Sunnyside La WA7 ....24 E4
Sunset Cotts CH64 ......67 A4
Surrey Dr CW12 ....156 E5
Surrey Rd Chester CH2 ..119 A5
Kidsgrove ST7 ....195 A2
Warren SK11 ....112 A4
Surrey St Crewe CW1 ...190 E4
9 Runcorn WA7 ....23 A2
Warrington WA4 ....16 D3
Surridge WA16 ....29 C5
Susan Dr WA5 ....14 D5
Susan St WA8 ....13 C2
Sussex Ave SK11 ....112 A5
Sussex Dr ST7 ....194 F2
Sussex Pl CW12 ....156 E5
Sussex Rd Chester CH2 ..118 F4
Irlam M44 ....11 C6
Partington M31 ....11 E2
Sussex St WA8 ....13 D1
Sussex Way CH2 ....118 F4
Sutch La WA13 ....19 A3
Sutherland Ct 5 WA7 ....23 B2
Sutherland Dr
Bebington CH62 ....43 D4
Macclesfield SK10 ....87 A1
Sutherland Way CH3 ...119 B3
Sutton Ave Culcheth WA3 ..4 F4
Neston CH64 ....66 E6
Sutton Cl Bebington CH62 .43 E3
Higher Wincham CW9 .....79 F6
Macclesfield SK11 ......112 D5
Mickle Trafford CH2 .....119 F8
Nantwich CW5 ....204 C5
Sutton Cswy WA6,WA7 ...49 E2
Sutton Dr CH2 ....118 E5
Sutton Green Prim Sch
CH66 ....69 C5
Sutton Hall Dr CH66 .....69 A6
Sutton Hall Gdns CH66 ..69 A6
Sutton High Sch CH66 ...69 E6
Sutton La CW10 ....151 C7
Sutton Quays Bsns Pk
WA7 ....49 E3
Sutton Rd
Alderley Edge SK9 ....59 F2
Poynton SK12 ....37 A2
Sutton St Runcorn WA7 ...23 B2
Warrington WA1 ....16 C4
Sutton Way
Ellesmere Port CH66 ......69 E4
1 Handforth SK9 ....34 E5
Sutton's La WA8 ....23 B7
Swale Cl SK9 ....34 E2
Swale Rd CH65 ....70 A7
Swaledale Ave CW12 ...157 A5
Swaledale Cl
Bebington CH62 ....43 E5
Warrington WA5 ....14 F7
Swallow Cl
1 Kidsgrove ST7 ....195 B2
Macclesfield SK10 ......113 A7
Warrington WA3 ....9 F4
Swallow Ct Handforth SK9 34 B1
Winsford CW7 ....149 D5
Swallow Dr Alsager ST7 .193 B3
Kelsall CW6 ....122 D5
Sandbach CW11 ....175 A8
Swallow Rd ST7 ....195 F1
Swallowfield Cl CW2 ...206 A8
Swallowfield Gdns WA4 .26 F5
Swallowfields CH3 .....180 E2
Swallowmore View ST7 .210 C8
Swan Ave WA9 ....1 A2
Swan Bank
Congleton CW12 ....156 D2
Talke ST7 ....210 D7
Swan Cl Poynton SK12 ...36 B4
Talke ST7 ....210 D8
Swan Ct CW8 ....101 E7
Swan Farm La CW3 .....232 B1
Swan Gr WA16 ....106 D7
Swan Ho ST7 ....210 D7
Swan La CW6 ....185 E8
Swan Rd WA12 ....1 E4
Swan St Congleton CW12 156 D2
Wilmslow SK9 ....60 B7
Swanage Cl WA4 ....16 E2
Swanage Ct 6 CW7 .....149 D6
Swanley La CW5 ....203 D4
Swanlow Ave CW7 ......149 D5
Swanlow Dr CW7 ....149 D6
Swanlow La CW7 ....149 E5
Swann Gr SK8 ....35 B8

Swann La SK8 ....35 B8
Swanscoe Ave SK10 ....88 A7
Swanscoe Cl CW10 ...151 B8
Swanscoe La SK10 ....88 B3
Sweet Briar Cres CW2 ..189 F3
Sweet Brier Cl CW8 ....78 B4
Sweetfield Gdns CH66 ..69 D7
Sweetfield Rd CH66 ....69 D7
Sweettooth La CW11 ...175 A7
Swettenham Cl
　Alsager ST7 ....193 C3
　Sandbach CW11 ......175 D7
Swettenham La CW12 ..131 E5
Swettenham Rd
　Handforth SK9 ....34 D5
　Swettenham CW12 ...132 B2
Swettenham St SK11 ...112 E7
Swift Cl Kidsgrove ST7 ..195 B2
　Warrington WA2 ....8 E3
　Wistaston CW2 ....205 F8
Swinburne Dr CW1 ....190 F4
Swindale Ave WA2 ......8 B3
Swinden Cl WA7 ....24 D2
Swine Market 2 CW5 ..204 E5
Swineyard La WA16 ....28 C4
Swinford Ave WA8 ......13 E2
Swinley Chase SK9 ....34 F1
Swinleys Hey CH3 .....142 A4
Swinnerton St CW2 ....190 C2
Swinton Sq 17 WA16 ...57 A2
Swireford Rd WA6 ......73 B2
Swiss Cott
　Alsager ST7 ....193 E2
Swiss Cott
　Alderley Edge SK9 ......60 C1
　Macclesfield SK10 ......87 B2
Swiss Hill SK9 ....60 B1
Swithin Rd M22 ....33 E8
Swynnerton Way WA8 ..13 B5
Sycamore Ave
　Alsager ST7 ....193 E2
　Congleton CW12 ......155 F4
　Crewe CW1 ....190 D6
　Haydock WA11 ....1 A5
　Newton-le-W WA12 .....2 C5
　Rode Heath ST7 ......193 F7
　Widnes WA8 ....13 B2
　Winsford CW7 ....149 A8
Sycamore Cl
　Audlem CW3 ....230 A4
　Biddulph ST8 ....179 E2
　Handforth SK9 ....34 B2
　Holmes Chapel CW4 ..130 D3
　Nantwich CW5 ....204 F7
　Talke ST7 ....210 E8
Sycamore Cres
　Barnton CW8 ....78 A4
　Hollinfare WA3 ....11 B2
　Macclesfield SK11 ....112 A4
Sycamore Dr
　Chester CH4 ....140 F5
　Ellesmere Port CH66 ..70 A4
　Lymm WA13 ....18 D4
　Middlewich CW10 .....151 E5
　Sutton WA7 ....50 B4
Sycamore Gr
　Broughton CH4 ....139 B3
　Sandbach CW11 ......175 A8
Sycamore La WA5 ......15 B5
Sycamore Lane Com Prim
Sch WA5 ....15 B5
Sycamore Lo SK7 ......35 F7
Sycamore Rd
　Morley Green WA16,SK9 ..59 C5
　Partington M31 ....11 E3
　Runcorn WA7 ....49 D6
Sycamore Rise SK11 ...112 B6
Sycamores The WA16 ..58 E2
Syddal Cl SK7 ....35 D5
Syddal Cres SK7 ....35 D4
Syddal Gn SK7 ....35 D5
Syddal Rd SK7 ....35 D5
Syddall Ave SK8 ....34 D8
Sydney Ave M90 ....33 A8
Sydney Rd Bramhall SK7 ..35 F5
　Chester CH1 ....118 B3
　Crewe CW1 ....190 F6
Sydney St
　Northwich CW8 ....103 C7
　Runcorn WA7 ....48 D7
Syers Ct WA1 ....16 E8
Sylvan Ave SK9 ....59 F5
Sylvan Cl CW8 ....103 C7
Sylvan Mews CH1 .....117 E6
Sylvia Cres WA2 ....8 D1
Symondley Rd SK11 ...112 F2
Synge St WA2 ....16 C7
Sytch Croft CH64 ......66 E8**

T

Tabley Ave WA8 ....12 D2
Tabley Cl Knutsford WA16 ..56 E3
　Macclesfield SK10 ....112 A8
　Sandbach CW11 ......174 E2
Tabley Ct WA16 ....56 B4
Tabley Gr WA16 ....56 E1
Tabley Hill La WA16 ...56 B2
Tabley Ho Knutsford WA16 ..81 B8
　★ Knutsford WA16 .....81 B8
Tabley Rd Crewe CW2 ..189 E3
　Handforth SK9 ....34 D5
　Knutsford WA16 ......56 E3

Tabley St CW9 ....79 A1
Tabley Stables WA16 ...81 A8
Tabor St SK11 ....112 E6
Tadgers La WA6 ....73 D8
Tailors View CW5 .....204 E6
Talbot Cl Neston CH64 ..66 F6
　Shavington CW2 ......206 B4
　Warrington WA3 ....9 E3
Talbot Gdns CH64 .....66 F6
Talbot Rd
　Alderley Edge SK9 .....60 B1
　Dunham-on-t-H WA6 ...97 E7
　Ellesmere Port CH66 ..69 F3
Talbot St Chester CH1 ..237 B4
　Golborne WA3 ....3 A8
Talbot Way CW5 ....205 A3
Talfryn Cl CH5 ....91 D1
Talisman Cl WA7 ....50 D7
Talke Rd Alsager ST7 ..193 E3
　High Carr ST5 ....210 F2
　Newcastle-u-Lyme ST7,
　ST5 ....210 D4
Tall Ash Ave CW12 ....157 A4
Tall Chys CW11 ....175 D4
Tall Trees Cl CW8 .....103 C6
Tally Ho La CW5 ....203 E3
Tamar Cl
　Congleton CW12 ......156 F1
　Macclesfield SK10 .....86 E1
Tamar Rd Haydock WA11 ..1 C6
　Kidsgrove ST7 ....195 B2
Tamar Wlk CW7 ....127 A2
Tame Cl Biddulph ST8 ..179 D1
　Sandbach CW11 ......174 E8
Tame Wlk 8 SK9 ....34 D2
Tamworth Cl SK7 ......36 D8
Tamworth St WA12 .....2 A3
Tan House La
　Burtonwood WA5 ....7 A5
　Widnes WA8 ....23 D8
Tanhouse WA7 ....23 E1
Tanhouse Ind Est WA8 ..23 C7
Tankersley Gr WA5 .....15 B6
Tanner St CW12 ....156 E2
Tanner's La WA3 ....3 B8
Tanners La WA2 ....16 A6
Tanners Way CW5 .....204 E4
Tannery La Neston CH64 ..66 E8
　Warrington WA5 ....14 D3
Tanning Ct 3 WA1 .....16 C5
Tanyard Dr WA8 ....32 C6
Tanyard La WA8 ....32 A5
Tapley Ave SK12 ....36 E2
Taplow Cl WA4 ....26 E6
Taporley War Meml Hospl
　CW6 ....146 D2
Target Cl ST7 ....210 E6
Target Rd CH60 ....40 C8
Tarn Cl CW7 ....126 C3
Tarn Ct WA1 ....17 F7
Tarn Mount SK11 .....112 A5
Tarnbeck WA7 ....50 D8
Tarnway WA3 ....3 F7
Tarporley Bsns Ctr
　CW6 ....168 C8
Tarporley CE Prim Sch
　CW6 ....146 D2
Tarporley Com High Sch
　CW6 ....146 D1
Tarporley Rd
　Duddon CH3 ....144 E7
　Ellesmere Port CH66 ..69 E4
　Little Budworth CW6,CW8 ..124 C5
　Lower Whitley WA4 ....52 C4
　Tarvin CH3 ....121 C1
　Utkinton CW6 ....146 E6
　Whitchurch SY13 .....225 F3
Tarporley Wlk SK9 .....34 E2
Tarrant Cl CH1 ....94 F1
Tarvin Ave CW2 ....189 D4
Tarvin Bridge CH3 .....119 A2
Tarvin Cl
　Ellesmere Port CH65 ..70 C4
　Golborne WA3 ....3 E7
　Macclesfield SK11 ....112 E5
　Middlewich CW10 .....151 D5
　Northwich CW9 ....103 F5
　Runcorn WA7 ....49 C6
Tarvin Prim Sch CH3 ..121 B1
Tarvin Rd Alvanley WA6 ..73 F4
　Bebington CH62 ....43 F3
　Chester, Boughton CH3 ..119 A2
　Chester,Vicarscross CH3 ..119 E2
　Christleton CH3 ....120 C3
　Manley WA6 ....99 A4
Tarvin Rdbt CH3 ....121 A2
Tarvin Sands Industries
　CH3 ....121 B4
Tarvin Way
　1 Handforth SK9 ......34 D5
　Winsford CW7 ....126 C2
Tasman Cl WA5 ....15 C8
Tate Cl WA8 ....12 D2
Tate Dr CW1 ....191 C4
Tattenhall La
　Beeston CW6 ....167 F2
　Tattenhall CH3 ....167 B3
Tattenhall Rd CH3 ....166 C4
Tatton Cl Alsager ST7 ..193 C3
　Chester CH4 ....140 E5
　Northwich CW9 ....103 F4
　Winsford CW7 ....126 C1
Tatton Ct
　2 Knutsford WA16 .....57 A2
Tatton Dr CW11 ....175 C7

Tatton Hall ★ WA16 ....56 E8
Tatton Lodge 16 WA16 ..57 A2
Tatton Pk ★ WA16 ......57 B7
Tatton Rd Crewe CW2 ..189 F2
　Handforth SK9 ....34 E5
Tatton St WA16 ....57 A2
Tatton Stile WA16 ......58 A4
Taurus Pk WA5 ....7 D3
Tavener Cl CH63 ....43 C5
Tavistock Rd WA5 ......14 E4
Tavlin Ave WA5 ....7 F1
Tawney Cl ST7 ....195 B2
Tawny Ct WA7 ....49 E7
Taxal & Fernilee CE Prim Sch
　SK23 ....65 D6
Taxal Moor Rd SK23 ...65 C3
Taxmere Cl CW11 ......174 F7
Tay Cl ST8 ....179 E1
Taylor Bsns Pk WA3 .....4 F1
Taylor Dr CW5 ....204 C5
Taylor Rd Altrincham WA14 ..20 F5
　Haydock WA11 ....1 F7
Taylor St Warrington WA4 ..16 A1
　Widnes WA8 ....13 C1
Taylors Row WA7 ....23 C2
Taylor's La
　Oakhanger CW1 ......192 C3
　Warrington WA5 ......14 A2
Teal Ave Knutsford WA16 ..57 B2
　Poynton SK12 ....36 A4
Teal Cl Warrington WA2 ..8 E3
　Winsford CW7 ....149 D5
Teal Gr WA3 ....9 F3
Tealby Cl CW9 ....104 B8
Teals Way CH60 ....40 E8
Tebay Rd CH62 ....43 E8
Tedder Dr M22 ....33 F7
Tedder Sq WA8 ....22 D8
Teddington Cl WA4 .....26 E5
Tees Ct CH65 ....70 A7
Teesdale Cl WA5 ....14 F7
Teesdale Rd WA11 ......1 C7
Tegg's Nose Ctry Pk ★
　SK11 ....113 D6
Teggsnose La SK11 ...113 C6
Tegid Way CH4 ....140 D5
Tegsnose Mount SK11 ..113 C4
Telegraph Rd CH60 ....41 A7
Telfer Ct CW10 ....151 E6
Telford Cl
　Congleton CW12 ......157 B2
　Macclesfield SK10 .....88 A1
　Talke ST7 ....210 E8
　Widnes WA8 ....12 D4
Telford Ct CH1 ....94 D6
Telford Gdns CW11 ....174 F3
Telford Pl CW5 ....204 C5
Telford Rd CH65 ....70 E4
Telford Way
　Audlem CW3 ....230 A3
　Chester CH4 ....140 F6
　Middlewich CW10 .....128 C1
Telford's Quay CH65 ...70 D7
Templeton Dr WA2 ......9 A2
Tempest Rd SK9 ....60 C1
Templar Ct SK10 ....87 A1
Temple Chambers CH1 ..237 B3
Temple Ct WA3 ....9 E6
Templeton Dr WA2 ......9 A3
Tenbury Cl WA5 ....15 A8
Tenby Cl WA5 ....7 F2
Tenby Dr WA7 ....23 D2
Tenby Rd SK11 ....111 F6
Tenchersfield CW5 ....205 A4
Tennyson Ave CW1 ....190 F4
Tennyson Cl Crewe CW2 ..190 A1
　Macclesfield SK11 ....111 E6
　Northwich CW9 ....104 C5
　Rode Heath ST7 ......193 E8
Tennyson Dr WA2 ....8 C2
Tennyson Rd
　Ellesmere Port CH65 ..70 A4
　Widnes WA8 ....13 A1
Tennyson Wlk CH1 .....118 A5
Tensing Cl WA5 ....15 B8
Tenth Ave CH5 ....92 D3
Terence Ave WA1 ......16 F6
Terminal Rd N M90 .....33 B7
Terminal Rd S M90 .....33 B7
Tern Ave ST7 ....195 C2
Tern Cl WA8 ....13 B4
Tern Dr SK12 ....36 B4
Terra Nova Sch CW4 ..108 D1
Terrace Rd WA8 ....23 A5
Terrick Mews SY13 ....226 B2
Terrick Rd SY13 ....226 A2
Tetchill Cl
　Ellesmere Port CH66 ..69 D2
　Runcorn WA7 ....50 D8
Tetton Cl 8 CW12 .....156 F3
Tetton La CW10 ......151 E3
Tewkesbury Cl
　Cheadle Hulme SK8 ...35 B6
　Chester CH2 ....118 F7
　Ellesmere Port CH66 ..94 E8
　Middlewich CW10 .....128 B1
　Poynton SK12 ....36 D4
Tewkesbury Dr SK10 ...87 E4
Tewkesbury Rd WA3 .....3 B8
Thackeray Dr CH3 .....119 C3
Thackery Ct 6 CW11 ..174 D6
Thames Cl
　Congleton CW12 ......156 F1
　Warrington WA3 ....9 E6
Thames Dr Biddulph ST8 ..179 D1
　Biddulph ST8 ....179 E1
Thames Gdns CH65 ....70 B3
Thames Pl CW7 ....127 B1

Thames Rd WA3 ....5 A2
Thames Side CH65 .....70 B3
Thames Trad Ctr M44 ..11 F7
Thamesdale CH65 ......70 B4
Thaxted Wlk M22 ......33 C8
The Verdin High Sch
　CW7 ....126 C1
Theatre Ct CW9 ....103 F8
Thelwall Com Inf Sch
　WA4 ....17 C3
Thelwall Com Jun Sch
　WA4 ....17 D3
Thelwall La
　Warrington WA4 ....16 F3
　Warrington WA4 ....17 B3
Thelwall New Rd WA4 ..17 C3
Thelwall New Rd Ind Est
　WA4 ....17 C3
Thelwall Rd CH66 ......69 E4
Thetford Cl SK10 ....87 C3
Thetford Rd WA5 ....14 E6
Thewlis St WA5 ....15 E5
Third Ave
　Connah's Quay CH5 ....92 F1
　Crewe CW1 ....190 F1
　Kidsgrove ST7 ....194 F1
　Poynton SK12 ....36 D1
　Runcorn WA7 ....49 F8
　Sandbach CW11 ......175 A5
Thirlemere SK11 ......112 A5
Thirlmere Ave WA2 ......8 C3
Thirlmere Cl
　Alderley Edge SK9 .....59 F1
　Frodsham WA6 ....49 D1
　Holmes Chapel CW4 ..130 A3
　Winsford CW7 ....126 F3
Thirlmere Ct CW12 ....156 A2
Thirlmere Dr WA13 .....18 F3
Thirlmere Lodge 5
　WA13 ....18 E3
Thirlmere Rd
　Chester CH2 ....119 A5
　Crewe CW2 ....190 A2
　Ellesmere Port CH65 ..70 C2
　Neston CH64 ....66 E6
　Partington M31 ....11 E4
Thirlmere Way WA8 ....22 D8
Thirsk Cl WA7 ....49 C6
Thirsk Way SK10 ....87 C3
Thistle Cl WA16 ....79 F7
Thistle Sq M31 ....11 E2
Thistle Wlk 4 M31 .....11 E2
Thistleton Cl SK11 ....112 D6
Thistlewood Dr SK9 ....60 D8
Thomas Ave CW5 .....205 A3
Thomas Brassey Cl CH2 ..237 C4
Thomas Cl Alsager ST7 ..193 E4
　Blacon CH1 ....117 F6
　Ellesmere Port CH65 ..70 B2
　Mickle Trafford CH2 ..119 F8
Thomas Ct WA7 ....49 F7
Thomas Ho CH1 ....118 A5
Thomas Hodges Ct
　CW4 ....130 D3
Thomas Row 8 CW5 ..204 E6
Thomas St Biddulph ST8 ..179 D1
　Congleton CW12 ......156 E3
　Crewe CW1 ....190 D4
　Golborne WA3 ....3 A8
　Packmoor ST7 ....195 F1
　Runcorn WA7 ....23 B3
　Talke ST7 ....210 D8
　2 Widnes WA8 ....23 A7
Thomas Wedge CE Jun Sch
　The CH1 ....94 A1
Thomasons Bridge La
　WA4 ....25 E6
Thompson Ave WA3 .....4 E3
Thompson Cl WA12 .....2 C1
Thomson Gdns CW12 ..156 A3
Thomson St WA3 ....9 E5
Thoresway Rd SK9 .....59 F5
Thorlby Rd WA3 ....9 F3
Thorley Gr CW2 ....190 A1
Thorley La M22 ....33 B8
Thorley Mews SK7 .....35 F7
Thorn Cl Runcorn WA7 ..49 C7
　Warrington WA5 ....14 F3
Thorn Dr M22 ....34 A8
Thorn Gr SK8 ....35 A7
Thorn Grove Prim Sch
　SK8 ....35 A7
Thorn Ho CH4 ....141 A6
Thorn La CH66 ....103 C5
Thorn Rd Bramhall SK7 ..35 E5
　Runcorn WA7 ....49 C7
　Warrington WA1 ......17 A8
Thorn Tree Cl L24 ......21 E2
Thorn Tree Dr CW1 ....173 A1
Thorn Wlk 8 M31 ......11 E2
Thornberry Cl CH1 ....117 B8
Thornbrook Way CW11 ..174 D5
Thornbury Ave WA3 .....3 E7
Thorne Cl SK10 ....87 A5
Thorne Dr CH66 ....69 B4
Thorney Dr SK7,SK8 ...35 C6
Thorneyholme Dr WA16 ..57 B2
Thornfield SK9 ....60 A4
Thornfield Hey SK9 .....60 E8
Thornfields CW1 ......173 B1
Thorngrove Dr SK9 .....60 C6
Thorngrove Hill SK9 ....60 C6
Thorngrove Rd SK9 .....60 C6
Thornhills WA8 ....12 A3
Thornleigh Ave CH62 ..43 F3
Thornleigh Dr CH66 ....69 E6

Thornley Cl 1 WA13 ...18 C3
Thornley Rd WA13 .....18 C3
Thornsgreen Rd M22 ...33 D8
Thornton WA8 ....22 E8
Thornton Ave SK11 ....112 A8
Thornton Bank CW6 ...169 D4
Thornton Cl CW7 ......127 A3
Thornton Common Rd
　CH63 ....42 D7
Thornton Cres CH60 ...41 B6
Thornton Dr
　Chester CH2 ....118 D5
　Handforth SK9 ....34 D3
　Wistaston CW2 ......206 A7
Thornton Green La CH2 ..71 E1
Thornton Ho
　Audlem CW3 ....230 A5
　Thornton Hough CH63 ..42 B6
Thornton Hough Prim Sch
　CH63 ....42 B7
Thornton Mews CH66 ..69 B8
Thornton Rd
　Ellesmere Port CH65 ..70 E3
　Heald Green SK8 ......34 C8
　Warrington WA5 ......15 B4
Thornton Sq SK11 ....112 A5
Thorntondale Dr WA5 ..14 F7
Thorntree Bglws SK11 ..132 A8
Thorntree Gn WA4 ......27 B5
Thornway Bollington SK10 ..88 A8
　Bramhall SK8 ....35 C7
　High Lane SK6 ....37 F7
Thornwythe Gr CH66 ...69 E4
Thornycroft CW7 ......126 A1
Thornycroft Cl SK11 ...111 E1
Thornycroft St 7 SK11 ..112 E7
Thorp St SK10 ....112 D8
Thorpe Cl CW1 ....189 F8
Thowler La WA4 ....30 A6
Threaphurst La SK7 ....37 C8
Three Acres La SK8 ....34 E7
Three Fields Cl CW12 ..156 A3
Threeways CW8 ....101 D4
Thrush Way CW7 ......126 F4
Thurlow WA3 ....3 E7
Thursfield Ave WA5 ....195 C3
Thursfield Ct CH1 .....118 B1
Thursfield Prim Sch
　ST7 ....195 B3
Thurstaston Rd CH60 ..40 F8
Thurston Cl WA5 ....15 D6
Thurston Gn SK9 ....60 A1
Thurston Rd CH4 ......140 E5
Thynne St WA1 ....16 A4
Tibb St ST7 ....209 F2
Tibbs Cross La WA8 ....13 D8
Tidal La WA1 ....16 F8
Tideswell Cl SK8 ....34 D8
Tideswell Rd SK7 ......36 E8
Tidnock Ave CW12 ....156 E5
Tiffield Ct CW7 ....127 A4
Tilbey Dr WA6 ....74 A8
Tilbury Pl WA7 ....50 E6
Tildsley Cres WA7 ......48 F6
Tilewright Cl ST7 .....195 B2
Tilley St WA1 ....16 C6
Tilman Cl WA5 ....15 B8
Tilston Ave WA4 ....17 A4
Tilston CE Prim Sch
　SY14 ....198 B3
Tilston Rd SY14 ....213 A5
Tilston Wlk 5 SK9 ......34 E1
Tilstone Cl Hough CW2 ..206 E2
　Northwich CW9 ......104 A5
Timber La 2 CW9 .....103 F8
Timber St SK10 ....87 F1
Timberfields Rd CH1 ...117 A8
Timbersbrook Gr 5 SK9 ..34 D2
Timberscombe Gdns
　WA1 ....17 E6
Timbrell Ave CW1 .....190 A6
Timmis Cl WA2 ....9 A3
Timmis Cres WA8 ......13 A1
Timperley Ave WA4 .....17 A4
Tinkersfield CW5 ......205 A4
Tinkwood La SY14 .....211 F1
Tinsley St WA4 ....16 F3
Tintagel Cl
　Macclesfield SK10 ....111 E8
　Runcorn WA7 ....50 B6
Tintern Ave CH2 ......118 F6
Tintern Cl Poynton SK12 ..36 D5
　Warrington WA5 ....7 E2
Tintern Rd SK8 ....35 B6
Tipping Brow WA16 ....58 C4
Tirley La CW6 ....123 A2
Tithebarn Cl CH60 .....40 F7
Tithebarn Dr CH64 ....41 B2
Tithebarn Rd WA15 ....32 C8
Tithings The WA7 ......23 E1
Tiverton Cl Chester CH2 ..118 F5
　Sandbach CW11 ......175 C7
　Widnes WA8 ....12 C3
Tiverton Ct 6 CW9 ....103 E5
Tiverton Dr SK9 ....34 D1
Tiverton Sq WA5 ....14 E4
Tiveton Ct CW7 ....103 F5
Tobermory Cl WA11 .....1 A5
Todbrook Cl SK23 ......65 D6
Todds Bldgs WA8 ......23 A6
Toft Cl Chester CH4 ...140 E5
　Widnes WA8 ....12 F1
Toft Rd WA16 ....82 B7
Toft Way SK9 ....34 E4
Toll Bar Ave SK11 .....112 F7
Toll Bar Pl WA2 ....8 A8
Toll Bar Rd Chester CH3 ..142 C8
　Macclesfield SK11 ....111 F8

Warrington WA2 ....8 A3
Tolland La WA15 ......31 F8
Tollard Cl SK8 ....35 B6
Tollemache Cotts CW5 .203 C8
Tollemache Dr CW1 ...190 A8
Tollemache Terr CH2 ...118 F2
Tollgate St ST7 ....210 C8
Tollgate Dr CW3 ......229 F4
Tollitt St CW1 ....190 C4
Tom Brads Croft SK23 ..65 E8
Tom Fields ST7 ....209 F1
Tom La WA14 ....30 E6
Tomkinson Cl CW1 ....189 F7
Tomkinson St CH2 ....237 C4
Tomlins Terr CH1 .....117 E5
Tomlinson Ave WA2 ...16 D8
Tommy's La
  Congleton CW12 ....156 F4
  Crewe CW1 ....190 D2
Tonbridge Cl SK10 ....87 B2
Toogood Cl CW2 .....119 F8
Top Farm La CW7 ....170 F2
Top Rd Frodsham WA6 ..74 D5
  Kingsley WA6 ....75 B1
Top Station Rd ST7 ...195 C7
Topgate Cl CH60 ......41 B8
Topping Ct WA3 ....9 B4
Torbrook Gr 1 SK9 ...34 D2
Torkington Rd SK9 ....60 D6
Toronto Ave M90 ......33 B7
Torr Dr CH62 ....44 A7
Torr Rd SK11 ....112 C4
Torr Rise CW6 ....146 D1
Torr Top St SK22 ......39 C7
Torridon Gr CH66 .....69 F3
Torrs Valley SK22 .....39 C7
Torrvale Rd SK22 .....39 B7
Totland Cl WA5 ....14 C7
Totland Gr CH2 ......118 E4
Totton Ct WA1 ....9 D1
Tourney Gn WA5 ....7 A2
Tower Hill SK10 ....88 D4
Tower Hill Rd ST7 ...195 F7
Tower Ho The 20 SK11 .112 C8
Tower La Lymm WA13 ...18 F2
  Runcorn WA7 ....50 D7
  Weaverham CW8 .....77 B1
Tower Rd CH1 ....118 B2
Tower Way CW1 ....190 C4
Towergate CH1 ......118 B1
Towers Cl Poynton SK12 .36 F5
  Wistaston CW2 .....206 A7
Towers Ct WA5 ....15 E7
Towers La WA6 ....98 C4
Towers Rd SK12 ....36 F5
Towers The 6 SK10 ...111 F8
Town Farm La WA6 ...100 E7
Town Gn The WA4 .....52 D5
Town Hill WA1 ....16 B5
Town La Hale L24,WA8 ..21 E2
  Mobberley WA16 ......58 B4
  Neston CH64 ....66 F6
Town Sq
  4 Northwich CW9 ...103 F8
  6 Runcorn WA7 ......49 F7
Town Well WA6 ....75 C2
Town Wlk 9 WA7 ......49 F7
Townbridge Ct 15 CW8 .103 F8
Towneley Ct WA8 ......13 A1
Townfield Ave CH3 ...180 E2
Townfield Cl ST7 .....194 D2
Townfield Ct CW8 .....78 A3
Townfield La
  Barnton CW8 ....78 A3
  Blacon CH1 ....117 F8
  Farndon CH3 ....180 D2
  Frodsham WA6 ....74 D7
  Lymm WA13 ....19 B7
  Mollington CH1 ....94 D2
  Swan Green WA16 ...106 E5
  Tarvin CH3 ....121 B2
  Tiverton CW6 ....168 C6
Townfield Rd
  Mobberley WA16 .....58 A4
  Runcorn WA7 ....24 C2
Townfield View WA7 ...24 C2
Townfield Villas CH2 ..72 B3
Townfields
  Knutsford WA16 ......57 C2
  Sandbach CW11 .....175 B5
Townfields Cotts 6
  CW7 ....149 C7
Townfields Cres CW7 .149 D7
Townfields Dr CW7 ...149 C7
Townfields Gdns CW7 .149 D7
Townfields Rd CW7 ...149 D7
Townley Mill 4 SK11 .112 D7
Townley Pl 5 SK11 ...112 C7
Townley St 4 SK11 ...112 C7
Townsend Farm ST7 ..193 E2
Townsend La ST7 ....194 A8
Townsend Rd CW12 ..156 E2
Townsfield Dr CW6 ...147 F7
Townsfield La WA2 .....8 A5
Townshend Rd CW9 ...80 A3
Township Cl CH3 .....182 C1
Townwell Ct CW5 ....204 D5
Trackside Bsns Pk
  CW11 ....174 C6
Tracy Dr WA12 ....2 E3
Trafalgar Ave SK12 ....37 A3
Trafalgar Cl
  Northwich CW9 .....103 E3
  Poynton SK12 ....37 A3
Trafalgar Ct
  8 Macclesfield SK11 .112 D7
  Widnes WA8 ....23 A6
Trafford Ave WA5 .....15 F7

Trafford Cres WA7 ....49 C6
Trafford Pl SK9 ....60 D6
Trafford Rd
  Alderley Edge SK9 ...60 B1
  Handforth SK9 ....34 B1
Trafford St CH1 ......237 B3
Tragan Dr WA5 ....14 D3
Tramway Rd M44 ......11 F7
Tramway St CH1 .....237 C3
Tranere Dr SK9 ....34 E2
Trap Rd CW12 ....132 C3
Trap St SK11 ....132 B6
Travellers Rest Cvn Pk
  CW7 ....150 C8
Travers' Entry WA9 ....6 A7
Travis St 10 WA8 .....23 B8
Treborth Rd CH1 ....117 D3
Tree Bank Cl WA7 ....49 A8
Tree Tops CH64 ......66 E4
Tree Way WA16 ....82 A7
Treen Cl SK10 ....86 D1
Treetops Cl WA1 ......16 F7
Trefoil Cl Huntington CH3 .142 B6
  Warrington WA3 ......9 C5
Tregele Cl CH1 ......117 D3
Trenance La CW7 .....50 C5
Trenchard Dr M22 .....33 F7
Trent Ave CW7 ......127 B1
Trent Cl Bramhall SK7 ..35 C6
  Widnes WA8 ....13 B4
  Winsford CW7 ....127 B1
Trent Way CH60 ....41 C6
Trentdale CH65 ....70 B3
Trentham Cl WA8 .....13 B4
Trentham St WA7 .....22 F3
Tresham Dr WA4 ......27 A8
Trevithick Cl CW11 ...191 A4
Trevone Cl WA16 ......57 A1
Trickett La CW8 .....102 A3
Tricketts La CW5 ....205 E5
Tricketts Mews CW5 .205 E5
Trident Ind Est WA3 ...9 E6
Trident Ret Pk WA7 ...49 E7
Trident Way SK11 ...112 A5
Trinity Cl CW2 ....190 A1
Trinity Ct
  Congleton CW12 ....157 B1
  1 Knutsford WA16 ...57 A2
  Warrington WA3 ......9 F5
Trinity Gdns 4 WA6 ..49 C1
Trinity La SK11 ......112 F3
Trinity Pl
  Congleton CW12 ....179 B8
  1 Widnes WA8 ......23 B7
Trinity Sq SK10 ....87 F1
Trinity St Chester CH1 .237 A2
  Runcorn WA7 ....23 B3
Trinity Terr 2 CW8 ..103 E8
Troon Cl Bebington CH63 .43 C5
  Bramhall SK7 ....36 A7
  Haydock WA11 ....1 A5
  Holmes Chapel CW4 .130 C2
Trossach Cl WA2 ......8 E2
Troutbeck Ave
  Congleton CW12 ....156 A2
  Newton-le-W WA12 ...1 E4
Troutbeck Cl WA7 ....50 A5
Troutbeck Gr CW7 ...126 D2
Trouthall La WA16 ....81 A2
Trubshaw Ct ST7 ....195 C3
Trubshaw Pl ST7 ....195 B3
Trumans La CH66 .....69 C7
Truro Cl Bramhall SK7 ..35 F7
  Congleton CW12 ....178 E8
  Ellesmere Port CH66 ..94 F8
  Macclesfield SK10 ...86 E1
  Runcorn WA7 ....50 C6
  Warrington WA1 .....17 B8
Tudor Cl
  Ellesmere Port CH66 ..94 F8
  Northwich CW9 .....104 E6
  Warrington WA4 .....17 A2
  Winsford CW7 ....149 D6
Tudor Ct
  Congleton CW12 ....156 D2
  4 Warrington WA4 ...16 E1
Tudor Dr SK10 ....86 D7
Tudor Gn Blacon CH1 .117 E6
  Handforth SK9 ....34 E1
Tudor Rd Handforth SK9 .34 E1
  Runcorn WA7 ....24 C3
Tudor Way Chester CH3 .142 A7
  Congleton CW12 ....156 D1
  Nantwich CW5 ......204 E3
Tudorway CH60 ....41 B8
Tue La WA8 ....12 B6
Tulip Rd Haydock WA11 ..1 F6
  Partington M31 ......11 E2
Tully Ave WA12 ....2 C3
Tulworth Rd SK12 .....36 D3
Tunbridge Cl
  Warrington WA5 .....15 A8
  Wistaston CW2 .....206 A8
Tunnel Rd CW8 ....78 B2
Tunnicliffe Rd SK11 ..112 F3
Tunnicliffe St 1 SK10 .112 D8
Tunstall Rd
  Bosley CW12,SK11 ..158 C7
  Congleton CW12 ....157 F2
Turf La SK11 ....112 C3
Turnall Rd WA8 ....22 B7
Turnberry Cl Lymm WA13 .18 C4
  Macclesfield SK10 ...87 C4
  Northwich CW9 .....104 E7
  Winsford CW7 ......126 C2
Turnberry Dr SK9 .....60 D8
Turner Ave ST7 .....210 A1

Turner Cl Crewe CW1 .190 A8
Turner Cl continued
  Widnes WA8 ....12 D3
Turner Rise SK10 .....88 C8
Turner St Bollington SK10 .88 B8
  Nantwich CW5 ......204 F5
Turner's View CH64 ...41 D2
Turnhurst Rd ST7 ...195 F1
Turnock St SK11 .....112 E7
Turnstone Ave WA12 ..2 C4
Turret Hall Dr 1 WA3 ..3 E8
Turriff Dr CH63 ....43 C4
Turrocks Cl CH64 .....66 E5
Turrocks Croft CH64 ..66 E5
Turton Cl Hale L24 ....21 E1
  Warrington WA3 ......9 C5
Turton St WA3 ....3 A8
Turville Ho SK9 ....34 D2
Tuscan Cl WA8 ....13 B5
Tushingham Cl CW9 ...4 F5
Tushingham-with-Grindley
  CE Prim Sch SY13 ..214 C1
Tuson Dr WA8 ....12 F4
Tutor Bank Dr WA12 ...2 D3
Tweedsmuir CH3 .....119 A2
Tweedsmuir Cl WA2 ...9 A4
Twemlow Ave CW11 ..175 B7
Twemlow La CW4 ....130 D6
Twenty Acre Rd WA5 .15 C8
Twinnies Rd SK9 ......34 B1
Twiss Green Com Prim Sch
  WA3 ....4 E4
Twiss Green Dr WA3 ...4 E4
Twiss Green La WA3 ...4 E4
Twist Ave WA3 ....3 C8
Two Acre Gr CH66 ....69 F1
Twyford Cl WA8 ....13 B5
Twyford La WA8 ......13 D6
Tyldesley Way CW5 ..204 D6
Tyler St SK9 ....60 A1
Tyne Cl WA2 ....8 E2
Tynedale Ave CW2 ...190 C2
Tynedale Cl SK11 ....112 C8
Tynemouth Rd WA7 ...50 C6
Tynesdale CH65 ....70 B3
Tynwald Cres WA8 ...12 F5
Tynwald Dr WA4 ......26 C7
Tyrer Rd WA12 ....2 C1
Tyrer Wlk 2 WA3 ......3 F8
Tytherington Bsns Pk
  SK10 ....87 D5
Tytherington Cl CW10 .151 C6
Tytherington Ct SK10 .87 D3
Tytherington Dr SK10 .87 E4
Tytherington Gn SK10 .87 C4
Tytherington High Sch
  SK10 ....87 D2
Tytherington La SK10 .87 D5
Tytherington Park Rd
  SK10 ....87 D3
Tytherington Sh Ctr 1
  SK10 ....87 D3

Ullapool Cl CH66 ......68 F6
Ullswater SK11 ......111 F5
Ullswater Ave
  Crewe CW2 ....189 E3
  Warrington WA2 ......8 D3
  Winsford CW7 ......126 C2
Ullswater Cres CH2 ..119 A6
Ullswater Dr SK9 .....83 F7
Ullswater Gr WA7 ....49 D5
Ullswater Mans SK11 .111 F6
Ullswater Rd
  Congleton CW12 ....156 A2
  Ellesmere Port CH65 ..70 C2
  Handforth SK9 ....34 C4
Ulverston Ave WA2 ....8 B4
Ulverston Cl WA11 .....1 A6
Ulviet Gate WA16 ....29 C7
Under Rainow Rd CW12 157 E1
Underbridge La WA4 ...25 E6
Undercliffe Ho WA4 ...26 D8
Underway The WA7 ...49 F8
Underwood Cl SK10 ...86 F1
Underwood Ct CW1 ..190 B6
Underwood Dr CH65 ...70 C2
Underwood Ind Pk CW1 190 A6
Underwood La CW1 ..190 B6
Underwood Rd SK9 ...60 C1
Underwood West Inf Sch
  CW1 ....190 A5
Underwood West Jun Sch
  CW1 ....190 A5
Unicorn Gateway 8
  SK10 ....112 D8
Union Cl CW12 ....156 D3
Union Ind Est SK11 ..112 E7
Union Pl CH1 ....237 A2
Union Rd
  Macclesfield SK11 ..112 E7
  New Mills SK22 ......39 C7
Union St Chester CH1 .237 C2
  Congleton CW12 ....156 D3
  Crewe CW2 ....190 D3
  Macclesfield SK11 ..112 D7
  Runcorn WA7 ....23 B2
  Sandbach CW11 .....175 B6
  Warrington WA1 .....16 B5
Union Terr CH1 .....237 B3
Union Wlk CH1 ......237 B2
Unity Way ST7 ......210 D8
Univ of Liverpool, Faculty of
  Veterinary Science
  (Leahurst) CH64 .....67 D8

University College Chester
  CH1 ....237 A4
University Way CW1 ..191 B2
Unsworth Ct WA2 .....8 F1
Upcast La SK9 ....59 E3
Uplands CW8 ....101 D4
Uplands Rd CW9 ......78 A4
Uplands The
  Biddulph ST8 ....179 E2
  Macclesfield SK11 ..112 A5
  Runcorn WA7 ....50 A7
Upper Cambrian Rd
  CH1 ....118 B2
Upper Haigh St CW7 .149 C8
Upper Mersey Rd WA8 .23 A5
Upper Mersey St SK11 .70 C7
Upper Northgate St
  CH1 ....237 A3
Upper Raby Rd CH64 ..42 A2
Upton Ave SK8 ....35 A8
Upton Bridle Path WA8 .12 F4
Upton Cl Golborne WA3 ..3 D8
  Winsford CW7 ......126 F4
Upton Dr Chester CH2 .118 C6
  Warrington WA5 .....14 F5
Upton Grange WA8 ...12 D4
Upton Heath CE Prim Sch
  CH2 ....118 E8
Upton La Chester CH2 .118 D7
  Widnes WA8 ....12 F4
Upton Mount SK10 ...87 A1
Upton Pk SK11 ......118 D6
Upton Priory Inf Sch
  SK10 ....86 F2
Upton Priory Jun Sch
  SK10 ....86 F2
Upton Rd CH66 ....69 D4
Upton Rocks Ave WA8 .12 E4
Upton Rocks Mews WA8 12 E4
Upton Way 12 SK9 ...34 D5
Upton Westlea Prim Sch
  CH2 ....118 E7
Upton-by-Chester High Sch
  CH2 ....118 E8
Upwood Rd WA3 ....3 D7
Ure Ct CH65 ....70 A7
Urmston Ave WA12 ....2 B5
Utkinton Cl WA6 .....146 E7
Utkinton Rd CW6 ....146 C5
Utkinton St Paul's CE Prim
  Sch CW6 ....146 B8

Vahler Terr WA7 ......23 C2
Vale Ave WA2 ....16 B8
Vale Bsns Ctr CW12 .156 D2
Vale Cl CH4 ....139 C3
Vale Ct WA4 ....51 A3
Vale Gdns Alsager ST7 .193 E4
  Ellesmere Port CH65 ..70 B4
  Helsby WA6 ....73 B4
Vale Head SK9 ....34 D2
Vale Owen Rd WA2 ....8 D1
Vale Rd Alpraham CW6 .169 A4
  Ellesmere Port CH65 ..70 B4
  Hartford CW8 ....103 C4
  Marston CW9 ....79 B6
  Wilmslow SK9 ....59 E8
Vale Royal Ctyd CW8 .126 B8
Vale Royal Dr CW8 ..126 A8
Vale Royal River Park Cvn
  Site CW9 ....126 E6
Vale View CW9 ....79 D4
Vale Wlk CW12 ......156 D2
Valebrook Dr CW5 ...220 A8
Valentine Rd
  Kidsgrove ST7 ......195 A1
  Newton-le-W WA12 ...1 F3
Valiant Cl WA2 ....8 F2
Valley Brook Bsns Ctr
  CW2 ....190 D3
Valley Cl Alsager ST7 .192 F3
  Knutsford WA16 .....82 A7
Valley Ct WA2 ....8 F1
Valley Dr Chester CH2 .118 D5
  Ellesmere Port CH66 ..69 D5
  Handforth SK9 ....34 C3
Valley La CW8 ....101 F3
Valley Rd Bebington CH62 .43 D8
  Bramhall SK8 ....35 F8
  Crewe CW2 ....189 F1
  Macclesfield SK11 ..112 A6
  Weaverham CW8 .....77 C1
Valley Sch SK7 ....35 C5
Valley View
  Congleton CW12 ....156 C3
  Ellesmere Port CH66 ..69 D5
  Newton-le-W WA12 ...2 B1
  Northwich CW9 .....104 C7
Valley Way WA16 .....82 A7
Vanguard Ct WA3 ......9 D4
Varden Rd SK12 ......36 E3
Varden Town Cotts SK10 .86 A4
Vardon Dr SK9 ....60 D6
Varey Rd WA12 ......156 F4
Vaudrey Cres CW12 .156 D2
Vaudrey Dr WA1 ......17 D2
Vaughan Rd SK23 .....65 C5
Vaughans La CH3 ....142 A8
Vauxhall Cl WA5 ......14 F4
Vauxhall Rd CW5 ....204 E7
Vauxhall Way CW7 ..149 C6
Vearows Pl CW8 .....103 F7
Venable's Rd CH1 ...117 F4
Venables Rd CW9 .....79 A1

Venables Way
  High Legh WA16 ......29 C4
  Middlewich CW10 ...151 E6
Venns Rd WA2 ....16 D7
Ventnor Cl
  Middlewich CW10 ...151 C6
  Warrington WA5 .....14 D7
Venture Ho SK11 ....112 D6
Venture Way SK12 ....36 F3
Verbena Cl Partington M31 11 F3
  Runcorn WA7 ....49 F4
Verdin Ave CW8 ....78 C4
Verdin Cl Moulton CW9 .126 F7
  Winsford CW7 ......126 C2
Verdin Ct CW1 ....190 A8
Verdin St CW9 ....104 C8
Vere St CW1 ....190 C5
Verity Cl CW1 ....191 C4
Vermont Cl WA5 ......15 C7
Vernay Gn CH4 ......141 B5
Vernon Ave Audley ST7 .209 D2
  Congleton CW12 ....178 F8
  Hooton CH66 ....44 A2
Vernon Cl Audley ST7 .209 D2
  Poynton SK12 ....36 D2
  Saughall CH1 ....117 A8
Vernon Dr CW3 ......230 F4
Vernon Inf Sch SK12 ..36 E3
Vernon Jun Sch SK12 ..36 E3
Vernon Lo SK12 ....36 D2
Vernon Rd Chester CH1 .118 B2
  Poynton SK12 ....36 E2
Vernon St Crewe CW1 .190 B5
  Macclesfield SK10 ..112 F8
  Warrington WA1 .....16 B4
Vernon Way CW1 ....190 D4
Veronica Way CH66 ...69 D7
Vetch Cl WA3 ....11 B5
Vetches The CH3 ....119 F5
Viaduct St WA12 ......2 A3
Vicar's Cl CH3 ......121 F7
Vicar's La CH1 ......237 B2
Vicarage Ave SK8 ....35 B7
Vicarage Cl
  Guilden Sutton CH3 .119 F5
  Hale L24 ....21 E1
Vicarage Ct LL13 ....196 E8
Vicarage Dr WA11 .....1 B7
Vicarage Gdns CW11 .174 E8
Vicarage Gr CW7 ....149 D5
Vicarage Hill WA6 ....73 C4
Vicarage La Audlem CW3 230 A4
  Bunbury CW6 ....168 F1
  Burton CH64 ....67 D2
  Frodsham WA6 ......74 C7
  Helsby WA6 ....73 C4
  Little Budworth CW6 .147 F7
  Poynton SK12 ....36 E5
  Sandbach CW11 ....174 E8
Vicarage Rd Chester CH2 118 F3
  Haslington CW1 ....191 D6
  Haydock WA11 ....1 A7
  Northwich CW9 .....104 B8
  Widnes WA8 ....23 A7
Vicarage Row CH62 ...44 A5
Vicarage Way 1 SK11 .111 F7
Vicarage Wlk
  Northwich CW9 .....104 B7
  Warrington WA4 .....26 C8
Vicars Cross Ct 2 CH3 .119 B2
Vicars Cross Rd CH3 .119 C2
Vickers Rd WA8 ....22 F4
Vickers Way CW9 ....104 A7
Victoria Ave Crewe CW2 .190 A4
  Haslington CW1 ....191 C4
  Heswall CH60 ....41 A6
  Holmes Chapel CW4 .130 C2
  Kidsgrove ST7 ......194 F2
  Warrington WA5 .....14 D6
  Warrington, Grappenhall
  WA4 ....17 A2
  Widnes WA8 ....13 A3
Victoria Bldgs 3 WA7 ..23 A2
Victoria Cl SK7 ....35 D6
Victoria Com Tech Sch
  CW1 ....190 C5
Victoria Cres
  Chester CH2 ....237 A4
  Chester,Queen's Park
  CH4 ....237 C1
Victoria Ct Chester CH2 .237 A4
  2 Crewe CW1 ......190 C4
  Haslington CW1 ....191 C4
  8 Kidsgrove ST7 ...195 A2
  Knutsford WA16 .....56 F1
  2 Widnes WA8 ......23 A8
Victoria Gr WA8 ......13 A3
Victoria Inf Sch CH1 .237 A4
Victoria Infmy CW8 ..103 E8
Victoria Mews CH65 ..70 B5
Victoria Mill Dr CW5 .205 D6
Victoria Pathway CH4 .237 C1
Victoria Pk CW8 ......78 F1
Victoria Pl CW8 .....237 B3
  Warrington WA4 .....16 C1
Victoria Rd
  Chester CH1,CH2 ...237 B3
  Chester CH7 ....237 A4
  Ellesmere Port CH65 ..70 C5
  Macclesfield SK10 ...87 A1
  Neston CH64 ....67 A6
  Newton-le-W WA12 ...2 C3
  Northwich CW9 .....104 B8

Victoria Rd *continued*
Runcorn WA7 .... 23 A2
Runcorn WA7 .... 23 B2
Saltney CH4 .... 140 D5
Warrington WA4 .... 16 F2
Warrington, Stockton Heath WA4 .... 16 D1
Warrington,Great Sankey WA5 .... 15 B4
Warrington,Penketh WA5 .. 14 D4
Widnes WA8 .... 23 A6
Wilmslow SK9 .... 60 A6
Victoria Road Prim Sch
Northwich CW9 .... 104 B8
Runcorn WA7 .... 23 A2
Victoria Sq
Warrington WA4 .... 16 C1
8 Widnes WA8 .... 23 A7
Winsford CW7 .... 149 A8
Victoria St
Congleton CW12 .... 156 D2
Crewe CW1 .... 190 C4
Knutsford WA16 .... 56 F2
New Mills SK22 .... 39 B6
Northwich CW9 .... 79 E2
Sandbach CW11 .... 175 B7
Warrington WA1 .... 16 C5
Widnes WA8 .... 23 B7
Victoria Stadium (Northwich Victoria FC) CW9 .... 79 D3
Victoria Trad Ctr WA8 .. 23 A6
Victoria Way SK7 .... 35 D6
Victoria Wlk SK10 .... 112 E8
Victory Rd M44 .... 11 C4
Viewlands Dr SK9 .... 34 D2
Villa Farm CW11 .... 176 B8
Villa Rd CH5 .... 116 B7
Village Cl
Lostock Green CW9 .... 105 A8
Runcorn WA7 .... 50 A8
Warrington WA4 .... 17 E4
Village Ct 8 SK9 .... 34 D1
Village Farm CW5 .... 172 A5
Village La WA4 .... 52 D4
Village Mews SK10 .... 87 A6
Village Rd
Christleton CH3 .... 142 E8
Great Barrow CH3 .... 120 E6
Heswall CH60 .... 40 F7
Waverton CH3 .... 143 C4
Village St WA7 .... 24 E2
Village Terr The 6 WA4 .. 16 C1
Village The
Astbury CW12 .... 178 B8
Burton CH64 .... 67 D1
Prestbury SK10 .... 86 F6
Village Way 12 SK9 .... 34 D1
Villars St WA1 .... 16 C5
Villas The CW4 .... 131 A8
Villiers Russell Cl CW1 .. 190 D5
Vincent Cl WA5 .... 15 C8
Vincent Dr CH4 .... 141 C6
Vincent St Crewe CW1 .. 190 E4
Macclesfield SK11 .... 112 D7
Vine Bank Rd ST7 .... 195 A1
Vine Cl SK11 .... 112 A6
Vine Cres WA5 .... 14 F6
Vine Rd CH66 .... 69 F1
Vine St Bollington SK10 .. 88 B8
12 Runcorn WA7 .... 23 A2
Widnes WA8 .... 23 A7
Vine Terr WA8 .... 12 A2
Vine Tree Ave
Crewe CW2 .... 190 B1
Shavington CW2 .... 206 B5
Vine Tree Prim Sch CW2 .... 190 A1
Violet Cl WA3 .... 9 C5
Violet St WA8 .... 23 A7
Virginia Chase SK8 .... 34 F8
Virginia Dr CH1 .... 117 C4
Virginia Gdns WA5 .... 15 B8
Virginia Terr CH66 .... 69 B8
Virtual Bsns Ctr CH1 .. 117 E2
Viscount Dr
Heald Green SK8 .... 34 D7
Woodhouse Park M90 .... 32 F7
Viscount Rd WA2 .... 8 E2
Vista Ave WA12 .... 2 A4
Vista Rd
Newton-le-W WA11,WA12 .. 2 A6
Runcorn WA7 .... 49 A8
Vista The M44 .... 11 C4
Vista Way WA12 .... 2 A4
Vixen Gr WA8 .... 12 F4
Volunteer Ave 7 CW5 .. 204 E6
Volunteer Fields CW5 .. 204 E6
Volunteer St
Chester CH1 .... 237 B2
Frodsham WA6 .... 49 D1
Vose Cl WA5 .... 15 D6
Vulcan Cl
Newton-le-W WA12 .... 2 C1
Warrington WA2 .... 8 F2
Vulcan Ind Est WA12 .... 2 D1
Vyrnwy Rd CH4 .... 140 D6

W

Wadbrook Trad Est CW9 .... 104 C8
Waddington Cl
Golborne WA3 .... 3 F8
Warrington WA2 .... 8 F1
Wade Cres CW8 .... 78 A3
Wade Ct ST7 .... 195 A1
Wade Deacon High Sch WA8 .... 13 A2
Wade St CW9 .... 79 B1
Wadebrook Gr 4 SK9 .. 34 D1
Wades La CW7 .... 126 D3
Wadeson Way WA3 .... 9 B7
Wadsworth Cl SK9 .... 34 E3
Wagg St CW12 .... 156 D2
Waggon Cotts ST7 .... 208 E1
Waggs Rd CW12 .... 156 C1
Wagon La WA11 .... 1 B6
Wain Ho CH1 .... 94 A1
Wain Lee ST7 .... 195 F4
Waine St CW1 .... 190 D5
Wakefield Cl CW1 .... 189 F7
Wakefield Ho WA5 .... 15 F6
Wakefield Rd CH66 .... 69 E1
Wakefield St WA3 .... 3 A7
Wakeham Chase 8 SK11 .... 111 F7
Wakes Mdw CW6 .... 185 E8
Walden Cl WA4 .... 17 D3
Walden Dr CH1 .... 93 D8
Waldon Rd SK11 .... 112 A5
Waldron Gdns CW2 .... 189 F1
Waldron Rd CW1 .... 191 D3
Waldron's La CW1 .... 173 D1
Walfield Ave CW12 .... 156 D5
Walford Ave CW2 .... 190 B3
Walgrave Cl CW12 .... 156 A3
Walker Cl CW1 .... 191 D4
Walker Dr CW10 .... 151 C8
Walker La SK11 .... 112 E2
Walker St Chester CH2 .. 237 C4
Crewe CW1 .... 190 B5
2 Macclesfield SK10 .... 112 C8
Warrington WA2 .... 16 A6
Walkers La
Ellesmere Port CH66 .... 69 C6
Farndon CH3 .... 180 F2
Scholar Green ST7 .... 177 B2
Tarporley CW6 .... 146 D1
Warrington WA5 .... 14 E3
Walkersgreen Rd ST5 .. 210 D2
Wall Fields Rd CW5 .... 204 E7
Wall Hill Way CW8 .... 76 F3
Wall La CW5 .... 204 E6
Wallace Ct CW7 .... 127 D1
Wallace St
Northwich CW8 .... 103 E7
Widnes WA8 .... 23 A8
Wallcroft CH64 .... 68 A7
Walled Gdn The CW10 .. 127 D5
Waller St SK11 .... 112 E6
Wallerscote Cl CW8 .... 102 E8
Wallerscote Com Sch CW8 .... 102 E8
Wallerscote Rd CW8 .. 102 E8
Walleys La CW5 .... 203 C7
Wallfields Cl CW5 .... 204 E7
Wallhill La CW11 .... 177 D7
Wallingford Rd SK9 .... 34 C5
Wallis St Crewe CW1 .. 190 D4
Warrington WA4 .... 16 B3
Wallrake CH60 .... 40 F7
Walls Ave CH1 .... 118 B1
Wallsend Ct WA8 .... 12 F3
Wallworth Terr SK9 .... 59 E8
Wallworth's Bank CW12 156 E2
Walmer Pl CW7 .... 149 C6
Walmoor Pk CH3 .... 119 A1
Walmsley St
Newton-le-W WA12 .... 2 D4
Widnes WA8 .... 23 C8
Walnut Ave CW8 .... 102 D7
Walnut Cl Chester CH2 .. 118 D7
Warrington WA1 .... 17 E7
Wilmslow SK9 .... 60 E8
Walnut Cotts LL13 .... 196 D8
Walnut Croft CH3 .... 180 F6
Walnut Dr CW7 .... 127 A1
Walnut Gr CH66 .... 70 A1
Walnut La CW8 .... 103 A5
Walnut Rd M31 .... 11 D3
Walnut Rise CW12 .... 156 B2
Walnut Tree La
Bradwall Green CW11 .. 153 A4
Warrington WA4 .... 26 F4
Walpole Cl CW1 .... 191 C5
Walpole Gr WA2 .... 8 C2
Walpole Rd WA7 .... 49 C6
Walpole St CH1 .... 237 A4
Walsh Cl WA12 .... 2 C5
Walsingham Dr WA7 .. 24 D2
Walsingham Rd WA5 .. 14 F5
Walter St Chester CH1 .. 237 B4
Warrington WA1 .... 16 E7
Widnes WA8 .... 13 D1
Walters Wood SK23 .... 65 F5
Walthall St CW2 .... 190 C2
Waltham Ave WA3 .... 5 C7
Waltham Ct WA7 .... 24 E4
Waltham Dr SK8 .... 35 B6
Waltham Pl CH4 .... 141 A6
Walton Ave WA5 .... 14 E5
Walton Gr ST7 .... 210 C8
Walton Hall★ WA4 .... 25 F7
Walton Hall Gdns★ WA4 .. 25 F6
Walton Heath Dr SK10 .. 87 B4
Walton Heath Rd WA4 .. 16 B1
Walton La WA3 .... 9 E5
Walton Lea Rd WA4 .... 26 A7
Walton New Rd WA4 .... 26 B8
Walton Pl CH1 .... 117 E4
Walton Rd Culcheth WA3 .. 4 F3
Warrington WA4 .... 26 C8
Walton St 15 WA7 .... 23 A2
Walton Way ST7 .... 210 C8
Waltons The CH4 .... 141 E6
Wandsworth Way WA8 .. 22 F5
Wansfell Pl WA2 .... 8 A3
Warburton Bridge Rd WA13,WA3 .... 11 A1
Warburton Cl
Altrincham WA15 .... 32 D6
Lymm WA13 .... 19 A4
Warburton Dr WA15 .... 32 D6
Warburton La M31,WA13 .. 11 E2
Warburton Rd SK9 .... 34 D4
Warburton St WA4 .... 16 D1
Warburton View WA3 .. 11 A2
Ward Ave SK10 .... 88 A8
Ward Cl WA5 .... 7 B1
Ward La SK12 .... 38 F4
Ward's La CW11 .... 153 C5
Ward's Terr CH2 .... 118 F3
Wardle Ave CW5 .... 187 C7
Wardle Cotts CW5 .... 187 C7
Wardle Cres SK11 .... 111 E1
Wardle Ind Est CW5 .. 187 A7
Wardle Mews CW10 .... 151 D8
Wardle St 7 SK11 .... 112 D7
Wardley Rd WA4 .... 16 B1
Wardour Cl 6 SK11 .... 111 F7
Wardour St WA5 .... 15 E6
Wards La CW12 .... 179 C8
Wareham Cl Haydock WA11 1 C7
Warrington WA1 .... 17 C8
Wareham Dr CW1 .... 190 B8
Warford Ave SK12 .... 37 A2
Warford Cres SK9 .... 84 B7
Warford Hall Dr SK9 .. 84 B6
Warford La WA16 .... 59 B1
Warford Terr WA16 .... 59 B2
Wargrave CE Prim Sch WA12 .... 2 C1
Wargrave Mews WA12 .... 2 C1
Wargrave Rd WA12 .... 2 C2
Warham St SK9 .... 60 B7
Waring Ave St Helens WA9 .. 1 B2
Warrington WA4 .... 16 F5
Warkick Rd CH1 .... 117 F5
Warkworth Cl WA8 .... 12 C3
Warkworth Ct CH65 .... 70 E3
Warmingham CE Prim Sch CW11 .... 173 E8
Warmingham Ct CW10 .. 151 D7
Warmingham La
Middlewich CW10 .... 151 D5
Sandbach CW11 .... 174 B8
Warmingham Rd CW1 .. 173 D4
Warnley Cl WA8 .... 12 D3
Warren Ave
Knutsford WA16 .... 56 E2
Lostock Gralam CW9 .... 80 A3
Warren Cl Knutsford WA16 56 F2
Middlewich CW10 .... 151 B7
Poynton SK12 .... 36 B4
Warren Croft WA7 .... 50 D7
Warren Ct
Ellesmere Port CH66 .... 69 D3
Frodsham WA6 .... 74 D6
Warren Dr
Altrincham WA15 .... 32 D7
Broughton CH4 .... 139 A3
Ellesmere Port CH66 .... 69 E7
Newton-le-W WA12 .... 2 F4
Warren SK11 .... 111 D1
Warrington WA4 .... 26 D8
Warren Gr SK11 .... 111 D1
Warren Hey SK9 .... 60 E8
Warren La Hartford CW8 .. 103 A4
Warrington WA1 .... 17 D8
Warren Lea SK12 .... 36 E5
Warren Rd
Warrington WA4 .... 26 C7
Warrington,Orford WA2 .. 8 D1
Warren The CW8 .... 101 D5
Warren Way CW6 .... 168 D8
Warrilow Heath Rd ST5 210 C1
Warrington Ave
Crewe CW1 .... 190 C6
Ellesmere Port CH65 .... 70 B2
Warrington Bank Quay Sta WA1 .... 15 F4
Warrington Bsns ctr WA2 .... 16 A6
Warrington Bsns Pk WA2 .. 8 C1
Warrington Central Sta WA2 .... 16 B6
Warrington Collegiate Inst WA2 .... 8 B1
Warrington Collegiate Inst (Padgate Campus) WA2 .. 9 B3
Warrington Hospl WA5 .. 15 F6
Warrington La WA13 .. 19 E2
Warrington Mus & Art Gallery★ WA1 .... 16 A4
Warrington Rd
Bold Heath L35,WA8 .... 13 D7
Comberbach CW9 .... 78 D7
Cronton L35 .... 12 E8
Cronton L35 .... 12 F8
Cuddington CW8 .... 102 A5
Fowley Common WA3,WN7 .. 5 C5
Golborne WA3,WA12 .... 3 A6
Hatton WA4 .... 25 F4
Little Leigh CW8 .... 77 A5
Lymm WA13 .... 18 B4
Mere WA16 .... 56 B7
Mickle Trafford CH2 .... 119 E7
Runcorn, Castlefields WA7 .. 23 E2
Runcorn, Manor Park WA7 .. 24 B4
Warrington WA5 .... 14 F4
Warrington Rd *continued*
Warrington,Risley WA3 .... 9 E7
Widnes WA8 .... 13 D1
Warrington St Ann's CE Prim Sch WA2 .... 16 C8
Warrington Trad Est WA2 .... 16 A6
Warton Cl Bramhall SK7 .. 36 A7
Warrington WA5 .... 15 A3
Warwick Ave
Newton-le-W WA12 .... 2 E2
Warrington,Bewsey WA5 .. 15 F7
Warrington,Great Sankey WA5 .... 14 D7
Warwick Cl
Kidsgrove ST7 .... 195 A3
Knutsford WA16 .... 57 C1
Macclesfield SK11 .... 111 F6
Neston CH64 .... 66 E5
Warwick Ct CH65 .... 70 E2
Warwick Dr SK7 .... 36 D8
Warwick Gr 1 WA7 .... 23 F1
Warwick Pl CW7 .... 149 C6
Warwick Rd Irlam M44 .. 11 D5
Macclesfield SK11 .... 111 E6
Warwick Wlk SK11 .... 111 F6
Wasdale Gr CW1 .... 173 B1
Wash La Allostock WA16 .. 106 E3
Warrington WA4 .... 16 E3
Washington Cl
Biddulph ST8 .... 179 C2
Cheadle Hulme SK8 .... 34 F8
Wasley Cl WA2 .... 8 F3
Waste La
Cuddington CW8 .... 101 E3
Delamere CW8 .... 123 F6
Kelsall CW6 .... 122 F4
Watch La CW11 .... 174 A6
Water La SK9 .... 60 A7
Water St Bollington SK10 .. 88 B8
Macclesfield SK11 .... 112 C8
Newcastle-u-Lyme ST5 .. 210 D2
Newton-le-W WA12 .... 2 C4
Northwich CW9 .... 104 A7
Runcorn WA7 .... 23 A3
Widnes WA8 .... 23 A6
Water's Reach SK6 .... 37 E7
Waterbank Row CW9 .. 103 F7
Waterbridge Ct
2 Lymm WA13 .... 18 C3
Warrington WA4 .... 26 D8
Waterfoot La SK23 .... 65 D6
Waterford Dr CH64 .... 67 A7
Waterford Pl SK8 .... 34 B8
Waterford Way WA7 .... 50 C6
Waterfowl Sanctuary★ SY13 .... 225 F6
Waterfront WA4 .... 50 F6
Watergate Row N CH1 .237 A2
Watergate Row S CH1 .237 A2
Watergate Sq CH1 .... 237 A2
Watergate St CH1 .... 237 A2
Waterhouse Ave SK10 .. 87 F8
Waterlode CW5 .... 204 E5
Waterloo Cl 5 CH65 .... 70 C5
Waterloo Cotts WA6 .... 99 F8
Waterloo Gr ST7 .... 195 A2
Waterloo Ho 16 CW8 .. 103 F8
Waterloo La WA6 .... 74 F1
Waterloo Rd Bramhall SK7 35 F8
Chester CH2 .... 118 C4
Haslington CW1 .... 191 D4
Northwich CW8 .... 103 E7
Poynton SK12 .... 37 A2
3 Runcorn WA7 .... 22 F2
Runcorn WA7 .... 22 F3
Widnes WA8 .... 23 A5
Waterloo St W SK11 .. 112 C8
Watermead Dr WA7 .... 50 F5
Watermill Dr SK11 .... 112 F7
Waters Edge
Anderton CW9 .... 78 D3
Chester CH1 .... 118 B2
Waters Edge Mews CW10 .... 151 C8
Waters Gn SK11 .... 112 D8
Waters Reach SK12 .... 36 F5
Waters Reams CH3 .... 142 B8
Watersedge WA6 .... 49 D2
Watersfield Cl SK8 .... 34 F8
Waterside Disley SK12 .... 38 E7
Macclesfield SK11 .... 112 E7
Warrington WA4 .... 26 D8
Whaley Bridge SK23 .... 39 E3
Waterside Cotts CW5 .. 216 E5
Waterside Dr WA6 .... 49 D2
Waterside La WA8 .... 22 C5
Waterside Mews CW11 .. 174 F3
Waterside Rd SK12 .... 38 F7
Waterside View
Chester CH1 .... 237 B3
Northwich CW9 .... 104 E6
Waterside Way CW10 .. 128 B2
Watertower View CH2 .. 118 F2
Waterway CH3 .... 143 B5
Waterways WA5 .... 15 D6
Waterworks La
Ellesmere Port CH66 .... 68 E8
Hooton CH66 .... 43 E1
Winwick WA2 .... 8 B7
Watery La Astbury CW12 .178 C5
Frodsham WA6 .... 74 E6
Winwick WA2 .... 7 E6
Watkin St
Sandycroft CH5 .... 116 A3
Warrington WA2 .... 16 B7
Watkins Ave WA12 .... 1 F3
Watkinson Way WA8 .... 13 C5
Watlands Rd ST7 .... 209 E2
Watling Cres CH4 .... 141 E7
Watling Ct Chester CH3 .. 119 C2
Cuddington CW8 .... 102 B2
Watling Dr CW6 .... 123 C6
Watling St CW9 .... 103 F8
Watson's Cl CH4 .... 139 C3
Watton Cl WA4 .... 17 C3
Wavell Ave WA8 .... 22 D8
Wavells Way CH3 .... 142 B5
Waveney Dr SK9 .... 34 D2
Waverley Ave WA4 .... 26 D8
Waverley Cl SK10 .... 113 A8
Waverley Ct 1 CW2 .... 190 D2
Waverley Dr SK8 .... 35 B7
Waverley Terr CH2 .... 118 E4
Waverton App CH3 .... 164 E6
Waverton Bsns Pk CH3 .142 F4
Waverton Cl Hough CW2 206 E2
Northwich CW9 .... 103 E4
Waverton Com Prim Sch CH3 .... 143 A5
Waverton Mill Quays CH3 .... 143 B5
Waverton Pk CH3 .... 143 B5
Waverton Rd CH66 .... 69 E5
Wavertree Ave
Scholar Green ST7 .... 194 E7
Widnes WA8 .... 23 A8
Wavertree Ct CH66 .... 69 F7
Wavertree Dr CW10 .... 151 B7
Wavertree Rd CH1 .... 117 C5
Way's Gn CW7 .... 149 E8
Waybutt La CW2 .... 221 D8
Wayfarers Ct CW9 .... 79 F7
Wayfarers Dr WA12 .... 2 E2
Wayford Cl WA6 .... 49 B1
Wayford Mews WA7 .... 49 B1
Wayside Cl WA13 .... 18 D2
Wayside Ct CH2 .... 119 F8
Wayside Dr SK12 .... 36 C4
Wayside Linley ST7 .... 193 F2
Wayside Rd SK10 .... 112 F8
Waystead Cl CW9 .... 103 F4
Waywell Cl WA2 .... 8 F3
Weald Dr CH66 .... 69 A6
Wealstone Ct CH2 .... 118 E5
Wealstone La CH2 .... 118 E6
Wearhead Cl WA3 .... 2 F7
Weaste La WA4 .... 17 E2
Weates Cl WA8 .... 13 F3
Weathercock La CW12 .157 E3
Weatherstones Cotts CH64 .... 67 D8
Weatherstones Mews CH64 .... 67 E8
Weaver Bank CW5 .... 204 D5
Weaver Cl Alsager ST7 .. 193 A3
Biddulph ST8 .... 179 D1
Sandbach CW11 .... 174 E7
Weaver Cres WA6 .... 49 D1
Weaver Ct
Macclesfield SK11 .... 112 C7
Northwich CW9 .... 103 F8
Weaver Gr
Mickle Trafford CH2 .... 119 F8
St Helens WA9 .... 1 A3
Weaver Grange CW9 .. 126 E8
Weaver Ho 19 CW8 .... 103 F8
Weaver La WA6 .... 49 B2
Weaver Park Ind Est WA6 .... 49 D2
Weaver Prim Sch CW5 .204 E3
Weaver Rd Culcheth WA3 .. 5 A2
Ellesmere Port CH65 .... 70 C2
Frodsham WA6 .... 49 D1
Moulton CW9 .... 126 E7
Nantwich CW5 .... 204 E6
Northwich CW8 .... 103 E7
Weaver St Chester CH1 .. 237 A2
Winsford CW7 .... 126 E1
Weaver Valley Rd CW7 .. 126 F3
Weaver View
Audlem CW3 .... 229 E3
Church Minshull CW5 .... 172 B6
Northwich CW8 .... 103 F7
Weaverham CW8 .... 77 D1
Weaver Way CW9 .... 78 F1
Weaverhall La CW7 .... 150 B5
Weaverham Forest Prim Sch CW8 .... 77 C1
Weaverham High Sch CW8 .... 102 C8
Weaverham Rd CW8 .. 102 B4
Weaverham Way SK9 .. 34 E4
Weavers Cotts 3 CW12 156 D3
Weavers La SK7 .... 35 D6
Weaverside CW5 .... 204 E2
Weaverside Ave WA7 .... 49 F4
Weavervale Pk CW8 .... 77 A6
Webb Dr WA5 .... 6 F6
Webb's Ct CW9 .... 103 F7
Webb's La CW10 .... 128 C2
Webbs Orch SK23 .... 65 D8
Webster Cl CH4 .... 139 C3
Websters La CH66 .... 69 F2
Weddell Cl WA5 .... 15 D7
Wedge Ave WA11 .... 1 A5
Wedgwood Ave ST7 .... 210 A1
Wedgwood Dr WA8 .... 13 B4
Wedgwood La ST8 .... 179 C2
Wedgwood Rd ST7 .... 210 D7
Wednesbury Dr WA5 .... 14 F6
Weedon Ave WA12 .... 2 B5
Weighbridge Rd
Connah's Quay CH5 .... 92 B4
Connah's Quay CH5 .... 92 C5
Weint The WA3 .... 11 B3

Weir Gr ST7 195 B2
Weir La WA1 17 E6
Weir St Northwich CW9 103 F7
Warrington WA4 16 A1
Welbeck Ave WA12 2 D2
Welbeck Cl CW10 128 B1
Welford Ave WA3 3 C7
Welford Cl SK9 60 E8
Well Ave SY14 213 B3
Well Bank CW11 175 B6
Well Bank Cotts WA16 108 C8
Well Bank La WA16, SK11 108 C7
Well Cl CH64 67 A4
Well Farm Cl
Malpas SY14 213 B3
Warrington WA1 17 D8
Well Field Cl WA16 80 A7
Well La Alsager ST7 193 C3
Antrobus CW9 53 A4
Biddulph ST8 179 D3
Chester CH2 118 E5
Heswall CH60 41 B6
Kingsley WA6 75 C2
Little Budworth CW6 147 F7
Macclesfield SK10 88 B2
Manley WA6 98 F3
Mollington CH1 94 F2
Neston CH64 66 F5
Prestbury SK10 87 C8
Stretton WA4 52 E8
Warrington WA5 14 F3
Weaverham CW8 77 C1
Well St Malpas SY14 213 B3
Mow Cop ST7 195 D7
New Mills SK22 39 B8
Winsford CW7 126 C1
Welland Cl CW11 174 C5
Welland Rd SK9 34 E2
Wellbank Ct CW12 156 E2
Wellbrook Cl WA7 50 C5
Wellcroft Cl CW2 206 B7
Weller Ave SK12 36 D2
Weller Cl SK12 36 D2
Welles St CW11 175 B6
Wellesbourne Cl
Macclesfield SK10 86 F1
Neston CH64 66 D6
Wellesley Ave
Ellesmere Port CH65 70 C5
Haslington CW1 191 C4
Wellesley Cl WA12 2 B5
Wellesley Wlk 6 CH65 70 C5
Wellfield Runcorn WA7 50 E5
Widnes WA8 13 A3
Winsford CW7 127 A2
Wellfield Rd WA3 4 F4
Wellfield St
Warrington WA5 15 E5
Warrington WA5 15 E6
Wellfield Way SY13 225 F1
Wellington Cir SK10 112 E8
Wellington Cl
Congleton CW12 156 D4
3 Ellesmere Port CH65 70 C5
Knutsford WA16 57 C4
Newton-le-W WA12 2 A3
Warrington WA2 8 F2
Wellington Gate L24 21 E2
Wellington Gdns WA12 2 A3
Wellington Pl CH1 237 B3
Wellington Rd
Bollington SK10 87 F8
Broughton CH4 139 B4
Ellesmere Port CH65 70 B4
Ellesmere Port CH65 70 C5
Hazel Grove SK7 37 B8
Kidsgrove ST7 195 A2
Nantwich CW5 204 E4
Wellington Rd N CH65 70 C5
Wellington St
15 Macclesfield SK11 112 D8
Newton-le-W WA12 2 A3
Northwich CW8 103 E7
3 Runcorn WA7 23 A3
Warrington WA1 16 C5
Widnes WA8 23 A6
Wellington St Wrkshps 4 WA1 16 C5
Wells Ave CW1 191 D5
Wells Cl
Ellesmere Port CH66 94 E8
Heald Green SK8 34 C7
Mickle Trafford CH2 119 F8
Warrington WA1 17 B8
Wellswood Dr CW2 205 F7
Wellswood Rd CH66 69 E7
Welsby Cl WA2 8 F3
Welsh La CW7 149 D6
Welsh Rd
Connah's Quay CH5 116 A7
Ellesmere Port CH66 68 E4
Hooton CH66 44 A1
Woodbank CH1 93 C6
Welsh Road Cotts CH1 93 D8
Welsh Row
Nantwich CW5 204 D5
Nether Alderley SK10 84 F6
Welshampton Cl CH66 69 D2
Welshmen's La CW5 204 C7
Welshpool Cl WA5 7 D2
Welton Cl SK9 59 F4
Welton Dr SK9 59 E4
Welton Gr SK9 59 E4
Welwyn Cl WA4 17 C3
Wem Gr ST5 210 E2
Wemyss Rd CH1 117 D4
Wendover Cl WA11 1 D7
Wenger Rd WA8 13 B5
Wenlock Cl
Macclesfield SK10 87 B2
Newcastle-u-Lyme ST5 210 E2
Warrington WA1 17 A8
Wenlock Gdns CH66 69 F2
Wenlock La CH66 69 F2
Wenlock Rd WA7 50 A4
Wenlock Way CH4 140 F6
Wensley Dr SK7 36 D7
Wensley Rd WA3 3 E7
Wensleydale Ave
Bebington CH62 43 E5
Congleton CW12 157 A5
Wensleydale Cl WA5 14 F8
Wentworth Ave
Macclesfield SK11 111 F6
Warrington WA1 17 B7
Wentworth Cl
Northwich CW9 104 E7
Widnes WA8 13 A5
Wentworth Dr
Bebington CH63 43 C5
Bramhall SK7 36 A7
Kidsgrove ST7 195 C3
Wentworth Gr CW7 126 A2
Wereton Rd ST7 209 D1
Wervin Rd CH2 96 A3
Wesley Ave Alsager ST7 193 D4
Haydock WA11 1 F7
2 Sandbach CW11 175 B6
Wesley Cl Nantwich CW5 204 E5
Neston CH64 66 D8
Wesley Ct
Congleton CW12 156 D2
Winsford CW7 126 F1
Wesley Gdns 7 ST7 195 A2
Wesley Pl Crewe CW2 190 D2
4 Northwich CW9 104 A8
Wesley St ST7 210 A1
Wessex Cl
Shavington CW2 206 C3
Warrington WA1 17 E7
Wessex Dr CW9 104 C6
West Ave Crewe CW1 190 B4
Kidsgrove ST7 194 C1
Middlewich CW10 128 C2
Northwich CW9 104 D7
Warrington WA2 16 B8
Warrington, Stockton Heath WA4 16 C1
Weston CW2 207 B5
West Bank
Alderley Edge SK9 85 A8
Chester CH2 118 C4
West Bank Dock Est WA8 22 E5
West Bank Prim Sch WA8 23 A4
West Bank Rd SK10 87 B1
West Bank St WA8 23 A5
West Bond St SK11 112 C7
West Cheshire Coll CH65 70 B5
West Cheshire Coll (Greenbank Ctr) CH4 141 D6
West Cheshire Coll (Handbridge Ctr) CH4 141 D7
West Cl SK10 87 F7
West Dr Heswall CH60 41 A7
Neston CH64 66 E6
Warrington WA5 15 B4
Winsford CW7 127 A2
West Dudley St CW7 126 F1
West End CH3 121 E7
West End Cotts CW12 156 C2
West End Gr WA11 1 A6
West End Rd WA11 1 A6
West Gn CH5 116 A6
West Gr Alsager ST7 193 E4
Heswall CH60 40 F8
West Hall Ct WA16 29 C5
West Heath Gr WA13 18 C4
West Heath Sh Ctr CW12 156 A3
West House Ct SK10 86 E1
West Hyde WA13 18 C3
West La Cuddington CW8 101 F3
High Legh WA16 29 C6
Runcorn WA7 49 F8
West Lorne St CH1 237 A3
West Mains L24 21 A3
West Park Ave SK12 36 A4
West Park Dr CH66 94 F8
West Park Mus★ SK10 87 C1
West Quay Rd WA2 7 F3
West Rd Congleton CW12 156 C3
Ellesmere Port CH65 70 C3
Runcorn WA7 48 D7
Weaverham CW8 77 B1
West Side Ave WA11 1 A6
West St Alderley Edge SK9 60 A1
Chester CH2 237 C4
Congleton CW12 156 D3
Crewe CW1 190 B5
Haslington CW1 191 C5
Macclesfield SK11 112 B8
Middlewich CW10 128 C1
Mount Pleasant ST7 195 B6
Warrington WA2 16 B7
West Vale CH64 66 E6
West View
Ellesmere Port CH66 69 A8
Northwich CW9 104 B8
Warrington WA2 9 A1
Antrobus WA4 53 A5
West View Rd WA6 101 A6
West Way
Holmes Chapel CW4 130 B3
West Way *continued*
Sandbach CW11 174 F4
Shavington CW2 206 D5
West Wing The CW10 127 D5
Westage La CW9 79 B8
Westbourne Ave CW1 190 A6
Westbourne Dr 17 SK9 34 D1
Westbourne Ho CW12 156 B2
Westbourne Mews CW12 156 B2
Westbourne Rd
Blacon CH1 118 A4
Warrington WA4 26 B7
Westbrook Ave WA4 16 D2
Westbrook Cres WA5 7 B2
Westbrook Ctr WA5 7 C1
Westbrook Dr SK10 87 C1
Westbrook Old Hall Prim Sch WA5 15 D8
Westbrook Rd WA6 75 B2
Westbrook Way WA5 7 B1
Westbury Cl Crewe CW2 206 C7
Middlewich CW10 151 B8
Warrington WA1 17 A8
Westbury Ct SK11 112 A7
Westbury Dr SK11 112 A7
Westbury Way CH4 140 F6
Westby Cl SK7 36 A7
Westcliffe Ct WA8 13 B4
Westcliffe Gdns WA4 26 E3
Westdale Rd WA1 17 A7
Westend Ct LL13 196 D8
Westenra Ave CH65 69 F6
Westerham Cl SK10 87 B2
Westerhope Way WA8 12 F3
Western App CH2 118 E4
Western Ave Blacon CH1 117 D4
Ellesmere Port CH65 69 F7
Macclesfield SK11 112 C5
Macclesfield SK11 112 D5
Milton Green CH3 165 C2
Nantwich CW5 204 E3
Western Ct CH2 118 E4
Western Dr SK11 112 C5
Western Pk CW11 191 F8
Westfield Ave ST7 209 C2
Westfield Cl Chester CH4 141 B7
Winsford CW7 149 C5
Westfield Cres WA7 22 E1
Westfield Dr
Knutsford WA16 56 E1
Willaston CW2 205 E8
Westfield Gr CW8 77 F4
Westfield Inf Sch CW2 205 E8
Westfield Mews WA7 22 F1
Westfield Prim Sch WA7 22 E1
Westfield Rd
Cheadle Hulme SK8 34 F8
Mow Cop ST7 195 C7
Northwich CW9 104 B7
Runcorn WA7 22 E1
Westfields WA15 31 F8
Westfields Ave SK10 87 B1
Westfields Rise CW3 232 C1
Westford Rd WA4 16 A1
Westgate Widnes WA8 22 B7
Wilmslow SK9 60 A5
Westgate Ave CW7 126 A1
Westgate Pk CW2 206 E2
Westhay Cres WA3 10 A5
Westholme Cl
Congleton CW12 156 C3
Crewe CW2 206 C8
Westholme Ct SK9 60 A2
Westhouse Cl CH63 43 C5
Westland Ct CW12 156 C2
Westlands ST7 209 F2
Westlands Cl CH64 41 F1
Westlands Rd CW10 128 B1
Westlands The CW12 156 C2
Westmere Cl CW2 207 B5
Westmere Dr CW1 190 F2
Westminster Ave CH4 141 B6
Westminster Cl
Middlewich CW10 128 B1
Warrington WA4 17 C2
Widnes WA8 22 B8
Westminster Ct CH2 118 F2
Westminster Dr
Bebington CH62 43 D7
Cheadle Hulme SK8 35 B6
Haydock WA11 1 F7
Wilmslow SK9 60 A4
Westminster Gn CH4 141 D7
Westminster Gr
Ellesmere Port CH65 70 C6
8 Winsford CW7 149 A8
Westminster Ind Pk CH65 69 F6
Westminster Pl 2 WA1 16 B5
Westminster Rd
Broughton CH4 139 B3
Chester CH2 118 F3
Ellesmere Port CH65 70 C6
4 Macclesfield SK10 112 C8
Macclesfield SK10 87 C1
Westminster St
Crewe CW2 190 C2
14 Macclesfield SK10 112 C8
Westminster Terr CH4 141 C7
Westmoreland Cl WA14 31 B8
Westmoreland Ave
Talke ST7 210 F7
Widnes WA8 13 B1
Westmorland Cl SK10 86 F2
Westmorland Rd M31 11 E2
Westmorland Terr CW4 130 B3
Weston Cl
Middlewich CW10 151 C7
Northwich CW9 103 F5
Weston Cres WA7 49 A6
Weston Ct Runcorn WA7 48 F7
Shavington CW2 206 C5
Weston Ctr The CW1 190 E1
Weston Gr Chester CH2 118 E7
Halewood L26 21 A6
Weston La CW2 206 E5
Weston Point Com Prim Sch WA7 48 E7
Weston Point Expressway
Runcorn WA7 22 E2
Runcorn,Rocksavage WA7 49 B5
Runcorn,Weston WA7 48 E6
Weston Prim Sch WA7 49 A6
Weston Rd Crewe CW1 190 F1
Runcorn WA7 48 E7
Weston CW1,CW2 207 B7
Wilmslow SK9 60 E6
Weston Sq SK11 111 F7
Weston View WA7 49 D4
Weston Village Prim Sch CW2 207 C5
Westover Rd WA1 16 F8
Westrees CW8 101 D5
Westville Dr CW12 156 A2
Westward Rd
Chester CH3 142 B8
Wilmslow SK9 59 F6
Westway CH60 40 F6
Westwood WA7 24 C1
Westwood Cl CW2 207 B1
Westwood Ct CH64 41 E2
Westwood Rd SK8 34 B8
Westy La WA4 16 F4
Wet Gate La WA13 19 E4
Wetheral Rd SK10 87 B2
Wetherby Cl
Chester CH1 118 B2
Newton-le-W WA12 2 C5
Wetherby Way CH66 69 B5
Wetreins La SY14,CH3 197 D6
Wettenhall Rd CW5 188 B4
Wetton La CW8 76 E4
Wexford Ave L24 21 D2
Weybourne Cl CH4 140 E5
Weybridge Cl WA4 26 E7
Weybridge Dr SK10 87 B3
Weygates Dr WA15 32 C7
Weymouth Cl WA7 50 E6
Weymouth Rd WA5 6 F6
Whaddon Dr CH4 140 F4
Whaley Bridge Prim Sch SK23 65 E7
Whaley Bridge Sta SK23 65 E8
Whaley Ct CH1 117 A4
Whaley La SK23 65 C8
Whalley Ave WA3 5 C7
Whalley Dr CW6 147 B3
Whalley Gr WA8 13 D3
Whalley Hayes SK10 112 C8
Whalley Rd CW9 104 A8
Whalley St WA1 16 C6
Wharams Bank CW11 176 F5
Wharburton Cl CW8 101 F2
Wharf Ct SK23 65 E7
Wharf La CW12 178 B3
Wharf Mill CW12 156 F1
Wharf Rd
Collins Green WA12 1 E2
Whaley Bridge SK23 65 E7
Wharf St WA1 16 C4
Wharf The Chester CH1 118 B1
Runcorn WA7 50 F6
Wharf Works SK22 39 B6
Wharfdale Ave CW1 173 B1
Wharfdale Cl WA5 15 A7
Wharfdale Rd CW12 157 A5
Wharfe Cl CW12 156 F1
Wharfe La CH65 70 A7
Wharfedale WA7 50 B6
Wharfedale Dr CH62 43 F5
Wharford La WA7 24 E3
Wharfside Ct 6 WA4 16 E1
Wharmby Rd WA11 1 E6
Wharton CE Jun Sch CW7 126 F1
Wharton Ct CH2 118 F2
Wharton Gdns CW7 127 A3
Wharton Hall CW7 127 A3
Wharton Ind Est CW7 126 F2
Wharton Park Rd CW7 126 F2
Wharton Rd CW7 127 A2
Wharton Ret Pk CW7 126 F3
Whatcroft Cl WA7 49 D6
Whatcroft Hall La CW9 104 F1
Wheat Moss SK11 84 B3
Wheatcroft Cl WA5 15 C6
Wheatfield Cl
Barnton CW8 78 A3
Ellesmere Port CH66 69 C3
Macclesfield SK10 87 C3
Wheatfield Rd WA8 12 C5
Wheatland Rd CH60 41 C7
Wheatlands WA7 23 E1
Wheatley Ave WA12 2 C5
Wheatley Rd CW1 190 E6
Wheatsheaf Cl SK23 65 E6
Wheatsheaf La CW9 53 B3
Wheatsheaf Rd SK23 65 E6
Wheelman Rd CW1 190 A7
Wheelock Cl Alsager ST7 193 A3
Handforth SK9 34 D1
Wheelock Ct CW11 175 A2
Wheelock Dr CW7 127 B1
Wheelock Prim Sch CW11 175 A4
Wheelock St CW10 128 C1
Wheelock Way 2 ST7 195 B2
Wheldon Cl CH2 118 E8
Wheldon Rd WA8 21 F7
Wheldrake Cl CH66 69 B5
Whernside WA8 12 C3
Whetstone Hey CH66 69 D5
Whetstone Rd ST8 179 C2
Wheycroft Mews CW1 190 C5
Whickham Cl WA8 12 F3
Whimbrel Ave WA12 2 C3
Whimbrel Cl WA7 49 F5
Whinchat Ave WA12 2 C4
Whinchat Cl WA3 3 E7
Whinchat Dr WA3 9 F3
Whinfell Gr WA7 49 E5
Whipcord La CH1 118 B2
Whirley Cl CW10 151 C7
Whirley La SK10 85 F1
Whirley Prim Sch SK10 86 D1
Whirley Rd SK10 86 C1
Whirlow Rd CW2 206 B7
Whisterfield La SK11 109 E3
Whiston Cl
High Legh WA16 29 C4
Winsford CW7 127 A4
Whiston Mews SK11 113 B4
Whiston St SK11 112 C7
Whitbarrow Rd WA13 18 D4
Whitby Ave Chester CH2 118 D5
Warrington WA2 8 D2
Whitby Cl Crewe CW1 190 B8
Poynton SK12 36 D4
Whitby Heath Prim Sch CH65 70 B3
Whitby High Sch The CH66 70 A2
Whitby La CH1 95 B6
Whitby Rd
Ellesmere Port CH65 70 C5
Runcorn WA7 23 A1
Whitby's La CW7 126 B1
Whitchurch Cl WA1 17 A8
Whitchurch Gr ST5 210 E2
Whitchurch Rd
Audlem CW3 229 C3
Broxton CH3 183 A3
Chester CH3 119 B1
Christleton CH3 142 E7
Edge Green SY14,CH3 199 B4
Handley CH3 182 D8
Milton Green CH3 165 C4
Newhall CW5,SY13 228 A6
Royal's Green CW3,SY13 228 C2
Sound CW5 217 E3
Waverton CH3 143 A3
Whitchurch Way WA7 49 D7
White Ave CW2 189 F4
White Bear Yd 12 WA16 57 A2
White Broom WA13 19 B4
White Friars CH1 237 A2
White Hall La CW11 151 E1
White Hart Gdns CW8 102 F4
White Hart La CW2 205 E8
White House Cl WA11 1 B6
White House Dr WA1 17 E7
White La CH3 142 D8
White Lodge Cl CH62 43 D5
White Lodge Mews CW8 102 A3
White Park Cl CW10 128 D2
White St
Macclesfield SK11 112 D6
Warrington WA1 16 A5
Warrington, Stockton Heath WA4 16 C1
Widnes WA8 23 A5
Whitebarn Rd SK9 85 B8
Whitebeam Ave 5 CH66 69 F1
Whitebeam Cl
Newcastle-u-Lyme ST5 210 D1
Runcorn WA7 24 C1
Whitebeam Row CW8 102 E7
Whitecroft Heath Rd SK11 109 B3
Whitecroft Rd CH66 69 E2
Whitecroft Villas M31 11 E2
Whitecross Rd WA5 15 E5
Whitefield WA13 19 A4
Whitefield Ave WA12 2 E2
Whitefield Cl
Golborne WA3 3 A8
Lymm WA13 19 A5
Whitefield Ct WA3 4 F2
Whitefield Gr WA13 19 A4
Whitefield Rd WA4 26 B8
Whitefields CH2 72 B3
Whitefriars Wlk M22 33 D8
Whitegate Ave WA3 4 F2
Whitegate CE Prim Sch CW8 125 F7
Whitegate Cl CW10 151 C6
Whitegate Fields LL13 180 D1
Whitegate La CH3 121 E7
Whitegate Rd CW7 125 F3
Whitegates CW12 179 D4
Whitegates Cl CH64 42 E1
Whitegates Cres CH64 42 E1
Whitegates Ho CW2 189 E2
Whitehall Ave ST7 194 F2
Whitehall Cl Barnton CW8 78 A4
Wilmslow SK9 60 A5
Whitehall Ct 3 CW5 204 D5

Whitehall Dr CW8 . . . . .103 C5
Whitehall La CW6 . . . . . .124 E1
Whitehall Pl **5** WA6 . . . . .74 B8
Whitehaven La CW5 . . . . . .203 A7
Whitehaven Rd SK7 . . . . .35 C5
Whitehill Rd ST7 . . . . . . .195 B2
Whitehouse Dr WA15 . . . .32 B8
Whitehouse Expressway
 WA7 . . . . .50 B5
Whitehouse Ind Est WA7 50 E4
Whitehouse La
 Nantwich CW5 . . . . .204 F7
 Partington WA14 . . . . .20 D8
 Plumley WA16 . . . . .80 F5
Whitehouse Rd WA16 . . . . .30 B3
Whiteleas Rd SK23 . . . . . . .65 D3
Whitemere Ct CH65 . . . . . .70 C7
Whitemore Rd CW10 . . . . .151 C6
Whiteridge Rd ST7 . . . . . .195 B2
Whites La CW2 . . . . .207 B6
Whites Mdw CH3 . . . . . . .142 A7
Whitesands Rd WA13 . . . . .18 C4
Whiteside Rd WA11 . . . . .1 B6
Whitesmead Cl SK12 . . . . . .38 D5
Whitethorn Ave WA5 . . . . .14 C5
Whitethorn Way ST5 . . . . .210 E1
Whitethroat Wlk WA3 . . . . . .9 F3
Whitewell Cl CW5 . . . . . . .204 F5
Whitewood La SY14 . . . . .212 D7
Whitfield Ave WA1 . . . . . . .16 F7
Whitfield Gr WA11 . . . . .1 A6
Whitfield Rd ST7 . . . . . . .195 B2
Whitfields The SK10 . . . . . .87 A1
Whitley Ave Barnton CW8 . .78 B3
 Warrington WA4 . . . . .17 A4
Whitley Cl
 Middlewich CW10 . . . . . . .151 B7
 Runcorn WA7 . . . . .48 F8
Whitley Dr CW8 . . . . .103 A6
Whitley La WA16 . . . . .55 B8
Whitley Village Sch WA4 52 D4
Whitlow Ave CW5 . . . . . . .204 F4
Whitlow La CW9 . . . . .126 F8
Whitney Croft SK10 . . . .113 A8
Whitstable Pk WA8 . . . . . . .12 E4
Whittaker Ave WA2 . . . . .8 D2
Whittaker Cl CW1 . . . . . . .190 A7
Whittington Gdns CW9 . . .104 A2
Whittle Ave Haydock WA11 . .1 A5
 Warrington WA5 . . . . .15 A7
Whittle Cl CH5 . . . . .116 A3
Whittle Hall La WA5 . . . . .14 F6
Whittlewood Cl WA3 . . . . .10 A5
Whitton Dr CH2 . . . . .118 E5
Whitwell Cl WA5 . . . . .14 D7
Whitworth Cl WA3 . . . . .9 E3
Wicker La
 Altrincham WA15 . . . . .32 C8
 Guilden Sutton CH3 . . . . . .120 A4
Wicklow Cl CH66 . . . . .69 A6
Wickson La CH3,CW6 . . . .167 D3
Wickstead Cl CW5 . . . . . .205 A4
Wicksten Dr WA7 . . . . .23 C2
Widdale Cl WA5 . . . . .14 F7
Widgeon Cl SK12 . . . . .36 B4
Widgeons Covert CH63 . . .41 F5
Widnes & Runcom Sixth
 Form Coll WA8 . . . . .12 E5
Widnes Rd
 Cuerdley Cross WA5,WA8 . .13 F2
 Warrington WA5 . . . . .14 C3
 Widnes WA8 . . . . .23 B8
Widnes Sta WA8 . . . . .13 A3
Wiend The CH2 . . . . .118 D4
Wight Cl CH65 . . . . .70 C1
Wightman Ave WA12 . . . . . .2 C5
Wigmore Cl WA3 . . . . .10 A6
Wigsey La WA13 . . . . .19 A7
Wigshaw La WA3 . . . . .4 D2
Wigwam Cl SK12 . . . . .36 C4
Wilbraham Cl CW5 . . . . . .204 A7
Wilbraham Rd
 Acton CW5 . . . . .204 A7
 Congleton CW12 . . . . .156 F3
 Weaverham CW8 . . . . .77 E1
Wilbraham's Wlk ST7 . .209 D2
Wilbrahams Way ST7 . .193 D4
Wilcock Rd WA11 . . . . .2 B8
Wilcote Cl WA8 . . . . .13 C4
Wilcott Dr SK9 . . . . .59 F4
Wild Ave Cl **8** WA3 . . . . . .3 E8
Wild Goose Ave ST7 . . . .195 D3
Wildenhall Cl WA5 . . . . . .15 B6
Wilderhope Cl CW2 . . . . .206 C7
Wilderspool Cres WA4 . . .16 B1
Wilderspool Cswy WA4 . .16 C3
Wilding Ave **8** WA7 . . . . .23 B2
Wilding Bsns Pk CH3 . . .119 C4
Wilding St CW1 . . . . .190 E4
Widings Old La WA3 . . . . . .9 A8
Wildmoor La CH3 . . . . .97 D1
Wildwood Gr WA1 . . . . . . .17 B7
Wilkin Croft **5** SK8 . . . . .34 E8
Wilkins La SK9 . . . . .33 E5
Wilkinson Ave WA1 . . . . . .16 F6
Wilkinson Cl WA8 . . . . . . .23 A5
Wilkinson Cl
 Ellesmere Port CH65 . . . . . .70 C6
 Warrington WA2 . . . . .16 C7
Wilkinson St N CH65 . . . .70 C6
Wilkinson Street Mews **1**
 CH65 . . . . .70 C6
Willan Rd CH1 . . . . .117 D4
Willaston CE Prim Sch
 CH64 . . . . .67 F8

Willaston Dr L26 . . . . .21 A6
Willaston Farm CH64 . . . .67 F8
Willaston Green Mews
 CH64 . . . . .67 F8
Willaston Hall Gdns
 CW5 . . . . .205 C6
Willaston Prim Sch
 CW5 . . . . .205 D6
Willaston Rd CH63,CH64 . .42 D4
Willaston Way **8** SK9 . .34 D5
Willbank La CW5 . . . . .202 D5
Willerby Cl **1** SK10 . . . .112 C8
Willeymoor La SY13 . . . . .225 D8
William Beamont Com High
 Sch WA4 . . . . .8 C1
William Ct CH64 . . . . .41 F2
William Johnson Gdns
 CH65 . . . . .70 C6
William Penn Cl WA5 . . . . .14 E5
William Rd ST7 . . . . .195 A2
William St Chester CH1 . .237 B3
 Chester,Hoole Park CH2 . .118 F3
 Congleton CW12 . . . . .157 A4
 Macclesfield SK10 . . . . . . .112 F8
 6 Northwich CW9 . . . .104 B8
 Widnes WA8 . . . . .13 C1
 Winsford CW7 . . . . .126 D3
William Stockton Com Sch
 CH65 . . . . .70 B5
Williams Ave WA12 . . . . . . .2 C5
Williams Cl CH2 . . . . .118 C4
Williams Way
 Frodsham WA6 . . . . .74 A8
 Henbury SK11 . . . . .111 C8
Williamson Cres SK23 . . .65 D8
Williamson Rd SK23 . . . . .65 D8
Willington Ave CH62 . . . . .43 E3
Willington La
 Duddon CW6 . . . . .145 E7
 Kelsall CW6 . . . . .122 D3
Willington Rd
 Duddon CW6 . . . . .145 B7
 Kelsall CW6 . . . . .122 C2
Willis St WA1 . . . . .16 C6
Willmer Cres ST7 . . . . . . .195 B6
Willotts Hill Rd ST5 . . . . .210 D1
Willoughby Cl WA5 . . . . . . .7 C1
Willow Ave
 Newton-le-W WA12 . . . . . . .2 E4
 2 Widnes WA8 . . . . .13 B2
Willow Bank
 Cheadle Hulme SK8 . . . . . .35 A6
 Helsby WA6 . . . . .73 D2
 Nantwich CW5 . . . . .204 F6
Willow Bank Est WA12 . . . .2 F4
Willow Cl Chester CH2 . . .118 D8
 Lymm WA13 . . . . .18 E4
 Morley Green WA16 . . . . . . .59 B5
 Newcastle-u-Lyme ST5 . . . .210 D1
 Poynton SK12 . . . . .36 E3
 Runcorn WA7 . . . . .49 C7
 Winsford CW7 . . . . .126 D3
Willow Cres Chester CH2 .119 A4
 Crewe CW2 . . . . .189 F2
 Moore WA4 . . . . .25 A7
 Warrington WA1 . . . . .17 B8
Willow Ct Alsager ST7 . . .193 E4
 Connah's Quay CH5 . . . . . . .91 D1
 Higher Kinnerton CH4 . . . . .161 A7
 Macclesfield SK10 . . . . .87 B2
 Middlewich CW10 . . . . .128 C2
 Nantwich CW5 . . . . .204 F7
 Newton-le-W WA12 . . . . . . .2 D4
 Winsford CW7 . . . . .127 B2
Willow Dr Blacon CH1 . . . .117 D5
 Bunbury CW6 . . . . .185 E8
 Handforth SK9 . . . . .34 D3
 Sandbach CW11 . . . . .175 E7
 Warrington WA4 . . . . .16 E1
Willow Gn Knutsford WA16 56 F3
 Weaverham CW8 . . . . .102 D8
Willow Gr Barnton CW8 . . .78 B4
 Chester CH2 . . . . .119 B4
 Ellesmere Port CH66 . . . . . .95 A8
 Elton CH2 . . . . .72 A3
Willow Green La CW8 . . . .77 B5
Willow Hayes CH3 . . . . . . .121 F7
Willow La Goostrey CW4 .107 E1
 Thornton Hough CH63,CH64 42 D3
 Warrington WA4 . . . . .26 E4
Willow Lea CH1 . . . . .94 F2
Willow Rd Chester CH4 . .140 F6
 Haydock WA11 . . . . .1 E7
 High Lane SK6 . . . . .37 F7
 Newton-le-W WA12 . . . . . . .2 E4
 Partington M31 . . . . .11 E2
Willow Sq CW7 . . . . .127 A2
Willow Tree Gr SK17 . . . .156 E3
Willow Way Bramhall SK7 . .35 D7
 Broughton CH4 . . . . .139 B3
 Prestbury SK10 . . . . .87 A5
Willow Wood Inf Sch
 CW7 . . . . .127 A2
Willow Wood Jun Sch
 CW7 . . . . .127 B2
Willoway Rd CH3 . . . . . . .119 B2
Willowbank Dr SK10 . . . . .88 C8
Willowbrow Rd CH63,
 CH64 . . . . .42 D3
Willowcroft Way ST7 . . . .195 E4
Willowdale WA12 . . . . .2 E3
Willowdale Way CH66 . . . .94 F8
Willowherb Cl CH3 . . . . . .142 A6
Willowmead Dr SK10 . . . . .87 A5
Willows SK9 . . . . .59 F6
Willows Cl CW2 . . . . .206 B7

Willows The
 Frodsham WA6 . . . . .74 C8
 Higher Wincham CW9 . . . . . .79 F6
 2 Northwich CW9 . . . . .103 E6
 Partington M31 . . . . .11 F3
 Sandbach CW11 . . . . .175 B7
 Warrington WA5 . . . . .14 F5
Wilmere La WA8 . . . . .13 A6
Wilmot Ave WA5 . . . . .14 F6
Wilmot Dr WA3 . . . . .2 F7
Wilmslow Ave CH66 . . . . . .69 E5
Wilmslow Cres WA4 . . . . .17 D4
Wilmslow Ct SK9 . . . . .34 D3
Wilmslow Dr CH66 . . . . . . .69 E5
Wilmslow Grange Prim Sch
 SK9 . . . . .34 C4
Wilmslow High Sch SK9 . .60 B6
Wilmslow Ho **6** SK9 . . . .60 B7
Wilmslow Old Rd
 Mottram St Andrew SK10 . . .61 A2
 Woodhouse Park M90,
 WA15 . . . . .33 A6
Wilmslow Park N SK9 . . . .60 D7
Wilmslow Park S SK9 . . . .60 C7
Wilmslow Prep Sch SK9 . .60 B7
Wilmslow Rd
 Alderley Edge SK9 . . . . .60 A2
 Handforth SK9 . . . . .34 D4
 Heald Green SK8,SK9 . . . . .34 C6
 Mottram St Andrew SK10 . . .61 A3
 Mottram St Andrew SK10 . . .61 D6
 Mottram St Andrew, Greendale
 SK10 . . . . .86 D8
 Woodford SK7 . . . . .35 C1
 Woodhouse Park M90,SK9,
 WA15 . . . . .32 F5
Wilmslow Sta SK9 . . . . . . .60 C7
Wilmslow Wlk **13** SK11 .112 E7
Wilsbury Grange CW8 . . .103 A5
Wilsden Rd WA8 . . . . .12 B1
Wilshaw Terr CH63 . . . . . .42 B6
Wilson Ct Warrington WA4 17 D3
 4 Widnes WA8 . . . . . . .13 C1
Wilson Cres CW9 . . . . .80 B3
Wilson Dr CW9 . . . . .126 F7
Wilson La WA3 . . . . .9 E5
Wilson Patten St WA1 . . . .16 A4
Wilson St WA5 . . . . .16 A7
Wilsons La CH65 . . . . .70 A3
Wilton Ave SK8 . . . . .34 C7
Wilton Cl CW9 . . . . .103 E4
Wilton Cres
 Alderley Edge SK9 . . . . .59 F2
 Macclesfield SK11 . . . . . . .111 E6
Wilton Dr WA15 . . . . .32 C8
Wilton La WA3 . . . . .4 B5
Wiltshire Cl
 Macclesfield SK10 . . . . .86 E2
 Warrington WA1 . . . . .17 D6
Wiltshire Dr CW12 . . . . . .156 E4
Wiltshire Rd M31 . . . . .11 E2
Wiltshire Wlk SK10 . . . . . .86 F2
Wilwick La SK11 . . . . .111 F7
Wimberry Dr ST5 . . . . . . .210 D1
Wimboldsley Com Prim Sch
 CW10 . . . . .150 F4
Wincham Ave CW9 . . . . . . .79 D3
Wincham Bsns Pk CW9 . . .79 D3
Wincham Com Prim Sch
 CW9 . . . . .79 E5
Wincham La CW9 . . . . .79 D3
Wincham Park (Witton
 Albion FC) CW9 . . . . .79 C2
Winchester Ave
 Ellesmere Port CH65 . . . . . .70 D4
 Warrington WA5 . . . . .15 C5
Winchester Cl
 Shavington CW2 . . . . .206 B3
 Wilmslow SK9 . . . . .59 E5
Winchester Dr SK10 . . . . .111 F8
Winchester Pl WA8 . . . . . .22 C8
Winchester Sq CH4 . . . . .140 F5
Wincle Ave SK12 . . . . .37 A2
Wincle CE Prim Sch
 SK11 . . . . .136 F1
Windermere Ave
 Chester CH2 . . . . .119 A6
 Warrington WA2 . . . . .8 D3
 Widnes WA8 . . . . .13 B4
Windermere Cl CH64 . . . .66 F7
Windermere Dr
 Alderley Edge SK9 . . . . .59 F1
 Congleton CW12 . . . . .156 A2
Windermere Rd
 Crewe CW2 . . . . .189 E2
 Ellesmere Port CH65 . . . . . .70 C2
 Handforth SK9 . . . . .34 C4
 Haydock WA11 . . . . .1 B6
 High Lane SK6 . . . . .37 E8
 Winsford CW7 . . . . .126 C2
Windermere St WA8 . . . . .13 B4
Windfield Gdns CH66 . . . .69 D7
Windings The CW10 . . . . .128 B2
Windle Ct Neston CH64 . . .41 E2
 Warrington WA3 . . . . .9 C4
Windlehurst Cl SK6 . . . . . .37 D7
Windlehurst Rd SK6 . . . . .37 D8
Windmill Cl
 Buerton CH3 . . . . .230 E4
 Warrington WA4 . . . . .26 C6
Windmill Ctr The WA8 . . .23 B8
Windmill Dr CW3 . . . . . . .229 F3
Windmill Hill Ave E WA7 24 D1
Windmill Hill Ave N WA7 24 D3
Windmill Hill Ave S WA7 24 D2
Windmill Hill Ave W
 WA7 . . . . .24 C2

Windmill Hill Prim Sch
 WA7 . . . . .24 C2
Windmill La
 Bollington SK10 . . . . .88 B6
 Christleton CH3 . . . . .142 D8
 Hankelow CW3 . . . . .230 F4
 Preston on t H WA4 . . . . . . .51 A6
 Warrington WA4 . . . . .26 C6
 Warrington,Penketh WA5 . . .14 C5
Windmill Rise CH2 . . . . . .118 D7
Windmill St
 Macclesfield SK11 . . . . . . .112 E6
 Runcorn WA7 . . . . .23 B2
Windscale Rd WA2 . . . . .9 A2
Windsor Ave Crewe CW1 190 B6
 Nantwich CW5 . . . . .204 F3
 Newton-le-W WA12 . . . . . . .2 D2
 Tarporley CW6 . . . . .146 D1
 Wilmslow SK9 . . . . .59 F7
Windsor Cl
 Bollington SK10 . . . . .87 E6
 Cuddington CW8 . . . . .101 F4
 Poynton SK12 . . . . .36 D4
Windsor Ct Chester CH1 . .237 B1
 1 Warrington WA4 . . . . . .16 E1
Windsor Dr Alsager ST7 . .192 F4
 Altrincham WA14 . . . . .20 F1
 Broughton CH4 . . . . .139 A3
 Ellesmere Port CH65 . . . . . .70 A3
 Faddiley CW5 . . . . .202 E7
 Haydock WA11 . . . . .2 A7
 Helsby WA6 . . . . .73 B2
 Warrington WA4 . . . . .17 B2
 Winsford CW7 . . . . .149 C5
Windsor Gdns SK7 . . . . . .35 E6
Windsor Gr
 Cheadle Hulme SK8 . . . . . .34 F8
 Runcorn WA7 . . . . .49 B8
Windsor Ho
 5 Northwich CW8 . . . . .103 C5
 Talke ST7 . . . . .210 D6
Windsor Pl CW12 . . . . . . .156 F2
Windsor Rd Chester CH4 140 F6
 Golborne WA3 . . . . .3 C8
 Widnes WA8 . . . . .13 A4
 Wistaston CW2 . . . . .205 E8
Windsor Sq SK11 . . . . . . .112 D4
Windsor St WA5 . . . . .15 E6
Windsor Way WA16 . . . . . .56 F2
Windways CH66 . . . . .69 D7
Windy Bank Ave WA3 . . . . .3 E8
Winfield Way WA8 . . . . . . .23 B8
Winfrith Rd WA2 . . . . .9 A2
Wingate Rd CH62 . . . . .43 E5
Wingfield Ave SK9 . . . . . . .59 E6
Wingfield Dr SK9 . . . . .59 E6
Wingfield Pl CW7 . . . . . . .149 B6
Winghay Rd ST7 . . . . .195 B2
Winifred St WA2 . . . . .16 C7
Winkwell Dr CH4 . . . . . . .141 A5
Winlowe SK11 . . . . .112 E7
Winmarith Dr WA15 . . . . . .32 D7
Winmarleigh St WA1 . . . . .16 A4
Winnington Ave CW8 . . . .103 C8
Winnington Ct **14** CW8 .103 F8
Winnington Hill CW8 . . . .103 F8
Winnington La CW8 . . . . . .78 D1
Winnington Park Com Prim
 Sch CW8 . . . . .103 D7
Winnington St
 Northwich CW8 . . . . .103 F8
 Winsford CW7 . . . . .126 E1
Winnows The WA7 . . . . . . .23 D1
Winscombe Dr CH3 . . . . .119 C2
Winsfield Rd SK7 . . . . .36 E8
Winsford Cl WA11 . . . . .1 F7
Winsford Cross Sh Ctr
 CW7 . . . . .126 D1
Winsford Dr WA5 . . . . .6 E7
Winsford Gr CH66 . . . . . . .69 C3
Winsford High Street Com
 Sch CW7 . . . . .126 E1
Winsford Ind Est CW7 . . .127 C3
Winsford Rd CW7 . . . . . . .170 F6
Winsford Sta CW7 . . . . . .127 C1
Winsford Way CH1 . . . . . .117 F2
Winslow Cl WA7 . . . . .50 D8
Winstanley Cl WA5 . . . . . .15 C5
Winstanley Ho WA16 . . . . .56 F2
Winstanley Ind Est WA2 . .8 B1
Winstanley Rd CH64 . . . . .66 E5
Winston Ave Alsager ST7 193 C5
 Newton-le-W WA12 . . . . . . .2 C3
 St Helens WA9 . . . . .1 B2
Winston Ct CH2 . . . . .119 A5
Winter Gr WA9 . . . . .1 B3
Winterbottom La WA16 . . .55 E8
Winterford La CW6 . . . . .147 B2
Wintergreen Wlk **3** M31 .11 F3
Winterley Dr L26 . . . . .21 A6
Winterton Way SK11 . . . .112 D3
Winterside Cl ST5 . . . . . . .210 D1
Winton Gr WA7 . . . . .24 D1
Winton Rd WA3 . . . . .3 E6
Winwick CE Prim Sch
 WA2 . . . . .8 B6
Winwick La WA3 . . . . .3 E1
Winwick Link Rd WA2,
 WA3 . . . . .8 C6
Winwick Park Ave WA2 . . .8 A5
Winwick Rd
 Newton-le-W WA12 . . . . . . .2 F1
 Warrington WA2 . . . . .8 A2
Winwick St WA2 . . . . .16 B6
Winwick View WA5 . . . . . . .1 D1
Wirksmoor Rd SK22 . . . . .39 B7
Wirral Cl WA3 . . . . .4 E4
Wirral Cres CH64 . . . . .66 F5

Wirral Ctry Pk **★** CH64 . .67 C7
Wirral Ed Ctr CH62 . . . . . .43 D8
Wirral Metropolitan Coll
 CH62 . . . . .44 A7
Wirswall Rd SY13 . . . . . . .226 C5
Wisenholme Cl WA7 . . . . .49 E5
Wistaston Ave CW2 . . . . .189 F2
Wistaston Green Cl
 CW2 . . . . .189 E2
Wistaston Green Inf Sch
 CW2 . . . . .189 F2
Wistaston Green Jun Sch
 CW2 . . . . .189 F2
Wistaston Green Rd
 CW2 . . . . .189 E2
Wistaston Jun Sch CW2 205 E8
Wistaston Pk CW2 . . . . . .189 F1
Wistaston Rd
 Crewe CW2 . . . . .190 C3
 Wistaston CW5 . . . . .205 E6
Wistaston Road Bsns Ctr
 CW2 . . . . .190 B4
Wisterdale Cl CW2 . . . . . .206 A7
Wisteria Way WA9 . . . . .6 A7
Witchingham SK9 . . . . .60 D6
Witham Cl CW2 . . . . .206 A8
Witham Way ST8 . . . . .179 E1
Withens Cl CW8 . . . . .102 D8
Withens La CW8 . . . . .102 D8
Withenshaw La SK11 . . . .136 E5
Wither's La
 High Legh WA16 . . . . .28 B4
 High Legh WA16 . . . . .28 C6
Withers Ave WA2 . . . . .16 D8
Witherwin Ave WA4 . . . . . .26 F7
Within Way L24 . . . . .21 E1
Withington Ave WA3 . . . . . .5 A4
Withington Cl
 Northwich CW9 . . . . .104 A6
 Sandbach CW11 . . . . .175 C7
Withinlee Rd SK10 . . . . . . .86 D6
Withins Rd Culcheth WA3 . .4 F3
 Haydock WA11 . . . . .1 F8
Withnall Dr CW2 . . . . .206 B4
Withy Cl WA6 . . . . .74 C8
Withy Croft CH3 . . . . .142 B7
Withycombe Rd WA5 . . . . .14 E4
Withyfold Dr SK10 . . . . . . .87 E1
Witney Gdns WA4 . . . . . . .26 E6
Witney La SY14 . . . . .213 D8
Witt Rd WA8 . . . . .23 A7
Wittenham Ho SK9 . . . . . .34 D2
Witter Pl CH1 . . . . .237 C3
Wittering La CH60 . . . . . . .40 D7
Witterings The WA4 . . . . . .41 E1
Witton Church Walk CE Prim
 Sch CW9 . . . . .104 A8
Witton St CW9 . . . . .79 A1
Witton Wlk **5** CW9 . . . .103 F8
Wivern Pl WA7 . . . . .23 B3
Wizard Country Pk SK10 .85 D6
Woburn Ave WA12 . . . . .2 D2
Woburn Cl Haydock WA11 . .1 F7
 Macclesfield SK10 . . . . .87 C2
 Northwich CW9 . . . . .103 E5
Woburn Ct SK12 . . . . .36 F4
Woburn Dr Chester CH2 . .118 F7
 Congleton CW12 . . . . .179 B8
 Cronton WA8 . . . . .12 D6
Woburn Rd WA2 . . . . .8 A4
Woking Rd SK8 . . . . .35 A7
Wolfe Cl
 Grappenhall Heys WA4 . . . .27 A8
 Knutsford WA16 . . . . .57 C3
Wolstanholme Cl CW12 .156 F1
Wolverham Prim Sch
 CH65 . . . . .70 D4
Wolverham Rd CH65 . . . . .70 D3
Wolverton Dr
 Handforth SK9 . . . . .34 D1
 Runcorn WA7 . . . . .24 D1
Wolvesey Pl CW7 . . . . . . .149 B6
Wood Croft CH3 . . . . .119 F4
Wood Dr ST7 . . . . .193 A4
Wood End Ct WA8 . . . . . . .13 D2
Wood End La CH64 . . . . . .67 E4
Wood Farm CW2 . . . . . . .189 B4
Wood Gdns SK9 . . . . .60 B2
Wood Heath Way CH62 . . .44 A7
Wood La Altrincham WA16 .32 D1
 Bradwall Green CW10,
 CW11 . . . . .152 E3
 Broughton CH4 . . . . .139 B4
 Burton CH64 . . . . .67 C2
 Duddon CW6 . . . . .145 E7
 Goostrey CW4 . . . . .107 C1
 Neston CH64 . . . . .41 D2
 Partington M31 . . . . .11 D3
 Runcorn WA7 . . . . .49 F5
 Runcorn, Brookvale WA7 . . .50 C6
 Sutton Weaver WA7 . . . . . . .49 F4
 Tattenhall CH3 . . . . .167 A1
 Warrington WA4 . . . . .26 E8
 Weaverham CW8 . . . . .102 E8
Wood La E SK10 . . . . .63 B8
Wood La N
 Fourlane-ends SK10 . . . . . . .63 B8
 Wardsend SK10 . . . . .37 B1
Wood La S SK10 . . . . .63 B7
Wood La W
 Fourlane-ends SK10 . . . . . . .63 A8
 Wardsend SK10 . . . . .36 F1
Wood Lane Prim Sch
 ST7 . . . . .210 A1
Wood Meml Sch CH4 . . . .140 F6
Wood Orchard La CW3 .230 A2
Wood Sorrel Way WA3 . . . .3 E8
Wood St Audley ST7 . . . . .209 E3

Wood St continued
Congleton CW12 . . . . .156 D3
Crewe CW2 . . . . .190 D2
Golborne WA3 . . . . .3 B8
Macclesfield SK11 . . . . . . .112 D7
Mow Cop ST7 . . . . .195 D7
New Mills SK22 . . . . .39 B7
Sandycroft CH5 . . . . .116 A2
Warrington WA1 . . . . .16 D6
Widnes WA8 . . . . .13 C1
Wood View ST7 . . . . .210 A1
Wood's Cl WA16 . . . . .82 F6
Wood's La CW8 . . . . .101 C5
Woodacre Gr CH66 . . . . . .69 F8
Woodacre Rd CH66 . . . . . .69 F8
Woodacres Ct SK9 . . . . . .59 F6
Woodale Cl WA5 . . . . .14 E7
Woodall Ave CH4 . . . . . .140 E6
Woodall Dr WA7 . . . . .23 B1
Woodavens Gr CW3 . . . . .229 A2
Woodbank SK9 . . . . .60 A2
Woodbank CW2 . . . . .206 A7
Woodbank La CH1 . . . . . . .93 D5
Woodbank Rd
Ellesmere Port CH65 . . . . . .70 B2
Warrington WA5 . . . . .15 A4
Woodbine Ave M44 . . . . . .11 D4
Woodbine Rd WA13 . . . . . .19 B4
Woodbourne Rd SK22 . . . . .39 A5
Woodbridge Cl WA4 . . . . . .26 E4
Woodbrook SK23 . . . . .65 E8
Woodbrook Ct SK23 . . . . . .65 E8
Woodbrook Rd SK9 . . . . . .60 C1
Woodburn Dr CH60 . . . . . .40 F6
Woodchurch La CH66 . . . . .69 E6
Woodclose CH66 . . . . .44 A1
Woodcock La ST7 . . . . . .195 C6
Woodcocks' Well CE Prim
Sch ST7 . . . . .195 C6
Woodcote Ave CH65 . . . . . .70 B1
Woodcote Cl WA2 . . . . .8 D1
Woodcote Pl CW11 . . . . . .191 F8
Woodcote View SK9 . . . . . .34 F1
Woodcotes The CH62 . . . . .43 D6
Woodcott Ave CW7 . . . . . .126 B1
Woodcott Cl CW2 . . . . . . .206 E2
Woodcott Gr ❸ SK9 . . . . . .34 E1
Woodcotthill La CW5 . . . . .217 B3
Woodcroft ST7 . . . . .210 A1
Woodcroft Gdns WA4 . . . . .26 E6
Woodend WA7 . . . . .50 E7
Woodend Cl CW10 . . . . . .151 C6
Woodend La
Altrincham WA16 . . . . .32 E1
Hollins Green WA3 . . . . . . .10 D2
Mobberley WA16 . . . . .58 E8
Woodend Rd CH65 . . . . . . .69 F6
Woodfall Cl CH64 . . . . .67 A6
Woodfall Gr CH64 . . . . . . .67 A6
Woodfall Inf Sch CH64 .67 A6
Woodfall Jun Sch CH64 .67 A6
Woodfall La CH64 . . . . . . .67 B6
Woodfield Cl CH4 . . . . . . .139 A3
Woodfield Gr CH2 . . . . . . .119 B5
Woodfield Ho CH2 . . . . . . .119 A5
Woodfield Prim Sch
CH2 . . . . .119 A5
Woodfield Rd
Cheadle Hulme SK8 . . . . . . .35 B7
Ellesmere Port CH65 . . . . . .70 C5
Woodfield Rd N ❷ CH65 .70 C5
Woodfields CH3 . . . . .142 E7
Woodfin Croft SK11 . . . . . .84 A3
Woodford Aerodrome
SK7 . . . . .36 A1
Woodford Ave WA3 . . . . . . .3 D7
Woodford Cl Crewe CW2 .189 F2
Helsby WA6 . . . . .73 B2
Runcorn WA7 . . . . .49 B6
Warrington WA4 . . . . .17 C3
Woodford Court Ind Est
CW7 . . . . .149 A8
Woodford La
Prestbury SK10 . . . . .61 D7
Winsford CW7 . . . . .149 B8
Woodford La W CW7 . . . .149 A7
Woodford Lodge High Sch
CW7 . . . . .149 A7
Woodford Park Ind Est
CW7 . . . . .148 F8
Woodford Rd
Bramhall SK7 . . . . .35 E4
Poynton SK12 . . . . .36 B6
Wilmslow SK9 . . . . .61 B8
Woodgate Ave ST7 . . . . . .194 A5
Woodhall Cl Bramhall SK7 .35 E3
Warrington WA5 . . . . .15 A8
Woodhall Rd ST7 . . . . . . .195 C3
Woodham Cl CH8 . . . . . . .103 C5
Woodham Gr CH66 . . . . . . .66 F5
Woodhatch Rd WA7 . . . . . .50 B5
Woodhey Hall La CW5 . . .202 B6
Woodhey La CW5 . . . . . . .202 C5
Woodhouse Cl WA3 . . . . . . .9 E3
Woodhouse End Rd
SK11 . . . . .135 C8
Woodhouse La
Biddulph ST8 . . . . .179 F2
Buerton CW3 . . . . .235 D8
Partington WA14 . . . . .20 C4
Warren SK11 . . . . .111 E1
Woodhouse Park M90 . . .33 D7
Woodhouse Mid Sch
ST8 . . . . .179 E2
Woodhouse Rd M22 . . . . . .33 D8
Woodhouses Pk WA6 . . . . .73 F5
Woodlan Ct CW6 . . . . . . .146 B6

Woodland Ave
Crewe CW1 . . . . .190 F4
Lymm WA13 . . . . .19 A2
Nantwich CW5 . . . . .205 A5
Newton-le-W WA12 . . . . .2 D2
Widnes WA8 . . . . .12 F1
Woodland Bank CH2 . . . . .96 F1
Woodland Cl SK11 . . . . . . .84 A3
Woodland Ct ST7 . . . . . . .193 D4
Woodland Dr WA13 . . . . . .19 A2
Woodland End WA13 . . . . .19 A2
Woodland Gdns CW1 . . . .190 D6
Woodland Rd
Ellesmere Port CH65 . . . . . .70 B2
Rode Heath ST7 . . . . .193 E8
Woodland View
Ellesmere Port CH66 . . . . . .69 B8
Whaley Bridge SK23 . . . . . . .65 F2
Woodland Wlk
Bebington CH62 . . . . .43 C8
Runcorn WA7 . . . . .24 A1
Woodlands
Hartford CW8 . . . . .103 B5
Kidsgrove ST7 . . . . .194 E3
Woodlands Ave
Chester CH1 . . . . .118 B4
Congleton CW12 . . . . .156 D4
Kidsgrove ST7 . . . . .194 D1
Woodlands Cl
Cheadle Hulme SK8 . . . . . . .35 A8
Eaton CW6 . . . . .147 A8
Neston CH64 . . . . .66 D8
Woodlands Ct
Alderley Edge SK9 . . . . .85 A8
❶❽ Knutsford WA16 . . . . . . .57 B2
Woodlands Cvn Pk
WA16 . . . . .106 E3
Woodlands Dr
Chester CH2 . . . . .118 E4
Chorlton CW2 . . . . .207 C3
Goostrey CW4 . . . . .107 C1
Knutsford WA16 . . . . .57 B2
Warrington WA4 . . . . .17 D3
Woodlands Gr CW8 . . . . . . .77 F3
Woodlands Ind Est WA12 .2 C6
Woodlands Inf Sch CH66 .69 F2
Woodlands Jun Sch
CH66 . . . . .69 F2
Woodlands La CH3 . . . . . .119 A2
Woodlands Pk CW12 . . . . .156 E3
Woodlands Rd
Chester CH4 . . . . .141 A7
Handforth SK9 . . . . .34 E3
High Lane SK12 . . . . .38 A6
Huntington CH3 . . . . .142 A6
Macclesfield SK11 . . . . . . .112 C6
Neston CH64 . . . . .66 D8
New Mills SK22 . . . . .39 A8
Northwich CW8 . . . . .103 C5
Wilmslow SK9 . . . . .33 F1
Woodlands Rd E ❶
CW8 . . . . .103 C5
Woodlands The
Higher Wincham CW9 . . . . . .80 A6
Winnington CW8 . . . . .78 E1
Woodlands Way CW6 . . . .146 D2
Woodlark Cl CW7 . . . . . . .150 A8
Woodlea Ave CH2 . . . . . . .118 F7
Woodlea Cl CH62 . . . . .43 D5
Woodlea Ct CW8 . . . . .103 D7
Woodlea Dr SK10 . . . . .87 E8
Woodleigh Ct SK9 . . . . . . .60 A2
Woodley Fold WA5 . . . . . . .14 F4
Woodnoth Dr CW2 . . . . . .206 C5
Woodpecker Cl WA3 . . . . . .9 F4
Woodpecker Dr
Northwich CW9 . . . . .103 F4
Packmoor ST7 . . . . .195 E1
Woodridge WA7 . . . . .24 C1
Woodrow Way Irlam M44 .11 F8
Newcastle-u-Lyme ST5 . . . .210 F1
Woodruff Cl ST7 . . . . .195 F1
Woods Cl WA3 . . . . .2 A3
Woods Gr SK8 . . . . .35 B7
Woods La SK8 . . . . .35 B7
Woods Rd M44 . . . . .11 D6
Woodsfin La CH3 . . . . . . .183 F7
Woodshutt's St ST7 . . . . .194 E1
Woodside
Ellesmere Port CH65 . . . . . .70 C2
Knutsford WA16 . . . . .57 B1
Lawton-gate ST7 . . . . .194 E4
Siddington SK11 . . . . .110 A3
Woodside Ave
Alsager ST7 . . . . .193 E4
Crewe CW2 . . . . .189 F2
Frodsham WA6 . . . . .74 D7
Kidsgrove ST7 . . . . .195 A1
Woodside Ct CH2 . . . . . . .118 C4
Woodside Dr
High Lane SK6 . . . . .37 F7
Sandbach CW11 . . . . .175 C6
Woodside La Crewe CW2 .189 F1
Lymm WA13 . . . . .19 B1
Poynton SK12 . . . . .36 E4
Woodside Prim Sch WA7 .49 D7
Woodside Rd
Blacon CH1 . . . . .117 C5
Haydock WA11 . . . . .1 E7
Warrington WA5 . . . . .14 F4
Woodside St SK22 . . . . . . .39 B6
Woodside Terr CW9 . . . . .104 B4
Woodsome Cl CH65 . . . . . .70 B1
Woodsome Dr CH65 . . . . . .70 B1
Woodstock Ave
Cheadle Hulme SK8 . . . . . . .35 A7

Woodstock Ave continued
Newton-le-W WA12 . . . . .2 D2
Woodstock Cl SK10 . . . . . .87 A2
Woodstock Ct ❹ SK9 . . . . .34 E5
Woodstock Dr CW10 . . . . .151 E5
Woodstock Gdns WA4 . . . .26 F6
Woodstock Gr WA8 . . . . . . .12 D2
Woodthorn Cl WA4 . . . . . . .24 F4
Woodvale Cl WA2 . . . . .8 E1
Woodvale Rd
Ellesmere Port CH66 . . . . . .69 D6
Knutsford WA16 . . . . .82 A8
Woodview Cres WA8 . . . . .22 A8
Woodview Rd WA8 . . . . . . .22 A8
Woodville Ho M31 . . . . . . .12 D1
Woodward St CW8 . . . . . . .77 D1
Woodward Wlk CH3 . . . . .121 C3
Woodwards Cotts CH64 . . .41 D6
Woodyear Rd CH62 . . . . . .43 E7
Woolacombe Cl WA4 . . . . .16 D2
Woolaston Dr ST7 . . . . . . .193 D3
Woolden Rd WA3 . . . . .11 B8
Woollam Dr CH66 . . . . .69 D7
Woolley Ave SK12 . . . . . . .36 D2
Woolley Cl WA6 . . . . .49 D2
Woolmer Cl WA3 . . . . .10 B6
Woolston Ave CW1 . . . . . .157 A2
Woolston CE Prim Sch
WA1 . . . . .17 D8
Woolston Com High Sch
WA1 . . . . .17 B7
Woolston Com Prim Sch
WA1 . . . . .17 C7
Woolston Dr CW2 . . . . . . .206 E2
Woolston Grange Ave
Warrington WA1 . . . . .9 D1
Warrington,Woolston WA1 . .17 F8
Woolston Hall WA1 . . . . . . .17 D7
Woolston Rd WA11 . . . . .1 C7
Woolton Ct CH66 . . . . .69 F8
Woore Prim Sch CW3 . . .232 C1
Woore Rd CW3 . . . . .230 D3
Worcester Ave WA3 . . . . . . .3 B8
Worcester Cl Talke ST7 . . .210 D7
Warrington WA5 . . . . .15 C5
Worcester Pl CH1 . . . . . . .118 A4
Worcester St CH65 . . . . . . .70 C6
Worcester Wlk ❻ CH65 . . .70 C6
Wordsworth Ave
Warrington WA4 . . . . .16 B2
Widnes WA8 . . . . .22 F4
Wordsworth Cl
Crewe CW2 . . . . .189 F1
❼ Sandbach CW11 . . . . . .174 D6
Wordsworth Cres CH1 . .118 A5
Wordsworth Dr CW1 . . . .190 F4
Wordsworth Ho SK10 . . . . .86 F1
Wordsworth Mews CH1 .118 A5
Wordsworth Sq CH1 . . . .118 A5
Wordsworth Way
Alsager ST7 . . . . .193 D4
Ellesmere Port CH66 . . . . . .69 E1
Works Cotts WA7 . . . . .49 E3
Works La CW9 . . . . .79 E1
World Way M90 . . . . .33 B8
Worleston Cl CW10 . . . . . .151 C6
Worley Ct CH3 . . . . .183 A8
Worrall St CW12 . . . . .156 E3
Worsborough Ave WA5 . . .15 B5
Worsley Ave
Saughall CH1 . . . . .117 A8
Warrington WA4 . . . . .16 F4
Worsley Dr CW12 . . . . . . .157 B1
Worsley Rd WA4 . . . . .16 B1
Worsley St Golborne WA3 . . .3 A8
Warrington WA5 . . . . .15 F7
Worth Prim Sch SK12 . . . .36 F2
Worthing St CW9 . . . . . . .104 C8
Worthington Ave ❾ M31 .11 F3
Worthington Cl
Henbury SK11 . . . . .111 C8
Nantwich CW5 . . . . .205 A5
Runcorn WA7 . . . . .50 A7
Worthington Ct CH2 . . . . .118 D4
Wr Twr (Mus) ★ CH1 . . . .118 B2
Wr Twr Rd CH64 . . . . .41 E1
Wr Twr St CH1 . . . . .237 A3
Wrekin Ho ❽ CW8 . . . . . .103 C5
Wrekin Way CH4 . . . . . . .140 F6
Wren Ave CW4 . . . . .129 C2
Wren Cl Macclesfield SK10 .87 A1
Runcorn WA7 . . . . .50 A6
Warrington WA3 . . . . .9 F4
Wrenbury Cl ST5 . . . . . . .210 D1
Wrenbury Dr ❸ CW9 . . . .103 E5
Wrenbury Frith CW5 . . . .216 B7
Wrenbury Hall Dr CW5 . .217 A5
Wrenbury Heath Rd
CW5 . . . . .217 D5
Wrenbury Ind Est CW5 .217 A3
Wrenbury Prim Sch
CW5 . . . . .216 F4
Wrenbury Rd Aston CW5 .217 B3
Marbury SY13 . . . . .226 E8
Marbury,Chorley Bank
SY14 . . . . .201 D1
Wrenbury SY13,CW5 . . . . .216 B1
Wrenbury Sta CW5 . . . . . .217 A3
Wrenmere Cl CW11 . . . . .174 E8
Wrenshot La WA16 . . . . . .29 D4
Wrexham Rd
Biddulph ST8 . . . . .179 D1
Malpas SY14 . . . . .7 E1
*Wrexham Ind Est/Ystad
Ddiwdiannol Wrecsam*
LL13 . . . . .196 A1
Wrexham Rd
Bickerton SY14 . . . . .200 A8

Wrexham Rd continued
Bulkeley SY14,CW6 . . . . . .184 E1
Burland CW5 . . . . .203 C8
Chester CH4 . . . . .141 B4
Faddiley CH4,CW6 . . . . . . .202 C5
Holt LL13 . . . . .196 B3
Malpas SY14 . . . . .212 E2
Pulford CH4 . . . . .162 E5
Roughhill CH4 . . . . .140 F1
Worthenbury SY14 . . . . . . .211 D1
Wright Ave CW9 . . . . .104 C6
Wright Cres WA8 . . . . .23 A5
Wright Ct CW5 . . . . .204 F5
Wright Lodge ❻ CW5 . . . .204 F5
Wright St ST7 . . . . .194 D1
Wright Tree Villas M44 . . .11 E5
Wright's La
Burtonwood WA5 . . . . .6 F3
Sandbach CW11 . . . . .175 D6
Wrights La CW5 . . . . .13 F2
Wrigley La SK10 . . . . .86 B3
Wrigley Rd WA11 . . . . .1 E6
Wrinehill Rd CW5 . . . . . . .220 E7
Wroxall Cl Chester CH2 .237 B4
Helsby WA6 . . . . .73 B4
Wroxham Rd WA5 . . . . .14 E6
Wrynose Rd CH62 . . . . . . .43 E8
Wybersley Rd SK6 . . . . . . .38 A8
*Wybunbury Delves CE Prim
Sch* CW5 . . . . .220 B7
Wybunbury La CW5 . . . . .205 E3
Wybunbury Rd
Willaston CW5 . . . . .205 D4
Wybunbury CW5 . . . . .220 B7
Wych House Bank CW5 .204 D5
Wych La SK10 . . . . .62 D5
Wych-House La CW10 . . . .128 C1
Wyche Ave CW5 . . . . .204 D5
Wyche Cl CW9 . . . . .104 E6
Wyche La CW6 . . . . .185 E3
Wyche Prim Sch CW5 . .204 E6
Wyche Rd CW6 . . . . .185 E8
Wychelm Rd M31 . . . . .11 F3
Wychwood Ave WA13 . . . . .18 C3
Wychwood Pk CW2 . . . . . .207 C1
Wycliffe Ave SK9 . . . . .60 A7
Wycliffe Ct CH2 . . . . .119 A2
Wycliffe Rd
Ellesmere Port CH65 . . . . . .69 F8
Haydock WA11 . . . . .1 E7
Wyedale CH65 . . . . .70 B3
Wyedale Rd WA11 . . . . .1 E6
Wyncroft Cl
Ellesmere Port CH65 . . . . . .70 B3
Widnes WA8 . . . . .22 C7
Wyncroft Ct CW8 . . . . .77 C1
Wyncroft Rd WA8 . . . . .22 C7
Wynd The CW6 . . . . .122 C4
Wyndham Cl
Northwich CW9 . . . . .103 F5
Wyndham Cres CH66 . . . . .69 E2
Wyndham Rd CH1 . . . . . . .117 C4
Wynfield Ave M22 . . . . . . .33 F7
Wyngate Rd WA15 . . . . . . .31 F8
Wynnstay Rd CH4 . . . . . . .139 C4
Wynter Cl SY14 . . . . .198 B3
Wynter La SY14 . . . . .198 B3
Wythburn Gr WA7 . . . . . . .49 E5
Wythens Rd SK8 . . . . .34 B8
Wythin St CW6 . . . . .168 D1

Y

**Y Berllan Geirios/Cherry
Orch** LL13 . . . . .196 D8
Yardley Ave WA5 . . . . .15 F8
Yarmouth Rd WA5 . . . . . . .14 E6
Yarrow Cl CH4 . . . . .139 C3
Yarwood Cl CW8 . . . . .103 F7
Yarwoodheath La WA14 . . .30 E7
Yatehouse La CW10 . . . . . .128 D7
Yates Cl WA5 . . . . .15 C5
Yates Rd New Mills SK22 . . .39 C7
Thornton-le-M CH2 . . . . . . .71 E1
Yates St CW2 . . . . .190 C2
Yeald Brow WA13 . . . . .18 B3
Yeardsley Ave SK23 . . . . . .39 D3
Yeardsley Gn SK23 . . . . . .65 D8
Yeardsley La SK23 . . . . . . .39 D3
Yearsleys La WA6 . . . . . . .101 A5
Yeld La CW6 . . . . .122 E8
Yeoman Way CH66 . . . . . . .69 F1
Yeovil Cl WA1 . . . . .17 C8
Yerburgh St CH2 . . . . .118 D4
Yew Tree Ave WA12 . . . . . . .2 A4
Yew Tree Ave / Lon yr Ywen
CH1 . . . . .116 F7
Yew Tree Bank CW6 . . . . .145 B5
Yew Tree Cl
Broughton CH4 . . . . .139 C3
Bulkeley SY14 . . . . .184 D2
Little Budworth CW6 . . . . .147 F7
Lymm WA13 . . . . .18 E4
Macclesfield SK11 . . . . . . .112 A6
Middlewich CW10 . . . . . . .128 B2
Prestbury SK10 . . . . .87 B7
Thornton-le-M CH2 . . . . . . .71 E1
Wilmslow SK9 . . . . .60 D7
Yew Tree Ct Alsager ST7 .193 E2
Wimboldsley CW10 . . . . . .150 F3
Yew Tree Dr Barnton CW8 .78 B3
Nantwich CW5 . . . . .204 D5
Yew Tree Farm Trad Est
WA11 . . . . .2 A8
Yew Tree La
Appleton Thorn WA4 . . . . . .27 C5
Astbury CW12 . . . . .178 C3

Yew Tree La continued
Bridgemere CW5 . . . . .232 A6
Poynton SK12 . . . . .36 F3
Yew Tree Park Rd SK8 . . . .35 B6
Yew Tree Way
Wardsend SK10 . . . . .37 B1
Wistaston CW2 . . . . .206 A8
Yew Tree Way
Golborne WA3 . . . . .3 B7
Prestbury SK10 . . . . .87 C6
Yew Wlk ❶ M31 . . . . .11 E3
Yewdale Dr CH66 . . . . .69 F1
Yewlands CW8 . . . . .101 D5
Yewlands Dr WA16 . . . . . . .57 C2
Yewtree Cl CH64 . . . . .66 F7
Yewtree Rd WA16 . . . . . . .80 F3
Yonne The CH1 . . . . .237 A2
York Ave Culcheth WA3 . . . .4 F2
Warrington WA5 . . . . .14 E7
York Cl Biddulph ST8 . . . . .179 C2
Talke ST7 . . . . .210 D7
York Cres SK9 . . . . .60 D8
York Ct ❷ WA4 . . . . .16 E1
York Dr
Mickle Trafford CH2 . . . . . .119 E8
Warrington WA4 . . . . .17 A2
Winsford CW7 . . . . .149 D6
Woodhouse Park M90 . . . . .32 F7
York Ho ❹ CW8 . . . . .103 C5
York Pl WA7 . . . . .23 A2
York Rd
Connah's Quay CH5 . . . . . .91 C1
Ellesmere Port CH65 . . . . . .70 C5
Irlam M44 . . . . .11 D5
Warrington WA4 . . . . .17 A2
Widnes WA8 . . . . .22 C5
York St Chester CH1 . . . . .237 B3
Macclesfield SK10 . . . . . . .112 E8
Runcorn WA7 . . . . .23 A2
Warrington WA4 . . . . .16 C4
Yorkshire Rd M31 . . . . .11 E2
Yorston Lodge Sch WA16 56 F1
Ysgol Derwen CH4 . . . . . .161 A7
*Ystad Ddiwdiannol
Wrecsam/Wrexham Ind Est*
LL13 . . . . .196 A1

Z

Zan Dr CW11 . . . . .175 A3
Zan Ind Pk CW11 . . . . . . .175 A3
Zara Ct WA11 . . . . .1 C7
Zinnia Dr M44 . . . . .11 E8
Zion St ❸ CW8 . . . . .103 E7

Addresses

Name and Address	Telephone	Page	Grid reference

Name and Address	Telephone	Page	Grid reference

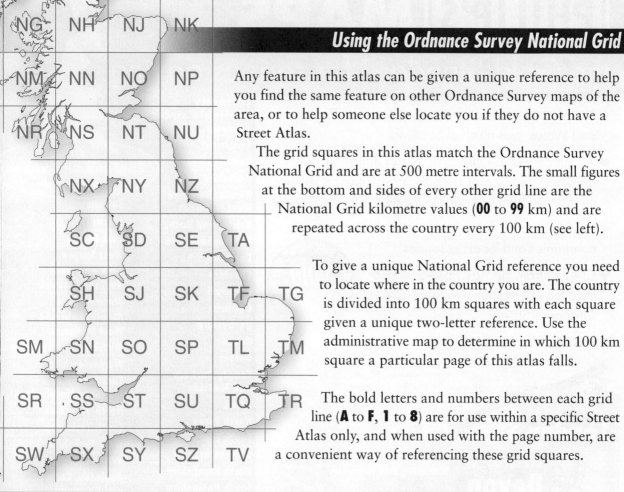

Any feature in this atlas can be given a unique reference to help you find the same feature on other Ordnance Survey maps of the area, or to help someone else locate you if they do not have a Street Atlas.

The grid squares in this atlas match the Ordnance Survey National Grid and are at 500 metre intervals. The small figures at the bottom and sides of every other grid line are the National Grid kilometre values (**00** to **99** km) and are repeated across the country every 100 km (see left).

To give a unique National Grid reference you need to locate where in the country you are. The country is divided into 100 km squares with each square given a unique two-letter reference. Use the administrative map to determine in which 100 km square a particular page of this atlas falls.

The bold letters and numbers between each grid line (**A** to **F**, **1** to **8**) are for use within a specific Street Atlas only, and when used with the page number, are a convenient way of referencing these grid squares.

Example   The railway bridge over DARLEY GREEN RD in grid square B1

Step 1: Identify the two-letter reference, in this example the page is in **SP**

Step 2: Identify the 1 km square in which the railway bridge falls. Use the figures in the southwest corner of this square: Eastings **17**, Northings **74**. This gives a unique reference: **SP 17 74**, accurate to 1 km.

Step 3: To give a more precise reference accurate to 100 m you need to estimate how many tenths along and how many tenths up this 1 km square the feature is (to help with this the 1 km square is divided into four 500 m squares). This makes the bridge about **8** tenths along and about **1** tenth up from the southwest corner.

This gives a unique reference: **SP 178 741**, accurate to 100 m.

Eastings (read from left to right along the bottom) come before Northings (read from bottom to top). If you have trouble remembering say to yourself "Along the hall, THEN up the stairs"!

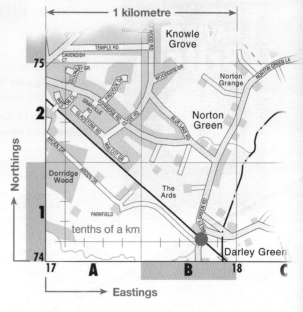